Nesbit Willoughby Wallace

A Regimental Chronicle and List of Officers of the 60th

The King's Royal Rifle Corps, formerly the 62nd, or the Royal American Regiment of Foot

Nesbit Willoughby Wallace

A Regimental Chronicle and List of Officers of the 60th
The King's Royal Rifle Corps, formerly the 62nd, or the Royal American Regiment of Foot

ISBN/EAN: 9783743408036

Manufactured in Europe, USA, Canada, Australia, Japa

Cover: Foto ©ninafisch / pixelio.de

Manufactured and distributed by brebook publishing software (www.brebook.com)

Nesbit Willoughby Wallace

A Regimental Chronicle and List of Officers of the 60th

A

REGIMENTAL CHRONICLE

AND

LIST OF OFFICERS

OF

THE 60TH, OR THE KING'S ROYAL RIFLE CORPS,

FORMERLY

THE 62ND, OR THE ROYAL AMERICAN REGIMENT
OF FOOT.

BY

NESBIT WILLOUGHBY WALLACE,

Captain, 60th Royal Rifles.

LONDON:

HARRISON, 59, PALL MALL,

Booksellers to the Queen and H.R.H. the Prince of Wales.

1879.

TO

FIELD-MARSHAL

HIS ROYAL HIGHNESS THE DUKE OF CAMBRIDGE,

K.G., G.C.B., K.P., G.C.S.I., G.C.M.G.,

COMMANDING-IN-CHIEF HER MAJESTY'S FORCES, &c., &c., &c.,

AND

COLONEL-IN-CHIEF OF H.M. 60TH KING'S ROYAL RIFLE CORPS,

THE ACCOMPANYING PAGES,

CONTAINING

A REGIMENTAL CHRONICLE AND LIST OF OFFICERS,

ARE, WITH PERMISSION, RESPECTFULLY DEDICATED BY

H.R.H.'S MOST OBEDIENT SERVANT,

NESBIT WILLOUGHBY WALLACE,

CAPTAIN, 60TH ROYAL RIFLES.

CONTENTS.

LIST OF PLATES.

PREFACE.

It has always been a matter of surprise to me that no book exists to which Riflemen can turn to trace the fortunes of a Regiment whose career has been so long and so distinguished as that of "The 60th, or King's Royal Rifle Corps;" but it may probably be accounted for by the peculiarity of the early history of the Regiment, its numerous battalions, and its singularly varied services.

It is not my object, in the present volume, to attempt a connected history of those services. The scanty and broken materials at my disposal make such an undertaking at present almost an impossibility; it will be enough if I can furnish those interested in the Regiment with a book of reference on most matters of importance in its eventful annals.

I am well aware that my information in many instances is fragmentary, and that I have not even been able always to assign the exact dates to the facts recorded, or to distinguish the separate services of the different battalions; nevertheless, I have thought it best to publish, without any more delay, what I have been able to collect, after careful research during the past five years, from private manuscripts and records, and from public offices and libraries in England and America.

Imperfect as this Regimental Chronicle is in too many respects, I believe that it will be found to contain some information that is new, and many things that have never before been brought together, in a convenient and accessible form.

I sincerely thank all those who have given me assistance, and especially Major-General Rigaud, who throughout has shown the liveliest interest in the work, and who, moreover, has greatly helped me in revising the proofs.

I am much indebted to Major-General Bedford, Captain Boyle (Rifle Brigade), Captain Astley Terry, Major Morrah, the Hon. Walter Pepys, and the Rev. Richard Davy, all of whom have lent me either valuable manuscripts or prints.

Most of the plates are from sketches (taken from old prints) by the Hon. F. Greville and another friend, to both of whom I am greatly obliged.

As there is still very much more to be done in working out the history of the Regiment, I earnestly ask all who are interested in the subject to help me, as far as they can, by furnishing me with any materials they may have collected, or by pointing out to me any fresh source of information, so that I may be able to make as complete as possible the volume which I hope to publish at some future time, containing the Historical Records of the 60th King's Royal Rifles.

Winchester,
        December, 1878.

60TH (OR ROYAL AMERICAN) REGIMENT OF FOOT
LIGHT INFANTRY.
2nd Battalion.

King's Colour

Regimental Colour

SKETCH OF THE HISTORY

60TH, OR THE KING'S ROYAL RIFLE CORPS.

THE formation of " The 62nd, or the Royal American Regiment of Foot," now called " The 60th, or King's Royal Rifle Corps," dates from the middle of the last century.

About that time it was thought advisable to augment the Army by eleven battalions, war between England and France seeming imminent, owing to the disregard of the treaty of Aix-la-Chapelle, and the frequent encroachments upon British territory in America by the latter power.

In May, 1756, war was declared by Great Britain against France, and, in order to strengthen the British Forces in America, the immediate attention of Parliament was turned towards raising in that country a new Regiment of Foot which was intended to combine the characteristics of a Colonial Corps with those of a Foreign Legion.

During the Parliament of 1755,* the sum of £81,000 was voted for the purpose of raising a Regiment of four battalions, each a thousand strong, for service in British North America.

By the same Parliament an Act was also passed " To enable His Majesty to grant commissions to a certain number of foreign Protestants, who have served abroad as officers or engineers, to act and rank as officers or engineers in America only, under certain restrictions and regulations."

The Earl of Loudoun, who had shortly before been nominated Commander-in-Chief of the Forces in North America, was appointed Colonel-in-Chief of the Regiment.

About fifty Officers' commissions, or rather less than a third of the whole, were given to Germans and Swiss ; and none were allowed to rise above the rank of Lieutenant-Colonel.

---

* 29th George II., cap. 5, November, 1755.

B

The men were chiefly German and Swiss Protestants, who, for some years past, had settled in America on the waste lands which had been assigned to them by the British Government. These men, from their religion, language, and race, were considered in every way suitable opponents to the French.

On enlistment for the requisite term of three years they were obliged to take the oath of allegiance, and to become naturalized subjects; but they were required to serve *only* in America.

This new Regiment was at first called "The 62nd, or the Royal American Regiment of Foot."

At the disbandment of Shirley's and Pepperel's Regiments in August, 1756, which were numbered the 50th and 51st Regiments, the title was changed to "The 60th, or the Royal American Regiment of Foot."

In 1757, General James Abercromby was appointed Colonel-in-Chief, and, in 1758, was succeeded by General Sir Jeffery Amherst, K.B.

In 1761,* an Act of Parliament was passed referring to Act 13 George II., naturalizing foreign Protestants, and giving further instructions on the subject.

At the conclusion of the seven years' war with France, the Third and Fourth Battalions were disbanded in England in 1763† and 1764.

In 1772,‡ another Act of Parliament, explanatory of the two former, was passed.

In 1775, owing to the outbreak of the Civil War in America, the British Government again decided to increase the Army.

Two more battalions of the 60th, numbered the Third and Fourth, were raised in England and ordered for service in the West Indies.

At the conclusion of the peace in 1783, these battalions were once more disbanded in Nova Scotia, and any of the men who chose were allowed to settle there.§

In 1787 they were again formed in England, almost entirely of foreigners, and sent to the West Indies.

In 1794, rifles were introduced into the English Army, and were first issued to a battalion of "The 60th Royal American Regiment of Foot."

---

* 2nd George III., cap. 25, November 3, 1761.
† Royal Warrant, St. James's, May 18, 1763.
‡ 13th George III., cap. 25, November 26, 1772.
§ Royal Warrant, St. James's, June 9, 1783.

In 1797, H.R.H. the Duke of York was appointed Colonel-in-Chief of the Regiment.

In the same year* another Act of Parliament was passed for the raising of a Fifth Battalion, in the Isle of Wight; about 400 of "Hompesch's Mounted Riflemen" were incorporated with it, and 500 of "Lowenstein's Chasseurs," a corps raised by a Prince of that name for the Dutch Republic, were also drafted into the battalion on its arrival in the West Indies.

The Colonel of the new battalion was Francis Baron de Rottenburg. About the same time Walstein's Foreign Light Infantry were drafted into the Fourth Battalion.

A clothing warrant of 1800 shows that for some time the Fifth Battalion had been dressed in green. This confirms the statement to that effect contained in the records of the First Battalion.

The Fifth Battalion was armed with rifles and carried leather rifle bags instead of knapsacks.

In 1799,† an Act of Parliament was passed for adding a Sixth and Seventh Battalion.

The Sixth Battalion was formed the same year, in the Isle of Wight, almost entirely of Germans.

The Seventh Battalion was raised in 1813, in the Channel Islands, from German prisoners of war, and consisted of 840 rank and file, 640 of which were called Light Infantry, and the remainder Rifles.

In the same year‡ an Act of Parliament was also passed to augment the Regiment still further by the addition of three more battalions.

The Eighth Battalion was formed at Lisbon in 1813, but the Ninth and Tenth do not appear to have been raised.

After the conclusion of the peace in 1815, six of the battalions were disbanded and drafted as follows:—

May, 1816. Drafts from the Eighth Battalion were sent to the Fifth Battalion at Gibraltar; the remainder were disbanded at Portsmouth.

June, 1817. The Seventh Battalion was disbanded at Halifax,

---

* 38th George III., cap. 13, December 30, 1797.
† 39th George III., cap. 104, July 12, 1799.
‡ 54th George III., cap. 12, December 6, 1813.

Nova Scotia, and drafted into the Second and Third Battalions, and lands were granted to all discharged men to settle on.

February, 1818. The Sixth Battalion was disbanded at Portsmouth, and the men drafted into the Third Battalion at Halifax, Nova Scotia.

July, 1818. The Fifth Battalion was disbanded at the Isle of Wight, and the men drafted into the Second Battalion at Quebec, which was renamed "The Rifle Battalion," whilst the Third Battalion was called "Light Infantry."

April, 1819. The First and Fourth Battalions were disbanded at Portsmouth, and drafted into the Second Battalion at Quebec ; the Second Battalion was again renamed and designated "The First, or the Rifle Battalion;" and the Third, "The Second, or Light Infantry."

Early in 1824 the Regiment was made a "British Corps," and its title changed to "The Duke of York's Own Rifle Corps" and "Light Infantry," and in July of the same year, both battalions were called "Rifle Battalions," and were ordered to be equipped as such.

In October the motto "*Celer et Audax*," granted to the Regiment for distinguished conduct and bravery under General Wolfe, in 1759, which had for some unaccountable reason fallen into disuse, was resumed by authority.

In 1830, the title was again changed to "The 60th, or the King's Royal Rifle Corps."

In 1855, during the Crimean War, a Third Battalion was once more raised in Dublin.

In 1857 the Indian Mutiny having caused the breaking up of the Native Army in the Bengal Presidency, second battalions were added to many of the Line Regiments, and a Fourth Battalion to "The 60th."

In 1827, H.R.H. the Duke of Cambridge was appointed Colonel-in-Chief of the Regiment, in succession to H.R.H. the Duke of York.

In 1850, H.R.H. the Duke of Cambridge died, and Field Marshal H.R.H. Prince Albert, the late Prince Consort, was appointed Colonel-in-Chief.

In 1852, General Viscount Beresford was gazetted Colonel-in-Chief.

In 1854, General Viscount Gough, &c., &c., became Colonel-in-Chief. At his death, in 1869, Field Marshal H.R.H. the Duke of Cambridge, &c., &c., &c., succeeded to the appointment.

ORIGIN OF THE REGIMENTAL MOTTO,
"*CELER ET AUDAX.*"

THE motto, "*Celer et Audax*," was given to the Regiment by General Wolfe for its distinguished bravery at the siege of Quebec, in 1759. It is not, indeed, possible *to produce contemporary evidence of this;* at least, I have failed to find any; but it will be seen that it was treated as a well-known fact by the Authorities at the Horse Guards. From some cause, which it is not easy to conceive of, this motto was either forgotten or disused, at what period I am unable to say. It was resumed on October 14, 1824, when, as the following letter shows, His Majesty George III. was pleased to authorise its being restored and worn on the Appointments of the Regiment :—

" HORSE GUARDS,

" *October* 11, 1824.

" SIR,

" I have the honor to acquaint you, by direction of the Commander-in-Chief, that His Majesty has been pleased to permit the 60th Regiment, 'The Duke of York's Own Rifle Corps,' to resume the motto, '*Celer et Audax*,' which was formerly worn by the Regiment in commemoration of its distinguished bravery whilst employed with the British Army in North America, under Major-General Wolfe, in the year 1759.

" I have the honor, &c.,

(Signed) " J. McDONALD,

" *D.A.G.*

" *To the Officer Commanding*
" 1*st Battalion,* 60*th Rifles.*"

A happier motto for a Rifle Regiment it would be difficult to find, but it is chiefly prized as being so closely connected with the early fortunes of the 60th in North America—a Regiment in whose history occurs the following curious and noteworthy coincidence :—

THE 2ND AND 3RD BATTALIONS OF THE 60TH, AS PART OF THE *first* ENGLISH GARRISON OF QUEBEC, WERE PRESENT IN SEPTEMBER, 1759, WHEN THE BRITISH ENSIGN WAS HOISTED OVER THE CITADEL BY AN OFFICER OF THE ROYAL ARTILLERY ; AND IN NOVEMBER, 1871, ONE HUNDRED AND TWELVE YEARS AFTERWARDS, A DETACHMENT OF THE 1ST BATTALION OF THE 60TH, THE REMNANT OF THE *last* ENGLISH GARRISON OF QUEBEC, CONSIGNED THE IMPERIAL FLAG TO THE KEEPING OF ANOTHER ARTILLERY OFFICER, WHILST THE FLAG OF THE DOMINION OF CANADA WAS HOISTED IN ITS STEAD.

PROBABLE ORIGIN OF THE MALTESE CROSS.

"A CROSS OF EIGHT POINTS OF THE FORM WORN BY HOSPITALLERS (AS A DECORATION) AND OTHER ORDERS OF KNIGHTHOOD."— *Chambers's Encyclopædia*, Vol. vi., page 287, 1874.

IT is difficult to discover the origin of the Maltese Cross as a Regimental Badge, but it probably was first adopted about 1797 when a Fifth Battalion was added to the Regiment composed principally of "Hompesch's Mounted Riflemen." As each battalion successively became a Rifle Battalion it was ordered to be equipped on the model of the Fifth Battalion, and it is therefore natural that they should have adopted the Badge which Hompesch's Battalion had in use at the time of its incorporation with the Fifth Battalion.

This theory is plausibly suggested in "Notes and Queries," July 14, 1870, by the writer, who signs himself H. A. St. J. M., where he says, "I suggest that Hompesch, who was a Bavarian, adopted the badge of the Maltese Cross either from the war medal then given to the Bavarian soldiers, or else because he was a relation of Ferdinand de Hompesch, Knight of Malta, who, in 1797, became grandmaster of the order."

That it was sanctioned as a Regimental Badge is certain, as it was worn by H.R.H. the Duke of York, Colonel-in-Chief of the Regiment, upon his own appointments, which were presented on H.R.H.'s death by His Majesty George IV. to the First Battalion, in whose possession they are still preserved.

Regimental Badge

LIST OF THE SERVICES OF THE
REGIMENT.

LIST OF THE SERVICES OF THE REGIMENT.

1757.

March to April. Five companies, First Battalion, 60th Royal American Regiment of Foot, under Lord Loudoun, were employed in skirmishes with the Indians about **Charlestown** and the back settlements. Five companies, First Battalion, under Colonel Stanwix, were employed in the back woods of Pennsylvania, and also in protecting the Canadian frontier.

May 3. Third Battalion, under Colonel **Webb**, was employed at Fort Hunter and Fort William Henry.

June 20 to August 1. Second and Fourth Battalions under Lord Loudoun, formed part of the force sent from New York and **Halifax** to Louisbourg (Cape Breton).

June 20 to August 1. Part of First Battalion under Colonel Bouquet was employed on an Expedition sent to the borders of South **Carolina**.

July 6. Six companies of *First and Fourth Battalions** formed part of the force sent under General Abercromby and Colonel Bradstreet to the southern frontier of Canada, Crown Point, Ticonderoga.

August 6. Third Battalion was present under Colonel Monro at the Capitulation and Massacre at Fort William Henry.

1758.

June 2. Second and Third Battalions formed part of the force sent under General Amherst, on the Second Expedition against Louisbourg.

July 8. Part of First and Fourth Battalions were present at the Defeat of the English under General Abercromby and Lord Howe at Ticonderoga.

---

* Where the word Battalion is printed in *italics* it signifies that it is not certain that the Battalion mentioned was engaged, though it is most probable.

July 26.   Second and Third Battalions were present at the Capture of Louisbourg by Generals Amherst and Wolfe.

July 27.   *First and Fourth Battalions* were present at the Capture of Fort Frontenac (Kingston), under Colonel Bradstreet.

August 7.   Detachments of Second and Third Battalions formed part of the Expeditions sent by General Amherst under Lieut.-Colonel Lord Rollo and Major Dalling, to reduce Prince Edward's Island.

August 28.   Detachments of Second and Third Battalions formed part of the Expeditions sent under General Wolfe to reduce the French Settlements in the Gulf of St. Lawrence, also of similar Expeditions under Colonel Monckton to the Bay of Fundy and Rivière, St. John's.

September 10.   First Battalion formed part of the force under Colonel Bouquet, a portion of which was defeated by the French, at Loyal Hannon, on the Ohio.

November 25.   Three hundred and fifty of First Battalion were present at the Capture of Fort du Quesne (Pittsburg), by General Forbes.

1759.

May 20.   Fourth Battalion formed part of a force sent under Brigadier-General Prideaux against Fort Niagara.

June 5.   Second and Third Battalions formed part of the force sent on the Expedition under General Wolfe from Louisbourg to Quebec.

July 5.   Fourth Battalion was present at Oswego under Colonel Haldiman when it was attacked by the French under Monsieur Lacome.

July 21.   First Battalion formed part of the force under General Amherst for the Invasion of Canada.

July 26.   First Battalion was present at the Capture of Fort Ticonderoga under General Amherst.

July 25.   Fourth Battalion was present at the Capture of Fort Niagara, under Sir William Johnston.

Fourth Battalion formed part of a force under Colonel Bouquet, sent by General Stanwix against the French posts to the westward.

July 31.   Two hundred of Second Battalion were engaged in the Attack and Repulse at the Montmorenci Falls (Quebec).

September 13.   Second and Third Battalions were engaged in the Battle on the Plains of Abraham, under General Wolfe.

September 17 *and* 18. Second and Third Battalions were present at the Capture of Quebec by Brigadier-General Townshend.

1760.

April 28. **First,** Second, and Third Battalions took part in the Second Battle on the Plains of Abraham, under General Murray.

May 16. First, Second, and Third Battalions composed part of the garrison at the Siege of Quebec by the French.

June 14. The Grenadiers of the Second and Third Battalions formed part of the force sent under General **Murray from Quebec,** to attack Montreal.

August 7. First and Fourth Battalions formed part of the force sent under Colonel Haldimand **and** General Amherst, **to** attack Montreal.

August 25. First Battalion was engaged at the **Capture of Fort** Isle Royale by General Amherst.

September 6. First and Fourth Battalions were present **at the** Siege of Montreal under **General** Amherst.

September **8. The** Grenadiers of Second **and** Third Battalions and the First and Fourth Battalions **were present at** the Capture **of** Montreal by General Amherst.

1761.

September. **Part** *of* **First** *Battalion* was employed on various expeditions against the Indians in Virginia.

1762.

January 7 *to February* 13. Third Battalion formed part of the force at the Capture of the Citadel of Fort Royal, Martinique, and at the Capture of the Island of Martinique, under General Monckton and Brigadier-General **Lord Rollo.**

August 13. Third Battalion was present at the Capture of Havannah, under the Earl of Albemarle.

1763.

First Battalion was employed in various skirmishes in the back woods near Forts Littleton, Bedford, and Pittsburg.

August 5. Part of First Battalion was engaged in the Action of Bushy Run, under Colonel Bouquet.

1764 to 1767.

Second Battalion was employed in various skirmishes in the back woods, under Colonel Bouquet.

1764.

August to November. First Battalion composed part of the garrison at Detroit, which was defended by Major Gladwin (80th Light Infantry).

1776.

First Battalion was engaged in quelling a rebellion in Jamaica.

1778.

November 27 to January 9, 1779. Part of Fourth Battalion was with the Expedition to Georgia, under Major-General Prevost, and was present at the Siege and Capture of Fort Sunbury, under Colonel Archibald Campbell, and together with Third Battalion was engaged in various skirmishes and affairs of outposts in Florida.

1779.

March 3. Three Grenadier Companies, Fourth Battalion, under Colonel Prevost, were engaged at Briar's Creek, Hudson Ferry.

June 18. Second Battalion formed part of the garrison at the Recapture of the Island of St. Vincent by the French, under Count D'Estaing.

September 16 to October 18. Part of Fourth Battalion was present under Major-General Prevost, at the Siege of Savannah, by Count D'Estaing and General Lincoln.

1780.

Four companies, Fourth Battalion, formed part of a force under Major-General Campbell and Captain Durnford, and were present at the Siege of Fort Mobile and Defence of Baton Rouge against Brigadier-General Galvez.

April 24 to 29. First Battalion was present at the Capture of Look-out Island and of Fort St. Juan, Nicaragua, under Colonel Polson.

August 15. Part of Second Battalion was in Carolina and Georgia under Lieut.-General the Earl of Cornwallis, and in West Florida under Major-General Campbell.

1781.

April 17. Part of Second and Third Battalions were engaged in a Skirmish at Hobkirks Hill, under Lord Rawdon, when he defeated the American General Green.

May 10. Part of Third Battalion, under Major-General Campbell, was present at the Capture of Fort George, West Florida, by the Spaniards under Brigadier-General Galvez.

January 31 *to October* 10. *Part of Second* **Battalion** formed **portion** of the force sent under the Earl of **Cornwallis to Carolina** and Georgia, and was present at the **Battle of Guildford, Capture** of New London, **Fort** Griswold, and Surrender of **York Town to** General Washington.

1784.

July. Light Company, Second Battalion, was sent from **Grenada to** St. Vincent to check a Carib insurrection.

1792.

June. Two companies, Third Battalion, were sent **from Antigua to Tortola to check a negro** insurrection.

1793.

Nine companies, **Fourth** Battalion, formed **part of** a force sent under General **Cuyler against the Island** of Tobago (Fort Castries).

1794.

March 15 *to* 23. *Part of First, Second,* Third, and Fourth Battalions were **present** at the Capture of the Island of Martinique by Lieut.-General Sir Charles Grey.

April 4. **Third** Battalion was present at the Capture of St. Lucia **under** Major-General Sir **Ralph** Abercromby. A detachment of Lowenstein's **Chasseurs** (afterwards drafted into the Fifth **Battalion**) **was present at the** Capture of St. Lucia.

April 10. A detachment of the regiment was engaged in quelling a Carib insurrection in Grenada.

April 21. Part of Fourth Battalion was present at the Capture of Guadaloupe by Lieut.-General Sir Charles Grey and Major-General Dundas.

October 14 *to December* 10. Two companies, Fourth Battalion, formed part of the garrison at the Siege of Fort Matilda, Guadaloupe.

1796.

June 10. Detachment of Lowenstein's Chasseurs afterwards drafted into Fifth Battalion) formed part of the force under Major-General Sir Ralph Abercromby, which defeated the Caribs at the Vigie, a stronghold in the Island of Grenada.

1797.

February 12. Four companies, Third Battalion, and a detachment Lowenstein's Chasseurs (afterwards drafted into Fifth Battalion) formed part of the force sent from Tobago against Trinidad.

May 2. Four companies, Third Battalion, and a detachment Lowenstein's Chasseurs (afterwards drafted into Fifth Battalion) were engaged in the Attack on Porto Rico, under Major-General Sir Ralph Abercromby.

1798.

June 21. Fifth Battalion served during the Rebellion in Ireland at Goff's Bridge, Wicklow, Vinegar Hill, and Enniscorthy, under General Sir J. Moore.

1799.

August 20 *to* 23. Four hundred of Fifth Battalion were employed at the Reduction of Surinam, under Lieut.-General Trigge.

October 2. The Rifle Company Sixth Battalion took part in the Battle of Bergen under H.R.H. the Duke of York.

1804.

April 30. The Rifle Company, Second Battalion, was present at the Capture of Surinam under Brigadier-General Hughes.

1807.

December 21. Third Battalion was present at the Capture of the Danish Isles, under Lieut.-Colonel Elliot.

1808.

June 15. Fifth or Rifle Battalion, formed part of the Expedition sent, under General Sir Arthur Wellesley, to Portugal and was present at the opening skirmish.

August 15. At Obidos.

August 16. Action of Lorinda.

August 17. Battle of Roliça.

August 21. Battle of Vimiera.

1809.

January 16. Second and Fifth Battalions formed part of the force sent under General Sir John Moore to Spain, and were present, *in reserve*, at the Battle of Corunna

February 8. Part of the **Third Battalion** was present at the Surrender of Fort Dessaix, Martinique, to Lieut.-Colonel Mackie.

April 12. The Rifle Companies, Third **and** Fourth Battalions, composed part of the force under General Maitland at the Capture of the Islands of Les Saintes, near Guadaloupe.

May 12. Fifth Battalion was engaged in **Passage of Douro** and Capture of Oporto.

July **27** and 28. **Battle** of Talavera.

1810.

January and February. Grenadier Companies, Second and Fourth Battalions, were engaged in the Capture of Guadaloupe, under General Sir G. Beckwith, K.B.

September 27. Fifth Battalion was engaged in the Battle of Busaco.

1811.

March 14. Skirmish at Pombol.

March 15. Action of Casal Nova.

April 15. One company at Surrender of **Olivenza to** Marshal Beresford.

May 3. Skirmish at Fuentes d'Onor.

May 5. Battle of Fuentes d'Onor.

May 10. Repulse of sortie at Badajos.

May 16. Battle of Albuera.

May 19. Third Battalion was employed in quelling a rebellion at St. Pierre, Martinique.

September 25. Fifth Battalion was engaged in the Combat at El Bodon.

September 27. Skirmish at Aldea de Ponte.

October 28. Action of Arroyo del Molino.

1812.

January 10 *to February.* Siege and Assault of Ciudad Rodrigo.

March 18 *to April* 7. Three companies at the Siege, Escalading, and Capture of the Castle of Badajos.

May 19. Action of Almarez.

June 18 *to* 24. The Siege of Forts St. Cayetano, San Vincente, La Merced, Salamanca.

July 18. Skirmish at Castragon.

July 22. Battle of Salamanca.

September 19.   Capture of Fort St. Michael, near Burgos.

September 27 to October 21.   Siege and Assault of the Castle of Burgos.

November 10.   Skirmish at Alba de Tormes.

November 11.   A detachment, Second Battalion, was sent on an Expedition, under Lieut. Adair, from Barbadoes to the coast of Demerara.

1813.

June 21.   Fifth Battalion was engaged in Battle of Vittoria.

July 25 to 31.   Battles of the Pyrenees.

October 7 and 8.   Passage of the Bidassoa, and Forcing of the French lines.

November 10.   Battle of Nivelle.

November 13.   Battle of St. Jean-de-Luz.

December 9 to 13.   Battle of Nive.

1814.

February 23.   Passage of the Adour.

February 27.   Battle of Orthes.

April 10.   Battle of Toulouse.

April 14.   Repulse of Sortie from Bayonne.

August 24.   Two companies, Seventh Battalion, were employed in the Expedition to the Penobscot River, State of Maine, under General Sherbrooke.

1816.

The Second Battalion was engaged in quelling riots in Barbadoes.

1826.

December 18.   First Battalion of 60th, or The Duke of York's Own Rifle Corps, formed part of the force sent under General Sir Edward Blakeney to Portugal.

1842.

July.   First Battalion was employed in quelling the riots in Lancashire.

1846.

March 24.   First Battalion was sent with the force under Colonel the Hon. H. Dundas, C.B., to Scinde.

1848.

October 7.   First Battalion, 60th, or The King's Royal Rifle Corps, was employed with the Bombay Column in the Punjaub

Campaign, under Colonel the Hon. Henry Dundas, C.B., 60th **Rifles**, which crossed (*December* 14) **the Sutlej at Pholadpore, took part in** the Siege of Mooltan (*December* 27 *to January* 22, 1849), and was present **at—**

1849.

January 22. **The Capture of Mooltan, under Major-General** Whish.

February 21. Battle of Goojerat, under Lord Gough.

February 22. With the column under **Sir** Walter **Gilbert,** K.C.B., which crossed the Jhelum to Hoor Munck, **Rawul Pindee,** Attock, and Peshawur, to the Khyber Pass.

December 3. Formed part of the force **under** Lieut.-Colonel Bradshaw, 60th Rifles, against the insurgent **tribes** in Barrydurrah, Luggoo, and Pallee, in the Euzuffzie Country, and was present **at—**

December 11. Capture of town of Luggoo.

December 14. Capture of Pallee Zoormundie **and** Thear **Khana.**

1850.

February 10 *to* 13. Formed part of the force under Brigadier-**General Sir Colin** Campbell, K.C.B., sent against the Affreedees **to the Kohat Pass, under Colonel Bradshaw,** C.B.

1851.

October. Second Battalion was employed in the Kaffir War of 1851 to 1853, under Generals Sir H. Smith and Honourable Sir George Cathcart, and was present at the Attack on the Kroomee Heights, and in various skirmishes in the Amatola Mountains.

October 29 *to January* 12, 1852. Three companies joined part of the force sent to the Kei and Bashee River, and were present at Passage of the Great Kei, under Lieut.-Colonel Eyre, 73rd Regiment.

At the same time Head-quarters were engaged in operations in Kreli's territory.

1852.

Second Battalion was employed in scouring the Water Kloof and Attack on the Iron Mountain.

1857.

May 10 *to* 31. First Battalion was present at the outbreak of the Indian Mutiny at Meerut, and was engaged in Action of the Hindun under Brigadier-General Wilson.

c

June 8. Battle of Badlee-ka-Serai, and Capture of Heights before Delhi, under General Barnard.

September 14 *to* 20. Siege, Assault, and Capture of Delhi, under Brigadier-General Wilson.

A wing of Second Battalion, under Major Butler, 60th Rifles, was engaged in watching the Fords of the Ganges near Aligurh.

1858.

April 14. First Battalion, under Brigadier-General Sir John Jones, K.C.B., was employed in the Rohilcund Campaign, and was present at—

April 17. Action of Bagawallah.

April 18. Capture of Nugeelabad.

April 21. Action of Nugena. Relief of Moradabad. Relief of Dojura.

May 6. Capture of Bareilly, with Flying Column, under Brigadier Sir John Jones, K.C.B.

May 11. Relief of Shahjehanpore.

May 24. Capture of Forts Bunnai and Mahomdee.

May 31. Capture of Shahabad, under Brigadier-General Taylor.

June 18. Right wing of Second Battalion was employed under Colonel Walter, 35th Regiment, in the Arrah District, and formed part of the field force patrolling the Jugdespoor jungles.

October 8. First Battalion formed part of the force sent under Brigadier-General Sir Thomas Seaton, and was engaged in the Action of Bunk-ka-Gong.

October 18. First Battalion formed part of the Oude field force under Brigadier-General Troup, and was present at—

October 19. Action of Pusgaon.

October 25. Action of Rissoolpore.

November 7. Capture of Fort Mittowlee.

November 26. Action of Dumeriagunge.

December 1. Action of Mehundee.

December 1. Action of Biswah.

December 25. Action of Toolsepore.

December 25. Formed part of the force under Colonel N. G Dennis, 60th Rifles, to the Kyreeghur Jungles.

1860.

February 28. **Second Battalion formed part of the force** under General Sir Hope Grant, sent to China, and **was present at—**

August 2. **Capture of** Peh-Tang.

August 13. Capture of Tang-Ku.

August 21. Capture of Taku Forts.

September **13.** Capture **of** Pekin.

1865.

First and Second Battalions were present **in Ireland during the Fenian disturbances.**

1870.

May 20 *to October* 12. **First** Battalion **formed** the main portion of the force sent, under Colonel Wolseley (Staff), on the Red River Expedition, to Fort Garry, in Upper Canada.

1878.

October. Second Battalion under orders to form part of the Afghan Expeditionary Force sent from Mooltan to Afghan.

NOTE.—Great difficulty has been experienced in tracing all the changes of quarters, owing to the numerous moves and detachments of the Regiment during its early service in America and the West Indies.

The following table is, however, believed to be correct.

In many instances where moves have been frequent and for short periods, only the head-quarters and principal stations have been named.

In *all* cases the stations have been verified by Regimental Records, Army Lists, and other Official Sources.

The Isle of Wight has been entered as the Regimental Depôt for all the Battalions from 1763 to 1824, as I have been unable to trace it to any other place; and as nearly all the Battalions were *raised*, *recruited*, and *disbanded* there, it is but reasonable to suppose that it was the Depôt during that period.

Before 1763 the Depôt was probably at Albany or New York.

N. W. W.

LIST SHOWING THE NUMBER OF BATTALIONS AND THEIR SEVERAL STATIONS FROM 1756 TO 1878.

THE 62ND, OR THE ROYAL AMERI-CAN REGIMENT OF FOOT.

1756.
Four Battalions.

1st. **2nd.** **3rd.** **4th.** New York, Albany, and Philadel-phia. Employed on different Ex-peditions to Forts Pitt, Lancaster, and William Henry, and on the Lakes.

Depôts—Albany and New York.

1757.
THE 60TH, OR THE ROYAL AMERI-CAN REGIMENT OF FOOT.
Four Battalions.

1st. New York, Charleston Expedition, Lancaster, Philadelphia.
2nd. New York, Halifax, Expedition to Louisbourg, Philadelphia.
3rd. Albany, Forts William Henry, Hun-ter, and Edward's.
4th. New York, Halifax, Expedition to Louisbourg, Expedition to Crown Point, Ticonderoga.

Depôts—America.

1758.
Four Battalions.

1st. Charleston, Philadelphia, Ticon-deroga, Pittsburg, New York, Niagara, Detroit, Frontenac, and Albany.
2nd. Halifax, Louisbourg, Expedition to Bay of Fundy.
3rd. Albany, New York, Boston, Halifax, and Louisbourg.
4th. Expedition to Ticonderoga and Fort Niagara, Crown Point, Frontenac, Albany.

Depôts—America.

1759.
Four Battalions.

1st. Albany, Niagara, Pittsburg, Ticon-deroga.
2nd. Louisbourg, Camp at Orleans Island, and Quebec.
3rd. Louisbourg, Camp at Orleans Island, and Quebec.
4th. Oswego, Niagara, and detachments.

Depôts—America.

1760.
Four Battalions.

1st. Pittsburg, Quebec; 4 Companies at Carlisle, Forts Bedford, Ligonier, and Niagara; 5 Companies at Montreal, and detachments.
2nd. Quebec.
3rd. Quebec.
4th. Oswego, Fort **Ontario, and detach-**ment at Montreal.

Depôts—America.

1761.
Four Battalions.

1st. 5 Companies at Pittsburg, Carlisle, Forts Bedford, Ligonier, and Niagara; 5 Companies at Montreal, and detach-ments.
2nd. Quebec and Pittsburg.
3rd. Quebec, New York, Barbadoes.
4th. Montreal, and detachments.

Depôts—America.

1762.
Four Battalions.

1st. Pittsburg, detachments on the Ohio, Philadelphia, and on Lakes Michigan, and Superior.
2nd. Quebec and Pittsburg.
3rd. Barbadoes, Martinique, Havannah, Pensacola.
4th. Montreal, and detachments.

Depôts—America.

1763.
Four Battalions.

1st. Pittsburg, Forts Littleton, Bedford, Presq'ile, and Niagara.
2nd. Quebec, Detroit, Pittsburg, Niagara, New York, and detachments.
3rd. Pensacola, and New York.
4th. Montreal, and detachments. D.

Depôts—Isle of Wight.

1764.
Three Battalions.

1st. Fort Pitt, New York, Expedition to the Lakes to Forts Ontario, Lancaster, and to Detroit, and detachments.
2nd. Quebec, and detachments.
3rd. New York. D.

Depôts—Isle of Wight.

NOTE.—D. opposite the number of a Battalion shows it was disbanded.

1765.
Two Battalions.
1st. Pittsburg, Fort Stanwix, Fort George, Albany, New York.
2nd. Quebec, Montreal, New York.
Depôt—Isle of Wight.

1766.
Two Battalions.
1st. New York, Quebec, Jamaica.
2nd. New York, and detachments.
Depôt—Isle of Wight.

1767.
Two Battalions.
1st. Jamaica, 3 Companies in South Carolina.
2nd. New York, Niagara, and detachments.
Depôt—Isle of Wight.

1768.
Two Battalions.
1st. Jamaica.
2nd. New York, Niagara, and detachments.
Depôt—Isle of Wight.

1769.
Two Battalions.
1st. Jamaica.
2nd. New York, Niagara, and detachments.
Depôt—Isle of Wight.

1770.
Two Battalions.
1st. Jamaica.
2nd. New York, Niagara, and detachments.
Depôt—Isle of Wight.

1771.
Two Battalions.
1st. Jamaica.
2nd. New York, Niagara, and detachments.
Depôt—Isle of Wight.

1772.
Two Battalions.
1st. Jamaica, New York.
2nd. New York, 6 Companies to St. Vincent, 4 to Antigua.
Depôt—Isle of Wight.

1773.
Two Battalions.
1st. Jamaica.
2nd. 6 Companies St. Vincent, 4 Antigua.
Depôt—Isle of Wight.

1774.
Two Battalions.
1st. Jamaica.
2nd. 6 Companies St. Vincent, 4 Antigua.
Depôt—Isle of Wight.

1775.
Four Battalions.
1st. Jamaica, Pensacola.
2nd. 6 Companies St. Vincent, 4 Antigua.
3rd and 4th. Raised this year in England, probably in Isle of Wight.
Depôt—Isle of Wight.

1776.
Four Battalions.
1st. Jamaica, 3 Companies South Carolina, Georgia.
2nd. St. Vincent, Antigua, St. Augustin, Isle of Wight.
3rd. Isle of Wight, Pensacola, St. Augustin, Jamaica.
4th. Isle of Wight, St. Augustin.
Depôt—Isle of Wight.

1777.
Four Battalions.
1st. Jamaica.
2nd. St. Vincent, Antigua, St. Augustin.
3rd. Pensacola, St. Augustin, Jamaica.
4th. St. Augustin.
Depôt—Isle of Wight.

1778.
Four Battalions.
1st. Jamaica.
2nd. St. Vincent, Antigua, St. Augustin.
3rd. Jamaica, Charleston.
4th. St. Augustin, Georgia.
Depôt—Isle of Wight.

1779.
Four Battalions.
1st. Jamaica.
2nd. St. Vincent, Antigua, St. Augustin, Georgia.
3rd. Charleston.
4th. St. Augustin, Georgia.
Depôt—Isle of Wight.

1780.
Four Battalions.
1st. Jamaica, Expedition to Nicaragua.
2nd. Antigua, St. Augustin, Georgia.
3rd. St. Augustin, New York.
4th. St. Augustin, Charleston, New York.
Depôt—Isle of Wight.

1781.
Four Battalions.
1st. Jamaica.
2nd. Barbadoes, St. Augustin, Georgia.
3rd. West Florida, New York.
4th. New York.
Depôt—Isle of Wight.

1782.
Four Battalions.
1st. Jamaica.
2nd. Barbadoes, St. Augustin.
3rd. New York.
4th. New York.
Depôt—Isle of Wight.

1783.
Four Battalions.
1st. Jamaica.
2nd. Barbadoes, St. Augustin, Grenada.
3rd. New York, Halifax. D.
4th. New York, Halifax. D.
Depôt—Isle of Wight.

1784.
Two Battalions.
1st. Jamaica.
2nd. Barbadoes, St. Augustin, Grenada,
St. Vincent.
Depôt—Isle of Wight.

1785.
Two Battalions.
1st. Jamaica.
2nd. Grenada, St. Vincent.
Depôt—Isle of Wight.

1786.
Two Battalions.
1st. Jamaica, Halifax.
2nd. Grenada.
Depôt—Isle of Wight.

1787.
Four Battalions.
1st. Halifax, Quebec, Niagara, Newfoundland.
2nd. Grenada, Montreal.
3rd and 4th. Raised this year at Chatham, England.
Depôt—Isle of Wight.

1788.
Four Battalions.
1st. Niagara, Montreal, Detroit, and detachments.
2nd. Detroit.
3rd. Chatham ; 4 Companies, and Head-quarters, Barbadoes ; 4 Companies at Dominica ; 2 Companies at Montserrat.
4th. Chatham, Barbadoes.
Depôt—Isle of Wight.

1789.
Four Battalions.
1st. Niagara.
2nd. Detroit, Montreal, Niagara.
3rd. Head-quarters and 4 Companies Barbadoes ; 4 Companies Dominica ; 2 at Montserrat.
4th. Barbadoes.
Depôt—Isle of Wight.

1790.
Four Battalions.
1st. Niagara, Montreal.
2nd. Detroit, Montreal, Niagara.
3rd. Barbadoes, Dominica, Montserrat, Antigua.
4th. Barbadoes.
Depôt—Isle of Wight.

1791.
Four Battalions.
1st. Montreal, and detachments.
2nd. Detroit, Montreal, Niagara.
3rd. Antigua.
4th. Barbadoes, Tobago.
Depôt—Isle of Wight.

1792.
Four Battalions.
1st. Montreal, and detachments.
2nd. Detroit, Montreal, Niagara.
3rd. Antigua, Tortola.
4th. Barbadoes, Tobago.
Depôt—Isle of Wight.

1793.
Four Battalions.
1st. Montreal, and detachments.
2nd. Detroit, Montreal, Niagara, Quebec.
3rd. Antigua, Tobago, Guernsey.
4th. Barbadoes, Tobago.
Depôt—Isle of Wight.

1794.
Four Battalions.
1st. Montreal, and detachments.
2nd. Detroit, Montreal, Niagara.
3rd. Guernsey.
4th. Tobago, Guadaloupe.
Depôt—Isle of Wight.

1795.
Four Battalions.
1st. Montreal.
2nd. Detroit, Montreal, Niagara.
3rd. Guernsey, Barbadoes, St. Vincent.
4th. Tobago.
Depôt—Isle of Wight.

1796.
Four Battalions.
1st. Montreal.
2nd. Quebec.
3rd. St. Vincent, Tobago.
4th. Tobago, Lymington, Guernsey.
Depôt—Isle of Wight.

1797.
Five Battalions.
1st. Montreal, Guernsey.
2nd. Quebec.
3rd. Tobago, Trinidad, Porto Rico.
4th. Guernsey, Grenada, Jamaica, Tobago, Martinique.
5th. Raised this year at Cowes.
Depôt—Isle of Wight.

1798.
Five Battalions.
1st. Guernsey.
2nd. Quebec.
3rd. Tobago.
4th. Martinique, St. Domingo.
5th. Cowes, God's Bridge, Clonmel.
Depôt—Isle of Wight.

1799.
Six Battalions.
1st. Guernsey, Barbadoes.
2nd. Quebec, Montreal.
3rd. Tobago.
4th. Martinique.
5th. Clonmel, Cork, Martinique, Surinam.
6th. Raised this year in Isle of Wight, 2 Companies in Holland.
Depôt—Isle of Wight.

1800.
Six Battalions.
1st. Barbadoes, Jamaica.
2nd. Quebec, Barbadoes.
3rd. Tobago.
4th. Martinique.
5th. Surinam.
6th. Cowes, Jamaica.
Depôt—Isle of Wight.

1801.
Six Battalions.
1st. Jamaica.
2nd. Barbadoes.
3rd. Tobago.
4th. Martinique.
5th. Surinam.
6th. Jamaica.
Depôt—Isle of Wight.

1802.
Six Battalions.
1st. Jamaica.
2nd. Barbadoes, Tobago.
3rd. Tobago, Grenada.
4th. Martinique, Jamaica.
5th. Surinam.
6th. Jamaica.
Depôt—Isle of Wight.

1803.
Six Battalions.
1st. Jamaica.
2nd. Barbadoes, Tobago, St. Vincent.
3rd. Tobago, Grenada, Antigua.
4th. Jamaica.
5th. Surinam, Halifax.
6th. Jamaica.
Depôt—Isle of Wight.

1804.
Six Battalions.
1st. Jamaica.
2nd. St. Vincent, Surinam.
3rd. Grenada.
4th. Jamaica.
5th. Halifax.
6th. Jamaica.
Depôt—Isle of Wight.

1805.
Six Battalions.
1st. Jamaica.
2nd. St. Vincent.
3rd. Grenada.
4th. Lymington.
5th. Halifax, Portsmouth.
6th. Jamaica.
Depôt—Isle of Wight.

1806.
Six Battalions.
1st. Jamaica.
2nd. St. Vincent.
3rd. Grenada, Portsmouth, Guernsey.
4th. Lymington, Cape of Good Hope.
5th. Portsmouth.
6th. Jamaica.
Depôt—Isle of Wight.

1807.
Six Battalions.
1st. Jamaica.
2nd. St. Vincent, Jersey.
3rd. Guernsey, Barbadoes, Danish Isles.
4th. Cape Town, and detachments.
5th. Portsmouth, Cork.
6th. Jamaica.
Depôt—Isle of Wight.

1808.
Six Battalions.
1st. Jamaica, Spain, Portugal.
2nd. Jersey.
3rd. Barbadoes.
4th. Cape of Good Hope, Barbadoes.
5th. Cork, Portugal, Spain.
6th. Jamaica, and detachments.
Depôt—Isle of Wight.

1809.
Six Battalions.
1st. Jamaica, Maroontown, Savannah.
2nd. Corunna, Guernsey, Barbadoes.
3rd. Antigua, Martinique, Les Saintes.
4th. Barbadoes, Martinique, Les Saintes.
5th. Corunna, and detachments in Spain.
6th. Jamaica.
Depôt—Isle of Wight.

1810.
Six Battalions.
1st. Jamaica, Guadaloupe, Cowes.
2nd. Barbadoes, Guadaloupe.
3rd. Martinique, Guadaloupe.
4th. Martinique, Guadaloupe, Dominica, Antigua, Lymington.
5th. Spain, and detachments.
6th. Jamaica.
Depôt—Isle of Wight.

1811.
Six Battalions.
1st. Cowes, Cape of Good Hope.
2nd. Barbadoes.
3rd. Martinique, Guadaloupe.
4th. Lymington.
5th. Spain, and detachments.
6th. Jamaica.
Depôt—Isle of Wight.

1812.
Six Battalions.
1st. Cape of Good Hope.
2nd. Barbadoes.
3rd. Martinique, Guadaloupe.
4th. Lymington, Dominica.
5th. Spain, and detachments.
6th. Jamaica.
Depôt—Isle of Wight.

1813.
Eight Battalions.
1st. Cape of Good Hope.
2nd. Barbadoes.
3rd. Martinique, Guadaloupe.
4th. Dominica.

5th. Spain and France.
6th. Jamaica.
7th and 8th. Raised this year; 7th at Guernsey, 8th at Lisbon.
Depôt—Isle of Wight.

1814.
Eight Battalions.
1st. Cape of Good Hope.
2nd. Barbadoes.
3rd. Martinique, Guadaloupe.
4th. Dominica.
5th. France, Cork.
6th. Jamaica.
7th. Guernsey, Halifax, Expedition to Penobscot.
8th. Lisbon, Gibraltar.
Depôt—Isle of Wight.

1815.
Eight Battalions.
1st. Cape of Good Hope.
2nd. Barbadoes.
3rd. Martinique, Guadaloupe, Dominica, St. Lucia.
4th. Dominica.
5th. Cork, Buttevant.
6th. Jamaica.
7th. Halifax, Annapolis.
8th. Gibraltar.
Depôt—Isle of Wight.

1816.
Eight Battalions.
1st. Cape of Good Hope.
2nd. Barbadoes.
3rd. Dominica, St. Lucia, Halifax, Annapolis, Prince Edward's Island.
4th. Demerara.
5th. Buttevant, Cowes, Gibraltar.
6th. Jamaica.
7th. Halifax.
8th. Gibraltar. D.
Depôt—Isle of Wight.

1817.
Seven Battalions.
1st. Cape of Good Hope.
2nd. Barbadoes, Halifax, Quebec.
3rd. Halifax.
4th. Demerara.
5th. Gibraltar.
6th. Jamaica, Portsmouth.
7th. Halifax, N.S. D.
Depôt—Isle of Wight.

1818.
Six Battalions.
1st. Cape of Good Hope.
2nd. RIFLE BATTALION, Quebec, and detachments.
3rd. LIGHT INFANTRY, Halifax.
4th. Demerara.
5th. Gibraltar, Isle of Wight. D.
6th. Portsmouth. D.
Depôt—Isle of Wight

1819.
Four Battalions.
1st. Cape of Good Hope, Demerara, Portsmouth. D.
2nd. RIFLE BATTALION, Quebec.
3rd. LIGHT INFANTRY, Halifax.
4th. Demerara, Portsmouth. D.
Depôt—Isle of Wight.

1820.
Two Battalions.
1st. RIFLE BATTALION, 5 Companies at Quebec, 3 at Isle aux Noix.
2nd. LIGHT INFANTRY, Halifax, Annapolis.
Depôt—Isle of Wight.

1821.
Two Battalions.
1st. Montreal, and detachments.
2nd. Right wing Annapolis, Left wing Bermuda.
Depôt—Isle of Wight.

1822.
Two Battalions.
1st. Montreal, and detachments.
2nd. Right wing Halifax, Left wing Bermuda.
Depôt—Isle of Wight.

1823.
Two Battalions.
1st. Kingston, Ontario.
2nd. Right wing, Halifax and Newfoundland; Left wing, Bermuda.
Depôt—Isle of Wight.

1824.
THE 60TH, OR THE DUKE OF YORK'S OWN RIFLE CORPS AND LIGHT INFANTRY.
Two Battalions.
1st. Kingston, Quebec, Chatham (England), Canterbury.
2nd. Right wing, Newfoundland, Barbadoes, and Demerara; Left wing, Bermuda and Demerara.
Depôts—1st, Chatham; 2nd, Isle of Wight.

1825.
Two Battalions.
1st. RIFLE BATTALION, Canterbury, Chatham, Weedon, Manchester.
2nd. RIFLE BATTALION, Right wing, Barbadoes, Berbice; Left wing, Demerara.
Depôt—Isle of Wight.

1826.
Two Battalions.
1st. Manchester, and detachments, Plymouth.
2nd. Right wing, Barbadoes, Berbice; Left wing, Demerara.
Depôt—2nd, Isle of Wight

1827.
Two Battalions.

1st. Lisbon.
2nd. Right wing, Barbadoes, Berbice; Left wing, Demerara.
Depôts—1st, Plymouth; 2nd, Isle of Wight.

1828.
Two Battalions.

1st. Lisbon, Fermoy, Limerick, and detachments.
2nd. Right wing, Berbice; Left wing, Demerara.
Depôts—1st, Plymouth; 2nd, Isle of Wight.

1829.
Two Battalions.

1st. Limerick, and detachments.
2nd. Right wing, Berbice; Left wing, Demerara. } Isle of Wight.
Depôt—2nd, Isle of Wight.

1830.
Two Battalions.

1st. Limerick, Cork, Gibraltar.
2nd. Isle of Wight, Weedon, Manchester.
Depôt—1st, Portsmouth.

1831.
THE 60TH, OR THE KING'S ROYAL RIFLE CORPS.
Two Battalions.

1st. Gibraltar.
2nd. Manchester, Dublin, and detachments.
Depôt—1st, Portsmouth.

1832.
Two Battalions.

1st. Gibraltar.
2nd. Naas, Templemore, and detachments.
Depôt—1st, Portsmouth.

1833.
Two Battalions.

1st. Gibraltar.
2nd. Naas, Templemore, Dublin.
Depôt—1st, Portsmouth.

1834.
Two Battalions.

1st. Gibraltar, Malta.
2nd. Mullingar, Kilkenny, and detachments.
Depôt—1st, Portsmouth.

1835.
Two Battalions.

1st. Malta.
2nd. Kilkenny, Buttevant, Cork, Gibraltar.
Depôt—1st, Stockport.

1836.
Two Battalions.

1st. Malta, Corfu, Vido.
2nd. Gibraltar.
Depôts—1st, Newcastle; 2nd, Jersey.

1837.
Two Battalions.

1st. Vido, Corfu.
2nd. Gibraltar, Corfu, Vido.
Depôts—1st, Sunderland; 2nd, Jersey.

1838.
Two Battalions.

1st. Corfu, Zante, Vido, and detachments.
2nd. Vido, Corfu.
Depôts—1st, Hull; 2nd, Jersey.

1839.
Two Battalions.

1st. Vido, Zante, and detachments.
2nd. Corfu.
Depôts—1st, Hull; 2nd, Jersey.

1840.
Two Battalions.

1st. Zante, Woolwich, Windsor.
2nd. Corfu.
Depôt—2nd, Clonmel.

1841.
Two Battalions.

1st. Windsor, Bolton, and detachments.
2nd. Corfu, Jamaica.
Depôt—2nd, Naas.

1842.
Two Battalions.

1st. Bolton, Manchester, and detachments.
2nd. Jamaica.
Depôt—2nd, Dublin.

1843.
Two Battalions.

1st. Manchester, Naas, and Dublin.
2nd. Jamaica.
Depôt—2nd, Newry.

1844.
Two Battalions.

1st. Dublin, Kilkenny, Waterford detachment, Fermoy.
2nd. Jamaica, Quebec.
Depôt—2nd, Belturbet.

1845.
Two Battalions.

1st. Fermoy, and detachments, Poonah.
2nd. Quebec, St. John, Lacrosse.
Depôts—1st, Chatham; 2nd, Dundee.

1846.
Two Battalions.

1st. Poonah, Kurrachee, Scinde.
2nd. St. John, Montreal, Halifax, N.S.
Depôts—1st, Chatham; 2nd, Paisley.

1847.
Two Battalions.
1st. Kurrachee.
2nd. Halifax, Portsmouth, Chichester, and detachments.
Depôt—1st, Chatham.

1848.
Two Battalions.
1st. Kurrachee, Punjaub.
2nd. Preston, Bolton, Manchester, Bury, Dublin, Kilkenny.
Depôt—1st, Chatham.

1849.
Two Battalions.
1st. Punjaub.
2nd. Dublin, Kilkenny, and detachments.
Depôt—1st, Chatham.

1850.
Two Battalions.
1st. Peshawur, Kussowlie.
2nd. Dublin, Templemore, and detachments.
Depôt—1st, Chatham.

1851.
Two Battalions.
1st. Kussowlie, Subattoo.
2nd. Templemore, Kilkenny, and detachments, Cork, British Kaffraria.
Depôts—1st, Chatham ; 2nd, Naas.

1852.
Two Battalions.
1st. Jullundur.
2nd. British Kaffraria.
Depôts—1st, Chatham ; 2nd, Naas.

1853.
Two Battalions.
1st. Jullundur.
2nd. British Kaffraria, King William's Town, and detachments.
Depôts—1st, Chatham ; 2nd, Birr.

1854.
Two Battalions.
1st. Jullundur.
2nd. King William's Town and detachments.
Depôts—1st, Chatham ; 2nd, Limerick.

1855.
Three Battalions.
1st. Jullundur, Meerut.
2nd. King William's Town, and detachments.
3rd. Raised this year at Dublin.
Depôts—1st, Chatham ; 2nd, Dublin.

1856.
Three Battalions.
1st. Meerut.
2nd. King William's Town, and detachments.
3rd. Curragh, Dublin.
Depôts—1st, Chatham ; 2nd, Athlone, Sligo, Curragh, Jersey.

1857.
Four Battalions.
1st. Meerut, Delhi.
2nd. King William's Town, and detachments.
3rd. Dublin, Madras, Bangalore, and detachments.
4th. Raised this year at Winchester.
Depôts—1st, Chatham ; 2nd, Jersey, Winchester ; 3rd, Jersey, Chatham.

1858.
Four Battalions.
1st. Delhi, Meerut, Rohilcund, Oude.
2nd. King William's Town, Armh.
3rd. Bangalore, Mysore, Bellary.
4th. Winchester, Dover.
Depôts—1st and 3rd, Colchester ; 2nd and 4th, Winchester.

1859.
Four Battalions.
1st. Benares, Allahabad, Dumdum, Calcutta.
2nd. Right wing, Benares ; Left wing, Armh.
3rd. Bangalore, Jackatalla.
4th. Dover.
Depôt—Winchester.

1860.
Four Battalions.
1st. Calcutta, Dover.
2nd. Benares, China.
3rd. Jackatalla.
4th. Dover, Waterford, Kilkenny, and detachments.
Depôt—Winchester.

1861.
Four Battalions.
1st. Dover, Aldershot.
2nd. Tien Tsin.
3rd. Jackatalla.
4th. Dublin, Quebec.
Depôt—Winchester.

1862.
Four Battalions.
1st. Aldershot.
2nd. Portsmouth.
3rd. Jackatalla, Thayet-Myo, Tonghoo.
4th. Quebec.
Depôt—Winchester.

1863.
Four Battalions.
1st. Aldershot, London.
2nd. Portsmouth, Aldershot.
3rd. Tonghoo, Rangoon, and detachments.
4th. Quebec, Montreal.
  Depôt—Winchester.

1864.
Four Battalions.
1st. London, Curragh, Dublin.
2nd. Aldershot.
3rd. Rangoon and detachments, Andaman Islands.
4th. Montreal.
  Depôt—Winchester.

1865.
Four Battalions.
1st. Dublin, Curragh, Newry, Enniskillen, Derry.
2nd. Dover.
3rd. Rangoon, Madras.
4th. Montreal, New London, N.B.
  Depôt—Winchester.

1866.
Four Battalions.
1st. Newry, Enniskillen, Dublin, Malta.
2nd. Dover, Dublin, Curragh, Cork.
3rd. Madras.
4th. New London.
  Depôt—Winchester.

1867.
Four Battalions.
1st. Malta, Montreal, Quebec.
2nd. Cork, Calcutta.
3rd. Madras, Bellary.
4th. New London.
  Depôt—Winchester.

1868.
Four Battalions.
1st. Point Levi (Quebec), Montreal.
2nd. Calcutta.
3rd. Madras, Bellary, Bangalore.
4th. New London, N.B.
  Depôt—Winchester.

1869.
Four Battalions.
1st. Montreal, Ottawa, Toronto.
2nd. Right wing, Seetapore; Left wing, Benares.
3rd. Bellary.
4th. New London, St. John, N.B., Aldershot.
  Depôt—Winchester.

1870.
Four Battalions.
1st. Ottawa, Toronto, Red River Expedition, Montreal, Quebec.
2nd. Right wing, Seetapore; Left wing, Benares, Peshawur.
3rd. Bellary.
4th. Aldershot, Colchester.
  Depôt—Colchester.

1871.
Four Battalions.
1st. Quebec, Halifax, N.S.
2nd. Peshawur.
3rd. Bellary, Aden.
4th. Colchester, Winchester.
  Depôt—Winchester.

1872.
Four Battalions.
1st. Halifax, N.S.
2nd. Peshawur, Nowshera.
3rd. Aden, Shorncliffe.
4th. Winchester.
  Depôt—Winchester.

1873.
Four Battalions.
1st. Halifax, N.S.
2nd. Rawul Pindee, Kuldunnah, and detachments.
3rd. Shorncliffe.
4th. Portland.
  Depôt—Winchester.

1874.
Four Battalions.
1st. Halifax.
2nd. Kuldunnah, and detachments.
3rd. Shorncliffe, Chatham.
4th. Portland, Devonport, Dublin.
  Depôt—Winchester.

1875.
Four Battalions.
1st. Halifax.
2nd. Kuldunnah and detachments, Delhi.
3rd. Chatham.
4th. Dublin.
  Depôt—Winchester.

1876.
Four Battalions.
1st. Halifax.
2nd. Delhi, Meerut, Futtehghur.
3rd. Winchester.
4th. Dublin, Agra.
  Depôt—Winchester.

1877.
Four Battalions.
1st. Portsmouth.
2nd. Delhi, Meerut, Futtehghur.
3rd. Aldershot.
4th. Agra.
  Depôt—Winchester.

1878.
Four Battalions.
1st. Portsmouth, Winchester.
2nd. Meerut, Futtehghur.
3rd. Aldershot, Colchester.
4th. Agra.
  Depôt—Winchester.

ACTS OF PARLIAMENT RELATING TO
THE REGIMENT.

29 GEO. II., Cap. 5.
2 GEO. III., Cap. 25.
13 GEO. III., Cap. 25.
38 GEO. III., Cap. 13.
39 GEO. III., Cap. 104.
54 GEO. III., Cap. 12.

ACTS OF PARLIAMENT RELATING TO THE REGIMENT.

Anno vicesimo nono
GEORGII II. REGIS.
29 Geo. II., cap. 5.

An Act to enable His Majesty to grant Commissions to a certain Number of Foreign Protestants **who have** served Abroad **as** Officers, or Engineers, to act and rank as Officers, **or** Engineers, in *America* only, under certain Restrictions and Qualifications.

WHEREAS by an Act made in **the** Thirteenth **Year of the Reign of** His present Majesty, intituled, An Act **for** Naturalizing **such** Foreign Protestants, **and** others therein mentioned, as are settled, or shall settle, in any **of** His Majesty's Colonies in *America*; all Persons born **out of the** Allegiance **of His Majesty, His Heirs or** Successors, who have inhabited and resided, or shall inhabit and reside, for **the Space of Seven Years, or** more, **in any of His** Majesty's Colonies in America, **or** shall not have been absent out of some of **the said Colonies for a longer** Space than Two Months, at any One Time **during the said Seven Years, are** upon the **Con**ditions prescribed by the said Act, naturalized and made **Partakers of all the Benefits and Privileges which the** natural-born **Subjects of this** Realm do enjoy, other than such as are specified in a **Pro**viso in the said Act contained: And whereas many **Foreigners,** being Protestants, have been induced by the Encouragement offered to them by the said Act, to reside and settle in some of **the said** Colonies (and particularly in the Provinces of Maryland **and Pen**sylvania) the natural-born Subjects of which last-mentioned Province do in great Part consist of the People called Quakers, whose Backwardness in their own Defence exposes themselves, and that Part of America, to imminent Danger: And whereas, for the better Defence of the said Colonies, it hath been proposed to raise a Regiment there, consisting of Four Battalions of One thousand

Men each, and to enlist as Soldiers in the said Regiment any of the said Foreign Inhabitants of the said Colonies, who, together with the Natives, shall voluntarily enter themselves in His Majesty's Service as Soldiers; which Foreigners cannot so well be raised or trained, without the Assistance of some Officers who are acquainted with their Manners and Language: And whereas it is expedient in the present Juncture of Affairs, to facilitate the speedy raising of such Regiment, and to enable a certain Number of Foreign Protestants who have served Abroad as Officers, or Engineers, and thereby acquired experience and knowledge, to serve and receive Pay as Officers in the said Regiment, or as Engineers in America; be it enacted by the King's most Excellent Majesty, by and with the Advice and Consent of the Lords Spiritual and Temporal, and Commons, in this present Parliament assembled, and by the Authority of the same, That all such Foreign Protestants who shall receive Commissions from His Majesty, His Heirs or Successors, to be Officers in the said Regiment, or to be Engineers in America (which Commissions it shall and may be lawful for His Majesty, His Heirs and Successors, to grant) and shall, in some of His Majesty's Colonies in America, take and subscribe the Oaths, and make, repeat, and subscribe the Declaration, appointed by an Act made in the First Year of the Reign of His late Majesty King George the First, intituled, An Act for the farther Security of His Majesty's Person and Government, and the Succession of the Crown in the Heirs of the late Princess *Sophia*, being Protestants; and for extinguishing the Hopes of the Pretended Prince of *Wales*, his open and secret Abettors; and shall at the Time of the taking and subscribing of the said Oaths, and making, repeating, and subscribing the said Declaration, produce Certificates signed in Manner directed by the said Act of the Thirteenth Year of His present Majesty, of their having received the Sacrament in some Protestant and reformed Congregation within the Kingdom of Great Britain, or within some of the said Colonies in America, within Six Months before that Time, shall and may be enabled to serve and receive Pay as Officers in the said Regiment, or as Engineers, in America.

Provided, nevertheless, That the Number of such Officers in the said Regiment shall not in the whole, at any Time, exceed Fifty; nor the Number of Engineers in the whole, at any time, exceed Twenty.

Provided also, That the Colonel of the said Regiment shall be

a natural-born Subject, **and not any Person naturalized or made**
Denizen.

Provided also, That no such foreign Officer shall **be enabled by**
this Act to serve as an Officer or Engineer in any **Place, except**
America only; **but every** such foreign Officer, when he shall **be**
reduced, shall be capable of receiving Half-pay, **according to the**
Rank in which he shall then serve.

Anno secundo

GEORGII III. REGIS.

2nd Geo. III. cap. 25.

An Act for Naturalizing such Foreign **Protestants as** have served,
or shall serve for the Time therein mentioned, as Officers **or**
Soldiers in His Majesty's **Royal** American Regiment, **or as**
Engineers in *America*.

WHEREAS by **an Act** made in the Thirteenth **Year** of the Reign of
His late Majesty **King** George the Second, intituled, An Act for
Naturalizing such Foreign Protestants, and others therein mentioned, as **are** settled, or shall settle, in any of His **Majesty's**
Colonies in *America*; all Persons born out of the Allegiance of
His Majesty, His Heirs or Successors, who shall have inhabited
and resided, or shall inhabit or reside, for the Space of Seven Years,
or more, in any of His Majesty's Colonies in America, or shall not
have been absent out of the said Colonies for a longer space than
Two Months at any One Time during the said Seven Years, are,
upon the Conditions prescribed by the said Act, Naturalized and
made Partakers of all the Benefits and Privileges which the
natural-born Subjects of this Realm do enjoy, other than such as
are specified in a Proviso in the said Act contained: And whereas
Commissions have been granted to a certain Number of Foreign
Protestants in America, in pursuance of a Power given by a subsequent Act of the Twenty-ninth Year of the Reign of His late
Majesty King George the Second, intituled, An Act to enable
His Majesty to grant Commissions to a certain Number of Foreign
Protestants, who have served abroad as Officers or Engineers, to
act and rank as Officers or Engineers in *America* only, under
certain Restrictions and Qualifications; which said Officers have

D

been very useful to His Majesty's Service, by the Raising of a
great Number of Men, and Training them to Discipline as Soldiers:
and whereas several of the said Officers, since the passing of the
above recited Acts, have purchased Estates in America, by which,
as well as by their faithful Services, they have given the strongest
Assurances of their Attachment and Fidelity to His Majesty's
Government: And whereas it is just to reward the past Services
of the said Officers and Soldiers, and to give Encouragement for
their future good Conduct; and it is likewise expedient to add
Inducements to such Foreign Protestants as have settled, or may
hereafter settle, in America, to engage in His Majesty's Service:
Be it therefore enacted by the King's most Excellent Majesty, by
and with the Advice and Consent of the Lords Spiritual and
Temporal, and Commons, in this present Parliament assembled,
and by the Authority of the same, That all such Foreign Protestants, as well Officers as Soldiers, who have served, or shall
hereafter serve, in the Royal American Regiment, or as Engineers
in America, for the Space of Two Years, and shall take and
subscribe the Oaths, and make, and repeat, and subscribe the
Declaration appointed by an Act made in the First Year of the
Reign of His Majesty King George the First, intituled, An Act
for the further Security of His Majesty's Person and Government,
and the Succession of the Crown in the Heirs of the late Princess
Sophia, being Protestants; and for extinguishing the Hopes of the
pretended Prince of *Wales*, his open and secret Abettors; and shall,
at the Time of subscribing the said Oaths, and making, repeating,
and subscribing the said Declaration, produce Certificates, signed
in Manner directed by the above recited Act of the Thirteenth of
His late Majesty, of their having received the Sacrament in some
Protestant and Reformed Congregation within the Kingdom of
Great Britain, or within some of the said Colonies in America,
within Six Months before that Time, shall be deemed, adjudged,
and taken to be, His Majesty's natural-born Subjects of this Kingdom, to all Intents, Constructions, and Purposes, as if they, and
every of them, had been or were born within this Kingdom; and
that no Estates, of what Nature or Kind soever, purchased by them,
or any of them, in any of His Majesty's Colonies in America, since
the passing of the above recited Act of the Twenty-ninth Year of
the Reign of His said late Majesty, shall be liable to Seizure into
the Hands of His Majesty, His Heirs or Successors, or their Titles

thereto be otherwise impeached by Reason of **their** having **been** Aliens at the Time of their making **the** said Purchases ; the above recited Acts, **or any** other Statute, **Law,** or **Thing whatsoever to** the contrary notwithstanding.

Provided always, and be it enacted by the Authority aforesaid. That nothing in this Act contained shall extend, or be construed **to** extend, **to** naturalize any Person or Persons whatsoever, **who, by** virtue of an Act made in the Fourth Year of the **Reign of His late Majesty King** George the First (intituled, **An Act to explain a** Clause in an Act made in the Seventh Year **of the Reign of Her** late Majesty Queen *Anne*, for Naturalizing **Foreign Protestants, which** relates **to** the Children of natural-born **Subjects of the** Crown of *England*, or of *Great Britain*) **are** declared and enacted **not to be entitled to** the Benefit of the said Act **of the** Seventh **Year of Her** said Majesty's Reign ; but that all such Persons shall **be** and remain in **the** same State, Plight, and Condition, to all Intents, Constructions, **and Purposes** whatsoever, as they would have been in if this **Act had never been made ;** any thing herein contained to the contrary **in any wise** notwithstanding.

Provided also, and be it **further enacted, That no** Person **who** shall become a natural-born **Subject of this Kingdom** by virtue of this **Act**, shall be thereby enabled to be of the Privy Council, or a Member of **either House of Parliament, or to be capable of taking,** having, or enjoying **any Office or Place of Trust within the King-** doms of Great Britain **or Ireland, either Civil or Military ; or of** having, **accepting, or taking any Grant from the Crown to himself,** or to any other **in Trust for him, of any Lands, Tenements, or Hereditaments, within the Kingdoms aforesaid ; anything herein** contained to the contrary thereof in any wise notwithstanding.

Anno decimo Tertio

GEORGII III. REGIS.

13th Geo. III. cap. 25.

An Act to explain Two Acts of Parliament, One of the Thirteenth Year of the Reign of His late Majesty, for Naturalizing such Foreign Protestants, and others, as are settled, or shall settle, in any of His Majesty's Colonies in *America* ; and the other of the

Second Year of the Reign of His present Majesty, for Naturalizing such Foreign Protestants as have served, or shall serve, as Officers or Soldiers in His Majesty's Royal *American* Regiment, or as Engineers, in *America*.

WHEREAS by an Act, made in the Thirteenth Year of the Reign of His late Majesty King George the Second (intituled, An Act for naturalizing such Foreign Protestants, and others therein mentioned, as are settled, or shall settle, in any of His Majesty's Colonies in *America*), all Persons born out of the Allegiance of His Majesty, His Heirs or Successors, who shall have inhabited and resided, or shall inhabit or reside, for the Space of Seven Years or more, in any of His Majesty's Colonies in America, or shall not have been absent out of the said Colonies for a longer Space than Two Months at any one time during the said Seven Years, are, upon the Conditions prescribed by the said Act, naturalized and made Partakers of all the Benefits and Privileges which the natural-born Subjects of this Realm do enjoy, other than such as are specified in a Proviso in the said Act contained: And whereas by an Act, made in the Second Year of the Reign of His present Majesty (intituled, An Act for naturalizing such Foreign Protestants as have served, or shall serve, for the Time therein mentioned, as Officers or Soldiers in His Majesty's Royal *American* Regiment, or as Engineers in *America*), it is enacted, That all such Foreign Protestants, as well Officers as Soldiers, who have served, or shall hereafter serve, in the Royal American Regiment, or as Engineers in America, for the Space of Two Years, shall, upon the Terms required by the said recited Act, be deemed, adjudged, and taken to be His Majesty's natural-born Subjects of this Kingdom, to all Intents, Constructions, and Purposes as if they and every of them had been, or were, born within this Kingdom; and in both which Acts respectively are contained Provisoes, That no Person, who shall become a natural-born Subject of this Kingdom by virtue of the said Acts, shall be thereby enabled to be of the Privy Council, or a Member of either House of Parliament, or to be capable of taking, having or enjoying any Office or Place of Trust within the Kingdom of Great Britain or Ireland, either Civil or Military, or of having, accepting or taking any Grant from the Crown, to himself or to any other in Trust for him, of any Lands, Tenements, or Hereditaments, within the Kingdoms aforesaid; and whereas Doubts may nevertheless arise,

whether such Persons as have been, or may be naturalized under
or by virtue of the said recited Acts, are capable of taking, having,
or enjoying any Office or Place of Trust, either Civil or Military, or
of taking any Grant of Lands, Tenements, and Hereditaments, from
the Crown whatsoever: Be it enacted and declared by the King's
most Excellent Majesty, by and with the Advice and Consent of
the Lords Spiritual and Temporal, and Commons, in this present
Parliament assembled, and by the Authority of the same, That all
and every Person and Persons that have become, or shall become
His Majesty's natural-born Subjects, by Force or Virtue of the said
Acts, or either of them, are and shall be deemed to be capable of
taking and holding any Office or Place of Trust, either Civil or
Military, and of taking and holding any Grant of Lands, Tenements, and Hereditaments, from the Crown, to himself or themselves,
or to any other or others in Trust for him or them, as well under
the Great Seal of Great Britain, as otherwise, other than and
except Offices and Places, and Grants of Lands, Tenements, and
Hereditaments, within the Kingdoms of Great Britain and Ireland;
any Law or Act of Parliament to the contrary notwithstanding.

Anno tricesimo octavo
GEORGII III. REGIS.
38th Geo. III. cap. 13.

An Act to amend an Act, made in the Twenty-ninth Year of the
Reign of His late Majesty King *George* the Second, intituled,
*An Act to enable His Majesty to grant Commissions to a certain
Number of Foreign Protestants, who have served Abroad as Officers
or Engineers, to act and rank as Officers or Engineers in America
only, under certain Restrictions and Qualifications.*

[*30th December,* 1797.]

WHEREAS it is judged expedient for the better Defence of His
Majesty's Colonies in *America*, to augment His Majesty's Sixtieth
Regiment of Infantry, now consisting of Four Battalions of One
Thousand Men each, by the Addition of a Fifth Battalion, to con-
sist in like Manner of One Thousand Men, and to inlist as Soldiers,
to serve in the said Fifth Battalion in *America*, any of the Foreign
Troops now in His Majesty's Pay, or other Foreigners who shall
voluntarily enter themselves to serve as Soldiers therein: And

whereas such Foreigners cannot so well be disciplined without the Assistance of some Officers who are acquainted with their Manners and Language : And whereas it is expedient, in the present Juncture of Affairs, to facilitate the speedy raising of such Fifth Battalion, and to enable a certain Number of Foreign Officers to serve and receive Pay as Officers in such Fifth Battalion : Be it enacted by the King's most Excellent Majesty, by and with the Advice and Consent of the Lords Spiritual and Temporal, and Commons, in this present Parliament assembled, and by the Authority of the same, That it shall and may be lawful for His Majesty, His Heirs and Successors, to augment the said Sixtieth Regiment of Infantry, by the Addition of a Fifth Battalion, to consist of One thousand Men, and to enlist as Soldiers, to serve in such Battalion, any of the Foreign Troops now in His Majesty's Pay, or other Foreigners who shall voluntarily enter themselves to serve as Soldiers therein in *America.*

II. And be it further enacted by the Authority aforesaid, That all such Foreign Officers who shall receive Commissions from His Majesty, His Heirs and Successors, to be Officers of such Fifth Battalion in *America* (which Commissions it shall and may be lawful for His Majesty, His Heirs and Successors, to grant), shall and may be enabled to serve and receive Pay as Officers in the said Regiment.

III. And whereas by an Act, passed in the Twenty-ninth Year of His late Majesty's Reign, intituled, *An Act to enable His Majesty to grant Commissions to a certain Number of Foreign Protestants, who have served Abroad as Officers or Engineers, to act and rank as Officers or Engineers in* America *only, under certain Restrictions and Qualifications,* it is amongst other Things enacted, that the Number of Officers in the said Regiment shall not, in the Whole, at any Time, exceed Fifty, nor the Number of Engineers, in the Whole, at any Time exceed Twenty : Be it therefore enacted, That the said recited Clause in the above-mentioned Act shall, from and after the Passing of this present Act, be, and it is hereby declared to be and stand totally repealed to all Intents and Purposes.

IV. Provided also, That no such Foreign Officer shall be enabled by this Act to serve as an Officer in any Place except *America* only ; but every such Foreign Officer, when he shall be reduced, shall be capable of receiving Half-pay according to the Rank in which he shall then serve.

Anno tricesimo nono
GEORGII III. REGIS.
39th Geo. III. cap. 104.

An Act to amend an Act, made in the Twenty-ninth Year of the Reign of King *George* the Second, intituled, *An Act to enable His* Majesty *to grant* Commissions to a certain Number of Foreign Protestants, who have served Abroad as Officers or Engineers, to act and rank as Officers or Engineers in America only, under certain Restrictions and Qualifications. [12*th July*, 1799.]

Whereas it is adjudged expedient, for the better Defence of His Majesty's Colonies in America, to augment His Majesty's Sixtieth Regiment of Infantry, now consisting of Five Battalions, of One thousand Men each, by the Addition of a Sixth and Seventh Battalions, to consist in like Manner of One thousand Men each, and to inlist as Soldiers, to serve in the said Sixth and Seventh Battalions in America, any of the Foreign Troops now in His Majesty's Pay, or other Foreigners who shall voluntarily enter themselves to serve as Soldiers therein: And whereas such Foreigners cannot be so well disciplined without the Assistance of some Officers who are acquainted with their Manners and Language: And whereas it is expedient, in the present Juncture of Affairs, to facilitate the speedy raising of such Sixth and Seventh Battalions, and to enable a certain Number of Foreign Officers to serve and receive Pay as Officers in such Sixth and Seventh Battalions: Be it enacted by the King's most Excellent Majesty, by and with the Advice and Consent of the Lords Spiritual and Temporal, and Commons, in this present Parliament assembled, and by the Authority of the same, That it shall and may be lawful for His Majesty, His Heirs and Successors, to augment the said Sixtieth Regiment of Infantry, by the Addition of a Sixth and Seventh Battalion, to consist of One thousand Men each, and to inlist as Soldiers, to serve in such Battalions, any of the Foreign Troops now in His Majesty's Pay, or other Foreigners who shall voluntarily enter themselves to serve as Soldiers therein in *America*.

II. And be it further enacted, That all such Foreign Officers who shall receive Commissions from His Majesty, His Heirs and Successors, to be Officers of such Sixth and Seventh Battalions, in *America* (which Commissions it shall and may be lawful for His

Majesty, His Heirs and Successors, to grant), shall be enabled to serve and receive Pay as Officers in the said Regiment.

III. Provided always, and be it further enacted, That no such Foreign Officer shall be enabled by this Act to serve as an Officer, in any Place except *America* only; but every such Foreign Officer, when he shall be reduced, shall be capable of receiving Half-pay according to the Rank in which he shall then serve.

Anno quinquagesimo quarto
GEORGII III. REGIS.
54th Geo. III. cap. 12.

An Act to enable His Majesty to augment the Sixtieth Regiment to Ten Battalions, by Enlistment of Foreigners.

[*6th December*, 1813.]

WHEREAS it is expedient, that His Majesty should be empowered to augment His Sixtieth Regiment of Infantry, now consisting of Seven Battalions, by the Addition of an Eighth, Ninth, and Tenth Battalion: Be it therefore enacted by the King's most Excellent Majesty, by and with the Advice and Consent of the Lords Spiritual and Temporal, and Commons, in this present Parliament assembled, and by the Authority of the same, That it shall be lawful for His Majesty, His Heirs and Successors, to augment the said Sixtieth Regiment of Infantry, by the Addition of an Eighth, Ninth, and Tenth Battalion, to consist of One thousand Men each, and to enlist as Soldiers to serve in such Battalions any Foreigners now in His Majesty's Pay, or other Foreigners who shall voluntarily enter themselves to serve as Soldiers therein, and to employ such Regiment, or any part thereof, in any Country or Place out of *Great Britain*, anything in any Act or Acts to the contrary notwithstanding.

II. And be it further enacted, That all Foreign Officers who shall receive Commissions from His Majesty, His Heirs and Successors, to be Officers in the said Regiment, for the Purpose of enabling His Majesty to augment the same to Ten Battalions (which Commissions it shall and may be lawful for His Majesty, His Heirs and Successors, to grant), shall be enabled to serve and receive Pay as Officers in the said Regiment; and when reduced shall be capable of receiving Half-pay, according to the Rank in which they shall serve at the Time of such Reduction.

CHRONOLOGICAL TABLE,

SHOWING

THE DATES OF THE PRINCIPAL ACTIONS, EVENTS, MOVES, CHANGES OF EQUIPMENTS, &c., ALTERATION OF TITLES, AND PERIODS OF THE RAISING AND DISBANDING OF THE DIFFERENT BATTALIONS,

FROM 1755 TO 1878.

CHRONOLOGICAL TABLE,

SHOWING

THE DATES OF THE PRINCIPAL ACTIONS, EVENTS, MOVES, CHANGES OF EQUIPMENTS, &c., ALTERATION OF TITLES, AND PERIODS OF THE RAISING AND DISBANDING OF THE DIFFERENT BATTALIONS.

FROM 1755 TO 1878.

1755.

November 13. Act of Parliament 29th George II., cap. 5, authorising the raising of a Regiment of Foot in British North America.

December 25. "The 62nd, or Royal American Regiment of Foot" raised.

December 25. The Earl of Loudoun appointed Colonel-in-Chief of the Regiment.

1756.

August. Title changed to "The 60th, or the Royal American Regiment of Foot."

1757.

July 26. The clothing warrant for the dress of the Regiment issued.

December 27. General James Abercromby appointed Colonel-in-Chief of the Regiment.

1758.

May 6. Sixteen rifled barrel fuzils, steel ramrods, screws, bayonets with scabbards, and sixteen bullet-moulds, issued to the First Battalion.

July 26. Capture of Louisbourg.

September 30. General Jeffery Amherst, Colonel-in-Chief in British North America, appointed Colonel-in-Chief of the Regiment.

1759.

February 20. Gold Medal for service against the Indians in the Campaign of 1758, issued to the Officers of Colonel Bouquet's Battalion (First) by General Forbes.

February. Green leggings with red gaiters issued.

March. First Light Infantry Company formed at Albany, one sergeant, one corporal, and twelve privates from each company.

July 31. Probable date of the granting of the motto, "*Celer et Audax*," by General Wolfe.*

September 13. Battle (on the Plains of Abraham) of Quebec.

September 17 *and* 18. Capture of Quebec.

1760.

April 28. Second battle (on the Plains of Abraham) of Quebec.

September 8. Capture of Montreal.

October. General the Hon. J. Murray was appointed the first English Governor of Quebec.

1761.

November 3. Act of Parliament, 2nd George III., cap. 25, for Naturalizing Foreign Protestants, &c., to serve in "The Royal American Regiment of Foot."

November. Third Battalion moved from North America to the West Indies.

1762.

February 4 *to* 13. Capture of Martinique.

June. Third Battalion moved from West Indies to West Florida.

August 13. Capture of Havannah.

1763.

June 27. Fourth Battalion was disbanded in England.†

1764.

February. Third Battalion was reduced in New York and sent to England to be disbanded.†

1766.

First Battalion moved from North America to the West Indies.

---

* The exact date is not known, but it was probably granted between July 1 and August 14. The Records of the 1st Battalion state that in consequence " of the Alertness and Intrepidity" of the Grenadiers of the 2nd and 3rd Battalions before Quebec, " the appropriate motto of *Celer et Audax*" was conferred upon them by General Wolfe. These records, of course, only give the regimental tradition.

† Royal Warrant, St. James's, May 18, 1763.

1768.

Clothing warrant for the dress of the Regiment, and Special Orders for the colours and devices issued.*   Black gaiters issued.

1770.

Standard for recruits for the Regiment fixed at 5 feet 6½ inches. One company of **Light** Infantry added to each battalion.

1772.

November 26, 1772.   Act of Parliament, 13th George III., **cap.** 25, to explain **Act** 29th George II., **cap.** 5, and **Act** 2nd George III., cap. 25.

Second Battalion moved from North America to the West Indies.

October.   New arms issued to Second Battalion.

1775.

August 25.   Third and **Fourth** Battalions were raised in England.

1776.

Third and Fourth **Battalions moved** from England **to** the West Indies.

1778.

Third and Fourth Battalions moved from the West Indies to the Floridas.

1780.

Fourth Battalion moved from the Floridas to New York.

1783.

September.   Third and Fourth Battalions moved from New York to Nova Scotia.

October 10.   Third and Fourth Battalions were disbanded at Halifax, Nova Scotia.†

1786.

First Battalion moved from the West Indies to Nova Scotia.

1787.

Second Battalion moved from the West Indies to North America.

September 22.   First and Second Battalions were each augmented by 1 sergeant, 1 drummer, and 14 privates per company. Two extra companies were also added, consisting of 1 captain, 1 lieu-

---

* General Order, George III., December 19, 1768.
† Royal Warrant, June 9, 1783.

tenant, 1 ensign, 3 sergeants, 3 corporals, 2 drummers, and 56 privates. One company especially for recruiting purposes was also formed, composed of 1 captain, 1 lieutenant, 1 ensign, 8 sergeants, 8 corporals, 4 drummers, and 30 privates.

September 22. Third and Fourth Battalions were raised at Chatham, and composed of foreign recruits.

1788.

October and November. Third and Fourth Battalions moved from England to the West Indies.

1792.

December. First, Second, Third, and Fourth Battalions were each augmented by 100 privates.

1793.

January. First, Second, Third, and Fourth Battalions were each augmented by 10 officers, 10 sergeants, and 170 rank and file.

December. Third Battalion was drafted into Fourth Battalion and the staff sent to England (to the Channel Islands).

1794.

Rifles first adopted in the British service, and first issued to *one* battalion of the Regiment (probably the First).*

1795.

April 8. Third Battalion moved from the Channel Islands to the West Indies.

1796.

Fourth Battalion moved from the West Indies to the Channel Islands.

1797.

Fourth Battalion moved from the Channel Islands to the West Indies.

June 25. First Battalion was drafted into Second Battalion at Quebec, and again re-formed at Guernsey.

August 23. H.R.H. Frederick, Duke of York, was appointed Colonel-in-Chief of the Regiment.

---

* Probably Baker rifle. Weighed 10½ lbs. with sword, sighted for 100 to 200 yards, seven grooves, a quarter turn in length of barrel, which was about 2 feet 6 inches in length. Total length of rifle, 3 feet 10 inches; weight of sword, 1 lb.; diameter of bore, .625; spherical bullet, with a mallet and greased patch.

December 30. Act of Parliament, 38th George III., cap. 13, to amend Act 29th George II., and add a Fifth Battalion.

December. Fifth Battalion was raised at Cowes, **Isle of** Wight; wore moustaches, **was** armed **with** rifles, dressed in **green,*** and carried rifle-bags made of leather, instead **of knapsacks.** Lieut.-General Baron de Rottenburg **was** appointed Colonel of the Fifth Battalion. Four hundred of Hompesch's **Mounted Riflemen were** drafted into Fifth Battalion at Cowes.

Three hundred **and ninety-three New** York Rangers were **drafted into** Third Battalion.

December 30. Walstein's Foreign Light Infantry were drafted into Fourth Battalion at Martinique.

1798.

April. Fifth **Battalion moved from the** Isle **of** Wight **to** Ireland.

1799.

January. First Battalion moved from Channel Islands to West Indies.

July 12. Act of Parliament, 39th George III., cap. 104, to amend Act 29th George II., cap. 5, and add a Sixth and Seventh Battalion.

August. Sixth Battalion was raised at the Isle of Wight, and composed of Germans.

February. Flank company of Sixth Battalion armed **with rifles.** Fifth Battalion moved from Ireland to West Indies and South America.

Five hundred of "Lowenstein's Chasseurs," a Corps raised by a prince of that name for the Dutch Republic, on the evacuation of Holland, entered the British Service, and were this year drafted into the Fifth Battalion.

October 2. Battle of Bergen.

1800.

Clothing warrant specially authorising a *green coat* for the Fifth Battalion.†

---

* Clothing Warrant, April, 1800.

† Regulations for clothing and half mountings of Infantry, George III., April 9, 1800.

May 1.   Second Battalion moved from Quebec to the West Indies.

November 28.   Sixth Battalion moved from England to the West Indies.

1802.

Third Battalion was temporarily drafted into the Second Battalion.

1803.

April 23.   Clothing warrant authorising green *jackets*, pantaloons, and short black gaiters for the Fifth Battalion.[*]

June 18.   Field Officers ordered not to command companies. Captain-Lieutenants to be promoted to, and command companies.

October 6.   Fifth Battalion moved from South America to Nova Scotia.

1805.

Fourth Battalion augmented by 44 officers, 22 sergeants, 800 rank and file, and moved from the West Indies to England in armed ships, "Suffolk" and "Perseverance."

November.   Fifth Battalion moved from Nova Scotia to England.

1806.

July 14.   Fourth Battalion moved from England to Africa.

Third Battalion drafted into Second in the West Indies, and part sent to England to recruit.

November 30.   Third Battalion augmented by 54 officers, 22 sergeants, 1,000 rank and file.

Five sergeants, 155 rank and file, armed with rifles, and moved from Portsmouth to the Channel Islands.

December.   Fifth Battalion augmented by 44 officers, 22 sergeants, and 800 rank and file.

1807.

April 20.   Third Battalion moved from the Channel Islands to the West Indies.

August 31.   Fifth Battalion moved from England to Ireland.

September 20.   Second Battalion moved from the West Indies to the Channel Islands.

December 21.   Capture of the Danish Isles.

1808.

March.   Fourth Battalion moved from Africa to the West Indies.

June 15.   Fifth Battalion moved from Ireland to Portugal in transports "Juliana," "Atlas," and "Malabar."

---

[*] Regulations, George III., April 23, 1803.

August 16 *and* 17.   Action of Lorinda.   Battle of Roliça.

August 21.   Battle of Vimiera.

October.   Second Battalion moved from the Channel Islands to Spain.

1809.

January 16.   Battle of Corunna.

January 17.   Second Battalion moved from Spain to the Channel Islands.

February 17.   Capture of Martinique.

May 11 *and* 12.   Passage of the Douro **and Capture of** Oporto.

July 27 *and* 28.   Battle **of** Talavera.

November 20.   Second Battalion moved from the Channel Islands to the **West** Indies in "La Loire" transport (from Portsmouth).

1810.

January and February.   Capture of Guadaloupe.

September 27.   Battle of Busaco.

April 28.   First Battalion moved from the West Indies to England.   Fourth Battalion moved from the West Indies to England.

1811.

May 5.   Battle of Fuentes d'Onor.

May 16.   Battle of Albuera.

May 30.   First Battalion moved from England to Africa. Fourth Battalion moved from England to West Indies.

1812.

January 10 *to February.*   Siege and Assault of Ciudad Rodrigo.

April 6.   Assault of Badajoz.

May 19.   Action of Almarez.

Clothing warrant, authorising green cloth pantaloons for Rifle Corps, and giving list of appointments for sergeants and rank and file.*

July 22.   Battle of Salamanca.

1813.

Fifth Battalion moved from Spain to France.

June 21.   Battle of Vittoria.

July 25 *to* 31.   Battles of the Pyrenees.

September 1.   Seventh Rifle Battalion was raised in Guernsey

* Regulations, George III., July 15, 1812.

and formed of the German prisoners of war. It consisted of 840 rank and file, *i.e.*, 640 Light Infantry, 200 Rifles.

November 10. Battle of Nivelle.

November 13. Battle of St. Jean-de-Luz.

November 14. Eighth Rifle Battalion was raised at Lisbon, out of a *provincial* battalion which existed there.

December 6. Act of Parliament, 54th George III., cap. 12, to augment the Regiment by an Eighth, Ninth, and Tenth Battalion.

December 9 *to* 13. Battle of Nive.

1814.

February 27. Battle of Orthes.

April 10. Battle of Toulouse.

May 28. Seventh Battalion moved from the Channel Islands to Halifax, N.S.

July. Fifth Battalion moved from France to Ireland.

August 24. Penobscot Expedition.

1815.

April 18. " Peninsula" granted to Fifth Battalion.*

1816.

February. Fifth Battalion moved from Ireland to England.

May 5. Fifth Battalion moved from England to Mediterranean in " Minerva," " Duncombe," and " Isabella " transports.

May 24. Third Battalion moved from West Indies to Nova Scotia in " Lord Eldon," " Mary and Dorothea," and " William and Ann " transports.

May 31. Most of the Eighth Battalion was drafted to the Fifth Battalion at Gibraltar, and the remainder disbanded at Portsmouth.

The dress of the Regiment was changed this year to green jacket with short skirts, lapels lined with scarlet, scarlet cuffs and collars, two buttons on each ; two rows of buttons in front, a gold bugle on the skirts, wings of gold chain and bullion, green pantaloons, and a cap of regulation pattern.

1817.

June 24. Seventh Battalion was disbanded at Halifax, N.S., and the men drafted into Second and Third Battalions at Quebec and Halifax.

* War Office Letter, 6th April, 1815.

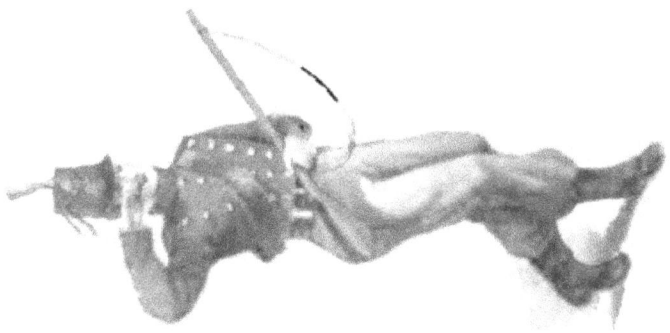

July 19.   **Second Battalion moved from the West Indies to** Nova Scotia, in " Queen " **and** " Retriever " transports.

September 17.   **"Martinique" granted.** *

Second Battalion moved from Nova Scotia to Quebec, **in brigs** " Earl of Dalhousie " and " George " transports.

October **28.**   Sixth Battalion moved from **Jamaica to England** in " Brailsford Glory " and " Christiana " transports.

1818.

February 9.   Sixth Battalion was disbanded at Portsmouth, and the men drafted **to** Third Battalion at Halifax.

May 10.   Fifth Battalion moved from the Mediterranean to **England, in** the " Borrodino," " Ocean," **and** " Kennedy Castle " **transports, and was** disbanded at the Isle of Wight, and **the men drafted into Second** Battalion at Quebec.

September 19.   **Second Battalion** called " Rifle Battalion," Third Battalion called " Light Infantry."

September 23.   Rifles issued **to Second Battalion** ; appointments of Fifth Battalion handed **over to Second Battalion, those of** Second to Third Battalion †

1819.

January 9.   First Battalion moved from Africa to **West Indies,** and thence to England, in transports " Minerva," " Nautilus," " William Pitt, " and " Astrea ;" and was disbanded at Portsmouth, and the men drafted **into** Second Battalion, at Quebec.

May 8.   Second Battalion **called The** First or Rifle Battalion ; **Third Battalion called The Second or Light** Infantry.‡

June.   Fourth Battalion moved from the West Indies to Portsmouth, and was disbanded there.

1820.

May 12.   Authority for the dress of the Officers of both battalions to be the same.§

* War Office Letter, September 17, 1817
† General Order, Letter, Quebec, September 23, 1818
‡ War Office Letter, April 28, 1819
§ General Order, Halifax, May 12, 1820

1821.

June 21. Left wing, Second (late Third) Battalion, moved from Nova Scotia to Bermuda, in transports "Albany" and "Impostor."

September 29. "Rolica," "Vimiera," "Talavera," "Fuentes d'Onor," "Ciudad Rodrigo," "Badajos," "Salamanca," "Vittoria," "Nivelle," "Orthes," "Toulouse" granted.*

1823.

June 18. Orders discontinuing breeches, leggings, and shoes, substituting trousers and half-boots, and authorising green trousers.†

August 23. Right wing, Second Battalion, moved from Nova Scotia to Newfoundland.

1824.

June. First Battalion moved from Canada to England.

June 25. Regiment made a British Corps, title changed to "The Duke of York's Own Rifle Corps and Light Infantry."‡

July 31. *Both* Battalions ordered to be trained and equipped as Rifle Battalions. *Both* to be called Rifle Battalions. The rank of Ensign abolished, and that of Second Lieutenant substituted.§ All British-born subjects to be sent to First Battalion, all not British-born to be sent to Second Battalion.

September 24. Right wing, Second Battalion, moved from Newfoundland, *vià* Halifax, to West Indies, in "Borrodino" and "Vibilia" transports. Left wing moved from Bermuda to the West Indies.

October 6. New pattern knapsack issued.

October 13. Steel scabbards instead of gilt sanctioned for Officers.

October 15. Motto, "*Celer et Audax*," resumed.‖

1825.

February 26. "Albuera," "Pyrenees," and "Nive" granted.

April 16. H.R.H. the Duke of York gave permission for his button, with "D. Y. O. R." on it, to be worn by First Battalion.

* Horse Guards Letter, September 21, 1821.
† General Order, 491, Horse Guards, 1823.
‡ Horse Guards Letter, June 19, 1824.
§ War Office Letter, July 15, 1824.
‖ Horse Guards Letter, 11th October, 1824.

R.Az.

1826.

June. New rifle, flint-lock with bayonet issued.*

August 24. Club exercises introduced.

December 18. First Battalion moved from England to Portugal in H.M.S. " Windsor Castle."

December 25. Jacket, pelisse, gilt-handled sword, black leather scabbard, scarlet sash, and black pouch-belt, sanctioned for all dismounted Officers. Sabretache, and steel scabbard for mounted Officers.†

1827.

January 5. H.R.H. the Duke of York died.

H.R.H. the Duke of Cambridge appointed Colonel-in-Chief of the regiment.

April. H.R.H. the Duke of York's appointments presented to the First Battalion, by order of George IV

August 7. New pattern knapsack issued.

1828.

March 5. First Battalion moved from Portugal to Ireland.

1829.

March 21. Hold-alls issued.

June 19. New pattern knapsack issued.

December 29. Second Battalion moved from the West Indies to the Isle of Wight.

1830.

June 17. Wings and tufts issued :

Four Companies Depôt of First Battalion formed at Portsmouth.

October 6. First Battalion moved from Ireland to the Mediterranean.

December 1. Title changed to " The 60th, or King's Royal Rifle Corps."§

1831.

December 27. Second Battalion moved from England to Ireland in " East Roden " and " Lee " steam packets

---

* Probably the Baker rifle, Delvigne pattern ; weight 9¼ lbs., 7 grooves, length of barrel 2½ feet, making ¼ turn in length of barrel ; calibre 20 bore, diameter .623, spherical bullet, wooden mallet, and greased patch, sighted to 100 to 200 yards.

† Dress Regulations for Army, George III , December 25, 1826.

‡ Addenda, General Regulations, June 17, 1824.

§ Horse Guards Letter, November 12, 1830

1834.

October 17. First Battalion moved from Gibraltar to Malta on board the troopship "Jupiter."

1835.

October 22. Second Battalion moved from Ireland to Mediterranean in "Sovereign" and "Moira" transports.

1836.

July 14. First Battalion moved from Malta to Corfu in "Barrossa" transport.

December 14. First Battalion moved from Corfu to Vido.

1837.

April 1. First Battalion moved from Vido to Corfu.

October 24. Second Battalion moved from Gibraltar to Corfu.

December 1. Second Battalion moved from Corfu to Vido.

1838.

January 6. First Battalion moved from Corfu to Zante and Vido on board transport steamer "Rhadamanthus."

March. Second Battalion moved from Vido to Corfu.

1840.

April 17, *June* 26. First Battalion moved from the Mediterranean to England on board "Horatio" and "Baretta, Junior" transports and H.M. troopship "Apollo."

1841.

January 30. Brunswick percussion rifle with swords, new accoutrements, and chacos with chains instead of straps issued to First Battalion.*

March 11. Second Battalion moved from Mediterranean to the West Indies.

1842.

July. New pattern shell jacket with braid and loops ordered for Officers, also black sheep-skins, edged with scarlet, instead of green saddle-cloths for mounted Officers.

---

* Brunswick rifle, with back-action book lock ; weight, with sword, bayonet, and ramrod 11 lbs. 5 oz. ; weight of barrel, 3 lbs. 11 oz. ; length of barrel, 2 feet 6 inches ; two grooves, making one turn in length ; weight of spherical-belted bullet, 557 grains ; diameter, ·696 ; charge of powder, 2½ drachms.

1846.   1867.   1846

1843.

April. Brunswick **rifle** with sword, new **accoutrements**, and chacos, with chains instead of straps, issued to Second Battalion.*

First Battalion moved from England to **Ireland**.

1844.

March 28. Second Battalion moved from the West Indies to **Canada** on board H.M. troopship " Apollo."

1845.

April. **New chacos of a** smaller pattern with black **straps** issued to Second **Battalion**.

May 8. **Companies** distinguished by letters instead of numbers.

June 1. **First Battalion** formed into nine **Service** and one Depôt Companies.

June 20. Permission granted **to retain Maltese** Cross on the **cap** ornaments.†

July 11. **First Battalion** moved from **Ireland to India** on board " **Stebbon Heath**," " **Neptune**," " Forfarshire," " Princess Royal," **and " Andromache " transports**.

1846.

August 21. Second Battalion moved from Canada to Nova Scotia in H.M.S. " Belleisle."

1847.

May 17. Second Battalion moved from Nova Scotia to England on board H.M.S. " Vengeance."

1848.

July 2. Second Battalion moved from England to Ireland

1849.

January 2 *to* 22. Siege and Capture of Mooltan.
Collars and cuffs of shell jacket altered.
February 21. Battle of Goojerat.

---

* Vide foot note, p. 54.
† Horse Guards Letter, 20th June, 1845.

1850.

May 13.   New pattern cap pocket issued to First Battalion.

July 8.   H.R.H. the Duke of Cambridge died.

August 15.   Field Marshal H.R.H. Prince Francis Albert Augustus Charles Emanuel, Duke of Saxe-Coburg and Gotha, K.G., &c., &c., appointed Colonel-in-Chief of the Regiment.

1851.

July 15.   Second Battalion moved from Ireland to British Kaffraria (South Africa) on board H.M.S. "Retribution" and "Sidon."

1851 to 1853.

Kaffir War.

1852.

February 26.   H.M. troopship "Birkenhead" was wrecked near Algoa Bay with 446 officers and men of various Regiments on board, among them a detachment of the Second Battalion; 1 sergeant, 2 lance sergeants, and 49 privates (1 sergeant and 9 privates saved).

September 23.   General Viscount Beresford, G.C.B., appointed Colonel-in-Chief of the Regiment.

October 7.   Medals for Mooltan and Goojerat issued.

December 30.   "Punjaub," "Mooltan," and "Goojerat" granted.*

1853.

September 22.   Authority granted for the decoration for "Punjaub," "Mooltan," and "Goojerat" to be worn on the pouch-belt ornaments, and Maltese Cross on the Officers' chacos. †

1854.

January 28.   General Viscount Gough, G.C.B., appointed Colonel-in-Chief of the Regiment.

June.   The rank of Ensign substituted for that of Second Lieutenant.

November.   Two companies added to Second Battalion at the Depôt.

---

* Horse Guards Letter, December 20, 1852.
† Horse Guards Letter, September 22, 1853.

1855.

March 31. Third Battalion was raised in Dublin.*

April. Double-breasted tunic instead of rifle jacket issued to Third Battalion.

1856.

August 1. Double-breasted tunic instead of rifle jacket issued to First and Second Battalions.

August 19. Third Battalion formed into Service and Depôt Companies. Short Enfield-Pritchett rifles with sword bayonet, and new accoutrements, issued to the Second Battalion. †

1857.

January 1. Long Enfield-Pritchett rifles with bayonets issued to First Battalion.

April 1. Single-breasted tunic issued to Third Battalion.

May 10. Outbreak of Indian Mutiny.

May 13. Third Battalion completed to the Indian establishment.

May 30. Battle of the Hindun.

June 8. Battle of Badlee-ka-Serai and Siege of Delhi commenced.

July 27. Fourth Battalion was raised at Winchester. ‡

August 4, 5, 7, 8, 14. Third Battalion moved from Ireland to India in "Defiance," "John Bull," "Liverpool," "Sussex," "Tyburnia," and "Ballarat" transports.

September 14 *to* 20. Assault and Capture of Delhi.

---

* Armed with long Enfield rifle and bayonet; weight with bayonet, 9lbs. 3 oz.; length of barrel, 3 feet 3 inches; weight, 4 lbs. 1½ oz.; diameter of bore, .577 inches; three grooves, one turn in 78 inches; charge, 2½ drs. Pritchett bullet, cylindro-conoidal form, lubricated, weight 530 grains, diameter .568, windage .009 inches. Dress: Albert chaco and coatee, black leathern waist-belt and spock, pouch-belt and pouch for 60 rounds, ball bag on waist-belt, small pouch for 20 rounds on waist-belt, latter returned into store in 1861

† Short Enfield-Pritchett rifle; three grooves, as above, weight 9 lbs.

‡ Armed with short Enfield-Pritchett rifles. Dress: tunic, red facings, black waist and pouch-belts, ball bag and cap pocket in front, former for 50 rounds, latter 10 rounds.

1858.

April 1 *to May* 27. Rohilcund Campaign.

May 6. Head-quarters and right wing, Second Battalion, moved from British Kaffraria to India in steamer " United Kingdom."

September 24. Left wing moved from British Kaffraria to India in H.M.S. " Megæra."

September 25. Short Enfield-Pritchett rifles issued to First Battalion.*

Medals for Kaffir War issued to Second Battalion.

October 18. Oudh Campaign.

December 18. Short Enfield-Pritchett rifles issued to Third Battalion.*

1859.

August. Serge frock issued to First Battalion in India.

1860.

February 28. Second Battalion moved from India to China in " Alfred," " Indomitable," and " Hougomont " transports.

March 17. First Battalion moved from India to England in " Aliquis " and " Monica " transports.

August 21. Capture of Taku Forts.

September 13. Capture of Pekin.

Fourth Battalion moved from England to Ireland.

September 20. Medals for Indian Mutiny issued to First Battalion.

October 5. New pattern chaco, cloth-stitched, without chin strap, issued to First Battalion.

1861.

April 10. Marine Service Rifle and sword bayonet issued to First Battalion.†

June 26. Fourth Battalion moved from Ireland to Canada in S.S. " Great Eastern."

September 30. Second Battalion moved from China to England in H.M.S. " Simoom," and " Flying Cloud," of New York transport.

---

* See foot note, p. 57.

† Similar to the short Enfield, with the following exceptions :— 577 diameter of bore ; five grooves, with one turn in 4 feet.

December 2. "Taku Forts" and "Pekin" granted.*

Medals for China issued to Second Battalion.

December 30. Third Battalion moved from India to Burmah.

1862.

January 17 *and February* 19. Third Battalion moved from the East Indies to Burmah in steamers "Sidney," "Tubal Cain," with "Sesostris" and "Commodore" in tow.

March. Medals for Indian Mutiny issued to the right wing Second Battalion.

June. Westley-Richards' breech-loading rifle, and Metford's explosive bullet, issued to marksmen First Battalion, for trial and report.

1863.

March 7. First Battalion was present at the public entry of Her Royal Highness the Princess Alexandra into London.

August 13. Authority for sword belts to be worn under tunic.†

September 1. Authority for scarlet facings to be substituted for red.‡

September 11. "Delhi" granted.§

1864.

May 28. Whitworth rifle issued to First Battalion.‖

Whitworth rifle issued to Second Battalion.

June 6. First Battalion moved from England to Ireland in H.M.S. "Aurora," "Geyser," and "Gladiator."

1865.

February 5. Depôt Companies First Battalion joined headquarters at Dublin from Winchester in steamer "Ceres."

Fourth Battalion was first on the roll of the British Army for shooting for the year 1865, figure of merit 126·39.

November 10 *and November* 17. Third Battalion moved from Burmah to India in troopships "Davenport" and "Star of India," were overtaken in a cyclone and nearly lost.

---

* War Office Letter, Horse Guards, December 2, 1861.

† Horse Guards Letter, August 13, 1863.

‡ Horse Guards Letter, 1st September, 1863.

§ General Order, 834, Horse Guards, September 3, 1863.

‖ Muzzle-loader, calibre across angles 0·4895 inches, sides 0·4195 inches; barrel, 39 inches long, 45 bore, one turn in 20 inches; either hexagonal or cylindrical bullet.

1866.

February 1. Second Battalion moved from England to Ireland.

February 23. First Battalion was formed into ten Service and two Depôt Companies.

March. First Battalion moved from Ireland to the Mediterranean in H.M.S. "Simoom."

November. Converted Snider breech-loading rifle issued to Second and Fourth Battalions.

1867.

Converted Snide breech-loading rifle issued to First Battalion.*

September 5. First Battalion moved from Mediterranean to Canada in H.M.S. "Himalaya."

September 14. Second Battalion moved from Ireland to India *viâ* Alexandria and rail to Suez, in H.M.S. "Crocodile," and from Suez in H.M.S. "Euphrates."

1868.

Twenty Martini-Henry rifles issued to First Battalion for trial and report.

1869.

March 3. Field Marshal H.R.H. the Duke of Cambridge appointed Colonel-in-Chief of the Regiment.

June 22. Fourth Battalion moved from Canada to England on board H.M.S. "Crocodile."

1870.

March 25. The Seventh or Rifle Depôt Battalion broken up. Depôts of First, Second, and Third Battalions attached to Fourth Battalion.

April 1. New pattern chaco with bronze chain issued to Fourth Battalion.

May 20 *and* 24. First Battalion proceeded on Red River Expedition.

October 5. First Battalion returned from Red River Expedition. New pattern tunic, and chaco with bronze chain issued to First Battalion.

December 5. Valise equipment, and Glengarry cap issued to Fourth Battalion.

* Marine service rifle as before described at p. 58, converted to a breech-loader by Jacob Snider.

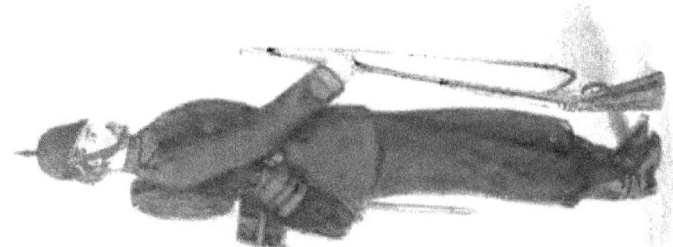

1873.

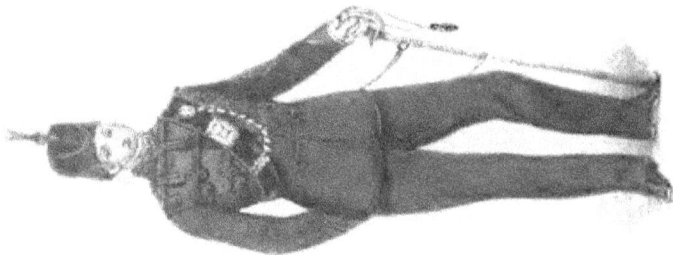

1873.

1878.

1871.

August.   Converted Snider breech-loading rifle issued to Third Battalion.

November 11.   First Battalion moved from Quebec to Halifax, N.S., in H.M.S. "Orontes."

November 29.   Third Battalion moved from India to Aden in H.M.S. "Serapis."

1872.

May 1.   Valise equipment issued to First Battalion.

November 29.   Third Battalion moved from Aden to England, *via* Suez Canal.

1873.

January.   Valise equipments, busbies, and Glengarry caps issued to Third Battalion.

January 15.   Martini-Henry breech-loading rifle issued to First Battalion.*

March 17.   First Battalion linked with Fourth, Second Battalion with the Third.

May 24.   Depôts of First and Second Battalions returned to Winchester.

July 7.   Glengarry caps issued to First Battalion.

October 1.   Busbies and Glengarry caps issued to Fourth Battalion.

1874.

April 1.   Busbies issued to First Battalion.

October 20.   Martini-Henry rifles issued to Third and Fourth Battalions.

December 4.   Fourth Battalion moved from England to Ireland.

1875.

November.   Water-bottles issued to First Battalion.

1876.

November.   Fourth Battalion moved from Ireland to India in H.M.S. "Serapis."

December 18.   First Battalion moved from Canada to England in H.M.S. "Tamar."

---

* Weight without sword, 8 lbs. 12 oz.; length without sword, 4ft. 1½ in.; weight, 3 lbs. 6 oz.; length, 2 ft. 9½ in.; calibre, 45 in., 7 grooves; turn of rifling, 1 inch in 22; range to 1,400 yards; charge, 85 grains; bullet, 480 grains. Extreme range 3,280 yards.

1877.

January 1.   Second Battalion was present at Delhi at the ceremony proclaiming Her Majesty the Queen Empress of India.*
Bronze Cross substituted for Rosette on Glengarry cap.

February 14.   New pattern haversack issued to First Battalion. Valise equipment, and Martini-Henry rifles issued to Second Battalion.

1878.

January 1.   Helmets issued to First Battalion.

April.   Two Company Depôts of First and Third Battalions joined the Rifle Depôt at Winchester.

April 20.   Militia and Army Reserves joined the First and Third Battalions on mobilisation.

July 31.   Militia and Army Reserves demobilised.

---

* In commemoration of which His Excellency the Viceroy granted a Silver Medal to the Battalion. It was presented, during the "Imperial assemblage" on the 1st January, to the Sergeant-Major, who is to retain it as long as he holds that position, after which it is to pass to his successors, in memory of the day.

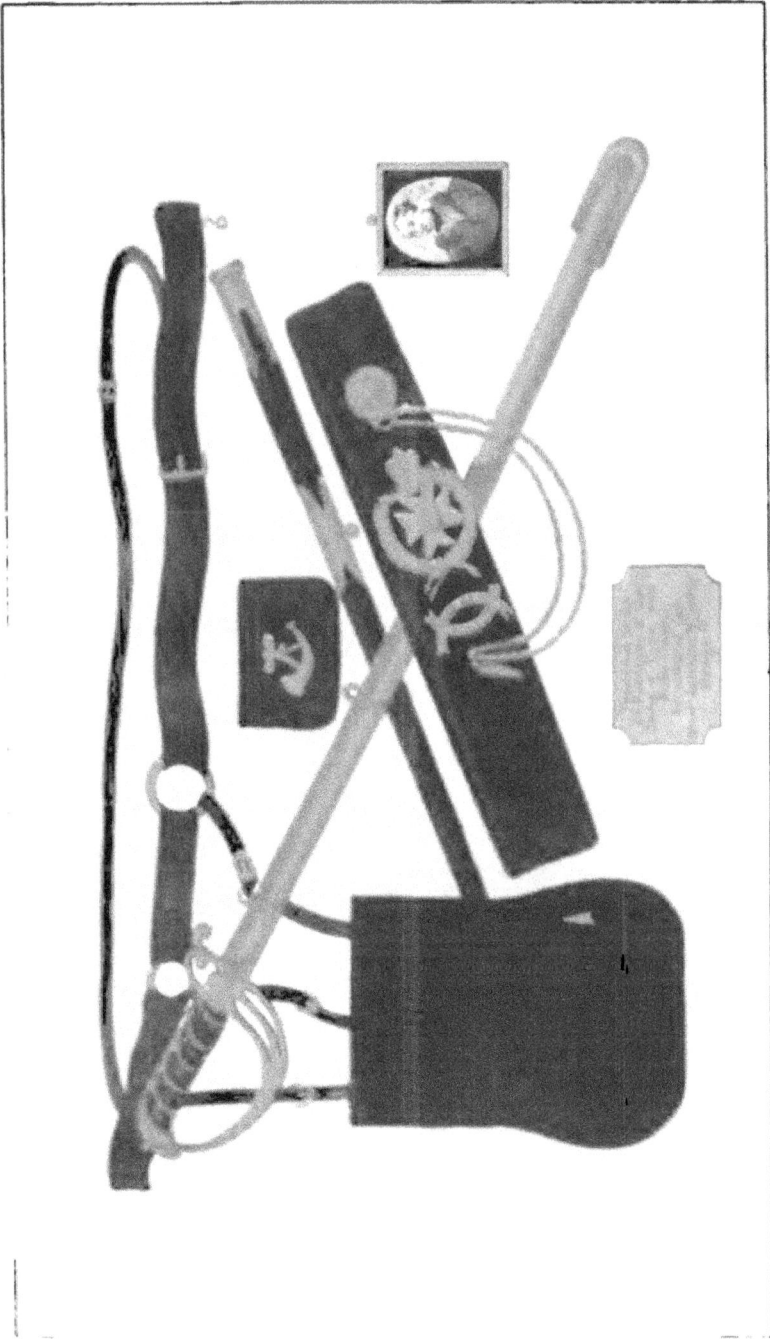

LISTS OF COLONELS-IN-CHIEF, COLONELS-COMMANDANT, LIEUTENANT-COLONELS COMMANDING, AND OFFICERS, WITH STATEMENT OF OFFICERS' SERVICES.

SUCCESSION LIST OF COLONELS-IN-CHIEF.

From—		From— (Date of Appointment.)	To—
1755 to 1757.	John Earl of Loudoun	25 Dec., 1755	26 Dec., 1757
1757 to 1758.	James Abercromby	27 Dec., 1757	30 Sept., 1758
1758 to 1797.	Jeffery Amherst, Sir Jeffery Amherst, K.B. (1761) Jefferr, Lord Amherst (1776)	30 Sept., 1758	23 Aug. 1797
	Hon. Thomas Gage	27 Sept., 1758	
1797 to 1827.	H.R.H. Fred., Duke of York, &c., K.G. (1812), G.C.B. (1816), G.C.H (1824)	23 Aug., 1797	25 Jan., 1827
1827 to 1850.	H.R.H. Duke of Cambridge, K.G., G.C.B., G.C.H., G.C.M.O. (1835), Field-Marshal (1844)	5 Jan., 1827	8 July, 1850
1850 to 1852.	Field-Marshal H.R.H. Francis Albert Augustus Charles Emanuel, Duke of Saxony, Prince of Saxe-Coburg and Gotha, K.G., K.T., K.P., G.C.B., G.C.M.O.	15 Aug., 1850	23 Sept., 1852
1852 to 1854.	General Viscount Beresford, G.C.B., G.C.H.	23 Sept., 1852	28 Jan., 1854
1854 to 1869.	General Hugh, Viscount Gough, G.C.B., K.P. (1857), Field-Marshal (1863), G.C.S.I. (1867)	28 Jan., 1854	3 Mar., 1869
1869.	Field-Marshal H.R.H. Duke of Cambridge, K.G., K.P., G.C.B., G.C.M.G.	3 Mar., 1869	

SUCCESSION LIST OF COLONELS-COMMANDANT.

Date of Appointment.

1756.

John Stanwix .. .. 1 Jan. 1756
Joseph Duffeaux .. .. 2 Jan. 1756
Charles Jeffereys .. .. 3 Jan. 1756
James Prevost .. .. 4 Jan. 1756

1757.

John Stanwix
Joseph Duffeaux
Joseph Haviland .. .. 2 Jan. 1756
James Prevost .. .. 4 Jan. 1756
George Vincent Howe .. 25 Feb. 1757

1758 to 1759.

John Stanwix
James Prevost
Charles Lawrence .. .. 28 Sept. 1757
Robert Monckton .. .. 20 Sept. 1757

1760.

John Stanwix
James Prevost
Charles Lawrence
Hon. James Murray .. .. 21 Oct. 1759

1761.

John Stanwix
James Prevost
Hon. James Murray
William Haviland .. .. 9 Dec. 1760
Marcus Smith .. .. .. 11 Nov. 1761

1762.

James Prevost
Hon. James Murray
William Haviland

1763 to 1768.

Hon. James Murray
James Prevost

1769 to 1772.

James Prevost
F'que Armstrong .. .. 16 Dec. 1767

1773 to 1776.

James Prevost
Fred. Haldiman.. .. .. 20 Oct. 1772
William Taylor .. .. .. 17 Sept. 1775

1777 to 1778.

Fred. Haldiman
James Robertson .. .. 11 Jan. 1776
John Dalling .. .. .. 16 Jan. 1776
Augustine Prevost .. .. 18 Sept. 1775

Date of Appointment.

1770 to 1783.

Fred. Haldiman
Gabriel Christie.. .. .. 14 May 1778
John Dalling
Augustus Prevost

1784 to 1786.

Fred. Haldiman, K.B. (1786)
Augustus Prevost

1787.

Fred. Haldiman, K.B.
Gabriel Christie

1788.

Fred Haldiman, K.B.
Gabriel Christie
William Rowley.. .. .. 3 Oct. 1787
Hon. William Gordon .. 3 Oct. 1787

1789 to 1791.

Fred. Haldiman, K.B.
Gabriel Christie
William Rowley
James Rooke .. .. .. 25 Oct. 1788

1792 to 1794.

Gabriel Christie
William Rowley
James Rooke
Alured Clarke .. .. .. 8 July 1791

1795 to 1796.

Gabriel Christie
William Rowley
James Rooke
Thomas Carleton .. .. 6 Aug. 1794

1797 to 1798.

Gabriel Christie
William Rowley
Thomas Carleton
Peter Hunter .. .. .. 2 Aug. 1796

1799.

Gabriel Christie
William Rowley
Thomas Carleton
Peter Hunter
William Morsland .. .. 30 Dec. 1797

Date of Appointment.

1800.

William Rowley
Thomas Carleton
Peter Hunter
William Morshead
William Gardiner .. .. 11 Nov. 1798
Robert Brownrigg .. .. 25 July 1799

1801 to 1804.

William Rowley
Thomas Carleton
Peter Hunter
William Gardiner
Robert Brownrigg
Thomas Staughton Stawix 9 May 1800

1805.

William Rowley
Thomas Carleton
Peter Hunter
William Gardiner
Robert Brownrigg
Lord Charles Fitzroy.. .. 15 June 1804
Hon. John Hope .. .. 3 Oct. 1805

1806 to 1807.

William Rowley
Thomas Carleton
Ed. Morrison .. .. .. 1 Jan. 1806
N. C. Burton .. .. .. 1 Jan. 1806
W. Keppel .. .. 1 Jan. 1806
Sir G. Prevost, Bart... .. 1 Jan. 1806

1808 to 1810.

Thomas Carleton
Edward Morrison
N. C. Burton
W. Keppel
Sir George Prevost, Bart.
Hon. Ed. Phipps .. .. 25 Aug. 1807

1811 to 1812.

Thomas Carleton
Edward Morrison
N. C. Burton
Sir G. Prevost, Bart.
Hon. E. Phipps
A. Whetham .. .. .. 7 Feb. 1811

1813 to 1815.

Thomas Carleton
N. C. Burton
Hon. E. Phipps
J. Robinson .. .. .. 2 Jan. 1813
Hon. C. Hope .. .. .. 15 Feb. 1813
Sir H. Clinton, K.B. .. 20 May 1813
Sir G. Murray, K.B. .. 9 Aug. 1813
J. Kempt .. .. 1 Nov. 1813

Date of Appointment.

1816 to 1817.

Thomas **Carleton**
N. C. Burton
Hon. E. Phipps
John Robinson
Hon. C. Hope
Sir G. Murray, G.C.B.
Sir J. Kempt, G.C.B.
Sir W. Pat. Acklund, K.C.B. 9 Aug. 1815

1818.

Napier C. Burton
Hon. E. Phipps
John Robinson
Hon. C. Hope
Sir James Kempt, G.C.B.

1819 to 1834.

N. C. Burton
Hon. E. Phipps

1835 to 1837.

Hon. E. Phipps
Sir John Maclean, K.C.B. 7 Jan. 1835

1838 to 1842.

Sir John Maclean, K.C.B. ..
Hon. Patrick Stuart .. .. 26 Sept. 1837

1843.

Hon. Patrick Stuart
Sir W. G. Davy, C.B., K.C.H. 2 Nov. 1842

1844 to 1855.

Sir W. G. Davy, K.B., K.C.H.
Sir W. C. Eustace,C.B.,K.C.H. 7 April 1843

1856.

Sir W. G. Davy, C.B., K.C.H.
Thomas Bunbury, K.H. .. 9 Feb. 1855

1857.

Thomas Bunbury, K.H.
Sir W. George Moore, K.C.B. 26 Jan. 1856

1858 to 1862.

Sir William Moore, K.C.B.
Joseph Paterson.. .. .. 14 April 1857

1863.

Joseph Paterson
Hon. G. Fred. Upton, C.B. 24 Oct. 1862

1864 to 1875.

G. F. Visc. Templetown, K.C.B. 24 Oct. 1862
H. Viscount Melville, G.C.B. 1 April 1863

1876 to 1878.

Sir A. A. T. Cunynghame, G.C.B. 24 Feb. 1876
Gen. Freeman Murray .. .. 11 Oct. 1876

F 2

SUCCESSION LIST OF LIEUTENANT-COLONELS COMMANDING.

Rank in Regiment.

1756 to 1757.

Henry Bouquet .. .. .. 3 Jan. 1756
Frederick Haldimaa .. .. 4 Jan. 1756
Russell Chapman .. .. 5 Jan. 1756
Sir John St. Clair, Bart. .. 6 Jan. 1756

1758 to 1760.

Henry Bouquet
Frederick Haldiman
Sir John St. Clair, Bart.
John Young .. .. .. 26 April 1756

1761 and 1762.

Henry Bouquet
Frederick Haldiman
Sir John St. Clair, Bart.
Augustine Prevost .. .. 20 Mar. 1761

1763 to 1765.

Henry Bouquet
Rank in Army, Col. 19 Feb. 1762
Frederick Haldiman
Rank in Army, Col. 19 Feb. 1762

1766.

Frederick Haldiman

1767 and 1768.

Frederick Haldiman
Augustine Prevost .. .. 13 Dec. 1765
Rank in Army, Col. 20 Mar. 1791

1769.

Frederick Haldiman
Gabriel Christie .. .. .. 14 Dec. 1768
Rank in Army, Col. 27 Jan. 1762

1770 to 1772.

Frederick Haldiman
Augustine Prevost .. .. 3 Nov. 1769

1773.

Augustine Prevost

1774 and 1775.

Augustine Prevost
Gabriel Christie.. .. .. 14 Aug. 1773

1776.

Gabriel Christie.. .. .. 18 Sept. 1775
George Etherington .. .. 19 Sept. 1775

Rank in Regiment.

1777 and 1778.

Gabriel Christie
George Etherington
William Stiell .. .. .. 21 Sept. 1775
Lewis Val. Fuser .. .. 20 Sept. 1775

1779 and 1780.

Stephen Kemble.. .. .. 14 May 1778
Rank in Army, 29 Aug. 1777
George Etherington
William Stiell
Lewis Val. Fuser

1781.

Stephen Kemble
George Etherington
William Stiell

1782.

Stephen Kemble..
Rank in Army, Col. 20 Nov. 1782
George Etherington
Rank in Army, Col. 16 May 1782
Archibald McArthur.. .. 24 April 1781
Beamsley Glazier .. .. 6 May 1778

1784 to 1787.

George Etherington
Stephen Kemble

1788 to 1790.

Stephen Kemble
Archibald McArthur
Rank in Army, Col. 24 April 1781
Peter Hunter .. .. .. 24 Sept. 1787
Rank in Army, Lt.-Col. 23 Nov. 1782
J. Adolphus Harris .. .. 16 Jan. 1788

1791 and 1792.

Stephen Kemble
Peter Hunter
James Adolphus Harris
Wm. Goodday Strutt .. 18 Nov. 1790

1793.

Stephen Kemble
Peter Hunter
James Adolphus Harris
Gerrit Fisher .. .. .. 25 April 1792

1794.

Peter Hunter
Rank in Army, Col. 12 Oct. 1793
James Adolphus Harris
Gerrit Fisher
Hon. Vere Poulett .. .. 13 May 1793

Rank in Regiment.

1795.

Peter Hunter
James Adolphus Harris
Hon. Vere Poulett
John Richie .. .. .. 17 Feb. 1794
Hon. John Elphinstone .. 20 July 1794
George Prevost .. .. .. 6 Aug. 1794
Rank in Army, 1 Mar. 1794

1796.

Peter Hunter
Rank in Army, M.-G. 26 **Feb.** 1795
James Adolphus Harris
Rank in Army, Col. 26 Feb. 1795
Hon. Vere Poulett
Hon. John Elphinstone
George Prevost
Duncan Mackintosh .. .. 1 Sept. 1795
Frederick Gottsched .. .. 2 Sept. 1795
Martin Hunter .. .. .. 12 Jan. 1796
Rank in Army, 19 July 1794

1797 and 1798.

James Adolphus Harris
Hon. John Elphinstone
George Prevost
Duncan Mackintosh
Frederick Gottsched
Martin Hunter
John de Berner .. .. .. 5 **Mar.** 1796
Rank in Army, 17 Feb. 1795
John Robert Napier .. .. 10 Aug. 1796

1799.

James Adolphus Harris
Rank in Army, Maj.-Gen. 1 Jan. 1798
George Prevost
Rank in Army, Col. 1 Jan. 1798
Duncan Mackintosh
Martin Hunter
John Robert Napier
George William Ramsay .. 30 Dec. 1797
Fr. Baron de Rottenburg .. 30 Dec. 1797
Robert Craufurd .. .. 30 Dec. 1797
Henry Couper .. .. .. 30 Dec. 1797
William Dowdeswell .. .. 18 Jan. 1798
Rank in Army, Col. 26 Jan. 1797
John Hughes .. .. .. 5 April 1798

1800.

James Adolphus Harris
George Prevost
Duncan Mackintosh
Martin Hunter
John Robert Napier
George William Ramsay ..
Fr. Baron de Rottenburg
Robert Craufurd
Henry Couper
William Dowdeswell
Thomas Philip Ainslie .. 20 June 1799
Lachlan McLean .. .. 25 July 1799
Rank in Army, 1 Jan. 1798
George Burgess Morden .. 26 July 1799
Rank in Army, 1 Jan. 1798

Rank in Regiment.

1801.

James Adolphus Harris
George Prevost
Duncan Mackintosh
George William Ramsay
Fr. Baron de Rottenburg
Robert Craufurd
Henry Couper
William Dowdeswell
Thomas Philip Ainslie
Lachlan McLean
George Burgess Morden
David Cunningham .. .. 8 Feb. 1800
Rank in Army, Col. 26 Jan. 1797

1802.

James Adolphus Harris
George Prevost
Duncan Mackintosh
George William Ramsay
Fr. Baron de Rottenburg
Rank in Army, 25 June 1796
Robert Craufurd
William Dowdeswell
Thomas Philip Ainslie
Lachlan McLean
George Burgess Morden
Frederick De Vos .. .. 15 Jan. 1801
Fitzroy J. Grafton **Maclean** 5 Feb. 1801
Rank in Army, 18 Nov. 1795

1803.

James Adolphus Harris
George Prevost
Duncan Mackintosh
George William Ramsay
Fr. Baron de Rottenburg
William Dowdeswell
Lachlan McLean
George Burgess Morden
Fitzroy J. Grafton Maclean
Robert Lethbridge .. .. 11 Feb. 1802
Rank in Army, 1 Jan. 1800
John Campbell .. .. .. 8 Mar. 1802
Gabriel Gordon .. .. .. 9 Mar. 1802
C. L. Theod. Schwehle .. 25 April 1802
Rank in Army, 16 May 1800

1804.

James Adolphus Harris
George Prevost
Duncan Mackintosh
George William Ramsay
Fr. Baron de Rottenburg
Lachlan McLean
Fitzroy J. Grafton Maclean
Robert Lethbridge
Gabriel Gordon
C. L. Theod. Schwehle
Gervaise Rainey .. .. .. 20 April 1803
Francis Streucler .. .. 30 April 1797
Rank in Army, Lt.-Col. 29 April 1802

1805.

James Adolphus Harris
George Prevost
Duncan Mackintosh

Rank in Regiment.

Geo. Wm. Ramsay
Fras. Baron de Rottenburg
Gabriel Gordon
C. L. Theod. Schoedde
Gervaise Rainey
John Hope .. .. 30 June 1804
   Rank in Army, 20 Feb. 1796
Lewis Mosheim .. .. .. 14 Sept. 1804
   Rank in Army, 29 April 1802
Edward Codd .. .. .. 26 Oct. 1804

1806 to 1808.

James Adolphus Harris
  Rank in Army { Maj.-Gen. 1 Jan. 1798
             { Lt.-Gen. 1 Jan. 1805
Geo. Wm. Ramsay
   Rank in Army, Col. 30 Jan. 1805
Fras. Baron de Rottenburg
   Rank in Army, Col. 1 Jan. 1805
Gabriel Gordon
Gervaise Rainey
John Hope
   Rank in Army, Col. 1 Jan. 1805
J. Wheeler Unwin .. .. 29 April 1802
Lewis Mosheim
   Rank in Army, 29 April 1802
Edward Codd
Edward Drummond .. .. 9 Dec. 1800
Thomas Austin .. .. .. 20 June 1805

1809.

James Adolphus Harris
George William Ramsay
Fras. Baron de Rottenburg
John Hope
Lewis Mosheim
Edward Codd
Thomas Austin
Paul Anderson .. .. .. 11 Jan. 1808
   Rank in Army, 17 Oct. 1805
Fr. Ger. Viscount Lake .. 10 May 1808
   Rank in Army, Col. 25 April 1808
William Dowdeswell .. .. 2 June 1808
   Rank in Army, Major-Gen. 25 Sept. 1803
George Mackie .. .. .. 22 Dec. 1808

1810.

James Adolphus Harris
George William Ramsay
Fras. Baron de Rottenburg
John Hope
Edward Codd
Thomas Austin
Paul Anderson
Fr. Ger. Viscount Lake
William Dowdeswell
George Mackie
William Williams .. .. 15 Nov. 1809
Anthony Wharton .. .. 16 Aug. 1810

1811.

James Adolphus Harris
George William Ramsay

Rank in Regiment.

Fras. Baron de Rottenburg
John Hope
Edward Codd
Thomas Austin
Paul Anderson
Fr. Ger. Viscount Lake
William Dowdeswell
George Mackie
William Williams
James Lomax .. .. .. 16 Nov. 1809
Anthony Wharton

1812.

James Adolphus Harris
George William Ramsay
Fras. Baron de Rottenburg
John Hope
Edward Codd
Thomas Austin
Paul Anderson
Fr. Ger. Viscount Lake
William Dowdeswell
George Mackie
William Williams
James Lomax
Anthony Wharton

1813 and 1814.

James Adolphus Harris
George William Ramsay
John Hope
Edward Codd
Thomas Austin
Paul Anderson
Fr. Ger. Viscount Lake
William Dowdeswell
George Mackie
James Lomax
Anthony Wharton
John Keane .. .. 25 June 1812
   Rank in Army, Col. 1 Jan. 1812
Henry John .. .. 9 Aug. 1813
John Philip Hunt .. .. 11 Nov. 1813

1815.

George William Ramsay
Edward Codd
Thomas Austin
Paul Anderson
Fr. Ger. Viscount Lake
George Mackie
James Lomax
Henry John
William Marlton.. .. .. 26 May 1814
   Rank in Army, 1 Jan. 1812
Adolphus J. Dalrymple .. 1 June 1814
William Woodgate .. .. 16 June 1814
   Rank in Army, 30 May 1811

1816.

Edward Codd
Thomas Austin
Paul Anderson, C.B.

Rank in Regiment.

George Mackie, C.B.
James Lomax
William Marlton
William Woodgate, C.B.
Edward Walker .. .. .. 9 Feb. 1815
    Rank in Army, 1 Oct. 1812
James Stopford .. .. .. 9 Mar. 1815

1817.

Edward Codd
    Rank in Army, Col. 4 June 1813
Thomas Austin
    Rank in Army, Col. 4 June 1813
Paul Anderson, C.B.
    Rank in Army, Col. 4 June 1813
George Mackie, C.B.
    Rank in Army, Col. 4 June 1813
James Lomax
William Woodgate, C.B.
James Stopford
Alexander Andrews .. .. 14 Dec. 1815

1818.

Edward Codd
George Mackie, C.B.
James Lomax
James Stopford
Alexander Andrews

1819.

Edward Codd
George Mackie, C.B.

1820 to 1823.

Edward Codd
    Rank in Army, Maj.-Gen. 12 Aug. 1819
George Mackie, C.B.
Alexander Andrews
    Rank in Army, 12 Aug. 1819

1824.

Edward Codd
George Mackie, C.B.
Thomas Bunbury .. .. 5 Feb. 1824

1825.

Edward Codd
George Mackie, C.B.
Thomas Bunbury
John Guliffe .. .. .. 18 June 1825

1826 to 1828.

Thomas Bunbury
    Rank in Army, 5 July 1821
Henry Fitzgerald .. .. 25 Dec. 1825

1829 to 1835.

Thomas Bunbury
Hon. H. A. F. Ellis .. .. 18 Dec. 1828

1830 to 1841.

Hon. H. A. F. Ellis
Hon. Hon. Rich. Molyneux 24 April 1835
    Rank in Army, 9 April 1825

Rank in Regiment.

1842.

Walter Trevelyan .. .. 10 Aug. 1841
Charles Markham .. .. 17 Aug. 1841

1843 to 1844.

Walter Trevelyan
Wemyss Thomas Cockburn, 23 April 1842

1845.

Hon. Henry Dundas, C.B.. 3 Dec. 1820
    Rank in Army, Col. 23 Nov. 1841
Cosby Lewis Nesbitt .. 26 July 1844
Hon. G. Augustus Spencer 30 Dec. 1844

1846 to 1851.

Hon. Henry Dundas, K.C.B. **1850**
Cosby Lewis Nesbitt
Joseph Bradshaw .. .. 27 Aug. 1841

1852.

Henry, Viscount Melville, K.C.B.
C. L. Nesbitt

1853.

Henry, Viscount Melville, K.C.B.
C. L. Nesbitt
Maurice Griffin Dennis .. 19 Oct. 1854

1854.

Henry, Viscount Melville, K.C.B.
Maurice Griffin Dennis
Charles Howe Spence .. 2 Oct. 1853

1855.

M. G. Dennis
    Rank in Army, Col. 28 Nov. 1854
C. H. Spence
John Jones .. .. .. 20 June 1854

1856 and 1857.

M. G. Dennis
C. H. Spence
John Jones
    Rank in Army, Col. 2 Oct. 1856
William Fanshawe Bedford 25 Mar. 1855

1858.

M. G. Dennis
C. H. Spence
J. Jones
W. F. Bedford
H. Bingham .. .. .. 19 June 1857
E. J. J. Vesey Brown .. .. 27 May 1856

1859.

M. G. Dennis
Sir John Jones, K.C.B.
    Rank in Army, Col. 19 Jan. 1858
W. F. Bedford
    Rank in Army, Col. 23 Mar. 1855
H. Bingham
E. J. V. Brown
Francis Roger Palmer, C.B. 22 June 1858
Webbe Butler .. .. .. 9 Sept. 1858

Rank in Regiment.

1860.
M. G. Dennis
Sir John Jones, K.C.B.
W. F. Bedford
H. Bingham
F. R. Palmer, C.B.
W. Butler
Wm. Pretyman *   ..   .. 29 April 1859

1861.
Sir John Jones, K.C.B.
H. Bingham
F. R. Palmer
Webbe Butler
Robert B. Hawley   ..   .. 18 May 1860
Peter Burton Roe   ..   .. 18 Sept. 1860

1862 to 1864.
H. Bingham
    Rank in Army, Col. 2 Feb. 1862
F. R. Palmer, C.B.
    Rank in Army, Col. 8 Aug. 1863
W. Butler
R. B. Hawley
P. B. Roe

1865.
Henry Bingham
F. R. Palmer, C.B.
R. B. Hawley
P. B. Roe
Randle Joseph Feilden   .. 1 Mar. 1864

1866 to 1870.
F. R. Palmer, C.B.
R. B. Hawley
    Rank in Army, Col. 18 May 1865
P. B. Roe
    Rank in Army, Col. 18 Sept. 1865
R. J. Feilden
    Rank in Army, Col. 1 Mar. 1869

Rank in Regiment.

1871.
F. R. Palmer, C.B.
R. B. Hawley
P. B. Roe
R. J. Feilden
Henry Friend Kennedy   .. 22 Nov. 1869

1872.
F. R. Palmer
R. B. Hawley
P. B. Roe
H. F. Kennedy
Chas. Alex. Boswell Gordon 9 Aug. 1871

1873.
Robert B. Hawley
P. B. Roe
C. A. B. Gordon
Gibbes Rigaud ..   ..   .. 24 April 1872
    Rank in Army, Col. 22 April 1868

1874 and 1875.
P. B. Roe
C. A. B. Gordon
Hugh Parker Montgomery 13 Aug. 1873
Charles Williamson ..   .. 18 Oct. 1873

1876 and 1877.
C. A. B. Gordon
    Rank in Army, Col. 13 Jan. 1876
H. P. Montgomery
W. L. Pemberton   ..   .. 10 Mar. 1875
R. W. Hinxman..   ..   .. 5 June 1875

1878.
H. P. Montgomery *
W. L. Pemberton
R. W. Hinxman
J. D. Douglas   ..   .. 19 Dec. 1877
J. J. Collins..   ..   .. 21 Aug. 1878

* Retired from command at expiration of five years.

LIST OF OFFICERS FROM 1756-1878.

The accompanying Lists have been taken from the Annual and Quarterly Army Lists published since the formation of the Regiment, and do not, therefore, necessarily include the names of all Officers who may have been gazetted to the Regiment, whose length of service in it may have been extremely short.

Great care has been taken to copy these Lists correctly, but in such a mass of names and dates some errors are almost unavoidable.

1756.

THE 62ND, OR THE ROYAL AMERICAN REGIMENT OF FOOT.

Four Battalions.

North America.

Rank and Name.	Rank in Regiment.
Col.-in-Chief—	
John, Earl of Loudoun	**25 Dec.** 1755
Cols.-Commandant—	
John Stanwix	1 Jan. 1756
Joseph Duffeaux	2 Jan. 1756
James Prevost	3 Jan. 1756
Lieut.-Colonels—	
Henry Bouquet	3 Jan. 1756
Frederick Haldimand	4 Jan. 1756
Russell Chapman	5 Jan. 1756
Sir John St. Clair, Bart.	6 Jan. 1756
Majors—	
John Young	25 Dec. 1755
James Robertson	26 Dec. 1755
John Rutherford	6 Jan. 1756
Augustine Prevost	9 Jan. 1756
Captains—	
John Tulliken	25 Dec. 1755
Thomas Oswald	26 Dec. 1755
Rodolph Fasch	27 Dec. 1755
Frederick Porter	28 Dec. **1755**
—— Munster	29 Dec. **1755**
Walter Rutherford	30 Dec. **1755**
—— Wittstein	31 Dec. **1755**
Charles Greme	1 Jan. 1756
Ralph Harding	2 Jan. 1756
—— Chambrier	3 Jan. 1756
Jeremiah Stanton	4 Jan. 1756
—— Knelling	5 Jan. 1756
Richard Mather	6 Jan. 1756
Gustavus Wetterstroom	7 Jan. 1756
Harry Charters	8 Jan. 1756
—— Steiner	10 Jan. 1756
Francis Lander	11 Jan. 1756
—— Rollas	12 Jan. 1756
John Innis	13 Jan. 1756
—— Schrader	14 Jan. 1756
Gavin Cochran	15 Jan. 1756
Joseph Prince	16 Jan. 1756
Marcus Prevost	17 Jan. 1756
Thomas Stanwix	18 Jan. 1756
Alexander Harbord	19 Jan. 1756
Abraham Bosomworth	20 Jan. 1756
John Fasch	21 Jan. 1756
—— de Schol (vice Castlemain 13th Foot)	22 Jan. 1756

Rank and Name.	Rank in Regiment.
Captain-Lieutenants—	
—— Schlosser	12 May 1756
John Dalrymple	26 Dec. 1755
Stephen Gradley	27 Dec. 1755
Edward Comberbach	28 Dec. 1755
Lieutenants—	
Gilbert M'Adam	26 Dec. 1755
Charles Crookshanks	28 Dec. 1755
Samuel Jas. Hollandt	29 Dec. 1755
George Brereton	30 Dec. 1755
Charles Forbes	31 Dec. 1755
Francis Pringle	31 Dec. 1755
Robert Brigstock	1 Jan. 1756
Peter von Ingen	2 Jan. 1756
Alexander M'Bean	3 Jan. 1756
Donald Campbell	4 Jan. 1756
Newsham Piers	5 Jan. 1756
—— Habberthorn	6 Jan. 1756
John Longsdon	7 Jan. 1756
Allan M'Lean	8 Jan. 1756
George Warburton	9 Jan. 1756
—— Barnstedt	10 Jan. 1756
Cunningham Cooper	11 Jan. 1756
Hazel Dunbar	12 Jan. 1756
John Evans	29 May 1756
—— Ourry	14 Jan. 1756
James Dalyell	15 Jan. 1756
Richard Wynne	16 Jan. 1756
James Allas	17 Jan. 1756
Thomas Lindsay (of 2 F.)	28 May 1756
William Baillie	19 Jan. 1756
John Swift	20 Jan. 1756
Christopher Spuesmacher	21 Jan. 1756
William Cook	22 Jan. 1756
Elias Meyer	23 Jan. 1756
Henry Sinnocks	24 Jan. 1756
Simson Ewyrer	25 Jan. 1756
Charles Willington	26 Jan. 1756
Charles Gallot	27 Jan. 1756
John Sealy	28 Jan. 1756
—— Girardidier	29 Jan. 1756
James Campbell	30 Jan. 1756
Simon Fraser	31 Jan. 1756
George Fullerton	1 Feb. 1756
William Stuart	2 Feb. 1756
Alexander Campbell	3 Feb. 1756
Joseph Ray	4 Feb. 1756
George Turnbull	5 Feb. 1756
William Abercrombie	6 Feb. 1756
David Ouchterlony	7 Feb. 1756
William Hazlewood	8 Feb. 1756
John Brown	9 Feb. 1756
Daniel M'Alpin	10 Feb. 1756

Rank and Name.	Rank in Regiment.
Lieutenants (continued)—	
Donald Forbes	11 Feb. 1756
Henry Gordon	12 Feb. 1756
—— Mackay	13 Feb. 1756
Thomas Basset	14 Feb. 1756
George Fresh	15 Feb. 1756
George Etherington ..	16 Feb. 1756
Emanuel Hesse	17 Feb. 1756
Rodolphus Bentinck ..	18 Feb. 1756
John Mulker	19 Feb. 1756
Bernard Ratzer	20 Feb. 1756
Dietrich Brehm	21 Feb. 1756
Fred. von Weissenfels ..	22 Feb. 1756
Jos. Frd. Wallet des Barres	23 Feb. 1756
Conrad Gugy	24 Feb. 1756
—— Kleinbeil.. ..	25 Feb. 1756
—— Zimmerman ..	26 Feb. 1756
—— Fuser	27 Feb. 1756
—— Winter	28 Feb. 1756
—— Von Ingen ..	29 Feb. 1756
John Williams Maier (vice Schlosser) ..	1 Mar. 1756
Ensigns—	
Brereton Poynton	25 Dec. 1755
—— Allen	25 Dec. 1755
Thomas Barnsley ..	26 Dec. 1755
—— M'Intosh ..	27 Dec. 1755
Thomas Campbell ..	28 Dec. 1755
Ralph Phillips ..	29 Dec. 1755
Samuel Mackay ..	30 Dec. 1755
Francis Mackay ..	31 Dec. 1755
George Archibald ..	1 Jan. 1756
James Monro	2 Jan. 1756
William Ridge ..	3 Jan. 1756
William Hay	4 Jan. 1756
Alexander Shaw ..	5 Jan. 1756
Thomas Meredith ..	6 Jan. 1756
Stair Campbell Carre	7 Jan. 1756
Walter Kennedy ..	8 Jan. 1756
Michael Davis.. ..	9 Jan. 1756
William Potts.. ..	10 Jan. 1756
Andrew Watson ..	11 Jan. 1756
William Jones ..	12 Jan. 1756
John Bell	13 Jan. 1756
Nicholas Sutherland ..	14 Jan. 1756
William Ryder ..	15 Jan. 1756
Abraham Hart ..	16 Jan. 1756
Robert Campbell ..	17 Jan. 1756
James Crofton ..	18 Jan. 1756
Townsend Guy ..	19 Jan. 1756
James Jeffries.. ..	20 Jan. 1756
Francis Hutchinson ..	21 Jan. 1756
James Herring ..	22 Jan. 1756
Edward Jenkins ..	23 Jan. 1756
James Ralfe	24 Jan. 1756
John Netterville ..	25 Jan. 1756
Allen Grant	1 Feb. 1756
Alexander Grant ..	2 Feb. 1756
Geo. Older (vice O'Brien)	3 Feb. 1756
Chaplains—	
Thomas Gawton ..	25 Dec. 1755
Wm. Nicholson Jackson..	4 Feb. 1756
Surgeons—	
George Tating.. ..	1 Feb. 1756
John M'Kenzie ..	2 Feb. 1756

Rank and Name.	Rank in Regiment.
Surgeons (continued)—	
George Wirgman	3 Feb. 1756
—— Stevenson	4 Feb. 1756

Regimentals—Red, facings blue, white lace, 2 blue stripes.

Agent—Mr. Calcraft, Channel Row, Westminster.

1757.

THE 60TH, OR THE ROYAL AMERICAN REGIMENT OF FOOT.

North America.

Four Battalions.

Rank and Name.	Rank in Regiment.
Col.-in-Chief—	
John, Earl of Loudoun..	25 Dec. 1755
Cols.-Commandant—	
John Stanwix..	1 Jan. 1756
Joseph Dufleaux	2 Jan. 1756
—— Haviland	
James Prevost	4 Jan. 1756
Lieut.-Colonels—	
Henry Bouquet	3 Jan. 1756
Frederick Haldiman ..	4 Jan. 1756
Russell Chapman.. ..	5 Jan. 1756
Sir John St. Clair, Bart..	6 Jan. 1756
Majors—	
John Young	25 Dec. 1755
James Robertson	26 Dec. 1755
John Rutherford	6 Jan. 1776
Augustine Prevost	9 Jan. 1776
Captains—	
John Tullikens	25 Dec. 1755
Thomas Oswald	26 Dec. 1755
Rodolph Fasch	27 Dec. 1755
Frederick Porter	28 Dec. 1755
—— Munster.. ..	29 Dec. 1755
Walter Rutherford.. ..	30 Dec. 1755
Hiacinthe de Bonneville	31 Dec. 1755
Charles Graham	1 Jan. 1756
Ralph Harding	2 Jan. 1756
—— Williams	3 Jan. 1756
Jeremiah Stanton	4 Jan. 1756
—— Gniebling	5 Jan. 1756
Richard Mather	6 Jan. 1756
Gustavus Wetterstrom..	7 Jan. 1756
Harry Charteris	8 Jan. 1756
—— Steiner	10 Jan. 1756
Francis Lander	11 Jan. 1756
—— Du Fer	12 Jan. 1756
John Innis	13 Jan. 1756
—— Burman	14 Jan. 1756
Gavin Cochran	15 Jan. 1756
Joseph Prince.. ..	16 Jan. 1756
Marcus Prevost	17 Jan. 1756
Thomas Stanwix	18 Jan. 1756
Alexander Harbard ..	19 Jan. 1756
Abraham Bosomworth ..	20 Jan. 1756
John Fresh	21 Jan. 1756
—— Little	22 Jan. 1756
Captain-Lieutenants—	
John Dalrymple	26 Dec. 1755
Stephen Gualley	27 Dec. 1755
Edward Cumberbach ..	28 Dec. 1755
—— Schlosser	12 May 1756

Rank and Name.	Rank in Regiment.
Lieutenants—	
Gilbert M'Adam	26 Dec. 1755
Charles Crookshanks	28 Dec. 1755
Samuel Jan. Hollandt	29 Dec. 1755
Charles Forbes	31 Dec. 1755
Francis Pringle	31 Dec. 1755
Robert Brigstock	1 Jan. 1756
Peter von Ingen	2 Jan. 1756
Alexander M'Bean	3 Jan. 1756
Donald Campbell	4 Jan. 1756
—— Le Noble	6 Jan. 1756
John Longsdon	7 Jan. 1756
Allan M'Lean	8 Jan. 1756
George Warburton	9 Jan. 1756
—— Rhein	10 Jan. 1756
Basil Dunbar	12 Jan. 1756
—— Gurry	14 Jan. 1756
James Dalyell	15 Jan. 1756
—— Allan	17 Jan. 1756
William Baillie	19 Jan. 1756
John Swift	20 Jan. 1756
Christ. Spriesmacher	21 Jan. 1756
Elias Meyer	23 Jan. 1756
Simeon Reuyier	25 Jan. 1756
Charles Willington	26 Jan. 1756
—— Gallot	27 Jan. 1756
—— Grandidier	29 Jan. 1756
James Campbell	30 Jan. 1756
Simon Fraser	31 Jan. 1756
George Fullerton	1 Feb. 1756
William Stuart	2 Feb. 1756
Alexander Campbell	3 Feb. 1756
Joseph Hay	4 Feb. 1756
George Turnbull	5 Feb. 1756
William Abercrombie	6 Feb. 1756
David Oughterlony	7 Feb. 1756
William Hazlewood	8 Feb. 1756
John Brown	9 Feb. 1756
Daniel M'Alpin	10 Feb. 1756
Donald Forbes	11 Feb. 1756
Henry Gordon	12 Feb. 1756
—— Mackay	13 Feb. 1756
Thomas Basset	14 Feb. 1756
George Fawell	15 Feb. 1756
George Etherington	16 Feb. 1756
Emanuel Hesse	17 Feb. 1756
Rudolphus Bentinck	18 Feb. 1756
Jacob Miller	19 Feb. 1756
Bernard Ratzer	20 Feb. 1756
Dietrich Brehm	21 Feb. 1756
Fred. von Weissenfels	22 Feb. 1756
Jos. P. Wallet des Barres	23 Feb. 1756
Conrad Gugy	24 Feb. 1756
—— Fanner	25 Feb. 1756
—— Desnouiles	26 Feb. 1756
C. F. Fuser	27 Feb. 1756
A. T. F. Winter	28 Feb. 1756
—— Von Ingen	29 Feb. 1756
James Williams	1 Mar. 1756
—— Miner	12 May 1756
Thomas Lindsey	28 May 1756
John Evans	29 May 1756
Ensigns—	
Brereton Poynton	25 Dec. 1755
James Allen	25 Dec. 1755
Thomas Barnsley	26 Dec. 1755

Rank and Name.	Rank in Regiment.
Ensigns (continued)—	
George M'Intosh	27 Dec. 1755
Thomas Campbell	28 Dec. 1755
Ralph Phillipe	29 Dec. 1755
Samuel Mackay	30 Dec. 1755
Francis Mackay	31 Dec. 1755
George Archibald	1 Jan. 1756
James Monro	2 Jan. 1756
William Ridge	3 Jan. 1756
William Hay	4 Jan. 1756
Alexander Shaw	5 Jan. 1756
Thomas Meredith	6 Jan. 1756
Stair Campbell Carre	7 Jan. 1756
Walter Kennedy	8 Jan. 1756
Michael Davis	9 Jan. 1756
William Potts	10 Jan. 1756
Andrew Watson	11 Jan. 1756
William Jones	12 Jan. 1756
John Bell	13 Jan. 1756
Nicholas Sutherland	14 Jan. 1756
William Rysler	15 Jan. 1756
Abraham Hart	16 Jan. 1756
Robert Campbell	17 Jan. 1756
James Crofton	18 Jan. 1756
Townsend Guy	19 Jan. 1756
James Jeffries	20 Jan. 1756
Francis Hutchinson	21 Jan. 1756
James Herring	22 Jan. 1756
Edward Jenkins	23 Jan. 1756
James Ralfe	24 Jan. 1756
John Netterville	25 Jan. 1756
Allen Grant	1 Feb. 1756
Alexander Grant	2 Feb. 1756
George Otter	3 Feb. 1756
Chaplains—	
Thomas Gaston	25 Dec. 1755
Wm. Nicholson Jackson	4 Feb. 1756
Surgeons—	
John M'Kenzie	2 Feb. 1756
George Wiegman	3 Feb. 1756
—— Stevenson	4 Feb. 1756

*Regimentals—*Red, facings blue, white laces, 2 blue stripes.

Agent—Mr Calcraft, Channel Row, Westminster.

1758.
Four Battalions
North America
Colonel-Chief—

James Abercromby	27 Dec. 1757
Rank in Army, Maj.-Gen.	31 Jan. 1756
Cols.-Commandant—	
John Stanwix	1 Jan. 1756
James Prevost	4 Jan. 1756
Charles Lawrence	28 Sept. 1757
Robert Monckton	20 Sept. 1757
Lieut.-Colonels—	
Henry Bouquet	3 Jan. 1756
Frederick Haldimand	4 Jan. 1756
Sir John St. Clair, Bart.	6 Jan. 1756
John Young	26 April 1756
Majors—	
James Robertson	26 Dec. 1755
Rank in Army, Lt.-Col.	8 July 1758

Rank and Names	Rank in Regiment.
Majors (continued)—	
John Rutherford	6 Jan. 1756
Augustine Prevost.. ..	9 Jan. 1756
John Tullikens	26 April 1757
Captains—	
Thomas Oswald	26 Dec. 1755
Rodolph Fæsch	27 Dec. 1755
Frederick Porter	28 Dec. 1755
D. Munster	29 Dec. 1755
Walter Rutherford.. ..	30 Dec. 1755
Charles Greene	1 Jan. 1756
Ralph Harding	2 Jan. 1756
Jeremiah Stanton	4 Jan. 1756
—— Onielling	5 Jan. 1756
Richard Mather	6 Jan. 1756
Gust. Wetterstroom ..	7 Jan. 1756
Harry Charteris	8 Jan. 1756
—— Steiner	10 Jan. 1756
Francis Lander	11 Jan. 1756
John Innis	13 Jan. 1756
—— Burmand	14 Jan. 1756
Gavin Cochran	15 Jan. 1756
Joseph Prince..	16 Jan. 1756
Marcus Prevost	17 Jan. 1756
Alexander Harbord ..	19 Jan. 1756
Abraham Bosomworth ..	20 Jan. 1756
John Bradstreet	8 Mar. 1757
Rank in Army,	5 Sept. 1745
Thomas Jocelyn	8 Mar. 1757
Rank in Army,	25 June. 1747
James Delancey	8 Mar. 1757
Rank in Army,	25 Nov. 1754
Samuel Wilyamoz	8 Mar. 1757
George du Fez	8 Mar. 1757
Stephen Gually	21 May 1757
William Stuart	21 May 1757
Captain-Lieutenants—	
Edward Comberbach ..	28 Dec. 1755
—— Schlosser	12 May 1756
Sam. Jun. Hollandt ..	21 May 1757
Charles Forbes	22 Mar. 1757
Lieutenants—	
Robert Brigstock	1 Jan. 1756
Rank in Army,	16 Feb. 1747-8
Peter von Ingen	2 Jan. 1756
Alexander M'Bean.. ..	3 Jan. 1756
Rank in Army,	17 May 1748
Donald Campbell	4 Jan. 1756
—— Le Noble	6 Jan. 1756
John Longsdon	7 Jan. 1756
Allan McLean..	8 Jan. 1756
Bazil Dunbar	12 Jan. 1756
Lewis Ourry	14 Jan. 1756
James Albany..	17 Jan. 1756
William Baillie	19 Jan. 1756
Christ. Spiessmacher ..	21 Jan. 1756
Elias Meyer	24 Jan. 1756
Simeon Ecuyer	25 Jan. 1756
Charles Wellington.. ..	26 Jan. 1756
Charles Galiot	27 Jan. 1756
—— Grundicker	29 Jan. 1756
James Campbell	30 Jan. 1756
George Fullerton	1 Feb. 1756
Alexander Campbell ..	3 Feb. 1756
Joseph Ray	4 Feb. 1756

Rank and Names	Rank in Regiment.
Lieutenants (continued)—	
George Turnbull	5 Feb. 1756
Wm. Abercrombie	6 Feb. 1756
David Ouchterlony.. ..	7 Feb. 1756
William Hazlewood ..	8 Feb. 1756
John Brown	9 Feb. 1756
Daniel M'Alpin	10 Feb. 1756
Donald Forbes..	11 Feb. 1756
Harry Gordon..	12 Feb. 1756
Rank in Army, Capt.	4 Jan. 1758
Thomas Basset	14 Feb. 1756
George Fæsch	15 Feb. 1756
George Etherington ..	16 Feb. 1756
Emanuel Hesse	17 Feb. 1756
Rodolphus Bentinck ..	18 Feb. 1756
Jacob Muller	19 Feb. 1756
Bernard Ratzer	20 Feb. 1756
Dietrich Brehm	21 Feb. 1756
Fred. von Weissenfels ..	22 Feb. 1756
Jos. Frd. Wallet des Barres	22 Feb. 1756
Conrad Gugy	24 Feb. 1756
—— Desmoiliez	26 Feb. 1756
L. T. Fuser	27 Feb. 1756
A. T. F. Winter	28 Feb. 1756
—— Von Ingen	29 Feb. 1756
—— Maier	12 May 1756
Thomas Lindsay	28 May 1756
John Evans	29 May 1756
Brereton Poynton	30 Nov. 1756
James Allen	1 Dec. 1756
Thomas Barnsley	2 Dec. 1756
George M'Intosh	3 Dec. 1756
Thomas Campbell	4 Dec. 1756
Ralph Phillips..	5 Dec. 1756
Samuel Mackay	6 Dec. 1756
Francis Mackay	7 Dec. 1756
George Archibald	8 Dec. 1756
James Monro..	9 Dec. 1756
William Ridge	10 Dec. 1756
William Hay	11 Dec. 1756
Alexander Shaw	12 Dec. 1756
Thomas Meredith	13 Dec. 1756
—— Chas	18 Dec. 1756
Beamsley Glazier	8 Mar. 1757
John Billings	8 Mar. 1757
Rank in Army,	21 Dec. 1754
John Rodolph Rhaus ..	8 Mar. 1757
Peter Penier	8 Mar. 1757
John Poison	5 May 1757
James Calder	6 May 1757
Stair Campbell Carre ..	7 May 1757
Walter Kennedy	8 May 1757
Michael Davis..	9 May 1757
William Potts..	10 May 1757
William Jones..	11 May 1757
John Bell..	12 May 1757
William Ryder	14 May 1757
Thomas Winter	25 May 1757
James Ralfe	25 May 1757
Charles de Widungen ..	23 July 1757
Townsend Guy	22 Mar. 1758
Robert Campbell	23 Mar. 1758
James Crofton	
James Jefferies	25 Mar. 1758
John Wilson	26 Mar. 1758
Francis Hutchinson.. ..	26 Mar. 1758

Rank and Name.　　Rank in Regiment.

Ensigns—

James Herring	22 Jan. 1756
Edward Jenkins	23 Jan. 1756
John Nuterville	25 Jan. 1756
Allen Grant	1 Feb. 1756
Alexander Grant	2 Feb. 1756
George Otter	3 Feb. 1756
Alexander Stephens	27 Nov. 1756
Archibald Blane	4 Dec. 1756
Donald Campbell	6 Dec. 1756
William Ramsay	7 Dec. 1756
Alexander Baillie	9 Dec. 1756
Simon Fraser	10 Dec. 1756
Lauchlan Forbes	11 Dec. 1756
Thomas Prickney	12 Dec. 1756
William Brown	13 Dec. 1756
John Mackie	14 Dec. 1756
Alexander Shaw	17 Dec. 1756
Isaac Motte	19 Dec. 1756
Rauthaer Schuyler	8 Mar. 1757
Peter De Witt	1 May 1757
John Daw	4 May 1757
Francis Gordon	7 May 1757
William M'Lure	11 May 1757
Arthur St. Clair	13 May 1757
Alexander M'Intosh	18 May 1757
Henry Peyton	25 May 1757
Charles Rice	24 July 1757
James Walter	16 Jan. 1758
Andrew Ross	16 Jan. 1758
John Bay	16 Jan. 1758
J. Charles St. Clair	16 Jan. 1758
—— Haldiman	28 Mar. 1758
George Bender	29 Mar. 1758
John James	30 Mar. 1758
Richard Faine	31 Mar. 1758
Louis Victor Dupuisoux	1 April 1758
John Bay	2 April 1758

Chaplains—

Thomas Gawton	25 Dec. 1755
W. Nicholson Jackson	4 Feb. 1756
John Ogilvie	1 Sept. 1756
Michael Schlaetter	25 Mar. 1757

Adjutants—

James Allen	18 Aug. 1756
Thomas Barnsley	18 Aug. 1756
James Herring	13 June 1757

Quartermasters—

Donald Campbell	18 Aug. 1756
Joseph Ray	18 Aug. 1756
James Samuel Engel	24 Feb. 1757
Donald Campbell	6 June 1757

Surgeons—

John M'Kenzie	2 Feb. 1756
George Wirgman	3 Feb. 1756
—— Stevenson	4 Feb. 1756
Arthur Nicholson	25 Dec. 1756

Regimentals—Red, facings blue, white lace, 2 blue stripes.

Agent—Mr Abercrombie, Craven Street, Strand.

1759.

Four Battalions.

North America.

Rank and Name.　　Rank in Regiment.

Col.-in-Chief—

Jeffery Amherst	30 Sept. 1758
Rank in Army, 25 June 1759	

Cols. Commandant—

John Stanwix	1 Jan. 1756
James Prevost	4 Jan. 1756
Charles Lawrence	28 Sept. 1757
Robert Monckton	29 Sept. 1757

Lieut.-Colonels—

Henry Bouquet	3 Jan. 1756
Frederick Haldiman	4 Jan. 1756
Sir John St. Clair, Bart.	6 Jan. 1756
John Young	26 April 1756

Majors—

James Robertson	26 Dec. 1755
Rank in Army, Lt.-Col. 8 July 1758	
Augustine Prevost	9 Jan. 1756
John Tullikens	26 April 1757
Herbert Munster	26 July 1758

Captains—

Thomas Oswald	26 Dec. 1755
Rodolph Faesch	27 Dec. 1755
Frederick Porter	28 Dec. 1755
Walter Rutherford	30 Dec. 1755
Charles Greene	1 Jan. 1756
Ralph Harding	2 Jan. 1756
Jeremiah Stanton	4 Jan. 1756
—— Onielling	5 Jan. 1756
Richard Mather	6 Jan. 1756
Gustav. Wetterstroom	7 Jan. 1756
Harry Charteris	8 Jan. 1756
Lewis Steiner	10 Jan. 1756
Francis Lander	11 Jan. 1756
John Innis	13 Jan. 1756
Dennis Ger. Burnaud	14 Jan. 1756
Gavin Cochran	15 Jan. 1756
Joseph Prince	16 Jan. 1756
Marcus Prevost	17 Jan. 1757
Abraham Bosomworth	24 Jan. 1756
John Bradstreet	8 Mar. 1757
Rank in Army, 5 Sept. 1745	
Samuel Willyamoz	8 Mar. 1757
George du Fez	8 Mar. 1757
Stephen Gually	21 May 1757
William Stuart	25 May 1757
—— Schlosser	20 July 1758
Edward Comberbach	23 Aug. 1758
John Parker	12 Feb. 1759

Captain-Lieutenants—

Sam. James Hollandt	21 May 1757
Alexander M'Bean	23 July 1758
Peter von Ingen	23 Aug. 1758
Donald Campbell	14 Apr. 1759

Lieutenants—

Robert Brigstock	1 Jan. 1756
Rank in Army, 16 Feb. 1747-48	
—— Le Noble	6 Jan. 1756

Lieutenants (continued)—

Rank and Name.	Rank in Regiment.
Bazil Dunbar	12 Jan. 1756
Lewis Ourry	14 Jan. 1756
James Allaz	17 Jan. 1756
William Baillie ..	19 Jan. 1756
Christ. Spiesmacher ..	21 Jan. 1756
Elias Meyer	23 Jan. 1756
Simeon Ecuvier ..	25 Jan. 1756
Charles Willington ..	26 Jan. 1756
Charles Gallot	27 Jan. 1756
—— Grandidier	29 Jan. 1756
James Campbell ..	30 Jan. 1756
George Fullerton ..	1 Feb. 1756
Alexander Campbell ..	3 Feb. 1756
George Turnbull ..	5 Feb. 1756
William Abercrombie ..	6 Feb. 1756
David Ouchterlony ..	7 Feb. 1756
John Brown	9 Feb. 1756
Daniel McAlpin ..	10 Feb. 1756
Donald Forbes	11 Feb. 1756
Harry Gordon	12 Feb. 1756
Rank in Army, Capt. 4 Jan. 1758.	
Thomas Basset	14 Feb. 1756
George Faesch.. ..	15 Feb. 1756
George Etherington ..	16 Feb. 1756
Rodolphus Bentinck ..	18 Feb. 1756
Jacob Muller	19 Feb. 1756
Bernard Ratzer ..	20 Feb. 1756
Dietrich Berlin	21 Feb. 1756
Fred. von Weissenfels ..	22 Feb. 1756
Jos. Frd. Wallet des Barres	22 Feb. 1756
Conrad Gugy	24 Feb. 1756
—— Desnoilles	26 Feb. 1756
L. F. Fuser	27 Feb. 1756
A. F. Winter	28 Feb. 1756
—— Von Ingen	29 Feb. 1756
—— Maier	12 May 1756
Thomas Lindsay ..	28 May 1756
John Evans	29 May 1756
Bereton Poynton ..	30 Nov. 1756
James Allen	1 Dec. 1756
Thomas Barnsley ..	2 Dec. 1756
George McIntosh ..	3 Dec. 1756
Thomas Campbell ..	4 Dec. 1756
Ralph Phillips	5 Dec. 1756
Samuel Mackay ..	6 Dec. 1756
Francis Mackay ..	7 Dec. 1756
George Archibald ..	8 Dec. 1756
James Monro.. ..	9 Dec. 1756
William Ridge	10 Dec. 1756
Alexander Shaw ..	12 Dec. 1756
Beamsley Glazier ..	8 Mar. 1757
John Rodolph Bhan ..	8 Mar. 1757
Peter Penier	8 Mar. 1757
John Polson	5 May 1757
James Calder	6 May 1757
Stair Campbell Carrie ..	7 May 1757
Walter Kennedy ..	8 May 1757
William Potts	10 May 1757
William Jones	11 May 1757
John Bell	12 May 1757
William Ryder	14 May 1757
James Balfe	25 May 1757
Charles De Wildungen ..	23 July 1757
Robert Campbell ..	23 Mar. 1758
Townsend Guy	24 Mar. 1758

Lieutenants (continued)—

Rank and Name.	Rank in Regiment.
James Jefferies.. ..	25 Mar. 1758
John Wilson	26 Mar. 1758
John Dowe	24 May 1758
Robert Bayard ..	16 July 1758
James Herring ..	24 July 1758
George Otter	25 July 1758
William Ramsey ..	26 July 1758
Alexander Baillie ..	27 July 1758
Allan Grant	28 July 1758
John Nordberg	28 July 1758
Harry Howarth ..	29 July 1758
Francis Hutchinson ..	23 Aug. 1758
Alexander Grant ..	23 Aug. 1758
John Netterville ..	23 Aug. 1758
Robert Stuart.. ..	15 Sept. 1758
Edward Jenkins ..	22 Oct. 1758
John Martin	25 Feb. 1759
Lauchlan Forbes ..	14 April 1759

Ensigns—

Rank and Name.	Rank in Regiment.
Alexander Stephens ..	27 Nov. 1756
Archibald Blane ..	4 Dec. 1756
Donald Campbell ..	6 Dec. 1756
Thomas Pinckney ..	12 Dec. 1756
William Brown ..	13 Dec. 1756
John Mackie	14 Dec. 1756
Alexander Shaw ..	17 Dec. 1756
Isaac Motte	19 Dec. 1756
Ransluer Schuyler ..	8 Mar. 1757
Peter De Witt ..	1 May 1757
Francis Gordon ..	7 May 1757
William McLure ..	11 May 1757
Arthur St. Clair ..	13 May 1757
Henry Peyton.. ..	25 May 1757
James Widder ..	16 Jan. 1758
J. Haldiman	28 Mar. 1758
George Demler ..	29 Mar. 1758
John Faint	30 Mar. 1758
Richard Fahie ..	31 Mar. 1758
Louis Victor Du Plessis	1 Apr. 1758
John Hay	2 Apr. 1758
William Hay	24 May 1758
Augustine Prevost ..	24 July 1758
Charles Rivers.. ..	25 July 1758
—— Monin	26 July 1758
Ulrich W. Riesberg..	27 July 1758
Samuel Johnston ..	28 July 1758
—— Christie	28 July 1758
James Hill	23 Aug. 1758
Alexander Graydon ..	23 Aug. 1758
Samuel Sears	23 Aug. 1758
Conrad Stockhausen ..	23 Aug. 1758
Francis Phister ..	15 Sept. 1758
William Leslie ..	22 Sept. 1758
Archibald Dow ..	6 April 1759
Philip Duperron ..	11 April 1759

Chaplains—

Rank and Name.	Rank in Regiment.
Thomas Gawton ..	25 Dec. 1755
W. Nicholson Jackson ..	4 Feb. 1756
John Ogilvie	1 Sept. 1756
Michael Schlachter ..	25 Mar. 1757

Adjutants—

Rank and Name.	Rank in Regiment.
James Allen	18 Aug. 1756
Thomas Barnsley ..	18 Aug. 1756
James Herring ..	13 June 1757
Daniel Forbes.. ..	23 Aug. 1758

Rank and Name.	Rank in Regiment.
Quartermasters—	
James Samuel Engel	.. 24 Feb. 1757
Donald Campbell ..	.. 6 June 1757
John Dawe	.. 22 Oct. 1758
William Baillie ..	.. 14 April 1759
Surgeons—	
John M'Kenzie ..	.. 2 Feb. 1756
—— Stevenson	4 Feb. 1756
Arthur Nicholson ..	.. 25 Dec. 1756
Samuel Collier ..	.. 6 Feb. 1759

Regimentals—Red, facings blue, **white** lace, 2 blue stripes.

Agent—Mr. Calcraft, Channel Row, Westminster.

1760.

Four Battalions.

North America.

Col.-in-Chief—	
Jeffery Amherst ..	.. 30 Sept. 1758
Rank in Army, Maj.-Gen. 25 June 1759	
Cols. Commandant—	
John Stanwix ..	.. 1 Jan. 1756
Rank in Army, Maj.-Gen. 25 June 1759	
James Prevost.. ..	.. 4 Jan. 1756
Charles Lawrence ..	.. 28 Sept. 1757
Hon. James Murray ..	.. 24 Oct. 1759
Lieut.-Colonels—	
Henry Bouquet ..	.. **3 Jan.** 1756
Fred. Haldimand ..	.. 4 Jan. 1756
Sir John St. Clair, Bart.	6 Jan. 1756
John Young	.. 26 April 1757
Majors—	
James Robertson ..	.. **26 Dec.** 1755
Rank in Army, Lt.-Col. **8 Jan.** 1758	
Augustine Prevost ..	.. **9 Jan.** 1756
John Tullikens ..	.. **26 April** 1757
Herbert Munster ..	.. **20 July** 1758
Captains—	
Thomas Oswald ..	.. **26 Dec.** 1755
Rudolph Fesch ..	.. **27 Dec.** 1755
Frederick Porter ..	.. **28 Dec.** 1755
Walter Rutherford ..	.. **30 Dec.** 1755
Jeremiah Stanton ..	.. **4 Jan.** 1756
—— Gaudling ..	.. **5 Jan.** 1756
Richard Mather ..	.. **6 Jan.** 1756
Gustav Wetterstrom ..	.. **7 Jan.** 1756
Harry Chistern ..	.. **8 Jan.** 1756
Lewis Stenec	.. **10 Jan.** 1756
John Innis	.. **13 Jan.** 1756
Dennis O. Burnand ..	.. **14 Jan.** 1756
Gavin Cochran ..	.. **15 Jan.** 1756
Marcus Prevost ..	.. **17 Jan.** 1756
Abraham Bosomworth ..	.. **20 Jan.** 1756
John Bradstreet ..	.. **8 Mar.** 1757
Rank in Army, **5 Sept. 1745**	
Samuel Willyamoz ..	.. **8 Mar.** 1757
Gus. du Fer	.. **8 Mar.** 1757
Stephen Gually ..	.. **21 May** 1757
—— Schlosser ..	.. **20 July** 1758
Edward Cumberland ..	.. **23 Aug.** 1758
John Parker	.. **12 Feb.** 1759
David Ouchterlony ..	.. **15 April** 1759
Henry Gordon. ..	.. **16 April** 1759
George Etherington	.. **17 April** 1759

Rank and Name.	Rank in Regiment.
Captains (continued)—	
Robert Bayard ..	.. **18 April 1759**
Thomas Barnsley ..	.. **30 May 1759**
Donald Campbell ..	.. **29 Aug. 1759**
Captain-Lieutenants—	
Sam. Jan. Hollandt..	.. **21 May 1757**
Alex. M'Bean	.. **23 July 1758**
Peter von Ingen ..	.. **23 Aug. 1758**
Lewis Ourry	.. **29 Aug. 1759**
Lieutenants—	
Robert Brigstock ..	.. 1 Jan. 1756
Rank in Army, 16 Feb. 1747–48	
—— Le Noble	.. 6 Jan. 1756
Basil Dunbar	.. 12 Jan. 1756
James Allan	.. 17 Jan. 1756
William Baillie ..	.. 19 Jan. 1756
Christ. Spierwacher	.. 21 Jan. 1756
Elias Meyer	.. **23 Jan.** 1756
Simeon Fourier ..	.. 25 Jan. 1756
Charles Willington	.. 26 Jan. 1756
Charles Oakes.. ..	.. 27 Jan. 1756
—— Grandidier ..	.. 29 Jan. 1756
James Campbell ..	.. 30 Jan. **1756**
Geo. Fullerton ..	.. 1 Feb. **1756**
Alex. Campbell ..	.. 3 Feb. **1756**
Geo. Turnbull ..	.. 5 Feb. **1756**
Wm. Abercrombie..	.. 6 Feb. **1756**
John Brown	.. 9 Feb. **1756**
Daniel M'Alpin ..	.. 10 Feb. **1756**
Donald Forbes ..	.. 11 Feb. **1756**
Thomas Basset ..	.. 14 Feb. **1756**
Geo. Fesch	.. 15 Feb. **1756**
Rodolphus Bentinck	.. 18 Feb. **1756**
Jacob Muller ..	.. 19 Feb. **1756**
Bernard Ratzer ..	.. 20 Feb. **1756**
Fred. von Wessenfels	.. 22 Feb. **1756**
Dietrich Brehm ..	.. 23 Feb. **1756**
Jos. Fred. Wallet des Barres	21 Feb. **1756**
Conrad Gugy	.. 24 Feb. **1756**
—— Desaulles ..	.. 26 Feb. **1756**
A. L. F. Winter ..	.. 28 Feb. **1756**
L. F. Euser	.. 27 Feb. **1756**
—— Von Ingen ..	.. 29 Feb. **1756**
—— Meuer	.. 12 May **1756**
Thomas Lindsay ..	.. 28 May **1756**
John Evans	.. 29 May **1756**
Alex. Stephens ..	.. 13 April **1759**
Arthur St. Clair ..	.. 17 April **1759**
William Leslie ..	.. 30 May **1759**
Brereton Poynton ..	.. 30 Nov. **1756**
James Allen	.. 1 Dec. **1756**
Geo. M'Intosh.. ..	.. 3 Dec. **1756**
Ralph Phillips.. ..	.. 5 Dec. **1756**
Samuel Mackay ..	.. 6 Dec. **1756**
Francis Mackay ..	.. 7 Dec. **1756**
Geo. Archibald ..	.. 8 Dec. **1756**
James Monro	.. 9 Dec. **1756**
William Ridge ..	.. 10 Dec. **1756**
Alex. Shaw	.. 12 Dec. **1756**
Beamsley Glazier ..	.. 8 Mar. **1757**
John Rudolph Rhan	.. 8 Mar. **1757**
Peter Pomer	.. 8 Mar. **1757**
John Polson	.. 5 May **1757**
James Calder	.. 6 May **1757**
Staat Campbell Carre	.. 7 May **1757**
Walter Kennedy ..	.. 8 May **1757**

Rank and Name.	Rank in Regiment.
Lieutenants (continued)—	
William Potts.. ..	.. 10 May 1757
William Jones ..	.. 11 May 1757
John Bell.. ..	.. 12 May 1757
William Ryder ..	.. 14 May 1757
James Ralfe ..	.. 25 May 1757
Robert Campbell ..	.. 23 Mar. 1758
Townsend Guy ..	.. 24 Mar. 1758
James Jeffries.. ..	.. 25 Mar. 1758
John Wilson ..	.. 26 Mar. 1758
John Dowe ..	.. 24 May 1758
James Herring ..	.. 24 July 1758
George Otter ..	.. 25 July 1758
William Ramsay ..	.. 26 July 1758
Alexander Baillie ..	.. 27 July 1758
Allan Grant ..	.. 28 July 1758
John Nordberg ..	.. 28 July 1758
Harry Howarth ..	.. 29 July 1758
Francis Hutchinson ..	23 Aug. 1758
Alexander Grant ..	.. 23 Aug. 1758
John Netterville ..	.. 23 Aug. 1758
Robert Stewart ..	.. 15 Sept.1758
Edward Jenkins ..	.. 22 Oct. 1758
John Martin ..	.. 25 Feb. 1759
Alexander Stephens ..	13 April 1759
Lauchlan Forbes ..	.. 14 April 1759
Isaac Motte ..	.. 15 April 1759
Arthur St. Clair ..	.. 17 April 1759
James Samuel Engel ..	11 May 1759
William Leslie ..	.. 30 May 1759
George M'Dougal ..	.. 30 May 1759
Ranaher Schuyler ..	.. 1 June 1759
Francis Gordon ..	.. 20 Aug. 1759
Ensigns—	
Archibald Blane ..	.. 4 Dec. 1756
Donald Campbell ..	.. 6 Dec. 1756
Thomas Pinckney ..	.. 12 Dec. 1756
William Brown ..	.. 13 Dec. 1756
John Mackie ..	.. 14 Dec. 1756
Peter De Witt ..	.. 1 May 1757
William McLure ..	.. 11 May 1757
Henry Peyton.. ..	.. 25 May 1757
James Welder ..	.. 16 Jan. 1758
I. Haldimann ..	.. 28 Mar. 1758
George Demler ..	.. 29 Mar. 1758
John Janiet ..	.. 30 Mar. 1758
Richard Fabie.. ..	.. 31 Mar. 1758
Louis Victor du Plessis	1 April 1758
John Hay	.. 2 April 1758
William Hay ..	.. 24 May 1758
Augustine Prevost ..	24 July 1758
Charles Rivez ..	.. 25 July 1758
—— Monin ..	.. 26 July 1758
Ulrich W. Riesberg ..	27 July 1758
Samuel Johnson ..	.. 28 July 1758
—— Christie ..	.. 28 July 1758
James Hill ..	.. 23 Aug. 1758
Alexander Graydon ..	23 Aug. 1758
Samuel Sears ..	.. 23 Aug. 1758
Conrad Stockhausen ..	23 Aug. 1758
Francis Phister ..	.. 15 Sept.1758
Archibald Dow ..	.. 6 April 1758
David Stewart ..	.. 13 April 1758
Philip Duperron ..	.. 14 April 1759
St. John Broderick.. ..	19 April 1759
James Gorrell ..	.. 30 April 1759

Rank and Name.	Rank in Regiment.
Ensigns (continued)—	
James McDonald ..	.. 30 April 1759
John Brittman ..	.. 1 June 1759
George Mackay ..	.. 2 June 1759
Francis Schlosser ..	.. 29 Aug. 1759
Chaplain—	
Thomas Gawton ..	.. 25 Dec. 1755
C. Nicholson Jackson ..	4 Feb. 1756
John Ogilvie ..	.. 1 Sep. 1756
Michael Schlaetler ..	.. 25 Mar. 1757
Adjutants—	
James Allen ..	.. 18 Aug. 1756
Thomas Barnsley ..	.. 18 Aug. 1756
James Herring ..	.. 13 June 1757
Daniel Forbes.. ..	.. 23 Aug. 1758
Quartermasters—	
Donald Campbell ..	.. 6 June 1757
John Dowe ..	.. 22 Oct. 1758
William Baillie ..	.. 14 April 1759
Lewis de Luz ..	.. 11 May 1759
Surgeons—	
James McKenzie ..	.. 2 Feb. 1756
—— Stevenson ..	.. 4 Feb. 1756
Samuel Collier ..	.. 6 Feb. 1759
William Mitchell ..	.. 20 April 1759

Regimentals—Red, facings blue, white lace, 2 blue stripes.

Agent—Mr. Calcraft, Channel Row, Westminster.

1761.

Four Battalions.

North America—West Indies.

Rank and Name.	Rank in Regiment.
Colonel-in-Chief—	
Sir Jeffery Amherst ..	30 Sept.1758
Rank in Army, Maj.-Gen.	25 June 1759
Cols. Commandant—	
John Stanwix ..	.. 1 Jan. 1756
Rank in Army, Maj.-Gen.	25 June 1759
James Prevost.. ..	.. 4 Jan. 1756
Hon. James Murray ..	21 Oct. 1759
William Haviland.. ..	9 Dec. 1760
Marcus Smith.. ..	.. 11 Nov. 1761
Lieut.-most Colonels—	
Henry Bouquet ..	.. 3 Jan. 1756
Frederick Haldiman ..	4 Dec. 1756
Sir John St. Clair, Bart.	6 Dec. 1756
Augustine Prevost ..	.. 20 Mar. 1761
Majors—	
Herbert Munster ..	.. 24 July 1758
William Walters ..	.. 25 Feb. 1760
John Munsell ..	.. 20 Mar. 1760
Captains—	
Rodolph Faesch ..	.. 27 Dec. 1755
Jeremiah Stanton ..	.. 4 Jan. 1756
—— Gnielling ..	.. 5 Jan. 1756
Richard Mather ..	.. 6 Jan. 1756
Gavin Cochran ..	.. 15 Jan. 1756
Marcus Prevost ..	.. 17 Jan. 1756
John Bradstreet ..	.. 8 Mar. 1756
Rank in Army,	5 Sept. 1743
—— Schlosser.. ..	.. 20 July 1758
Edmond Cumberbach ..	23 Aug. 1758

Rank and Name.	Rank in Regiment.
Captains (continued)—	
Henry Gordon ...	16 April 1759
Rank in Army,	4 Jan. 1758
George Etherington	17 April 1759
Robert Bayard	18 April 1759
Thomas Barnsley	30 May 1759
Sam. Jas. Hollandt	24 Aug. 1759
Donald Campbell	29 Aug. 1759
Fr. Gab. de Ruvynes	25 Dec. 1759
Robert Brigstock	14 Feb. 1760
John Carden	25 Feb. 1760
Beamsley Glazier	16 June 1760
Henry Alt	12 Sept. 1760
John Brown	15 Sept. 1760
John Wharton	17 Sept. 1760
John Gordon	18 Sept. 1760
William Ridge	18 Sept. 1760
William Baillie	4 Oct. 1760
Lewis Ourry	12 Dec. 1760
Henry Brown	18 April 1761
Daniel Claus	7 July 1761
Alexander M'Bean	13 July 1761
Captain-Lieutenants—	
Simeon Ecuyier	14 Feb. 1760
Ralph Phillips	12 Dec. 1760
James Allen	6 May 1761
Fred. Christ. Spiessmacher	13 July 1761
Lieutenants—	
—— Le Noble	6 Jan. 1756
Elias Meyer	23 Jan. 1756
Charles Willington	26 Jan. 1756
Charles Gallas	27 Jan. 1756
—— Graudsleir	29 Jan. 1756
James Campbell	30 Jan. 1756
George Fullerton	1 Feb. 1756
George Turnbull	5 Feb. 1756
William Abercrombie	6 Feb. 1756
Daniel M'Alpin	10 Feb. 1756
George Fawch	15 Feb. 1756
Jacob Muller	19 Feb. 1756
Bernard Ratzer	20 Feb. 1756
Dietrich Bredin	21 Feb. 1756
Fred. von Weissenfels	22 Feb. 1756
Jas. Fred. Wallet des Barres	22 Feb. 1756
Conrad Gugy	23 Feb. 1756
—— Desnoudes	26 Feb. 1756
L. F. Fuser	27 Feb. 1756
A. T. F. Winter	28 Feb. 1756
—— Von Ingen	29 Feb. 1756
—— Maire	12 May 1756
Thomas Lindsay	28 May 1756
John Evans	29 May 1756
Brereton Poynton	30 Nov. 1756
George M'Intosh	3 Dec. 1756
Samuel Mackay	6 Dec. 1756
Francis Mackay	7 Dec. 1756
George Archibold	8 Dec. 1756
Alexander Shaw	12 Dec. 1756
John Rodolph Rhan	8 Mar. 1757
John Polson	5 May 1757
James Cabler	6 May 1757
Stair Campbell Carre	7 May 1757
William Potts	10 May 1757
William Jones	11 May 1757
John Bell	12 May 1757
James Rolfe	25 May 1757

Rank and Name.	Rank in Regiment.
Lieutenants (continued)—	
Robert Campbell	23 Mar. 1758
Townsend Guy	24 Mar. 1758
James Jeffries	25 Mar. 1758
John Dows	24 May 1758
James Herring	24 July 1758
George Otter	25 July 1758
William Ramsey	26 July 1758
Alexander Baillie	27 July 1758
Allan Grant	28 July 1758
John Nordberg	28 July 1758
Francis Hutchinson	28 Aug. 1758
John Netterville	23 Aug. 1758
Robert Stewart	15 Sept. 1758
Edward Jenkins	22 Oct. 1758
John Martin	25 Feb. 1759
Alexander Stephens	13 April 1759
Lauchlan Forbes	14 April 1759
Isaac Motte	15 April 1759
Arthur St. Clair	17 April 1759
James Samuel Engel	11 May 1759
William Leslie	30 May 1759
George M'Dougal	30 May 1759
Baptiste Schuyler	1 June 1759
Alexander Shaw	2 June 1759
Donald Campbell	20 Aug. 1759
Francis Gordon	29 Aug. 1759
William Brown	31 Oct. 1759
Lewis de Mestral	31 Mar. 1760
John M'Dougal	29 April 1760
Thomas Pinckney	29 April 1760
James Webber	29 May 1760
William M'Lure	16 June 1760
William Snow Steel	23 June 1760
Alexander Graydon	14 Sept. 1760
James Hill	15 Sept. 1760
Francis Pfister	18 Sept. 1760
Charles River	4 Oct. 1760
Frederick Haldiman	8 Dec. 1760
Archibald Dow	12 Dec. 1760
David Stewart	
George Mackey	20 Mar. 1761
Phillip Duceros	16 April 1761
Augustine Prevost	6 May 1761
James M'Donald	18 May 1761
Daniel W. Rexberg	18 July 1761
George Dendr	14 July 1761
John Ormsby Doncellan	31 July 1761
Ensigns—	
Archibald Blane	4 Dec. 1756
John Jones	30 Mar. 1758
Lewis Victor du Plessis	1 April 1758
John Hay	2 April 1758
—— Moran	26 July 1758
—— Christie	28 July 1758
Samuel Sears	24 Aug. 1758
St. John Broderick	19 April 1759
James Gimmel	30 May 1759
Francis Schlosser	29 Aug. 1759
———	3 Sept. 1759
Donald M'Donald	14 Feb. 1760
James Danster	31 Mar. 1760
Robert M Pherson	22 April 1760
John Mann	29 April 1760
David M'Kee	29 April 1760
Thomas Beard	16 June 1760

Rank and Name.	Rank in Regiment.
Ensigns (continued)—	
Robert Nott	.. 16 June 1760
John Amiel	.. 26 June 1760
Angus M'Donald	.. 8 July 1760
Nicholas Power	.. 14 Sept. 1760
David Barry	.. 15 Sept. 1760
John Gregorson	.. 17 Sept. 1760
John Charlton	.. 4 Oct. 1760
Robert Holmes	.. 12 Dec. 1760
Christopher Pauli	.. 8 Feb. 1761
Benjamin Strodtman	.. 20 Mar. 1761
Samuel Stewart	.. 16 April 1761
James Brigstock	.. 24 April 1761
Daniel Tucker	.. 6 May 1761
George Price	.. 18 May 1761
Frederick Winter	.. 7 July 1761
Edward Hubbard	..
James M'Dougal	.. 24 Feb. 1761
Chaplains—	
Thomas Gawton	.. 25 Dec. 1755
W. Nicholson Jackson	.. 4 Feb. 1756
John Ogilvie	.. 1 Sept. 1756
Michael Schlatter	.. 25 May 1757
Adjutants—	
Thomas Barnsley	.. 18 Aug. 1756
James Herring	.. 13 June 1757
Patrick M'Alpin	.. 26 April 1760
Edward Barrow	.. 1 May 1760
Quartermasters—	
John Dowe	.. 22 Oct. 1758
John Peter Rochat	.. 1 May 1760
Francis Hutchinson	.. 4 Oct. 1760
Lime Phill	.. 27 July 1761
Surgeons—	
James M'Kenzie	.. 2 Feb. 1756
—— Stevenson	.. 4 Feb. 1756
Samuel Collier	.. 6 Feb. 1759
William Mitchell	.. 20 April 1759

Regimentals—Red, facings blue, white
lace, 2 blue stripes.

Agent—Mr. Calcraft, Channel Row,
Westminster.

1762.

Four Battalions.

North America—West Indies.

Col.-in-Chief—	
Sir Jeffery Amherst	.. 30 Sep. 1758
Rank in Army, Maj.-Gen. 25 June 1759	
Cols.-Commandant—	
James Prevost	.. 4 Jan. 1756
Hon. James Murray	.. 24 Oct. 1759
William Haviland	.. 9 Dec. 1760
Lieut.-Colonels—	
Henry Bouquet	.. 3 Jan. 1756
Fred. Haldimand	.. 4 Jan. 1756
Sir John St. Clair	.. 6 Jan. 1756
Augustine Prevost	.. 20 Mar. 1761
Majors—	
Herbert Munster	.. 20 July 1758
Thomas Oswald	.. 29 Oct. 1759
William Walters	.. 25 Feb. 1760
John Mansell	.. 20 Mar. 1761

Rank and Name.	Rank in Regiment.
Captains—	
Rodolph Fæsch	.. 27 Dec. 1755
Walter Rutherford	.. 30 Dec. 1755
Jeremiah Stanton	.. 4 Jan. 1756
—— Gnielling	.. 5 Jan. 1756
Richard Mather	.. 6 Jan. 1756
Harry Charteris	.. 8 Jan. 1756
Gavin Cochran	.. 15 Jan. 1756
Marcus Prevost	.. 17 Jan. 1756
John Bradstreet	.. 8 Mar. 1757
Rank in Army, 5 Sept. 1745	
Samuel Wilyamos	.. 8 Mar. 1757
—— Schlosser	.. 20 July 1758
Edward Comberbach	.. 23 Aug. 1758
Henry Gordon	.. 26 April 1759
Rank in Army, 4 Jan. 1758	
George Etherington	.. 17 April 1759
Robert Baynd	.. 18 April 1759
Thomas Barnsley	.. 30 May 1759
Sam. Jan. Holland	.. 24 Aug. 1759
Donald Campbell	.. 29 Aug. 1759
F. Gab. de Ravynes	.. 25 Dec. 1759
Robert Brigstock	.. 14 Feb. 1760
John Carden	.. 25 Feb. 1760
Beamsley Glazier	.. 16 June 1760
Henry Alt	.. 12 Sept. 1760
John Brown	.. 15 Sept. 1760
John Wharton	.. 17 Sept. 1760
John Gordon	.. 18 Sept. 1760
William Ridge	.. 18 Sept. 1760
William Baillie	.. 4 Oct. 1760
Lewis Ourry	.. 12 Dec. 1760
Captain-Lieutenants—	
Alexander M'Bean	.. 23 July 1758
Simeon Ecuyier	.. 14 Feb. 1760
Alex. Campbell	.. 8 Oct. 1760
Lieutenants—	
—— Le Noble	.. 6 Jan. 1756
James Allaz	.. 17 Jan. 1756
Christ. Spiesmacher	.. 21 Jan. 1756
Elias Meyer	.. 23 Jan. 1756
Charles Willington	.. 26 Jan. 1756
Charles Gallot	.. 27 Jan. 1756
—— Grandidier	.. 29 Jan. 1756
James Campbell	.. 30 Jan. 1756
George Fullerton	.. 1 Feb. 1756
George Turnbull	.. 5 Feb. 1756
William Abercrombie	.. 6 Jan. 1756
Daniel M'Alpin	.. 10 Jan. 1756
Thomas Bassett	.. 14 Feb. 1756
George Fæsch	.. 15 Feb. 1756
Rodolphus Beufinck	.. 18 Feb. 1756
Jacob Muller	.. 19 Feb. 1756
Bernard Ratzer	.. 20 Feb. 1756
Dietrich Brehm	.. 21 Feb. 1756
Fred. von Weissenfels	.. 22 Feb. 1756
J. F. Wallet des Barres	.. 22 Feb. 1756
Conrad Gugy	.. 24 Feb. 1756
—— Desmoilles	.. 26 Feb. 1756
L. F. Fuser	.. 27 Feb. 1756
A. T. F. Winter	.. 28 Feb. 1756
—— Von Ingen	.. 29 Feb. 1756
—— Maier	.. 12 May 1756
Thomas Lindsay	.. 28 May 1756
John Evans	.. 29 May 1756
Brereton Poynton	.. 30 Nov. 1756

Rank and Name.	Rank in Regiment.	Rank and Name.	Rank in Regiment.
Lieutenants (continued)—		*Ensigns* (continued)—	
George M'Intosh	.. 3 Dec. 1756	Francis Phister	.. 15 Sept. 1758
Ralph Phillips ..	.. 5 Dec. 1756	Archibald Dow ..	.. 6 April 1759
Samuel Mackay ..	.. 6 Dec. 1756	David Stewart.. ..	.. 13 April 1759
Francis Mackay ..	.. 7 Dec. 1756	Phillip Duperron ..	.. 14 April 1759
George Archbold ..	.. 8 Dec. 1756	St. John Broderick..	.. 19 April 1759
James Munro.. ..	.. 9 Dec. 1756	James Gorrell ..	.. 30 May 1759
Alexander Shaw ..	12 Dec. 1756	James M'Donald ..	.. 30 May 1759
John Rodolph Rhan	.. 8 Mar. 1757	George Mackay ..	.. 2 June 1759
John Polson	.. 5 Mar. 1757	Francis Schlosser ..	.. 20 Aug. 1759
James Calder	.. 6 Mar. 1757	Henry Coxeter ..	.. 3 Sept. 1759
Stair Campbell Carre	.. 7 Mar. 1757	Donald M'Donald ..	.. 14 Feb. 1760
William Potts.. ..	.. 10 Mar. 1757	James Dunster ..	.. 31 Mar. 1760
William Jones.. ..	.. 11 Mar. 1757	**Robert** M'Pherson..	.. 22 April 1760
John Bell.. ..	.. 12 Mar. 1757	John Mouin	.. 29 April 1760
James Ralfe	.. 25 May 1757	David M'Kenzie ..	.. 29 April 1760
Robert Campbell ..	.. 23 Mar. 1758	Thomas Ricard ..	.. 16 June 1760
Townshend Guy ..	.. 24 Mar. 1758	Robert Nott	.. 16 June 1760
James Jeffries.. ..	.. 25 Mar. 1758	George Fraser.. ..	.. 23 June 1760
John Dowe	.. 24 May 1758	John Amiel	.. 26 June 1760
James Herring ..	.. 24 July 1758	Angus M'Donald ..	.. 8 July 1760
George Otter	.. 25 July 1758	Nicholas Power ..	.. 14 Sept. 1760
William Ramsay ..	.. 26 July 1758	David Borry	.. 15 Sept. 1760
Alexander Baillie ..	.. 27 July 1758	John Gregorson ..	.. 17 Sept. 1760
Allan Grant	.. 28 July 1758	John Charlton ..	.. 4 Oct. 1760
John Nordberg.. ..	.. 28 July 1758	*Chaplains*—	
Francis Hutchinson	.. 23 Aug. 1758	Thomas Omston ..	.. 25 Dec. 1755
John Netterville ..	.. 23 Aug. 1758	W. Nicholson Jackson	.. 4 Feb. 1756
Robert Stewart ..	.. 15 Sept. 1758	**John** Ogilvie	.. 1 Sept. 1756
Edward Jenkins ..	.. 22 Oct. 1758	Michael Schlacttier ..	.. 25 May 1757
John Martin	.. 25 Feb. 1759	*Adjutants*—	
Alexander Stephens	.. 13 April 1759	Thomas Barnsley ..	.. 18 Aug. 1756
Lauchlan Forbes ..	.. 14 April 1759	James Herring ..	.. 13 June 1757
Isaac Morie	.. 15 April 1759	Patrick M'Alpin ..	.. 26 April 1760
Arthur St. Clair ..	.. 17 April 1759	Edward Barrow ..	.. 1 May 1760
James Samuel Engel	.. 11 May 1759	*Quartermasters*—	
William Leslie ..	.. 30 May 1759	Donald Campbell ..	.. 6 June 1757
George M'Dougal ..	.. 30 May 1759	John Dowe	.. 22 Oct. 1758
Ranslaer Schuyler ..	.. 1 June 1759	John Peter Rochat..	.. 1 May 1760
Alexander Shaw ..	.. 2 June 1759	Francis Hutchinson	.. 4 Oct. 1760
Donald Campbell ..	.. 20 Aug. 1759	*Surgeons*—	
Francis Gordon ..	.. 29 Aug. 1759	James M'Kenzie ..	.. 2 Feb. 1756
William Brown ..	.. 31 Oct. 1759	—— Stevenson ..	.. 4 Feb. 1756
Lewis de Montrai ..	.. 31 Mar. 1760	Samuel Collier ..	.. 6 Feb. 1759
John M'Dougal ..	.. 29 April 1760	William Mitchell ..	.. 20 April 1759
Thomas Pinckney ..	.. 22 April 1760		
James Wilder.. ..	.. 29 May 1760	*Regimentals*—Red, facings blue, white	
William M'Clare ..	.. 16 June 1760	lace, 2 blue stripes.	
William Snow Steel	.. 23 June 1760		
Alexander **Graydon**	.. 14 Sept. 1760	*Agent*—Mr. Calcraft, Channel Row,	
James Hill	.. 15 Sept. 1760	Westminster.	
Samuel Sears	.. 4 Oct. 1760		
John Ormsby	.. 31 July 1761		
Ensigns—			
Archibald Blane ..	.. 4 Dec. 1756		
Frederick Hallinan	.. 28 Mar. 1758	**1763.**	
George Denller ..	.. 29 Mar. 1758		
John Jamet	.. 30 Mar. 1758	*Four Battalions.*	
Louis Victor du Plessis	1 April 1758		
John Hay	.. 2 April 1758	North America.	
William Hay	.. 24 May 1758	*Colonel-in-Chief*	
Augustine Prevost ..	.. 24 July 1758	Sir Jeffery Amherst .. 30 Sept. 1758	
Charles Rivez	.. 25 July 1758	*Rank in Army,* Maj.-Gen. 25 June 1759	
—— Monin	.. 26 July 1758	*Cols. Commandant*—	
Ullrich W. Reisberg	.. 27 July 1758	Hon. James Murray .. 24 Oct. 1759	
—— Christie	.. 28 July 1758	James Prevost .. .. 28 Oct. 1756	
		Rank in Army, 4 Jan. 1756	

Rank and Name.	Rank in Regiment.
Lieut.-Colonels—	
Henry Bouquet	3 Jan. 1756
Rank in Army, Col. 19 Feb. 1762	
Fred. Haldiman	4 Jan. 1756
Rank in Army, Col. 19 Feb. 1762	
Majors—	
Herbert Munster	20 July 1758
Rank in Army, Lt.-Col. 14 Jan. 1762	
Samuel Mackay	30 Sept. 1761
Captains—	
Rodolph Fræsch	27 Dec. 1755
Geo. Gnielling	5 Jan. 1756
Gavin Cochran	15 Jan. 1756
Marcus Prevost	17 Jan. 1756
John Bradstreet	8 Mar. 1757
Rank in Army, 5 Sept. 1745	
Jno. Jos. Schlosser	20 July 1758
Henry Gordon	16 April 1759
Rank in Army, 4 Jan. 1758	
George Etherington	17 April 1759
Robert Bayard	18 April 1759
Thomas Barnsley	30 May 1759
Sam. Jan. Hollandt	24 Aug. 1759
Robert Brigstock	14 Feb. 1760
Rank in Army, 16 Feb. 1748-9	
Captain-Lieutenants—	
Ralph Phillips	12 Dec. 1760
Fred. Chr. Spiesmacher.	13 July 1761
Lieutenants—	
Charles Gallot	27 Jan. 1756
—— Grandidier	29 Jan. 1756
George Turnbull	5 Feb. 1756
Daniel M'Alpin	10 Feb. 1756
Bernard Ratzer	20 Feb. 1756
Dietrich Brehm	21 Feb. 1756
Jos. Fred. Wallet des Barres	22 Feb. 1756
Conrad Gugy	24 Feb. 1756
A. T. F. Winter	28 Feb. 1756
Von Ingen	29 Feb. 1756
Brereton Poynton	30 Nov. 1756
George M'Intosh	3 Dec. 1756
Samuel Mackay	6 Dec. 1756
Francis Mackay	7 Dec. 1756
George Archbold	8 Dec. 1756
Alexander Shaw	12 Dec. 1756
John Rodolph Rhau	8 Mar. 1757
John Polson	5 May 1757
Ensigns—	
—— Christie	28 July 1758
Francis Schlosser	29 Aug. 1759
Donald M'Donald	14 Feb. 1760
John Antel	26 June 1760
Angus M'Donald	8 June 1760
John Gregorson	17 Sept. 1760
John Charlton	4 Oct. 1760
Christopher Pauli	8 Feb. 1761
Benjam. Strcatman	20 Mar. 1761
James Brigstock	24 April 1761
Daniel Tucker	6 May 1761
George Price	18 May 1761
Frederick Winter	7 July 1761
Thomas Hutchinson	2 Mar. 1762
James Leighton	22 April 1762
John Fraser	25 Aug. 1762
Chaplains—	
Thomas Gawton	25 Dec. 1755
W. Nicholson Jackson	1 Feb. 1756

Rank and Name.	Rank in Regiment.
Adjutant—	
Patrick M'Alpin	26 April 1760
William Potts	
Quartermasters—	
John Peter Rochat	1 May 1760
Francis Hutchinson	4 Oct. 1760
Surgeons—	
—— Stevenson	4 Feb. 1756
Samuel Collier	6 Feb. 1759

*Regimentals—*Red, facings blue, white lace, 2 blue stripes.

Agent—Mr. Calcraft, Channel Row, Westminster.

1764.

Three Battalions.

North America.

Col.-in-Chief—	
Sir Jeffery Amherst	30 Sept. 1758
Rank in Army, M.-Gen. 25 June 1759	
Cols.-Commandant—	
Hon. James Murray	24 Oct. 1759
James Prevost	28 Oct. 1756
Lieut.-Colonels—	
Henry Bouquet	3 Jan. 1756
Rank in Army, Col. 19 Feb. 1762	
Fred. Haldiman	4 Jan. 1756
Rank in Army, Col. 19 Feb. 1762	
Majors—	
Herbert Munster	20 July 1758
Rank in Army, Lt.-Col. 14 Jan. 1762	
Samuel Mackay	30 Sept. 1761
Captains—	
Rodolph Fræsch	27 Dec. 1755
Geo. Gnielling	5 Jan. 1756
Gavin Cochran	15 Jan. 1756
Marcus Prevost	17 Jan. 1756
John Bradstreet	8 Mar. 1757
Rank in Army, 5 Sept. 1745	
Jno. Jos. Schlosser	20 July 1758
Henry Gordon	16 April 1759
Rank in Army, 4 Jan. 1758	
George Etherington	17 April 1759
Robert Bayard	18 April 1759
Thomas Barnsley	30 May 1759
Sam. Jan. Hollandt	24 Aug. 1759
Robert Brigstock	14 Feb. 1760
Rank in Army, 16 Feb. 1748-9	
Captain-Lieutenants—	
Ralph Phillips	12 Dec. 1760
Fred. Chr. Spiesmacher	13 July 1761
Lieutenants—	
Charles Gallot	27 Jan. 1756
—— Grandidier	29 Jan. 1756
George Turnbull	5 Feb. 1756
Daniel M'Alpin	10 Feb. 1756
Bernard Ratzer	20 Feb. 1756
Dietrich Brehm	24 Feb. 1756
Jos. Fred. Wallet des Barres	22 Feb. 1756
Conrad Gugy	24 Feb. 1756
A. T. F. Winter	28 Feb. 1756
Von Ingen	29 Feb. 1756

Rank and Name.	Rank in Regiment.
Lieutenants (continued)—	
Brereton Poynton	**30 Nov. 1756**
George M'Intosh	**3 Dec. 1756**
Samuel Mackay	**6 Dec. 1756**
Francis Mackay	**7 Dec. 1756**
George Archbold	**8 Dec. 1756**
Alexander Shaw	**12 Dec. 1756**
John Rodolph **Rhan** ..	**8 Mar. 1757**
John Polsen	**5 May 1757**
Ensigns—	
—— Christie	.. 28 July 1758
Francis Schlosser ..	.. 29 Aug. 1759
Donald M'Donald ..	.. 14 Feb. 1760
John Amiel	.. 26 June 1760
Angus M'Donald ..	.. 8 July 1760
John Gregorson ..	.. 17 Sept. 1760
John Charlton ..	.. 4 Oct. 1760
Christopher Pauli ..	.. 8 Feb. 1761
Benjamin Strodinson	.. 20 Mar. 1761
James Brigstock ..	.. 24 April 1761
Daniel Tucker	.. 6 May 1761
George Price	.. 18 May 1761
Frederick Winter ..	.. 7 July 1761
Thomas Hutchinson ..	.. 2 Mar. 1762
James Leighton ..	.. 22 April 1762
John Fraser	.. 25 Aug. 1762
Chaplain—	
Thomas Gaveton ..	.. 25 Dec. 1755
W. Nicholson **Jackson** ..	4 Feb. 1756
Adjutant—	
Patrick M'Alpin ..	.. 26 April 1760
William Potts	
Quartermasters—	
John Peter Rochat ..	.. 1 May 1760
Francis Hutchinson ..	.. 4 Oct. 1760
Surgeon—	
—— Stevenson	.. 4 Feb. 1756
Samuel Collier ..	.. 6 Feb. 1759
Regimentals—Red, facings blue, white lace, 2 blue stripes.	

Agent—Mr. Calcraft, Channel Row, Westminster.

1765.

Two Battalions.
North America.
Col.-in-Chief—
Sir Jeffery Amherst .. 30 Sept. 1757
  Rank in Army, Maj.-Gen. 25 June 1759
Cols.-Commandant—
Hon. James Murray .. 24 Oct. 1759
James Prevost .. .. 28 Oct. 1761
Lieut.-Colonels—
Henry Bouquet .. .. 3 Jan. 1756
  Rank in Army, Col. 19 Feb. 1762
Fred. Haldimand .. 1 Jan. 1756
  Rank in Army, Col. 19 Feb. 1762
Majors—
John Wilkins .. .. 15 Aug. 1761
  Rank in Army, 9 June 1762
Horatio Gates .. .. 27 Oct. 1761
  Rank in Army, 24 April 1762
Captains—
Gavin Cochran .. .. 15 Jan. 1756
Marcus Prevost .. .. 17 Jan. 1756

Rank and Name.	**Rank in Regiment.**
Captains (continued)—	
John Bradstreet	8 Mar. 1757
Rank in Army, 5 Sept. 1745	
John Jos. Schlosser ..	29 July 1768
Henry Gordon ..	16 April 1759
Rank in Army, 4 Jan. 1758	
George Etherington ..	17 April 1759
Robert Bayard	18 April 1759
Sam. Jas. Holland ..	24 Aug. 1759
Thomas Barnsley ..	30 May 1759
Robert Brigstock ..	14 Feb. 1760
Rank in Army, 16 Feb. 1758-9	
Lewis Val. Faser ..	30 Dec. 1763
Rank in Army, 27 Sept. 1763	
John Brown	14 Jan. 1764
Rank in Army, 25 Sept. 1760	
Captain Lieutenants—	
Ralph Phillips ..	12 Dec. 1760
Fred. Chr. Spiesmacher ..	14 July 1761
Lieutenants—	
Tho. Armsdeber ..	29 Jan. 1756
George Turnbull	5 Feb. 1756
Daniel M'Ayin ..	10 Feb. 1756
Bernard Batzer ..	20 Feb. 1756
Dietrich Brehm ..	21 Feb. 1756
Jos. Fri Wallrabe Barres	22 Feb. 1756
Conrad Gings	24 Feb. 1756
A. F. Winter	28 Feb. 1756
J. von Ingen	29 Feb. 1756
Brereton Poynton ..	30 Nov. 1756
George M'Intosh ..	3 Dec. 1756
George Archbold ..	8 Dec. 1756
John Polsen ..	5 May 1756
Allan Grant	7 Oct. 1763
Rank in Army, 28 July 1758	
Stair Campbell Carre ..	8 May 1764
Rank in Army, 7 May 1757	
Francis Hutchinson ..	9 May 1764
Rank in Army, 13 Aug. 1758	
Augustine Prevost ..	10 May 1764
Rank in Army, 6 May 1761	
Henry Congalton	18 May 1764
Rank in Army, 11 Feb. 1761	
Ensigns—	
John Christie	.. 28 July 1758
Francis Schlosser ..	.. 29 Aug. 1759
Donald M'Donald ..	.. 14 Feb. 1760
John Amiel	.. 26 June 1760
Angus M'Donall ..	.. 8 July 1760
Christopher Pauli ..	.. 8 Feb. 1761
Benjamin Strodinson ..	.. 20 Mar. 1761
James Brigstock ..	.. 24 April 1761
Daniel Tucker ..	.. 6 May 1761
George Price	.. 18 May 1761
Frederick Winter ..	.. 7 July 1761
Thomas Hutchinson ..	.. 2 Mar. 1762
James Leighton ..	.. 22 April 1762
John Fraser	.. 25 Aug. 1762
Mathew Keough ..	.. 31 Oct. 1763
Kenneth M'Culloch ..	.. 15 Dec. 1763
Chaplains—	
W. Nicholson Jackson ..	4 Feb. 1756
John Thomas	.. 15 Aug. 1764
Adjutants—	
Patrick M'Alpin ..	.. 26 April 1760
William Potts	.. 26 April 1760

Rank and Name.   *Rank in Regiment.*

Quartermasters—
John Peter Rochat..   .. 1 May 1760
Francis Hutchinson   .. 4 Oct. 1760

Surgeons—
James Stevenson ..   .. 4 Feb. 1756
Samuel Collier ..   .. 6 Feb. 1759

Regimentals—Red, facings blue, white lace, 2 blue stripes.

Agent—Mr. Calcraft, Channel Road, Westminster.

1766.

Two Battalions.

North America—West Indies.

Col.-in-Chief—
Sir Jeffery Amherst .. 30 Sept. 1759
   Rank in Army, Lt.-Gen. 19 Jan. 1761

Cols.-Commandant—
Hon. James Murray .. 24 Oct. 1759
   Rank in Army, Maj.-Gen. 10 July 1762
James Prevost ..   .. 28 Oct. 1761
   Rank in Army, Maj.-Gen. 3 June 1762

Lieut.-Colonel—
Fred. Haldiman ..   .. 4 Jan. 1756
   Rank in Army, Col. 19 Feb. 1762

Majors—
Hon. Luc. Fred. Cary .. 4 April 1765
   Rank in Army, 3 Feb. 1762
Robert Bayard ..   .. 4 Oct. 1765

Captains—
Gavin Cochran ..   .. 15 Jan. 1756
Marcus Prevost ..   .. 17 Jan. 1756
John Bradstreet ..   .. 8 Mar. 1757
   Rank in Army, Col. 19 Feb. 1762
John Jos. Schlosser .. 20 July 1758
George Etherington .   .. 17 April 1759
Thomas Barnsley ..   .. 30 May 1759
Sam. Jan. Holland .. 24 Aug. 1759
Lewis Val. Fuser ..   .. 30 Dec. 1763
   Rank in Army, 27 Sept. 1762
John Brown .. ..   .. 14 Jan. 1762
   Rank in Army, 15 Sept. 1760
Stephen Kemble ..   .. 24 Jan. 1765
John Wharton ..   .. 19 June 1765
   Rank in Army, 17 Sept. 1760
George Turnbull ..   .. 15 Nov. 1765

Captain-Lieutenants—
Ralph Phillips   .. 12 Dec. 1760
Fred. Chr. Spiesmacher.. 13 July 1761

Lieutenants—
Thos. Grandidier ..   .. 29 Jan. 1756
Daniel M'Alpin ..   .. 10 Feb. 1756
Bernard Ratzer ..   .. 20 Feb. 1756
Dietrich Brehm ..   .. 21 Feb. 1756
Jos. Fred.Wallet des Barres 22 Feb. 1756
A. T. F. Winter ..   .. 28 Feb. 1756
J. von Ingen ..   .. 29 Feb. 1756
Brereton Poynton ..   .. 30 Nov. 1756
George M'Intosh ..   .. 3 Dec. 1756
George Archibold ..   .. 8 Dec. 1756
John Polson ..   .. 5 May 1757
Allan Grant ..   .. 7 Oct. 1768
   Rank in Army, 28 July 1758

Rank and Name.   *Rank in Regiment.*

Lieutenants (continued)—
Staire Campbell Carre .. 8 May 1764
   Rank in Army, 7 May 1757
Francis Hutchinson .. 9 May 1764
   Rank in Army, 23 Aug. 1758
Augustine Prevost .. 10 May 1764
   Rank in Army, 6 May 1766
Henry Congalton ..   .. 18 May 1764
   Rank in Army, 11 Feb. 1761
Frederick Haldiman .. 13 April 1765
   Rank in Army, 8 Dec. 1760
John Christie..   .. 15 Nov. 1765

Ensigns—
Francis Schlosser ..   .. 29 Aug. 1759
Donald M'Donald ..   .. 14 Feb. 1760
John Amiel ..   .. 26 June 1760
Angus M'Donald ..   .. 8 July 1760
Christopher Pauli ..   .. 8 Feb. 1761
James Brigstock ..   .. 24 April 1761
Daniel Tucker ..   .. 6 May 1761
George Price ..   .. 18 May 1761
Frederick Winter ..   .. 7 July 1761
Thomas Hutchins ..   .. 2 Mar. 1762
John Fraser ..   .. 25 Aug. 1762
Mathew Keough ..   .. 31 Oct. 1763
Kenneth M'Culloch .. 15 Dec. 1763
Thomas Meadows ..   .. 16 Jan. 1765
Robert Johnson ..   .. 25 April 1765
   Rank in Army, 20 April 1761
Thomas Delamaine .. 12 Nov. 1765

Chaplains —
W. Nich. Jackson ..   .. 4 Feb. 1756
William Winder ..   .. 4 April 1765

Adjutants—
Patrick M'Alpin ..   .. 26 April 1760
William Potts.. .. ..

Quartermasters—
John Peter Rochat..   .. 1 May 1760
Francis Hutchinson   .. 4 Oct. 1760

Surgeons—
James Stevenson ..   .. 4 Feb. 1756
Samuel Collier ..   .. 6 Feb. 1759

Regimentals—Red, facings blue, white lace, 2 blue stripes.

Agent—Mr. Ross, Conduit Street.

1767

Two Battalions.

North America—West Indies.

Col.-in-Chief.—
Sir Jeffery Amherst .. 30 Sept. 1758
   Rank in Army, Lt.-Gen. 19 Jan. 1761

Cols.-Commandant—
Hon. James Murray .. 24 Oct. 1759
   Rank in Army, Maj.-Gen. 10 July 1762
James Prevost ..   .. 28 Oct. 1761
   Rank in Army, Maj.-Gen. 3 June 1762

Lieut.-Cols.—
Fred. Haldiman ..   .. 4 Jan. 1756
   Rank in Army, Col. 19 Feb. 1762
Augustine Prevost ..   .. 13 Dec. 1765
   Rank in Army, Col. 20 Mar. 1761

Rank and Name.	Rank in Regiment.
Majors—	
Hon. Luc. Fred. Cary ..	4 April 1765
Rank in Army, Lt.-Col.	8 Feb. 1762
Robert Bayard	4 Oct. 1765
Captains—	
Gavin Cochran	15 Jan. 1756
John Bradstreet ..	8 Mar. 1757
Rank in Army, Col.	19 Feb. 1762
John Jos. Schlosser ..	20 July 1758
George Etherington ..	17 April 1759
Thomas Barnsley	30 May 1759
Sam. Jan. Hollandt ..	24 Aug. 1759
Lewis Val Fuser	30 Dec. 1763
Rank in Army,	27 Sept. 1762
John Brown	14 June 1764
Rank in Army,	15 Sept. 1760
Stephen Kemble	24 Jan. 1765
John Wharton	19 June 1765
Rank in Army,	17 Sept. 1760
Courtland Schuyler ..	8 Nov. 1765
Rank in Army,	21 Jan. 1760
George Turnbull	15 Nov. 1765
John Carden	25 Dec. 1765
Rank in Army,	25 Feb. 1760
Beamsley Glazier	25 Dec. 1765
Rank in Army,	16 June 1760
Captain-Lieutenants—	
Ralph Phillips	12 Dec. 1765
Fred. Spitzmacher	13 July 1761
Lieutenants—	
Thos. Grandidier	29 Jan. 1756
Daniel M'Alpin	10 Feb. 1756
Bernard Ratzer	20 Feb. 1756
Dietrich Brehm	21 Feb. 1756
Jos. Fred. Wallet des Barres	22 Feb. 1756
J. von Ingen	29 Feb. 1756
Brereton Poynton ..	30 Nov. 1756
George M'Intosh	3 Dec. 1756
George Archbold ..	8 Dec. 1756
John Polson	5 May 1757
Allan Grant	7 Oct. 1763
Rank in Army,	28 July 1758
Staire Campbell Carre ..	8 May 1761
Rank in Army,	18 May 1757
Francis Hutchinson ..	9 May 1761
Rank in Army,	23 Aug. 1758
Augustine Prevost ..	10 May 1761
Rank in Army,	6 May 1761
John Christie ..	15 Nov. 1762
John Nordberg ..	27 Mar. 1762
Rank in Army,	28 June 1758
Lewis de Mestral ..	13 Sept. 1762
Rank in Army,	31 Mar. 1761
Thomas Etherington ..	13 Sept 1762
Rank in Army,	27 May 1761
Ensigns—	
Francis Schlosser	29 Aug. 1759
Donald M'Donald	14 Feb. 1761
John Ambel	26 June 1761
Angus M'Donald	8 July 1761
Christopher Carre ..	8 Feb. 1761
James Bergesen	24 April 1761
George Prevost	18 May 1761
Frederick Winter	7 July 1761
Thomas Hutchins	2 Mar. 1762
Mathew **Keough**	31 Oct. 1763

Rank and Name.	Rank in Regiment.
Ensigns (continued)—	
Robert Johnson	25 April 1765
Rank in Army,	10 April 1761
Thomas Delannine.. ..	15 Nov. 1765
James Christie	25 Dec. 1765
Rank in Army,	10 Oct. 1762
Jn. Geo. Gobbrup ..	21 Mar. 1766
David Alex. Grant.. ..	3 Sept. 1766
Charles Duncan	3 Sept. 1766
John K. Muller	11 Oct. 1766
Chaplains—	
W. Nich. Jackson	**4 Feb. 1756**
William Winder	**4 April 1765**
Adjutants—	
Patrick M'Alpin	**26 April 1766**
William Potts..	**26 April 1766**
Quartermasters—	
John Peter Rochat.. ..	**1 May 1760**
Francis Hutchinson ..	**4 Oct. 1760**
Surgeons—	
James Stevenson	4 Feb. 1756
John Graham..	12 Mar. 1766

Regimentals—Red, facings blue, white lace, 2 blue stripes.

Agent—Mr. Ross, Conduit Street.

1768.

Two Battalions.

North America—West Indies.

Col.-in-Chief—	
Sir Jeffery Amherst ..	30 Sept. 1758
Rank in Army, Lt.-Gen.	19 Jan. 1761
Hon. Thos. Gage	27 Sept. 1768
Cols. Commandant—	
Hon. James Murray ..	24 Oct. 1759
Rank in Army, Maj. Gen.	10 July 1762
James Prevost	28 Oct. 1761
Rank in Army, Maj.-Gen.	3 June 1762
Lieut.-Colonels—	
Fred. Haldimand	4 Jan. 1756
Rank in Army, Col.	9 Feb. 1762
Augustine Prevost ..	13 Dec. 1765
Rank in Army,	20 Mar. 1761
Majors—	
Hon. Luc. Fred. Carr ..	4 April 1768
Rank in Army,	8 Feb. 1762
Robert Bayard	4 Oct. 1765
Captains—	
Gavin Cochran..	15 June 1756
John Bradstock	8 Mar. 1757
Rank in Army, Col.	19 Feb. 1762
John Jos. Schlosser.. ..	20 July 1758
George Etherington ..	17 April 1759
Sam. Jan. Hollandt ..	24 Aug. 1759
Lewis Val Fuser	30 Dec. 1763
Rank in Army,	27 Sept. 1762
John Brown	14 Jan. 1764
Rank in Army,	15 Sept. 1760
Stephen Kemble	24 Jan. 1765
John Wharton	19 June 1765
Rank in Army,	17 Sept. 1760
Courtland Schuyler ..	8 Nov. 1765
Rank in Army,	21 Jan. 1760

Rank and Name.	Rank in Regiment.
Captains (continued)—	
George Turnbull	.. 16 Nov. 1765
John Carden	.. 25 Dec. 1765
Rank in Army, 25 Feb. 1760	
Beamsley Glazier	.. 25 Dec. 1765
Rank in Army, 10 June 1760	
James Stevenson	.. 4 Dec. 1767
Rank in Army, 15 June 1764	
Captain-Lieutenants—	
Ralph Phillips..	.. 12 Dec. 1760
Fred. Chr. Spiesmacher ..	3 July 1761
Lieutenants—	
Thos. Grandidier	.. 29 Jan. 1756
Daniel M'Alpin ..	.. 10 Feb. 1756
Bernard Ratzer ..	.. 20 Feb. 1746
Dietrich Brehm ..	.. 21 Feb. 1756
Jos. Frd. Wallet des Barres	22 Feb. 1756
J. von Ingen	.. 22 Feb. 1756
Brereton Poynton ..	.. 30 Nov. 1756
George M'Intosh ..	.. 3 Dec. 1756
George Archbold ..	.. 8 Dec. 1756
John Polson	.. 5 May 1757
Allan Grant	.. 7 Oct. 1763
Rank in Army, 28 July 1758	
Francis Hutchinson.. ..	9 Oct. 1763
Rank in Army, 23 Aug. 1758	
John Christie	.. 15 Nov. 1765
John Nordberg.. ..	.. 29 Mar. 1766
Rank in Army, 28 July 1758	
Thomas Etherington ..	29 Mar. 1766
Rank in Army, 27 May 1760	
Francis Phister	9 Oct. 1767
Rank in Army, 18 Sept. 1760	
George Demler	9 Oct. 1767
Rank in Army, 13 July 1761	
James Hughes..	9 Oct. 1767
Rank in Army, 9 Nov. 1761	
Ensigns—	
Francis Schlosser ..	.. 29 Aug. 1759
Donald M'Donald ..	.. 14 Feb. 1760
John Amiel	.. 26 June 1760
Angus M'Donald ..	.. 8 July 1760
Christopher Pauli ..	.. 8 Feb. 1761
James Brig-tock ..	.. 24 April 1761
George Price ..	.. 18 May 1761
Frederick Winter ..	.. 7 July 1761
Thomas Hutchins ..	.. 2 Mar. 1762
Mathew Keough ..	.. 31 Oct. 1763
Robert Johnson ..	.. 25 April 1765
Rank in Army, 20 April 1761	
Thomas Delamaine..	.. 15 Nov. 1765
Jn. Geo. Goldstrap..	.. 21 Mar. 1766
David Alexander Grant..	3 Sept. 1766
Charles Duncan ..	.. 3 Sept. 1766
John McMullin ..	.. 11 Oct. 1766
John Strickland ..	.. 13 April 1767
Rank in Army, 10 Nov. 1762	
Chaplains—	
W. Nich. Jackson ..	.. 4 Feb. 1756
William Winder ..	.. 4 April 1765
Adjutants—	
Patrick M'Alpin ..	.. 26 April 1766
John Bursent ..	.. 7 June 1761
Quartermasters—	
John Peter Rochat..	.. 1 May 1760
Francis Hutchinson..	.. 4 Oct. 1760

Rank and Name.	Rank in Regiment
Surgeons—	
John Graham.. ..	.. 12 Mar. 1766
Peter Welch	.. 19 April 1767

Regimentals— Red, facings blue, white lace, 2 blue stripes.

Agent—Mr. Ross, Conduit Street.

1769.

Two Battalions.

North America—West Indies.

Col.-in-Chief—	
Sir Jeffery Amherst.. ..	30 Sept. 1758
Rank in Army, Lt.-Gen. 19 Jan. 1761	
Cols.-Commandant—	
James Prevost.. ..	.. 28 Oct. 1761
Rank in Army, Maj.-Gen. 3 Jan. 1762	
Thque Armstrong ..	.. 16 Dec. 1767
Rank in Army, Maj.-Gen. 10 July 1762	
Lieut.-Colonels—	
Fred. Haldiman ..	.. 4 Jan. 1756
Rank in Army, Col. 10 Feb. 1762	
Gabriel Christie ..	.. 14 Dec. 1768
Rank in Army, 27 Jan. 1762	
Majors—	
Robert Bayard ..	.. 4 Oct. 1765
Hon. Thomas Bruce ..	27 May 1768
Rank in Army, 13 Jan. 1763	
Captains—	
Gavin Cochran ..	.. 15 Jan. 1756
John Bradstreet ..	.. 8 Mar. 1757
Rank in Army, Col. 19 Feb. 1762	
John Jos. Schlosser ..	20 July 1758
Geo. Etherington ..	17 April 1758
Sam. Jas. Hollandt ..	24 Aug. 1759
Lewis Val. Fuser ..	.. 30 Dec. 1763
Rank in Army, 27 Sept. 1763	
John Brown	14 June 1764
Rank in Army, 15 Sept. 1760	
Stephen Kemble ..	.. 24 Jan. 1765
John Wharton	19 June 1765
Rank in Army, 17 Sept. 1760	
Courtland Schuyler ..	8 Nov. 1765
Rank in Army, 21 Jan. 1760	
George Turnbull ..	.. 15 Nov. 1765
John Carden	25 Dec. 1765
Rank in Army, 25 Feb. 1760	
Beamsley Glazier	25 Dec. 1765
Rank in Army, 16 June 1760	
James Stevenson	4 Dec. 1767
Rank in Army, 15 June 1764	
Captain-Lieutenants—	
Ralph Phillips.. ..	.. 12 Dec. 1760
Fred. Chr. Spiesmacher ..	13 July 1761
Lieutenants—	
Thomas Grandidier ..	29 Jan. 1756
Daniel M'Alpin ..	.. 10 Feb. 1756
Bernard Ratzer ..	.. 20 Feb. 1756
Dietrich Brehm ..	.. 21 Feb. 1756
Jos. Frd. Wallet des Barres	22 Feb. 1756
J. von Ingen	.. 22 Feb. 1756
Brereton Poynton ..	.. 10 Nov. 1756
George M'Intosh ..	.. 3 Dec. 1756
George Archbold ..	.. 8 Dec. 1756

Rank and Name.	Rank in Regiment.
Lieutenants (continued)—	
John Polson	5 May 1767
Allan Grant	7 Oct. 1763
Rank in Army, 28 July 1758	
Francis Hutchinson	9 Oct. 1763
Rank in Army, 24 Aug. 1758	
John Christie ..	15 Nov. 1763
John Nordberg	29 Mar. 1766
Rank in Army, 28 July 1758	
Thomas Etherington	29 Mar. 1766
Rank in Army, 27 May 1761	
Francis Pfister ..	9 Oct. 1767
Rank in Army, 18 Sept. 1760	
George Demler	9 Oct. 1767
Rank in Army, 13 July 1761	
James Hughes.. ..	9 Oct. 1767
Rank in Army, 9 Nov. 1761	
Ensigns—	
Donald M'Donald ..	14 Feb. 1760
John Amiel ..	26 June 1760
Angus M'Donald ..	8 July 1760
Christopher Pauli ..	8 Feb. 1761
James Brigstock ..	24 April 1761
George Price ..	18 May 1761
Frederick Winter ..	7 July 1761
Thomas Hutchinson ..	2 Mar. 1762
Mathew Keough ..	31 Oct. 1762
Robert Johnson ..	25 April 1765
Rank in Army, 20 April 1762	
Thomas Delamater ..	15 Nov. 1765
Jn. Geo. Goldstrap ..	21 Mar. 1766
David Alex. Grant ..	3 Sept. 1766
Charles Baucus ..	3 Sept. 1766
John K. Muller ..	11 Oct. 1767
John Strickland ..	13 April 1768
Rank in Army, 10 Nov. 1762	
Richard Rodyeed ..	27 July 1768
Chaplains—	
W. Nich. Jackson	4 Feb. 1756
William Winder	4 April 1756
Adjutants—	
John Burrent	7 June 1764
Patrick M'Alpin ..	26 April 1762
Quartermasters—	
John Peter Rochat.. ..	1 May 1762
Francis Hutchinson ..	4 Oct. 1763
Surgeons—	
John Graham	12 Mar. 1761
Peter Welch ..	22 April 1762

Regimentals—Red, facings blue, white lace, 2 blue stripes.

Agent—Mr. Ross, Conduit Street.

1770.

Two Battalions,
West Indies—North America.

Col.-in-Chief—
Sir Jeffery Amherst .. 7 Nov. 1768
Rank in Army, Lt.-Gen. 19 June 1761
Col.-Commandant—
James Prevost .. .. 28 Oct. 1761
Rank in Army, Maj.-Gen. 3 June 1761
Bogue Armstrong .. .. 16 Dec. 1767
Rank in Army, Maj.-Gen. 10 July 1762

Rank and Name.	Rank in Regiment.
Lieut.-Colonels—	
Frederick Haldimand.. ..	4 Jan. 1756
Rank in Army, Col. 19 Feb. 1762	
Augustine Prevost	3 Nov. 1769
Rank in Army, 20 Mar. 1761	
Majors—	
Hon. Thomas Bruce ..	27 Mar. 1768
Rank in Army, 13 Jan. 1763	
John Wharton..	17 Mar. 1769
Captains—	
Gavin Cochran	15 Jan. 1756
John Bradstreet ..	8 Mar. 1757
Rank in Army, Col. 19 Feb. 1762	
John Jos. Schlosser..	20 July 1758
George Etherington ..	17 April 1759
Sam. Jas. Holland ..	24 Aug. 1759
Lewis Val. Finey	30 Dec. 1763
Rank in Army, 17 Sept. 1762	
John Brown	14 Jan. 1764
Rank in Army, 15 Sept. 1760	
Stephen Kemble	24 Jan. 1765
Courtland Schuyler..	8 Nov. 1765
Rank in Army, 21 June 1760	
George Turnbull	15 Nov. 1765
John Carden	29 Dec. 1765
Rank in Army, 25 Feb. 1760	
Beamsley Glazier ..	25 Dec. 1765
Rank in Army, 16 June 1760	
James Stephenson	4 Dec. 1767
Rank in Army, 15 June 1764	
Francis Hutchinson ..	17 Mar. 1768
Captain-Lieutenants—	
Ralph Phillips	12 Dec. 1760
Fred. Chr. Spanenacker.	13 July 1761
Lieutenants—	
Thos. Grosvalder ..	29 Jan. 1756
Daniel M'Alpin ..	10 Feb. 1756
Bernard Ratzer ..	20 Feb. 1756
Dietrich Brehm ..	21 Feb. 1756
J. Fred. Wallet des Barres	22 Feb. 1756
James von Inger ..	22 Feb. 1756
Brereton Poynton ..	30 Nov. 1756
George M'Intosh ..	3 Dec. 1756
George Archbold ..	8 Dec. 1756
John Polson	5 May 1767
Allan Grant	7 Oct. 1763
Rank in Army, 28 July 1758	
John Christie	17 Nov. 1763
John Nordberg ..	29 Mar. 1766
Rank in Army, 28 July 1758	
Thomas Etherington ..	29 Mar. 1766
Rank in Army, 27 May 1761	
Francis Pfister ..	9 Oct. 1767
Rank in Army, 18 Sept. 1760	
George Demler	9 Oct. 1767
Rank in Army, 13 July 1761	
James Hughes.. ..	9 Oct. 1767
Rank in Army, 9 Nov. 1761	
George Burns	14 July 1769
Rank in Army, 14 Aug. 1759	
Ensigns—	
Donald M'Donald ..	14 Feb. 1760
James Amiel ..	26 June 1760
Angus M'Donald ..	8 July 1760
Christopher Pauli ..	8 Feb. 1761
James Brigstock ..	24 April 1761

Rank and Name.	Rank in Regiment.
Ensigns (continued)—	
George Price	18 May 1761
Thomas Hutchins	2 Mar. 1762
Robert Johnson ..	25 April 1765
Rank in Army, 20 April 1761	
Thomas Delamaine.. ..	15 Nov. 1765
Jn. Geo. Goldstrap ..	21 Mar. 1766
David Alex. Grant.. ..	3 Sept. 1766
Charles Duncan ..	3 Sept. 1766
John K. Muller	14 Oct. 1766
John Strickland	13 April 1767
Rank in Army, 10 Nov. 1761	
William Kelly.. ..	17 Mar. 1769
Francis Duffield ..	20 April 1769
Maurice Fitzgerald.. ..	21 June 1769
Chaplains—	
W. Nich. Jackson	4 Feb. 1755
William Winder	4 April 1765
Adjutants—	
John Barrent	7 June 1764
Francis M'Alpin	6 April 1766
Quartermasters—	
John Peter Rochat.. ..	1 May 1760
John Polson	10 June 1769
Surgeons—	
John Graham	17 Mar. 1755
Peter Welch	29 April 1767

Regimentals—Red, facings blue, white lace, 2 blue stripes.

Agent—Mr. Ross, Conduit Street.

1771.

Two Battalions.

West Indies—North America.

Rank and Name.	Rank in Regiment.
Col.-in-Chief—	
Sir Jeffery Amherst ..	7 Nov. 1768
Rank in Army, Lt.-Gen. 19 Jan. 1761	
Cols.-Commandant—	
James Prevost.. ..	28 Oct. 1761
Rank in Army, Maj.-Gen.	
in America 3 June 1762	
Bique Armstrong	16 Dec. 1767
Rank in Army, Maj.-Gen. 10 July 1762	
Lieut.-Colonels—	
Fred. Haldiman	4 Jan. 1756
Rank in Army, Col. 19 Feb. 1762	
Augustine Prevost	3 Nov. 1769
Rank in Army, 20 Mar. 1761	
Majors—	
John Wharton	17 Mar. 1769
George Etherington ..	4 Oct. 1770
Captains—	
Gavin Cochran	15 June 1756
John Bradstreet	8 Mar. 1757
Rank in Army, Col. 19 Feb. 1762	
John Jos. Schlosser ..	20 July 1768
Sam. Jan. Hollandt ..	21 Aug. 1759
Lewis Val. Fuser ..	30 Dec. 1763
Rank in Army, 27 Sept. 1762	
John Brown	14 Jan. 1764
Rank in Army, 15 Sept. 1769	
Stephen Kemble ..	24 Jan. 1763
Courtland Schuyler ..	8 Nov. 1763
Rank in Army, 24 Jan. 1769	
George Turnbull	15 Nov. 1763

Rank and Name.	Rank in Regiment.
Captains (continued)—	
John Carden	25 Dec. 1763
Rank in Army, 25 Feb. 1760	
Beamsley Glazier	25 Dec. 1763
Rank in Army, 16 June 1760	
James Stevenson	4 Dec. 1767
Rank in Army, 15 June 1764	
Francis Hutchinson ..	17 Mar. 1769
Fred. Chr. Spiesmacher..	4 Oct. 1770
Captain-Lieutenants—	
Ralph Phillips	12 Dec. 1760
Thomas Grandidier ..	4 Oct. 1770
Lieutenants—	
Daniel M'Alpin	10 Feb. 1756
Bernard Ratzer	20 Feb. 1756
Dietrich Brehm	21 Feb. 1756
Jos.Frei.Wallet des Barres	22 Feb. 1756
James von Ingen	22 Feb. 1756
Brereton Poynton	30 Nov. 1756
George M'Intosh	3 Dec. 1756
George Archbold	8 Dec. 1756
John Polson	5 May 1757
Allan Grant	7 Oct. 1763
Rank in Army, 28 July 1758	
John Christie	15 Nov. 1765
John Nordberg	29 Mar. 1766
Rank in Army, 28 July 1758	
Thomas Etherington ..	29 Mar. 1766
Rank in Army, 27 May 1760	
Francis Phister	9 Oct. 1767
Rank in Army, 18 Sept. 1760	
George Demler	9 Oct. 1767
Rank in Army, 13 July 1761	
James Hughes	9 Oct. 1767
Rank in Army, 9 Nov. 1764	
Donald M'Donald	3 Oct. 1770
George Price	4 Oct. 1770
Daniel W. Reisberg ..	25 Dec. 1770
Rank in Army, July 1761	
Patrick Murray	26 Dec. 1770
Rank in Army, 21 Sept. 1762	
Angus M'Donald	27 Dec. 1770
Christopher Pauli	28 Dec. 1770
Ensigns—	
James Brigstock	24 April 1761
Thomas Hutchins	2 Mar. 1762
Robert Johnson ..	25 April 1765
Rank in Army, 20 April 1761	
Thomas Delamaine.. ..	15 Nov. 1765
David Alex. Grant.. ..	3 Sept. 1766
Charles Duncan ..	3 Sept. 1766
John K. Muller	11 Oct. 1766
John Strickland	13 April 1767
Rank in Army, 10 Nov. 1762	
William Kelly	17 Mar. 1769
Francis Duffield	10 April 1769
Samuel Rutherford ..	2 Mar. 1770
Rank in Army, 2 May 1762	
Peter Graham	11 May 1770
Spencer Briscoe	4 Oct. 1770
John Charles Schlosser..	31 Oct. 1770
Thomas Reeves	24 Dec. 1770
Marcus Pictet	27 Dec. 1770
Chaplains—	
W. Nich. Jackson	4 Feb. 1756
William Winder	4 April 1765

Rank and Name.	Rank in Regiment.
Adjutants—	
John Barrent	7 June 1764
Patrick M'Alpin	26 April 1766
Quartermasters—	
John Peter Rochat ..	1 May 1760
John Polson	10 June 1769
Surgeons—	
John Graham..	12 Mar. 1766
Peter Welch	29 April 1767

Regimentals—Red, facings blue, white
lace, 2 blue stripes.

Agent—Mr. Ross, Conduit Street.

1772.

Two Battalions.

West Indies—North America.

Col.-in-Chief—
Sir Jeffery Amherst, K.B. 7 Nov. 1768
  Rank in Army, Lt.-Gen. 19 Jan. 1761

Col.-Commandants—
James Prevost .. .. 28 Oct. 1761
  Rank in Army, Maj.-Gen. 3 June 1762
Bique Armstrong .. 16 Dec. 1767
  Rank in Army, Maj.-Gen. 10 July 1762

Lieut.-Colonels—
Fred. Haldiman .. .. 4 Jan. 1756
  Rank in Army, Col. 19 Feb. 1762
Augustine Prevost .. 3 Nov. 1760
  Rank in Army, 20 Mar. 1761

Majors—
George Etherington .. 4 Oct. 1770
Lewis Valentine Fuser .. 7 Aug. 1771

Captains—
Gavin Cochran .. .. 15 Jan. 1756
John Bradstreet .. .. 8 Mar. 1757
  Rank in Army, Col. 19 Feb. 1762
John Jas. Schlosser .. 24 July 1758
Sam. Jas. Holland .. 24 Aug. 1759
John Brown .. .. 14 Jan. 1761
  Rank in Army, 15 Sept. 1760
Stephen Kemble .. 24 Jan. 1765
Courtland Schuyler .. 8 Nov. 1765
  Rank in Army, 21 Jan. 1762
George Turnbull .. .. 15 Nov. 1765
John Carden .. .. .. 25 Dec. 1766
  Rank in Army, 25 Feb. 1760
Beamsley Glazier .. .. 25 Dec. 1765
  Rank in Army, 10 June 1760
James Stevenson .. .. 4 Dec. 1767
  Rank in Army, 15 June 1761
Francis Hutchinson .. 17 Mar. 1769
Fred. Chr. Spiessmacher.. 4 Oct. 1770
Daniel M'Alpin .. .. 7 Aug. 1771

Captain-Lieutenants—
Ralph Phillips .. .. 12 Dec. 1769
Thomas Grandidier .. 4 Oct. 1770

Lieutenants—
Bernard Ratzer .. .. 20 Feb. 1756
Dietrich Brehm .. .. 21 Feb. 1756
Jos. Fred. Wallet des Barres 22 Feb. 1756

Rank and Name.	Rank in Regiment.
Lieutenants (continued)—	
James von Ingen	22 Feb. 1756
Brereton Poynton	30 Nov. 1756
George M'Intosh	3 Dec. 1756
George Archbold	8 Dec. 1756
John Polson	5 May 1757
Allan Grant	7 Oct. 1763

  Rank in Army, 28 July 1758
John Christie .. .. 15 Nov. 1765
John Nordberg .. .. 29 Mar. 1766
  Rank in Army, 28 July 1758
Thomas Etherington .. 29 Mar. 1766
  Rank in Army, 27 May 1760
Francis Phister .. .. 9 Oct. 1767
  Rank in Army, 18 Sept. 1760
James Hughes .. .. 9 Oct. 1767
  Rank in Army, 9 Nov. 1764
Donald M'Donald .. 3 Oct. 1770
Patrick Murray .. .. 26 Dec. 1770
  Rank in Army, 21 Sept. 1762
Angus M'Donald .. .. 27 Dec. 1770
Christopher Pauli .. 28 Dec. **1770**
James Brigstock .. .. 3 June **1771**
Augustine Prevost .. 25 June **1771**
  Rank in Army, 6 May **1765**
Thomas Hutchins .. .. 7 Aug. **1771**
Charles Dixon .. .. 21 Dec. **1771**
  Rank in Army, 21 Mar. **1765**

Ensigns—
Thomas Delamaine .. 15 Nov. 1765
David Alex. Grant .. 3 Sept. 1767
Charles Duncan .. .. 3 Sept. 1766
John K. Muller .. .. 11 Oct. 1766
John Strickland .. .. 13 April 1767
  Rank in Army, 10 Nov. 1762
William Kelly .. .. 17 Mar. 1769
Francis Duffield .. .. 10 April 1770
Samuel Rutherford .. 2 Mar. 1770
  Rank in Army, 2 May 1762
Peter Graham .. .. 14 May 1770
Spencer Browne .. .. 4 Oct. 1770
John Charles Schlosser .. 31 Oct. 1770
Thomas Reeves .. .. 24 Dec. 1770
Marcus Perci .. .. 27 Dec. 1770
Jeffery Amherst .. .. 3 June 1771
John Carden .. .. .. 7 Aug. 1771
George Balson .. .. 29 Nov. 1771

Chaplains—
W. Nich. Jackson .. .. 4 Feb. 1756
William Winder .. .. 4 April 1765

Adjutants—
Patrick M'Alpin .. .. 26 April 1766
Augustine Prevost .. 25 June 1771

Quartermasters—
John Peter Rochat.. .. 1 May 1760
John Polson .. .. .. 10 June 1769

Surgeons—
John Graham.. .. .. 12 Mar. 1766
Peter Welch .. .. .. 29 April 1767

Regimentals—Red, facings blue, white
lace, 2 blue stripes.

Agents—Messrs. Ross and Grey, Conduit
Street.

1773.

Two Battalions.
West Indies.
1st Battalion.

Rank and Name.	Rank in Regiment.
Col.-in-Chief—	
Sir Jeffery Amherst, K.B.	7 Nov. 1768
Rank in Army, Lt.-Gen. 19 Jan. 1761	
Col.-Commandant—	
James Prevost	28 Oct. 1761
Rank in Army, Lt.-Gen. 25 May 1772	
Lieut.-Colonel—	
Augustine Prevost	3 Nov. 1769
Rank in Army, 30 Mar. 1761	
Major—	
Lewis Valentine Fuser ..	7 Aug. 1771
Captains.-	
Gavin Cochran	15 Jan. 1756
Rank in Army, Major, 23 July 1772	
Stephen Kemble	24 Jan. 1765
John Cardew	25 Dec. 1765
Rank in Army, 25 Feb. 1760	
James Stevenson	4 Dec. 1767
Rank in Army, 15 June 1764	
Fred. Chr. Spiesmacher..	4 Oct. 1770
George Archbold	23 Jan. 1772
Thomas Etherington ..	14 Aug. 1772
Captain-Lieutenant—	
Ralph Phillips	12 Dec. 1760
Rank in Army, Capt. 25 May 1772	
Lieutenants—	
Bernard Ratzer	20 Feb. 1756
Jos. F. Wallet des Barres	22 Feb. 1756
George M'Intosh	3 Dec. 1756
John Nordberg	29 Mar. 1766
Rank in Army, 28 July 1758	
Patrick Murray	26 Dec. 1770
Rank in Army, 21 Sept. 1762	
Christopher Pauli	28 Dec. 1770
Augustine Prevost	25 June 1771
Rank in Army, 6 May 1761	
Charles Dixon	21 Dec. 1771
Rank in Army, 24 Mar. 1765	
Thomas Delannaine ..	4 April 1772
John K. Muller	13 April 1772
James Bom	6 May 1772
Rank in Army, 11 Dec. 1761	
Ensigns—	
Samuel Rutherford ..	2 Mar. 1770
Rank in Army, 2 May 1762	
Spencer Briscoe	4 Oct. 1770
Jeffery Amherst	3 June 1771
George Hallam	29 Nov. 1771
George Brown	4 April 1772
John Peter Rochat.. ..	26 Aug. 1772
Chaplain—	
W. Nich. Jackson	4 Feb. 1756
Adjutant—	
Augustine Prevost.. ..	25 June 1771
Quartermaster—	
John Peter Rochat.. ..	1 May 1760
Surgeon—	
Peter Welch	29 April 1767

2nd Battalion.

Col.-in-Chief—	
Sir Jeffery Amherst, K.B.	7 Nov. 1768

Rank and Name.	Rank in Regiment.
Col.-Commandant—	
Fred. Haldimand	20 Oct. 1772
Rank in Army, Maj.-Gen., 25 May 1772	
Lieut.-Colonel—	
	.. ..
Major—	
George Etherington ..	4 Oct. 1770
Captains—	
John Bradstreet	8 Mar. 1757
Rank in Army, Maj.-Gen. 25 May 1772	
John Brown	14 Jan. 1764
Rank in Army, 15 Sept. 1760	
George Turnbull	15 Nov. 1765
Beamsley Glazier	25 Dec. 1765
Rank in Army, 16 June 1760	
Francis Hutchinson ..	17 Mar. 1763
Daniel M'Alpin	7 Aug. 1771
Brereton Poynton	13 April 1772
Captain-Lieutenants—	
Thomas Grandidier ..	4 Oct. 1770
Rank in Army, Capt. 25 May 1772	
Dietrich Brehm	21 Feb. 1756
Lieutenants—	
James von Ingen	22 Feb. 1756
John Polson	5 May 1757
John Christie	15 Nov. 1765
Donald M'Donald	3 Oct. 1770
Angus M'Donald	27 Dec. 1770
Thomas Hutchins	7 Aug. 1771
Charles Duncan	23 Jan. 1772
David Alex. Grant.. ..	11 May 1772
Benjamin Wickham ..	3 June 1772
Rank in Army, 28 Sept. 1762	
William Kelly..	14 Aug. 1772
Ensigns—	
John Strickland	13 April 1767
Rank in Army, 10 Nov. 1762	
Francis Duffield	11 April 1769
Peter Graham..	14 May 1770
John Charles Schlosser..	31 Oct. 1770
Marcus Pictet..	27 Dec. 1770
John Cardew	7 Aug. 1771
Joseph Hodgkinson ..	13 Mar. 1772
Bartholomew Unacke ..	31 July 1772
Chaplain—	
William Winder	4 April 1765
Adjutant—	
David Alex. Grant.. ..	23 Sept. 1772
Quartermaster—	
John Polson	10 June 1769
Surgeon—	
John Graham..	12 Mar. 1766

Regimentals- Red, facings blue, white
lace, 2 blue stripes.

Agents- Messrs. Ross and Gray, Conduit
Street.

1774.

Two Battalions.
West Indies.
1st Battalion.

Col.-in-Chief—	
Sir Jeffery Amherst, K.B.	7 Nov. 1768
Rank in Army, Lt.-Gen. 19 Jan. 1761	

Rank and Name.	Rank in Regiment.

Col.-Commandant—
James Prevost.. .. .. 28 Oct. 1761
  Rank in Army, Lt.-Gen. 25 May 1772
Lieut.-Colonel—
Augustine Prevost.. .. 3 Nov. 1769
  Rank in Army, 20 Mar. 1761
Major—
Lewis Valentine Fuser .. 7 Aug. 1771
Captains—
Stephen Kemble .. .. 24 Jan. 1765
Fred. Chr. Spiesmacher.. 4 Oct. 1770
George Archbold .. .. 23 Jan. 1772
Thomas Etherington .. 14 Aug. 1772
Ralph Phillips .. .. 25 May 1773
John Polson .. .. 16 June 1773
Marcus Prevost .. .. 13 Sept. 1773
  Rank in Army, 17 Dec. 1756
Captain-Lieutenant and Captain—
Bernard Ratzer .. .. 14 Aug. 1773
Lieutenants—
Jos. Fred. Wallet des Barres 22 Feb. 1756
George M'Intosh .. .. 3 Dec. 1756
John Nordberg .. .. 29 Mar. 1766
  Rank in Army, Capt. 31 Aug. 1773
Patrick Murray .. .. 26 Dec. 1770
  Rank in Army, 21 Sept. 1762
Christopher Pauli .. 28 Dec. 1770
Augustine Prevost.. .. 25 June 1771
  Rank in Army, 6 May 1763
Charles Dixon.. .. 21 Dec. 1771
  Rank in Army, 21 Mar. 1765
John K. Muller .. .. 13 April 1772
James Bant .. .. 6 May 1772
  Rank in Army, 11 Dec. 1761
Jeffery Amherst .. .. 12 April 1773
Francis Duffield .. .. **14 Aug. 1773**
Ensigns—
Samuel Rutherford .. **2 Mar.** 1770
  Rank in Army, **2 May** 1762
Spencer Briscoe .. .. **4** Oct. 1770
George Hallam .. .. **29 Nov.** 1771
George Browne .. .. 4 April 1772
John Peter Rochat.. .. 26 Aug. 1772
Robert Palmer .. .. 4 Mar. 1773
Charles Butter .. .. 11 April 1773
James Faly .. .. 12 April 1773
Chaplain—
W. Nich. **Jackson** .. .. 4 Feb. 1756
Adjutant—
Augustine Prevost .. 25 June 1771
Quartermaster—
John Peter Rochat .. .. 1 May 1769
Surgeon—
Peter **Walsh** .. .. .. 29 April 1767
2nd Battalion.
Col.-in-Chief—
Sir Jeffery Amherst, K.B. 1 Nov. 1768
  Rank in Army, Lt.-Gen. 19 Jan. 1761
Col.-Commandant—
Fred. Haldimand .. .. 29 Oct. 1772
  Rank in Army, Maj.-Gen. 25 May 1772
Lieut.-Colonels—
Gabriel Christie .. .. 14 Aug. 1772
  Rank in Army, 27 Jan. 1762
Major—
George Etherington .. 4 Oct. 1770

Rank and Name	Rank in Regiment.

Captains—
John Bradstreet .. .. 8 Mar. 1757
  Rank in Army, Maj.-Gen. 25 May 1772
John Brown .. .. .. 14 Jan. 1764
  Rank in Army, 15 Sept. 1765
George Turnbull .. .. 15 Nov. 1765
Beamsley Glazier .. .. 25 Dec. 1760
  Rank in Army, 16 June 1769
Francis Hutchinson .. 17 Mar. 1761
Daniel M'Alpin .. .. 7 Aug. 1770
Brereton Poynton.. .. 13 April 1772
Captain-Lieutenant—
Thomas Grandidier .. 4 Oct. **1770**
  Rank in Army, Capt. 25 May **1772**
Lieutenants—
Dietrich Brehm .. .. 21 Feb. **1756**
James von Ingen .. .. 22 Feb. **1756**
John Christie .. .. 15 Nov. **1765**
Donald M'Donald .. .. 3 Oct. **1770**
Angus M'Donald .. .. 27 Dec. **1770**
Thomas Hutchins .. .. 7 Aug. **1771**
David Alex. Grant .. 11 May **1772**
Benjamin Wickham .. 3 June **1772**
  Rank in Army, 28 Sept. 1762
William Kelly.. .. .. 14 Aug. 1772
Peter Graham.. .. .. 6 Jan. 1773
Marcus Pictet.. .. .. 16 June 1773
Ensigns—
John Charles Schlosser .. **31 Oct.** 1770
John Carden .. .. .. **7 Aug.** 1771
Joseph Hodgkinson .. 13 Mar. 1772
—— Ricketts.. .. .. 6 Jan. 1773
John Bayard .. .. .. 6 Jan. 1773
Hans Carden .. .. .. 16 June 1773
Thomas Allen .. .. 12 Aug. 1773
—— Worseley .. .. **14 Aug.** 1773
Chaplain—
William Winder .. .. **4 April 1765**
Adjutant—
David Alex. Grant .. **23 Sept. 1772**
Quartermaster—
John **Polson** .. .. **10 June 1769**
Surgeon—
John Graham .. .. **12 Mar. 1766**
*Regimentals—*Red, facings blue, white lace, 2 blue stripes

Agents Messrs. Ross and Gray, Conduit Street.

1775.

Four Battalions.

West Indies North America England.
1st Battalion.
Col.-in-Chief—
Sir Jeffery Amherst, K.B. 7 Nov. 1768
  Rank in Army, Lt.-Gen. 19 Jan. 1761
Col.-Commandant—
James Prevost.. .. .. 28 Oct. 1761
  Rank in Army, Lt.-Gen. 25 May 1772
William Taylor .. .. 17 July 1775
Lieut.-Colonel—
Augustine Prevost.. .. 3 Nov. 1769
  Rank in Army, 20 Mar. 1761

Rank and Name.	Rank in Regiment.
Major—	
Lewis Valentine Fuser ..	7 Aug. 1771
Captains—	
Stephen Kemble	24 Jan. 1765
Rank in Army, Major 7 Aug. 1772	
Fred. Chr. Spiesmacher..	4 Oct. 1770
George Archbold	23 Jan. 1772
Ralph Phillips	25 May 1772
Thomas Etherington ..	14 Aug. 1772
John Polson	16 June 1773
James Mark Prevost ..	13 Sept. 1773
Rank in Army, Major 23 July 1772	
Captain-Lieut. and Captain—	
Bernard Ratzer	14 Aug. 1773
Lieutenants—	
Jos. Frd. Wallet des Barres	23 Feb. 1756
George M'Intosh	3 Dec. 1756
Patrick Murray	26 Dec. 1770
Rank in Army, 21 Sept. 1762	
Christopher Pauli	28 Dec. 1770
Augustine Prevost	25 June 1771
Rank in Army, 6 May 1761	
Charles Dixon..	21 Dec. 1771
Rank in Army, 21 Mar. 1765	
John K. Muller	13 April 1772
James Cain	6 May 1772
Rank in Army, 11 Dec. 1761	
Jeffery Amherst	12 April 1773
Francis Dutfield	14 Aug. 1773
Samuel Rutherford.. ..	16 Feb. 1774
Ensigns—	
Spencer Briscoe	14 Oct. 1770
George Hallam	29 Nov. 1771
George Brown..	4 April 1772
John Peter Rochat ..	26 Aug. 1772
Robert Palmer	4 Mar. 1773
Charles Butter	11 April 1773
James Faby	12 April 1773
Hans Carden	12 April 1773
Rank in Army, 16 June 1773	
Chaplain—	
W. Nich. Jackson	4 Feb. 1756
Adjutant—	
Augustine Prevost.. ..	25 June 1771
Quartermaster—	
John Peter Rochat ..	1 May 1760
Surgeon—	
Peter Walsh	22 April 1767

2nd Battalion.

Col.-in-Chief—	
Sir Jeffery Amherst, K.B.	7 Nov. 1768
Rank in Army, Lt.-Gen. 19 Jan. 1761	
Col.-Commandant—	
Fred. Haldimand	20 Oct. 1772
Rank in Army, Maj.-Gen.	
in America 25 May 1772	
Lieut.-Colonel—	
Gabriel Christie	14 Aug. 1773
Rank in Army, 27 Jan. 1761	
Major—	
George Etherington ..	4 Oct. 1770

Rank and Name.	Rank in Regiment.
Captains—	
John Brown	14 Jan. 1764
Rank in Army, 15 Sept. 1760	
George Turnbull	15 Nov. 1765
Beamsley Glazier	25 Dec. 1765
Rank in Army, 16 June 1760	
Francis Hutchinson ..	17 Mar. 1769
Daniel M'Alpin	7 Aug. 1771
Brereton Poynton	13 April 1772
Thomas Grandidier ..	25 May 1772
Captain-Lieut. and Captain—	
Dietrich Brehm	16 Nov. 1774
Lieutenants—	
James von Ingen	19 Feb. 1756
John Christie..	15 Nov. 1765
Donald M'Donald	27 Oct. 1770
Angus M'Donald	27 Dec. 1770
Thomas Hutchins	7 Aug. 1771
David Alex. Grant.. ..	11 May 1772
Benjamin Wickham ..	3 June 1772
Rank in Army, 28 Sept. 1762	
William Kelly	14 Aug. 1772
Peter Graham..	6 Jan. 1773
Marcus Pictet	16 June 1773
John Chr. Schlosser ..	16 Nov. 1774
John Carden	7 Aug. 1771
—— Ricketts..	6 Jan. 1773
John Bayard	6 Jan. 1773
—— Worsley	14 Aug. 1773
Thomas Flucker	16 Feb. 1774
Ensigns—	
Richard Hansard	11 April 1774
Rank in Army, 14 Jan. 1772	
Charles Southby	23 May 1774
Louis Haldimand	16 Nov. 1774
Chaplain—	
William Winder	4 April 1765
Adjutant—	
Donald M'Donald	16 Feb. 1774
Quartermaster—	
John Fleming..	9 Nov. 1774
Surgeon—	
Joseph Price	8 Dec. 1774

Regimentals—Red, facings blue, white lace, 2 blue stripes.

Agents—Messrs. Ross and Gray, Conduit Street.

1776.

*Four Battalions.**

West Indies—North America—England.

1st Battalion.

Col.-in-Chief—	
Sir Jeffery Amherst, K.B.	7 Nov. 1768
Rank in Army, Lt.-Gen. 19 Jan. 1761	
Col.-Commandant—	
James Prevost	28 Oct. 1761
Rank in Army, Lt.-Gen. 25 May 1772	

* Although the 3rd and 4th Battalions were raised in 1775, they do not appear in Army List till 1777.

Rank and Name.	Rank in Regiment.
Lieut.-Colonel—	
Gabriel Christie	18 Sept. 1775
Rank in Army,	27 Jan. 1762
Major—	
Stephen Kemble	20 Sept. 1775
Rank in Army,	7 Aug. 1772
Captains—	
Fred. Chr. Spiesmacher ..	4 Oct. 1770
George Archbold	23 Jan. 1772
Ralph Phillips	25 May 1772
Thomas Etherington ..	14 Aug. 1772
John Polson	16 June 1773
Bernard Ratzer	14 Aug. 1773
Jos. Fr. Wallet des Barres	23 Sept. 1775
Captain-Lieut. and Captain—	
Augustine Prevost	20 Sept. 1775
Lieutenants—	
Charles Dixon	21 Dec. 1771
Rank in Army,	21 Mar. 1765
John K. Muller	13 April 1772
James Bain	6 May 1772
Rank in Army,	11 Dec. 1761
Jeffery Amherst	12 April 1773
Francis Duffield	14 Aug. 1773
Samuel Rutherford ..	6 Feb. 1774
Spencer Brisson	23 Sept. 1775
George Hallam	28 Sept. 1775
George Brown	29 Sept. 1775
John Peter Rochat ..	30 Sept. 1775
Ensigns—	
Robert Palmer	4 Mar. 1773
Charles Butter	11 April 1773
James Fahy	12 April 1773
Hans Carden	
Rank in Army,	16 June 1773
Thos. Milward Smith ..	28 Sept. 1775
William Muir	29 Sept. 1775
Thomas Sentence	30 Sept. 1775
Chaplain—	
W. Nich. Jackson	4 Feb. 1756
Adjutant—	
Augustine Prevost	25 June 1771
Quartermaster—	
John Peter Rochat ..	1 May 1760
Surgeon—	
Peter Walsh	29 April 1767

2nd Battalion.

Col.-in-Chief—	
Sir Jeffery Amherst, K.B.	7 Nov. 1768
Rank in Army, Lt.-Gen.	19 Jan. 1761
Col. Commandant —	
Fred. Haldiman	20 Oct. 1772
Rank in Army, Maj.-Gen.	25 May 1772
Lieut.-Colonel—	
George Etherington ..	19 Sept. 1775
Major —	
James Mark Prevost ..	21 Sept. 1775
Rank in Army,	23 July 1772
Captains—	
Francis Hutchinson ..	17 Mar. 1762
Daniel M'Alpin	7 Aug. 1772
Brereton Poynton	13 April 1772
Thomas Gransbhier ..	25 May 1772
Dietrich Brehm	16 Nov. 1774

Rank and Name.	Rank in Regiment.
Captains (continued)—	
William Kelly	28 April 1775
James von Ingen	24 Sept. 1775
Captain-Lieut. and Captain—	
Thomas Hutchins	21 Sept. 1775
Lieutenants—	
Angus M'Donald	27 Dec. 1770
David Alex. Grant ..	11 May 1772
Benjamin Wickham ..	3 June 1772
Rank in Army,	26 Sept. 1772
Peter Graham	6 Jan. 1773
Marcus Pictet	16 June 1773
John Chr. Schlosser ..	16 Nov. 1774
John Carden	28 April 1775
Poyntz Ricketts	1 Oct. 1775
John Bayard	2 Oct. 1775
John Worseley	3 Oct. 1775
Thomas Flucker	
Ensigns—	
Richard Hansard	11 April 1774
Rank in Army,	14 Jan. 1772
Charles Southby	25 May 1774
Louis Haldiman	16 Nov. 1774
Thomas Walker	28 April 1775
David Gordon	1 Oct. 1775
Chaplain—	
William Winder	4 April 1765
Adjutant—	
Donald M'Donald	16 Feb. 1774
Quartermaster—	
John Fleming	4 Nov. 1774
Surgeon—	
William Notter	28 June 1775

Regimentals—Red, facings blue, white lace, 2 blue stripes.

Agents—Messrs. Ross and Gray, Conduit Street.

1777.

Four Battalions.

West Indies—North America.

Col.-in-Chief—	
Jeffery, Ld. Amherst, K.B.	17 Nov. 1768
Rank in Army, Lt.-Gen.	19 Jan. 1761
Col. Commandant—	
Frederick Haldiman ..	11 Jan. 1776
Rank in Army, Maj.-Gen.	25 May 1772
Lieut.-Colonel—	
Gabriel Christie	18 Sept. 1775
Rank in Army,	27 Jan. 1762
Major—	
Stephen Kemble	20 Sept. 1775
Rank in Army,	7 Aug. 1772
Captains—	
Fred. Chr. Spiesmacher ..	4 Oct. 1770
George Archbold	23 Jan. 1771
Brereton Poynton	13 April 1771
Ralph Phillips	25 May 1771
Bernard Ratzer	13 Nov. 1771
John Polson	16 June 1775
Jos. Fr. Wallet des Barres	3 Sept. 1775
Captain-Lieut. and Captain—	
Chas. Dixon	12 Nov. 1776

Rank and Name.	Rank in Regiment.

Lieutenants—

James Bain	6 May 1772
Rank in Army, 11 Dec. 1762	
David Alex. Grant	11 May 1772
Francis Duffield	13 Nov. 1772
Jeffery Amherst	12 April 1773
Samuel Rutherford ..	16 Feb. 1774
Spencer Briscoe	23 Sept. 1775
George Ballam	28 Sept. 1775
John Peter Rochat ..	30 Sept. 1775
Robert Palmer.	12 Nov. 1776
Charles Butter	13 Nov. 1776

Ensigns—

James Fahy	6 May 1772
Hans Carden	
Rank in Army, 16 June 1773	
Thos. Milward Smith ..	28 Sept. 1775
William Mair	29 Sept. 1775
Thomas Sentence	30 Sept. 1775
John Henry Wolfe ..	1 Mar. 1776
Simon Ecuyier	13 Mar. 1776

Chaplain—

| James Manesty .. .. | 18 May 1776 |

Adjutant—

| Jeffery Amherst .. .. | 21 Nov. 1776 |

Quartermaster—

| John Peter Rochat .. | 1 May 1760 |

Surgeon—

| Peter Walsh .. .. .. | 29 April 1767 |

2nd Battalion.

Col.-in-Chief—

| Jeffrey, Ld. Amherst, K.B. | 7 Nov. 1768 |
| *Rank in Army,* Lieut.-Gen. 19 Jan. 1761 | |

Col.-Commandant—

| James Robertson .. .. | 11 Jan. 1776 |
| *Rank in Army,* 25 May 1772 | |

Lieut.-Colonel—

| George Etherington .. | 19 Sept. 1775 |

Major—

| James Mark Prevost .. | 21 Sept. 1775 |
| *Rank in Army,* 23 July 1772 | |

Captains—

Francis Hutchinson ..	27 Mar. 1769
Daniel McAlpin	7 Aug. 1771
Thomas Graudidier ..	25 May 1772
Thomas Etherington ..	14 Aug. 1772
Dietrich Brehm	16 Nov. 1774
William Kelly..	28 April 1775
James van Ingen	24 Sept. 1775

Captain-Lieut. and Captain—

| John K. Muller .. .. | 13 Nov. 1776 |

Lieutenants—

Benjamin Wickham ..	3 June 1772
Rank in Army, 26 Sept. 1772	
Peter Graham	6 Jan. 1773
Marcus Pictet	16 June 1773
John Chas. Schlosser ..	16 Nov. 1774
Poentz Ricketts	1 Oct. 1774
John Bayard	2 Oct. 1774
Thomas Flucker	4 Oct. 1774
James Wakeley	18 April 1776
Rank in Army, 28 Oct. 1760	
Charles Scuthby	14 Aug. 1776
Richard Hansard	14 Nov. 1776
Thomas Walker	15 Nov. 1776

Rank and Name.	Rank in Regiment.

Ensigns—

David Gordon..	1 Oct. 1775
John Charlton	5 Feb. 1776
Richard Bennet	6 Feb. 1776
John Gottsched	29 Feb. 1776
J. O. Degernann	17 May 1776
John Sharpe	14 Aug. 1776
Charles Crochley	14 Nov. 1776
Phillip Priddie	15 Nov. 1776

Chaplain—

| William Winder .. .. | 4 April 1765 |

Adjutant—

| John Charlton .. .. | 5 Feb. 1776 |

Quartermaster—

| John Fleming.. .. .. | 9 Nov. 1774 |

Surgeon—

| William Notter .. .. | 28 June 1765 |

3rd Battalion.

Col.-in-Chief—

| Jeffery, Ld. Amherst, K.B. | 25 Aug. 1775 |
| *Rank in Army,* Lt.-Gen. 19 Jan. 1761 | |

Col.-Commandant—

| John Dalling .. .. .. | 16 Jan. 1776 |
| *Rank in Army,* 25 May 1772 | |

Lieut.-Colonel—

| William Stiell.. .. .. | 21 Sept. 1775 |

Major—

| John Brown .. | 22 Sept. 1775 |

Captains—

Jacob Van Braam	31 Aug. 1775
Rank in Army, 19 Sept. 1761	
Jacob Muller	3 Sept. 1775
Rank in Army, 11 April 1763	
George McIntosh	25 Sept. 1775
Donald M'Donald	27 Sept. 1775
Christopher Pauli	29 Sept. 1775
Augustine Prevost	12 Nov. 1776
Rank in Army, 24 Sept. 1775	
George Bruere	15 Nov. 1776

Captain-Lieutenant—

Lieutenants—

Archibald Lamont	2 Sept. 1775
Rank in Army, 15 May 1757	
George Mackay	3 Sept. 1775
Rank in Army, 20 Mar. 1761	
George Sneyder	5 Sept. 1775
Rank in Army, 27 Sept. 1762	
James Robertson	5 Feb. 1776
H. Christ. Fenner	7 Feb. 1776
Fred. de Gentzkow ..	1 Nov. 1776
N. F. C. Lockell	24 Nov. 1776

Ensigns—

Lewis Mattay..	1 Sept. 1775
James Gordon	2 Sept. 1775
Robert Lowe	3 Sept. 1775
Imbert de Traytorrens ..	7 Feb. 1776
Ferdinand Brock	8 Feb. 1776
Isaac Besselburg	9 Feb. 1776
James Finlay	13 Feb. 1776

Chaplain—

| Michael Schlueter .. | 1 Sept. 1775 |

Adjutant—

| George Eberhard .. | 1 Sept. 1775 |

Rank and Name.	Rank in Regiment.
Quartermaster—	
Lewis Genevay	1 Sept. 1775
Surgeon—	
John Summers	10 Nov. 1775
4th Battalion.	
Col.-in-Chief—	
Jeffery, Ld. Amherst, K.B.	25 Aug. 1775
Rank in Army, Lt.-Gen.	19 Jan. 1761
Col.-Commandant—	
Augustine Prevost ..	18 Sept. 1775
Lieut.-Colonel—	
Lewis Val. Fuser	20 Sept. 1775
Major—	
Beaumsley Glazier	23 Sept. 1775
Captains—	
James Allaz	1 Sept. 1775
Rank in Army,	2 Oct. 1761
Simon Fenvier	2 Sept. 1775
Rank in Army,	22 April 1762
George Fusch..	22 Sept. 1775
John Christie..	26 Sept. 1775
Patrick Murray	28 Sept. 1775
William Wolffe	30 Sept. 1775
Thomas Hutchins	13 Nov. 1776
Rank in Army,	24 Sept. 1775
Captain-Lieut. and Captain—	
Alexander Shaw	14 Nov. 1776
Lieutenants—	
James Edwards	4 Sept. 1775
Rank in Army,	23 June 1762
David Monins..	6 Sept. 1775
Rank in Army,	14 Jan. 1763
William Lochcowitz ..	4 Oct. 1775
Harry Burrard	6 Feb. 1776
Fred. de Montrond ..	20 Mar. 1776
—— Graham	21 Nov. 1776
Ensigns—	
Alexander M'Donald ..	2 Sept. 1775
George M'Kenzie ..	3 Sept. 1775
William Probick	4 Sept. 1775
Maria Vemper..	4 Oct. 1775
John Campbell	10 Feb. 1776
James Irwin	11 Feb. 1776
Robert Lethbridge.. ..	12 Feb. 1776
C. L. Theod. Schossido ..	18 May 1776
Chaplain—	
George Bone	5 Feb. 1776
Adjutant—	
Alexander Shaw	1 Sept. 1775
Quartermaster—	
John Clark	5 Feb. 1776
Surgeon—	
James Henderson	10 Nov. 1775

Regimentals—Red, facings Blue, white lace, 2 blue stripes.
Agents—Messrs. Ross and Gray, Conduit Street.

1778.

Four Battalions.

West Indies North America.

1st Battalion.

Col.-in-Chief—
Jeffery, Ld. Amherst, K.B. 7 Nov. 1768
Rank in Army, Lt.-Gen. 19 Jan. 1761

Rank and Name.	Rank in Regiment.
Col.-Commandant—	
Frederick Haldiman ..	11 Jan. 1776
Rank in Army, Lt.-Gen.	29 Aug. 1777
Lieut.-Colonel—	
Gabriel Christie	18 Sept. 1775
Rank in Army, Col.	27 Jan. 1762
Major—	
Stephen Kemble	**20 Sept. 1775**
Rank in Army,	**7 Aug. 1772**
Captains—	
Fred. Chr. Spiessmacher..	4 Oct. 1770
Ralph Phillips	25 May 1772
Bernhard Ratzer	13 Nov. 1772
John Folsen	16 June 1773
Jos. Fr. Wallet des Barres	23 Sept. 1775
Charles Dixon	12 Nov. 1776
Geo. Montg. Metham ..	25 Feb. 1777
Rank in Army,	26 May 1776
Captain-Lieut. and Captain—	
Jeffery Amherst	2 Aug. 1777
Lieutenants—	
James Bain	6 May 1772
Rank in Army,	11 Dec. 1761
David Alexander Grant ..	11 May 1772
Samuel Rutherford ..	16 Feb. 1774
George Hallam	28 Sept. 1775
George Brown..	29 Sept. 1775
John Peter Rochat.. ..	30 Sept. 1775
Robert Palmer	12 Nov. 1776
James Faby	31 Jan. 1777
Thos. Milward Smith ..	2 Aug. 1777
William Mair..	3 Aug. 1777
Joshua Wolfe..	28 Nov. 1777
Ensigns—	
Thomas Sentence	30 Sept. 1775
Simon Fenvier	13 Nov. 1776
John Charlton	27 Dec. 1776
Edward Davis..	31 Jan. 1777
James Paquet	6 Feb. 1777
Christian Pless	29 Aug. 1777
Phillip Penfche	28 Nov. 1777
Rank in Army,	15 Nov. 1776
Chaplain—	
James Mancely	18 May 1776
Adjutant—	
Jeffery Amherst	21 Nov. 1776
Quartermaster—	
John Peter Rochat.. ..	1 May 1760
Surgeon—	
Peter Walsh	29 April 1767

2nd Battalion.

Col.-in-Chief—
Jeffery Ld. Amherst, K.B. 7 Nov. 1768
Rank in Army, Lt.-Gen. 19 Jan. 1761
Col.-Commandant—
James Robertson .. 11 Jan. 1776
Rank in Army, Maj.-Gen. 29 Aug. 1777
Lieut.-Colonel—
George Etherington .. 19 Sept. 1775
Major—
James Mark Prevost .. 21 Sept. 1775
Rank in Army, 23 July 1772
Captains—
Francis Hutchinson .. 27 Mar. 1769
Daniel M'Alpin .. .. 7 Aug. 1771

H

Rank and Name.	Rank in Regiment.
Captain (continued)—	
Thomas Graudidier ..	.. 25 May 1772
Thomas Etherington ..	14 Aug. 1772
Dietrich Brehm ..	.. 16 Nov. 1774
William Kelly.. ..	.. 28 Apr. 1775
James von Ingen ..	.. 2? Sept. 1775
Captain-Lieutenant and Captain—	
John K. Muller ..	.. 13 Nov. 1776
Lieutenants—	
Benjamin Pictet ..	.. 16 June 1773
Marcus Wickham ..	.. 3 June 1772
Rank in Army, 28 Sept. 1762	
Poyntz Ricketts ..	.. 1 Oct. 1774
John Bayard	.. 2 Oct. 1774
Thomas Flucker ..	.. 4 Oct. 1774
James Wak ley ..	.. 18 April 1776
Rank in Army, 28 Oct. 1760	
Charles Southby ..	.. 14 Aug. 1776
Richard Hansard ..	.. 14 Nov. 1776
Thomas Walker ..	.. 15 Nov. 1776
John Charlton ..	.. 6 Mar. 1777
David Gordon.. ..	.. 17 Mar. 1777
Ensigns—	
Richard Bennet ..	.. 6 Feb. 1776
John Gottsched ..	.. 29 Feb. 1776
J. O. Degermann ..	.. 17 May 1776
John Sharpe	.. 14 Aug. 1776
Charles Crochley ..	.. 14 Nov. 1776
Wm. John Davis ..	.. 6 Mar. 1777
—— Van Hamell ..	.. 17 Mar. 1777
Wm. Henry Rickets ..	28 Nov. 1777
Chaplain—	
William Winder ..	.. 4 April 1765
Adjutant—	
John Charlton ..	.. 5 Feb. 1776
Quartermaster—	
John Fleming.. ..	.. 9 Nov. 1774
Surgeon—	
William Notter ..	.. 28 June 1775

3rd Battalion.

Col.-in-Chief—	
Jeffery, Ld. Amherst, K.B.	25 Aug. 1775
Rank in Army, Lt.-Gen. 19 Jan. 1761	
Col.-Commandant—	
John Dalling	.. 16 Jan. 1776
Rank in Army, Maj.-Gen. 29 Aug. 1777	
Lieut.-Colonel—	
William Stiell.. ..	.. 21 Sept. 1775
Major—	
Jacob Van Braam ..	.. 14 June 1777
Captains—	
Jacob Muller	.. 3 Sept. 1775
Rank in Army, Major 29 Aug. 1777	
George M'Intosh ..	.. 25 Sept. 1775
Donald M'Donald ..	.. 27 Sept. 1775
Christopher Pauli ..	.. 29 Sept. 1775
Augustine Prevost ..	.. 12 Nov. 1776
Rank in Army, 23 Sept. 1775	
George Bruere ..	.. 15 Nov. 1776
Francis Duffield ..	.. 3 Aug. 1777
Lieutenants—	
George Mackay ..	.. 3 Sept. 1775
Rank in Army, 20 Mar. 1761	
George Snevder ..	.. 5 Sept. 1775
Rank in Army, 27 Sept. 1762	

Rank and Name.	Rank in Regiment.
Lieutenants (continued)—	
James Robertson ..	.. 5 Feb. 1776
Rank in Army, 15 Sept. 1763	
Fred. de Gentzkow ..	1 Nov. 1776
N. F. C. Lockell ..	.. 21 Nov. 1776
Robert Sutherland..	.. 21 Jan. 1777
Rank in Army, 6 Jan. 1760	
Hans Carden	.. 6 Feb. 1777
Nathaniel Farnall ..	.. 13 Mar. 1777
Rank in Army, 27 Jan. 1773	
Lewis Mattay	.. 29 May 1777
Peter Haldiman ..	.. 9 Sept. 1777
Ensigns—	
James Gordon ..	.. 2 Sept. 1775
Robert Lowe	.. 3 Sept. 1775
Frederick Brock ..	.. 8 Feb. 1776
Isaac Hesselburg ..	.. 9 Feb. 1776
James Finlay	.. 13 Feb. 1776
William Floyer ..	.. 24 Feb. 1776
Charles Ward.. ..	.. 29 May 1777
Samuel Devisme ..	.. 9 Sept. 1777
Chaplain—	
Michael Schlaetter ..	.. 1 Sept. 1775
Adjutant—	
George Eberhard ..	.. 1 Sept. 1775
Quartermaster—	
Lewis Genevay ..	.. 1 Sept. 1775
Surgeon—	
John Summers ..	.. 10 Nov. 1775

4th Battalion.

Col.-in-Chief—	
Jeffery, Ld. Amherst, K.B.	25 Aug. 1775
Rank in Army, Lt.-Gen. 19 Jan. 1761	
Col.-Commandant—	
Augustine Prevost ..	.. 18 Sept. 1775
Lieut.-Colonel—	
Lewis Val. Fuser ..	.. 20 Sept. 1775
Major—	
Beamsley Glazier ..	.. 23 Sept. 1775
Captains—	
James Allaz	.. 1 Sept. 1775
Rank in Army, Major 29 Aug. 1777	
Simon Fenzier ..	.. 2 Sept. 1775
Rank in Army, Major 29 Aug. 1777	
George Fesch	.. 22 Sept. 1775
John Christie	.. 26 Sept. 1775
Patrick Murray ..	.. 28 Sept. 1775
William Wolff ..	.. 30 Sept. 1775
Thomas Hutchins ..	.. 13 Nov. 1776
Rank in Army, 24 Sept. 1775	
Captain-Lieutenant and Captain—	
Alexander Shaw ..	.. 14 Nov. 1775
Lieutenants—	
James Edwards ..	.. 4 Sept. 1775
Rank in Army, 23 June 1762	
David Munns	.. 6 Sept. 1775
Rank in Army, 14 Jan. 1763	
William Lachenwitz ..	4 Oct. 1775
Harry Barrard ..	.. 6 Feb. 1776
Fred. de Montreuil ..	29 Mar. 1776
John J. Graham ..	.. 21 Nov. 1776
William Keppel ..	.. 7 Feb. 1777
Ernest Aug. de Hellfeld .	4 Aug. 1777
Geo. Fred. Loup ..	.. 11 Sept. 1777
—— Breitenbach ..	.. 21 Nov. 1777

Rank and Name.	Rank in Regiment.
Ensigns—	
Alexander M'Donald ..	2 Sept. 1775
George M'Kenzie	3 Sept. 1775
William Probick	4 Sept. 1775
Marin Vaniper	4 Oct. 1775
John Campbell	10 Feb. 1776
Robert Lethbridge.. ..	12 Feb. 1776
C. L. Throd. Schoedde ..	18 Mar. 1776
Lewis Bardo	29 June 1776
Chaplain—	
George Bowe	5 Feb. 1776
Adjutant—	
Alexander Shaw	1 Sept. 1775
Quartermaster—	
John Clarke	5 Feb. 1776
Surgeon—	
James Henderson ..	10 Nov. 1775

Regimentals—Red, facings **blue**, white lace, 2 blue stripes.

Agents—Messrs. Ross and Gray, Conduit Street.

1779.

Four Battalions.

West Indies—North America.

1st Battalion.

Col.-in-Chief—	
Jeffery, Ld. Amherst, K.B.	7 Nov. 1768
Rank in Army, Gen. 19 Mar. 1778	
Col.-Commandant—	
Frederick Haldimand ..	11 Jan. 1776
Rank in Army, Gen. 1 Jan. 1776	
Lieut.-Colonel—	
Stephen Kemble	14 May 1778
Rank in Army, 29 Aug. 1777	
Major—	
James Mark Prevost ..	6 June 1778
Rank in Army, Lieut.-Col. 29 Aug. 1777	
Captains—	
Ralph Phillips.. ..	25 May 1772
Bernard Ratzer	13 Nov. 1772
John Polson	16 June 1773
Jos. Frd. Wallet des Barres	23 Sept. 1775
Charles Dixon.. ..	12 Nov. 1776
Geo. Montg. Metham ..	26 Feb. 1777
Rank in Army, 24 May 1776	
Jeffery Amherst	2 Aug. 1777
James Bain	14 May 1778
Samuel Rutherford.. ..	26 Dec. 1778
Capt.-Lieutenant and Captain -	
George Hallam	27 Dec. 1778
Lieutenants—	
George Brown.. ..	29 Sept. 1775
John Peter Rochat.. ..	30 Sept. 1775
Robert Palmer.. ..	12 Nov. 1776
James Fahy	31 Jan. 1777
Joshua Wolfe.. ..	28 Nov. 1777
Simon Ecuyer	10 April 1778
John Charlton	11 April 1778
Edward Davis.. ..	14 May 1778
Marin Vaniper	25 Dec. 1778
John Campbell	26 Dec. 1778
Robert Lethbridge.. ..	27 Dec. 1778
Louis Paquet	28 Dec. 1778

Rank and Name.	Rank in Regiment.
Ensigns—	
Christian Plees	29 Aug. 1777
Phillip Priddie	28 Nov. 1777
Rank in Army, 15 Nov. 1776	
Wm. Henry Ricketts ..	10 April 1778
Rank in Army, 28 Nov. 1777	
Charles Brown.. ..	11 April 1778
J. Phillip Jeserick ..	14 May 1778
Thomas Foy	5 June 1778
Daniel Muller.. ..	26 Dec. 1778
Louis Correront ..	21 April 1779
T. Berclay Scriven.. ..	12 Mar. 1779
Rank in Army, 27 Dec. 1778	
Chaplain—	
James Manesty	18 May 1776
Adjutant—	
Jeffery Amherst	21 Nov. 1776
Quartermaster—	
John Peter Rochat.. ..	1 May 1760
Surgeon—	
Peter Walsh	29 April 1767

2nd Battalion.

Col.-in-Chief—	
Jeffery, Ld. Amherst, K.B.	7 Nov. 1768
Rank in Army, Gen. 19 Mar. 1778	
Col.-Commandant—	
Gabriel Christie	14 May 1778
Rank in Army, 19 Aug. 1777	
Lieut.-Colonel—	
George Etherington ..	10 Sept. 1775
Major—	
Fred. Chr. Spiesmacher	6 June 1778
Rank in Army, 14 May 1778	
Captains—	
Francis Hutchinson ..	27 Mar. 1769
Thomas Grauchder ..	25 May 1771
Thomas Etherington ..	14 Aug. 1771
Dietrich Brehm ..	16 Nov. 1774
William Kelly.. ..	28 April 1775
John K. Muller ..	15 Nov. 1776
Benjamin Wickham ..	16 Aug. 1777
Marcus Paeter ..	26 Dec. 1778
Alexander Wright ..	28 Mar. 1779
Captain-Lieut. and Captain—	
Poynts Ricketts	27 Dec. 1778
Lieutenants—	
John Bassell	2 Oct. 1774
Thomas Flunter	4 Oct. 1774
James Wakeley	18 April 1776
Rank in Army, 28 Oct. 1760	
Richard Hansard	14 Nov. 1776
Thomas Walker	15 Nov. 1776
John Charlton	6 Mar. 1777
David Gordon.. ..	17 Mar. 1777
John Gottschol	20 May 1778
Thomas Barker	31 July 1778
Rank in Army, 3 April 1777	
C. L. Theod. Schoedde ..	25 Dec. 1778
John Sharp	26 Dec. 1778
Charles Crotchley ..	17 Dec. 1778
Wm. John Davis ..	28 Dec. 1778
—— Van Hancell ..	17 Mar. 1777
Samuel Wills	10 Aug. 1777
Charles Levell	27 Jan. 1778
John Irving	10 April 1778

Rank and Name.	Rank in Regiment.

Ensigns—
Gabriel Forrester .. .. 20 May 1778
William Porter .. .. 25 Dec. 1778
—— Young .. .. .. 26 Dec. 1778
Rich. Tyrrel Barnes .. 21 April 1779
James Barrick.. .. .. 20 May 1779

Chaplain—
William Winder .. .. 4 April 1765

Adjutant—
John Charlton.. .. .. 5 Feb. 1776

Quartermaster—
John Fleming.. .. .. 9 Nov. 1774

Surgeon—
George Clark .. .. .. 25 April 1779

3rd Battalion.

Col.-in-Chief—
Jeffery, Ld. Amherst, K.B. 25 Aug. 1775
    Rank in Army, Gen. 19 Mar. 1778

Col.-Commandant—
John Dalling .. .. .. 16 Jan. 1776
    Rank in Army, Maj.-Gen. 29 Aug. 1777

Lieut.-Colonel—
William Stiell.. .. .. 21 Sept. 1775

Major—
Jacob Van Braam .. .. 14 June 1777

Major-General—
Augustine Prevost .. .. 12 Nov. 1776
    Rank in Army, 23 Sept. 1775

Captains—
George Bruere.. .. .. 15 Nov. 1776
Francis Duffield .. .. 3 Aug. 1777
Thomas Taylor Byrd .. 17 Jan. 1778
Thomas Barron .. .. 27 April 1778
Frederick de Diemar .. 20 June 1778
James Rivers .. .. .. 10 Oct. 1778
George Sneyder .. .. 26 Dec. 1778

Captain-Lieut. and Captain—
James Robertson .. .. 12 Jan. 1779

Lieutenants—
N. F. C. Lockell .. .. 21 Nov. 1776
Hans Carden .. .. .. 6 Feb. 1777
Lewis Mattay .. .. .. 29 May 1777
Peter Haldiman .. .. 9 Sept. 1777
James Gordon .. .. 21 May 1778
George Meggs.. .. .. 22 May 1778
Robert Lowe .. .. .. 19 Aug. 1778
    Rank in Army, 20 June 1778
Ferdinand Brock .. .. 25 Dec. 1778
Isaac Hesselburg .. .. 26 Dec. 1778
James Finlay .. .. .. 15 Mar. 1779
Charles Ward .. .. .. 16 Mar. 1779

Ensigns—
William Floyer .. .. 21 Feb. 1776
Samuel Devisme .. .. 9 Sept. 1777
Lewis de Crowsax .. .. 21 May 1778
Enoch Planner .. .. 20 June 1778
—— Rudow .. .. .. 19 Aug. 1778
John Wm. Dalling.. .. 12 Feb. 1779
Geo. W. Augt. Prevost .. 15 Mar. 1779
Luke Walsh .. .. .. 21 April 1779
Luke Rogers .. .. .. 29 May 1779

Chaplain—
Michael Schlaeter .. .. 1 Sept. 1775

Adjutant—
George Eberhard .. .. 1 Sept. 1775

Rank and Name.	Rank in Regiment.

Quartermaster—
Lewis Genevay .. .. 1 Sept. 1775

Surgeon—
John Summers .. .. 10 Nov. 1775

4th Battalion.

Col.-in-Chief—
Jeffery, Ld. Amherst, K.B. 25 Aug. 1775
    Rank in Army, Gen. 19 Mar. 1778

Col.-Commandant—
Augustine Prevost . .. 18 Sept. 1775
    Rank in Army, Maj.-Gen. 19 Feb. 1779

Lieut.-Colonel—
Lewis Val. Fuser .. .. 20 Sept. 1775

Major—
Beamsley Glazier .. .. 23 Sept. 1775

Captains—
George Fresch.. .. .. 22 Sept. 1775
John Christie .. .. .. 26 Sept. 1775
Patrick Murray .. .. 28 Sept. 1775
William Wolff .. .. .. 30 Sept. 1775
Thomas Hutchins .. .. 13 Nov. 1776
    Rank in Army, 24 Sept. 1775
Alexander Shaw .. .. 14 Nov. 1776
Harry Burrard .. .. 18 Sept. 1776
James Stevenson .. .. 25 Dec. 1778
    Rank in Army, 15 June 1764
Francis Erskine .. .. 30 Dec. 1778

Captain-Lieutenant and Captain—

Lieutenants—
James Edwards .. .. 4 Sept. 1775
    Rank in Army, 23 June 1762
David Monins.. .. .. 6 Sept. 1775
    Rank in Army, 14 Jan. 1763
William Lachenwitz .. 4 Oct. 1775
Fred. de Montrond .. 20 Mar. 1776
John J. Graham .. .. 21 Nov. 1776
Ernest Augt. de Hellfeld 4 Aug. 1777
Geo. Ferd. Loup .. .. 11 Sept. 1777
Alexander M'Donald .. 18 Sept. 1777
—— Breitenbach .. .. 21 Nov. 1777
Rowland Hosleton.. .. 30 May 1778
George M'Kenzie .. .. 25 Dec. 1778
William Porbick .. .. 26 Dec. 1778

Ensigns—
Lewis Barde .. .. .. 29 June 1770
John Kearsley.. .. .. 18 Sept. 1770
William Fickle .. .. 20 May 1779

Chaplain—
George Bowe .. .. .. 5 Feb. 1776

Adjutant—
George M'Kenzie.. .. 18 Sept. 1777

Quartermaster—
James Wright.. .. .. 18 Sept. 1777

Surgeon—
James Henderson .. .. 10 Nov. 1775

Regimentals— Red, facings blue, white
    lace, 2 blue stripes.

Agents—Messrs. Ross and Gray, Conduit
    Street.

1780.

Four Battalions.

West Indies—North America.

1st Battalion.

Rank and Name.   Rank in Regiment.

Col.-in-Chief—
Jeffery, Ld. Amherst,K.B.   7 Nov. 1768
    Rank in Army, Gen. 19 Mar. 1778
Col.-Commandant—
Frederick Haldiman ... 11 Jan. 1776
    Rank in Army, Gen. 1 Jan. 1776
Lieut.-Colonel—
Stephen Kemble ... .. 14 May 1778
    Rank in Army, 29 Aug. 1777
Major—
James Mark Prevost ... 6 June 1774
    Rank in Army, Lt. Col. 29 Aug. 1777
Captains—
Ralph Phillips .. .. 25 May 1772
Bernard Ratzer .. .. 13 Nov. 1772
John Polson .. .. .. 16 June 1773
Jos. Fr. Wallet des Barres 23 Sept. 1775
Charles Dixon .. .. 12 Nov. 1776
Geo. Montague Metham 25 Feb. 1777
    Rank in Army, 24 May 1776
Jeffery Amherst .. .. 2 Aug. 1777
James Bain .. .. 14 May 1778
Samuel Rutherford .. 26 **Dec.** 1778
Captain-Lieut. and **Captain**—
George Hallam .. .. **27 Dec. 1778**
Lieutenants—
George Brown .. .. 29 Sept. 1775
John Peter Rochat .. 30 Sept. 1775
Robert Palmer .. .. 12 Nov. 1776
James Fahy .. .. 31 Jan. 1777
Joshua Wolfe .. .. **28 Nov.** 1777
Simon Ecuyier .. .. **10 April** 1778
John Charlton .. .. **11 April** 1778
Edward Davis .. .. **14 May** 1778
Martin Vaniper .. .. **25 Dec.** 1778
John Campbell .. .. **26 Dec.** 1778
Robert Lethbridge .. **27 Dec.** 1778
Louis Paquet .. .. **28 Dec.** 1778
Ensigns—
Christian Pleos .. .. **29 Aug. 1777**
Phillip Priddle .. .. **28 Nov. 1777**
    Rank in Army, 15 Nov. 1776
Wm. Henry Rickets .. **10 April** 1778
    Rank in Army, 28 Nov. 1777
Charles Brown .. .. 11 April 1778
J. Phillip Jeserick .. 14 May 1778
Thomas Foy .. .. 5 June 1778
Louis Corrivaut .. .. 24 April 1779
J. Berclay Scriven .. 12 Mar. 1779
    Rank in Army, 17 Dec. 1779
Lorentz Greenholme .. 3 Mar. 1781
Chaplain—
James Manesty .. 18 May 1776
Adjutant—
Robert Lethbridge.. .. 25 Sept. 1779
Quartermaster—
John Peter Rochat.. 1 May 1769
Surgeon—
Peter Walsh .. .. 29 April 1780

2nd Battalion.

Rank and Name.   Rank in Regiment.

Col.-in-Chief—
Jeffery, Ld. Amherst,K.B. 7 Nov. 1768
    Rank in Army, Gen. 19 Mar. 1778
Col.-Commandant—
Gabriel Christie ... 14 May 1778
    Rank in Army, 29 Aug. 1777
Lieut.-Colonel—
George Etherington .. **19 Sept. 1775**
Major—
Fred. Chr. Spiesmacher.. 6 June 1778
    Rank in Army, 14 May 1778
Captains—
Francis Hutchinson .. 27 Mar. 1769
Thomas Grandidier .. 25 May 1772
Thomas Etherington .. 14 Aug. 1772
Dietrich Brehm .. 16 Nov. 1774
William Kelly.. .. .. 28 April 1775
John K. Muhle .. .. 13 Nov. 1776
Benjamin Wickham .. 10 Aug. 1777
Marcus Pictet .. .. 26 Dec. 1778
Alexander Wright .. 28 Mar. 1779
Captain-Lieut. and Captain—
Peyntz Hickets .. .. 27 Dec. 1778
Lieutenants—
John Bayard .. .. .. 2 Oct. 1774
Thomas Flucker .. .. 4 Oct. 1774
James Wakeley .. .. 18 April 1776
    Rank in Army, 28 Oct. 1769
Richard Hannard .. .. 14 Nov. 1776
Thomas Walker .. .. 15 Nov. 1776
John Charlton.. .. .. 6 Mar. 1777
David Gordon .. .. 17 Mar. 1777
John Gottschal .. .. 20 May 1778
Thomas Barker .. .. 31 July 1778
    Rank in **Army**, 3 April 1777
C. L. Theod. **Schoedde** .. **26** Dec. 1778
John Sharpe .. .. .. 26 Dec. 1778
Charles Craitchley .. 27 Dec. 1778
William John Davis .. 28 Dec. 1778
Ensigns—
----- Van Bunnell .. .. 17 Mar. 1777
Samuel Willis .. .. 10 Aug. 1777
Charles Levett .. .. 27 Jan. 1774
Gabriel Forrester .. 20 May 1778
William Foster .. .. 25 Dec. 1778
----- Young .. .. 26 Dec. 1778
Rich. Tyrrell Barnes .. 24 April 1779
James Barrick .. .. 20 May 1779
Harris Power .. .. 22 Mar. 1780
Chaplain—
William Winder .. .. 4 April 1765
Adjutant—
John Charlton.. .. 5 Feb. 1776
Quartermaster—
John Fleming .. .. 9 Nov. 1774
Surgeon—
George Clarke.. .. 25 April 1779

3rd Battalion.

Col.-in-Chief—
Jeffery, Ld. Amherst,K.B. 25 Aug. 1775
    Rank in Army, Gen. 19 Mar. 1778
Col.-Commandant—
John Dalling .. .. 16 Jan. 1776
    Rank in Army, M. Gen. 29 Aug. 1777

Rank and Name.	Rank in Regiment.
Lieut.-Colonel—	
William Stiell..	21 Sept. 1775
Major—	
John Loyd	22 Oct. 1779
Captains—	
Augustine Prevost	12 Nov. 1776
Rank in Army, 23 Sept. 1775	
George Bruere	15 Nov. 1776
Thomas Taylor Byrd ..	27 Jan. 1778
Thomas Barron	27 April 1778
Frederick de Diemar ..	20 June 1778
James Rivers	10 Oct. 1778
George Schneider	26 Dec. 1778
W. Carlyon Hughes ..	12 Jan. 1779
Hans Carden	1 Feb. 1780
Captain-Lieut. and Captain—	
Alexander Broley	2 Feb. 1780
Lieutenants—	
N. F. C. Lockell	21 Nov. 1776
Lewis Mattay	29 May 1777
Peter Haldiman	9 Sept. 1777
James Gordon..	21 May 1778
George Meggs..	22 May 1778
Robert Lowe	19 Aug. 1778
Rank in Army, 20 June 1778	
Isaac Hesselburg	26 Dec. 1778
Charles Ward	16 Mar. 1779
William Flover	17 Mar. 1779
Samuel Davison	1 April 1779
Enoch Plumer..	23 Sept. 1779
Ensigns—	
Louis de Crowfax	21 May 1778
—— Rudow	19 Aug. 1778
John W. Dalling	12 Feb. 1779
Geo. M. Aug. Prevost ..	15 Mar. 1779
Luke Walsh	21 April 1779
Simon Bradstreet	21 April 1779
Luke Rogers	20 May 1779
Augustus Gould	21 May 1779
George Eberhard	22 May 1779
William Hewlett	23 Sept. 1779
Chaplain—	
Michael Schlaetler.. ..	1 Sept. 1775
Adjutant—	
James Gordon	22 May 1779
Quartermaster—	
Lewis Genevay	1 Sept. 1775
Surgeon—	
John Summers	10 Nov. 1775

4th Battalion.

Rank and Name.	Rank in Regiment.
Col.-in-Chief—	
Jeffery, Ld. Amherst, K.B.	25 Aug. 1775
Rank in Army, Gen. 19 Mar. 1778	
Col.-Commandant—	
Augustine Prevost	18 Sept. 1775
Rank in Army, Maj.-Gen. 19 Feb. 1779	
Lieut.-Colonels—	
Lewis Val. Fuser	20 Sept. 1775
Major—	
Peamsby Glazier	23 Sept. 1775
Captains—	
George Forsch..	22 Sept. 1775
John Christie	26 Sept. 1775
Patrick Murray	28 Sept. 1775
Thomas Hutchins	13 Nov. 1776
Rank in Army, 24 Sept. 1775	

Rank and Name.	Rank in Regiment.
Captains (continued)—	
Alexander Shaw	14 Nov. 1776
Harry Burrard	18 Sept. 1777
James Stevenson	25 Dec. 1778
Rank in Army, 15 June 1764	
Francis Erskine	30 Dec. 1778
James Robertson	25 Aug. 1779
Rank in Army, 12 Jan. 1779	
Captain-Lieut. and Captain—	
Fred. de Montreond.. ..	24 May 1779
Lieutenants—	
James Edwards	4 Sept. 1775
William Lachenwitz ..	4 Oct. 1775
Rank in Army, 23 June 1762	
John James Graham ..	21 Nov. 1776
Geo. Ferd. Loup	11 Sept. 1777
Alexander M'Donald ..	18 Sept. 1777
—— Breitenbach	21 Nov. 1777
George M'Kenzie	25 Dec. 1778
William von Borbeck ..	26 Dec. 1778
Fred. Chr. Robinson ..	1 Sept. 1779
Lewis Barde	2 Sept. 1779
John Kearsley..	3 Sept. 1779
Francis Boniface	4 Sept. 1779
James Wright..	Feb. 1780
Ensigns—	
John Manning	24 April 1779
James Sinclair..	24 April 1779
William Field..	20 May 1779
F. P. Fatio	2 Sept. 1779
George Prevost	3 Sept. 1779
Edward Cartwright ..	4 Sept. 1779
Thomas Clarke	5 Sept. 1779
John Elphinstone	6 Sept. 1779
William Martin	7 Dec. 1779
—— Muller	5 Jan. 1780
Chaplain—	
George Bowe	5 Feb. 1776
Adjutant—	
George Mackenzie.. ..	18 Sept. 1777
Quartermaster—	
James Wright..	18 Sept. 1775
Surgeon—	
James Henderson	10 Nov. 1775

Regimentals – Red, facings blue, white lace, 2 blue stripes.

Agents – Messrs. Ross and Gray, Conduit Street.

1781.

Four Battalions.

West Indies—North America.

1st Battalion.

Rank and Name.	Rank in Regiment.
Col.-in-Chief—	
Jeffery, Ld. Amherst, K.B.	7 Nov. 1768
Rank in Army, Gen. 19 Mar. 1778	
Col.-Commandant—	
Frederick Haldiman ..	11 Jan. 1776
Rank in Army, Gen. 1 Jan. 1776	
Lieut.-Colonel—	
Stephen Kemble	14 May 1778
Rank in Army, 29 Aug. 1777	
Major—	
James Mark Prevost ..	6 June 1778
Rank in Army, Lt.-Col. 29 Aug. 1777	

Rank and Name.	Rank in Regiment.

Captains—

Bernard Ratzer	.. .. 13 Nov. 1772
John Polson	.. .. 16 June 1773
Jos. Fr. Wallet des Barres	23 Sept. 1775
Charles Drion	.. .. 12 Nov. 1776
Jeffery Amherst	.. 2 Aug. 1777
James Bain	.. .. 14 May 1778
Samuel Rutherford	.. 26 Dec. 1778
George Hallam	.. 27 Dec. 1778
John Peter Rochat	.. 8 June 1780

Captain-Lieut. and Captain—

| George Brown | .. .. 4 Oct. 1780 |

Lieutenants—

Robert Palmer	.. .. 12 Nov. 1776
James Fahy	.. .. 31 Jan. 1777
Joshua Wolfe	.. .. 28 Nov. 1777
Simon Ecuyier	.. .. 10 April 1778
Edward Davis	.. .. 14 May 1878
Martin Vaniper	.. .. 25 Dec. 1778
John Campbell	.. .. 26 Dec. 1778
Robert Lethbridge	.. 27 Dec. 1778
Louis Paquet	.. .. 28 Dec. 1778
Wm. Henry Rickets	.. 8 June 1780
Charles Brown	.. 23 Sept. 1780
Thomas Fry	.. 24 Sept. 1780
J. Barclay Scriven	.. 4 Oct. 1780
Rank in Army, 18 Sept. 1780

Ensigns—

| Phillip Priddie | .. 28 Nov. 1777 |
| Rank in Army, 15 Nov. 1776 |
Louis Correvont	.. 21 April 1779
Lorenz Greenhalme	3 Mar. 1780
John Gordon	.. 23 Sept. 1780
Samuel Dalrymple	.. 24 Sept. 1780
John Brownrigg	.. 26 Sept. 1780
James Gray Tucker	26 Sept. 1780
Samuel Kempthorne	13 June 1781

Chaplain—

| James Manesty | 18 May 1776 |

Adjutant—

| Robert Lethbridge | .. 25 Sept. 1779 |

Quartermaster—

| John Peter Rochat | .. 1 May 1780 |

Surgeon—

| Peter Walsh | .. .. 19 April 1767 |

2nd Battalion.

Col.-in-Chief—

| Jeffery 1st Amherst, K B | 7 Nov. 1768 |
| Rank in Army, Gen. 19 Mar. 1778 |

Col.-Commandant—

| Gabriel Christie | .. 14 May 1778 |
| Rank in Army, 29 Aug. 1777 |

Lieut.-Colonel—

| George Etherington | .. 19 Sept. 1775 |

Major—

| Fred. Chr. Spiesmacher | 6 June 1778 |
| Rank in Army, 14 May 1778 |

Captains—

| Francis Hutchins | .. 27 Mar. 1769 |
| Rank in Army, Major 17 Nov. 1780 |
Thomas Grandidier	.. 25 May 1772
Thomas Etherington	14 Aug. 1772
Dietrich Brehm	.. 16 Nov. 1774
William Kelly	.. 28 April 1775
Benjamin Wickham	.. 10 Aug. 1777

Rank and Name.	Rank in Regiment.

Captains (continued)—

Marcus Pictet	.. .. 26 Dec. 1778
Alexander Wright	.. 83 Mar. 1779
William Richardson	.. 30 May 1780
Rank in Army, 24 April 1779

Captain-Lieut. and Captain—

| Poynte Ricketts | .. 27 Dec. 1778 |

Lieutenants—

John Bayard	.. .. 2 Oct. 1774
Thomas Flucker	.. 4 Oct. 1774
James Wakeley	.. .. 8 April 1776
Rank in Army, 28 Oct. 1763
Ed. Massey Hassard	.. 14 Nov. 1776
Thomas Walker	.. 15 Nov. 1776
John Charlton	.. .. 6 Mar. 1777
David Gordon	.. .. 17 Mar. 1777
John Gottsched	.. 20 May 1778
C. L. Theod. Schoedde	25 Dec. 1778
John Sharpe	.. .. 26 Dec. 1778
Charles Crotchley	.. 27 Dec. 1778
William John Davis	.. 28 Dec. 1778
Gilbert Hillock	.. 27 April 1781
Rank in Army, 12 June 1780

Ensigns—

Von Barnell	.. .. 17 Mar. 1777
Samuel Willis	.. .. 10 Aug. 1777
Charles Levett	.. 27 Jan. 1778
Gabriel Forrester	.. 20 May 1778
—— Young	.. .. 26 Dec. 1778
Rich. Tyrrel Barnes	.. 21 April 1779
James Barrick	.. 29 May 1779
Harris Tower	.. 22 Mar. 1780
John Campbell	.. 27 April 1781
William Mackinnon	13 June 1781

Chaplain—

| William Winder | .. .. 4 April 1765 |

Adjutant—

| Ed. Massey Hassard | .. 9 Mar. 1780 |

Quartermaster—

| John Fleming | .. .. 9 Nov. 1774 |

Surgeon—

| George Clarke | .. .. 25 April 1779 |

3rd Battalion.

Col.-in-Chief—

| Jeffery 1st Amherst, K B | 25 Aug. 1775 |
| Rank in Army, Gen. 19 Mar. 1778 |

Col.-Commandant—

| John Darling | .. 16 June 1776 |
| Rank in Army Maj.-Gen. 19 Aug. 1777 |

Lieut.-Colonel—

| William Stuhl | .. 21 Sept. 1775 |

Major—

| John Loyd | .. .. 22 Oct. 1779 |

Captains—

| Augustine Prevost | .. 12 Nov. 1776 |
| Rank in Army, 23 Sept. 1775 |
George Bruere	.. 15 Nov. 1776
Thomas Taylor Byrd	27 Jan. 1778
Thomas Barron	.. 27 April 1778
Frederick de Diemar	.. 20 June 1778
James Rivers	.. 10 Oct. 1778
George Schroeder	.. 26 Dec. 1778
W. Carlton Hughes	12 Jan. 1779
Hans Carlen	.. .. 1 Feb. 1780

Captain-Lieut. and Captain—

| Alexander Brdey | .. .. 2 Feb. 1780 |

Rank and Name.	Rank in Regiment.
Lieutenants—	
Jo. F. C. Lockell	21 Nov. 1776
Peter Haldiman	9 Sept. 1777
James Gordon	21 May 1778
George Meggs..	22 May 1778
Robert Lowe	19 Aug. 1778
Rank in Army,	20 June 1778
Isaac Hesselburg	26 Dec. 1778
Charles Ward..	16 Mar. 1779
William Floyer	17 Mar. 1779
Samuel Devisme	1 April 1779
Henry de Crowfax.. ..	21 Sept. 1779
Enoch Plumer	22 Sept. 1779
Ensigns—	
Enoch Rudow..	19 Aug. 1778
John Wm. Dalling.. ..	12 Feb. 1779
Geo. W. Aug. Prevost ..	15 Mar. 1779
Luke Walsh	21 April 1779
Simon Bradstreet	24 April 1779
Luke Rogers	20 May 1779
Augustus Gould	21 May 1779
George Eberhard	22 May 1779
William Hewlett	23 Sept. 1779
James Mackenzie	21 Sept. 1780
Chaplain—	
Michael Schlaetler.. ..	1 Sept. 1775
Adjutant—	
James Gordon	22 May 1779
Quartermaster—	
Lewis Genevay	4 Sept. 1775
Surgeon—	
John Summers	10 Nov. 1775

4th Battalion.

Col.-in-Chief—	
Jeffery, Ld. Amherst, K.B.	25 Aug. 1775
Rank in Army, Gen.	19 Mar. 1778
Col.-Commandant—	
Augustine Prevost.. ..	18 Sept. 1775
Rank in Army, Maj.-Gen.	19 Feb. 1779
Lieut.-Colonel—	
Major—	
Beamsley Glazier	23 Sept. 1775
Rank in Army, Lt.-Col.	17 Nov. 1780
Captains—	
John Christie	26 Sept. 1775
Patrick Murray	28 Sept. 1775
Thomas Hutchins	13 Nov. 1776
Rank in Army,	24 Sept. 1775
Alexander Shaw	11 Nov. 1776
Harry Burrard	18 Sept. 1777
James Stevenson	25 Dec. 1778
Rank in Army, Major	10 Nov. 1780
Francis Erskine	30 Dec. 1778
James Robinson	25 Aug. 1779
Rank in Army,	12 Jan. 1779
Captain-Lieut. and Captain—	
Fred. de Montrond.. ..	24 May 1779
Lieutenants—	
James Edwards	4 Sept. 1775
William Lachenwitz ..	4 Oct. 1775
Rank in Army,	24 June 1762
John Ja. Graham	21 Nov. 1776
Geo. Ferd. Loup	11 Sept. 1777
Alexander M'Donald ..	18 Sept. 1777

Rank and Name.	Rank in Regiment.
Lieutenants (continued)—	
—— Breitenbach	21 Nov. 1777
George M'Kenzie	25 Dec. 1778
William von Borbeck ..	26 Dec. 1778
Lewis Barde	2 Sept. 1779
John Kearsley..	3 Sept. 1779
Francis Boniface	4 Sept. 1779
James Wright..	Feb. 1780
Edward Moncrieffe.. ..	4 Nov. 1780
Rank in Army,	12 Sept. 1777
Ensigns—	
John Manning	24 April 1779
James Sinclair	24 April 1779
William Field	20 May 1779
F. P. Fatio	2 Sept. 1779
George Prevost	3 Sept. 1779
Edward Cartwright ..	4 Sept. 1779
Thomas Clarke	5 Sept. 1779
John Elphinstone	6 Sept. 1779
William Martin	7 Dec. 1779
—— Muller	5 Jan. 1780
Chaplain—	
George Bowe	5 Feb. 1776
Adjutant—	
George Mackenzie	18 Sept. 1777
Quartermaster—	
James Wright	18 Sept. 1777
Surgeon—	
James Henderson	10 Nov. 1775
Regimentals—Red, facings blue, white lace, 2 blue stripes.	
Agents—Messrs. Gray and Ogilvie, Terrace, Spring Gardens.	

1782.

Four Battalions.

West Indies—North America.

1st Battalion.

Col.-in-Chief—	
Jeffery, Ld. Amherst, K.B.	7 Nov. 1768
Rank in Army, Gen.	19 Mar. 1778
Col.-Commandant—	
Frederick Haldiman ..	11 Jan. 1776
Rank in Army, Gen.	1 Jan. 1776
Lieut.-Colonel—	
Stephen Kemble	14 May 1778
Rank in Army,	29 Aug. 1777
Major—	
Peter Hunter	20 Oct. 1781
Rank in Army,	25 Aug. 1779
Captains—	
Gerrard Ratzer	13 Nov. 1772
J. Fr. Wallet des Barres.	24 Sept. 1775
Charles Dixon..	12 Nov. 1776
Jeffery Amherst	2 Aug. 1777
James Bain	14 May 1778
Samuel Rutherford ..	26 Dec. 1778
Alexander Derimon ..	10 Aug. 1781
Rank in Army,	8 Dec. 1780
James Faby	11 Aug. 1781
Thos. Gunter Brown ..	24 Oct. 1781
Rank in Army,	20 Sept. 1781
Captain-Lieut. and Captain—	
John James Kenyer ..	20 Oct. 1781

Rank and Name.	Rank in Regiment.
Lieutenants—	
Edward Davis..	14 May 1778
Martin Vaniper	25 Dec. 1778
Robert Lethbridge.. ..	27 Dec. 1778
Wm. Henry Rickets ..	8 June 1780
Charles Brown	28 Sept. 1780
Thomas Foy	24 Sept. 1780
Louis Correvont	25 Sept. 1780
O. Berclay Scriten.. ..	4 Oct. 1778
Rank in Army,	18 Sept. 1780
Lorentz Greenholme ..	20 Nov. 1780
James Grey Tucker ..	11 Aug. 1781
—— M'Lean	4 Sept. 1781
Roger Coghlan	24 Sept. 1781
Henry Graydon	20 Oct. 1781
Ensigns—	
Aug. Fred. Prevost ..	25 Sept. 1780
J. Barton Prevost.. ..	29 Dec. 1780
W. James Stevenson ..	2 June 1781
John Watson	29 June 1781
John Barber	11 Aug. 1781
George Mackay	24 Sept. 1781
John Marsh	20 Oct. 1781
John Farrell	5 Dec. 1781
Duncan M'Intosh ..	4 Jan. 1782
Chaplain—	
James Mauesty	18 May 1776
Adjutant—	
Roger Coghlan	5 Dec. 1781
Quartermaster—	
John Kaston	4 Oct. 1780
Surgeon—	
Peter Walsh	29 April 1767

2nd Battalion.

Rank and Name.	Rank in Regiment.
Col.-in-Chief—	
Jeffery Ld. Amherst, K.B.	7 Nov. 1768
Rank in Army, Gen.	19 Mar. 1778
Col.-Commandant—	
Gabriel Christie	14 May 1778
Rank in Army, Maj.-Gen.	19 Oct. 1781
Lieut.-Colonel—	
George Etherington ..	19 Sept. 1775
Major—	
Fred. Chr. Sphnemacher..	6 June 1778
Rank in Army,	14 May 1778
Captains—	
Thomas Grandidier ..	25 May 1772
Thomas Etherington ..	14 Aug. 1772
Dietrich Brehm	16 Nov. 1773
William Kelly	28 April 1775
Benjamin Wickham ..	10 Aug. 1777
Marcus Petet	26 Dec. 1778
Alexander Wright ..	28 Mar. 1779
William Richardson ..	30 May 1780
Rank in Army,	24 April 1779
Teesdale Cockell	17 Sept. 1780
Captain-Lieut. and Captain—	
Richard Carrigue	19 Oct. 1780
Lieutenants—	
John Baynel	2 Oct. 1780
James Wakeley	8 April 1776
Rank in Army,	14 Oct. 1780
Rd. Massey Hansard ..	14 Nov. 1776
Thomas Walker	15 Nov. 1776

Rank and Name.	Rank in Regiment.
Lieutenants (continued)—	
John Charlton..	6 Mar. 1777
David Gordon..	17 Mar. 1777
John Gottsched	20 May 1778
C. L. Theo. Schoedde ..	25 Dec. 1778
Charles Crotchley	27 Dec. 1778
William John Davis ..	28 Dec. 1778
Gilbert Hillock	27 April 1781
Rank in Army,	12 June 1780
Ashton Warner	10 Aug. 1781
Hubert von Hanxell ..	15 Aug. 1781
Ensigns—	
Samuel Willis..	10 Aug. 1777
Charles Levett	27 Jan. 1778
James Barrick..	20 May 1779
William Grant	13 Oct. 1780
Gabriel Gordon	6 Jan. 1781
John Campbell	27 April 1781
William M'Kinnon ..	13 June 1781
Joseph Pasquals	25 June 1781
John Randall Foster ..	11 July 1781
George Evans	15 Aug. 1781
Chaplain—	
William Winder	4 April 1765
Adjutant—	
Rd. Massey Hansard ..	9 Mar. 1780
Quartermaster—	
John Fleming..	9 Nov. 1774
Surgeon—	
George Clark	25 April 1779

3rd Battalion.

Rank and Name.	Rank in Regiment.
Col.-in-Chief—	
Jeffery Ld. Amherst, K.B.	25 Aug. 1775
Rank in Army, Gen.	19 Mar. 1778
Col.-Commandant—	
John Dalling	16 Jan. 1776
Rank in Army, Maj.-Gen.	29 Aug. 1777
Lieut.-Colonel—	
Archibald M'Arthur ..	24 April 1781
Major—	
John Loyd	22 Oct. 1779
Captains—	
Thomas Taylor Byrd ..	16 July 1776
Augustine Prevost ..	12 Nov. 1776
Rank in Army,	23 Sept. 1775
George Beaver	15 Nov. 1776
Thomas Barrow	27 April 1778
Frederick de Ronner ..	20 June 1778
James Rivers	10 Oct. 1778
George Schoedde	26 Dec. 1778
James Auchie	1 Feb. 1780
James Rickets	19 Oct. 1780
Rank in Army,	27 Dec. 1778
Capt.-Lieut. and Captain—	
Mungo Noble	9 June 1781
Lieutenants—	
N. F. C. Lockell	21 Nov. 1776
Peter Hallman	9 Sept. 1777
George Meggs..	22 May 1778
Robert Lowe	13 Aug. 1778
Rank in Army,	20 June 1778
Isaac Hess Burg	26 Dec. 1778
Charles Ward	16 Mar. 1779
William Howe	17 Mar. 1779
Samuel Devignie	1 April 1779
Henry de Crowfax.. ..	21 Sept. 1779

Rank and Name.	Rank in Regiment.
Lieutenants (continued)—	
Enoch Pinner ..	.. 22 Sept. 1779
John Wm. Dalling..	.. 8 July 1781
Anthony Pasqualda..	.. 25 June 1781
Ensigns—	
—— Rudow ..	.. 19 Aug. 1778
Geo. W. Aug. Prevost ..	15 Mar. 1779
Luke Walsh	.. 21 April 1779
Simon Bradstreet ..	.. 24 April 1779
Luke Rogers	.. 20 May 1779
Augustus Gould ..	.. 21 May 1779
George Eberard ..	.. 22 May 1779
Robert A. Farmer ..	8 Jan. 1781
William Johnson ..	27 Sept. 1781
Chaplain—	
Michael Schlaetter..	.. 1 Sept. 1775
Adjutant—	
James Gordon.. ..	.. 22 May 1779
Quartermaster—	
Lewis Genevay ..	.. 1 Sept. 1775
Surgeon—	
John Summers ..	.. 10 Nov. 1775

4th Battalion.

Col.-in-Chief—	
Jeffery, Ld. Amherst, K.B. 25 Aug. 1775	
Rank in Army, Gen. 19 Mar. 1778	
Col.-Commandant—	
Augustine Prevost ..	.. 18 Sept. 1775
Rank in Army, Maj.-Gen. 19 Feb. 1779	
Lieut.-Colonel—	
Beamsley Glazier ..	.. 6 May 1780
Major—	
Timothy Newmarsh	.. 10 Aug. 1780
Captains—	
John Christie.. ..	.. 26 Sept. 1775
Patrick Murray ..	.. 28 Sept. 1775
Thomas Hutchins ..	.. 13 Nov. 1776
Rank in Army, 24 Sept. 1775	
Alexander Shaw ..	14 Nov. 1776
Harry Burnard ..	.. 18 Sept. 1777
James Stevenson ..	.. 25 Dec. 1778
Rank in Army, Major 10 Nov. 1780	
Francis Erskine ..	.. 30 Dec. 1778
James Robertson ..	.. 25 Aug. 1779
Rank in Army, 12 Jan. 1779	
Captain-Lieut. and Captain—	
Fred. de Montrond ..	24 May 1779
Lieutenants—	
James Edwards ..	.. 4 Sept. 1775
William Lachenwitz ..	4 Oct. 1775
Rank in Army, 23 June 1782	
John James Graham ..	24 Nov. 1776
George Ferd. Loup ..	11 Sept. 1777
Alexander M'Donald ..	18 Sept. 1777
—— Breitenbach ..	.. 21 Nov. 1777
George MacKenzie..	.. 25 Dec. 1778
William von Borbeck ..	26 Dec. 1778
Lewis Barde	2 Sept. 1779
John Kearsley	3 Sept. 1779
Francis Boniface ..	.. 4 Sept. 1779
James Wright.. ..	.. Feb. 1780
Edward Motschelle..	.. 4 Nov. 1780
Rank in Army, 12 Sept. 1777	
Ensigns—	
James Sinclair ..	24 April 1779

Rank and Name.	Rank in Regiment.
Ensigns (continued)—	
William Field.. ..	.. 20 May 1779
F. P. Fatio	.. 2 Sept. 1779
George Prevost ..	.. 3 Sept. 1779
Edward Cartwright ..	4 Sept. 1779
Thomas Clarke ..	.. 8 Sept. 1779
William Martin ..	.. 7 Dec. 1779
—— Darby	.. 25 June 1781
James Peutz	.. 8 Mar. 1782
Chaplain—	
George Bowe	5 Feb. 1776
Adjutant—	
George M'Kenzie ..	.. 18 Sept. 1777
Quartermaster—	
James Wright.. ..	.. 18 Sept. 1777
Surgeon—	
James Henderson ..	.. 10 Nov. 1775

Regimentals—Red, facings blue, white lace, 2 blue stripes.

Agents—Messrs. Gray and Ogilvie, Spring Gardens.

1783.

Four Battalions.

West Indies—North America.

1st Battalion.

Col.-in-Chief—	
Jeffery, Ld. Amherst, K.B. 7 Nov. 1768	
Rank in Army, Gen. 19 Mar. 1778	
Col.-Commandant—	
Frederick Haldimand ..	11 Jan. 1776
Rank in Army, Gen. 1 Jan. 1776	
Lieut.-Colonel—	
Stephen Kemble ..	.. 14 May 1778
Rank in Army, Col. 20 Nov. 1782	
Major—	
Peter Hunter.. ..	.. 20 Oct. 1781
Rank in Army, Lt.-Col. 23 Nov. 1782	
Captains—	
Bernard Ratzer ..	.. 13 Nov. 1772
Rank in Army, Maj. 19 Mar. 1783	
J. F. Walke Desbarres ..	23 Sept. 1775
Rank in Army, Maj. 19 Mar. 1783	
Charles Dixon.. ..	.. 12 Nov. 1776
James Bain	.. 14 May 1778
Samuel Rutherford ..	26 Dec. 1778
Alexander Dennison ..	10 Aug. 1781
Rank in Army, 8 Dec. 1780	
James Fahy	.. 11 Aug. 1781
Thomas Gunter Brown..	24 Oct. 1781
Rank in Army, 20 Sept. 1781	
Captain-Lieut. and Captain—	
John James Ecuyer ..	20 Oct. 1781
Lieutenants—	
Edward Davis.. ..	.. 14 May 1778
Martin Vamper ..	.. 25 Dec. 1778
Robert Lethbridge..	.. 27 Dec. 1778
Charles Brown ..	.. 23 Sept. 1780
Louis Correvont ..	.. 25 Sept. 1780
J. Berclay Scriven..	.. 4 Oct. 1780
Rank in Army, 18 Sept. 1780	
Lorentz Greenholme ..	20 Nov. 1780
James Grey Tucker ..	11 Aug. 1781
George M'Lean ..	.. 4 Sept. 1781

Rank and Name.	Rank in Regiment.
Lieutenants (continued) —	
Roger Coghlan	24 Sept. 1781
Henry Graydon	30 Oct. 1781
James Campbell ..	30 April 1782
Rank in Army, 5 Dec. 1781	
W. James Stevenson ..	5 July 1782
Ensigns—	
Augustus Fred. Prevost..	25 Sept. 1780
J. Barlow Prevost ..	29 Dec. 1780
John Watson	29 June 1781
John Barber	11 Aug. 1781
William Sands	4 Sept. 1781
George Mackay	24 Sept. 1781
John Marsh	20 Oct. 1781
John Farreil	5 Dec. 1781
Alexander Simpson ..	5 Jan. 1782
Chaplain—	
James Manesty	18 May 1776
Adjutant—	
Roger Coghlan	5 Dec. 1781
Quartermaster—	
John Keaton	4 Oct. 1780
Surgeon—	
Everard Home	2 Dec. 1782

2nd Battalion.

Col.-in-Chief—	
Jeffery, Ld. Amherst, K.B.	7 Nov. 1768
Rank in Army, Gen. 19 Mar. 1778	
Col.-Commandant—	
Gabriel Christie	14 May 1778
Rank in Army, Maj.-Gen. 19 Oct. 1781	
Lieut.-Colonel—	
George Etherington ..	19 Sept. 1775
Rank in Army, Col. 16 May 1782	
Major—	
Jeffery Amherst	1 Oct. 1782
Captains—	
Thomas Grandulier ..	25 May 1772
Rank in Army, Maj. 19 Feb. 1783	
Thomas Etherington ..	14 Aug. 1772
Rank in Army, Maj. 19 Mar. 1783	
Dietrich Urehn	16 Nov. 1774
William Kelly	28 April 1775
Benjamin Wickham ..	10 Aug. 1777
Marcus Pictet	26 Dec. 1778
Alexander Wright	28 May 1781
Rank in Army, 24 April 1778	
Teesdale Cockell	18 Oct. 1780
Captain-Lieut. and Captain—	
Richard Carrique	19 Oct. 1780
Lieutenants—	
John Bayard	2 Oct. 1774
James Wakeley	18 April 1776
Rank in Army, 28 Oct. 1760	
R. Massey Hansard ..	14 Nov. 1776
Thomas Walker	15 Nov. 1776
John Charlton	6 Mar. 1777
David Gordon..	17 Mar. 1777
John Gottsched	20 May 1778
C. L. Theo Schoedle ..	25 Dec. 1778
Charles Crotchley	27 Dec. 1778
Ashton Warner	10 Aug. 1781
Hubert von Hamell ..	15 Aug. 1781
Charles Levett	2 Jan. 1782

Rank and Name.	Rank in Regiment.
Lieutenants (continued)—	
Robert Holland	12 Mar. 1783
Rank in Army, 29 June 1780	
Ensigns—	
Samuel Willis..	10 Aug. 1777
James Barrick	20 May 1779
Gabriel Gordon	6 Jan. 1781
John Campbell	27 April 1781
William M'Kinnon ..	18 June 1781
Joseph Pasquada	25 June 1781
John Randall Forster ..	11 July 1781
George Holmes	2 Jan. 1782
John Lewis Prevost ..	20 Feb. 1782
John Lennox	3 July 1782
Chaplain—	
William Winder	4 April 1705
Adjutant—	
Richard Massey Hansard	9 Mar. 1780
Quartermaster—	
John Fleming..	9 Nov. 1774
Surgeon—	
George Clarke..	26 Mar. 1779

3rd Battalion.

Col.-in-Chief—	
Jeffery, Ld. Amherst, K.B.	25 Aug. 1775
Rank in Army, Gen. 19 Mar. 1778	
Col.-Commandant—	
John Dalling, Bt.	16 Jan. 1776
Rank in Army, Lt.-Gen. 20 Nov. 1782	
Lieut.-Colonel—	
Archibald M'Arthur ..	24 April 1781
Major—	
George Thompson	24 Oct. 1781
Rank in Army, Lt.-Col. 19 Feb. 1783	
Captains—	
Thomas Taylor Byrd ..	14 July 1776
Augustine Prevost	12 Nov. 1776
Rank in Army, 23 Sept. 1775	
George Bruere	15 Nov. 1776
Thomas Barron	27 April 1778
Frederick de Diemar ..	20 June 1778
James Rivers	10 Oct. 1778
George Schneider	26 Dec. 1778
James Ricketts..	19 Oct. 1780
Rank in Army, 27 Dec. 1778	
Thomas Sweetland.. ..	28 April 1782
Captain-Lieut. and Captain—	
N. F. Lockell	1 Oct. 1781
Lieutenants—	
Isaac Hesselburg	26 Dec. 1778
Charles Ward	16 Mar. 1779
William Floyer	17 Mar. 1779
Samuel Devisme	1 April 1779
Henry de Crostas.. ..	21 Sept. 1779
Enoch Plumer	22 Sept. 1779
John William Dalling ..	8 Jan. 1781
Anthony Pasquala	25 June 1781
Luke Walsh	2 Oct. 1781
John Campbell	3 Oct. 1781
James Apthorpe	1 Mar. 1782
William Sealy	3 Dec. 1782
Rank in Army, 8 Nov. 1781	
Duncan M'Intosh	13 Feb. 1783
Ensigns	
—— Rudow	19 Aug. 1778

Rank and Name.	Rank in Regiment.
Ensigns (continued)—	
Luke Rogers	.. 20 May 1779
Augustus Gould ..	.. 21 May 1779
George Ebenard ..	.. 22 May 1779
Robert A. Farmer ..	8 Jan. 1781
Fred. C. Diemar ..	1 Oct. 1781
Charles Willcocks ..	2 Oct. 1781
Charles Lemoine ..	3 Oct. 1781
Chaplain—	
Michael Schlaetler ..	.. 18 Sept. 1775
Adjutant—	
Charles Ward	.. 8 June 1781
Quartermaster—	
Lewis Genevay ..	.. 1 Sept. 1775
Surgeon—	
John Sumners.. ..	.. 10 Nov. 1775

4th Battalion.

Col.-in-Chief—	
Jeffery, Ld. Amherst, K.B. 25 Aug. 1775	
Rank in Army, Gen. 19 Mar. 1778	
Col.-Commandant—	
Augustine Prevost .. .. 18 Sept. 1775	
Rank in Army, Maj.-Gen. 19 Feb. 1779	
Lieut.-Colonel—	
Beamsley Glazier .. .. 6 May 1778	
Major—	
Timothy Newmarsh .. 10 Aug. 1780	
Captains—	
Patrick Murray .. .. 28 Sept. 1775	
Alexander Shaw .. .. 14 Nov. 1770	
Harry Burrard .. .. 18 Sept. 1777	
James Stevenson .. .. 25 Dec. 1778	
Rank in Army, Maj. 10 Nov. 1780	
Francis Erskine .. .. 30 Dec. 1778	
Fred. de Montrond .. 24 May 1779	
James Robertson .. .. 25 Aug. 1779	
Rank in Army, 12 Jan. 1779	
George Meggs.. .. .. 1 Mar. 1782	
John Rotton .. .. .. 1 July 1782	
Captain-Lieut. and Captain—	
Hon. Charles Curzon .. 11 Oct. 1782	
Rank in Army, Capt. 11 Oct. 1781	
Lieutenants—	
James Edwards .. .. 4 Sept. 1775	
William Lachenwitz .. 4 Oct. 1775	
Rank in Army, 23 June 1762	
George Ferdinand Laup 11 Sept. 1777	
Alexander M'Donald .. 18 Sept. 1777	
—— Breitenbach .. .. 21 Nov. 1777	
George Mackenzie .. .. 25 Dec. 1778	
William von Borbeck .. 26 Dec. 1778	
Lewis Barde .. .. .. 2 Sept. 1779	
John Kearsley .. .. 3 Sept. 1779	
Francis Boniface .. .. 4 Sept. 1779	
Edward Menerieffe .. 4 Nov. 1780	
Rank in Army, 12 Sept. 1777	
William Field.. .. .. 3 April 1782	
F. P. Fatio .. .. .. 1 Dec. 1782	
Ensigns—	
Edward Cartwright .. 4 Sept. 1779	
Thomas Clarke .. .. 5 Sept. 1779	
William Martin .. .. 7 Dec. 1779	
William Darby .. .. 25 June 1781	
James Pentz .. .. .. 8 Mar. 1782	
Thomas Francis Burdett 5 June 1782	

Rank and Name.	Rank in Regiment.
Ensigns (continued)—	
Thos. Gainsforth ..	.. 21 Sept. 1782
Chaplain—	
George Bowe	.. 5 Feb. 1776
Adjutant—	
George Mackenzie ..	.. 18 Sept. 1777
Quartermaster—	
James Wright.. ..	.. 18 Sept. 1777
Surgeon—	
James Henderson ..	.. 10 Nov. 1775

Regimentals — Red, facings blue, white lace, 2 blue stripes.

Agents—Messrs. Gray and Ogilvie, Terrace, Spring Gardens.

LIST OF OFFICERS OF 3RD AND 4TH BATTALION DISBANDED AND ADDITIONAL OFFICERS OF 1ST AND 2ND BATTALION REDUCED, 1783-84.

Cols.-Commandant—
John Dalling, Bt.
Gabriel Christie
Lieut.-Colonels—
Beamsley Glazier
Archibald McArthur
Lieut.-Cols. and Majors—
William Gooshy Strutt
Ludovick Colquhoun
Thos. Etherington
Captains—
James Bain
Fred. de Diemar
James Stevenson
Samuel Rutherford
Marcus Pictet
George Schneider
Francis Erskine
Alexander Wright
Fred. de Montrond
James Robertson
Teesdale Cockell
Alexander Dirom
James Fahy
T. Gunter Brown
George Miggs
Thomas Sweetland
John Rotton
Samuel de Visme
Duncan M'Intosh
George Prevost
W. Bladen Tinker
Henry Thurston Shadwell
Charles Dixon
H. J. Kearny
William Gossip
Captain-Lieutenants—
N. F. Cockell
James Ecuvier
Hon. Charles Curzon
Lieutenants—
Lewis Barde
John Kearsley
Francis Boniface

Lieutenants (continued)—
Henry de Crowfax
Enoch Plumer
Charles Brown
Lewis Correvont
J. Barclay Scriven
Edward Moncrieffe
Lorentz Grunholme
John William Dalling
Anthony Pasquada
Ashton Warner
James Grey Tucker
Herbert von Hamell
George M'Lean
Roger Coghlan
Luke Walsh
John Campbell
Henry Grayslan
James Apthorp
William Field
W. J. Stevenson
F. P. Fatio
William Scaly
H. Lomck
Charles de Damas
Robert Holland
John Watson
William M'Kinnen
Charles Ventuern
Frederick West
John Young
Thos. Booker
John Bard

Ensigns—
William Darby
John Randall Forster
John Barker
William Sands
Charles Willcocks
Charles Lemoine
John Marsh
John Farrell
George Holmes
John Lewis Prevost
James Petrie
John Leaner
George Glover
Thomas Gainsforth
Ruth Clarke
Enens Sloss
W. Vassel Mac
F. R. Bromfield
Robert Barclay
W. Brabham Chuton
T. W. Prince
Ambrose Lane
William West
Robert Sutherland
John Holiday Laule
Adolphus Ross
John Mackinnon
Robert Simpson
John Wilson
John Dockray
Hugh Mackay
John Conolly
W. Ross Darby

Ensigns (continued)—
George Fenton
Augustus Gould
John Goodall
Thomas de Jersey
Henry Synes

Chaplains—
James Manesty
Charles Mongau

Adjutants—
George Westphal
Colin MacKenzie

Quartermasters—
William Fitzgerald
Robert Burton

Surgeons—
George Clarke
Isaac Tilford

1784.

Two Battalions.

West Indies.

1st Battalion.

Rank and Name.	Rank in Regiment.
Colonel-in-Chief—	
Jeffery, Ld. Amherst, K.B.	7 Nov. 1768
Rank in Army, Gen.	19 Mar. 1778
Col.-Commandant—	
Frederick Baldwan	23 Oct. 1772
Rank in Army, Gen.	1 Jan. 1776
Lieut.-Colonel—	
George Etherington	19 Sept. 1775
Rank in Army, Col.	16 May 1782
Major—	
Peter Hunter	20 Oct. 1781
Rank in Army, Lt.-Col.	23 Nov. 1782
Captains—	
James Grandidier	25 May 1772
Rank in Army, Major	19 Feb. 1783
Bernard Ratzer	13 Nov. 1772
Rank in Army,	19 Mar. 1783
William Kelly	28 April 1775
Patrick Murray	23 Sept. 1775
Tho. Taylor Byrd	14 July 1776
George Bruere	15 Nov. 1776
Harry Burrard	28 Sept. 1777
Captain-Lieut. and Captain—	
Richard Carrique	12 Oct. 1780
Lieutenants—	
James Edwards	4 Sept. 1775
Rank in Army,	13 June 1762
William Loudenwatg	4 Oct. 1775
E. Massey Hannard	14 Nov. 1776
John Charlton	6 Mar. 1777
Geo. Ford Loup	11 Sept. 1777
— Breitenbach	21 Nov. 1777
Frederick Gottached	26 May 1778
Martin Vamper	25 Dec. 1778
Wm. von Borbeck	26 Dec. 1778
Robert Lethbridge	17 Dec. 1778
William Floyer	17 Mar. 1779
Ensigns—	
Samuel Willis	10 Aug. 1777
Luke Rogers	20 May 1779
Augustus Gould	21 May 1779

Rank and Name.	Rank in Regiment.
Ensigns (continued)—	
Edward Cartwright ..	4 Sept. 1779
Tho. Fra. Bardell	5 June 1780
J. Barlow Prevost	29 Dec. 1780
Robert A. Farmer	8 Jan. 1781
William McKinnon ..	13 June 1781
Chaplain—	
William Winder	4 April 1765
Adjutant—	
Rd. Massey Hansard ..	9 Mar. 1780
Quartermaster—	
James Wright..	10 Sept. 1777
Surgeon—	
John Summers	10 Nov. 1775

2nd Battalion.

Col.-in-Chief—	
Jeffery, Ld. Amherst, K.B.	7 Nov. 1768
Rank in Army, Gen.	19 Mar. 1778
Col.-Commandant—	
Augustine Prevost	18 Sept. 1775
Rank in Army, Maj.-Gen.	19 Feb. 1779
Lieut.-Colonel—	
Stephen Kemble	14 May 1778
Rank in Army, Col.	20 Nov. 1782
Major—	
George Thompson	24 Oct. 1781
Rank in Army, Lieut.-Col.	19 Feb. 1783
Captains—	
Tho. Etherington	14 Aug. 1772
Rank in Army, Major	19 Mar. 1783
Dietrich Brehm	16 Nov. 1774
Rank in Army,	19 Mar. 1783
J. Fr. Wallet des Barres	23 Sept. 1775
Rank in Army,	19 Mar. 1783
Augustine Prevost	23 Sept. 1775
Charles Dixon..	12 Nov. 1776
Benjamin Wickham ..	19 Aug. 1777
Thomas Barrow	27 April 1778
Captain-Lieut. and Captain—	
N. F. Lockell	1 Oct. 1781
Lieutenants—	
John Bayard	2 Oct. 1775
James Wakeley	18 April 1776
Rank in Army.	28 Oct. 1760
Thomas Walker	15 Nov. 1776
David Gordon	17 Mar. 1777
Alexander M'Donald ..	18 Sept. 1777
Edward Davis..	14 May 1778
George McKenzie	25 Dec. 1778
C. L. Theo. Schoedde ..	25 Dec. 1778
Isaac Hesselburg	26 Dec. 1778
Charles Crotchley	27 Dec. 1778
Charles Ward	16 Mar. 1779
Ensigns—	
—— Rudow	19 Aug. 1778
James Barrick..	20 May 1779
George Eberlard	22 May 1779
Thomas Carke..	5 Sept. 1779
Aug. Fred. Prevost.. ..	25 Sept. 1780
Gabriel Gordon	6 Jan. 1781
John Campbell	27 April 1781
Joseph Pusquada	25 June 1781
Chaplain—	
George Bowe	5 Feb. 1776

Rank and Name.	Rank in Regiment.
Adjutant—	
Charles Ward..	8 Jan. 1781
Quartermaster—	
John Fleming..	9 Nov. 1774
Surgeon—	
James Henderson	10 Nov. 1775

Regimentals—Red, facings blue, white lace, 2 blue stripes.

Agents—Messrs. Gray and Ogilvie, Terrace, Spring Gardens.

1785.

Two Battalions.

West Indies.

1st Battalion.

Col.-in-Chief—	
Jeffery, Ld. Amherst, K.B.	7 Nov. 1768
Rank in Army, Gen.	19 Mar. 1778
Col.-Commandant—	
Frederick Haldiman, K.B.	28 Oct. 1768
Rank in Army, Lieut.-Gen.	29 Aug. 1777
Lieut.-Colonel—	
Geo. Etherington	19 Sept. 1775
Rank in Army, Col.	16 May 1782
Major—	
Peter Hunter	20 Oct. 1781
Rank in Army, Lieut.-Col.	23 Nov. 1782
Captains—	
James Grandidier	24 May 1772
Rank in Army, Major	19 Feb. 1783
William Kelly..	28 April 1775
Thos. Taylor Byrd.. ..	14 July 1776
George Bruere	15 Nov. 1776
Harry Bernard	18 Sept. 1777
Geo. Ferd. Loup	6 Oct. 1784
Captain-Lieut. and Captain—	
Richard Carrique	19 Oct. 1780
Lieutenants—	
James Edwards	4 Sept. 1775
Rank in Army,	23 June 1762
William Lichenwitz ..	4 Oct. 1775
Rd. Massey Hansard ..	14 Nov. 1776
—— Breitenbach	21 Nov. 1777
Fred. Gottsched	20 May 1778
Wm. von Borbeck.. ..	26 Dec. 1778
R. Lethbridge..	27 Dec. 1778
W. Floyer	17 Mar. 1779
Roger Coghlan	6 Oct. 1784
Rank in Army,	24 Sept. 1781
John Campbell	26 Nov. 1784
Ensigns—	
Samuel Willis	10 Aug. 1777
Augustus Gould	21 May 1779
Edward Cartwright ..	4 Sept. 1779
J. Barlow Prevost	29 Dec. 1780
Robt. A. Farmer	8 Jan. 1781
William Mackinnon ..	13 June 1781
James Bruere	19 Jan. 1785
Rank in Army,	25 Nov. 1782
Francis Quarme	25 Feb. 1785
Chaplain—	
William Winder	4 April 1765
Adjutant—	
Rd. Massey Hansard ..	9 Mar. 1780

Rank and Name.	Rank in Regiment.
Quartermaster—	
William Fitzgerald.. .. 30 April 1784	
Surgeon—	
James Wright.. .. .. 28 April 1784	

2nd Battalion.

Col.-in-Chief—
Jeffery, Ld. Amherst, K.B. 7 Nov. 1768
   Rank in Army, Gen. 19 Mar. 1778
Col.-Commandant—
Augustine Prevost .. .. 18 Sept. 1775
   Rank in Army, Maj.-Gen. 19 Feb. 1779
Lieut.-Colonel—
Stephen Kemble .. .. 14 May 1778
   Rank in Army, Col. 20 Nov. 1782

Major—
Patrick Murray .. .. 6 Oct. 1784
Captains—
Dietrich Brehm .. .. 16 Nov. 1774
   Rank in Army, Major 19 Mar. 1783
J. Fr. Wallet des Barres.. 23 Sept. 1775
   Rank in Army, 19 Mar. 1783
Charles Dixon . .. 12 Nov. 1776
Benjamin Wickham .. 10 Aug. 1777
Thomas Barron .. .. 27 April 1778
Richard Porter .. .. 26 Nov. 1784
Mark Pictet .. .. 2 Feb. 1785
   Rank in Army, 26 Dec. 1778
Captain-Lieut. and Captain—
N. F. Lockell .. .. .. 1 Oct. 1781
Lieutenants—
James Wakeley .. .. 18 April 1776
   Rank in Army 28 Oct. 1760
Thomas Walker .. .. 15 Nov. 1776
David Gordon .. .. 17 Mar. 1777
Alex. M'Donald .. .. 18 Sept. 1777
Edward Davis.. .. .. 14 May 1778
George Mackenzie .. 25 Dec. 1778
C. L. Theo. Schoedde .. 25 Dec. 1778
Isaac Hesselburg .. .. 26 Dec. 1778
Charles Crotchley .. .. 27 Dec. 1778
Gabriel Gordon .. .. 26 Nov. 1784
John Lennox .. .. .. 26 Nov. 1784
Ensigns—
—— Rudow .. .. 19 Aug. 1778
James Barrick .. .. 20 May 1779
George Eberhard .. .. 22 May 1779
Thomas Clarke .. .. 5 Sept. 1779
Aug. Fred. Prevost .. 25 Sept. 1780
Joseph Pasquada .. .. 25 June 1781
Chaplain—
George Bowe .. .. 5 Feb. 1776
Adjutant—
George Westphall .. 26 Nov. 1784
Quartermaster—
John Fleming.. .. 9 Nov. 1774
Surgeon—
James Henderson .. .. 10 Nov. 1775
Regimentals— Red, facings blue, white lace and 2 blue stripes.
Agents—Messrs. Gray and Ogilvie, Terrace, Spring Gardens.

1786.

Two Battalions.

West Indies—North America.

Rank and Name.	Rank in Regiment.

Col.-in-Chief—
Jeffery, Ld. Amherst, K.B. 7 Nov. 1768
   Rank in Army, Gen. 19 Mar. 1778
Cols.-Commandant—
Fred. Haldimand, K.B. .. 28 Oct. 1772
   Rank in Army, Lt.-Gen. 20 Aug. 1777
Augustine Prevost .. .. 18 Sept. 1775
   Rank in Army, Maj.-Gen. 19 Feb. 1779
Lieut.-Colonels—
George Etherington .. 19 Sept. 1775
   Rank in Army, Col. 26 May 1782
Stephen Kemble .. .. 14 May 1778
   Rank in Army, Col. 20 Nov. 1782
Majors—
Peter Hunter .. .. .. 20 Oct. 1781
   Rank in Army, Lt.-Col. 23 Nov. 1782
Patrick Murray .. .. 6 Oct. 1784
Captains—
Dietrich Brehm .. .. 16 Nov. 1774
   Rank in Army, Major 19 Mar. 1783
J. F. Wallet des Barres.. 23 Sept. 1775
   Rank in Army, Major 19 Mar. 1783
Charles Dixon .. .. 12 Nov. 1776
Benjamin Wickham .. 10 Aug. 1777
Harry Burrard .. .. 18 Sept. 1777
Geo. Ferd. Loup .. .. 6 Oct. 1784
Richard Porter .. .. 26 Nov. 1784
Mark Pictet .. .. .. 2 Feb. 1785
   Rank in Army, 26 Dec. 1778
Edward Davis.. .. .. 23 Mar. 1785
Hon. George Fraser .. 20 Apr. 1785
Lachlan Maclean .. .. 8 Feb. 1786
   Rank in Army, 17 Oct. 1782
Captain-Lieuts. and Captains—
Ed. Mercer Hammond .. 23 Mar. 1785
Thomas Walker .. .. 4 Nov. 1785
Lieutenants—
William Lochenowtz .. 4 Oct. 1775
James Wakeley .. .. 18 April 1776
   Rank in Army, 28 Oct. 1760
David Gordon .. .. 17 Mar. 1777
Alexander M'Donald .. 18 Sept. 1777
—— Greutenbach .. 21 Nov. 1777
Frederick Gottschol .. 20 May 1778
C. L. Theo. Schoedde .. 25 Dec. 1778
William von Borbeck .. 26 Dec. 1778
Isaac Hesselburg .. .. 26 Dec. 1778
Robert Lethbridge .. 27 Dec. 1778
Charles Crotchley .. .. 27 Dec. 1778
William Floyer .. .. 17 Mar. 1779
Roger Coghlan .. .. 6 Oct. 1784
   Rank in Army, 24 Sep. 1781
Gabriel Gordon .. .. 26 Nov. 1784
John Campbell .. .. 26 Nov. 1784
John Lennox .. .. 26 Nov. 1784
James Bruce.. .. .. 6 April 1785
M Perkins .. .. 27 April 1785
Robert Booker .. .. 18 May 1785
F. P. Fatio .. .. .. 4 Nov. 1785
   Rank in Army, 1 Dec. 1782

Rank and Name.	Rank in Regiment.
Ensigns—	
Samuel Willis.. ..	.. 10 Aug. 1777
James Barrick.. ..	.. 20 May 1779
Augustine Gould ..	.. 21 May 1779
George Eberard ..	.. 22 May 1779
Edward Cartwright ..	4 Sept. 1779
Thomas Clarke ..	5 Sept. 1779
Robert A. Farmer ..	.. 8 Jan. 1781
William Darby ..	.. 25 June 1781
Joseph Pasquada ..	.. 25 June 1781
Francis Quarme ..	.. 25 Feb. 1785
Dorrell Cope	.. 6 April 1785
William Tireman ..	.. 15 April 1785
J. Randall Forster..	.. 2 Nov. 1785
Rank in Army, 11 July 1781	
Jacob Jordan	.. 11 Jan. 1780
Chaplains—	
William Winder ..	.. 4 April 1765
George Bowe	.. 5 Feb. 1776
Adjutants—	
Rd. Massey Hansard	.. 9 Mar. 1780
George Westphall ..	.. 26 Nov. 1784
Quartermasters—	
John Fleming.. ..	.. 9 Nov. 1774
William Fitzgerald	.. 30 April 1784
Surgeons—	
James Henderson ..	.. 10 Nov. 1775
James Wright ..	.. 28 April 1784

Regimentals— Red, facings blue, white laces, 2 blue stripes.

*Agents—*Messrs. Gray and Ogilvie, Argyle Street.

1787.

Two Battalions.

North America— Newfoundland— West Indies— England.

Col.-in-Chief—	
Jeffery, Ld. Amherst, K.B.	7 Nov. 1768
Rank in Army, Gen. 19 Mar. 1778	
Cols.-Commandant—	
F. Haldimand, K.B. ..	.. 28 Oct. 1772
Rank in Army, Lt.-Gen. 29 Aug. 1777	
Gabriel K. Christie ..	10 May 1786
Rank in Army, Maj.-Gen. 19 Oct. 1781	
Lieut.-Colonels—	
George Etherington	.. 19 Sep. 1775
Rank in Army, Col. 16 May 1782	
Stephen Kemble ..	.. 14 May 1778
Rank in Army, Col. 20 Nov. 1782	
Majors—	
Peter Hunter	.. 20 Oct. 1781
Rank in Army, Lt.-Col. 23 Nov. 1782	
Patrick Murray ..	.. 6 Oct. 1784
Captains—	
J. F. Wallet des Barres..	23 Sep. 1775
Rank in Army, Major 19 Mar. 1783	
Benjamin Wickham ..	10 Aug. 1777
Geo. Ford, Lesp ..	.. 6 Oct. 1784
Richard Porter ..	.. 26 Nov. 1784
Mack Piatt	.. 2 Feb. 1785
Rank in Army, 26 Dec. 1778	
Edward Davis ..	.. 23 Mar. 1785
Hon. George Fraser ..	20 April 1785

Rank and Name.	Rank in Regiment.
Captains (continued)—	
Lachlan Maclean ..	.. 8 Feb. 1786
Rank in Army, 17 Oct. 1782	
Duncan M'Intosh ..	.. 2 June 1786
Rank in Army, 29 April 1783	
John Parr	.. 5 July 1786
Captain-Lieuts. and Captains—	
Rd. Massey Hansard	.. 23 Mar. 1785
Thomas Walker ..	.. 4 Nov. 1785
Lieutenants—	
William Lachenwitz	.. 4 Oct. 1775
James Wakeley ..	.. 18 April 1776
Rank in Army, 28 Oct. 1760	
David Gordon.. ..	.. 17 Mar. 1777
Alexander McDonald	.. 18 Sep. 1777
—— Breitenbach ..	.. 21 Nov. 1777
Frederick Gottsched	.. 20 May 1778
C. L. Theo. Schoedde ..	25 Dec. 1778
William von Borbeck	.. 26 Dec. 1778
Isaac Hesselburg ..	.. 26 Dec. 1778
Robert Lethbridge ..	.. 27 Dec. 1778
Charles Crotchley ..	.. 27 Dec. 1778
William Floyer ..	.. 17 Mar. 1779
Roger Coghlan ..	.. 6 Oct. 1784
Rank in Army, 24 Sep. 1781	
Gabriel Gordon ..	.. 26 Nov. 1784
John Campbell ..	.. 26 Nov. 1784
John Lennox	.. 26 Nov. 1784
James Bruere	.. 6 April 1785
Robert Rankes ..	.. 18 May 1785
Robert McWorth ..	.. 3 May 1786
Rank in Army, 9 Sep. 1783	
Samuel Kempthorne ..	10 Jan. 1787
Rank in Army, 20 Mar. 1783	
Ensigns—	
Samuel Willis ..	.. 10 Aug. 1777
James Barrick ..	.. 20 May 1779
Augustus Gould ..	.. 21 May 1779
George Eberard ..	.. 22 May 1779
Edward Cartwright ..	4 Sep. 1779
Thomas Clarke ..	5 Sep. 1779
Robert A. Farmer ..	.. 8 Jan. 1781
William Darby ..	.. 25 June 1781
Joseph Pasquada ..	.. 25 June 1781
Francis Quarme ..	.. 25 Feb. 1785
Dorrell Cope	.. 6 April 1785
William Tireman ..	.. 15 April 1785
J. Randall Forster ..	2 Nov. 1785
Rank in Army, 11 July 1781	
Jacob Jordan	.. 11 Jan. 1786
Chaplains—	
William Winder ..	.. 4 April 1765
George Bowe	.. 5 Feb. 1776
Adjutants—	
Rd. Massey Hansard	.. 9 Mar. 1780
George Westphall ..	.. 26 Nov. 1784
Quartermasters—	
John Fleming ..	.. 9 Nov. 1774
Robert Burton ..	.. 12 April 1786
Surgeons—	
James Henderson ..	.. 10 Nov. 1775
James Wright ..	.. 28 April 1784

Regimentals— Red, facings blue, white laces, 2 blue stripes.

*Agents—*Messrs. Ross and Ogilvie, Argyle Street.

1787.

LIST OF OFFICERS APPOINTED TO THE 3RD BATTALION 60TH REGIMENT ON ITS BEING RAISED.

Rank and Name.	Rank in Regiment.
Col.-Commanding—	
William Rowley ..	.. 24 Sept. 1787
Lieut.-Colonel—	
Arch. MacArthur ..	.. 24 Sept. 1787
Major—	
Wm. Gooday Strutt	.. 24 Sept. 1787
Captains—	
Fred. de Diemar ..	.. 24 Sept. 1787
James Erayer	.. 24 Sept. 1787
Wm. Lechmere ..	.. 24 Sept. 1787
Wm. Martin	.. 27 Sept. 1787
James Bain	.. 16 April 1788
Robt. Bowker Jebb ..	14 May 1788
Francis Erskine ..	.. 1 Oct. 1788
Captain-Lieutenant—	
Joseph Breitenbach ..	. 30 Sept. 1787
Lieutenants—	
Henry Crowfax ..	.. 24 Sept. 1787
Anthony Pasquale ..	.. 24 Sept. 1787
John Watson	.. 24 Sept. 1787
John Young, senr...	.. 25 Sept. 1787
John Lewis Prevost	.. 25 Sept. 1787
James Bold	.. 7 Nov. 1787
Wm. Robins	.. 5 Dec. 1787
John Lewis Cornveet	.. 7 May 17-8
John de Laney ..	.. 28 May 1788
John Young, junr. ..	.. 3 Sept. 1788
A. G. Tucker	.. 10 Oct. 1787
Ensigns—	
C. F. Piquet	.. 2 Oct. 1787
W. H. Banbury ..	.. 24 Oct. 1787
James Browse ..	.. 7 Nov. 1787
Thomas de Jersey ..	.. 16 Nov. 1787
Thomas Martin ..	.. 22 Jan. 1788
Wm. Jevon	.. 25 Jan. 1788
Richd. Maitland ..	.. 1 Oct. 1788
John Kenny	.. 1 Oct. 1788
Chaplain—	
James Maxwell ..	.. 24 Sept. 1787
Adjutant—	
Wentworth Tonge ..	.. 24 Sept. 1787
Quartermaster—	
Wm. Cook	.. 9 July 1788
Surgeon—	
J. Dickson Reade ..	7 May 1788

LIST OF OFFICERS OF THE 4TH BATTALION 60TH REGIMENT.

Col.-Commanding—	
James Keoke ..	.. 20 Oct. 1788
Lieut.-Colonel—	
Peter Hunter ..	.. 24 Sept. 1787
Major—	
John Whitelock	2 Oct. 1788
Captains—	
Thomas Walker ..	.. 1 Nov. 1785
Geo. Schneider ..	.. 24 Sept. 1787
Sam. Devisme ..	.. 24 Sept. 1787
James Wakeley ..	.. 25 Sept. 1787
Philip Skene	.. 27 Sept. 1787

Rank and Name.	Rank in Regiment.
Captains—	
Robert Lethbridge..	.. 27 Sept. 1787
Geo. Meggs	.. 18 June 1788
Captain-Lieutenant—	
Fred. Gottsched ..	.. 30 Sept. 1787
Lieutenants—	
Lorentz Greenholme	.. 24 Sept. 1787
Hubert von Hamell	.. 24 Sept. 1787
Charles Diemar ..	.. 24 Sept. 1787
Joseph Pasquale ..	.. 25 Sept. 1787
John Manners Kerr ..	24 Sept. 1787
Jno. Randall Forster	.. 25 June 1788
James Panton	.. 2 July 1788
D—— Walker	.. 1 Aug. 1788
Hender Molesworth ..	1 Oct. 1788
Ashton Warner ..	.. 10 Oct. 1788
F. J. Grafton Maclean ..	15 Oct. 1788
Ensigns—	
Geo. Carl Schneider	.. 30 Sept. 1787
Cavendish Nugent ..	.. 6 Oct. 1787
Hugh Fraser	.. 12 Nov. 1787
Francis Slater.. ..	.. 14 Nov. 1787
Robt. Gordon	.. 17 Nov. 1787
Robt. Tyler	.. 23 Jan. 1788
John Vireher	.. 24 Jan. 1788
Thomas Walcott ..	.. 9 April 1788
Chaplain—	
Charles Morgan ..	.. 24 Sept. 1787
Adjutant—	
J. H. Gordon	.. 24 Sept. 1787
Quartermaster—	
John Clarke	.. 24 Sept. 1787
Surgeon—	
Isaac Titford	.. 24 Sept. 1787

1788.

Four Battalions.

North America—England—West Indies.

Col. in Chief—	
Jeffery, 1st Amherst, K.B.	7 Nov. 1768
Rank in Army, Gen. 19 Mar. 1778	
Cols.-Commandant—	
Fred. Haldimand, K.B. ..	18 Oct. 1772
Rank in Army, Lt.-Gen. 29 Aug. 1777	
Gabriel Christie ..	.. 1st May 1786
Rank in Army, Maj.-Gen. 19 Oct. 1781	
William Rowley	3 Oct. 1787
Rank in Army, Maj.-Gen. 19 Oct. 1781	
Hon. William Gordon ..	3 Oct. 1787
Rank in Army, Maj.-Gen. 19 Oct. 1781	
Lieut.-Colonels—	
Stephen Kemble	14 May 1778
Rank in Army, Col. 20 Nov. 1782	
Archibald M'Arthur ..	24 Sept. 1787
Rank in Army, 24 April 1781	
Peter Hunter	24 Sept. 1787
Rank in Army, Lt.-Col. 23 Nov. 1782	
Jas. Adolphus Harris ..	16 Jan. 1788
Majors—	
Patrick Murray	5 Oct. 1784
Wm. Gooday Strutt ..	24 Sept. 1787
Rank in Army, 9 Aug. 1783	
John Moore	16 Jan. 1788
Rank in Army, 23 Nov. 1785	
George Benson	16 Jan. 1788

i

Rank and Name.	Rank in Regiment.
Captains—	
J. F. Wallet des Barres ..	23 Sept. 1775
Rank in Army, Major 19 Mar. 1783	
Benjamin Wickman ..	10 Aug. 1777
Geo. Ferdinand Loup ..	6 Oct. 1784
Richard Porter ..	26 Nov. 1784
Mark Pictet	2 Feb. 1785
Rank in Army, 26 Dec. 1778	
Rich. Massey Hansard ..	23 Mar. 1785
Edward Davis	23 Mar. 1785
Thomas Walker	4 Nov. 1785
Lachlan Maclean	8 Feb. 1786
Rank in Army, 17 Oct. 1782	
Duncan M'Intosh	2 June 1786
Rank in Army, 29 April 1783	
John Parr	5 July 1786
Frederick de Diemar ..	24 Sept. 1787
Rank in Army, 20 June 1778	
George Schneider	24 Sept. 1787
Rank in Army, 26 Dec. 1778	
Frederick de Montrond ..	24 Sept. 1787
Rank in Army, 24 May 1779	
Hon. Charles Curzon ..	24 Sept. 1787
Rank in Army, 11 Oct. 1781	
James Ecuyer	24 Sept. 1787
Rank in Army, 20 Oct. 1781	
Samuel Devismes	24 Sept. 1787
Rank in Army, 15 Dec. 1782	
William Lachenwitz ..	24 Sept. 1787
James Wakeley	25 Sept. 1787
William Freemantle ..	26 Sept. 1787
Rank in Army, 24 May 1783	
Alexander Phillip Forbes	26 Sept. 1787
James Lowe	26 Sept. 1787
Charles Ingram ..	26 Sept. 1787
H. Thurloe Shadwell ..	27 Sept. 1787
Rank in Army, 2 Dec. 1779	
Andrew Philip Skene ..	27 Sept. 1787
Rank in Army, 19 Mar. 1783	
William Martin ..	27 Sept. 1787
Robert Lethbridge	27 Sept. 1787
Fred. de Chambauth ..	16 Jan. 1788
Rank in Army, 27 Sept. 1787	
Captain-Lieut. and Captains—	
David Gordon ..	30 Sept. 1787
Archibald M'Donald ..	30 Sept. 1787
Joseph Breitenbach ..	30 Sept. 1787
Frederick Gottsched ..	30 Sept. 1787
Lieutenants—	
C. L. Theo. Schoedde ..	25 Dec. 1778
William von Borbeck ..	26 Dec. 1778
Isaac Hesselburg ..	26 Dec. 1778
Charles Crotchley	27 Dec. 1778
William Flover	17 Mar. 1779
Gabriel Gordon ..	26 Nov. 1784
John Campbell ..	26 Nov. 1784
John Lennox	26 Nov. 1784
James Bruere ..	6 April 1785
Robert Bowker Jebb ..	18 May 1785
Robert McWorth ..	3 May 1786
Rank in Army, 9 Sept. 1783	
Samuel Kempthorne ..	10 Jan. 1787
Rank in Army, 20 Mar. 1783	
John Kearsley	24 Sept. 1787
Rank in Army, 3 Sept. 1779	

Rank and Name.	Rank in Regiment.
Lieutenants (continued)—	
Henry Crasny	24 Sept. 1787
Rank in Army, 21 Sept. 1779	
Enoch Plummer	24 Sept. 1787
Rank in Army, 22 Sept. 1779	
Robert Hollandt	24 Sept. 1787
Rank in Army, 29 June 1780	
Charles Brown	24 Sept. 1787
Rank in Army, 23 Sept. 1780	
Lorentz Greenholme ..	24 Sept. 1787
Rank in Army, 20 Nov. 1780	
Anthony Pasqunda ..	24 Sept. 1787
Rank in Army, 25 June 1781	
Hubert von Hamell ..	24 Sept. 1787
Rank in Army, 15 Aug. 1781	
Henry Graydon	24 Sept. 1787
Rank in Army, 22 Oct. 1781	
Charles de Diemar ..	24 Sept. 1787
Rank in Army, 15 Dec. 1782	
John Watson	24 Sept. 1787
Rank in Army, 16 Mar. 1783	
Samuel Willis ..	24 Sept. 1787
James Barrick ..	24 Sept. 1787
John Young	25 Sept. 1787
Rank in Army, 15 May 1780	
Edward Cartwright ..	25 Sept. 1787
Thomas Clarke ..	25 Sept. 1787
Robert Adolphus Farmer	25 Sept. 1787
Joseph Pasquada ..	25 Sept. 1787
John Lewis Prevost ..	25 Sept. 1787
John Manners Kerr ..	25 Sept. 1787
John Jones	25 Sept. 1787
Frederick de Vos ..	26 Sept. 1787
Phillip Masserin ..	27 Sept. 1787
William Claus ..	31 Oct. 1787
John Robert Nolon ..	24 Oct. 1787
James Dodds	7 Nov. 1787
Rank in Army, 1 May 1781	
William Robins ..	5 Dec. 1787
Francis Quarme ..	16 Jan. 1788
Ensigns—	
Dorrell Cope	6 April 1785
William Tireman ..	15 April 1785
John Randall Forster ..	2 Nov. 1785
Rank in Army, 11 July 1781	
Jacob Jordan	11 Jan. 1786
Henry Le Moine ..	7 Feb. 1787
Rank in Army, 3 Oct. 1781	
Hercules Molesworth ..	28 June 1787
Augustus Gould ..	24 Sept. 1787
Rank in Army, 21 May 1779	
Alexander Fraser ..	24 Sept. 1787
Rank in Army, 17 Oct. 1782	
R. Campbell McPherson	24 Sept. 1787
R. Chance Nixon ..	26 Sept. 1787
John Dupuy	27 Sept. 1787
Lewis Muller	29 Sept. 1787
—— Schneider ..	30 Sept. 1787
George Fourneret ..	1 Oct. 1787
C. Frederick Piquett ..	2 Oct. 1787
James Peachey ..	3 Oct. 1787
Samuel Hollandt ..	1 Oct. 1787
Cavendish Nugent ..	6 Oct. 1787
Robert Gordon ..	17 Nov. 1787
Rank in Army, 2nd Lieut. 3 Dec. 1781	
Hamilton Fawcett ..	6 Dec. 1787

Rank and Name.	Rank in Regiment.
Ensigns (continued)—	
Alexander John Goldie	8 Jan. 1788
Daniel Nixon	16 Jan. 1788
Thomas Martin	22 Jan. 1788
Rank in Army, 25 Sept. 1787	
Robert Tyler	23 Jan. 1788
John J. Vischer	24 Jan. 1788
Chaplains—	
William Winder	4 April 1765
George Bowe	5 Feb. 1765
James Manesty	24 Sept. 1787
Charles Morgan	24 Sept. 1787
Adjutants—	
Richard Massey Hansard	9 Mar. 1780
George Westphall	26 Nov. 1784
T. Hamilton Gordon	12 Dec. 1787
Quartermasters—	
John Fleming	9 Nov. 1775
Robert Burton	12 April 1786
John Summers	24 Sept. 1787
John Clarke	24 Sept. 1787
Surgeons—	
James Henderson	10 Nov. 1775
James Wright	28 April 1784
John Clarke	24 Sept. 1787
Isaac Titford	

Regimentals—Red, facings blue, white lace, 2 stripes.

Agents—Messrs. Ross and Ogilvie, Argyle Street.

1789.

Four Battalions.

North America—West Indies

Col.-in-Chief—
Jeffery, Lord Amherst,
K.B. ... ... 7 Nov. 1768
Rank in Army, Gen. 19 Mar. 1778

Cols.-Commandant—
Fred. Haldimand, K.B. ... 20 Oct. 1772
Rank in Army, Lt.-Gen. 29 Aug. 1777
Gabriel Christie ... 10 May 1780
Rank in Army, Maj.-Gen. 19 Oct. 1781
William Rowley ... 3 Oct. 1787
Rank in Army, 19 Oct. 1781
James Rooke ... 30 Oct. 1788
Rank in Army, 25 Sept. 1787

Lieuts.-Colonels—
Stephen Kemble ... 14 May 1778
Rank in Army, Col. 20 Nov. 1782
Archibald M'Arthur ... 24 Sept 1787
Rank in Army, 24 April 1781
Peter Hunter ... 24 Sept. 1787
Rank in Army, 23 Nov 1782
J. Adolphus Harris ... 16 Jan. 1788

Majors—
Patrick Murray ... 6 Oct. 1781
Wm. Gosslay Strutt ... 24 Sept 1787
Rank in Army, 9 Aug. 1780
George Benson ... 16 Jun. 1788
John Whitelocke ... 2 Oct. 1788

Captains—
J. F. Wallet des Barres ... 23 Sept 1775
Rank in Army, Major 19 Mar. 1783

Rank and Name.	Rank in Regiment.
Captains (continued)—	
Benjamin Wickham	10 Aug. 1777
Geo. Ferdinand Loup	6 Oct. 1784
Richard Farter	26 Nov. 1784
Mark Pictet	2 Feb. 1785
Rank in Army, 26 Dec. 1778	
Edward Davis	23 Mar. 1785
Thomas Walker	4 Nov. 1785
Lachlan Maclean	8 Feb. 1786
Rank in Army, 17 Oct. 1728	
Duncan M'Intosh	2 June 1786
Rank in Army, 29 April 1783	
John Parr	5 July 1786
Frederick de Diemar	24 Sept. 1787
Rank in Army, 20 June 1778	
George Schoedler	24 Sept. 1787
Rank in Army, 26 Dec. 1778	
James Rouvier	24 Sept. 1787
Rank in Army, 20 Oct. 1781	
Samuel Delisaes	24 Sept. 1787
Rank in Army, 15 Dec. 1782	
William Lochrowitz	24 Sept. 1787
James Wakeley	25 Sept. 1787
James Lane	26 Sept. 1787
Charles Ingram	26 Sept. 1787
Rank in Army, 19 Mar. 1783	
Andrew Philip Skene	27 Sept. 1787
William Martin	27 Sept. 1787
Robert Lethbridge	27 Sept. 1787
Fred. de Chambault	16 Jan. 1788
Rank in Army, 27 Sept. 1787	
James Bain	16 April 1788
Rank in Army, 14 May 1778	
Robert Bowles Jebb	14 May 1788
John Thomas Roller	2 June 1788
John Wm. Aug. Ranser	18 June 1788
Rank in Army, 6 Mar. 1776	
George Meggs	18 June 1788
Rank in Army, 1 Mar. 1782	
Robert Farmer	9 April 1789
Rank in Army, 12 June 1782	
Captains-Lieut. and Captains—	
David Gordon	30 Sept. 1787
Archibald M'Donald	30 Sept. 1787
Joseph Breitenbach	30 Sept. 1787
Frederick Gretschel	30 Sept. 1787
Lieutenants—	
C. Lewis T. Schoedle	25 Dec. 1778
William von Borbeck	26 Dec. 1778
Isaac Hesselburg	26 Dec. 1778
Charles Crotchley	26 Dec. 1778
William Floyer	17 Mar. 1780
Gabriel Gordon	26 Nov. 1784
John Campbell	26 Nov. 1784
John Lennox	26 Nov. 1784
James Bruere	6 April 1785
Robert Mackworth	3 May 1789
Rank in Army, 9 Sept. 1783	
Samuel Kempthorne	10 Jan. 1787
Rank in Army, 29 Mar. 1784	
John Kearsley	24 Sept. 1787
Rank in Army, 3 Sept. 1779	
Henry Crassy	24 Sept. 1787
Rank in Army, 24 Sept. 1779	
Enoch Plummer	24 Sept. 1787
Rank in Army, 22 Sept. 1779	

I 2

Rank and Name.	Rank in Regiment.

Lieutenants (continued)—

- Lorentz Greenholme .. .. 24 Sept. 1787
  - *Rank in Army,* 20 Nov. 1780
- Anthony Pasquada.. .. 24 Sept. 1787
  - *Rank in Army,* 25 June 1781
- Hubert von Hamell .. 24 Sept. 1787
  - *Rank in Army,* 15 Aug. 1781
- Charles de Diemar.. .. 24 Sept. 1787
  - *Rank in Army,* 15 Dec. 1782
- James Barrick.. .. .. 24 Sept. 1787
- Edward Cartwright .. .. 24 Sept. 1787
- Thomas Clarke .. .. 24 Sept. 1787
- Robt. Adolphus Farmer.. 24 Sept. 1787
- Joseph Pasquada .. .. 24 Sept. 1787
- John Lewis Prevost .. 24 Sept. 1787
- John Manners Kerr .. 24 Sept. 1787
- Frederick de Vos .. .. 26 Sept. 1787
- William Claus .. .. 31 Oct. 1787
  - *Rank in Army,* 1 May 1781
- James Dodds.. .. .. 7 Nov. 1787
- William Robins .. .. 5 Dec. 1787
- Francis Quarme .. .. 16 Jan. 1788
- John Robertson .. .. 16 April 1788
  - *Rank in Army,* 28 Feb. 1787
- Lewis Corretout .. .. 7 May 1788
  - *Rank in Army,* 25 Sept. 1780
- William Tireman .. .. 14 May 1788
- John de Lancey .. .. 28 May 1788
  - *Rank in Army,* 7 Feb. 1783
- J. Randall Forster.. .. 25 June 1788
- Jones Ponton .. .. .. 2 July 1788
- David Walker.. .. .. 1 Aug. 1788
  - *Rank in Army,* 28 Feb. 1788
- John Young .. .. .. 3 Sept. 1788
  - *Rank in Army,* 27 April 1781
- Hender Molesworth .. 1 Oct. 1788
- Ashton Warner .. .. 10 Oct. 1788
  - *Rank in Army,* 10 Oct. 1781
- James Grey Tucker .. 10 Oct. 1788
  - *Rank in Army,* 11 Aug. 1781
- Fitzroy J. G. Maclean .. 15 Oct. 1788
  - *Rank in Army,* 19 June 1788
- William Edmonston .. 12 Mar. 1789
  - *Rank in Army,* 2 Feb. 1782
- Edward Poytt.. .. .. 2 April 1789
  - *Rank in Army,* 4 Jan. 1786

Ensigns—

- Dorrell Cope .. .. 6 April 1785
- Jacob Jordan .. .. 14 Jan. 1786
- Henry Le Moine .. .. 7 Feb. 1787
  - *Rank in Army,* 3 Oct. 1781
- Alexander Fraser .. .. 24 Sept. 1787
  - *Rank in Army,* 17 Oct. 1782
- Robt. Campl. M'Pherson 24 Sept. 1787
- John Dupuy .. .. 27 Sept. 1787
- Lewis Muller .. .. .. 29 Sept. 1787
- —— Schneider .. .. 30 Sept. 1787
- George Fourneret .. .. 1 Oct. 1787
- Chas. Frederick Piquett.. 2 Oct. 1787
- James Peachey .. .. 3 Oct. 1787
- Samuel Holland .. .. 4 Oct. 1787
- J. Cavendish Nugent .. 6 Oct. 1787
- Welsh Hamilton Bunbury 21 Oct. 1787
- James Brown.. .. .. 7 Nov. 1787
- Hugh Frazer .. .. .. 12 Nov. 1787
- Francis Slater.. .. .. 14 Nov. 1787

Rank and Name.	Rank in Regiment.

Ensigns (continued)—

- Thomas de Jeffery .. .. 16 Nov. 1787
- Robert Gordon .. .. 17 Nov. 1787
  - *Rank in Army,* 2nd Lieut. 3 Dec. 1781
- Hamilton Fweett .. .. 6 Dec. 1787
- Daniel Nixon .. .. .. 16 Jan. 1788
- Thomas Martin .. .. 22 Jan. 1788
  - *Rank in Army,* 25 Sept. 1787
- Robert Tyler .. .. .. 23 Jan. 1788
- John J. Visscher .. .. 24 Jan. 1788
- William Jevers .. .. 25 Jan. 1788
- Thomas Wellcott .. .. 9 April 1788
- James Abernethy .. .. 25 June 1788
- Samuel Cates .. .. .. 27 Aug. 1788
- Richard Maitland .. .. 1 Oct. 1788
  - *Rank in Army,* 31 Aug. 1780
- John Kenney .. .. .. 1 Oct. 1788
- Samuel Gibbs.. .. .. 29 Oct. 1788
  - *Rank in Army,* 8 Oct. 1783
- —— Fitzgerald .. .. 12 Mar. 1789

Chaplains—

- William Winder .. .. 4 April 1765
- George Howe .. .. .. 5 Feb. 1776
- James Manesty .. .. 24 Sept. 1787
- Charles Morgan .. .. 24 Sept. 1787

Adjutants —

- George Westphall .. .. 26 Nov. 1784
- Ja. Hamilton Gordon .. 24 Sept. 1787
- Winkworth Tonge .. .. 24 Sept. 1787
- William Warburton .. 24 Sept. 1787

Quartermasters—

- Robert Barton .. .. 12 April 1786
- John Clarke .. .. .. 24 Sept. 1787
- William Cook.. .. .. 9 July 1788
- Robert Eyre .. .. .. 12 Mar. 1789

Surgeons—

- James Henderson .. .. 10 Nov. 1775
- James Wright.. .. .. 28 April 1784
- Thos. Dickson Reide .. 7 May 1788
- Edward Shannon .. .. 19 Mar. 1789

Regimentals—Red. facings blue, white lace, 2 blue stripes.

Agents—Messrs. Ross and Ogilvie, Argyle Street.

1790.

Four Battalions.

North America—West Indies.

Col.-in-Chief—

- Jefferys, Lord Amherst, K.B. .. .. .. 7 Nov. 1768
  - *Rank in Army,* Gen. 19 Mar. 1783

Cols.-Commandant—

- Fred. Haldiman, K.B. .. 20 Oct. 1772
  - *Rank in Army,* Lt.-Gen. 29 Aug. 1777
- Gabriel Christie .. .. 10 May 1785
  - *Rank in Army,* Maj.-Gen. 19 Oct. 1781
- William Rowley .. .. 3 Oct. 1787
  - *Rank in Army,* 19 Oct. 1781
- James Rooke .. .. .. 20 Oct. 1788
  - *Rank in Army,* 28 Sept. 1787

Lieut.-Colonels—

- Stephen Kemble .. .. 11 May 1778
  - *Rank in Army,* Col. 20 Nov. 1782

Rank and Name.	Rank in Regiment.
Lieut.-Colonels (continued)—	
Archibald M'Arthur ..	24 Sept. 1787
Rank in Army, 24 April	1781
Peter Hunter	24 Sept. 1787
Rank in Army, 23 Nov.	1782
James Adolphus Harris..	16 Jan. 1788
Majors—	
Patrick Murray	6 Oct. 1784
Wm. Gooday Strutt ..	24 Sept. 1787
Rank in Army, 9 Aug.	1783
George Benson	16 Jan. 1718
John Whitelocke	2 Oct. 1788
Captains—	
J. F. Wallet des Barres	23 Sept. 1775
Rank in Army, Major 19 Mar.	1783
Benjamin Wickham ..	10 Aug. 1777
George Ferdinand Loup	6 Oct. 1784
Richard Porter	26 Nov. 1784
Mark Pictet	2 Feb. 1785
Rank in Army, 26 Dec.	1778
Edward Davis	24 Mar. 1785
Thomas Walker	8 Nov. 1785
Lachlan Maclean	8 Feb. 1786
Rank in Army, 17 Oct.	1782
Duncan Mackintosh ..	2 June 1786
Rank in Army, 29 April	1783
John Parr	5 July 1786
Frederick de Diesoar ..	24 Sept. 1787
Rank in Army, 24 June	1778
George Schneider ..	24 Sept. 1787
Rank in Army, 26 Dec.	1778
James Eccyier	24 Sept. 1787
Rank in Army, 20 Oct.	1781
Samuel Deviaines ..	24 Sept. 1787
Rank in Army, 15 Dec.	1786
William Lachenoure ..	24 Sept. 1787
James Wakeley ..	25 Sept. 1787
James Lowe	26 Sept. 1787
Charles Ingram ..	26 Sept. 1787
William Martin ..	27 Sept. 1787
Robert Leithbridge ..	27 Sept. 1787
Fred. de Chambault ..	16 Jan. 1788
Rank in Army, 27 Sept.	1789
James Bain	16 April 1788
Rank in Army, 14 May	1777
Robert Bowker Jebb ..	14 May 1788
John Thomas Buller ..	2 June 1788
John Will. Aug. Romer	18 June 1788
Rank in Army, 6 Mar.	1776
George Megis	18 June 1788
Rank in Army, 1 Mar.	1782
Robert Mackworth ..	8 Oct. 1789
William Casby	14 Nov. 1789
Rank in Army, 18 Feb.	1782
Captains-Lieut. and Captains—	
David Gordon	30 Sept. 1787
Joseph Breitenbach ..	30 Sept. 1787
Frederick Gottschal ..	30 Sept. 1787
Frederick Maitland ..	2 Dec. 1789
Lieutenants—	
C. Lewis T. Schoedde ..	25 Dec. 1775
William von Borleyk ..	26 Dec. 1775
Isaac Hesselburg ..	26 Dec. 1775
Charles Cretchley ..	27 Dec. 1775
William Floyer ..	17 Mar. 1779
Gabriel Gordon ..	26 Nov. 1784

Rank and Name.	Rank in Regiment.
Lieutenants (continued)—	
John Campbell	26 Nov. 1784
John Lennox	26 Nov. 1784
James Bruere.. ..	6 April 1785
Samuel Kempthorne ..	10 Jan. 1787
Rank in Army, 20 Mar.	1783
John Kearsley	24 Sept. 1787
Rank in Army, 3 Sept.	1779
Henry Crusy	24 Sept. 1787
Rank in Army, 21 Sept.	1779
Lorentz Greenholmo ..	24 Sept. 1787
Rank in Army, 20 Nov.	1780
Anthony Pasquada.. ..	24 Sept. 1787
Rank in Army, 25 June	1781
James Garrick.. ..	24 Sept. 1787
Edward Cartwright ..	
Thomas Clarke ..	24 Sept. 1787
Joseph Pasquala ..	24 Sept. 1787
John Lewis Prevost ..	24 Sept. 1787
John Mumers Kerr ..	24 Sept. 1787
Frederick de Vos ..	26 Sept. 1787
William Claus.. ..	31 Oct. 1787
James Dodds	7 Nov. 1787
Rank in Army, 1 May	1781
William Robins ..	5 Dec. 1787
Francis Quarme ..	16 Jan. 1788
John Robertson ..	16 April 1788
Rank in Army, 28 Feb.	1787
Lewis Correvont ..	7 May 1788
Rank in Army, 25 Sept.	1780
William Tireman ..	14 May 1788
John de Lancey ..	28 May 1788
Rank in Army, 7 Feb.	1783
J. Randall Forster..	25 June 1788
David Walker.. ..	1 Aug. 1788
Rank in Army, 28 Feb.	1788
Hender Molesworth ..	1 Oct. 1788
Ashton Warner ..	10 Oct. 1788
Rank in Army, 10 Aug.	1781
Fitzroy J. G. Maclean ..	15 Oct. 1788
Rank in Army, 19 June	1789
William Edmonsiton ..	12 Mar. 1789
Rank in Army, 2 Feb.	1782
Hugh Fraser	24 April 1789
Alexander Maclean ..	5 June 1789
Rank in Army, 23 Sept.	1788
James Apthorpe ..	21 June 1789
Rank in Army, 1 Mar.	1782
Solomon Hen. Durell ..	21 June 1789
Jacob Jordan	8 Oct. 1789
Francis Slater.. ..	14 Oct. 1789
John Bard	25 Nov. 1789
Rank in Army, 2 Sept.	1779
Charles Frederick Piquett	26 Nov. 1789
George Fontraed	9 Dec. 1789
Ensigns—	
Darell Cape	6 April 1785
Henry Le Mane	7 Feb. 1787
Rank in Army, 3 Oct.	1781
Alexander Fraser ..	24 Sept. 1787
Rank in Army, 17 Oct.	1782
Lewis Muller	29 Sept. 1787
—— Schneider ..	30 Sept. 1787
James Pemby.. ..	3 Oct. 1787
Samuel Hollredt ..	4 Oct. 1787
Welsh Hamilton Bunbury	24 Oct. 1787

Rank and Name.	Rank in Regiment.

Ensigns (continued)—

Name	Rank in Regiment
James Brown	7 Nov. 1787
Thomas de Jersey	16 Nov. 1787
Robert Gordon	17 Nov. 1787
Rank in Army, 2nd Lieut.	3 Dec. 1781
Hamilton Fawcett.. ..	6 Dec. 1787
Daniel Nixon	16 Jan. 1788
Thomas Martin	22 Jan. 1788
Rank in Army, 25 Sept. 1787	
Robert Tyler	23 Jan. 1788
William Jevers	25 Jan. 1788
Thomas Walcott	9 April 1788
James Abernethy	25 June 1788
Samuel Cates	27 Aug. 1788
John Kenney	1 Oct. 1788
Samuel Gibbs..	29 Oct. 1788
Rank in Army, 8 Oct. 1783	
—— Fitzgerald	12 Mar. 1789
Pinson Bonham	24 April 1789
Robert Robertson	9 May 1789
Rank in Army, 20 Sept. 1779	
William Fraser	5 June 1789
John Campbell	28 Aug. 1789
Rank in Army, 23 Sept. 1787	
William Prichard	8 Oct. 1789
Henry Powell	14 Oct. 1789
John Clunes	3 Nov. 1789
Rank in Army, 20 Sept. 1780	
William Thomas	26 Nov. 1789
George Sproule	9 Dec. 1789
Rank in Army, 26 June 1784	
Edward Codd..	9 Dec. 1789

Chaplains—

Name	Rank
William Winder	4 April 1765
George Bowe	5 Feb. 1776
James Manesty	24 Sept. 1787
Charles Morgan	24 Sept. 1787

Adjutants—

Name	Rank
George Westphall	26 Nov. 1784
Jas. Hamilton Gordon ..	24 Sept. 1787
Winkworth Tonge.. ..	24 Sept. 1787
William Warburton ..	24 Sept. 1787

Quartermasters—

Name	Rank
Robert Burton	12 April 1786
John Clarke	24 Sept. 1787
William Cooke	9 July 1788
Robert Eyre	12 Mar. 1789

Surgeons—

Name	Rank
James Henderson	10 Nov. 1775
James Wright	28 April 1784
Thos. Dickson Reid ..	7 May 1788
Edward Shannon	19 Mar. 1789

Regimentals—Red, facings blue, white
lace, 2 blue stripes.

Agents—Messrs. Ross and Ogilvie, Argyle
Street.

1791.

Four Battalions.

North America—West Indies.

Col.-in-Chief—

Name	Rank
Jeffery, Ld. Amherst, K.B.	7 Nov. 1768
Rank in Army, Gen.	19 Mar. 1778

Rank and Name.	Rank in Regiment.

Cols.-Commandant at—

Name	Rank in Regiment
Fred. Haldiman, K.B. ..	20 Oct. 1772
Rank in Army, Lt.-Gen.	29 Aug. 1777
Gabriel Christie	10 May 1786
Rank in Army, M.-Gen.	19 Oct. 1781
William Rowley	3 Oct. 1787
Rank in Army, M.-Gen.	19 Oct. 1781
James Rooke	20 Oct. 1788
Rank in Army, M.-Gen.	28 Sept. 1787

Lieut.-Colonels—

Name	Rank
Stephen Kemble	14 May 1778
Rank in Army, Col.	20 Nov. 1782
Peter Hunter	24 Sept. 1787
Rank in Army, 23 Nov. 1782	
James Adolphus Harris..	16 Jan. 1788
Wm. Goolay Strutt ..	18 Nov. 1790

Majors—

Name	Rank
Patrick Murray	6 Oct. 1784
George Benson	16 Jan. 1788
John Whitelocke	2 Oct. 1788
George Prevost	18 Nov. 1790

Captains—

Name	Rank
J. F. Wallet des Barres..	23 Sept. 1775
Rank in Army, Major	19 Mar. 1783
Benjamin Wickham ..	10 Aug. 1777
Geo. Ferdinand Loup ..	6 Oct. 1784
Richard Porter	26 Nov. 1784
Edward Davis..	23 Mar. 1785
Thomas Walker	4 Nov. 1785
Lachlan Maclean	8 Feb. 1786
Rank in Army, 17 Oct. 1782	
Duncan Mackintosh ..	2 June 1786
Rank in Army, 29 April 1783	
John Parr	5 July 1786
Frederick de Diemar ..	24 Sept. 1787
Rank in Army, 20 June 1778	
George Schneider	24 Sept. 1787
Rank in Army, 26 Dec. 1778	
James Eenyier	24 Sept. 1787
Rank in Army, 20 Oct. 1781	
Samuel Deviaines	24 Sept. 1787
Rank in Army, 15 Dec. 1782	
William Lachenwitz ..	24 Sept. 1787
Charles Ingram	26 Sept. 1787
William Martin	27 Sept. 1787
Robert Lethbridge.. ..	27 Sept. 1787
Frederick Gottsched ..	30 Sept. 1787
Fred. de Chambault ..	16 Jan. 1788
Rank in Army, 27 Sept. 1787	
James Bain	16 April 1788
Rank in Army, 14 May 1778	
John Thomas Buller ..	2 June 1788
John Will. Aug. Rouer..	18 June 1788
Rank in Army, Major	18 Nov. 1790
William Casby	11 Nov. 1789
Rank in Army, 18 Feb. 1789	
Frederick Maitland.. ..	2 Dec. 1789
Richard Dodgson	14 July 1790
Rank in Army, 27 Jan. 1783	
Alexander Graham ..	1 Sept. 1790
Rank in Army, 30 June 1790	
John Manners Kerr ..	10 Nov. 1790
John Lewis Prevost ..	26 Jan. 1791

Captain-Lieut. and Captains—

Name	Rank
David Gordon	30 Sept. 1787
Joseph Breitenbach ..	30 Sept. 1787

Rank and Name.	Rank in Regiment.
Capt.-Lieut. and Captains (contd.)—	
Isaac Hesselburg	17 Nov. 1790
Hon. Andrew Cochrane	10 Nov. 1790
Lieutenants—	
Ch. Lewis Th. Schoeckle	25 Dec. 1778
William von Borbeck	26 Dec. 1778
Charles Cratchley	27 Dec. 1778
William Floyer	17 Mar. 1779
Gabriel Gordon	26 Nov. 1784
John Campbell	26 Nov. 1784
John Lennox	26 Nov. 1784
James Bruere	6 April 1785
Samuel Kempthorne	10 Jan. 1787
Rank in Army,	20 Mar. 1783
Anthony Pasquada	24 Sept. 1787
Rank in Army,	25 June 1784
James Barnett	24 Sept. 1787
Edward Cartwright	25 Sept. 1787
Thomas Clarke	25 Sept. 1787
Frederick de Ver	26 Sept. 1787
William Claus	31 Oct. 1787
James Doskin	7 Nov. 1787
Rank in Army,	1 May 1781
William Robins	5 Dec. 1787
Francis Quarme	16 Jan. 1788
John Robertson	16 April 1788
Rank in Army,	28 Feb. 1787
Lewis Correvont	7 May 1788
Rank in Army,	15 Sept. 1780
William Tireman	14 May 1788
John de Lancey	28 May 1788
Rank in Army,	7 Feb. 1783
J. Randall Forster	25 June 1788
David Walker	1 Aug. 1788
Rank in Army,	28 Feb. 1788
Hender Molesworth	1 Oct. 1788
Ashton Warner	10 Oct. 1788
Fitzroy J. G. Maclean	15 Oct. 1788
Rank in Army,	19 June 1788
Hugh Fraser	24 April 1789
James Apthorpe	21 June 1789
Rank in Army,	1 Mar. 1782
Jacob Jordan	8 Oct. 1789
Francis Slater	14 Oct. 1789
Chas. Frederi A Piquett	26 Nov. 1789
George Fourneret	3 Dec. 1789
Samuel Oates	17 Mar. 1790
Andrew M'Can	14 April 1790
Rank in Army,	25 Dec. 1782
Robert Gordon	5 May 1790
Thomas Wallcott	30 July 1790
Edward Walsh	18 Aug. 1790
Rank in Army,	1 Feb. 1782
Rob. Adolphus Farmer	6 Oct. 1790
Rank in Army,	15 Sept. 1787
James Brown	2 Nov. 1790
Gordon Maxwell	5 Jan. 1791
Pinson Bonham	26 Jan. 1791
Ensigns—	
Derrell Cope	6 Apr. 17
Henry Le Moine	7 Feb. 1787
Rank in Army,	3 Oct. 1781
Alexander Fraser	24 Sept. 1787
Rank in Army,	17 Oct. 1782
Lewis Muller	29 Sept. 1787

Rank and Name.	Rank in Regiment.
Ensigns (continued)—	
—— Schneider	30 Sept. 1787
James Peachey	3 Oct. 1787
Samuel Hollandt	4 Oct. 1787
Welsh Hamilton Bunbury	24 Oct. 1787
Hamilton Fawcett	6 Dec. 1787
Daniel Nixon	16 Jan. 1788
Thomas Martin	22 Jan. 1788
Rank in Army,	25 Sept. 1787
James Abernethy	23 June 1788
John Kenney	1 Oct. 1788
Samuel Gibbs	20 Oct. 1788
Rank in Army,	8 Oct. 1783
—— Fitzgerald	12 Nov. 1789
Robert Robertson	9 May 1789
Rank in Army,	20 Sept. 1779
William Fraser	5 June 1789
John Campbell	28 Aug. 1789
Rank in Army,	24 Sept. 1787
William Pritchard	8 Oct. 1789
Henry Powlett	14 Oct. 1789
William Thomas	26 Oct. 1789
George Sproule	9 Dec. 1789
Rank in Army,	16 June 1783
Edward Cudd	9 Dec. 1789
Jenkins Cogan Williams	17 Mar. 1790
Peter Stewart Barclay	31 Mar. 1790
Clement Briggs	21 April 1790
Edmond Spalding	19 May 1790
Rank in Army,	12 Mar. 1781
William Neville Hurt	7 July 1790
Edward Draper	30 July 1790
Henry Pickering	8 Dec. 1790
Chaplains—	
George Bowe	5 Feb. 1770
James Manesty	24 Sept. 1787
William Leslie	29 Sept. 1790
Jean Fra. Micoville	10 Nov. 1790
Adjutants—	
George Westphall	26 Nov. 1784
Winkworth Tonge	24 Sept. 1787
William Warburton	24 Sept. 1787
Robert Gordon	7 April 1790
Quartermasters—	
Robert Burton	12 April 1786
John Clark	24 Sept. 1787
William Cook	9 July 1788
Isaac Germain	20 Dec. 1790
Surgeons—	
James Henderson	10 Nov. 1775
James Wright	28 April 1784
Thos. Dickson Reide	7 May 1789
Edward Shannon	19 Mar. 1789
Regimentals—Red, facings blue, white lace, 2 blue stripes.	
Agents—Messrs. Ross and Ogilvie, Argyle Street.	

1792.

Four Battalions.

North America—West Indies.

Colonel-in-Chief—
Jeffery, Lord Amherst,
K.B. .. 7 Nov. 1768
Rank in Army, Gen. 19 Mar. 1778

Rank and Name.	Rank in Regiment.
Col.-Commandant—	
Gabriel Christie	10 May 1786
Rank in Army, Maj.-Gen.	19 Oct. 1781
William Rowley	3 Oct. 1787
Rank in Army,	19 Oct. 1781
James Rooke	20 Oct. 1788
Rank in Army,	28 Sept. 1787
Alured Clarke..	8 July 1791
Rank in Army,	28 April 1790
Lieut.-Colonels—	
Stephen Kemble	14 May 1778
Rank in Army, Col.	20 Nov.
Peter Hunter	24 Sept. 1787
Rank in Army,	23 Nov. 1782
James Adolphus Harris..	16 Jan. 1788
(D) William Goodday Strutt	18 Nov. 1790
Majors—	
Patrick Murray	6 Oct. 1784
George Benson	16 Jan. 1788
George Prevost	18 Nov. 1790
William Gordon	30 Mar. 1791
Captains -	
J. F. Wallet des Barres..	23 Sept. 1775
Rank in Army, Major	19 Mar. 1783
Benjamin Wickham ..	10 Aug. 1777
George Ferdinand Loup..	6 Oct. 1784
Richard Porter	26 Nov. 1784
Edward Davis..	23 Mar. 1785
Thomas Walker	4 Nov. 1785
Lachlan Maclean	8 Feb. 1786
Rank in Army,	17 Oct. 1782
Duncan Mackintosh ..	2 June 1786
Rank in Army,	29 April 1783
John Parr	5 July 1786
Frederick de Diemar ..	24 Sept. 1787
Rank in Army,	20 June 1778
George Schneider	24 Sept. 1787
Rank in Army,	26 Dec. 1778
James Ecuyer	24 Sept. 1787
Rank in Army,	20 Oct. 1781
Samuel Devismes	24 Sept. 1787
Rank in Army,	15 Dec. 1782
William Lachenwitz ..	24 Sept. 1787
Charles Ingram	26 Sept. 1787
William Martin	27 Sept. 1787
Robert Lethbridge ..	27 Sept. 1787
Frederick Gottsched ..	30 Sept. 1787
Fred. de Chambault ..	16 Jan. 1788
Rank in Army,	27 Sept. 1787
James Bain	16 April 1788
Rank in Army,	14 May 1778
John Will. Aug. Romer..	18 June 1788
Rank in Army, Major	18 Nov. 1790
Frederick Maitland.. ..	2 Dec. 1789
Richard Dodgson	14 July 1790
Rank in Army,	27 Jan. 1783
John Manners Kerr ..	10 Nov. 1790
John Lewis Prevost ..	26 Jan. 1791
Henry Bethune Starke ..	31 Mar. 1791
Rank in Army,	3 Aug. 1785
Geo. Townsend Walker..	4 May 1791
Rank in Army,	13 Mar. 1789
John Bonamy..	10 Aug. 1791
Rank in Army,	24 Nov. 1790
Captain-Lieut. and Captains—	
David Gordon..	30 Sept. 1787

Rank and Name.	Rank in Regiment.
Capt.-Lieut. and Captains (contd.)—	
Joseph Breitenbach ..	30 Sept. 1787
Isaac Hesselberg	17 Mar. 1790
Hon. Andrew Cochran ..	10 Nov. 1790
Lieutenants—	
C. Lewis T. Schoedde ..	25 Dec. 1788
William von Borbeck ..	26 Dec. 1788
Gabriel Gordon	26 Nov. 1784
John Campbell	26 Nov. 1784
John Lennox	26 Nov. 1784
James Bruere..	6 April 1785
Samuel Kempthorne ..	10 Jan. 1787
Rank in Army,	20 Mar. 1783
Anthony Pasquada.. ..	24 Sept. 1787
Rank in Army,	25 June 1781
James Barrick..	24 Sept. 1787
Edward Cartwright ..	25 Sept. 1787
Thomas Clarke	25 Sept. 1787
Frederick de Vos	26 Sept. 1787
William Claus..	31 Oct. 1787
James Dodds	7 Nov. 1787
Rank in Army,	1 May 1781
William Robins	5 Dec. 1787
John Robertson	16 April 1788
Rank in Army,	28 Feb. 1787
Louis Correvont	17 May 1788
Rank in Army,	15 Sept. 1780
William Tireman	14 May 1788
John de Lancey	28 May 1788
Rank in Army,	7 Feb. 1783
J. Randall Forster.. ..	25 June 1788
David Walker..	1 Aug. 1788
Rank in Army,	28 Feb. 1788
Hender Molesworth ..	1 Oct. 1788
Ashton Warner	10 Oct. 1788
Rank in Army,	10 Aug. 1781
Fitzroy J. G. Maclean ..	15 Oct. 1788
Rank in Army,	19 June 1788
Hugh Fraser	24 April 1789
James Apthorpe	24 June 1789
Rank in Army,	1 Mar. 1782
Jacob Jordan	8 Oct. 1789
Francis Slater..	14 Oct. 1789
Chas. Fred. Piquett ..	26 Nov. 1789
George Fourneret	9 Dec. 1789
Samuel Cates	17 Mar. 1790
Andrew M'Can	14 April 1790
Rank in Army,	25 Dec. 1782
Robert Gordon	5 May 1790
Edward Walsh	18 Aug. 1790
Rank in Army,	1 Feb. 1782
James Brown	2 Nov. 1790
Gordon Maxwell	5 Jan. 1791
Pinson Bonham	26 Jan. 1791
Welsh Hamilton Bunbury	29 Mar. 1791
Henry Powlett	29 Mar. 1791
Julius Herring	30 Mar. 1791
Rank in Army,	12 Feb. 1783
William Thomas	13 April 1791
William Henry Mackenzie	13 July 1791
Rank in Army,	26 Mar. 1783
Alexander Fraser	20 July 1791
Archibald Grant	7 Sept. 1791
Rank in Army,	27 June 1777
Ensigns—	
Dorrell Cope	6 April 1785

Rank and Name.		Rank in Regiment.
Ensigns (continued)—		
Henry Le Mesne	..	7 Feb. 1778
Rank in Army,		3 Oct. 1781
Lewis Muller	..	29 Sept. 1787
—— Schneider	..	30 Sept. 1787
James Peachey	..	3 Oct. 1787
Samuel Hollandt	..	4 Oct. 1787
Hamilton Fawcett	..	6 Dec. 1787
Daniel Nixon	..	16 Jan. 1788
Thomas Martin	..	22 Jan. 1788
Rank in Army,		25 Sept. 1787
James Abernethy	..	25 June 1788
John Kenney	..	1 Oct. 1788
Samuel Gibbs	..	29 Oct. 1788
Rank in Army,		8 Oct. 1788
Robert Robertson	..	9 May 1789
Rank in Army,		29 Sept. 1779
William Fraser	..	5 June 1789
John Campbell	..	28 Aug. 1789
Rank in Army,		24 Sept. 1787
William Prachard	..	8 Oct. 1789
George Sprowle	..	9 Dec. 1789
Rank in Army,		26 June 1784
Edward Cobb	..	9 Dec. 1789
Jenkin Cogan Williams	..	17 Mar. 1790
Peter Stewart Barclay	..	31 Mar. 1790
Edmund Spalding	..	19 May 1790
Rank in Army,		12 Mar. 1781
William Neville Hart	..	7 June 1790
Edward Draper	..	30 July 1790
Henry Pickering	..	8 Dec. 1790
Jacob Topson	..	3 Feb. 1791
Thomas M'Kee	..	29 Mar. 1791
Robert Glynn Griffith	..	30 Mar. 1791
Rank in Army,		10 Oct. 1787
Lucius Burne	..	5 Oct. 1791
The Hipolite Des Rivieres		12 Oct. 1791
Peter Long Conway	..	19 Oct. 1791
Jas. Ad. Oughton Clarke		16 Nov. 1791
Rank in Army,		23 July 1782
Chaplains—		
George Bowe	..	5 Feb. 1776
James Manesty	..	24 Sept. 1787
William Leslie	..	29 Sept. 1789
Jean Fra Muserville	..	10 Nov. 1789
Adjutants—		
George Westphall	..	26 Nov. 1784
Wadsworth Tonge	..	24 Sept. 1787
William Warburton	..	2 Sept. 1787
Robert Gordon	..	7 April 1790
Quartermasters—		
Robert Barton	..	12 April 1786
John Clark	..	24 Sept. 1787
William Cook	..	9 July 1789
Isaac Germain	..	29 Dec. 1789
Surgeons—		
James Henderson	..	10 Nov. 1775
James Wright	..	28 April 1784
Thos. Parkson Reale	..	7 May 1788
Edward Shannon	..	19 Mar. 1789

Regimentals: Red, facings blue, white lace, 2 blue stripes.
Agents—Messrs. Ross and Ogilvie, Argyle Street.

1793.

Four Battalions.

North America—West India—England.

Rank and Name.		Rank in Regiment.
Col.-in-Chief—		
Jeffery, Ld. Amherst, K.B.		7 Nov. 1768
Rank in Army, Gen.		19 Mar. 1778
Cols.-Commandant—		
Gabriel Christie	..	10 May 1786
Rank in Army, Maj.-Gen.		19 Oct. 1781
William Rowley	..	3 Oct. 1787
Rank in Army, Maj.-Gen.		19 Oct. 1781
James Rooke	..	20 Oct. 1788
Rank in Army,		28 Sept. 1787
Alured Clarke	..	8 July 1788
Rank in Army,		28 April 1790
Lieut.-Colonel—		
Stephen Kemble	..	14 May 1778
Rank in Army, Col.		20 Nov. 1782
Peter Hunter	..	24 Sept. 1787
Rank in Army,		23 Nov. 1782
James Adolphus Harris	..	16 Jan. 1788
Gerrit Fisher	..	25 April 1792
Majors—		
Patrick Murray	..	6 Oct. 1784
George Prevost	..	18 Nov. 1790
William Gordon	..	30 Mar. 1791
Hon. John Elphinstone	..	14 Sept. 1792
Captains—		
J. F. Wallet des Barres	..	23 Sept. 1775
Rank in Army, Major		19 Mar. 1783
Benjamin Wackham	..	10 Aug. 1777
George Ferdinand Loup	..	6 Oct. 1784
Richard Porter	..	26 Nov. 1784
Edward Davis	..	13 Mar. 1785
Lachlan Maclean	..	8 Feb. 1786
Rank in Army,		17 Oct. 1782
Duncan Mackintosh	..	2 June 1786
Rank in Army,		23 April 1782
John Parr	..	5 July 1786
Frederick de Diemar	..	24 Sept. 1787
Rank in Army,		29 June 1778
George Schneider	..	24 Sept. 1787
Rank in Army,		26 Dec. 1778
James Kenyon	..	24 Sept. 1787
Rank in Army,		20 Oct. 1781
Samuel Devismes	..	24 Sept. 1787
Rank in Army,		15 Dec. 1782
William Luckenwitz	..	24 Sept. 1787
Charles Ingram	..	26 Sept. 1787
Wm. Martin	..	27 Sept. 1787
Robert Lethbridge	..	27 Sept. 1787
Frederick Gottschoel	..	30 Sept. 1787
Fred de Chambault	..	16 Jan. 1788
Rank in Army,		27 Sept. 1787
James Bain	..	16 April 1788
Rank in Army,		14 May 1788
John Will. Aug. Romer	..	18 June 1788
Rank in Army, Major		18 Nov. 1790
Frederick Maitland	..	2 Dec. 1789
Richard Dodgson	..	14 July 1790
Rank in Army,		27 Jan. 1783
John Manners Kerr	..	10 Nov. 1790
Geo. Townsend Walker	..	4 May 1791
Rank in Army,		13 Mar. 1789

Rank and Name.	Rank in Regiment.

Captains (continued)—

John Bonamy .. .. .. 10 Aug. 1791
   Rank in Army, 21 Nov. 1790
Lewis Briggs .. .. .. 24 Aug. 1792
   Rank in Army, 27 Aug. 1785
George Dunlop .. .. 13 Sept. 1792
   Rank in Army, 14 Sept. 1783
Francis Slater .. .. .. 18 Sept. 1792

Capt.-Lieut. and Captains—

David Gordon.. .. .. 30 Sept. 1787
Joseph Breitenbach .. 30 Sept. 1787
Isaac Hesselburg .. .. 17 Mar. 1790
Hon. Andrew Cochrane.. 10 Nov. 1790

Lieutenants—

Ch. Lewis Th. Schoelde.. 25 Dec. 1778
William von Borbeck .. 26 Dec. 1778
Gabriel Gordon .. .. 26 Nov. 1784
John Campbell .. .. 26 Nov. 1784
John Lennox .. .. .. 26 Nov. 1784
James Bruere.. .. .. 6 April 1715
Anthony Pasquala .. 24 Sept. 1787
   Rank in Army, 25 June 1784
James Barrick.. .. .. 24 Sept. 1787
Edward Cartwright .. 25 Sept. 1787
Thomas Clarke .. .. 25 Sept. 1787
Frederick de Vos .. .. 26 Sept. 1787
William Claus .. .. 31 Oct. 1787
James Dodds .. .. .. 7 Nov. 1787
   Rank in Army, 1 May 1784
William Robins .. .. 5 Dec. 1787
John Robertson .. .. 16 April 1788
   Rank in Army, 28 Feb. 1787
William Tireman .. .. 14 May 1788
John de Lancey .. .. 28 May 1788
   Rank in Army, 7 Feb. 1784
J. Randall Forster .. 25 June 1788
David Walker.. .. .. 1 Aug. 1788
   Rank in Army, 28 Feb. 1788
Hender Molesworth .. 1 Oct. 1788
Fitzroy J. G. Maclean .. 15 Oct. 1788
   Rank in Army, 19 June 1788
James Apthorpe .. .. 21 June 1789
   Rank in Army, 1 Mar. 1782
Jacob Jordan .. .. .. 8 Oct. 1789
Chas. Frederick Piquett.. 26 Nov. 1789
George Fourneret .. .. 9 Dec. 1789
Samuel Cates .. .. .. 17 Mar. 1790
Andrew M'Lean .. .. 14 April 1790
   Rank in Army, 25 Dec. 1782
Robert Gordon .. .. 5 May 1790
Edward Walsh .. .. 18 Aug. 1790
   Rank in Army, 1 Feb. 1782
James Brown .. .. .. 2 Nov. 1790
Gordon Maxwell .. .. 5 Jan. 1791
Pinson Bonham .. .. 26 Jan. 1791
Welsh Hamilton Bunbury 29 Mar. 1791
Henry Powlett .. .. 29 Mar. 1791
Julines Herring .. .. 30 Mar. 1791
   Rank in Army, 12 Feb. 1783
Wm. Hen. Mackenzie .. 13 July 1791
   Rank in Army, 26 Mar. 1783
Alexander Fraser .. .. 20 July 1791
Archibald Grant .. .. 7 Sept. 1791
   Rank in Army, 27 June 1783
Cogan Williams .. .. 25 April 1792

Rank and Name.	Rank in Regiment.

Lieutenants (continued)—

James Abernethy .. .. 8 Aug. 1792
John Clements .. .. 18 Sept. 1792
   Rank in Army, 21 June 1783
William Neville Hart .. 18 Sept. 1792
Henry Pickering .. .. 4 Oct. 1792
William Prichard .. .. 5 Dec. 1792

Ensigns—

Dorrell Cope .. .. .. 6 April 1785
Henry Le Moine .. .. 7 Feb. 1787
   Rank in Army, 3 Oct. 1781
Lewis Muller .. .. .. 29 Sept. 1787
——— Schneider .. .. 30 Sept. 1787
James Peachey .. .. 3 Oct. 1787
Samuel Hollandt .. .. 4 Oct. 1787
Hamilton Fawcett .. .. 6 Dec. 1787
Daniel Nixon .. .. .. 16 Jan. 1788
Thomas Martin .. .. 22 Jan. 1788
   Rank in Army, 25 Sept. 1787
John Kenney .. .. .. 1 Oct. 1788
Robert Robertson .. .. 9 May 1789
   Rank in Army, 30 Sept. 1779
William Fraser .. .. 5 June 1789
John Campbell .. .. 28 Aug. 1789
   Rank in Army, 24 Sept. 1787
George Sproule .. .. 9 Dec. 1789
   Rank in Army, 26 June 1783
Edward Codd .. .. .. 9 Dec. 1790
Jacob Tonson .. .. .. 9 Feb. 1791
Thomas M'Kee .. .. 29 Mar. 1791
Robert Glynn Griffith .. 30 Mar. 1791
   Rank in Army, 10 Oct. 1787
Lucius Barne .. .. .. 5 Oct. 1791
Tho. Hipolite des Rivieres. 12 Oct. 1791
Peter Luny Conway .. 19 Oct. 1791
Jas. Ad. Oughton Clarke. 16 Nov. 1791
   Rank in Army, 24 July 1792
Fra. G. de Montmollin .. 20 Jan. 1792
William Cunningham .. 30 May 1792
Joseph Peters .. .. .. 22 Oct. 1792
Alexander Campbell .. 21 Nov. 1792
Martin Falkes Edgell .. 22 Nov. 1792
Benj. King Lavicount .. 28 Nov. 1792
Henry Barston .. .. 5 Dec. 1792
John M. Reid.. .. ..

Chaplains—

George Bowe .. .. .. 5 Feb. 1776
James Maucely .. .. 24 Sept. 1787
William Leslie .. .. 29 Sept. 1790
Jean Fra. Mieoville .. 10 Nov. 1790

Adjutants—

George Westphall .. .. 26 Nov. 1784
Winkworth Tonge.. .. 24 Sept. 1787
William Warburton .. 28 Sept. 1787
Robert Gordon .. .. 7 April 1790

Quartermasters—

Robert Barton .. .. 12 April 1786
John Clarke .. .. .. 24 Sept. 1787
William Cook .. .. .. 9 July 1788
Isaac Germain .. .. 28 Dec. 1790

Surgeons—

James Henderson .. .. 10 Nov. 1775
James Wright.. .. .. 28 April 1774

Rank and Name.	Rank in Regiment.
Surgeons (continued)—	
Joseph Dowse	8 Aug. 1792
Edward Shannon	19 Mar. 1789

Regimentals—Red, facings blue, white lace, 2 blue stripes.

Agents—Messrs. Ross and Ogilvie, **Argyle** Street.

1794.

Four Battalions.

North America—West Indies—England.

Col.-in-Chief—
Jeffery, 1st **Amherst**, K.B. 7 Nov. 1768
 Rank in Army, Gen. 19 Mar. 1778

Cols.-Commandant—
Gabriel Christie .. .. 10 May 1786
 Rank in Army, Lt.-Gen. 12 Oct. 1793
William Rowley .. .. 3 Oct. 1787
 Rank in Army, 12 Oct. 1793
James Rooke .. .. .. 20 Oct. 1788
 Rank in Army, Maj.-Gen. 28 Sep. 1787
Alured Clarke .. .. 8 July 1791
 Rank in Army, 28 Apr. 1790

Lieut.-Colonels—
Peter Hunter .. .. 24 Sept. 1787
 Rank in Army, Col. 12 Oct. 1793
James Adolph. Harris .. 16 Jan. 1788
Gerrit Fisher .. .. 25 April 1792
Hon. Vere Poulett .. .. 13 May 1793

Majors—
George Prevost .. .. 18 Nov. 1790
Hon. John Elphinstone .. 14 Sept. 1792
Duncan Mackintosh .. 20 April 1793
Frederick Gottschied .. 15 July 1793

Captains—
J. F. Wallet des Barres.. 23 Sept. 1775
 Rank in Army, Major 19 Mar. 1784
Benjamin Wickham .. 10 Aug. 1777
Richard Porter .. .. 26 Nov. 1784
Edward Davis .. .. 13 Mar. 1785
Lachlan Maclean .. .. 8 Feb. 1786
 Rank in Army, 17 Oct. 1782
John Parr .. .. 5 July 1786
James Ecuyer .. .. 24 Sept. 1787
 Rank in Army, 20 Oct. 1781
William Lacheuwitz .. 24 Sept. 1787
Charles Ingram .. .. 26 Sept. 1787
William Martin .. .. 27 Sept. 1787
Robert Lethbridge .. 27 Sept. 1787
Fred. de Chanteault .. 16 Jan. 1788
 Rank in Army, 27 Sept. 1787
Jn. Will. Aug. Renner .. 18 June 1788
 Rank in Army, Major 18 Nov. 1790
Frederick Maitland .. 2 Dec. 1789
 Rank in Army, 24 Aug. 1793
Isaac Hesselburg .. .. 17 Mar. 1790
Richard Dodgson .. .. 14 July 1790
 Rank in Army, 27 Jan. 1784
John Manners Kerr .. 14 July 1790
G. Townsend Walker .. 4 May 1791
 Rank in Army, 13 Mar. 1790
John Bonamy .. .. 10 Aug. 1791
 Rank in Army, 24 Nov. 1790

Rank and Name.	Rank in Regiment.
Captains (continued)—	
Lewis Briggs	24 Aug. 1792
Rank in Army,	27 Aug. 1785
Francis Slater	18 Sept. 1792
Daniel Robertson	27 Feb. 1793
Rank in Army, Major	18 Nov. 1790
Julius Herring	19 Mar. 1793
J. Randall Forster ..	22 May 1793
James Dodd	7 June 1793
Pinson Bonham	9 June 1793
John de Lancey	5 July 1793
David Walker	14 July 1793

Capt.-Lieut. and Captains—
David Gordon .. .. 30 Sept. 1787
C. Lewis T. Schoedde .. 20 April 1793
F. R. J. G. Maclean .. 15 July 1793
William Robins .. .. 7 Nov. 1793

Lieutenants—
William de Barbeck .. 27 Dec. 1787
Gabriel Gordon .. .. 26 Nov. 1784
John Campbell .. .. 26 Nov. 1784
John Lennox .. .. 26 Nov. 1784
James Barrick.. .. 24 Sept. 1787
Edward Cartwright .. 25 Sept. 1787
Thomas Clarke .. .. 25 Sept. 1787
Frederick de Vos .. 26 Sept. 1787
William Claus.. .. 31 Oct. 1787
John Robertson .. .. 16 April 1788
William Freeman .. 14 May 1788
 Rank in Army, 28 Feb. 1787
Hender Molesworth .. 1 Oct. 1788
Jacob Jordan .. .. 8 Oct. 1789
C. Frederick Picquett .. 26 Nov. 1789
George Fourneret .. 9 Dec. 1789
Samuel Oates .. .. 17 Mar. 1790
Andrew M'Can .. .. 14 April 1790
 Rank in Army, 25 Dec. 1782
Robert Gordon .. .. 5 May 1790
Edward Walsh .. .. 18 Aug. 1790
 Rank in Army, 1 Feb. 1782
James Brown .. .. 2 Nov. 1790
Gordon Maxwell .. 5 Jan. 1791
W. H. Bunbury .. .. 29 Mar. 1791
Henry Poulett .. .. 29 Mar. 1791
W. H. Mackenzie .. 13 July 1791
 Rank in Army, 26 Mar. 1783
Alexander Fraser .. 20 July 1791
Archibald Grant .. .. 7 Sept. 1791
 Rank in Army, 27 June 1777
Cogan Williams .. .. 25 April 1792
James Abernethy .. 8 Aug. 1792
John Clement .. .. 18 Sept. 1792
 Rank in Army, 21 June 1783
William Neville Hart .. 18 Sept. 1792
William Prichard .. 5 Dec. 1792
Jacob Freeson .. .. 19 Mar. 1793
Edward Codd .. .. 20 April 1793
Lewis Mailer .. .. 22 May 1793
George Sproule .. .. 9 June 1793
Darrell Cope .. .. 21 June 1793
G. C. Schoeder .. .. 11 July 1793
P. Lucy Conway .. .. 15 July 1793
John Campbell .. .. 24 July 1793
F. G. de Montmollin .. 24 July 1793
Benj. K. Lavosseur .. 15 Aug. 1793

Rank and Name.	Rank in Regiment.

Lieutenants (continued)—

Richard H. Temple	.. 30 Oct. 1793
	Rank in Army, 22 Sept. 1784
M. Folkes Edgell ..	.. 7 Nov. 1793

Ensigns—

Henry Le Moine	.. 7 Feb. 1787
	Rank in Army, 3 Oct. 1781
Samuel Hollandt ..	.. 4 Feb. 1787
Daniel Nixon ..	.. 16 Jan. 1788
Robert Robertson ..	.. 9 May 1789
	Rank in Army, 20 Sept. 1779
William Fraser	.. 5 June 1789
Thomas M'Kee ..	.. 29 Mar. 1789
Roll. Glynn Griffith	.. 30 Mar. 1789
	Rank in Army, 10 Oct. 1787
Lucius Burne ..	.. 5 Oct. 1789
T. Hip. des Rivieres	.. 22 Oct. 1789
J. A. Oughton Clarke	.. 16 Nov. 1789
	Rank in Army, 24 July 1782
Wm. Cunningham ..	.. 30 May 1792
Joseph Peters.. ..	.. 22 Oct. 1792
Henry Barstow	.. 5 Dec. 1792
John M. Reid ..	.. 19 Dec. 1792
William Cooke ..	.. 16 Jan. 1793
Joseph Kelly	.. 19 Mar. 1793
Kenelm Chandler ..	.. 20 Mar. 1793
Chas. de Salaberry..	.. 10 April 1793
Wm. Plenderleath ..	.. 20 April 1793
Lewis Schneider ..	.. 15 May 1793
Rl. Edwin Worsley ..	.. 11 June 1793
Gab. Plenderleath ..	.. 24 July 1793
John B. Vischer ..	.. 25 July 1793
W. S. Plenderleath	.. 7 Nov. 1793
Charles Skene.. ..	.. 7 Nov. 1793

Chaplains—

Charles Bowe	.. 5 Feb. 1776
James Manesty ..	.. 24 Sept. 1787
William Leslie ..	.. 29 Sept. 1787
Jean Fra. Mieoville ..	.. 10 Nov. 179

Adjutants—

George Westphall ..	.. 26 Nov. 1784
Winkworth Tonge.. ..	.. 24 Sept. 1787
William Warburton ..	.. 2 Sept. 1787
Robert Gordon ..	.. 7 April 1790

Quartermasters—

Robert Burton ..	.. 12 April 1786
Isaac Germain ..	.. 28 Dec. 1790
George Johnstone ..	.. 16 Jan. 1793
—— Bell..	.. 12 June 1793

Surgeons—

James Henderson ..	.. 10 Nov. 1775
Joseph Dowse ..	.. 8 Aug. 1792
Edward Shannon ..	.. 19 Mar. 1789
Thomas Wright ..	.. 16 Oct. 1793

Regimentals Red, facings blue, white lace, 2 blue stripes.

Agents—Messrs. Ross and Ogilvie, Argyle Street.

1795.

North America West Indies—England.

Four Battalions.

Col.-in-Chief—

| Jeffery, Ld. Amherst, K.B. | 7 Nov. 1768 |
| | *Rank in Army,* Gen. 19 Mar. 1778 |

Rank and Name.	Rank in Regiment.

Cols.-Commandant—

Gabriel Christie ..	.. 10 May 1786
	Rank in Army, Lt.-Gen. 12 Oct. 1793
William Rowley	.. 3 Oct. 1787
	Rank in Army, 12 Oct. 1793
James Rooke	.. 20 May 1788
	Rank in Army, Maj.-Gen .28 Sept. 1787
Thomas Carleton	.. 6 Aug. 1794
	Rank in Army, 12 Oct. 1793

Lieut.-Colonels—

Peter Hunter	.. 24 Sept. 1787
	Rank in Army, Col. 12 Oct. 1793
James Adolph. Harris ..	16 Jan. 1788
Hon. Vere Poulett.. ..	.. 13 May 1793
John Ritchie	.. 17 Feb. 1794
Hon. John Elphinstone..	20 July 1794
George Prevost	.. 6 Aug. 1794
	Rank in Army, 1 Mar. 1794

Majors—

Duncan Mackintosh	.. 20 April 1793
Frederick Gottschel	.. 15 July 1793
Lachlan Maclean ..	.. 5 Aug. 1793
John Bommny.. ..	.. 27 Aug. 1793

Captains—

J. F. Wallet des Barres..	23 Sept. 1775
	Rank in Army, Lt.-Col. 1 Mar. 1794
Richard Porter ..	.. 29 Nov. 1784
Edward Davis.. ..	.. 13 Mar. 1785
John Parr	.. 5 July 1786
James Ecuyer ..	.. 24 Sept. 1787
	Rank in Army, Major 1 Mar. 1794
William Lachenwitz ..	.. 24 Sept. 1787
Charles Ingram ..	.. 26 Sept. 1787
William Martin ..	.. 27 Sept. 1787
Robert Lethbridge ..	.. 27 Sept. 1787
Fredl. de Chambault ..	16 Jan. 1788
	Rank in Army, 27 Sept. 1787
John Wm. Aug. Romer..	18 June 1788
	Rank in Army, Lt.-Col. 1 Mar. 1794
Frederick Maitland ..	2 Dec. 1789
	Rank in Army, Major 21 Aug. 1783
Richard Dodgson ..	11 July 1790
	Rank in Army, Major 1 Mar. 1794
G. Townsend Walker ..	4 May 1791
	Rank in Army, 13 Mar. 1789
Francis Slater.. ..	.. 18 Sept. 1792
Daniel Robertson ..	.. 27 Feb. 1793
	Rank in Army, Lt.-Col. 1 Mar. 1794
James Herring ..	.. 19 Mar. 1793
C. Lewis T. Schoside ..	20 April 1793
Randall Forster ..	.. 22 May 1793
James Dodd	.. 7 June 1793
John de Lancey ..	.. 5 July 1793
David Walker.. ..	.. 14 July 1793
F. J. G. Maclean ..	.. 15 July 1793
James Bruere	.. 9 Oct. 1793
Henry Powlett ..	.. 2 July 1794
Warren Johnston	.. 27 Aug. 1794
	Rank in Army, 15 Feb. 1794
Dorrell Cope	.. 27 Aug. 1794
Pat. Chas. O'Connor ..	15 Oct. 1794
	Rank in Army, 8 May 1793

Captain-Lieut. and Captains—

| Robert Gordon .. .. | .. 2 Nov. 1793 |
| Gabriel Gordon .. | .. 10 July 1794 |

Rank and Name.	Rank in Regiment.
Capt.-Lieut. and Captains (contd.)—	
Robert Owen	11 July 1794
Frederick de Vos	7 Aug. 1794
Lieutenants—	
John Campbell	26 Nov. 1784
John Lennox	26 Nov. 1784
James Barrick.. ..	24 Sept. 1787
Edward Cartwright ..	25 Sept. 1787
Thomas Clarke	25 Sept. 1787
William Claus.. ..	31 Oct. 1787
John Robertson	16 April 1788
Rank in Army, 28 Feb. 1787	
William Tronson ..	14 May 1788
Jacob Jordan	8 Oct. 1789
C. Frederick Piquett ..	26 Nov. 1789
George Fourneret ..	9 Dec. 1789
Samuel Cates	17 Mar. 1790
Andrew M'Can ..	14 April 1790
Rank in Army, 25 Dec. 1782	
Edward Walsh	18 Aug. 1790
Rank in Army, 1 Feb. 1782	
James Brown	2 Nov. 1790
Gordon Maxwell ..	5 Jan. 1791
W. H. Bunbury	29 Mar. 1791
Alexander Fraser ..	29 July 1791
Archibald Grant ..	7 Sept. 1791
Rank in Army, 27 June 1777	
James Abernethy ..	8 Aug. 1792
William Pritchard..	5 Dec. 1792
Jacob Tonson	19 Mar. 1793
Edward Codd	20 April 1793
Lewis Muller	22 May 1793
John Campbell ..	24 July 1793
F. G. de Montenollin ..	24 July 1793
Benj. K. Lovecount ..	15 Aug. 1793
Daniel Nixon	9 Oct. 1793
Richard H. Temple ..	30 Oct. 1793
Rank in Army, 22 Sept. 1793	
Geo. William Barr..	18 Dec. 1784
Rank in Army, 4 May 1785	
William Cunningham ..	2 Jan. 1794
Joseph Peters	24 Mar 1794
John Alexander Reid ..	2 April 1794
Lewis Schreuder ..	8 May 1794
Samuel Hollandt ..	10 July 1794
James Christie ..	25 July 1794
Lucius Burne	7 Aug 1794
Henry Harstow ..	12 Aug 1794
Charles de Salaberry ..	25 Aug 1794
Ensigns—	
Henry Le Moine ..	7 Feb 1787
Rank in Army, 31 Oct. 1781	
Robert Robertson ..	9 May 1789
Rank in Army, 20 Sept 1779	
William Fraser ..	5 June 1789
Thomas M'Kee ..	29 Mar 1794
Robt. Glyan Griffith ..	30 Mar 1794
Rank in Army, 10 Oct. 1787	
J. Hip. des Rivieres ..	22 Oct 1793
Joseph Kelly.. ..	19 Mar 1794
Kenelm Chandler ..	29 Mar 1794
William Plenderleath ..	29 April 1793
Wm. S. Plenderleath ..	7 Nov 1793
J... Ross	1 Feb 1794
A'xdan E. Gough ..	14 Feb 1794
—— Chalmers ..	24 Mar 1794

Rank and Name.	Rank in Regiment.
Ensigns (continued)—	
Chidley Coote.. ..	8 May 1794
Thomas Fothergill ..	13 May 1794
William Powell ..	20 Aug. 1794
Henry Hendy.. ..	25 Aug. 1794
James Rivers	3 Sept. 1794
—— Thompson ..	1 Oct. 1794
Chaplains—	
George Bowe	5 Feb. 1776
James Manesty ..	24 Sept. 1787
William Leslie	29 Sept. 1787
Jean Frn. Micoville..	10 Nov. 1790
Adjutants—	
George Westphall ..	26 Nov. 1784
William Warburton ..	2 Sept. 1787
Robert Gordon ..	7 April 1790
James Brown	24 Feb. 1794
Quartermasters—	
Robert Burton	12 April 1786
Isaac Germain.. ..	28 Dec. 1790
George Johnstone ..	26 Jun. 1793
William Marlton ..	7 Jan. 1794
Surgeons—	
James Henderson ..	10 Nov. 1775
Joseph Bowne.. ..	8 Aug. 1792
Edward Shannon ..	19 Mar. 1789
Thomas Wright ..	26 Oct. 1793

Regimentals—Red, facings blue, white lace, 2 blue stripes.

Agents—Messrs Ross and Ogilvie, Argyle Street.

1796.

North America—West Indies—England.

Four Battalions.

Col. in Chief—	
Jeffery, Ld Amherst, K.B.	7 Nov. 1768
Rank in Army, Gen. 19 Mar. 1778	
Cols.-Commandant—	
Gabriel Christie ..	10 May 1786
Rank in Army, Lt.-Gen. 12 Oct. 1793	
William Rowley ..	3 Oct. 1787
Rank in Army, Maj-Gen. 12 Oct. 1793	
James Rooke	20 Oct. 1788
Rank in Army, Maj.-Gen 28 Sept. 1787	
Thomas Carleton ..	6 Aug. 1794
Rank in Army, 12 Oct. 1793	
Lieut. Colonels—	
Peter Hunter	24 Sept. 1787
Rank in Army, Maj.-Gen. 26 Feb. 1795	
James Adolp. Harris ..	16 Jan. 1778
Rank in Army, Col. 26 Feb. 1795	
Hon. Vere Poulett ..	13 May 1793
Hon. John Elphinstone..	29 July 1794
George Prevost ..	6 Aug. 1794
Rank in Army, 1 Mar. 1794	
Duncan Mackintosh ..	1 Sept. 1795
Frederick Gottschol ..	2 Sept. 1795
Martin Hunter ..	12 Jan. 1796
Rank in Army, 19 July 1794	
Majors—	
Lachlan Maclean ..	5 Aug. 1794
Rank in Army, 1 Mar. 1794	

Rank and Name.	Rank in Regiment.	Rank and Name.	Rank in Regiment.
Majors (continued)—		**Lieutenants** (continued)—	
John Bonnmy	27 Aug. 1794	Benj. K. Laviecount ..	15 Aug. 1793
Richard Porter	1 Sept. 1795	Daniel Nixon	9 Oct. 1773
Rank in Army, 6 May 1795		Richard H. Temple ..	30 Oct. 1793
James Ecuyier	2 Sept. 1795	*Rank in Army,* 22 Sept. 1783	
Rank in Army, 1 Mar. 1794		Geo. William Barr	18 Dec. 1793
William Lachenwitz ..	3 Sept. 1795	*Rank in Army,* 4 May 1785	
Rank in Army, 6 May 1795		James Christie	25 July 1794
Charles Ingram	4 Sept. 1795	Lucius Burne	7 Aug. 1794
Rank in Army, 6 May 1795		Henry Barlow	12 Aug. 1794
William Martin	5 Sept. 1795	Francis M. Miller ..	16 Nov. 1794
Rank in Army, 6 May 1795		Thomas M'Kee	5 Feb. 1795
Robert Lethbridge	25 Nov. 1795	Henry Lemoine	18 Mar. 1795
Rank in Army, 6 May 1795		William Fraser	18 Mar. 1795
George Townsend Walker 25 Nov. 1795		Adrain E. Gough	18 Mar. 1795
Captains—		Chidley Coote	18 Mar. 1795
J. F. Wallet des Barres ..	23 Sept. 1775	John Lewis Bontems ..	2 July 1795
Rank in Army, Lt.-Col. 1 Mar. 1794		Kenelm Chandler	8 July 1795
Fred. de Chambault ..	16 Jan. 1788	J. Hip. des Rivieres ..	12 Aug. 1795
Rank in Army, Maj. 6 May 1795		William Plenderleath ..	15 Aug. 1795
J. Wm. Aug. Romer ..	18 June 1788	Thomas Fothergill	15 Aug. 1795
Rank in Army, Lt.-Col. 1 Mar. 1794		Henry Hendy	14 Sept. 1795
Richard Dodgson	11 July 1790	William Warburton ..	15 Sept. 1795
Rank in Army, Major 1 Mar. 1794		Frederick Holland	16 Sept. 1795
Francis Slater	18 Sept. 1792	Edward Cope	17 Sept. 1795
Daniel Robertson	27 Feb. 1793	Robert Hazen	18 Sept. 1795
Rank in Army, Lt.-Col. 1 Mar. 1794		Charles Hitch Woolley ..	5 Oct. 1795
Julines Herring	19 Mar. 1793	John Gunthorpe	17 Oct. 1795
C. Lewis T. Schoedde ..	20 April 1793	George Westphall	21 Oct. 1795
James Dodd	7 June 1793	William Muelton	2 Dec. 1795
John de Lancey	5 July 1793	James Ximenes	15 Dec. 1795
David Walker	11 July 1793	William Floyer	16 Dec. 1795
James Bruere	9 Oct. 1793	*Rank in Army,* 17 Mar. 1779	
Gabriel Gordon	10 July 1794	Louis Foy	16 Dec. 1795
Frederick de Vos ..	7 Aug. 1794	*Rank in Army,* 10 July 1782	
Warren Johnston ..	27 Aug. 1794	David Joly	16 Dec. 1795
Rank in Army, 15 Feb. 1794		George Johnstone	16 Dec. 1795
Dorrell Cope	27 Aug. 1794	Henry Jeffrey Flower ..	16 Dec. 1795
James Cockburne ..	10 Nov. 1794	Henry Austin	16 Dec. 1795
Edward Walsh	16 Nov. 1794	Nicholas Maigny	16 Dec. 1795
William Claus	5 Feb. 1795	William Abram	16 Dec. 1795
Edward Codd	15 Aug. 1795	John Heslop	16 Dec. 1795
John Lennox	1 Sept. 1795	J. Parry Jones	30 Dec. 1795
Edward Cartwright ..	8 Sept. 1795	*Rank in Army,* 2 April 1795	
Thomas Clarke	9 Sept. 1795	John Reynolds	12 Jan. 1796
Alex. Jekyll Chalmers ..	9 Sept. 1795	*Rank in Army,* 31 Aug. 1795	
John Robertson	10 Sept. 1795	V. G. de Hompesch ..	12 Jan. 1796
James Brown	12 Sept. 1795	**Ensigns—**	
Jacob Tonson	13 Sept. 1795	Robert Glynn Griffith ..	30 Mar. 1791
Lewis Muller	14 Sept. 1795	*Rank in Army,* 10 Oct. 1787	
John Campbell	15 Sept. 1795	—— Thompson	1 Oct. 1794
Charles St. Ours	2 Dec. 1795	Peter M'Arthur	10 Jan. 1795
Rank in Army, 22 May 1783		James M'Arthur	10 Jan. 1795
William Tireman	16 Dec. 1795	James Massey	1 July 1795
Jacob Jordan	16 Dec. 1795	Thomas Penton	15 July 1795
George Fourneret ..	16 Dec. 1795	Rich. Jackson Mapender 15 July 1795	
Samuel Cates	16 Dec. 1795	—— Norton	4 Sept. 1795
Andrew M'Can	16 Dec. 1795	John Fraser	16 Sept. 1795
Capt.-Lieut. and Captains—		M. S. Walrund	17 Oct. 1795
Gordon Maxwell	16 Dec. 1795	Charles Shearer	21 Oct. 1795
Alexander Fraser	16 Dec. 1795	Richard Hudson	4 Nov. 1795
Archibald Grant	16 Dec. 1795	*Rank in Army,* 31 July 1795	
William Pritchard	16 Dec. 1795	Nobles Johnson	4 Nov. 1795
Lieutenants—		George Morse	4 Nov. 1795
James Abernethy	8 Aug. 1792	R. B. Sullivan	4 Nov. 1795
F. G. de Montmellin ..	24 July 1793	Thomas Ferrar	2 Dec. 1795

Rank and Name.	Rank in Regiment.
Ensigns (continued)—	
—— Clarke	.. 16 Dec. 1795
James O'Neil	.. 16 Dec. 1795
Robert Paterson ..	.. 16 Dec. 1795
James Cuthbertson..	.. 16 Dec. 1795
Charles Cranstone Dixon	16 Dec. 1795
Meenor Scholey ..	.. 16 Dec. 1795
Arthur O'Neil.. ..	.. 16 Dec. 1795
Edward Cooke ..	.. 16 Dec. 1795
John Campbell ..	.. 16 Dec. 1795
John Fred. Townley ..	.. 23 Dec. 1795
Rank in Army, 31 Dec. 1794	
Donald O'Neil ..	.. 23 Dec. 1795
John Monro ..	.. 23 Dec. 1795
M. Rosa M'Pherson ..	27 Dec. 1795
Bartholomew Naigle ..	.. 30 Dec. 1795
Rank in Army, 10 July 1794	
John Watson	30 Dec. 1795
Rank in Army, 22 Aug. 1794	
Hon. George M'Donald..	30 Dec. 1795
Rank in Army, 28 Aug. 1794	
—— Gillespie ..	.. 30 Dec. 1795
Rank in Army, 22 Dec. 1794	
—— Nares	.. 30 Dec. 1795
Rank in Army, 1 July 1795	
Richard Wall ..	.. 12 Jan. 1796
Thomas Bunting ..	.. 12 Jan. 1796

Chaplains—

George Rowe	.. 6 Feb. 1776
James Morecly ..	.. 24 Sept. 1787
Jean Francois Micoulh..	10 Nov. 1789
—— Archer	.. 16 Sept. 1795

Adjutants—

William Warburton ..	2 Sept. 1787
William Bell ..	10 Dec. 1794
James Brown ..	1 Mar. 1795
George Johnston ..	2 July 1795

Quartermasters—

Isaac Vernson ..	.. 28 Dec. 1780
—— Fitzgerald ..	2 July 1795
Allan Cameron ..	9 Sept. 1795
B. Radou ..	6 Jan. 1796

Surgeons—

James Henderson ..	10 Nov. 1775
Joseph Dowse ..	8 Aug. 1792
Thomas Wright ..	16 Oct. 1793
James Anderson ..	7 Nov. 1794

Regimentals— Red, facings blue, white lace and 2 blue stripes.

Agents—Messrs. Ross and Ogilvie, Argyle Street.

1797.

Four Battalions.

North America—West Indies—England

Col.-in-Chief—
Jeffery Ld Amherst, K.B. 7 Nov. 1768
Rank in Army, Field Mar. 30 July 1796

Rank and Name.	Rank in Regiment.
Cols.-Commandant—	
Gabriel Christie	10 May 1786
Rank in Army, Lt.-Gen. 12 Oct. 1793	
William Rowley	3 Oct. 1787
Rank in Army, 12 Oct. 1793	
Thomas Carleton ..	6 Aug. 1794
Rank in Army, Maj.-Gen. 12 Oct. 1793	
Peter Hunter	2 Aug. 1796
Rank in Army, 26 Feb. 1795	
Lieut.-Colonels—	
James Adolphus Harris..	16 Jan. 1788
Rank in Army, Col. 26 Feb. 1795	
Hon. John Elphinstone,.	20 July 1794
George Prevost ..	6 Aug. 1794
Rank in Army, 1 Mar. 1794	
Duncan Mackintosh ..	1 Sept. 1795
Frederick Gottschied ..	2 Sept. 1795
Martin Hunter ..	12 Jan. 1796
Rank in Army, 19 July 1794	
John de Berniere	5 Mar. 1796
Rank in Army, 17 Feb. 1795	
John Robert Napier ..	10 Aug. 1796
Majors—	
Lachlan Maclean	5 Aug. 1794
Rank in Army, 1 Mar. 1794	
John Bonamy.. ..	27 Aug. 1794
Geo. Townsend Walker..	28 Aug. 1794
Richard Porter ..	1 Sept. 1795
Rank in Army, 6 May 1795	
William Martin	5 Sept. 1795
Rank in Army, 6 May 1795	
Robert Lethbridge ..	25 Nov. 1795
Rank in Army, 6 May 1795	
Francis Slater Rebow ..	20 Feb. 1796
Fredl. de Choubault ..	3 Aug. 1796
Rank in Army, 6 May 1795	
Captains—	
J. F. Wallet des Barres	23 Sept. 1775
Rank in Army, Lt.-Col. 1 Mar. 1794	
Jas. Wm. Aug. Romer ..	18 June 1788
Rank in Army, Lt.-Col. 1 Mar. 1794	
Richard Dodgson ..	14 July 1790
Rank in Army, Major 1 Mar. 1794	
Daniel Robertson ..	27 Feb. 1793
Rank in Army, Lt.-Col. 1 Mar. 1794	
James Herring ..	19 Mar. 1793
C. Lewis T. Schoedde ..	20 April 1793
James Dodd	7 June 1793
John de Lancey ..	5 July 1793
David Walker ..	11 July 1793
James Bruere.. ..	9 Oct. 1793
Gabriel Gordon ..	10 July 1794
Frederick de Vos ..	7 Aug. 1794
Warren Johnston ..	27 Aug. 1794
Rank in Army, 15 Feb. 1784	
Dowell Cope	27 Aug. 1794
James Cockburne ..	10 Nov. 1794
Edward Walsh ..	16 Nov. 1794
William Claus ..	5 Feb. 1795
Edward Cobb.. ..	15 Aug. 1795
Edward Cartwright ..	8 Sept. 1795
Thomas Clarke ..	9 Sept. 1795
Alex. Jekyll Chalmers..	9 Sept. 1795
John Robertson	10 Sept. 1795
James Brown	12 Sept. 1795
Jacob Tonson	13 Sept. 1795

Rank and Name.	Rank in Regiment.
Captains (continued)—	
Lewis Muller	14 Sept. 1795
John Campbell	15 Sept. 1795
John Lennox	21 Oct. 1795
William Tireman	16 Dec. 1795
Jacob Jordan	16 Dec. 1795
George Fourneret	16 Dec. 1795
Samuel Cates	16 Dec. 1795
Andrew M'Can	16 Dec. 1795
Thomas M'Kee	20 Feb. 1796
James Faly	27 Feb. 1796
Rank in Army, Major	1 Mar. 1794
John Bradshaw	5 April 1796
George Sinclair	12 April 1796
Colin Campbell	8 June 1796
Rank in Army,	17 Feb. 1794
Thomas Lidderdale ..	29 July 1796
Rank in Army,	5 Sept. 1794
Malcolm Fraser	18 Aug. 1796
Rank in Army, Major	1 Mar. 1794
Capt.-Lieut. and Captains—	
Gorman Maxwell	16 Dec. 1795
Alexander Fraser	16 Dec. 1795
Archibald Grant	16 Dec. 1795
William Pritchard	20 Jan. 1796
Lieutenants—	
Benj. K. Lavicount ..	15 Aug. 1793
Daniel Nixon	9 Oct. 1793
Richard H. Temple ..	30 Oct. 1793
Rank in Army,	22 Sept. 1783
Geo. William Barr ..	18 Dec. 1793
Rank in Army,	4 May 1783
James Christie	25 July 1794
Lucius Burne	7 Aug. 1794
Henry Barstow	12 Aug. 1794
Charles de Saluberry ..	25 Aug. 1794
Francis M. Miller	16 Nov. 1794
Henry Lemoine	18 Mar. 1795
William Fraser	18 Mar. 1795
Adrian F. Gough	18 Mar. 1795
Chidley Coote	18 Mar. 1795
John Lewis Bontems ..	2 July 1795
Kenelm Chandler	8 July 1795
T. Hip. des Rivieres ..	12 Aug. 1795
William Plenderleath ..	15 Aug. 1795
Thomas Fothergill	15 Aug. 1795
Henry Hendy	14 Sept. 1795
William Warburton ..	15 Sept. 1795
Frederick Holland	16 Sept. 1795
Edward Cope	17 Sept. 1795
James Masse	17 Sept. 1795
Robert Hazen	18 Sept. 1795
John Gunthrope	17 Oct. 1795
George Westphall	21 Oct. 1795
William Marlton	2 Dec. 1795
James Ximines	15 Dec. 1795
William Floyer	16 Dec. 1795
Rank in Army,	17 Mar. 1779
Thomas Foy	16 Dec. 1795
Rank in Army,	24 Sept. 1782
David Joly	16 Dec. 1795
Hon. Henry Jeff. Flower	16 Dec. 1795
Henry Austin	16 Dec. 1795
Nicholas Maigny	16 Dec. 1795
John Heslop	16 Dec. 1795
J. Parry James	30 Dec. 1795
Rank in Army,	2 April 1798

Rank and Name.	Rank in Regiment.
Lieutenants (continued)—	
John Reynolds	12 Jan. 1796
Rank in Army,	31 Aug. 1795
Daniel Gordon	18 Jan. 1796
Chr. Francis Schneider ..	18 Jan. 1796
Theod. Christ. Esaw ..	18 Jan. 1796
Edward Charles Stuart ..	18 Jan. 1796
V. G. de Hompesch ..	20 Jan. 1796
James O'Neal	2 Feb. 1796
Rank in Army,	29 June 1780
George B. Little	2 Feb. 1796
Rank in Army,	11 Oct. 1794
William B. Montford ..	2 Feb. 1796
Rank in Army,	11 Oct. 1794
George Patrick Sutton ..	2 Feb. 1796
Rank in Army,	1 Nov. 1794
John Bealy	2 Feb. 1796
John Cummings	5 Mar. 1796
Rank in Army,	10 Feb. 1780
John O'Reily	5 Mar. 1796
Rank in Army,	30 Dec. 1794
Charles Thompson	5 Mar. 1796
Thomas Penton	5 Mar. 1796
Charles Shearer	5 Mar. 1796
Richard Henry Turner ..	5 Mar. 1796
William Parker	12 Mar. 1796
Rank in Army,	16 June 1794
William Disney	19 Mar. 1796
—— Haverkam	19 Mar. 1796
Alexander Andrews ..	5 April 1796
John Holland	12 April 1796
Edward Norton	14 May 1796
Hubert Seymour	17 May 1796
Rank in Army,	24 June 1795
James Gillespie	18 May 1796
John Campbell	15 June 1796
John Cummings	29 July 1796
Edward Cook	5 Oct. 1796
M. S. Walrond	5 Oct. 1796
Ensigns—	
Robert Glynn Griffith ..	30 Mar. 1791
Rank in Army,	10 Oct. 1787
Peter M'Arthur	10 June 1795
James M'Arthur	10 June 1795
John Fraser	16 Sept. 1795
Thomas Durham	1 Dec. 1795
—— Clarke	16 Dec. 1795
James O'Neil	16 Dec. 1795
Robert Paterson	16 Dec. 1795
James Curbutbson	16 Dec. 1795
Charles Cranstoun Dixon	16 Dec. 1795
Meeson Scholey	16 Dec. 1795
Arthur O'Neil	16 Dec. 1795
—— Espre	16 Dec. 1795
John Fred. Townley ..	23 Dec. 1795
Rank in Army,	31 Dec. 1794
Donald O'Neil	23 Dec. 1795
M. Ross M'Pherson ..	23 Dec. 1795
Anthony Wall	12 Jan. 1796
Thomas Bunting	20 Jan. 1796
John D. Plancher	5 Mar. 1796
John L. Gallie	5 Mar. 1796
—— Williams	5 Mar. 1796
Emanuel Harcourt	19 Mar. 1796
Henry Winchcombe ..	19 Mar. 1796
Richard Carrique	5 April 1796
Alexander Fordyce	3 May 1796

Rank and Name.	Rank in Regiment.
Ensigns (continued)—	
—— Bolime	19 May 1796
Dennis Maguire ..	17 May 1796
George Murray ..	15 June 1796
Rank in Army,	2 Dec. 1795
D. Faggart	2 July 1796
Francis Polhill ..	10 Aug. 1796
—— German ..	26 Aug. 1796
—— Whiting ..	5 Oct. 1796
George Pearson ..	11 Oct. 1796
Charles Hazlewood..	11 Oct. 1796
Chaplains—	
George Bowe	5 Feb. 1776
James Mancety ..	24 Sept. 1787
Jean Francis Micoville .	10 Nov. 1790
—— Archer ..	16 Sept. 1795
Adjutants—	
William Warburton ..	2 Sept. 1787
William Bell	10 Dec. 1794
James Brown	1 Mar. 1795
George Johnston ..	2 July 1795
Quartermasters—	
Isaac Germain.. ..	28 Dec. 1790
—— Fitzgerald ..	2 July 1795
Allan Cameron ..	9 Sept 1795
B. Radon	6 Jan. 1796
Surgeons—	
James Henderson ..	10 Nov. 1775
Joseph Dowse.. ..	8 Aug. 1792
Thomas Wright ..	16 Oct. 1793
James Anderson ..	7 Nov. 1794

Regimentals—Red, facings blue, white
lace, 2 blue stripes.

Agents—Messrs. Ross and Ogilvie, Argyle
Street.

1798.

Four Battalions.

England—North America   West Indies
Ireland.

Col.-in-Chief

H.R.H. Fred., Duke of	
York, K.G...	23 Aug. 1797
Rank in Army, Field-Mar	10 Feb. 1795

Cols.-Commandant—

Gabriel Christie	10 May 1786
Rank in Army, Lt. Gen.	12 Oct. 1793
William Rowley	3 Oct. 1787
Rank in Army,	12 Oct. 1793
Thomas Carleton	6 Aug. 1794
Rank in Army, Maj.-Gen.	12 Oct. 1793
Peter Hunter	2 Aug. 1796
Rank in Army,	26 Feb. 1795

Lieut.-Colonels

James Adolph Harris ..	16 Jan. 1788
Rank in Army, Col.	26 Feb. 1795
Hon. John Elphinstone..	20 July 1791
George Prevost	6 Aug. 1794
Rank in Army,	1 Mar. 1794
Duncan Mackintosh ..	1 Sept. 1795
Frederick Gottsched ..	2 Sept. 1795
Martin Hunter	12 Jan. 1796
Rank in Army,	19 July 1794
John de Bernicre	5 Mar. 1796
Rank in Army,	17 Feb. 1795

Rank and Name.	Rank in Regiment.
Lieut.-Colonel (continued)—	
John Robert Napier ..	10 Aug. 1796
Majors—	
Lachlan Maclean	5 Aug. 1794
Rank in Army,	1 Mar. 1794
John Bonamy	27 Aug. 1794
George Townsend Walker	28 Aug. 1794
Robert Lethbridge.. ..	25 Nov. 1795
Rank in Army,	6 May 1795
John Hughes	16 Feb. 1797
Rank in Army,	6 June 1794
Frederick de Vos	22 May 1797
Tho. Phillip Ainslie ..	17 Aug. 1797
Rank in Army,	19 Sept. 1795
Julius Herring	25 Oct. 1797
Captains—	
J. F. Wallet des Barres..	23 Sept. 1775
Rank in Army, Lt.-Col.	1 Mar. 1794
Jn. Will. Aug. Romer ..	18 June 1788
Rank in Army, Lt.-Col.	1 Mar. 1794
Richard Dodgson	14 July 1790
Rank in Army, Major	1 Mar. 1794
Daniel Robertson	27 Feb. 1793
Rank in Army, Lt.-Col.	1 Mar. 1794
C. Lewis T. Schoedde ..	20 April 1793
James Dodd	7 June 1793
John De Lancey	5 July 1793
David Walker.. ..	14 July 1793
James Bruere	9 Oct. 1793
Gabriel Gordon	10 July 1794
Warren Johnson	27 Aug. 1794
Rank in Army,	15 Feb. 1794
Dorrell Cope	27 Aug. 1794
James Cockburne	10 Nov. 1794
Edward Walsh	16 Nov. 1794
William Chas.. ..	5 Feb. 1795
Edward Codd	15 Aug. 1795
John Lennox	7 Sept. 1795
Edward Cartwright ..	8 Sept. 1795
Thomas Clarke	9 Sept. 1795
Alex. Jekyll Chalmers ..	9 Sept. 1795
John Robertson	10 Sept. 1795
John Campbell	15 Sept. 1795
William Tireman	16 Dec. 1795
George Fourneret	16 Dec. 1795
Samuel Cates	16 Dec. 1795
Andrew M'Can	16 Dec. 1795
Gordon Maxwell	16 Dec. 1795
Thomas M'Kee	20 Feb. 1796
James Fahy	27 Feb. 1796
Rank in Army, Major	1 Mar. 1794
John Bradshaw	5 April 1796
Colin Campbell	8 June 1796
Rank in Army,	17 Feb. 1794
Thomas Ladderdale ..	29 July 1796
Rank in Army,	5 Sept. 1794
Malcolm Fraser	18 Aug. 1796
Rank in Army, Major	1 Mar. 1794
T. Hippes des Rivieres..	23 Mar. 1797
Cottrel Mercer	22 May 1797
Rank in Army, Major	1 Mar. 1794
Henry Young..	7 June 1797
Rank in Army,	6 Nov. 1794
Hon. Henry Jeff. Flower	26 July 1797
Robert Forsyth	20 Sept. 1797
Rank in Army,	10 June 1795
M. Walrund	11 Oct. 17..

K

Captain-Lieut. and Captain—

Rank and Name.	Rank in Regiment.
Alexander Fraser	16 Dec. 1795
Archibald Grant	16 Dec. 1795
William Pritchard.. ..	20 Jan. 1796
James Grant	25 April 1797
Rank in Army,	1 April 1795

Lieutenants—

Benj. K. Lavicount ..	15 Aug. 1793
Daniel Nixon	9 Oct. 1793
Richard H. Temple ..	30 Oct. 1793
Rank in Army,	22 Sept. 1783
Geo. William Barr.. ..	18 Dec. 1793
Rank in Army,	4 May 1785
James Christie	25 July 1794
Henry Barstow	12 Aug. 1794
Charles du Saluberry ..	25 Aug. 1794
Francis M. Miller	16 Nov. 1794
Henry Lemoine	18 Mar. 1795
William Fraser	18 Mar. 1795
Adrian K. Gough	18 Mar. 1795
Chidley Coote..	18 Mar. 1795
John Lewis Bontems ..	2 July 1795
Kenelem Chandler.. ..	8 July 1795
William Plenderleath ..	15 Aug. 1795
Thomas Fothergill	15 Aug. 1795
William Warburton ..	15 Sept. 1795
James M'Arthur	17 Sept. 1795
James Massey..	17 Sept. 1795
Robert Hazen..	18 Sept. 1795
John Greenthorpe	17 Oct. 1795
William Marlton	2 Dec. 1795
James Ximines	15 Dec. 1795
William Floyer	16 Dec. 1795
Rank in Army,	17 Mar. 1779
Thomas Foy	16 Dec. 1795
Rank in Army,	24 Sept. 1782
David Joly	16 Dec. 1795
Henry Austin..	16 Dec. 1795
Nicolas Magny	16 Dec. 1795
John Heslop	16 Dec. 1795
John Reynolds	12 Jan. 1796
Rank in Army,	31 Aug. 1795
Daniel Gordon	18 Jan. 1796
Theo. Christopher Esaw.	18 Jan. 1796
V. G. de Hompesch ..	20 Jan. 1796
John Beatty	2 Feb. 1796
John Cummings	5 Mar. 1796
Rank in Army,	10 Feb. 1780
John O'Reily	5 Mar. 1796
Rank in Army,	30 Dec. 1794
Charles Thompson.. ..	5 Mar. 1796
Thomas Penton	5 Mar. 1796
Charles Shearer	5 Mar. 1796
Richard Henry Turner ..	5 Mar. 1796
William Parker	12 Mar. 1796
Rank in Army,	16 June 1794
William Disney	19 Mar. 1796
Alexander Andrews ..	5 April 1796
Edward Norton	14 May 1796
Hubert Seymour	17 May 1796
Rank in Army,	24 June 1795
James Gillespie	18 May 1796
John Campbell	15 June 1796
John Cummings	29 July 1796
Thomas Durham	1 Sept. 1796
Edward Cook	5 Oct. 1796

Lieutenants (continued)—

Rank and Name.	Rank in Regiment.
Peter M'Arthur	4 Jan. 1797
James Cuthbertson.. ..	5 Jan. 1797
Arthur O'Neale	26 Jan. 1797
Francis Polhill	9 Feb. 1797
George Cartwright.. ..	2 Mar. 1797
Anthony Wall	6 April 1797
James Bunting	7 April 1797
William M'Intosh	12 April 1797
Benjamin Clarke	11 May 1797
—— de Visme	12 May 1797
—— de Mangin	14 May 1797
Louis d'Espres	22 May 1797
Alexander Ross	22 May 1797
W. H. Queast	23 May 1797
Thomas Cates..	15 June 1797
George Holmes	9 Aug. 1797
Thomas Henderson ..	9 Aug. 1797
Cha. Cranstoun Dixon ..	24 Aug. 1797
J. Edwards	9 Nov. 1799

Ensigns—

Robert Glynn Griffiths..	30 Mar. 1791
Rank in Army,	10 Oct. 1787
John Fraser	16 Sept. 1795
Donald M'Neil	23 Dec. 1795
John D. Plancher	5 Mar. 1796
John L. Gillie	5 Mar. 1796
—— Williams	5 Mar. 1796
Henry Winchcombe ..	19 Mar. 1796
—— Bolme	10 May 1796
Dennis Maguire	17 May 1796
George Murray	15 June 1796
Rank in Army,	2 Dec. 1795
—— German..	26 Aug. 1796
—— Whiling..	5 Oct. 1796
Charles Haslewood.. ..	20 Oct. 1796
John Fargues..	23 Nov. 1796
—— Rogers	23 Nov. 1796
William Walther	5 Jan. 1797
Thos. Rowley Swiney ..	6 Jan. 1797
John P. Walker	30 Mar. 1797
James Erskine Bell ..	6 April 1797
—— De Cameres	6 April 1797
John Donaldson	7 April 1797
William Fitzgerald ..	1 May 1797
John Allan	3 May 1797
Rank in Army,	26 Oct. 1796
—— Kennart	11 May 1797
William Peacock	23 May 1797
Timothy Thornhill.. ..	25 June 1797
Henry Pringle	1 July 1797
Samuel Brewster	24 Aug. 1797
Rank in Army,	6 Sept. 1795
Lewis Amédée de Noé ..	24 Aug. 1797
Falkner Phillips	18 Oct. 1797
Thomas Hutchins	25 Oct. 1797
Thomas Walsh	25 Oct. 1797

Adjutants—

William Warburton ..	2 Sept. 1787
William Bell	10 Dec. 1794
—— Fitzgerald	1 Sept. 1796
John Heslop..	23 Feb. 1797

Quartermasters—

Isaac Germain	28 Dec. 1790
Allan Cameron	9 Sept. 1795
B. Radon	6 Jan. 1796
C. Ludam	1 Sept. 1796

Rank and Name.	Rank in Regiment.
Surgeons—	
James Henderson	10 Nov. 1775
Thomas Wright ..	16 Oct. 1793
Alexander M'Dougall ..	1 Sept. 1796
Thomas Carter	7 June 1797
Assistant-Surgeons—	
Thomas Hutton ..	25 April 1797
Anthony Murray	25 June 1797
Regimentals—Red, facings blue, white	
lace and blue stripes.	
Agents—Messrs. Cox and Greenwood,	
Craig's Court.	

1799.

Six Battalions.

England—West Indies—North America—
Ireland.

Col.-in-Chief—	
H.R.H. Fred., Duke **of**	
York, K.G.	23 Aug. 1797
Rank in Army, Field-Mar.	10 Feb. 1793
Cols.-Commandant—	
Gabriel Christie	10 May 1786
Rank in Army, Gen.	1 Jan. 1798
William Rowley ..	3 Oct. 1787
Rank in Army, Gen.	1 Jan. 1798
Thomas Carleton	6 Aug. 1794
Rank in Army, Lt.-Gen.	1 Jan. 1798
Peter Hunter ..	2 Aug. 1796
Rank in Army, Maj.-Gen.	26 Feb. 1795
William Morshead ..	30 Dec. 1797
Rank in Army, Maj. Gen.	26 Feb. 1795
Lieut.-Colonels—	
James Adolph. Harris ..	16 Jan. 1788
Rank in Army, Maj.-Gen.	1 Jan. 1798
George Prevost ..	6 Aug. 1794
Rank in Army, Col.	1 Jan. 1798
Duncan Mackintosh ..	1 Sept. 1795
Martin Hunter ..	12 Jan. 1796
Rank in Army,	19 July 1794
John Robert Napier ..	10 Aug. 1796
George William Ramsay	30 Dec. 1797
Fred Barnade Rottenburg	30 Dec. 1797
Robert Crauford ..	30 Dec. 1797
Henry Cooper.. ..	30 Dec. 1797
William Dowdeswell ..	18 Jan. 1798
Rank in Army, Col.	26 Jan. 1797
John Hughes	5 April 1798
Majors—	
Lachlan Maclean	5 Aug. 1794
Rank in Army, Lt.-Col.	1 Jan. 1798
Robert Lethbridge ..	25 Nov. 1795
Rank in Army,	6 May 1795
Frederick de Vos ..	22 May 1792
Thomas Philip Amslie ..	17 Aug. 1797
Rank in Army,	19 Sept. 1795
George Lewis de Virnis .	30 Dec. 1797
—— Dorsner ..	30 Dec. 1797
—— Mosheim	30 Dec. 1797
—— Creznelky	30 Dec. 1797
—— Streicher.. ..	30 Dec. 1797
Gervase Ramey ..	8 Mar. 1798
Edmund Burke ..	19 Mar. 1798
Warren Johnson ..	6 Sept. 1798
John Campbell	20 Dec. 1798

Rank and Name.	Rank in Regiment.
Captains—	
J. F. Wallet des Barres..	23 Sept. 1775
Rank in Army, Col.	1 Jan. 1798
Julines Herring	19 Mar. 1793
C. Lewis T. Schoedde ..	20 April 1793
James Dodd	7 June 1793
John de Lancey	5 July 1793
David Walker..	14 July 1793
Gabriel Gordon	10 July 1794
Dorrell Cope	27 Aug. 1794
James Cockburne	10 Nov. 1794
William Claus..	5 Feb. 1795
Edward Codd.. ..	15 Aug. 1795
John Lennox	7 Sept. 1795
Edward Cartwright ..	8 Sept. 1795
Thomas Clarke	9 Sept. 1795
John Robertson	10 Sept. 1795
William Tireman	16 Dec. 1795
George Fourneret	16 Dec. 1795
Samuel Cates	16 Dec. 1795
Andrew McCan	16 Dec. 1795
Gordon Maxwell	16 Dec. 1795
Thomas McKee	20 Feb. 1796
James Fahy	27 Feb. 1796
Rank in Army, Lt.-Col.	1 Jan. 1798
John Bradshaw	5 April 1796
Colin Campbell	8 June 1796
Rank in Army,	17 Feb. 1794
Thomas Lidderdale ..	29 July 1796
Rank in Army,	5 Sept. 1794
Malcolm Fraser	18 Aug. 1796
Rank in Army, Maj.	1 Mar. 1794
T. Hippo. des Rivieres ..	23 Mar. 1797
Robert Forsyth	20 Sept. 1797
Rank in Army,	10 June 1795
Maine Walrond	11 Oct. 1797
—— Rumpler.. ..	30 Dec. 1797
—— Desgranges	30 Dec. 1797
G. Paulus de Gitens ..	30 Dec. 1797
Lumb. Lewis de Weire ..	30 Dec. 1797
—— Glutner	30 Dec. 1797
Henry Roberfeld	30 Dec. 1797
Fred. Ernest de Gerardy	30 Dec. 1797
L. de Villers Masburgh..	30 Dec. 1797
Ant. Aug. Baron d'Erp..	30 Dec. 1797
Lewis Schneider	30 Dec. 1797
—— Veroli	30 Dec. 1797
—— Huxle	30 Dec. 1797
—— Mortmann	30 Dec. 1797
—— Gintl	30 Dec. 1797
—— Grautt	30 Dec. 1797
—— Ronnige	30 Dec. 1797
—— Subock	30 Dec. 1797
—— Emmenhausen ..	30 Dec. 1797
—— Galalle	30 Dec. 1797
Rank in Army,	13 Oct. 1796
—— Haberkorn	30 Dec. 1797
—— de Gitens	30 Dec. 1797
—— Valnort.. ..	30 Dec. 1797
—— de la Houssaye ..	30 Dec. 1797
—— Count Byland ..	30 Dec. 1797
—— Schwartz.. ..	30 Dec. 1797
—— Bernll	30 Dec. 1797
—— Intorm	30 Dec. 1797
—— Vorstadt	30 Dec. 1797
—— Crest	30 Dec. 1797

K 2

Rank and Name.	Rank in Regiment.
Captains (continued) —	
—— St. Mart	30 Dec. 1797
—— Raymond ..	30 Dec. 1797
—— Turiac	30 Dec. 1797
—— Maissaig.. ..	30 Dec. 1797
—— Count Rouvray ..	30 Dec. 1797
—— Fogasse	30 Dec. 1797
—— Schouberg ..	30 Dec. 1797
—— de Estenne ..	30 Dec. 1797
Count de Seyn and Witt-	30 Dec. 1797
genstein	
—— de Blumenstein	29 Mar. 1798
A. F. Duncker ..	29 Mar. 1798
—— de Roggendorff	24 April 1798
—— Francis Gomer	25 April 1798
Thomas Morrison ..	31 May 1798
Benedict Simon ..	19 July 1798
G. Bussche ..	13 Sept. 1798
William Raymond ..	11 Oct. 1798
Thomas Walker ..	24 Oct. 1798
William Marlton ..	25 Oct. 1798
Edward Kelly.. ..	22 Nov. 1798
George Pearson ..	20 Dec. 1798
Thomas Kavanagh	
Rank in Army,	1 Oct. 1794
Charles Lloyd	
Anthony de Berzel	
Robert Beresford	
Rank in Army,	25 Sept. 1796
Captain-Lieut. and Captains—	
Alexander Fraser ..	16 Dec. 1795
Archibald Grant ..	16 Dec. 1795
William Pritchard ..	20 Jan. 1796
James Grant	25 April 1797
Rank in Army,	1 April 1795
—— Hellerick.. ..	30 Dec. 1797
Lieutenants—	
Daniel Nixon	9 Oct. 1793
Richard H. Temple ..	30 Oct. 1793
Rank in Army,	22 Sept. 1783
James Christie ..	25 July 1794
Henry Barstow ..	12 Aug. 1794
Charles de Salaberry ..	25 Aug. 1794
Henry Lemoine ..	18 Mar. 1795
William Fraser ..	18 Mar. 1795
Adrian E. Gough ..	18 Mar. 1795
John Lewis Bontems ..	2 July 1795
Kenelm Chandler ..	8 July 1795
William Plenderleath ..	15 Aug. 1795
William Warburton ..	15 Sept. 1795
James M'Arthur ..	17 Sept. 1795
James Massey.. ..	17 Sept. 1795
Robert Hazen	18 Sept. 1795
John Gunthorpe ..	17 Oct. 1795
William Floyer ..	16 Dec. 1795
Rank in Army,	17 Mar. 1779
Thomas Fox	16 Dec. 1795
Rank in Army,	24 Sept. 1782
David Joly	16 Dec. 1795
John Heslop	16 Dec. 1795
Theod. Christ. Esaw ..	18 Jan. 1796
John Beatty	2 Feb. 1796
John O'Reilly.. ..	5 Mar. 1796
Rank in Army,	30 Dec. 1794
Charles Thompson..	5 Mar. 1796
Thomas Penton	5 Mar. 1796

Rank and Name.	Rank in Regiment
Lieutenants (continued) —	
Charles Shearer ..	5 Mar. 1796
William Disney ..	19 Mar. 1796
Alexander Andrews ..	5 April 1796
Edward Norton ..	14 May 1796
Hubert Seymour ..	17 May 1796
Rank in Army,	24 June 1795
James Gillespie ..	18 May 1796
John Campbell ..	15 June 1796
John Cummings ..	29 July 1796
Thomas Durham ..	1 Sept. 1796
Edward Cook	5 Oct. 1796
Peter M'Arthur ..	4 Jan. 1797
George Cartwright..	2 Mar. 1797
Anthony Wall ..	6 April 1797
James Bunting ..	7 April 1797
Benjamin Clarke ..	11 May 1797
—— De Visme ..	12 May 1797
—— De Mangin ..	14 May 1797
Louis D'Espres ..	22 May 1797
Alexander Ross ..	22 May 1797
W. H. Queast.. ..	23 May 1797
Thomas Cates.. ..	15 June 1797
Thomas Henderson ..	9 Aug. 1797
Charles Cranstoun Dixon	24 Aug. 1797
Falkener Phillips ..	7 Dec. 1797
Charles de Kinzinger ..	30 Dec. 1797
—— Patier	30 Dec. 1797
—— de Renauld ..	30 Dec. 1797
Gabriel Burer.. ..	30 Dec. 1797
—— Schmidt	30 Dec. 1797
William Lewis de Virna .	30 Dec. 1797
Peter W. de Haren ..	30 Dec. 1797
George Frederick de Virna	30 Dec. 1797
—— McLeod	30 Dec. 1797
Aug. Viscount de Maim-	30 Dec. 1797
bourg	
L. de Bosse	30 Dec. 1797
L. Baron de H. Hugenpoet	30 Dec. 1797
John Anthony Woolff ..	30 Dec. 1797
Peter Frederick Blassire .	30 Dec. 1797
Frederick William B. de	30 Dec. 1797
Gilse	
Adolphus Munsthal ..	30 Dec. 1797
—— Vendt	30 Dec. 1797
—— Erhardt	30 Dec. 1797
—— Sister	30 Dec. 1797
—— Franchufin ..	30 Dec. 1797
—— Ratsenhausen ..	30 Dec. 1797
—— Bertner	30 Dec. 1797
—— Hoffman.. ..	30 Dec. 1797
—— Krien	30 Dec. 1797
—— Hauffeger ..	30 Dec. 1797
—— Suger	30 Dec. 1797
—— Langsdorff ..	30 Dec. 1797
—— Ellett	30 Dec. 1797
—— Wackenstein ..	30 Dec. 1797
—— Vanderbrouch ..	30 Dec. 1797
—— Berzel	30 Dec. 1797
—— Bader	30 Dec. 1797
Lewis Inturn	30 Dec. 1797
Frederick Inturn ..	30 Dec. 1797
—— Colbert	30 Dec. 1797
—— Bennat	30 Dec. 1797
—— Saurberg	30 Dec. 1797
—— Apenlier	30 Dec. 1797

Rank and Name.	Rank in Regiment.
Lieutenants (continued)—	
—— Hamelin	30 Dec. 1797
—— de Conders ..	30 Dec. 1797
—— Hantz	30 Dec. 1797
—— Maleuffe	30 Dec. 1797
—— Scheding.. ..	30 Dec. 1797
—— Mauriage ..	30 Dec. 1797
—— de Bellot.. ..	30 Dec. 1797
—— de Vigny.. ..	30 Dec. 1797
Sebastian Crozant ..	30 Dec. 1797
—— Killenpach ..	30 Dec. 1797
—— Stapleton ..	30 Dec. 1797
John Crozant	30 Dec. 1797
—— Connesin.. ..	30 Dec. 1797
—— d'Arequi.. ..	30 Dec. 1797
—— d'Haleu	30 Dec. 1797
—— Craft	30 Dec. 1797
—— Ammon	23 Jan. 1798
W. Wright	8 Mar. 1798
Rank in Army, 25 Mar. 1796	
James Burkett ..	8 Mar. 1798
Rank in Army, 5 Sept. 1796	
Hubert de Salve ..	29 Mar. 1798
—— Frankisson ..	29 Mar. 1798
—— Brook ..	29 Mar. 1798
Charles Hinckeldy..	26 April 1798
Joseph Baron Munster ..	25 April 1798
—— Hugon ..	25 April 1798
John Fergurs	17 May 1798
Patrick O'Brien ..	24 May 1798
Rank in Army, 27 May 1796	
John Thomas Cussack ..	31 May 1798
Rank in Army, 2 Feb. 1798	
Alexander McLachlan ..	6 Sept. 1798
Rank in Army, 11 Dec. 1797	
Peter King	27 Sept. 1798
Rank in Army, 3 Mar. 1797	
Henry Winchcombe ..	27 Sept. 1798
John Fox.. ..	18 Oct. 1798
Rank in Army, 7 Sept. 1796	
John Christopher Bekout	11 Nov. 1798
Ensigns—	
Robert Glynn **Griffith** ..	30 Mar. 1791
Rank in Army, 10 Oct. 1787	
John Fraser	16 Sept. 1795
Donald McNeil ..	23 Dec. 1795
John D. Fletcher ..	5 Mar. 1796
John L. Gillie ..	5 Mar. 1796
—— Williams.. ..	5 Mar. 1796
—— Bohme ..	10 May 1796
—— German ..	26 Aug. 1796
—— Whiting	5 Oct. 1796
—— Rogers ..	23 Nov. 1796
William Walther ..	5 Jan. 1797
Thomas Rowley Swiney	6 Jan. 1797
John P. Walker ..	30 Mar. 1797
James Erskine Bell ..	6 April 1797
—— De Carenen ..	6 April 1797
John Donaldson ..	7 April 1797
William Fitzgerald..	1 May 1797
John Alison ..	3 May 1797
Rank in Army, 16 Oct. 1796	
—— Kemmt ..	11 May 1797
William Peacock ..	23 May 1797
Samuel Brewster ..	24 Aug. 1797
Rank in Army, 6 Sept. 1796	

Rank and Name.	Rank in Regiment.
Ensigns (continued)—	
—— Campbell	7 Oct. 1797
Rank in Army, 1 Sept. 1796	
Thomas Walsh ..	15 Nov. 1797
Charles Sankey ..	30 Dec. 1797
William Medhurst..	30 Dec. 1797
—— Villedon ..	30 Dec. 1797
—— Bachmann ..	30 Dec. 1797
—— Mayer	30 Dec. 1797
Charles Osbrand ..	30 Dec. 1797
—— Oatman	30 Dec. 1797
Frank Hay	30 Dec. 1797
—— Allard	30 Dec. 1797
M. Frederick Henckel ..	30 Dec. 1797
Cha. William Henry Koch	30 Dec. 1797
George Henry Zulkie ..	30 Dec. 1797
George Philip Schneider	30 Dec. 1797
—— Kemmeter ..	30 Dec. 1797
—— Kilener ..	30 Dec. 1797
—— Hul.. ..	30 Dec. 1797
—— Stamba ..	30 Dec. 1797
—— Kellerman ..	30 Dec. 1797
—— Berger	30 Dec. 1797
—— Mertens ..	30 Dec. 1797
—— Weissenbach ..	30 Dec. 1797
—— Jonnnes	30 Dec. 1797
—— du Sable ..	30 Dec. 1797
—— Loth ..	30 Dec. 1797
—— Noell ..	30 Dec. 1797
—— Petrie ..	30 Dec. 1797
—— Talouillot ..	30 Dec. 1797
—— Muller	30 Dec. 1797
—— Jockell ..	30 Dec. 1797
—— Winckler ..	30 Dec. 1797
—— Fries	23 Jan. 1798
—— Ingwersen ..	23 Mar. 1798
C. L. Mergel ..	29 Mar. 1798
George W. Avenar..	29 Mar. 1798
—— Baron d'Ovn ..	25 April 1798
H. Baron d'Adelsheim ..	25 April 1798
John Ormsby ..	4 May 1798
Rank in Army, 8 June 1796	
Charles Hawke ..	17 May 1798
Charles Dickson Green ..	1 June 1798
Rank in Army, 5 Mar. 1797	
Paymasters—	
Frederick Samuel Pohl ..	28 Feb. 1798
James Lawson.. ..	5 April 1798
James Fitzmaurice.. ..	6 Dec. 1798
Adjutants—	
William Warburton ..	2 Sept. 1787
William Bell ..	10 Dec. 1794
—— Fitzgerald ..	1 Sept. 1796
John Bestep ..	23 Feb. 1797
—— Ammon ..	30 Dec. 1797
L. de Besse ..	22 Mar. 1798
—— Hamelin.. ..	4 July 1798
Quartermasters—	
Isaac Germain.. ..	28 Dec. 1790
B. Radou	6 Jan. 1796
C. Luchau	1 Sept. 1796
—— Kemmeter ..	30 Dec. 1797
Surgeons—	
James Henderson ..	10 Nov. 1778
Thomas Wright ..	16 Oct. 1793
Alexander McDougall ..	1 Sept. 1796

Rank and Name.		Rank in Regiment.
Surgeons (continued)—		
Thomas Carter	.. ..	7 June 1797
—— Beaujean	..	30 Dec. 1797
Anthony Reifer	..	30 Dec. 1797
Lewis Poitier	.. ..	30 Dec. 1797
Charles Woelfing	..	30 Dec. 1797
—— Reifer	.. ..	30 Dec. 1797
Assistant-Surgeons—		
Anthony Murray	..	25 June 1797
Philip Mulheran	..	11 Sept. 1797
—— Kelhuandt	..	30 Dec. 1797
—— Wortwick	..	30 Dec. 1797
—— Bruckmann	..	30 Dec. 1797
—— Gabriel	.. ..	30 Dec. 1797
—— Muller	.. ..	30 Dec. 1797
—— Gineke	..	30 Dec. 1797
—— Bucker	..	30 Dec. 1797
—— Felling	.. ..	30 Dec. 1797
John Farris	..	18 Jan. 1798
—— Grant	.. ..	31 May 1798
—— Tockens		

Regimentals—Red, facings blue, white lace, two blue stripes.

5th Rifle Battalion, green.

Agents—Messrs. Cox. Greenwood, and Cox, Craig's Court.

1800.

Six Battalions.

West Indies—North America—England—South America.

Col.-in-Chief—

H.R.H. Fred., Duke of York, K.G.	.. ..	23 Aug. 1797
Rank in Army, Field-Mar. 10 Feb. 1795		
Cols.-Commandant—		
William Rowley	.. ..	3 Oct. 1787
Rank in Army, Gen. 1 Jan. 1798		
Thomas Carleton	..	6 Aug. 1794
Rank in Army, Lt.-Gen. 1 Jan. 1798		
Peter Hunter	.. ..	2 Aug. 1796
Rank in Army, Maj.-Gen. 26 Feb. 1795		
William Morshead	..	30 Dec. 1797
Rank in Army, Maj.-Gen. 26 Feb. 1795		
William Gardiner	..	11 Nov. 1798
Rank in Army, Lt.-Gen. 26 June 1799		
Robert Browning	..	25 July 1799
Rank in Army, 3 May 1796		
Lieut.-Colonels—		
James Adolph Harris	..	16 Jan. 1788
Rank in Army, M.-Gen. 1 Jan. 1798		
George Prevost	.. ..	6 Aug. 1794
Rank in Army, Col. 1 Jan. 1798		
Duncan Mackintosh	..	1 Sept. 1795
Martin Hunter	..	12 Jan. 1796
Rank in Army, 19 July 1794		
John Robert Napier	..	10 Aug. 1796
Geo. William Ramsay	..	30 Dec. 1797
F. Baron de Rottenburg	..	30 Dec. 1797
Robert Crauford	..	30 Dec. 1797
Henry Cooper	..	30 Dec. 1797
William Dowdeswell	..	18 Jan. 1798
Rank in Army, Col. 26 Jan. 1797		
Thomas Philip Ainslie	..	20 June 1799

Rank and Name.		Rank in Regiment.
Lieut.-Colonels (continued)—		
Lachlan McLean	.. ..	25 July 1799
Rank in Army, 1 Jan. 1798		
George Burgess Morden	. 26 July 1799
Rank in Army, 1 Jan. 1798		
Majors—		
Robert Lethbridge	..	25 Nov. 1795
Rank in Army, 6 May 1795		
Frederick de Vos	..	22 May 1797
George Lewis de Virna	. 30 Dec. 1797
—— Dorsner	.. ..	30 Dec. 1797
—— Mosheim	..	30 Dec. 1797
—— Crezielsky	..	30 Dec. 1797
—— Streicher	..	30 Dec. 1797
Gervase Rainey	..	8 Mar. 1798
Warren Johnston	..	6 Sept. 1798
John Campbell	..	20 Dec. 1798
George Lewis T. Schoedde	20 June 1799
John Bryng	.. ..	20 June 1799
Captains—		
J. F. Wallet des Barres	. 23 Sept. 1775
Rank in Army, Col. 1 Jan. 1798		
John de Lancey	..	5 July 1793
Gabriel Gordon	..	10 July 1794
Dorrell Cove	.. ..	27 Aug. 1794
James Cockburne	..	10 Nov. 1794
William Claus	..	5 Feb. 1795
Edward Codd	..	15 Aug. 1795
John Lennox	..	7 Sept. 1795
Thomas Clarke	..	9 Sept. 1795
John Robertson	..	10 Sept. 1795
William Tircman	..	16 Dec. 1795
George Fourneret	..	16 Dec. 1795
Andrew M'Can	..	16 Dec. 1795
Goram Maxwell	..	16 Dec. 1795
Thomas M'Kee	..	20 Feb. 1796
James Fahy	.. ..	27 Feb. 1796
Rank in Army, Lt.-Col. 1 Jan. 1798		
John Bradshaw	..	5 Apr. 1796
Colin Campbell	..	8 June 1796
Rank in Army, 17 Feb. 1794		
T. Hip. des Rivieres	..	23 Mar. 1797
Robert Forsyth	..	20 Sept. 1797
Rank in Army, 10 June 1795		
Maine Walrond	..	11 Oct. 1797
—— Rumpler	..	30 Dec. 1797
—— Desgranges	..	30 Dec. 1797
G. Paulus de Gheus	..	30 Dec. 1797
Laub. Lewis de Weise	. 30 Dec. 1797
—— Glumar	.. ..	30 Dec. 1797
Henry Roberfeld	..	30 Dec. 1797
Fred. Ernest de Genardy	. 30 Dec. 1797
Ant. Aug. Baron d'Erp	..	30 Dec. 1797
Lewis Schneider	..	30 Dec. 1797
—— Vendt	.. ..	30 Dec. 1797
—— Hurdt	.. ..	30 Dec. 1797
—— Mortmain	..	30 Dec. 1797
—— Gaud	.. ..	30 Dec. 1797
—— Braun	.. ..	30 Dec. 1797
—— Donags	..	30 Dec. 1797
—— Emmenhausen	..	30 Dec. 1797
—— Galliffe	.. ..	30 Dec. 1797
Rank in Army, 13 Oct. 1796		
—— Haberkorn	..	30 Dec. 1797
—— Valmont	.. ..	30 Dec. 1797
—— de la Houssaye	..	30 Dec. 1797

Rank and Name.	Rank in Regiment.
Captains (continued)—	
—— Count Byland	.. 30 Dec. 1797
—— Schwartz	.. 30 Dec. 1797
—— Imturn	.. 30 Dec. 1797
—— Vorstadt	.. 30 Dec. 1797
—— Crest	.. 30 Dec. 1797
—— St. Mart	.. 30 Dec. 1797
—— Turnc	.. 30 Dec. 1797
—— Maiszig	.. 30 Dec. 1797
—— Count Rouvray	30 Dec. 1797
—— Fognasse	.. 30 Dec. 1797
—— Schouberg	.. 30 Dec. 1797
—— de Estenne	.. 30 Dec. 1797
—— Count de Seyn and 30 Dec. 1797	
Wittgenstein	
Anthony de Berzel	.. 30 Dec. 1797
Benedict Simon	.. 1 Mar. 1798
—— de Blumenstein	.. 29 Mar. 1798
Francis Gomer	.. 25 Apr. 1798
Thomas Morrison	.. 31 May 1798
Rank in Army, 27 Nov. 1794	
Thomas Walker	.. 24 Oct. 1798
Rank in Army, 15 Mar. 1798	
William Machen	.. 25 Oct. 1798
Robert Drummond	.. 8 Nov. 1798
Edward Cooke	.. 19 Dec. 1798
Thomas Kavanagh	.. 1 Jan. 1799
Rank in Army, 1 Oct. 1794	
William J. O'Connor	.. 24 Jan. 1799
Rank in Army, 1 Oct. 1794	
William Shewbridge	.. 24 Jan. 1799
Rank in Army, 6 Mar. 1795	
John Pringle Dalrymple	24 Jan. 1799
John Farquer	.. 17 June 1799
Holland Leckey	.. 20 June 1799
Rank in Army, 6 Apr. 1797	
Francis Vyvyan	.. 26 June 1799
William Fraser	.. 15 July 1799
Rank in Army, 26 Feb. 1797	
William Richards	.. 15 July 1799
Rank in Army, 20 Oct. 1796	
Archibald Bertram	.. 24 Oct. 1799
George Maugles	.. 24 Oct. 1799
Thomas Austin	.. 24 Oct. 1799
James Lomax	.. 24 Oct. 1799
Rank in Army, 15 June 1798	
Captain-Lieut. and Captains—	
Alexander Fraser	.. 16 Dec. 1795
Archibald Grant	.. 16 Dec. 1795
—— Hellerick	.. 30 Dec. 1797
Daniel Nixon	.. 25 Nov. 1798
Charles du Salaberry	.. 13 July 1799
William Fraser	.. 13 July 1799
Lieutenants—	
Adrian E. Gough	.. 18 Mar. 1795
Kenelm Chandler	.. 8 July 1795
William Plenderleath	.. 15 Aug. 1795
William Warburton	.. 15 Sept. 1795
James M'Arthur	.. 17 Sept. 1795
James Massey	.. 17 Sept. 1795
Robert Hazen	.. 18 Sept. 1795
John Gunthrope	.. 17 Oct. 1795
John Heslop	.. 15 Dec. 1795
William Floyer	.. 16 Dec. 1795
Rank in Army, 17 Mar. 1779	

Rank and Name.	Rank in Regiment.
Lieutenants (continued)—	
Thomas Foy	.. 16 Dec. 1795
Rank in Army, 24 Sept. 1782	
David Joly	.. 16 Dec. 1795
Charles Thompson	.. 5 Mar. 1796
Thomas Penton	.. 5 Mar. 1796
Charles Shearer	.. 5 Mar. 1796
William Disney	.. 19 Mar. 1796
Alexander Andrew	.. 5 Apr. 1796
Edward Norton	.. 14 May 1796
Hubert Seymour	.. 17 May 1796
Rank in Army, 24 June 1795	
John Campbell	.. 15 June 1796
John Cummings	.. 29 July 1796
Thomas Durham	.. 1 Sept. 1796
Peter M'Arthur	.. 4 Jan. 1797
George Cartwright	.. 2 Mar. 1797
Anthony Wall	.. 6 Apr. 1797
James Bunting	.. 7 Apr. 1797
Benjamin Clarke	.. 11 May 1797
—— de Visme	.. 14 May 1797
—— de Mangin	.. 12 May 1797
Alexander Kess	.. 22 May 1797
W. H. Quenet	.. 23 May 1797
Thomas Cates	.. 15 June 1797
Thomas Henderson	.. 9 Aug. 1797
Charles Cranstoun Dixon	24 Aug. 1797
Falkener Philps	.. 7 Dec. 1797
Charles de Kinsinger	.. 30 Dec. 1797
—— Potter	.. 30 Dec. 1797
—— de Renauld	.. 30 Dec. 1797
Gabriel Burer	.. 30 Dec. 1797
—— Schmidt	.. 30 Dec. 1797
William Lewis de Virм	30 Dec. 1797
Peter William de Hazen	30 Dec. 1797
George Fred de Virм	.. 30 Dec. 1797
—— M'Leod	.. 30 Dec. 1797
L. de Rosse	.. 30 Dec. 1797
L. Baron de H. Hugenguet	30 Dec. 1797
John Anthony Wisdff	.. 30 Dec. 1797
Peter Fred. Blassire	.. 30 Dec. 1797
Fred. William B. de Gilse	30 Dec. 1797
Adolphus Munsthul	.. 30 Dec. 1797
—— Vendt	.. 30 Dec. 1797
—— Luster	.. 30 Dec. 1797
—— Franchuffin	.. 30 Dec. 1797
—— Ratsenhausen	.. 30 Dec. 1797
—— Bertner	.. 30 Dec. 1797
—— Hoffmann	.. 30 Dec. 1797
—— Krem	.. 30 Dec. 1797
—— Hausseger	.. 30 Dec. 1797
—— Suger	.. 30 Dec. 1797
—— Langsdorff	.. 30 Dec. 1797
—— Ellert	.. 30 Dec. 1797
—— Winkerstein	.. 30 Dec. 1797
—— Vanderbroteh	.. 30 Dec. 1797
—— Bader	.. 30 Dec. 1797
Louis Inturn	.. 30 Dec. 1797
Frederick Inturn	.. 30 Dec. 1797
—— Colbert	.. 30 Dec. 1797
—— Pennut	.. 30 Dec. 1797
—— Apentier	.. 30 Dec. 1797
—— Hanselin	.. 30 Dec. 1797
—— de Couders	.. 30 Dec. 1797
—— Handz	.. 30 Dec. 1797
—— Malcaffe	.. 30 Dec. 1797

Rank and Name.	Rank in Regiment.	Rank and Name.	Rank in Regiment.
Lieutenants (continued) —		*Ensigns* (continued) —	
—— Scheding..	.. 30 Dec. 1797	Thomas Walsh ..	.. 15 Nov. 1797
—— Mauriage	.. 30 Dec. 1797	Charles Shankey ..	.. 30 Dec. 1797
—— de Bellot	.. 30 Dec. 1797	—— Villedon.. ..	.. 30 Dec. 1797
—— de Vigny	.. 30 Dec. 1797	—— Bachmann ..	.. 30 Dec. 1797
Sebastian Chozant ..	.. 30 Dec. 1797	—— Mayer	.. 30 Dec. 1797
—— Killenpach ..	.. 30 Dec. 1797	Charles Osbrand ..	.. 30 Dec. 1797
—— Stapelton ..	.. 30 Dec. 1797	—— Ostman	.. 30 Dec. 1797
John Crozant	.. 30 Dec. 1797	—— Allard	.. 30 Dec. 1797
—— Connesin.. ..	.. 30 Dec. 1797	Chas. Wm. Henry Koch.	30 Dec. 1797
—— d'Arequi.. ..	.. 30 Dec. 1797	George Henry Zulkie ..	30 Dec. 1797
—— d'Halem	.. 30 Dec. 1797	George Philip Schneider	30 Dec. 1797
—— Craft	.. 30 Dec. 1797	—— Kemmeter ..	.. 30 Dec. 1797
—— Ammon	.. 23 Jan. 1798	—— Kilener	.. 30 Dec. 1797
James Burkett ..	.. 8 Mar. 1798	—— Hul..	.. 30 Dec. 1797
Rank in Army, 5 Sept. 1796		—— Stamba	.. 30 Dec. 1797
Hubert de Salve ..	.. 29 Mar. 1798	—— Kellerman ..	.. 30 Dec. 1797
—— Frankisson ..	.. 29 Mar. 1798	—— Berger	.. 30 Dec. 1797
—— Brook	.. 29 Mar. 1798	—— Mertens	.. 30 Dec. 1797
Charles Hinckeldy ..	.. 29 Mar. 1798	—— Joannes	.. 30 Dec. 1797
Joseph Barrow Munster .	29 Mar. 1798	—— du Sable.. ..	.. 30 Dec. 1797
—— Hugon	.. 29 Mar. 1798	—— Loth	.. 30 Dec. 1797
—— Schulties.. ..	.. 29 Mar. 1798	—— Noel	.. 30 Dec. 1797
Patrick O'Brien ..	.. 24 May 1798	—— Petrie	.. 30 Dec. 1797
Rank in Army, 29 May 1796		—— Tabouillot ..	.. 30 Dec. 1797
Alexander McLachlan ..	6 Sept. 1798	—— Jockell	.. 30 Dec. 1797
Rank in Army, 11 Dec. 1797		—— Friess	.. 23 Jan. 1798
Peter King	.. 27 Sept. 1798	C. L. Mergel	29 Mar. 1798
Rank in Army, 3 Mar. 1797		George W. Avenar ..	29 Mar. 1798
Henry Winchcombe ..	27 Sept. 1798	—— Baron d'Ota ..	.. 25 Apr. 1798
John William Aldred ..	2 Apr. 1799	H. Baron Adelsheim ..	25 Apr. 1798
Rank in Army, 17 Aug. 1797		John Ormsby.. ..	.. 4 May 1798
John Bourne	.. 6 Apr. 1799	*Rank in Army*, 8 June 1796	
Rank in Army, 26 Dec. 1796		Charles Hauke ..	.. 17 May 1798
—— Prater	.. 19 Apr. 1799	Charles Dickson Green..	1 June 1798
James Campbell ..	.. 19 May 1799	*Rank in Army*, 5 Mar. 1797	
Ch. Baron de Selchow ..	1 June 1799	Florence M'Carthy.. ..	2 Dec. 1798
James Hamilton ..	.. 5 Aug. 1799	Robert Kelly	22 Feb. 1799
Rank in Army, 14 Nov. 1798		Bysse Molesworth ..	.. 24 Dec. 1799
Dugald Cameron ..	.. 5 Aug. 1799	*Rank in Army*, 21 Dec. 1797	
Thomas Gells	.. 12 Sept. 1799	Thomas Stratham ..	.. 25 Apr. 1799
James Finucane ..	.. 17 Oct. 1799	*Rank in Army*, 10 Nov. 1788	
Rank in Army, 19 Nov. 1796		—— Barclay	.. 18 July 1799
Lord Charles Kerr.. ..	13 Nov. 1799	Thadey Grehan ..	.. 1 June 1799
Rank in Army, 1 July 1795		*Rank in Army*, 1 Oct. 1796	
Harry John Murray ..	13 Nov. 1799	Louis La Roche ..	.. 23 Aug. 1799
James Erskine Bell ..	13 Nov. 1799	—— Ooulzac	.. 5 Sept. 1799
—— Bramer	.. 13 Nov. 1799	Frederick des Barres ..	12 Sept. 1799
Ensigns —		John Jeffries	.. 26 Sept. 1799
John Fraser	.. 16 Sept. 1795	James Le Grice ..	.. 13 Nov. 1799
Donald M'Neil ..	.. 23 Dec. 1795	John Moore	.. 13 Nov. 1799
John D. Plancher ..	.. 5 Mar. 1796	*Paymasters* —	
John L. Gallie ..	.. 5 Mar. 1796	Fredk. Samuel Pohl.. ..	28 Feb. 1798
—— Williams ..	.. 5 Mar. 1796	James Lawson.. ..	.. 5 Apr. 1798
—— Behme	.. 10 May 1796	James Fitzmaurice ..	6 Dec. 1798
—— German	.. 26 Aug. 1796	Robert Wilson ..	.. 26 Sept. 1799
—— Whiling.. ..	.. 5 Oct. 1796	Lewis Foy	.. 17 Oct. 1799
—— Rogers	.. 23 Nov. 1796	*Adjutants* —	
William Walther ..	.. 5 Jan. 1797	William Warburton ..	2 Sept. 1787
Thomas Rowley Swiney .	6 Jan. 1797	—— Fitzgerald ..	.. 1 Sept. 1796
—— de Carneres ..	.. 6 Apr. 1797	John Heslop	.. 23 Feb. 1797
William Fitzgerald ..	1 May 1797	—— Ammon	.. 30 Dec. 1797
—— Kemart	.. 11 May 1797	L. de Bosse	.. 22 Mar. 1798
William Peacock ..	.. 23 May 1797	—— Hamelin.. ..	.. 4 July 1798
Samuel Brewster ..	.. 24 Aug. 1797	—— Jabouillot ..	.. 10 May 1799
Rank in Army, 6 Sept. 1795		John Moore	.. 9 Aug. 1799

Rank and Name.	Rank in Regiment.
Quartermasters—	
Isaac Germain	28 Dec. 1790
B. Baden..	6 Jan. 1796
C. Ludam..	1 Sept. 1796
—— Kemmeter	30 Sept. 1797
Dennis Alexander ..	5 Sept. 1799
Surgeons—	
James Henderson ..	10 Nov. 1775
Thomas Wright	16 Oct. 1793
Alexander McDougall ..	1 Sept. 1796
—— Beaujean	30 Dec. 1797
Anthony Reifer	30 Dec. 1797
Lewis Pottier	30 Dec. 1797
Charles Worling	30 Dec. 1797
—— Reifer	30 Dec. 1797
—— Franklin.. ..	25 July 1799
Alexander Stewart ..	30 Aug. 1799
Assistant-Surgeons—	
Philip Mulberan	11 Sept. 1797
—— Kellmundt	30 Dec. 1797
—— Wortwick	30 Dec. 1797
—— Bruckmann	30 Dec. 1797
—— Gabriel	30 Dec. 1797
—— Muller	30 Dec. 1797
—— Gineke	30 Dec. 1797
—— Bucker	30 Dec. 1797
—— Felling	30 Dec. 1797
John Farris	18 Jan. 1798
—— Fockens	1 Jan. 1799
John Cole Price	19 Apr. 1799
William King..	25 May 1799
John Molle	7 Nov. 1799

Regimentals—Red, facings blue, white lace, 2 blue stripes.

6th Rifle Battalion, green.

Agents—Messrs. Cox and Greenwood, Craig's Court.

1801.

Six Battalions.

West Indies—South America.

Rank and Name.	Rank in Regiment.
Col.-in-Chief—	
H.R.H. Fred., Duke of York, K.G...	23 Aug. 1797
Rank in Army, Field-Mar.	10 Feb. 1795
Cols.-Commandant—	
William Rowley	3 Oct. 1787
Rank in Army, Gen.	1 Jan. 1798
Thos. Carleton	6 Aug. 1794
Rank in Army, Lt.-Gen.	1 Jan. 1798
Peter Hunter	2 Aug. 1794
Rank in Army, Maj.-Gen.	26 Feb. 1795
Commandants—	
William Gardner ..	11 Nov. 1798
Rank in Army, Lt.-Gen.	26 June 1799
Robert Brownrigg ..	25 July 1799
Rank in Army,	3 May 1796
Thos. Slaughter Stanwix..	9 May 1800
Rank in Army, Lt.-Gen.	26 June 1799
Lieut.-Colonels—	
James Adolph Harris ..	16 Jan. 1788
Rank in Army, Maj.-Gen.	1 Jan. 1798
George Prevost	6 Aug. 1794
Rank in Army, Col.	1 Jan. 1798
Duncan Mackintosh ..	1 Sept. 1795

Rank and Name.	Rank in Regiment.
Lieut.-Colonels (continued)—	
Geo. W. Ramsay	30 Dec. 1797
F. Baron de Rottenburg	30 Dec. 1797
Rank in Army,	25 June 1796
Robert Crauford	30 Dec. 1797
Henry Couper..	30 Dec. 1797
William Dowdeswell ..	18 Jan. 1798
Rank in Army, Col.	26 Jan. 1797
Thos. Philip Ainslie ..	20 June 1799
Lachlan M'Lean	25 July 1799
Rank in Army,	1 Jan. 1798
Geo. Burgess Morden ..	26 July 1799
Rank in Army,	1 Jan. 1798
David Cuningham.. ..	8 Feb. 1800
Rank in Army, Col.	26 Jan. 1797
Majors—	
Robert Lethbridge.. ..	25 Nov. 1795
Rank in Army, Lt.-Col.	1 Jan. 1800
Fred. de Vos	22 May 1797
Geo. Lewis de Virna ..	30 Dec. 1797
—— Dorsner	30 Dec. 1797
—— Mosheim	30 Dec. 1797
—— Crezielsky	30 Dec. 1797
—— Streicher..	30 Dec. 1797
Gervase Ramey	8 Mar. 1798
Warren Johnston	6 Sept. 1798
John Campbell	20 Dec. 1798
Robt. Forsyth..	28 Mar. 1800
Gabriel Gordon	16 May 1800
Captains—	
J. F. Wallet des Barres..	23 Sept. 1775
Rank in Army, Col.	1 Jan. 1798
John de Lancey	5 July 1793
Dorrell Cope	27 Aug. 1794
James Cockburne	10 Nov. 1794
William Claus	5 Feb. 1795
Edwd. Codd	15 Aug. 1795
John Lennox	7 Sept. 1795
Thos. Clarke	9 Sept. 1795
John Robertson	10 Sept. 1795
Wm. Tireman	18 Dec. 1795
Geo. Fourneret	16 Dec. 1795
Andrew M'Can	16 Dec. 1795
Gordon Maxwell	16 Dec. 1795
Thos. M'Kee	29 Feb. 1796
John Bradshaw	5 April 1796
Colin Campbell	8 June 1796
T. Hippo. des Rivieres ..	23 Mar. 1797
—— Rumpler..	30 Dec. 1797
—— Desgranges	30 Dec. 1797
G. Paulus de Gibans ..	30 Dec. 1797
Lamb. Lewis de Weise..	30 Dec. 1797
—— Glauser	30 Dec. 1797
Henry Roberfeld	30 Dec. 1797
Frd. Ernest de Gerardy	30 Dec. 1797
Lewis Schneider	30 Dec. 1797
—— Vendt	30 Dec. 1797
—— Mortmain	30 Dec. 1797
—— Ginol	30 Dec. 1779
—— Braun	30 Dec. 1797
—— Douags	30 Dec. 1797
—— Enonenhausen ..	30 Dec. 1797
—— Gulhile	30 Dec. 1797
Rank in Army,	13 Oct. 1796
—— Haberkorn	30 Dec. 1797
—— Valmont..	30 Dec. 1797

Rank and Name.	Rank in Regiment.
Captains (continued)—	
—— De la Houssaye	.. 30 Dec. 1797
—— Count Byland	.. 30 Dec. 1797
—— Schwartz	.. 30 Dec. 1797
—— Beruff ..	.. 30 Dec. 1797
—— Inturn	.. 30 Dec. 1797
—— Vorstadt..	.. 30 Dec. 1797
—— Crest ..	.. 30 Dec. 1797
—— St. Mart ..	.. 30 Dec. 1797
—— Turine ..	.. 30 Dec. 1797
—— Count Rouvray	.. 30 Dec. 1797
—— Fogasse ..	.. 30 Dec. 1797
—— Count de Seyn and	
Wittgenstein	.. 30 Dec. 1797
Charles Berzel	.. 30 Dec. 1797
Benedict Simon	.. 30 Dec. 1797
Lewis Kinnan..	.. 30 Dec. 1797
—— de Blumenstein	.. 29 Mar. 1798
Francis Gomer	.. 25 April 1798
Thos. Morrison	.. 31 May 1798
Rank in Army, 27 Nov. 1794	
Thos. Walker ..	.. 24 Oct. 1798
Rank in Army, 15 Mar. 1798	
William Marlton ..	.. 25 Oct. 1798
Robt. Drummond ..	.. 8 Nov. 1798
Thos. Kavanagh ..	.. 1 Jan. 1799
Rank in Army, 1 Oct. 1794	
W. J. O'Connor ..	.. 24 Jan. 1799
Rank in Army, 1 Oct. 1794	
John Pringle Dalrymple	24 Jan. 1799
John Fargues ..	.. 17 June 1799
William Fraser ..	.. 15 July 1799
Rank in Army, 26 Feb. 1797	
Wm. Richards ..	.. 16 Aug. 1799
Rank in Army, 20 Oct. 1796	
James Lomax ..	.. 8 Oct. 1799
Rank in Army, 15 June 1798	
George Mangles	.. 5 Dec. 1799
Thos. Austin ..	.. 11 Dec. 1799
Rank in Army, 1 Dec. 1794	
James Myburn	.. 11 April 1800
Thos. Geils ..	.. 7 Aug. 1800
John W. Aldred	.. 7 Aug. 1800
Captain-Lieut. and Captain—	
Archibald Grant ..	.. 16 Dec. 1795
—— Hellerick .	.. 30 Dec. 1797
Daniel Nixon ..	.. 25 Nov. 1798
Charles du Saluberry	10 July 1799
William Fraser ..	.. 25 July 1799
Walter Johnson ..	.. 5 Jan. 1800
Lieutenants—	
Kenelm Chandler ..	.. 8 July 1795
W. Plenderleath ..	.. 15 Aug. 1795
W. Warburton ..	.. 15 Sept. 1795
James M'Arthur ..	.. 17 Sept. 1795
James Massey..	.. 17 Sept. 1795
Robert Hazen..	.. 18 Sept. 1795
John Gunthorpe ..	.. 17 Oct. 1795
John Heslop ..	.. 15 Dec. 1795
William Floyer ..	.. 16 Dec. 1795
Rank in Army, 17 Mar. 1779	
Thos. Foy ..	.. 16 Dec. 1795
Rank in Army, 24 Sept. 1782	
David Joly ..	.. 16 Dec. 1795
Charles Thompson..	.. 5 Mar. 1796
Thos. Penton..	.. 5 Mar. 1796

Rank and Name.	Rank in Regiment.
Lieutenants (continued)—	
Charles Shearer ..	.. 5 Mar. 1796
Wm. Disney ..	.. 19 Mar. 1796
Alex. Andrews ..	.. 5 April 1796
Edwd. Norton . ..	.. 14 May 1796
Hubert Seymour ..	.. 17 May 1796
Rank in Army, 24 June 1795	
John Campbell .	.. 15 June 1796
Donald M'Neil. ..	.. 28 July 1796
John Cummings ..	.. 29 July 1796
Thos. Durham . ..	.. 1 Sep. 1796
Peter M'Arthur ..	.. 4 Jan. 1797
George Cartwright .	.. 2 Mar. 1797
Anthony Wall . ..	.. 6 April 1797
James Bunting. ..	.. 7 April 1797
—— De Visme. ..	.. 14 May 1797
—— De Mangin ..	.. 12 May 1797
Alex. Ross.. ..	.. 22 May 1797
W. H. Queast.. ..	.. 23 May 1797
Thos. Cates ..	.. 15 June 1797
Thos. Henderson ..	.. 9 Aug. 1797
Charles Cranstoun Dixon	24 Aug. 1797
Falkener Philips ..	.. 7 Dec. 1797
Charles de Kinsinger ..	30 Dec. 1797
—— de Reynauld ..	.. 30 Dec. 1797
Gabriel Burer.. ..	.. 30 Dec. 1797
—— Schmidt	.. 30 Dec. 1797
Wm. Lewis de Virna ..	.. 30 Dec. 1797
Peter Wm. de Hazen ..	.. 30 Dec. 1797
Geo. Frederick de Virna .	30 Dec. 1797
—— MacLeod	.. 30 Dec. 1797
L. de Bosse ..	.. 30 Dec. 1797
L. Baron de H. Hugenpoet	30 Dec. 1797
John Anthony Wooliff ..	.. 30 Dec. 1797
Peter Fredk. Blassire ..	.. 30 Dec. 1797
Fred. Wm. B. de Gilse..	.. 30 Dec. 1797
Adolphus Munsthal ..	.. 30 Dec. 1797
—— Vendt ..	.. 30 Dec. 1797
—— Lister ..	.. 30 Dec. 1797
—— Franckassin ..	.. 30 Dec. 1797
—— Ratzenhausen ..	.. 30 Dec. 1797
—— Bertner ..	.. 30 Dec. 1797
—— Hoffman.. ..	.. 30 Dec. 1797
—— Krein ..	.. 30 Dec. 1797
—— Hausseger ..	.. 30 Dec. 1797
—— Ellert ..	.. 30 Dec. 1797
—— Wackenstein..	.. 30 Dec. 1797
—— Vanderbrouch .	.. 30 Dec. 1797
—— Bader ..	.. 30 Dec. 1797
Lewis Inturn.. ..	.. 30 Dec. 1797
Fredk. Inturn ..	.. 30 Dec. 1797
—— Colbert ..	.. 30 Dec. 1797
—— Bennat ..	.. 30 Dec. 1797
—— Apentier ..	.. 30 Dec. 1797
—— Hamelin ..	.. 30 Dec. 1797
—— de Conders ..	.. 30 Dec. 1797
—— Hantz ..	.. 30 Dec. 1797
—— Maleiffe ..	.. 30 Dec. 1797
—— Scheding ..	.. 30 Dec. 1797
—— Maurriage .	.. 30 Dec. 1797
—— de Bellot ..	.. 30 Dec. 1797
—— de Vigny .	.. 30 Dec. 1797
—— Killempuch ..	.. 30 Dec. 1797
—— Stapleton ..	.. 30 Dec. 1797
—— Connesin ..	.. 30 Dec. 1797
—— Craft ..	.. 30 Dec. 1797

Rank and Name.	Rank in Regiment.
Lieutenants (continued)—	
Hubert de Salve	29 Mar. 1798
—— Frankisson	29 Mar. 1798
—— Brook	29 Mar. 1798
Charles Hinckeldy	25 April 1798
—— Schulties	25 April 1798
Alex. M'Lachlan	6 Sept. 1798
Rank in Army, 11 Dec. 1797	
Peter King	27 Sept. 1798
Rank in Army, 3 Mar. 1797	
Henry Winchcombe ..	27 Sept. 1798
John Bourne	6 April 1799
Rank in Army, 26 Dec. 1796	
—— Prater	19 April 1799
James Campbell	19 May 1799
Ch. Baron de Selchow ..	1 June 1799
Dougald Cameron	5 Aug. 1799
Harry John Murray ..	25 Sept. 1799
James Erskine Bell ..	9 Oct. 1799
James Finucane	17 Oct. 1799
Rank in Army, 19 Nov. 1796	
Lord Chas. Kerr	13 Nov. 1799
Rank in Army, 1 July 1795	
Alex. Rattray	8 Dec. 1799
Rank in Army, 10 July 1799	
—— Bramer	19 Dec. 1799
Isaac Ogden	11 Jan. 1800
Wm. Peacock	14 Feb. 1800
John D. Plancher	11 July 1800
John L. Gallic	12 July 1800
—— German	13 July 1800
—— Rogers	14 July 1800
—— de Carseres	15 July 1800
Wm. Fitzgerald	16 July 1800
Thos. Walsh	18 July 1800
W. H. Johans..	19 July 1800
Chas. du Sable	20 July 1800
J. N. Loth	21 July 1800
Charles Sankey	22 July 1800
Henry Boone Hall ..	23 July 1800
Rank in Army, 11 Oct. 1797	
Geo. Philip Schneider ..	24 July 1800
Anthony Stamba	25 July 1800
Francis Noel	26 July 1800
—— Villedon	27 July 1800
—— Mertens	28 July 1800
—— Kellerman	29 July 1800
Leonard Koellner	31 July 1800
Conrad Heel	1 Aug. 1800
Charles W. H. Koch ..	2 Aug. 1800
—— Kemmeter	3 Aug. 1800
—— Myers	5 Aug. 1800
Geo. Henry Zulklic ..	6 Aug. 1800
—— Berger	7 Aug. 1800
—— Friess	8 Aug. 1800
Geo. W. Aveusr	9 Aug. 1800
—— Baron d'Ora	10 Aug. 1800
H. Baron Adelsheim ..	10 Aug. 1800
Chas. Hawke	13 Aug. 1800
Chas. Dixon Green . ..	14 Aug. 1800
Wm. M'Kinnon	18 Sept. 1800
Rank in Army, 28 May 1783	
Florence M'Carthy.. ..	16 Oct. 1800
Geo. Bent	16 Oct. 1800
Robert Kelly	17 Oct. 1800
Dougald Cameron	18 Oct. 1800

Rank and Name.	Rank in Regiment.
Lieutenants (continued)—	
P. Lindsay	19 Oct. 1800
Fredk. des Barres	20 Oct. 1800
James Le Grice	21 Oct. 1800
John Moore	22 Oct. 1800
Geo. Mason Teale	23 Oct. 1800
Wm. Yates Johnson ..	24 Oct. 1800
Peter Montoniere	25 Oct. 1800
Allan Maclean	26 Oct. 1800
Anthony Suaffo	27 Oct. 1800
Peter French	28 Oct. 1800
Wm. M'Veagh	29 Oct. 1800
A. Oatman	..
John Law	..
Ensigns—	
Wm. Walther..	5 Jan. 1797
Thos. Rowley Swincy ..	6 Jan. 1797
—— Kemart	11 May 1797
—— Bachmann	30 Dec. 1797
Chas. Osbrand	30 Dec. 1797
—— Petrie	30 Dec. 1797
C. L. Mergel	29 Mar. 1798
—— Barclay	18 July 1799
Toulzac	5 Sept. 1799
Godrick Sarda	18 June 1800
Caesar Colclough	7 July 1800
Daniel Page	8 July 1800
Richard Daly	10 July 1800
Geo. F. Gibson	11 July 1800
—— Landells	12 July 1800
Carew Reynell	13 July 1800
Thos. Blofeld Kerrison..	14 July 1800
Rank in Army, 13 Dec. 1799	
Orange Balnervis, sen. ..	20 July 1800
David Balnervis, jun. ..	21 July 1800
Robert Thompson	22 July 1800
Atwood Henry Kelsey ..	23 July 1800
Edward John Watson ..	24 July 1800
Rank in Army, 27 Aug. 1799	
Alex James Schoedde ..	25 July 1800
Riddell Campbell	26 July 1800
Edward Llewellyn.. ..	27 July 1800
Charles Fozard	28 July 1800
Valentine J. Ravenscroft	29 July 1800
Thos. Frazer	30 July 1800
James Fahy	31 July 1800
J. C. Cameron..	1 Aug. 1800
Donald Campbell	3 Aug. 1800
David Gordon	4 Aug. 1800
Dundas Blackball	5 Aug. 1800
Redmond Walsh	6 Aug. 1800
—— Miller	9 Aug. 1800
Howell Harris Pritchard	4 Sept. 1800
Robert Gordon.	2 Oct. 1800
Godfred Stark..	16 Oct. 1800
Thos. Coleman	17 Oct. 1800
Abraham Logan	20 Oct. 1800
John Jackson	21 Oct. 1800
—— Glenie	23 Oct. 1800
F. A. Seanne	24 Oct. 1800
—— Redmond	25 Oct. 1800
Charles Penn	26 Oct. 1800
—— Dodsworth	27 Oct. 1800
Alex. Macbun	28 Oct. 1800
John Custice	29 Oct. 1800
Charles Seton	29 Oct. 1800

Rank and Name.	Rank in Regiment.

Paymasters—
Fred. Samuel Pohl.. .. 28 Feb. 1798
James Lawson .. .. 5 April 1798
Robert Wilson . .. 26 Sept. 1799
James Newland .. .. 2 Oct. 1800
John Munro .. .. 9 Oct. 1800

Adjutants—
Wm. Warburton .. .. 2 Sept. 1787
—— Fitzgerald .. .. 1 Sept. 1796
L. de Bosse .. .. 22 Mar. 1798
—— Hamelin . .. .. 4 July 1798
John Moore .. .. 9 Aug. 1799
Henry Dibbly.. .. .. 5 Feb. 1800
Wm. Murray .. .. 24 Mar. 1800
Fred. W. B. Gilae .. .. 14 April 1800

Quartermasters—
B. Radon.. .. .. 6 Jan. 1796
—— Kemmeter .. .. 30 Dec. 1797
Dennis Alexander .. .. 5 Sept. 1799
Joseph Chattoway .. .. 3 July 1800
Robert Waugh . .. .. 7 Aug. 1800

Surgeons –
James Henderson .. .. 10 Nov. 1775
Thos. Wright .. .. .. 16 Oct. 1793
—— Beaujean . .. .. 30 Dec. 1797
Anthony Reifer .. .. 30 Dec. 1797
Lewis Poitier .. .. .. 30 Dec. 1797
Charles Woelling .. .. 30 Dec. 1797
—— Reifer .. .. .. 36 Dec. 1797
John Lindsay .. .. 25 Jan. 1800
Edward Caldwell .. .. 24 June 1800
John Glasco .. .. 26 June 1800

Assistant-Surgeons—
Philip Mulberan .. .. 11 Sept. 1797
—— Kelbnandt .. .. 30 Dec. 1797
—— Wortwick .. .. 30 Dec. 1797
—— Bruckmann .. .. 30 Dec. 1797
—— Gabriel .. .. .. 30 Dec. 1797
—— Muller .. .. .. 30 Dec. 1797
—— Gincke .. .. .. 30 Dec. 1797
—— Bucker .. .. .. 30 Dec. 1797
—— Felling .. .. .. 30 Dec. 1797
John Farris .. .. 18 Jan. 1798
—— Fockens .. .. .. 1 Jan. 1799
John Cole Price .. .. 19 April 1799
Wm. King .. .. .. 25 May 1799
Fredk. Midike . .. .. 1 Mar. 1800
—— Doughty .. .. 30 Oct. 1800
—— Cooper .. .. .. 30 Oct. 1800

*Regimentals—*Red, facings blue, white lace, 2 blue stripes.

5th Rifle Battalion, green.

*Agents—*Messrs. Cox and Greenwood, Craig's Court.

1802.

Six Battalions.
West Indies South America.
Col.-in-Chief—
H.R.H. Fred., Duke of York, K.G... .. .. 23 Aug. 1797
Rank in Army, Field-Mar. 10 Feb. 1795
Cols.-Commandant—
William Rowley .. .. 3 Oct. 1787
Rank in Army, Gen. 1 Jan. 1798

Rank and Name.	Rank in Regiment.

Cols.-Commandant (continued)—
Thomas Carleton .. .. 6 Aug. 1794
Rank in Army, Lt.-Gen. 1 Jan. 1798
Peter Hunter .. .. .. 2 Aug. 1796
Rank in Army, Maj.-Gen. 26 Feb. 1795
William Gardiner .. .. 11 Mar. 1799
Rank in Army, Lt.-Gen. 26 June 1799
Robert Brownrigg .. .. 25 July 1799
Rank in Army, 3 May 1796
Tho. Slaughter Stanwix.. 9 May 1800
Rank in Army, Lt.-Gen. 26 June 1799

Lieut.-Colonels—
James Adolph. Harris .. 16 Jan. 1788
Rank in Army, Maj.-Gen. 1 Jan. 1798
George Prevost .. .. 6 Aug. 1794
Rank in Army, Col. 1 Jan. 1798
Duncan Mackintosh .. 1 Sept. 1795
George William Ramsay 30 Dec. 1797
Fran. Baron Rottenburg. 30 Dec. 1797
Rank in Army, 25 Jan. 1796
Wm. Dowdeswell .. .. 18 Jan. 1798
Rank in Army, Col. 26 Jan. 1797
Tho. Philip Ainslie .. 20 June 1799
Lachlan Maclean .. .. 25 July 1799
Rank in Army, 1 Jan. 1798
Geo. Burgess Morden .. 26 July 1799
Rank in Army, 1 Jan. 1798
Frederick de Vos .. .. 15 Jan. 1801
Fitzroy J. Cuf. Maclean. 5 Feb. 1801
Rank in Army, 18 Nov. 1795
Robert Lethbridge.. .. 10 Feb. 1801

Majors—
F. Streicher .. .. .. 30 Dec. 1797
L. Mosheim .. .. .. 30 Dec. 1797
William Crezielsky.. .. 30 Dec. 1797
Gervaise Rainey .. .. 8 Mar. 1798
John Campbell .. .. 20 Dec. 1798
Robert Forsyth .. .. 28 Mar. 1800
Gabriel Gordon .. .. 16 May 1800
Edward Codd .. .. 25 Dec. 1800
Edward Drummond .. 11 June 1801
Thomas Austin .. .. 3 July 1801
John Lennox .. .. 19 Oct. 1801

Captains—
J. F. W. des Barres .. 23 Sept. 1775
Rank in Army, Col. 1 Jan. 1798
John de Lancey .. .. 5 July 1793
William Claus.. .. .. 5 Feb. 1795
Thomas Clarke .. .. 9 Sept. 1795
John Robertson .. .. 10 Sept. 1795
William Tiranian .. .. 16 Dec. 1795
George Fourneret .. .. 16 Dec. 1795
Andrew M'Can .. .. 16 Dec. 1795
Gordon Maxwell .. .. 16 Dec. 1795
Thomas McKee .. .. 20 Feb. 1796
John Bradshaw .. .. 5 April 1796
Colin Campbell .. .. 8 June 1796
Rank in Army, 17 Feb. 1794
—— Glaner .. .. .. 30 Dec. 1797
Benedict Simon .. .. 30 Dec. 1797
Joseph de Wendt .. .. 30 Dec. 1797
Chris. de Morimain .. 30 Dec. 1797
Ferdinand Crusé .. .. 30 Dec. 1797
Francis St. Mart .. .. 30 Dec. 1797
Anthony Rumpler .. .. 30 Dec. 1797
—— Vorstadt.. .. .. 30 Dec. 1797

Rank and Name.	Rank in Regiment.	Rank and Name.	Rank in Regiment.
Captains (continued) —		Lieutenants (continued)—	
John de Granges	30 Dec. 1797	Alexander Andrews	5 April 1796
Charles de la Houssaye	30 Dec. 1797	Edward Norton	14 May 1796
Fred. de Gerhardy	30 Dec. 1797	John Campbell	15 June 1796
—— Schwartz	30 Dec. 1797	Donald M'Neill	28 July 1796
—— Imturn	30 Dec. 1797	John Cummings	29 July 1796
John Gausse	30 Dec. 1797	Thomas Durham	1 Sept. 1796
Rank in Army,	31 Oct. 1796	George Cartwright	2 Mar. 1797
Henry Valmont	30 Dec. 1797	Anthony Wall	6 April 1797
C. Paulus de Gheus	30 Dec. 1797	James Bunting	7 April 1797
—— Tauriac	30 Dec. 1797	—— De Mangin	14 May 1797
—— Gaaa	30 Dec. 1797	W. H. Queast	23 May 1797
Lamb. Lewis de Weise	30 Dec. 1797	Thomas Henderson	9 Aug. 1797
Lewis Schmuder	30 Dec. 1797	Chas. Cranstoun Dixon	24 Aug. 1797
Gasper Rompny	30 Dec. 1797	Lewis de Ratsenhausen	30 Dec. 1797
Lewis Fognass	30 Dec. 1797	Michael de Wendt	30 Dec. 1797
Lewis Keenau	30 Dec. 1797	—— Hamelin	30 Dec. 1797
—— Braun	30 Dec. 1797	A. Malaasye	30 Dec. 1797
Charles Herzel	30 Dec. 1797	Hubert de Salve	30 Dec. 1797
Count de Seyn and Witt-		Alexander de Conders	30 Dec. 1797
genstein	30 Dec. 1797	—— Sebeling	30 Dec. 1797
Francis Gomer	25 April 1798	Adolphus Munstal	30 Dec. 1797
Thomas Walker	24 Oct. 1798	Charles Mackensten	30 Dec. 1797
Rank in Army,	15 Mar. 1798	John Beder	30 Dec. 1797
William Marlton	25 Oct. 1798	Charles Kinzinger	30 Dec. 1797
Thomas Kavenagh	1 Jan. 1799	Lewis Inturn	30 Dec. 1797
Rank in Army,	1 Oct. 1794	—— Colbert	30 Dec. 1797
William J. O'Connor	24 Jan. 1799	Francis Vanderbrock	30 Dec. 1797
Rank in Army,	1 Oct. 1794	Charles Kmast	30 Dec. 1797
John Pringle Dalrymple	24 Jan. 1799	Francis Hugenpoet	30 Dec. 1797
John Farques	17 June 1799	Adam Kruen	30 Dec. 1797
William Fraser	15 July 1799	Peter Blassire	30 Dec. 1797
Rank in Army,	26 Feb. 1797	Peter Wm. de Huzen	30 Dec. 1797
James Lomax	8 Oct. 1799	George Fred. de Virna	30 Dec. 1797
Rank in Army,	15 June 1798	—— Killenpsch	30 Dec. 1797
George Mangles	5 Dec. 1799	John Woolff	30 Dec. 1797
James Wyburn	11 April 1800	F. de Renauld	30 Dec. 1797
John William Aldred	19 Nov. 1800	—— Hoffman	30 Dec. 1797
Hugh Maclean	25 Dec. 1800	Frederick Gilse	30 Dec. 1797
William Bayard	15 Jan. 1801	Jacob Hauffeger	30 Dec. 1797
James W. Cowin	10 July 1801	Charles de Vigny	30 Dec. 1797
Rank in Army, Major,	6 May 1795	—— Schmidt	
Daniel Hutchon Cairns	24 July 1801	—— Lister	30 Dec. 1797
Hugh Montgomery	24 July 1801	—— Franchaffen	30 Dec. 1797
William Goodlad	19 Oct. 1801	Claude Bertner	30 Dec. 1797
Augustus Warburton	20 Dec. 1801	Philip Mauriage	30 Dec. 1797
James G. Wright		F. H. de Bellot	30 Dec. 1797
William Gabriel Davy	5 Jan.	—— De Bosse	30 Dec. 1797
Captain-Lieut. and Captains—		—— Brook	29 Mar. 1798
James Grant	25 April 1797	—— Schulties	25 April 1798
Ambrose Hellerick	30 Dec. 1797	Peter King	27 Sept. 1798
Daniel Nixon	25 Nov. 1798	Rank in Army,	3 Mar. 1797
Charles de Salisberry	10 July 1799	John Fitzmaurice	14 Feb. 1799
William Fraser	25 July 1799	Rank in Army,	24 Dec. 1796
Walter Johnson	5 Jan. 1800	John Bourne	6 April 1799
Lieutenants—		Rank in Army,	26 Dec. 1796
Kenelm Chandler	8 July 1795	—— Penter	19 April 1799
William Plenderleath	15 Aug. 1795	James Campbell	13 May 1799
William Warburton	15 Sept. 1795	Ch. Baron de Selchow	1 June 1799
James M'Arthur	17 Sept. 1795	James Erskine Bell	8 Oct. 1799
Robert Hazen	18 Sept. 1795	Lord Charles Kerr	13 Nov. 1799
David Jely	16 Dec. 1795	Rank in Army,	1 July 1795
Charles Thompson	5 Mar. 1796	Alexander Rattray	8 Dec. 1799
Thomas Penton	5 Mar. 1796	Rank in Army,	10 July 1799
Charles Shearer	5 Mar. 1796	—— Bramer	19 Dec. 1799
William Disney	19 Mar. 1796	John D. Plaucher	11 July 1800

Rank and Name.	Rank in Regiment.
Lieutenants (continued) —	
John L. Gallie	12 July 1800
—— German	13 July 1800
—— Rogers	14 July 1800
—— de Caraeres ..	15 July 1800
Thomas Walsh	18 July 1800
W. H. Johans.. ..	19 July 1800
Charles du Sable ..	20 July 1800
J. N. Loth	21 July 1800
Henry Boone Hall..	23 July 1800
Rank in Army, 11 Oct. 1797	
George P. Schneider ..	24 July 1800
Anthony Stauba ..	25 July 1800
Francis Noel	26 July 1800
—— Villedon	27 July 1800
—— Mertens	28 July 1800
—— Kellerman ..	29 July 1800
Leonard Koellner ..	30 July 1800
Henry Petrie	30 July 1800
Conrad Heel	1 Aug. 1800
C. W. H. Koch ..	2 Aug. 1800
—— Kemmeter ..	3 Aug. 1800
—— Myers	5 Aug. 1800
George Henry Zulke ..	6 Aug. 1800
—— Berger	7 Aug. 1800
—— Friess	8 Aug. 1800
George W. Avenar..	9 Aug. 1800
A. Ostman	11 Aug. 1800
Baron de Oya	10 Aug. 1800
H. Baron Adelsheim ..	11 Aug. 1800
Charles Hainke ..	13 Aug. 1800
Charles Dixon Green ..	14 Aug. 1800
William M'Kinnon ..	18 Sept. 1800
Rank in Army, 28 May 1783	
Florence M'Carthy..	16 Oct. 1800
Robert Kelly	17 Oct. 1800
Dougald Cameron ..	18 Oct. 1800
Peter Lindsay.. ..	19 Oct. 1800
Frederick des Barres ..	20 Oct. 1800
James Le Grice ..	21 Oct. 1800
James Moore	22 Oct. 1800
George Mason Teale ..	23 Oct. 1800
Wm. Yates Johnson ..	24 Oct. 1800
Peter Montoniere ..	25 Oct. 1800
Allan Maclean.. ..	26 Oct. 1800
Anthony Suasso ..	27 Oct. 1800
George Brent	27 Oct. 1800
Peter French	28 Oct. 1800
John Herbert	25 Dec. 1800
Rank in Army, 4 Nov. 1795	
Henry Fischbach ..	28 Jan. 1801
J. Blashfield	5 Feb. 1801
Wm. Ackland Gilland ..	14 May 1801
Rank in Army, 21 Dec. 1796	
Thomas Ellis	15 May 1801
Rank in Army, 29 Jan. 1801	
William Morton ..	25 June 1801
Rank in Army, 21 Feb. 1800	
Joseph Carruthers..	26 June 1801
Rank in Army, 3 May 1800	
Abraham Logan ..	17 July 1801
William Murray ..	17 Sept. 1801
Eneas Anderson ..	17 Sept. 1801
Rank in Army, 23 Sept. 1799	
Thomas Hassal ..	8 Oct. 1801
Rank in Army, 26 Dec. 1795	

Rank and Name.	Rank in Regiment.
Lieutenants (continued) —	
Richard R. Nugent ..	8 Oct. 1801
Ensigns —	
David Barclay.. ..	18 July 1799
Godrick Sarda.. ..	18 June 1800
J. B. Kerrison ..	14 July 1800
Rank in Army, 13 Dec. 1799	
Orange Balneavis ..	20 July 1800
David Balneavis ..	21 July 1800
Robert Thompson ..	22 July 1800
A. Henry Kelsey ..	23 July 1800
Alex. Ja. Schoedde..	25 July 1800
Riddell Campbell ..	26 July 1800
Edward Llewellyn..	27 July 1800
V. J. Ravenscroft ..	29 July 1800
Thomas Frazer ..	30 July 1800
James Fahy	31 July 1800
David Gordon.. ..	4 Aug. 1800
Redmond Walsh ..	6 Aug. 1800
Daniel Page	8 Aug. 1800
Geo. F. Gibson ..	11 Aug. 1800
James Landells ..	12 Aug. 1800
Carew Reynells ..	13 Aug. 1800
Robert Gordon ..	2 Oct. 1800
Godfred Stark.. ..	16 Oct. 1800
Thomas Coleman ..	17 Oct. 1800
John Jackson ..	21 Oct. 1800
—— Glenie	23 Oct. 1800
—— Redmond ..	25 Oct. 1800
Charles Dean ..	26 Oct. 1800
Alexander Maclean..	28 Oct. 1801
Archibald Campbell ..	12 Mar. 1801
Rank in Army, 24 July 1800	
Hugh Ross	12 Mar 1801
William Farrand ..	19 May 1801
Rank in Army, 16 Dec. 1799	
Thomas Rowland ..	27 May 1801
—— Pillersdorff ..	26 June 1801
William Blacken ..	3 July 1801
Robert Thompson ..	25 July 1801
Rank in Army, 14 May 1801	
Rich. Hen. Hughes ..	15 Aug. 1801
Thomas Fernyhough ..	3 Sept. 1801
Rank in Army, 21 May 1783	
Peter Irwine	2 Oct. 1801
Rank in Army, 12 June 1800	
John Boardman ..	2 Oct. 1801
G. Ramsay	6 Feb. 1801
Paymasters—	
Fred. Sam. Pohl ..	28 Feb. 1798
James Lawson ..	5 April 1798
Robert Wilson ..	26 Sept. 1799
James Nolan ..	2 Oct. 1800
John Munro	9 Oct. 1800
Brian Leigh	1 Jan. 1801
Adjutants—	
William Warburton ..	2 Sept. 1787
L. de Bosse	22 Mar. 1798
—— Hamelin.. ..	4 July 1798
John Moore	9 Aug. 1799
Henry Dibbly.. ..	5 Feb. 1800
William Murray ..	24 Mar. 1800
Frederick Gilse ..	14 April 1800
John Watson	25 Oct. 1800
Quartermasters—	
Denis Alexander ..	5 Sept. 1799

Rank and Name.	Rank in Regiment.
Quartermasters (continued)—	
——Kemmeter	30 Dec. 1797
Joseph Chattoway	3 July 1800
Peter Child	3 July 1801
Francis de la Chana ..	19 July 1801
Surgeons—	
James Henderson	10 Nov. 1775
Anthony Reifer	30 Dec. 1797
—— Fockens	4 Sept. 1800
John Feries	21 Dec. 1800
William Kilgour	29 Jan. 1801
Samuel Cathcart	28 Mar. 1801
Thomas Fitzgerald.. ..	28 Mar. 1801
Assistant Surgeons—	
Philip Mulheran	11 Sept. 1797
—— Felling	30 Dec. 1797
Frederick Midike	1 Mar. 1800
—— Doughty..	30 Oct. 1800
J. S. England	21 Dec. 1800
David Brown	6 Feb. 1800
Edw. Jarvis	16 Feb. 1800
John Freeman	16 Feb. 1800

Regimentals — Red, facings blue, white lace, 2 blue stripes.

5th **Rifle** Battalion, green.

Agents—Messrs. Cox, Greenwood, and Cox, Craig's Court.

1803.

Six Battalions.

West Indies—North America—South America.

Col.-in-Chief—	
H.R.H. Fred., Duke of York, K.G.	23 Aug. 1797
Rank in Army, Field-Mar. 10 Feb. 1795	
Cols.-Commandant—	
William Rowley	3 Oct. 1787
Rank in Army, Gen. 1 Jan. 1798	
Thos. Carleton	6 Aug. 1794
Rank in Army, Lt.-Gen. 1 Jan. 1798	
Peter Hunter	2 Aug. 1795
Rank in Army, Lt.-Gen. 29 April 1802	
Wm. Gardiner	11 Mar. 1799
Rank in Army, Lt.-Gen. 26 Jan. 1799	
Robert Brownrigg ..	25 July 1799
Rank in Army, Maj.-Gen. 29 April 1802	
Tho. Slaughter Stanwix ..	9 May 1800
Rank in Army, Lt.-Gen. 20 June 1799	
Lieut.-Colonels—	
James Adolph. Harris ..	16 Jan. 1788
Rank in Army, Maj.-Gen. 1 Jan. 1798	
George Prevost	6 Aug. 1794
Rank in Army, Col. 1 Jan. 1798	
Duncan Mackintosh ..	1 Sept. 1795
Geo. Wm. Ramsay ..	30 Dec. 1797
Francis Baron de Rottenburg	30 Dec. 1797
Rank in Army, 25 June 1796	
William Dowdeswell ..	18 Jan. 1798
Rank in Army, Col. 26 Jan. 1797	
Lachlan McLean	25 July 1799
Rank in Army, 1 Jan. 1798	
George Burgess Morden	26 July 1799
Rank in Army, 1 Jan. 1798	

Rank and Name.	Rank in Regiment.
Lieut.-Colonels (continued)—	
Fitz. J. Grafton Maclean	5 Feb. 1801
Rank in Army, 18 Nov. 1795	
Robert Lethbridge.. ..	11 Feb. 1802
Rank in Army, 1 Jan. 1800	
John Campbell	8 Mar. 1802
Gabriel Gordon	9 Mar. 1802
C. L. Theod. Schoedde ..	25 April 1802
Rank in Army, 16 May 1800	
Majors—	
Francis Streicher	30 Dec. 1797
Rank in Army, Lt.-Col. 29 April 1802	
L. Mosheim	30 Dec. 1797
Rank in Army, Lt.-Col. 29 April 1802	
Gervase Rainey	8 Mar. 1798
Edward Codd	25 Dec. 1800
Edward Drummond ..	11 June 1801
Thomas Austin	3 July 1801
James Maitland	5 Mar. 1802
George Mackie	8 Mar. 1802
John Pringle Dalrymple	13 Mar. 1802
William Forster	15 April 1802
John Keane	27 May 1802
Thomas Clarke	24 June 1802
Captains—	
J. F. W. des Barres ..	23 Sept. 1795
Rank in Army, Col. 1 Jan. 1798	
John Robertson	10 Sept. 1795
William Tireman	16 Dec. 1795
George Fourneret	16 Dec. 1795
Thos. McKee	20 Feb. 1796
Colin Campbell	8 June 1796
Rank in Army, 17 Feb. 1794	
—— Glasier	30 Dec. 1797
Benedict Simon	30 Dec. 1797
Ferdinand Crist	30 Dec. 1797
Francis St. Mart	30 Dec. 1797
Anthony Rumpler	30 Dec. 1797
—— Verstadt	30 Dec. 1797
John des Granges	30 Dec. 1797
Charles de la Houssaye..	30 Dec. 1797
—— Inturn	30 Dec. 1797
John Galiffe	30 Dec. 1797
—— Taurnac	30 Dec. 1797
—— Gaul	30 Dec. 1797
Lewis Schneider	30 Dec. 1797
Gasper Rousray	30 Dec. 1797
—— Braun	30 Dec. 1797
Francis Gomer	25 April 1798
William Marlton	25 Oct. 1798
Thomas Kavenagh.. ..	1 Jan. 1799
Rank in Army, 1 Oct. 1794	
Wm. J. O'Connor	24 Jan. 1799
Rank in Army, 1 Oct. 1794	
John Farques..	17 June 1799
William Fraser	15 July 1799
Rank in Army, 26 Feb. 1797	
James Lomax..	8 Oct. 1799
Rank in Army, 15 June 1798	
James Wyburn	11 April 1800
John William Aldred ..	19 Nov. 1800
James W. Unwin	10 July 1801
Rank in Army, Lt.-Col. 29 April 1802	
Daniel Hutchins Cairns..	24 July 1801
William Goodlad	11 Dec. 1801
Augustus Warburton ..	12 Dec. 1801

Rank and Name.	Rank in Regiment.		Rank and Name.	Rank in Regiment.
Captains (continued)—			*Lieutenants* (continued)	
William Gabriel Davy ..	1 Jan. 1802		Franchassen	30 Dec. 1797
Guy G. C. L'Estrange ..	13 Mar. 1802		Claude Bertner	30 Dec. 1797
Joseph Twigg..	31 Mar. 1802		Philip Mauriage	30 Dec. 1797
Rank in Army,	28 Mar. 1800		L. de Bosse	30 Dec. 1797
H. C. Appebus	25 April 1802		Gabriel Burer..	30 Dec. 1797
Rank in Army,	21 Aug. 1801		*Rank in Army,*	27 June 1800
Edward Broughton ..	13 May 1802		—— Brook	29 Mar. 1798
James Hall	3 June 1802		Charles Hinkeldy	25 April 1798
Rank in Army,	1 July 1801		—— Schultics	25 April 1798
William Drummond ..	16 July 1802		John Fitzmaurice	14 Feb. 1799
Charles Gordon	6 Aug. 1802		*Rank in Army,*	21 Dec. 1796
Allan Maclean..	13 Aug. 1802		John Bourne	6 April 1799
George Bent	1 Oct. 1802		*Rank in Army,*	26 Dec. 1796
Cornelius Cuyler	1 Oct. 1802		James Campbell . ..	19 May 1799
Rank in Army,	8 May 1796		Charles Baron de Selchow	1 June 1799
Captain-Lieut. and Captain—			James Erskine Bell ..	8 Oct. 1799
James Grant	25 April 1797		—— Brauer	19 Dec. 1799
Ambrose Hellerick.. ..	30 Dec. 1797		John D. Plancher	11 July 1800
Daniel Nixon	25 Nov. 1798		John L. Gallie	12 July 1800
Charles De Salaberry ..	10 July 1799		—— Rogers	14 July 1800
William Fraser	25 July 1799		—— de Carneres	15 July 1800
Walter Johnson	5 Jan. 1800		Thomas Walsh	18 July 1800
Lieutenants—			W. H. Johns..	19 July 1800
Kenelm Chandler	8 July 1795		J. N. Loth	21 July 1800
William Plenderleath ..	15 Aug. 1795		Henry Boone Hall.. ..	23 July 1800
James M'Arthur	17 Sept. 1795		*Rank in Army,*	11 Oct. 1797
Robert Hazen	18 Sept. 1795		George P. Schneider ..	24 July 1800
David Joly	16 Dec. 1795		Anthony Stamba	25 July 1800
Charles Thompson,. ..	5 Mar. 1796		—— Mertens..	28 July 1800
William Disney	19 Mar. 1796		—— Kellerman	29 July 1800
Alexander Andrews ..	5 April 1796		Henry Petrie	30 July 1800
John Campbell	15 June 1796		Conrad Heel	1 Aug. 1800
Donald M'Neill	28 July 1796		C. W. H. Koch	2 Aug. 1800
John Cummings	29 July 1796		—— Kewmeter	3 Aug. 1800
Thomas Durham	1 Sept. 1796		—— Myers	5 Aug. 1800
George Cartwright.. ..	2 Mar. 1797		George Henry Zulke ..	6 Aug. 1800
James Bunting	7 April 1797		—— Berger	7 Aug. 1800
—— De Mangin	14 May 1797		—— Friess	8 Aug. 1800
W. H. Quenet..	23 May 1797		George W. Avenar.. ..	9 Aug. 1800
Thomas Henderson.. ..	9 Aug. 1797		A. Ostman	9 Aug. 1800
Charles Craustoun Dixon	24 Aug. 1797		Baron D'Oya	10 Aug. 1800
Lewis de Ratzenhausen ..	30 Dec. 1797		H. Baron Adelsheim ..	11 Aug. 1800
Michael de Wendt.. ..	30 Dec. 1797		Charles Hawke	13 Aug. 1800
—— Hamelin..	30 Dec. 1797		Charles Dixon Green ..	14 Aug. 1800
Rank in Army, Adjutant			William M'Kinnon.. ..	18 Sept. 1800
Hubert de Salve	30 Dec. 1797		*Rank in Army,*	28 May 1783
Alexander de Conders ..	30 Dec. 1797		Florence M'Carthy.. ..	16 Oct. 1800
—— Scheding	30 Dec. 1797		Robert Kelly	17 Oct. 1800
Adolphus Munstal.. ..	30 Dec. 1797		Frederick des Barres ..	20 Oct. 1800
John Basler	30 Dec. 1797		James Le Grice	21 Oct. 1800
Charles Kinsinger	30 Dec. 1797		James Moore	22 Oct. 1800
Lewis Inturn..	30 Dec. 1797		William Yates Johnson..	24 Oct. 1800
Francis Vanderbruck ..	30 Dec. 1797		Peter Montemiere	25 Oct. 1800
Charles Kraust	30 Dec. 1797		Anthony Stausso	27 Oct. 1800
Adam Krien	30 Dec. 1797		Richard R. Nugent.. ..	20 Dec. 1799
Peter Blossiere	30 Dec. 1797		John Herbert	25 Dec. 1800
Peter William de Hazen	30 Dec. 1797		*Rank in Army,*	4 Nov. 1795
George Fred. de Virun..	30 Dec. 1797		Henry Fischbach	28 Jan. 1801
—— Killenpach	30 Dec. 1797		J. Blathfield	5 Feb. 1801
John Woolff	30 Dec. 1797		William Ackland Gilland	11 May 1801
F. de Remauld	30 Dec. 1797		*Rank in Army,*	21 Dec. 1796
—— Hoffman..	30 Dec. 1797		Thomas Ellis	15 May 1801
Frederick Gilse	30 Dec. 1797		*Rank in Army,*	29 Jan. 1801
Charles de Vigny	30 Dec. 1797		Abraham Logan	17 July 1801
—— Schmidt	30 Dec. 1797		William Murray	17 Sept. 1801

Rank and Name.	Rank in Regiment.
Lieutenants (continued)—	
John White	6 April 1802
Rank in Army, 29 Jan. 1801	
William Walther	25 April 1802
Rank in Army, 28 June 1800	
J. H. Schoedde	25 April 1802
Rank in Army, 8 Oct. 1801	
Lewis Runsson	25 April 1802
Rank in Army, 7 Aug. 1801	
Alexander Mackenzie ..	25 June 1802
Rank in Army, 27 Feb. 1796	
John M'Mahon	16 July 1802
Francis Holmes	13 Aug. 1802
Rank in Army, 28 Aug. 1801	
John Kirwan	20 Aug. 1802
Richard Philbin	29 Oct. 1802
Rank in Army, 22 Oct. 1799	
Henry Vernon.. ..	25 Nov. 1802
***Rank in Army*, 15 Mar.** 1802	
Ensigns—	
David Barclay.. ..	18 July 1799
Godrich Sarda	18 June 1800
J. D. Kerrison	14 July 1800
Rank in Army, 15 Dec. 1799	
Orange Baheuvis ..	20 July 1800
David Baheuvis ..	21 July 1800
Robert Thompson ..	22 July 1800
A. Henry Kelsey ..	23 July 1800
Ruddell Campbell ..	26 July 1800
Edward Llewellyn ..	27 July 1800
V. J. Ravenscroft ..	28 July 1800
Thomas Fraser ..	30 July 1800
James Fahy	31 July 1800
David Gordon.. ..	4 Aug. 1800
Redmond Walsh ..	6 Aug. 1800
Daniel Page ..	8 Aug. 1800
George F. Gibson ..	11 Aug. 1800
James Landells ..	12 Aug. 1800
Carew Reynell ..	13 Aug. 1800
Robert Gordon ..	2 Oct. 1800
Godfred Stark ..	16 Oct. 1800
Thomas Coleman ..	17 Oct. 1800
John Jackson ..	21 Oct. 1800
—— Glenie ..	23 Oct. 1800
—— Redmond ..	25 Oct. 1800
Archibald Campbell ..	12 Mar. 1801
Rank in Army, 23 July 1800	
William Forrard ..	19 May 1801
Rank in Army, 16 Dec. 1799	
Thomas Rowland ..	27 May 1801
—— Pillersdorff ..	26 June 1801
Robert Thompson ..	25 July 1801
Rank in Army, 14 May 1801	
Richard Henry Hughes..	15 Aug. 1801
Thomas Fernyhough ..	25 Sept. 1801
Rank in Army, 21 May 1783	
Peter Irwine	2 Oct. 1801
Rank in Army, 12 June 1800	
John Beardman ..	30 Oct. 1801
G. Ramsay	30 Nov. 1801
J. Trundock	25 April 1802
J. Hanmer	25 April 1802
J. Rimer	25 April 1802
Rank in Army, 7 Aug. 1801	
J. Eckhard	25 April 1802
Rank in Army, 8 Aug. 1801	

Rank and Name.	Rank in Regiment.
Ensigns (continued)—	
Henry Dibbey.. ..	25 June 1802
John Watson	25 June 1802
James Nethery.. ..	1 July 1802
Henry Henrage St. Paul	12 Nov. 1802
Paymasters—	
Fred. Sam. Pehl ..	28 Feb. 1798
James Lawson ..	5 April 1798
James Nolan ..	2 Oct. 1800
Thomas Pierce **Harte** ..	1 Oct. 1802
John Munro ..	1 Oct. 1802
Adjutants—	
L. de Boose	22 Mar. 1798
Rank in Army, Lieut. 30 Dec. 1797	
—— Hamelin.. ..	4 July 1798
Rank in Army, Lieut. 30 Dec. 1797	
John Moore	9 Aug. 1799
Henry Dibbly.. ..	8 Feb. 1800
Rank in Army Ensign, 25 June 1802	
William Murray ..	24 Mar. 1800
Rank in Army, Lieut. 17 Sept. 1801	
Frederick Giles ..	14 April 1800
Rank in Army, Lieut. 30 Dec. 1797	
John Watson	25 Oct. 1800
Rank in Army, Ensign 25 June 1802	
Quartermasters—	
—— Kenneter ..	30 Dec. 1797
Denis Alexander ..	5 Sept. 1799
Joseph Chattowsy ..	3 July 1800
Peter Child	3 July 1801
Joseph Piercy.. ..	25 Nov. 1802
Surgeons—	
James Henderson ..	10 Nov. 1775
Anthony Reifer ..	30 Dec. 1797
John Feries	21 Dec. 1800
Samuel Cathcart ..	28 Mar. 1801
Robert M'Intyre ..	1 Oct. 1801
—— Stewart	13 Aug. 1802
Assistant-Surgeons—	
—— Felling	30 Dec. 1797
Fred. Mishke ..	1 Mar. 1800
—— Doughty ..	30 Oct. 1800
David Brown ..	30 Sept. 1801
Edward Jarvis ..	13 Dec. 1801
John Murton.. ..	13 Aug. 1802
—— Little	15 Oct. 1802
Gilles Tucks	18 Nov. 1802
John Carroll	18 Nov. 1802

Regimentals—Red, facings blue, white lace, 2 blue stripes.

5th Rifle Battalion, green.

Agents—Messrs. Cox, Greenwood, & Cox, Craig's Court.

1804.

Six Battalions.

West Indies—North America—South America.

Colonel-in-Chief—

H.R.H. Fred. Duke of York, K.G.	23 Aug. 1797

Rank in Army, Field-Mar. 10 Feb. 1795.

L.

Rank and Name.	Rank in Regiment.
Cols.-Commandant—	
William Rowley	3 Oct. 1787
Rank in Army, Gen.	1 Jan. 1798
Thomas Carleton	6 Aug. 1794
Rank in Army, 25 Sept. 1803	
Peter Hunter	2 Aug. 1796
Rank in Army, Lt.-Gen. 29 April 1802	
William Gardiner	11 Mar. 1799
Rank in Army, Lt.-Gen. 26 June 1799	
Robert Brownrigg	25 July 1799
Rank in Army, Maj.-Gen. 29 April 1802	
Tho. Slaughter Stanwix..	9 May 1800
Rank in Army, Lt.-Gen. 26 June 1799	
Lieut.-Colonels—	
James Adolph. Harris ..	16 Jan. 1788
Rank in Army, Maj.-Gen. 1 Jan. 1798	
George Prevost	6 Aug. 1794
Rank in Army, Col. 1 Jan. 1798	
Duncan Macintosh.. ..	1 Sept. 1795
Rank in Army, Col. 25 Sept. 1803	
Geo. William Ramsay ..	30 Dec. 1797
Rank in Army, Col. 25 Sept. 1803	
Fra., Baron de Rottenburg	30 Dec. 1797
Rank in Army, 25 June 1796	
Lachlan Maclean	25 July 1799
Rank in Army, 1 Jan. 1798	
Fitz. J. Grafton Maclean.	5 Feb. 1801
Rank in Army, Col. 25 Sept. 1803	
Robert Lethbridge.. ..	11 Feb. 1802
Rank in Army, 1 Jan. 1800	
Gabriel Gordon	9 Mar. 1802
Rank in Army, 1 Jan. 1800	
C. L. Theod. Schoedde ..	28 April 1802
Rank in Army, 16 May 1800	
Gervase Rainy	20 April 1803
Francis Streicher	30 Dec. 1797
Rank in Army, Lt.-Col. 29 April 1802	
Majors—	
L. Mosheim	30 Dec. 1797
Rank in Army, Lt.-Col. 29 April 1802	
Edward Codd	25 Dec. 1800
Edward Drummond ..	11 June 1801
Thomas Austin	3 July 1801
George Mackie	8 Mar. 1802
John Pringle Dalrymple.	13 Mar. 1802
Thomas Clarke	24 June 1802
James Lomax	20 April 1803
James Wheeler Unwin ..	21 April 1803
Rank in Army, Lt.-Col. 29 April 1802	
James Bathurst	1 Oct. 1803
Robert Campbell	24 Nov. 1803
Rank in Army, Lt.-Col. 1 Jan. 1800	
Captains—	
John Robertson	10 Sept. 1795
George Fourneret	16 Dec. 1795
Thomas McKee	20 Feb. 1796
Colin Campbell	8 June 1796
Rank in Army, Major 25 Sept. 1803	
James Grant	25 April 1797
John Galiffe	30 Dec. 1797
Rank in Army, 31 Oct. 1796	
Benedict Simon	30 Dec. 1797
Ferdinand Creest	30 Dec. 1797
Francis St. Mart	30 Dec. 1797
Anthony Rumpler	31 Dec. 1797

Rank and Name.	Rank in Regiment.
Captains (continued)—	
—— Vorstadt	30 Dec. 1797
Francis Gomer	30 Dec. 1797
Charles de la Houssaye..	30 Dec. 1797
—— Inturn	30 Dec. 1797
Charles Tauriac	30 Dec. 1797
—— Gand	30 Dec. 1797
Lewis Schneider	30 Dec. 1797
Gasper Rouvray	30 Dec. 1797
—— Braun	30 Dec. 1797
Ambrose Hillerick	30 Dec. 1797
William Marlton	25 Oct. 1798
Daniel Dixon	25 Nov. 1798
William J. O'Connor ..	24 Jan. 1799
Rank in Army, 1 Oct. 1794	
Charles de Salaberry ..	10 July 1799
William Fraser	15 July 1799
Rank in Army, 26 Feb. 1797	
William Fraser	25 July 1799
Walter Johnson	5 Jan. 1800
John William Aldred ..	19 Nov. 1800
Daniel Hutchins Cairns..	24 July 1801
William Goodlad	11 Dec. 1801
William Gabriel Davy ..	1 Jan. 1802
Joseph Twigg	31 Mar. 1802
Rank in Army, 28 Mar. 1800	
H. C. Appelius	28 April 1802
Rank in Army, 21 Aug. 1801	
William Drummond ..	16 July 1802
Charles Gordon	6 Aug. 1802
George Bent	8 Sept.1802
William Batteley	15 Mar. 1803
Rank in Army, 5 Oct. 1795	
John Welsford	16 Mar. 1803
Rank in Army, 27 Dec. 1796	
William Woodgate.. ..	6 April 1803
William White	26 May 1803
Rank in Army, 25 Oct. 1794	
Kenelm Chandler	28 May 1803
William Plenderleath ..	29 May 1803
James McArthur	30 May 1803
Robert Hazen	31 May 1803
David Joly	1 June 1804
Alexander Andrews ..	2 June 1803
Alexander Deiken	22 June 1803
Rank in Army, Lt.-Col. 22 June 1803	
John Campbell	25 June 1803
Donald McNeill	25 June 1803
John Cummings	25 June 1803
George Cartwright.. ..	25 June 1803
James Bunting	25 June 1803
—— De Mangou	25 June 1803
Philip Maurrage	2 July 1803
William Williams	3 July 1803
Richard Buthe	4 July 1803
—— Grun	12 Aug. 1803
Rank in Army, 24 Nov. 1800	
Geo. H. Duckworth ..	17 Aug. 1803
John MacMahon	20 Aug. 1803
Thomas Hames	12 Nov. 1803
Lieutenants—	
Thomas Durham	1 Sept. 1796
W. H. Quist	23 May 1797
Thomas Henderson ..	9 Aug. 1797
Chn. Cranstoun Dixon ..	24 Aug. 1797
Lewis de Ratzenhausen..	30 Dec. 1797

Rank and Name.	Rank in Regiment.	Rank and Name.	Rank in Regiment.
Lieutenants (continued)—		*Lieutenants* (continued)—	
Michael de Wendt ..	.. 30 Dec. 1797	Henry Fischbach ..	.. 28 Jan. 1801
—— Hamelin ..	.. 30 Dec. 1797	C. Blathfield ..	.. 5 Feb. 1801
Hubert de Salve ..	.. 30 Dec. 1797	Wm. Ackland Gilland	.. 14 May 1801
Alexander de Conders	.. 30 Dec. 1797	*Rank in Army*, 21 Dec. 1796	
—— Scheding. ..	.. 30 Dec. 1797	Thomas Ellis ..	.. 15 May 1801
Adolphus Munstal ..	.. 30 Dec. 1797	*Rank in Army*, 29 Jan. 1801	
Charles Kinsinger ..	.. 30 Dec. 1797	Abraham Logan ..	.. 17 July 1801
Lewis Inturn ..	.. 30 Dec. 1797	William Murray ..	.. 17 Sept. 1801
Adam Krien ..	.. 30 Dec. 1797	John White ..	.. 6 April 1802
Peter Blassiere ..	.. 30 Dec. 1797	*Rank in Army*, 29 Jan. 1801	
George Fred. de Virna	.. 30 Dec. 1797	William Walther ..	.. 25 April 1802
—— Killenpach ..	.. 30 Dec. 1797	*Rank in Army*, 28 June 1800	
John Wootlf ..	.. 30 Dec. 1797	Lewis Runnan ..	.. 25 April 1802
F. de Reynauld ..	.. 30 Dec. 1797	*Rank in Army*, 7 Aug. 1801	
Frederick Odce ..	.. 30 Dec. 1797	J. H. Schoedde ..	.. 25 April 1802
Charles de Vigny ..	.. 30 Dec. 1797	*Rank in Army*, 8 Oct. 1801	
—— Schmidt ..	.. 30 Dec. 1797	Alexander Mackenzie	.. 29 June 1802
—— Franchasson ..	.. 30 Dec. 1797	*Rank in Army*, 27 Feb. 1796	
L. de Bosne ..	.. 30 Dec. 1797	Francis Holmes ..	.. 18 Aug. 1802
—— Brock ..	.. 29 Mar. 1798	*Rank in Army*, 28 Aug. 1801	
Charles Hinkelly ..	.. 25 April 1798	Richard Philbin ..	.. 29 Oct. 1802
—— Schultics ..	.. 25 April 1798	*Rank in Army*, 22 Oct. 1799	
John Fitzmaurice ..	.. 14 Feb. 1799	Richard Cochran ..	.. 18 Dec. 1802
Rank in Army, 21 Dec. 1796		*Rank in Army*, 19 Sept. 1801	
James Campbell ..	.. 19 May 1799	Godrick Sarda. ..	.. 19 Dec. 1802
Ch. Baron de Selchow	.. 1 June 1799	J. B. Kerrison. ..	.. 20 Dec. 1802
James Erskine Bell	.. 8 Oct. 1799	Orange Balneavis ..	.. 21 Dec. 1802
John D. Plancher ..	.. 11 July 1800	David Balneavis ..	.. 22 Dec. 1802
John L. Gallie ..	.. 12 July 1800	Robert Thompson ..	.. 23 Dec. 1802
—— Rogers ..	.. 14 July 1800	A. Henry Kelsey ..	.. 24 Dec. 1802
—— de Carneros ..	.. 15 July 1800	Richard Daly ..	.. 10 Feb. 1803
Thomas Walsh ..	.. 18 July 1800	*Rank in Army*, 26 June 1801	
Charles du Sable ..	.. 20 July 1800	Francis Cockburne. ..	.. 6 April 1803
C. N. Loth ..	.. 21 July 1800	Edward Byrne. ..	.. 4 May 1803
Henry Boone Hall. ..	.. 23 July 1800	*Rank in Army*, 12 Aug. 1801	
Rank in Army, 1 May 1797		J. N. Muller ..	.. 5 May 1803
George P. Schneider	.. 24 July 1800	Robert Hawthorne. ..	.. 26 May 1803
Anthony Stanba ..	.. 25 July 1800	*Rank in Army*, 27 June 1801	
—— Mortens ..	.. 28 July 1800	V. J. Ravenscroft ..	.. 28 May 1803
——Kellerman ..	.. 29 July 1800	Thomas Frazer ..	.. 29 May 1803
Henry Petrie . ..	.. 30 July 1800	David Gordon. ..	.. 30 May 1803
C. W. H. Koch ..	.. 2 Aug. 1800	Redmond Walsh ..	.. 31 May 1803
—— Kemmeter ..	.. 3 Aug. 1800	Daniel Page ..	.. 1 June 1803
—— Myers ..	.. 5 Aug. 1800	George F. Gibson ..	.. 2 June 1803
George Henry Zulke	.. 6 Aug. 1800	William Brooke ..	.. 25 June 1803
—— Berger ..	.. 7 Aug. 1800	James Lambdils ..	.. 25 June 1803
—— Friess ..	.. 8 Aug. 1800	Carew Reynell ..	.. 26 June 1803
George W. Avenar. ..	.. 9 Aug. 1800	Robert Gordon ..	.. 27 June 1803
A. Ostman ..	.. 10 Aug. 1800	Godfrey Stark. ..	.. 28 June 1803
Baron D'Oyn ..	.. 10 Aug. 1800	Thomas Coleman ..	.. 29 June 1803
H. Baron Adelsheim	.. 11 Aug. 1800	Melville Gleme ..	.. 30 June 1803
Charles Haeke ..	.. 13 Aug. 1800	—— Redmond ..	.. 1 July 1803
Charles Dixon Green	.. 14 Aug. 1800	Archibald Campbell	.. 2 July 1803
William McKinnon ..	.. 18 Sept. 1800	Everard Baring ..	.. 12 Nov. 1803
Rank in Army, 28 May 1783		*Rank in Army*, 7 Aug. 1801	
Florence McCarthy ..	.. 16 Oct. 1800	C. F. Baring ..	.. 12 Nov. 1803
Frederick des Barres	.. 20 Oct. 1800	James Nottory ..	.. 12 Nov. 1803
James Le Geyer ..	.. 21 Oct. 1800	Edward Llewellyn ..	.. 27 July 1803
James Moore ..	.. 22 Oct. 1800	John Jackson ..	.. 21 Oct. 1800
William Yates Johnson.	.. 24 Oct. 1800	William Farrand ..	.. 19 May 1804
Allan Maclean ..	.. 26 Oct. 1800	*Rank in Army*, 16 Dec. 1799	
Anthony Sousso ..	.. 27 Oct. 1800	Thomas Rowland ..	.. 27 May 1804
Richard R. Nugent. ..	.. 20 Dec. 1800	Robert Thompson ..	.. 28 July 1804
John Herbert ..	.. 25 Dec. 1800	*Rank in Army*, 14 May 1804	
Rank in Army, 1 Nov. 1795		Richard Henry Hughes.	15 Aug. 1804

L 2

Rank and Name.	Rank in Regiment.

Lieutenants (continued)—

Peter Irwine	2 Oct. 1801
Rank in Army, 12 June 1800	
John Boardman	30 Oct. 1801
G. Ramsay	30 Nov. 1801
J. Rimer	25 April 1802
Rank in Army, 7 Aug. 1801	
J. Eckhard	25 April 1802
Rank in Army, 8 Aug. 1801	
J. Trumback	28 April 1802
J. Hammer	28 April 1802
J. Bartoli..	28 April 1802
Henry Dibbly.. ..	25 June 1802
John Watson	25 June 1802
William Hobart ..	17 Dec. 1802
T. Franchini	22 Dec. 1802
Francis Bretze ..	23 Dec. 1802
Charles Appelius ..	24 Dec. 1802
Robert Johnson ..	24 Mar. 1803
Jacobus Hazel.. ..	19 June 1803
John Terry	20 June 1803
Edward Schultz ..	22 June 1803

Ensigns—

Valentine Ricchard ..	23 June 1803
—— Malaspina ..	24 June 1803
—— Schemmelkehl ..	3 Aug. 1803
—— Von Lindenberg ..	4 Aug. 1803
R. K. Mews	6 Aug. 1803
Frederick W. Kyth ..	12 Aug. 1803
Rank in Army, 28 Sept. 1803	
Charles Richardson ..	27 Aug. 1803
Rank in Army, 13 Nov. 1799	
George Jack	3 Sept. 1803
—— Klinkerfuss ..	13 Nov. 1803
William Willermin..	14 Nov. 1803
Henry Lodge	15 Nov. 1803
—— McIntire.. ..	16 Nov. 1803
Lewis Poincey.. ..	17 Nov. 1803
—— Sawarsky ..	19 Nov. 1803
Charles Rausch ..	8 Dec. 1803

Paymasters —

Fred. Sam. Pohl ..	28 Feb. 1798
James Lawson.. ..	5 April 1798
James Nolan	2 Oct. 1800
Fra. E. Matz	2 May 1803

Adjutants—

L. de Bosso	22 Mar. 1798
Rank in Army, Lieut. 30 Dec. 1797	
—— Hamelin	4 July 1798
Rank in Army, Lieut. 30 Dec. 1797	
John Moore	9 Aug. 1799
Henry Dibbly.. ..	5 Feb. 1800
Rank in Army, Ensign 2 June 1802	
William Murray ..	24 Mar. 1800
Rank in Army, Lieut. 17 Sept. 1801	
Frederick Gilse ..	14 April 1800
Rank in Army, Lieut. 30 Dec. 1797	
John Watson	25 Oct. 1800
Rank in Army, Ensign 25 June 1802	

Quartermasters —

—— Kennecter ..	30 Dec. 1797
Denis Alexander ..	5 Sept. 1798
Joseph Chattoway ..	3 July 1800

Rank and Name.	Rank in Regiment.

Quartermasters (continued)—

Peter Child	3 July 1801
Richard Marriott ..	31 Mar. 1803

Surgeons—

Anthony Reifer ..	30 Dec. 1797
John Feries	21 Dec. 1800
Samuel Cathcart ..	28 Mar. 1801
Robert McIntire ..	1 Oct. 1801
F. Fielder	25 Dec. 1802
William Powell ..	25 Mar. 1803

Assistant-Surgeons—

—— Felling	31 Dec. 1797
Frederick Midike ..	1 Mar. 1800
—— Little	3 Jan. 1801
David Browne.. ..	30 Sept. 1801
Edward Jarvis ..	13 Dec. 1801
John Marton.. ..	13 Aug. 1802
John Carroll	25 Sept. 1802
J. Adolphus	10 Oct. 1802
—— Jackson	12 Oct. 1802
Gilles Tucks	18 Nov. 1802

Regimentals—Red, facings blue, white, lace, 2 blue stripes.

5th Rifle Battalion, green.

Agent—Messrs. Greenwood and Cox, Craig's Court.

1805.

Six Battalions.

West Indies—England.

Col.-in-Chief—

H.R.H. Fred., Duke of York, K.G.	23 Aug. 1797
Rank in Army, Field-M. 10 Feb. 1795	

Cols.-Commandant—

William Rowley	3 Oct. 1787
Rank in Army, Gen. 1 Jan. 1798	
Thomas Carleton	6 Aug. 1794
Rank in Army, Gen. 25 Sept. 1883	
William Gardiner	11 Mar. 1799
Rank in Army, Lt.-Gen. 26 June 1799	
Robert Brownrigg	25 July 1799
Rank in Army, Maj.-Gen. 29 April 1802	
Thos. Slaughter Stanwix	9 May 1800
Rank in Army, Lt.-Gen. 29 June 1799	
Lord Charles Fitzroy ..	15 June 1804
Rank in Army, Maj.-Gen. 1 Jan. 1798	
Hon. John Hope	3 Oct. 1805

Lieut.-Colonels—

James Adolphus Harris	16 Jan. 1788
Rank in Army, Maj.-Gen. 1 Jan. 1798	
George Prevost	6 Aug. 1794
Rank in Army, Col. 1 Jan. 1798	
Duncan Mackintosh ..	1 Sept. 1795
Rank in Army, Col. 25 Sept. 1803	
George William Ramsay	30 Dec. 1797
Rank in Army, Col. 25 Sept. 1803	
Fra. Baron de Rottenburg	30 Dec. 1797
Rank in Army, 25 June 1796	

Rank and Name.	Rank in Regiment.

Lieut.-Colonels (continued)--

| Gabriel Gordon | .. .. 9 Mar. 1802 |
| *Rank in Army,* 25 June 1796 |
| **C.** L. Theod. Schoedde .. 25 April 1802 |
| *Rank in Army,* 16 May 1800 |
| Gervaise Rainey .. .. 20 April 1803 |
| *Rank in Army,* 16 May 1800 |
| John Hope .. .. .. 30 June 1804 |
| *Rank in Army,* 20 Feb. 1796 |
| L. Mosheim .. .. .. 14 Sept. 1804 |
| *Rank in Army,* 29 April 1802 |
| Edward Codd .. .. .. 26 Oct. 1804 |

Majors--

| Edmund Drummond .. 11 June 1801 |
| Thomas Austin .. .. 3 July 1801 |
| George Mackie .. .. 8 Mar. 1802 |
| Thomas Clarke .. .. 24 June 1802 |
| James Lomax .. .. 20 April 1803 |
| James Wheeler Unwin . 21 April 1803 |
| *Rank in Army,* Lt.-Col. 29 April 1802 |
| James Bathurst .. .. 1 Oct. 1803 |
| Anthony Wharton .. 26 July 1803 |
| **Rank in Army,** 3 Feb. 1803 |
| **John Robertson** .. .. 14 Sept. 1804 |

Captains--

| George Fourmerett .. .. 16 Dec. 1795 |
| Thomas Mackes .. .. 20 Feb. 1796 |
| Colin Campbell .. 8 June 1796 |
| *Rank in Army,* **Major** 25 Sept. 1803 |
| James Grant .. .. .. 25 April 1797 |
| John Galiffe .. .. 30 Dec. 1797 |
| *Rank in Army,* 31 Oct. 1796 |
| Benedict Sutton .. .. 30 Dec. 1797 |
| Ferdinand Creset .. .. 30 Dec. 1797 |
| Francis St. Mart .. 30 Dec. 1797 |
| Anthony Rumpler .. .. 30 Dec. 1797 |
| —— Vorstadt .. .. 30 Dec. 1797 |
| Francis Comer .. .. 30 Dec. 1797 |
| Charles de la Houssaye.. 30 Dec. 1797 |
| Charles Taurine .. .. 30 Dec. 1797 |
| —— **Gaud** .. .. 30 Dec. 1797 |
| **Gaspar Rouvray** .. .. 30 Dec. 1797 |
| —— **Braun** .. .. 30 Dec. 1797 |
| Ambrose Hilderick .. 30 Dec. 1797 |
| William Mariton .. .. 25 Oct. 1798 |
| Daniel Nixon .. .. 25 Nov. 1798 |
| William J. O'Connor .. 24 Jan. 1799 |
| *Rank in Army,* 1 Oct. 1794 |
| Charles de Salaberry .. 10 July 1799 |
| William Fraser .. .. 15 July 1799 |
| *Rank in Army,* 26 Feb. 1797 |
| William Fraser .. .. 25 July 1799 |
| Walter Johnson .. .. 5 Jan. 1800 |
| John William Morel .. 19 Nov. 1800 |
| William Goodlad .. .. 11 Dec. 1801 |
| William Gabriel Davy .. 1 Jan. 1802 |
| Joseph Twigg .. .. 31 Mar. 1802 |
| *Rank in Army,* 28 Mar. 1800 |
| H. C. Appelius .. .. 25 April 1802 |
| *Rank in Army,* 21 Aug. 1801 |
| William Drummond .. 16 July 1802 |
| William Batteley .. .. 15 Mar. 1803 |
| *Rank in Army,* 5 Oct. 1799 |
| John Welsford .. .. 16 Mar. 1803 |
| *Rank in Army,* 27 Dec. 1799 |

Rank and Name.	Rank in Regiment.

Captains (continued)--

| William Woodgate.. .. 6 April 1803 |
| William White .. .. 26 May 1803 |
| *Rank in Army,* 25 Oct. 1794 |
| Kenelm Chandler .. .. 28 May 1803 |
| William Plenderleath .. 29 May 1803 |
| James M'Arthur .. .. 30 May 1803 |
| Robert Hazen .. .. 31 May 1803 |
| Alexander Andrews .. 2 June 1803 |
| John Campbell .. .. 25 June 1803 |
| Donald M'Neill .. .. 25 June 1803 |
| George Cartwright.. .. 25 June 1803 |
| James Bunting .. .. 25 June 1803 |
| —— De Mangon .. .. 25 June 1803 |
| Philip Mauriage .. .. 2 July 1803 |
| William Williams .. .. 3 July 1803 |
| —— Gran .. .. 12 Aug. 1803 |
| *Rank in Army,* 24 Nov. 1800 |
| John MacMahon .. .. 29 Aug. 1803 |
| Thomas Hames .. .. 12 Nov. 1803 |
| Samuel Courtenay .. .. 31 Dec. 1803 |
| *Rank in Army,* 24 May 1802 |
| Nathaniel Humphries .. 6 July 1804 |
| Thomas Henderson .. 7 July 1804 |
| Hon. Leveson Blackwood 5 Oct. 1804 |
| *Rank in Army,* 15 Nov. 1794 |
| Charles Vigny .. .. 1 Nov. 1804 |
| **C. Lane** Murphy .. .. 23 Nov. 1804 |
| *Rank in Army,* 4 Mar. 1801 |

Lieutenants--

| Charles Cranstoun Dixon 24 Aug. 1797 |
| Michel de Wendt .. .. 30 Aug. 1797 |
| —— Hamelin .. .. 30 Aug. 1797 |
| Hubert de Salon .. .. 30 Aug. 1797 |
| —— Scheling .. .. 30 Aug. 1797 |
| Charles Kinsinger .. .. 30 Dec. 1797 |
| Lewis Inturn.. .. .. 30 Dec. 1797 |
| Adam Krieu .. .. .. 30 Dec. 1797 |
| Peter Blassiere .. .. 30 Dec. 1797 |
| Geo. Fred. de Virna .. 30 Dec. 1797 |
| —— Killeaguch .. .. 30 Dec. 1797 |
| John Woolf .. .. .. 30 Dec. 1797 |
| L. de Reynauld .. .. 30 Dec. 1797 |
| —— Schmidt.. .. .. 30 Dec. 1797 |
| L. de Bosse .. .. .. 30 Dec. 1797 |
| Charles Hinkeldy .. .. 25 April 1798 |
| —— Schultzs .. .. 25 April 1798 |
| Ch. Baron de Selchow .. 1 June 1798 |
| James Erskine Bell .. 8 Oct. 1798 |
| John de Plancher .. .. 11 July 1800 |
| —— Rogers .. .. .. 14 July 1800 |
| —— de Cumeres .. .. 15 July 1800 |
| Thomas Walsh .. .. 18 July 1800 |
| Charles du Sable .. .. 20 July 1800 |
| J. N. Loth .. .. .. 21 July 1800 |
| Anthony Straube .. .. 25 July 1800 |
| —— Mertens.. .. .. 28 July 1800 |
| —— Kellermann .. .. 29 July 1800 |
| Henry Petrie.. .. .. 30 July 1800 |
| C. W. H. Koch .. .. 2 Aug. 1800 |
| —— Myers .. .. .. 5 Aug. 1800 |
| George Henry Zulke .. 6 Aug. 1800 |
| —— Berger .. .. .. 7 Aug. 1800 |
| William Friess .. .. 8 Aug. 1800 |
| A. Ostman .. .. .. 9 Aug. 1800 |
| H. Baron Ade Germ .. 11 Aug. 1800 |

Rank and Name.	Rank in Regiment.
Lieutenants (continued)—	
Charles Hawke	13 Aug. 1800
Charles Dixon Green ..	14 Aug. 1800
William M'Kinnon,. ..	18 Sept. 1800
Rank in Army, 28 May 1783	
Florence M'Carthy.. ..	16 Oct. 1800
Frederick Desbarres ..	20 Oct. 1800
James Moore..	22 Oct. 1800
William Yates Johnson..	24 Oct. 1800
Allan Maclean..	26 Oct. 1800
Anthony Suasso	27 Oct. 1800
Richard R. Nugent ..	20 Dec. 1800
John Herbert..	25 Dec. 1800
Rank in Army, 4 Nov. 1795	
Henry Fischbach	28 Jan. 1801
William Ackland Gillan	14 May 1801
Rank in Army, 21 Dec. 1796	
Thomas Ellis	15 May 1801
Rank in Army, 29 Jan. 1801	
William Murray	17 Sept. 1801
John White	6 April 1802
Rank in Army, 29 Jan. 1801	
William Walther	25 April 1802
Rank in Army, 28 June 1800	
Lewis Runnan	25 April 1802
Rank in Army, 7 Aug. 1801	
J. H. Schoe.de	25 April 1802
Rank in Army, 8 Oct. 1801	
Alexander Mackenzie ..	25 June 1802
Rank in Army, 27 Feb. 1796	
Francis Holmes	13 Aug. 1802
Rank in Army, 28 Aug. 1801	
Richard Philbin	29 Oct. 1802
Rank in Army, 22 Oct. 1799	
Orange Balneavis	21 Dec. 1802
Rank in Army, 2 June 1801	
Richard Daly	10 Feb. 1803
Rank in Army, 26 June 1801	
Edward Byrne	4 May 1803
Rank in Army, 12 Aug. 1801	
David Gordon..	30 May 1803
Redmond Walsh	31 May 1803
Daniel Page	1 June 1803
George F. Gibson	2 June 1803
William Brooke	25 June 1803
Carew Reynell	26 June 1803
Robert Gordon	27 June 1803
Godfrey Stark..	28 June 1803
Melville Glenie	30 June 1803
Archibald Campbell ..	2 July 1803
Everard Baring	12 Nov. 1803
Rank in Army, 7 Aug. 1801	
C. F. Baring	12 Nov. 1803
Rank in Army, 1 Aug. 1801	
Richard Henry Hughes..	3 Mar. 1804
Lewis Ritter	24 Mar. 1804
Rank in Army, 17 Mar. 1804	
John Boardman	25 Mar. 1804
Matthew Towes	14 May 1804
Rank in Army, 2 Dec. 1796	
G. Ramsay	19 May 1804
J. Reignier	20 May 1804
J. Turnbuck	21 May 1804
Henry Dibbly..	23 May 1804
John Watson	24 May 1804
Frederick Steitz	9 June 1804

Rank and Name.	Rank in Regiment.
Lieutenants (continued)—	
John Blair	30 June 1804
Rank in Army, 1 Oct. 1794	
William Hobart	30 Aug. 1804
George West Barnes ..	14 Sept. 1804
Rank in Army, 5 May 1800	
J. Franchin	8 Nov. 1804
Ensigns—	
Edward Llewellyn.. ..	27 July 1800
Francis Bretze	23 Dec. 1802
Charles Appellius	24 Dec. 1802
Jacobus Hojel..	19 June 1803
John Toore	30 June 1803
Edward Schultze	22 June 1803
Valentine Ricchard ..	23 June 1803
—— Malafpina	24 June 1803
R. K. Mews	6 Aug. 1803
Charles Richardson ..	27 Aug. 1803
Rank in Army, 13 Nov. 1799	
—— Deckner..	8 Sept. 1803
—— Klinkerfuss	13 Nov. 1803
—— M'Intire..	16 Nov. 1803
Lewis Poincey..	17 Nov. 1803
—— Sawarsky	19 Nov. 1803
Charles Rausch	8 Dec. 1803
Charles Cartwright.. ..	17 Dec. 1803
Ern. F. C. B. Richter ..	4 Jan. 1804
Ern. A. Baron D'Eberstein	2 Feb. 1804
George Germain	3 Mar. 1804
Richard Campbell	4 Mar. 1804
Lewis de Saluberry ..	5 Mar. 1804
F. Dunker	17 Mar. 1804
Rank in Army, 9 July 1803	
John August Dietrichsen	14 May 1804
James M'Kay..	21 May 1804
Lewis Appelius	1 June 1804
Ernest C. Kersting.. ..	2 June 1804
J. F. Galbraith	14 July 1804
M. Francis A. Tresson ..	19 July 1804
Rank in Army, 19 Nov. 1796	
—— Morphew	4 Aug. 1804
John Correvant	30 Aug. 1804
—— Schriewe..	7 Sept. 1804
Henry Muller..	8 Sept. 1804
Benjamin Keyfer	14 Sept. 1804
James Gubbins	12 Oct. 1804
Peter Warren	19 Oct. 1804
—— Kageneck	1 Nov. 1804
Paymasters—	
Frederick Sam. Pohl ..	28 Feb. 1798
James Nolan	2 Oct. 1800
Fra. E. Matz	2 May 1803
John Tapp	21 May 1804
Michael Byrne	19 Oct. 1804
Edward Hansler	1 Dec. 1804
Adjutants—	
L. de Busse	22 Mar. 1798
Rank in Army, Lieut. 30 Dec. 1797	
—— Hamelin	4 July 1798
Rank in Army, Lieut. 30 Dec. 1797	
John Moore	9 Aug. 1799
Henry Dibbly..	5 Feb. 1800
Rank in Army, Lieut. 23 May 1804	
John Watson	25 Oct. 1800
Rank in Army, Lieut. 21 May 1804	

Rank and Name.	Rank in Regiment.
Adjutants (continued)—	
—— Decknor..	8 Sept. 1803
Rank in Army, Ensign	8 Sept. 1803
Quartermasters—	
Kemmeter	30 Dec. 1797
Joseph Chattoway	3 July 1800
Peter Child	3 July 1801
Richard Marriott	31 Mar. 1803
Joseph Wilson	25 May 1804
Surgeons—	
John Feries	21 Dec. 1800
Samuel Cathcart	28 Mar. 1801
F. Fielder	25 Dec. 1802
—— Von **Malden** ..	28 Oct. 1804
Assistant Surgeons—	
Frederick Midike	1 Mar. 1800
—— Little	3 Jan. 1801
David Browne.. ..	30 Sept. 1801
Edward Jarvis	13 Dec. 1801
John Carroll	25 Sept. 1802
J. Adolphus	19 Oct. 1802
—— Jackson	12 Oct. 1802
J. A. du Moulin	28 April 1804
Augustus Kreich	25 June 1804

Regimentals—Red, facings blue, white lace, 2 blue stripes.

5th Rifle Battalion, green.

Agents—**Messrs.** Greenwood and Cox, Craig's Court.

1806.*

Six Battalions

West Indies—England—Africa.

Colonel-in-Chief—	
H.R.H. Fred., Duke **of** York .. Field Mar. **23 Aug** 1797
Cols. Commandant—	
W. Rowley .. .. G. 3 Oct. 1797
F. Carleton .. .. G. 6 Aug. 1799
Ed. Morrison .. .. 1 Jan. 1800
N. C. Burton .. .. 1 Jan. 1800
W. Keppel .. .. 1 Jan. 1805
Sir G. Prevost, Bart .. 1 Jan. 1805
Lieut.-Colonels—	
J. A. Harris .. L. G. 16 Jan. 1795
G. W. Ramsay .. .. 30 Dec. 1797
F. Baron de Rottenburg 25 June 1798
Gab. Gordon .. .. 9 Mar. 1801
Ger. Raney .. .. 20 April 1803
John Hope .. .. 30 June 1804
L. von Mosheim .. 14 Sept. 1804
Edw. Cold .. .. 26 Oct. 1804
Edw. Drummond .. 29 Dec. 1804
Thos. Austin .. .. 20 June 1805
Majors—	
Geo. Mackie .. .. 8 Mar. 1802
Thos. Clarke .. .. 24 June 1802
Jas. Lomax .. .. 20 April 1803

Rank and Name.	Rank in Regiment.
Majors (continued)—	
J. W. Unwin	.. 21 April 1803
Ja. Bathurst	.. 1 Oct. 1803
And. Wharton	.. 26 July 1804
John Robertson	.. 28 July 1804
Fras. S. Mart	.. 5 Jan. 1805
W. Marlton	.. 25 July 1806
Captains—	
G. Fourneret	.. 16 Dec. 1795
C. Campbell	.. 8 June 1796
Jas. Grant	.. 25 April 1797
J. Galiffe	.. 30 Dec. 1797
Ant. Rumpler	.. 30 Dec. 1797
Ferd. Vorstadt	.. 30 Dec. 1797
F. Gomer..	.. 30 Dec. 1797
C. Bouverie	.. 30 Dec. 1797
Gust. Brown	.. 30 Dec. 1797
W. C. O'Connor ..	M. 24 Jan. 1799
C. de Saluberry ..	.. 10 July 1799
Wm. Fraser	.. 15 July 1799
John Wm. Aldred ..	.. 19 Nov. 1800
W. G. Davy	.. 1 Jan. 1802
J. Twigg	.. 28 Mar. 1802
Wm. Drummond ..	.. 16 July 1802
Wm. Batteley	.. 15 Mar. 1803
John Welsford ..	.. 18 Mar. 1803
W. Woodgate	.. 6 April 1803
Kenelm Chandler ..	.. 28 May 1803
W. Plenderleath ..	.. 29 May 1803
Jas. McArthur ..	.. 30 May 1803
Rob. Hazen	.. 31 May 1803
A. Andrews	.. 2 June 1803
E. Norton	.. 24 June 1803
Wm. Fraser	.. 25 June 1803
J. Campbell	.. 25 June 1803
Donald McNeill ..	.. 25 June 1803
J. Hunting	.. 25 June 1803
D. de Mangon.. ..	.. 25 June 1803
P. Maurage	.. 2 July 1803
Wm. Williams ..	.. 3 July 1803
Geo. Gran	.. 12 April 1803
J. McMahon	.. 20 April 1803
Thomas Hames ..	.. 12 Nov. 1803
S. Courtenay	.. 31 Dec. 1802
W. Humphries ..	.. 31 July 1804
C. de Vigny	.. 1 Nov. 1804
C. C. Dixon	.. 6 Dec. 1804
M. de Wendt	.. 7 Dec. 1804
John Hamelin ..	.. 8 Dec. 1804
F. Souter..	.. 1 Jan. 1805
J. A. Dolling	.. 31 Jan. 1805
Jacob Jordan	.. 15 Dec. 1805
H. de Salve	.. 23 April 1805
C. Kissinger	.. 24 April 1805
Lewis Tintorn ..	.. 25 April 1805
A. Kreu	.. 23 May 1805
A. Livingstone ..	.. 8 April 1805
J. H. Schnuble ..	.. 19 Sept. 1805
H. Retnell.. ..	.. 3 Jan. 1805
F. Inturn	.. 1st Dec. 1805
P. Blassere	.. 30 Dec. 1805
F. Killepps	.. 30 Dec. 1805
Hon. F. C. Ponsonby ..	2 April 1806

* For Rank on Army, see Note referred to at foot of the page 149 and 143.

Rank and Name.	Rank in Regiment.
Captains (continued)—	
J. A. Wolff	.. 5 June 1806
W. Fairfield	.. 25 July 1806
O. de Tripp	.. 22 Aug. 1806
T. Howard	.. 9 Oct. 1806
Lieutenants—	
John Woolff	.. 30 Dec. 1797
L. de Boffe Schmidt	.. 30 Dec. 1797
J. de Reynauld ..	.. 30 Dec. 1797
Ch. Hinckledy ..	.. 25 April 1798
James E. Bell.. ..	.. 8 Oct. 1799
J. de Plancher ..	.. 11 July 1800
Benj. Rogers	.. 14 July 1800
De Carneres	.. 20 July 1800
Chas. du Sable ..	.. 21 July 1800
John L'Hoste.. ..	.. 21 July 1800
A. P. Stamba	.. 25 July 1800
Erdman Mertens ..	.. 28 July 1800
—— Kellerman ..	.. 30 July 1800
Henry Petrie	.. 30 July 1800
Chas. W. B. Koch..	.. 2 Aug. 1800
Philip Mayer	.. 5 Aug. 1800
Geo. H. Zulke.. ..	.. 6 Aug. 1800
—— Berger	.. 8 Aug. 1800
Wm. Friess	.. 8 Aug. 1800
Chas. D. Green ..	.. 14 Aug. 1800
—— M'Kinnon ..	.. 18 Sept. 1800
Florence McCarthy ..	.. 16 Oct. 1800
J. Moore.. .. Adjutant	22 Oct. 1800
W. Yates Johnson..	.. 24 Oct. 1800
Anthony Susson ..	.. 27 Oct. 1800
Rich. Nugent.. ..	.. 20 Dec. 1800
John Herbert	.. 25 Dec. 1800
Henry Fischbach ..	.. 28 Jan. 1801
Robert Kelly	.. 28 Jan. 1801
John White	.. 6 April 1802
Wm. Walther	.. 25 April 1802
Lewis Romann ..	.. 25 April 1802
Alex. McKenzie ..	.. 25 June 1802
Francis Holmes ..	.. 13 Aug. 1802
Richard Philbin ..	.. 29 Oct. 1802
Orange Balneavis ..	.. 21 Dec. 1802
David Gordon.. ..	.. 30 May 1803
Redmond Walsh ..	.. 31 May 1803
Daniel Page	.. 1 June 1803
George F. Gibson ..	.. 2 June 1803
Carew Reynell ..	.. 26 June 1803
Godfrey Starck ..	.. 28 June 1803
Melville Glenie ..	.. 30 June 1803
Arch. Campbell ..	.. 2 July 1803
Everard Baring ..	.. 12 Nov. 1803
C. F. Baring	.. 12 Mar. 1804
Henry Hughes ..	.. 3 Mar. 1804
Lewis Ritter	.. 21 Mar. 1804
John Boardman ..	.. 25 Mar. 1804
Matthew Towes ..	.. 14 May 1804
G. Ramsay	.. 19 May 1804
J. Reigner	.. 20 May 1804
Fred. Tomback ..	.. 21 May 1804
Henry Dibbly Adjutant	23 May 1804
John Watson.. ..	.. 24 May 1804
E. F. Steiby	.. 9 June 1804
John Blair	.. 30 June 1804
J. Franchou	.. 8 Nov. 1804
John McArthur ..	.. 8 Nov. 1804
—— Hagenbach ..	.. 8 Nov. 1804

Rank and Name.	Rank in Regiment.
Lieutenants (continued)—	
Aubrey C. Bowers..	.. 22 Aug. 1805
Henry O'Grady ..	.. 22 Aug. 1805
Ben. Cathel. Harte..	.. 12 Sept. 1805
Fras. Beretzo	.. 16 Oct. 1805
Chas. Appelius ..	.. 17 Nov. 1805
Edward Schultze ..	.. 19 Nov. 1805
Valentine Reichard ..	.. 20 Nov. 1805
—— Malafpina ..	.. 20 Nov. 1805
—— E. Deckner ..	.. 23 Nov. 1805
R. K. Mews	.. 23 Nov. 1805
Val. Klinkerfuss ..	.. 24 Nov. 1805
—— Sawarsky ..	.. 25 Nov. 1805
Chas. Rausch	.. 26 Nov. 1805
Ernest A. Baron D'Eber-	
stein	.. 27 Nov. 1805
Geo. Germain . ..	.. 28 Nov. 1805
Godfrey de Romance ..	12 Dec. 1805
J. B. J. Duchesnay ..	2 Jan. 1806
Rich. Campbell ..	.. 20 Jan. 1806
F. Duncker	.. 21 Jan. 1806
E. C. Kersting ..	.. 22 Jan. 1806
J. F. Galbraith ..	.. 23 Jan. 1806
John Correvont ..	.. 4 Feb. 1806
Henry Muller.. ..	.. 5 Feb. 1806
Fred. Shrieue ..	.. 6 Feb. 1806
J. Perry	.. 12 Feb. 1806
Geo. Turner	.. 13 Feb. 1806
H. Hoffman	.. 25 April 1806
Archibald Mair ..	.. 19 June 1806
Benj. Keyser	.. 11 Sept. 1806
John Gregory.. ..	.. 9 Oct. 1806
Ensigns—	
Jacobus Hojel.. ..	.. 19 June 1803
Lewis Poiney ..	.. 17 Nov. 1803
Che. Cartwright ..	.. 17 Dec. 1803
—— Steiger	.. 17 Dec. 1803
F. Deckner	.. 17 Dec. 1803
M. A. Tresson.. ..	.. 19 July 1804
Geo. Gilbert	.. 19 July 1804
G. H. Clements ..	.. 12 Jan. 1805
F. Hammond	.. 12 Jan. 1805
M. L. J. Duchesnay ..	9 May 1805
Wm. Simpson .. Adjt.	23 May 1805
Jos. Cosley Lewis ..	.. 6 June 1805
Jas. La Roche ..	.. 25 July 1805
Jas. von König ..	.. 29 Aug. 1805
Max du Chatelet ..	.. 12 Sept. 1805
Tho. Liddell	.. 17 Oct. 1805
J. Pauton Passley ..	.. 31 Oct. 1805
Jas. Cath. Antrobus ..	16 Nov. 1805
—— Muller	.. 20 Nov. 1805
John Lyons Cane ..	.. 25 Nov. 1805
Wm. Linston ..	.. 27 Nov. 1805
F. Baron Elverstein ..	28 Nov. 1805
Johann Voltz	.. 28 Nov. 1805
J. Wilson..	.. 28 Nov. 1805
J. G. Schmidt.. ..	.. 5 Feb. 1806
F. de Güse .. Adjt.	6 Feb. 1806
C. Steiby..	.. 10 April 1806
E. de la Bourdonnaye ..	25 April 1806
J. H. Adair	.. 26 April 1806
G. Plenderleath ..	.. 27 April 1806
N. A. Orgell	.. 15 May 1806
—— Thibullier ..	.. 3 July 1806
W. Bidgood	.. 25 July 1806

Rank and Name.	Rank in Regiment.
Ensigns (continued)—	
J. F. Schultz	25 July 1806
Baron Thüler	27 Aug. 1806
J. Green	Adjt. 28 Aug. 1806
John Carlos	11 Sept. 1806
Geo. Meadley	11 Sept. 1806
Thos. Page	9 Oct. 1806
Geo. Ramsay	9 Oct. 1806
J. W. Reader	9 Oct. 1806
Paymasters—	
Fras. E. Matz	2 May 1803
John Tapp	21 May 1804
Mich. Byrne	19 Oct. 1804
Edw. Hassler	1 Dec. 1804
G. Gilbert	1 Dec. 1805
R. T. Raynes	10 April 1806
Adjutants—	
John Moore	9 Aug. 1799
H. Dibbly	6 Feb. 1800
F. de Gilse	Ens. 5 Feb. 1805
W. Simpson	23 May 1805
G. Starck	24 May 1804
J. Green	28 Aug. 1806
Quartermasters—	
J. Kemmeter	30 Dec. 1797
Jos. Chattoway	Jan. 1800
Peter Child	3 Jan. 1801
R. Marriott	31 Mar. 1803
J. Wilson	25 May 1804
G. E. Stern	12 Oct. 1805
Surgeons—	
J. Faries	21 Dec. 1800
Thos. Jones	25 April 1805
J. Adolphus	25 April 1806
J. Carrol	22 Aug. 1806
John Bennett	15 May 1806
M. E. Parker	12 June 1806
Assistant-Surgeons—	
Frederick Mudke	1 Nov. 1800
J. A. du Moulin	28 April 1804
Aug. Krench	25 June 1804
Chas. Welsarg	6 Feb. 1805
H. B. Marse	22 Sept. 1802
Wm. Gordon	1 Jan. 1806
Edw. Kelis	11 Nov. 1802
Thos. Talbot	15 Jan. 1803
Wm. Thornton	23 Jan. 1803
J. Modshein	8 May 1806
D. P. Noble	8 May 1806

Regimentals—Red, facings blue, white lace, 2 white stripes.

5th Rifle Battalion, green.

Agents—Messrs. Greenwood and Cox, Craig's Court.

1807.

Six Battalions.

West Indies—England—Africa—Ireland.

Col.-in-Chief—
H.R.H. Fred., Duke of York, K.G. ... 23 Aug. 1797
Rank in Army, Field.-Mar. 10 Feb. 1795

Rank and Name.	Rank in Regiment.
Cols.-Commandant—	
Wm. Rowley	3 Oct. 1787
Rank in Army, Gen.	1 Jan. 1789
Thomas Carleton	6 Aug. 1794
Rank in Army, Gen.	25 Sept. 1802
Edward Morrison	1 Jan. 1805
Rank in Army, Lt.-Gen.	1 Jan. 1805
Napier Christie Burton	3 Jan. 1806
Rank in Army, Lt.-Gen.	1 Jan. 1805
Wm. Keppel	24 April 1806
Rank in Army, Lt.-Gen.	25 Sept. 1803
Sir George Prevost, Bart.	8 Sept. 1806
Rank in Army, Maj.-Gen.	1 Jan. 1805
Lieut.-Colonels—	
John Adolphus Harris	16 Jan. 1788
Rank in Army, Lt.-Gen.	1 Jan. 1805
Geo. Wm. Ramsay	30 Dec. 1797
Rank in Army, Col.	3 Oct. 1805
Fras., Baron de Rottenburg	30 Dec. 1797
Rank in Army, Col.	1 Jan. 1805
Gabriel Gordon	9 Mar. 1802
Gervais Rainey	20 April 1803
John Hope	30 June 1804
Rank in Army, Col.	1 Jan. 1805
L. Mosheim	11 Sept. 1804
Rank in Army,	22 April 1802
Edward Cold	20 Oct. 1804
Edward Drummond	22 Dec. 1804
Thomas Austin	20 June 1805
Majors—	
Geo. Mackie	8 Mar. 1802
Thos. Clarke	24 June 1802
James Lomax	20 April 1803
James Wheeler Unwin	21 April 1803
Rank in Army, Lt.-Col.	29 April 1802
James Bathurst	1 Oct. 1803
Rank in Army, Lt.-Col.	10 Oct. 1805
Anthony Wharton	26 July 1804
Rank in Army,	3 Feb. 1804
Thos. Robertson	14 Sept. 1804
Francis St Mart	5 Jan. 1805
Wm. Marlton	25 July 1805
Captains -	
Geo. Fourneret	16 Dec. 1795
Colin Campbell	8 June 1796
Rank in Army, Major	25 Sept. 1803
James Grant	25 April 1797
Rank in Army,	1 April 1795
John Galifle	30 Dec. 1797
Rank in Army,	31 Oct. 1796
Anthony Rumpler	30 Dec. 1797
— Vorstadt	30 Dec. 1797
Francis Gomer	30 Dec. 1797
Charles de la Houssaye Bouverie	30 Dec. 1797
— Braun	30 Dec. 1797
Wm. J. O'Connor	24 Jan. 1799
Rank in Army, Major	1 Jan. 1805
Charles De Salaberry	10 July 1799
Wm. Fraser	15 July 1799
Rank in Army,	26 Feb. 1797
Wm. Fraser	25 July 1799
John Wm. Aldred	19 Nov. 1800
Wm. Gabriel Davy	1 Jan. 1802
Joseph Twigg	31 Mar. 1802
Rank in Army,	28 Mar. 1802

Rank and Name.	Rank in Regiment.
Captains (continued)—	
Wm. Drummond	16 July 1802
Wm. Batteley..	15 Mar. 1803
Rank in Army,	5 Oct. 1795
John Welsford ..	16 Mar. 1803
Rank in Army,	27 Dec. 1796
Wm. Woodgate	6 April 1803
Kenelm Chandler ..	28 May 1803
Wm. Penderleath ..	29 May 1803
James M'Arthur ..	30 May 1803
Robert Hazen.. ..	31 May 1803
Alexander Andrews ..	2 June 1803
Edward Norton ..	24 June 1803
John Campbell	25 June 1803
Donald M'Neill ..	25 June 1803
James Bunting ..	25 June 1803
—— de Mangon	25 June 1803
Philip Mauriage	2 July 1803
Wm. Williams	3 July 1803
—— Grau	12 Aug. 1803
Rank in Army,	24 Nov. 1800
John MacMahon ..	20 Aug. 1803
Thos. Hawes	12 Nov. 1803
Samuel Courtenay ..	31 Dec. 1803
Rank in Army,	24 May 1802
Nathaniel Humphries ..	6 July 1804
Charles Vigny	1 Nov. 1804
Rank in Army,	4 Mar. 1801
Charles Cranston Dixon..	6 Dec. 1804
Michael de Wendt	7 Dec. 1804
J. Hamelin	8 Dec. 1804
Thomas Souter	11 Jan. 1805
Rank in Army,	28 April 1805
James A. Dolling	31 Jan. 1805
Jacob Jordan	28 Mar. 1805
Rank in Army,	16 Dec. 1795
Hubert de Salve ..	23 April 1805
Charles Kinsinger ..	24 April 1805
Lewis Inturn ..	25 April 1805
Adam Krein	28 May 1805
Alexander Livingstone ..	8 Aug. 1805
John Schoedde	19 Sept. 1805
Henry Rennells ..	2 Dec. 1805
Rank in Army,	13 July 1803
Frederick Inturn	3 Dec. 1805
Peter Blassiere ..	4 Dec. 1805
—— Killenbach	5 Dec. 1805
Hon. Fred. C. Ponsonby	2 April 1806
Rank in Army,	20 Aug. 1803
John Anthony Wolff ..	5 June 1806
Wm. Fairfield.. ..	25 July 1806
Ernest Otto de Pripper..	21 Aug. 1806
Rank in Army,	4 Dec. 1804
Thomas Howard ..	9 Oct. 1806
Rank in Army,	20 Dec. 1804
Lieutenants —	
F. de Reznmayd	30 Dec. 1797
L. de Bosse	30 Dec. 1797
Charles Himkledy ..	25 April 1798
James Erskine Gill ..	8 Oct. 1799
John D. Plancher ..	11 July 1800
—— Rogers	11 July 1800
Charles du Sable ..	20 July 1800
J. N. L'Hoste ..	21 July 1800
Anthony Stamba ..	25 July 1800
—— Mertens	28 July 1800

Rank and Name.	Rank in Regiment.
Lieutenants (continued)—	
Henry Petrie	30 July 1800
C. W. H. Koch	2 Aug. 1800
—— Myers	5 Aug. 1800
Geo. Henry Zulke ..	6 Aug. 1800
Wm. Friess	8 Aug. 1800
Charles Dixon Green ..	14 Aug. 1800
Florence M'Carthy..	16 Oct. 1800
Robert Kelly	17 Oct. 1800
James Moore	22 Oct. 1800
Wm. Yates Johnson ..	24 Oct. 1800
Anthony Sunsso	27 Oct. 1800
Richard Nugent ..	20 Dec. 1800
Henry Fischbach ..	28 Jan. 1801
John White	6 April 1802
Rank in Army,	29 Jan. 1801
Wm. Walther.. ..	25 April 1802
Rank in Army,	28 June 1800
Alexander McKenzie ..	25 June 1802
Rank in Army,	27 Feb. 1796
Francis Holmes	13 Aug. 1802
Rank in Army,	28 Aug. 1801
Richard Philbin ..	29 Oct. 1802
Rank in Army,	22 Oct. 1799
Orange Balneavis ..	21 Dec. 1802
David Gordan.. ..	30 May 1803
Redmond Walsh ..	31 May 1803
Daniel Page	1 June 1803
Geo. F. Gibson ..	2 June 1803
Carew Reynell.. ..	26 June 1803
Godfrey Starck ..	28 June 1803
Melville Glenie ..	30 June 1803
Archibald Campbell ..	2 July 1803
Everard Baring ..	12 Nov. 1803
Rank in Army,	7 Aug. 1801
C. F. Baring	12 Nov. 1803
Richard Henry Hughes..	3 Mar. 1804
Lewis Ritter	24 Mar. 1804
Rank in Army,	17 Mar. 1804
John Boardman ..	25 Mar. 1804
Matthew Towes ..	14 May 1804
Rank in Army,	2 Dec. 1796
C. Ramsay	19 May 1804
J. Reignier	20 May 1804
J. Tautbuck	21 May 1804
Henry Dibbly.. ..	23 May 1804
John Watson	24 May 1804
Frederick Steitz ..	9 June 1804
John Blair	30 June 1804
Rank in Army,	1 Oct. 1794
J. Franchini	8 Nov. 1803
Aubrey Carteret Bowers	22 Aug. 1805
Rank in Army,	26 Oct. 1804
Henry Casthall Harte ..	12 Sept. 1805
Rank in Army,	27 Feb. 1805
Francis Bretze	10 Oct. 1805
Charles Appdius ..	17 Oct. 1805
Edward Schultze ..	19 Nov. 1805
Valentine Reichard ..	20 Nov. 1805
—— Decker	23 Nov. 1805
—— Klinkerfuss ..	24 Nov. 1805
—— Sawarsky	25 Nov. 1805
Charles Bausch ..	26 Nov. 1805
Ern. A. Baron Eberstein	27 Nov. 1805
Geo. Germain	28 Nov. 1805
Godfrey de Romance ..	12 Dec. 1805

Rank and Name.	Rank in Regiment.
Lieutenants (continued)—	
Jean Bapt. J. Duchesnay	2 Jan. 1806
Richard Campbell	20 Jan. 1806
F. Duncker	21 Jan. 1806
Ernest C. Kersting	22 Jan. 1806
J. F. Galbraith	23 Jan. 1806
John Carrevout	4 Feb. 1806
Henry Muller	5 Feb. 1806
—— Schriene	6 Feb. 1806
John Perry	12 Feb. 1806
Geo. Turner	13 Feb. 1806
Henry Hoffman	25 April 1806
Rank in Army, 30 Dec. 1797	
Archibald Mair	19 June 1800
Rank in Army, 26 Sept. 1809	
Benjamin Keyser	11 Sept. 1806
John Gregory	9 Oct. 1806
Ensigns—	
Jacobus Hojel	10 June 1803
Lewis Pednuy	17 Nov. 1803
Charles Cartwright	17 Dec. 1803
M. Francis A. Tresson	10 July 1804
Rank in Army, 19 Nov. 1798	
O. H. Clements	13 Jan. 1806
M. L. Inch. Duchesnay	9 May 1806
Wm. Simpson	23 May 1806
James Cosley **Lewis**	6 June 1806
James La Roche	25 July 1806
Rank in Army, 30 Aug. 1804	
Joseph von König	29 Aug. 1806
Johannes Valtz	30 Aug. 1806
Maximilian du Chatelet	12 Sept. 1806
Thomas Liddell	17 Oct. 1806
John Panton Pasley	31 Oct. 1806
James Wilson	16 Nov. 1806
James Cuthbert Antrobus	20 Nov. 1806
—— Muller	24 Nov. 1806
John Lyons Cave	25 Nov. 1806
Wm. Lawton	27 Nov. 1806
Francis Baron Eberstein	28 Nov. 1806
James Grolley Schnooch	5 Feb. 1806
Frederick de Gilse	6 Feb. 1806
Charles Stetz	10 April 1806
Edm. de la Bourdonnaye	25 April 1806
Rank in Army, 16 Aug. 1806	
Johann Hein. Adair	26 April 1806
Rank in Army, 19 Sept. 1806	
Geo. Plenderleath	27 April 1806
Wm. Anderson Orgell	15 May 1806
—— Thetollier	3 July 1806
Wm. Bidgood	25 July 1806
John. Frederick Schultz	25 July 1806
—— Baron Hinuer	27 Aug. 1806
John Green	28 Aug. 1806
John Carhee	11 Sept. 1806
—— Mendley	11 Sept. 1806
Thomas Page	9 Oct. 1806
George Ramsay	9 Oct. 1806
Paymasters—	
Francis E. Matz	2 May 1804
John Tapp	21 May 1804
Michael Byrne	19 Oct. 1804
Edward Hausler	1 Dec. 1804
George Gilbert	6 Feb. 1806
Robert Taylor-Royser	10 April 1806

Rank and Name.	Rank in Regiment.
Adjutants—	
John Moore	9 Aug. 1799
Henry Dibbly	5 Feb. 1800
Rank in Army, Lieut. 20 May 1804	
Godfrey Starck	24 Mar. 1804
Rank in Army, Lieut. 28 June 1803	
Wm. Simpson	23 May 1805
Rank in Army, Ensign 23 May 1805	
Frederick de Gilse	15 Mar 1806
Rank in Army, Ensign 6 Feb. 1806	
John Green	28 Aug. 1806
Rank in Army, Ensign 28 Aug. 1806	
Quartermasters—	
—— Kenmaster	30 Dec. 1797
Joseph Cinttoway	3 July 1800
Peter Child	3 July 1801
Richard Marriott	31 Mar. 1803
Joseph Wilson	16 Aug. 1804
Geo. Frederick Stern	12 Oct. 1806
Surgeons—	
John Fanls	21 Dec. 1800
Thomas Jones	25 April 1805
Jacob Adolphus	25 April 1805
John Carrol	22 Aug. 1815
John Bennet	15 May 1806
Michael Edward Parker	12 June 1806
Assistant-Surgeons—	
Frederick Middle	1 Mar. 1800
H. B. Marte	22 Sept. 1802
Edward Kelly	11 Nov. 1802
Thomas Talbot	15 Jan. 1803
Wm. Thornton	23 July 1803
J. A. de Mocha	28 April 1804
Augustus Kresch	25 June 1804
Wm. Gordon	1 Jan. 1805
Charles Welberg	6 Feb. 1805
Francois Madelmont	8 May 1805
D. Noble	8 May 1806

Regimentals Red, facings blue, white lace, 2 blue stripes.

5th Rifle Battalion, green.

*Agents—*Messrs. Greenwood and Cox, Craig's Court.

1808.

Six Battalions.

West Indies England Portugal Spain — Africa Ireland.

Colonel-in-Chief—

H.R.H. Fred., Duke of
York, K.G. ... 23 Aug. 1797
Rank in Army Field-Mar. 10 Feb. 1795

Cols. Commandant—

Thomas Carleton ... 6 Aug. 1794
Rank in Army, Gen. 25 Sept. 1803
Edward Morrison ... 1 Jan. 1805
Rank in Army, Lt.-Gen. 25 Sept. 1805
Napier Christie Burton .. 3 Jan. 1804
Rank in Army, Lt.-Gen. 1 Jan. 1805
William Keppel ... 24 April 1806
Rank in Army, Lt.-Gen. 25 Sept. 1803

Rank and Name.	Rank in Regiment.
Col's.-Commandant (continued)—	
Sir George Prevost, Bart..	8 Sept. 1806
Rank in Army, Maj.-Gen.	1 Jan. 1805
Hon. Edmund Phipps ..	25 Aug. 1807
Rank in Army, Maj.-Gen.	29 April 1802
Lieut.-Colonels—	
James Adolphus Harris..	16 Jan. 1788
Rank in Army, Lt.-Gen.	1 Jan. 1805
George William Ramsay.	30 Dec. 1797
Rank in Army, Col.	30 Oct. 1805
Francis, Baron de Rotten-	
burg	30 Dec. 1797
Gabriel Gordon	9 Mar. 1802
Gervaise Rainey	20 April 1803
John Hope	30 June 1804
Rank in Army, Col.	1 Jan. 1805
Lewis Mosheim ..	14 Sept. 1804
Rank in Army,	29 April 1802
Edward Codd	26 Oct. 1804
Edward Drummond ..	29 Dec. 1804
Thomas Austin	29 June 1805
Majors—	
George Mackie	8 Mar. 1802
James Lomax	20 April 1803
James Bathurst	1 Oct. 1803
Rank in Army, Lt.-Col.	10 Oct. 1805
Anthony Wharton ..	26 July 1804
Rank in Army,	3 Feb. 1804
Francis St. Mart	5 Jan. 1805
William Marlton ..	25 July 1805
William Gabriel Davy ..	5 Feb. 1807
William Drummond ..	12 Mar. 1807
William Woodgate.. ..	13 Aug. 1807
Captains—	
George Fourneret	16 Dec. 1795
James Grant	25 April 1797
Rank in Army,	1 April 1795
John Galiffe	30 Dec. 1797
Rank in Army,	31 Oct. 1796
Anthony Rumpler ..	30 Dec. 1797
Ferdinand Vorstadt ..	30 Dec. 1797
Francis Gomer	30 Dec. 1797
Charles de la Houssaye	
Bouverie	30 Dec. 1797
Gustavus Braun	30 Dec. 1797
William J. O'Connor ..	24 Jan. 1800
Rank in Army, Major	1 Jan. 1805
Charles De Salaberry ..	10 July 1799
William Fraser	15 July 1799
Rank in Army,	26 Feb. 1797
William Fraser	25 July 1799
John William Aldred ..	19 Nov. 1800
Joseph Twigg	31 Mar. 1802
Rank in Army,	28 Mar. 1800
William Battesley ..	15 Mar. 1803
Rank in Army,	5 Oct. 1795
Kenelm Chandler ..	28 May 1803
William Plenderleath ..	29 May 1803
James M'Arthur ..	30 May 1803
Robert Hazen.. ..	31 May 1803
Alexander Andrews ..	2 June 1803
Edward Norton	24 June 1803
John Campbell ..	25 June 1803
Donald M'Neill ..	25 June 1803
James Bunting ..	25 June 1803
—— De Mangou ..	25 June 1803

Rank and Name.	Rank in Regiment.
Captains (continued)—	
Phillip Mauringe	2 July 1803
—— Grau	12 Aug. 1803
Rank in Army,	24 Nov. 1800
John MacMahon	20 Aug. 1803
Thomas Hames	12 Nov. 1803
Nathaniel Humphries ..	6 July 1804
Charles Vigny..	1 Nov. 1804
Rank in Army,	4 Mar. 1801
Michael de Wendt.. ..	7 Dec. 1804
J. Hammelin	8 Dec. 1804
James A. Dolling	31 Jan. 1805
Jacob Jordan	28 Mar. 1805
Rank in Army,	16 Dec. 1795
Hubert de Salve	23 April 1805
Charles Kinsinger	24 April 1805
Lewis Inturn	25 April 1805
Adam Krien	23 May 1805
Alexander Livingstone ..	8 Aug. 1805
John Schoedde	19 Sept. 1805
Henry Remmells	2 Dec. 1805
Rank in Army,	13 July 1803
Frederick Inturn	3 Dec. 1805
Peter Blassiere	4 Dec. 1805
Frederick Killenbach ..	5 Dec. 1805
John Anthony Wolff ..	5 June 1806
Thomas Howard	9 Oct. 1806
Rank in Army,	20 Dec. 1804
F. Reymuld	11 Dec. 1806
William Lupton	8 Jan. 1807
Rank in Army,	23 May 1805
Thomas Farrar	22 Jan. 1807
Rank in Army,	9 July 1803
James Prevost..	26 Feb. 1807
Rank in Army,	2 Dec. 1806
Francis Cockburne.. ..	23 April 1807
Rank in Army,	3 Mar. 1804
Charles Hinckledy.. ..	7 May 1807
John Henry Ellington ..	25 June 1807
Rank in Army,	12 June 1800
Richard Henry Shaw ..	16 July 1807
Edward Purdon	27 Aug. 1807
William Henry Virgo ..	17 Sept. 1807
John Boardman	29 Oct. 1807
Lieutenants—	
James Erskine Bell ..	8 Oct. 1799
John Douglas Plancher..	11 July 1800
Benjamin Rogers	11 July 1800
Charles du Sable	20 July 1800
Anthony Stamba	25 July 1800
—— Mertens..	28 July 1800
Henry Petrie..	30 July 1800
C. W. H. Koch	2 Aug. 1800
Philip Myers	5 Aug. 1800
George Henry Zulke ..	6 Aug. 1800
William Friess..	8 Aug. 1800
Charles Dixon Green ..	14 Aug. 1800
Florence M'Carthy.. ..	16 Oct. 1800
Robert Kelly	17 Oct. 1800
John Moore	22 Oct. 1800
Anthony Suasso	27 Oct. 1800
Henry Fischbach	28 Jan. 1801
William Walther	25 April 1802
Rank in Army,	28 June 1802
Alexander McKenzie ..	25 June 1802
Rank in Army,	27 Feb. 1796

Rank and Name.	Rank in Regiment.
Lieutenants (continued)—	
Francis Holmes	13 Aug. 1802
Rank in Army,	28 Aug. 1801
Richard Philbin	29 Oct. 1802
Rank in Army,	22 Oct. 1799
David Gordon	30 May 1803
Redmond Walsh	31 May 1803
Daniel Page	1 June 1803
George F. Gibson	2 June 1803
Carew Reynell	26 June 1803
Melville Glenie	30 June 1803
Archibald Campbell	2 July 1803
Everard Baring	12 Nov. 1803
Rank in Army,	7 Aug. 1801
C. F. Baring	22 Nov. 1803
Richard Henry Hughes	3 Mar. 1804
Lewis Ritter	24 Mar. 1804
Rank in Army,	17 Mar. 1804
George Ramsay	19 May 1804
Jacob Regnier	20 May 1804
J. Tunback	21 May 1804
Henry Dibby	23 May 1804
John Watson	24 May 1804
Frederick Steitz	9 June 1804
John Blair	30 June 1804
Rank in Army,	1 Oct. 1794
J. Franchini	8 Nov. 1804
Aubrey Carteret Bowers	22 Aug. 1805
Rank in Army,	26 Oct. 1804
Henry Cashell Harte	12 Sept. 1805
Rank in Army,	27 Feb. 1805
Francis Bereton	16 Oct. 1805
Charles Appelius	17 Oct. 1805
Edward Schultze	19 Nov. 1805
Valentine Reichard	23 Nov. 1805
—— Deckarr	23 Nov. 1805
Valentine Klinkerfuss	24 Nov. 1805
—— Saxarsky	25 Nov. 1805
Charles Rausch	26 Nov. 1805
Ern. A. Baron Eberstein	27 Nov. 1805
George German	28 Nov. 1805
Godfrey de Rottance	12 Dec. 1805
Jean Bapt. J. Duchesnay	2 Jan. 1806
Richard Campbell	20 Jan. 1806
Frederick Puncker	21 Jan. 1806
Ernest Charles Kersting	22 Jan. 1806
John Correvont	4 Feb. 1806
Henry Muller	5 Feb. 1806
Frederick Schriener	6 Feb. 1806
John Perry	12 Feb. 1806
Henry Hoffman	25 April 1806
Rank in Army,	30 Dec. 1806
Benjamin Keyser	11 Sept. 1806
John Gregory	23 Oct. 1806
O. H. Clements	11 Dec. 1806
Alexander Webster	7 May 1807
Rank in Army,	27 Aug. 1803
John Fitzgerald	12 June 1807
Rank in Army,	11 Aug. 1804
John Baden	3 Sept. 1807
Rank in Army,	30 Dec. 1797
Andrew Skene	1 Oct. 1807
Rank in Army,	8 Aug. 1805
M. F. A. Tresson	29 Nov. 1807
M. L. J. Duchesnay	30 Nov. 1807
William Simpson	1 Dec. 1807

Rank and Name.	Rank in Regiment.
Lieutenants (continued)—	
Joseph von Konig	2 Dec. 1807
M. du Chatelet	3 Dec. 1807
Thomas Liddell	4 Dec. 1807
John P. Passley	5 Dec. 1807
James Wilson	6 Dec. 1807
J. C. Antrobus	7 Dec. 1807
Henry Muller	8 Dec. 1807
William Linston	9 Dec. 1807
Francis Baron Eberstein	10 Dec. 1807
Ensigns—	
Jacobus Hojel	19 June 1803
Lewis Poincey	17 Nov. 1803
James Godley Schmidt	5 Feb. 1806
Frederick du Gilse	6 Feb. 1806
Charles Steiby	10 April 1806
Johann Hein Adsir	26 April 1806
Rank in Army,	19 Sept. 1805
George Pleuderleuth	27 April 1806
Wm. Anderson Orgell	15 May 1806
William Ridgeod	25 July 1806
John Frederick Schultz	25 July 1806
Baron Thuler	27 Aug. 1806
John Carlos	11 Sept. 1806
George Meadley	11 Sept. 1806
George Ramsay	30 Oct. 1806
Frederick Strobeck	20 Nov. 1806
J. Pooler	11 Dec. 1806
Julio Sprecher	22 Jan. 1807
Isaac Rabatean d'Arcy	15 April 1807
William Wynne	16 April 1807
—— Zuche	23 April 1807
William Hake	25 June 1807
John Jory	2 July 1807
Daniel Farier	6 Aug. 1807
James Lewis	27 Aug. 1807
Richard Grout	9 Sept. 1807
John Schwartz	10 Sept. 1807
Charles Lorentz	1 Oct. 1807
Julius von Boeck	7 Dec. 1807
John Louis Barloz	8 Dec. 1807
—— Baron Plesse	9 Dec. 1807
—— de Bree	10 Dec. 1807
John Frederick Schultz	11 Dec. 1807
Andrew Ellison	
Paymasters—	
John Tapp	21 May 1804
Edward Hansler	1 Dec. 1805
George Gilbert	6 Feb. 1804
Robert Taylor Raynes	10 April 1806
George Robertson	15 Oct. 1807
Adjutants—	
John Moore	9 Aug. 1799
Rank in Army, Lieut.	22 Oct. 1800
Henry Dibbly	5 Feb. 1800
Rank in Army, Lieut.	23 May 1804
William Simpson	23 May 1805
Rank in Army, Lieut.	1 Dec. 1807
Frederick d. Gilse	15 May 1806
Rank in Army, Ensign	6 Feb. 1806
Frederick Strobeck	20 Nov. 1806
Rank in Army, Ensign	20 Nov. 1806
—— Luchs	23 April 1807
Rank in Army, Ensign	23 April 1807

Rank and Name.	Rank in Regiment.
Quartermasters—	
J. Adolphus Kemmeter..	30 Dec. 1797
Joseph Chattoway	3 July 1800
Peter Child	3 July 1801
Richard Marriott ..	31 Mar. 1803
Joseph Wilson	25 May 1804
George Frederick Stern..	12 Oct. 1805
Surgeons—	
John Faries	21 Dec. 1800
Jacob Adolphus	5 Oct. 1804
Thomas Jones..	25 April 1805
John Carrol	22 Aug. 1805
John Bennett	15 May 1806
Michael Edward Parker..	12 June 1806
Assistant-Surgeons—	
Frederick Midiko	1 Mar. 1800
H. B. Marie	22 Sept. 1802
Edward Kelly..	11 Nov. 1802
Thomas Talbot	15 Jan. 1803
William Thornton	23 July 1803
J. A. du Moulin	28 April 1804
Augustus Kreich	25 June 1804
William Gordon	1 Jan. 1805
Charles Wehsarg	6 Feb. 1805
Francis Madeheim.. ..	8 May 1806
A. B. Ross	29 Oct. 1807

*Regimentals—*Red, facings blue, white lace, 2 blue stripes.

5th Rifle Battalion, green.

*Agents—*Messrs. Greenwood, Cox, and Co., Craig's Court.

1809.

Six Battalions.

West Indies—England—Spain.

Col.-in-Chief—
H.R.H. Fredk., Duke of
  York, K.G... .. .. 23 Aug. 1797
  Rank in Army, Field-Mar. 10 Feb. 1795

Cols.-Commandant—
Thomas Carleton .. .. 6 Aug. 1794
  Rank in Army, Gen. 25 Sept. 1803
Edward Morrison .. .. 1 Jan. 1805
  Rank in Army, Lt.-Gen. 1 Jan. 1805
Napier Christie Burton.. 3 Jan. 1806
  Rank in Army, Lt.-Gen. 1 Jan. 1805
William Keppel .. .. 24 April 1806
  Rank in Army, Lt.-Gen. 25 Sept. 1803
Sir George Prevost, Bart. 8 Sept. 1806
  Rank in Army, Maj.-Gen. 1 Jan. 1805
Hon. Edmund Phipps .. 25 Aug. 1807
  Rank in Army, Lt.-Gen. 25 April 1808

Lieut.-Colonels—
John Adolphus Harris .. 16 Jan. 1788
  Rank in Army, Lt.-Gen. 1 Jan. 1805
George William Ramsay 30 Dec. 1797
  Rank in Army, Col. 30 Oct. 1805

Lieut.-Colonels (continued)—
Francis, Baron de Rotten-
  burg .. .. 30 Dec. 1797
  Rank in Army, Col. 1 Jan. 1805
John Hope .. .. .. 30 June 1804
  Rank in Army, Col. 1 Jan. 1805
Lewis Masheim .. .. 14 Sept. 1804
  Rank in Army, 29 April 1802
Edward Codd.. .. .. 26 Oct. 1804
Thomas Austin .. .. 20 June 1805
Paul Anderson .. .. 14 Jan. 1808
  Rank in Army, 17 Oct. 1805
Fra. Ger., Viscount Lake 10 May 1808
  Rank in Army, Col. 25 April 1808
William Dowdeswell .. 2 June 1808
  Rank in Army, Maj.-Gen. 25 Sept. 1803
George Mackie .. .. 22 Dec. 1808

Majors—
James Loumax.. .. .. 20 April 1803
James Bathurst .. .. 1 Oct. 1803
  Rank in Army, Lt.-Col. 10 Oct. 1805
Anthony Wharton .. .. 26 July 1804
  Rank in Army, 3 Feb. 1804
Francis St. Mart .. .. 5 Jan. 1805
William Marlton .. .. 25 July 1805
William Gabriel Davy .. 5 Feb. 1807
William Drummond .. 12 Mar. 1807
William Woodgate.. .. 13 Aug. 1807

Captains—
George Fourneret .. .. 16 Dec. 1795
  Rank in Army, Major 25 April 1808
John Bradshaw .. .. 5 April 1796
  Rank in Army, Major 25 April 1808
James Grant .. .. .. 25 April 1797
  Rank in Army, Major 25 April 1808
John Galiffe .. .. .. 30 Dec. 1797
  Rank in Army, Major 25 April 1808
Anthony Rumpler.. .. 30 Dec. 1797
Francis Gosner .. .. 30 Dec. 1797
  Rank in Army, Major 9 June 1808
Charles de la Houssaye
  Bouverie .. .. .. 30 Dec. 1797
Gustavus Braun .. .. 30 Dec. 1797
William J. O'Connor .. 24 Jan. 1799
  Rank in Army, Major 1 Jan. 1805
Charles De Salaberry .. 10 Jan. 1799
William Fraser .. .. 15 Jan. 1799
  Rank in Army, 26 Feb. 1797
William Fraser .. .. 25 Jan. 1799
John William Aldred .. 19 Nov. 1800
William Batteley .. .. 15 Mar. 1803
  Rank in Army, Major 25 April 1808
Kenelm Chandler .. .. 28 May 1803
William Plenderleath .. 29 May 1803
James M'Arthur .. .. 30 May 1803
Robert Hazen.. .. .. 31 May 1803
Alexander Andrews .. 2 June 1803
Edward Norton .. .. 24 June 1803
Donald O'Neill .. .. 25 June 1803
James Bunting .. .. 25 June 1803
Lewis de Mangeon .. 25 June 1803
Phillip Mauriage .. .. 2 July 1803
George Grau .. .. .. 12 Aug. 1803
  Rank in Army, 24 Nov. 1803

Rank and Name.	Rank in Regiment.
Captains (continued)—	
John MacMahon	.. 20 Aug. 1803
Thomas Haines	.. 12 Nov. 1803
Nathaniel Humphries	.. 6 July 1804
Charles Vigny	.. 1 Nov. 1804
Rank in Army, 4 Mar. 1804	
Michael de Wendt	.. 7 Dec. 1804
James A. Dölling	.. 31 Jan. 1805
Jacob Jordan	.. 28 Mar. 1805
Rank in Army, Major 25 April 1808	
Hubert de Salve	.. 23 April 1805
Charles Kissinger	.. 24 April 1805
Lewis Intturn	.. 25 April 1805
Adam Krien	.. 23 May 1805
Alexander Livingstone	.. 8 Aug. 1805
John Schoeble	.. 19 Sept. 1805
Henry Rennells	.. 2 Dec. 1805
Rank in Army, 13 July 1803	
Frederick Intturn	.. 3 Dec. 1805
Peter Bassiere	.. 4 Dec. 1805
Frederick Kellenbach	.. 5 Dec. 1805
John Anthony Wolff	.. 5 June 1806
Thomas Howard	.. 9 Oct. 1806
Rank in Army, 20 Dec. 1804	
Galenius Reynauld	.. 11 Dec. 1806
William Lupton	.. 8 Jan. 1807
Rank in Army, 23 May 1805	
Thomas Farmar	.. 22 Jan. 1807
Rank in Army, 9 July 1801	
James Prevost	.. 26 Feb. 1807
Rank in Army, 2 Dec. 1804	
Francis Cockburne	.. 23 April 1807
Rank in Army, 3 Mar. 1804	
Charles Hinckledy	.. 7 May 1807
Edward Purdon	.. 27 Aug. 1807
William Henry Virgo	.. 17 Sept. 1807
John Boardman	.. 29 Oct. 1807
James Erskine Bell	.. 20 Jan. 1808
John D. Plancher	.. 21 Jan. 1808
Benjamin Rogers	.. 12 May 1808
Alexander Campbell	.. 15 May 1808
C. Frederick	.. 6 Oct. 1808
George Grigby	.. 29 Oct. 1808
Lieutenants -	
Charles du Sable	.. 20 July 1800
Anthony Stamler	.. 25 July 1800
Henry Petrie	.. 30 July 1800
C. W. H. Koch	.. 2 Aug. 1800
Phillip Myer	.. 5 Aug. 1800
George Henry Zulke	.. 6 Aug. 1800
William Friess	.. 8 Aug. 1800
Charles Dixon Green	.. 14 Aug. 1800
Florence M'Carthy	.. 16 Oct. 1800
Robert Kelly	.. 17 Oct. 1800
John Moore	.. 22 Oct. 1800
Anthony Snasso	.. 27 Oct. 1800
Henry Frschbach	.. 28 Jan. 1801
William Walcher	.. 25 April 1802
Rank in Army, 28 June 1800	
Alexander Mckenzie	.. 25 June 1802
Rank in Army, 27 Feb. 1795	
Francis Holmes	.. 13 Aug. 1802
Rank in Army, 28 Aug. 1801	
Richard Philbin	.. 29 Oct. 1802
Rank in Army, 22 Oct. 1799	
David Gordon	.. 30 May 1803

Rank and Name.	Rank in Regiment.
Lieutenants (continued)—	
Daniel Page	.. 1 June 1803
George F. Gibson	.. 2 June 1803
Carew Reynell	.. 26 June 1803
Archibald Campbell	2 July 1803
Everard Baring	.. 12 Nov. 1803
Rank in Army, 7 Aug. 1801	
C. T. Baring	.. 12 Nov. 1803
Richard Henry Hughes	3 Mar. 1804
Lewis Ritter	.. 24 Mar. 1804
Rank in Army, 17 Mar. 1804	
George Ronsoy	.. 19 May 1804
Jacob Reigner	.. 20 May 1804
J. Tumbock	.. 21 May 1804
Henry Dibbly	.. 23 May 1804
John Watson	.. 24 May 1804
Frederick Steitz	.. 9 June 1804
John Blair	.. 30 June 1804
Rank in Army, 1 Oct. 1794	
John Franchini	.. 8 Nov. 1804
Aubrey Carteret Bowers	22 Aug. 1805
Rank in Army, 26 Oct. 1804	
Henry Codell Harte	.. 12 Sept. 1805
Rank in Army, 27 Feb. 1805	
Francis Beretze	.. 10 Oct. 1805
Charles Appelius	.. 17 Oct. 1805
Edward Schultze	.. 19 Nov. 1805
Valentine Reichard	.. 20 Nov. 1805
Charles Deckner	.. 23 Nov. 1805
Valentine Klinkerfuss	.. 24 Nov. 1805
Charles Sawatsky	.. 25 Nov. 1805
Charles Rausch	.. 26 Nov. 1805
Ern. A. Baron Eberstein	27 Nov. 1805
George Oermann	.. 28 Nov. 1805
Godfrey de Ronmore	.. 12 Dec. 1805
Frederick Duncker	.. 21 Jan. 1806
Ernest Charles Kersting	22 Jan. 1806
John Correvont	.. 4 Feb. 1806
Henry Muller	.. 5 Feb. 1806
Frederick Schriene	.. 6 Feb. 1806
John Perry	.. 12 Feb. 1806
Henry Hoffman	.. 25 April 1806
Rank in Army, 30 Dec. 1797	
Alexander Webster	.. 7 May 1807
Rank in Army, 27 Aug. 1803	
John Fitzgerald	.. 12 June 1807
Rank in Army, 11 Aug. 1804	
M. Francis A. Tresson	.. 23 Nov. 1807
William Simpson	.. 1 Dec. 1807
Joseph von Konig	.. 2 Dec. 1807
Maximilian du Chatelet	.. 3 Dec. 1807
John Pardon Passley	.. 5 Dec. 1807
James Wilson	.. 6 Dec. 1807
John Cuthbert Antrobus	7 Dec. 1807
William Luston	.. 9 Dec. 1807
Francis Baron Eberstein	10 Dec. 1807
H. C. Brown	.. 14 Jan. 1808
Colin Campbell	.. 18 Feb. 1808
Rank in Army, 3 Sept. 1795	
James Godfrey Schmidt	.. 5 May 1808
Robert Mitchell	.. 22 Sept. 1808
Robert Thoburn	.. 12 Jan. 1809
Ensigns—	
Lewis Poincey	.. 17 Nov. 1805
Frederick de Gilse	.. 6 Feb. 1806
Charles Steitz	.. 19 April 1806

Rank and Name.	Rank in Regiment.
Ensigns (continued)—	
Johann Hein. Adair	.. 26 April 1806
Rank in Army,	19 Sept. 1805
George Pleuderleath	.. 27 April 1806
William Anderson Orgill	15 May 1806
William Balgood ..	.. 25 July 1806
John Carlos ...	.. 11 Sept. 1806
George Meadley ..	.. 11 Sept. 1806
George Ramsay ..	.. 30 Oct. 1806
Frederick Strobeck..	.. 20 Nov. 1806
John S. de Bernegg	.. 22 Jan. 1807
Isaac Raboteau d'Arcy	.. 15 April 1807
William Wynne ..	.. 16 April 1807
Andrew Lache ..	.. 23 April 1807
John Joyce ..	.. 2 July 1807
Daniel Faries ..	.. 6 Aug. 1807
James Lewis ..	.. 27 Aug. 1807
Charles Lorentz ..	.. 1 Oct. 1807
Julius von Boeck ..	.. 7 Dec. 1807
John Louis Bartaz..	.. 8 Dec. 1807
—— de Bree ..	.. 10 Dec. 1807
Andrew Ellison ..	.. 25 Dec. 1807
R. B. Hislop ..	.. 14 Jan. 1808
Leopold de Froger..	.. 15 Jan. 1808
William Gregory ..	.. 3 Mar. 1808
William Morgenthal	.. 21 April 1808
J. T. Allinson ..	.. 19 May 1808
Rank in Army,	21 April 1808
J. Pelt ..	.. 19 May 1808
Mathew Furst..	.. 23 June 1808
James Fontaine	.. 14 July 1808
Richard Pasley ..	.. 8 Sept. 1808
George Robinson ..	.. 15 Sept. 1808
—— Crozier ..	.. 19 Oct. 1801
Edward M'Arthur..	.. 27 Oct. 1808
Augustine F. Evans	.. 19 Nov. 1808
Rank in Army,	10 Mar. 1808
Von Stein Alteustein	.. 19 Jan. 1809
Paymasters—	
Edward Hausler ..	.. 1 Dec. 1804
George Gilbert ..	.. 6 Feb. 1806
Robert Taylor Raynes ..	10 April 1806
George Robertson ..	.. 15 Oct. 1807
Patrick Heyns..	.. 19 Jan. 1809
Adjutants—	
John Moore ..	.. 9 Aug. 1799
Rank in Army, Lieut.	22 Oct. 1800
Henry Dibbly..	.. 5 Feb. 1800
Rank in Army, Lieut.	23 May 1804
William Simpson ..	.. 23 May 1805
Rank in Army, Lieut.	1 Dec. 1807
Frederick de Gilse..	.. 15 May 1806
Rank in Army, Ensign	6 Feb. 1806
Frederick Strobeck..	.. 20 Nov. 1806
Rank in Army, Ensign	20 Nov. 1806
Andrew Lachs ..	.. 23 April 1807
Rank in Army, Ensign	23 April 1807
Quartermasters—	
J. Adolphus Kennacter ..	30 Dec. 1797
Joseph Chattoway ..	.. 3 July 1800
Joseph Wilson ..	.. 25 May 1804
George Ered. Stern	.. 12 Oct. 1805
Augustus Hennerhofer ..	25 Nov. 1807
Henry Heartsoake ..	.. 25 Nov. 1808
John Faries ..	.. 21 Dec. 1800

Rank and Name.	Rank in Regiment.
Surgeons—	
John Carroll ..	.. 22 Aug. 1805
John Bennett ..	.. 15 May 1806
Michael Edward Parker	. 12 June 1806
Thomas O'Mealy ..	.. 6 Oct. 1808
Edward Doughty ..	.. 3 Nov. 1808
Assistant-Surgeons—	
Frederick Mislike ..	.. 1 Mar. 1800
William Marie..	.. 22 Sept. 1802
James du Moulin ..	.. 28 April 1804
William Gordon ..	.. 1 Jan. 1805
Charles Welsarg ..	.. 6 Feb. 1805
Francis Madeheim ..	.. 8 May 1806
A. B. Ross ..	.. 29 Oct. 1807
Robert Punshon ..	.. 2 Feb. 1809

Regimentals—Red, facings blue, white lace, 2 blue stripes.

5th Rifle Battalion, green.

Agents—Messrs. Greenwood, Cox, & Co., Craig's Court.

1810.

Six Battalions.

West Indies—England—Spain.

Col.-in-Chief—	
H.R.H. the Duke of York,	
K.G., K.B. ..	.. 23 Aug. 1797
Rank in Army, Field-Mar.	10 Feb. 1795
Cols.-Commandant—	
T. Carleton ..	.. 6 Aug. 1794
Rank in Army, Gen.	25 Sept. 1803
E. Morrison ..	.. 1 Jan. 1805
Rank in Army, Lt.-Gen.	1 Jan. 1805
N. C. Burton ..	.. 3 Jan. 1806
Rank in Army, Lt.-Gen.	1 Jan. 1805
W. Keppel ..	.. 24 April 1806
Rank in Army, Lt.-Gen.	25 Sept. 1803
Sir G. Prevost, Bart.	.. 8 Sept. 1806
Rank in Army, Maj.-Gen.	1 Jan. 1805
Hon. E. Phipps ..	.. 25 Aug. 1807
Rank in Army, Lt.-Gen.	25 April 1808
Lieut.-Colonels—	
J. A. Harris ..	.. 16 Jan. 1788
Rank in Army, Lt.-Gen.	1 Jan. 1805
G. W. Ramsay ..	.. 30 Dec. 1797
Rank in Army, Col.	30 Oct. 1805
Fra. Baron de Rottenburg	30 Dec. 1797
Rank in Army, Col.	1 Jan. 1805
J. Hope ..	.. 30 June 1794
Rank in Army, Col.	1 Jan. 1805
Lewis Mosheim ..	.. 14 Sept. 1804
Rank in Army,	29 April 1802
Edward Codd..	.. 26 Oct. 1804
T. Austin ..	.. 20 June 1805
P. Anderson ..	.. 14 Jan. 1808
Rank in Army,	17 Oct. 1805
F. Viscount Lake ..	.. 10 May 1808
Rank in Army, Col.	25 April 1808
W. Dowdeswell ..	.. 2 June 1808
Rank in Army, M.-Gen.	25 Sep. 1803

Rank and Name	Rank in Regiment.	Rank and Name	Rank in Regiment.
Lieut.-Colonels (continued)—		*Captains* (continued):—	
G. Mackie	22 Dec. 1808	A. Ligertwood	30 Mar. 1809
Wm. Williams	15 Nov. 1809	C. H. Tyler	20 April 1809
Anthony Wharton	16 Aug. 1810	T. R. Swyney	23 May 1809
Majors—		C. du Sable	29 June 1809
F. St. Mart	5 Jan. 1805	Anthony Stambo	10 Oct. 1809
W. Marlton	25 July 1805	Henry Petrie	11 Oct. 1809
W. Woodgate	13 Aug. 1807	C. W. H. Koch	12 Oct. 1809
G. Fourneret	9 Feb. 1809	Philip Myer	23 Nov. 1809
Rank in Army, 25 April 1808		C. Mackenzie	12 Dec. 1799
James Grant	8 Nov. 1809	G. H. Zulke	11 Jan. 1810
Rank in Army, 25 April 1808		J. Coningham	23 Jan. 1810
J. F. Fitzgerald	9 Nov. 1809	F. M'Carthy	24 May 1810
Rank in Army, 25 Sept. 1803		W. J. Alexander	12 July 1810
John Galiffe	15 Mar. 1810	Robert Kelly	26 Aug. 1810
Rank in Army, 25 April 1808		Archibald Taylor	20 Sep. 1810
Robert Hazen	14 June 1810	*Lieutenants*—	
A. Rumpler	16 Aug. 1810	William Friess	8 Aug. 1800
Captains—		John Moore	22 Oct. 1800
C. D. D. Bouverie		Anthony Suasso	27 Oct. 1800
Gustav Brown		H. Fischbach	28 Jan. 1801
W. J. O'Connor	24 Jan. 1799	W. Walther	28 June 1800
Rank in Army, Major 1 Jan. 1806		F. Holmes	28 Aug. 1801
C. De Salaberry	18 July 1799	R. Philbin	22 Oct. 1799
W. Fraser	25 July 1799	David Gordon	30 May 1803
Rank in Army, Major 25 Oct. 1809		Daniel Page	1 June 1803
J. W. Aldred	19 Nov. 1800	G. F. Gibson	2 June 1803
W. Batteley	15 Mar. 1803	Carew Reynell	26 June 1803
Rank in Army, Major 25 April 1808		G. Baring	7 Aug. 1801
K. Chandler	28 May 1803	C. F. Baring	12 Nov. 1803
W. Flenderleath	29 May 1803	R. H. Hughes	3 Mar. 1804
Alexander Andrews	2 June 1803	Lewis Batter	17 Mar. 1804
Edward Norton	24 June 1803	J. Regnier	20 May 1804
James Bunting	25 June 1803	J. Trumbeck	21 May 1804
L. de Maugon	25 June 1803	H. Dibbly	23 May 1804
P. Maurioge	2 July 1803	John Watson	24 May 1804
George Gray	24 Nov. 1803	Frederick Stitz	9 June 1804
J. MacMahon	20 Aug. 1803	John Blair	1 Oct. 1794
Thomas Bowes	12 Nov. 1804	J. Franchine	8 Nov. 1804
N. Humphreys	6 July 1804	A. C. Bowers	26 Oct. 1804
Charles Vigus	4 Mar. 1804	H. C. Harte	27 Feb. 1805
M. de Wendt	7 Dec. 1804	Francis Beritz	10 Oct. 1805
F. Jordan		Charles Appelius	17 Oct. 1805
H. de Salis	23 April 1805	Valentine Reichard	20 Nov. 1805
C. Kissinger	24 April 1805	Charles Decause	23 Nov. 1805
Lewis Inchurn	25 April 1805	Valentine Kinkerfuss	24 Nov. 1805
Adam Krien	23 May 1805	C. Sawatsky	25 Nov. 1805
A. Livingstone	8 Aug. 1805	Charles Rausch	26 Nov. 1805
J. Schoedde	19 Sept. 1805	E. A. Baron Elerstein	27 Nov. 1805
H. Rennells	13 July 1806	George Germain	28 Nov. 1805
F. Inturn	3 Dec. 1805	Frederick Duncker	21 Jan. 1806
P. Blassiere	4 Dec. 1805	J. F. Galbraith	23 Jan. 1806
J. A. Wolff	5 Jan. 1805	John Correvont	4 Feb. 1806
Thomas Howard	20 Dec. 1804	Frederick Schroene	6 Feb. 1806
G. A. Reynauld	11 Dec. 1806	John Perry	12 Feb. 1806
W. Lupton	23 May 1805	H. Hoffmann	30 Dec. 1797
J. Prevost	2 Dec. 1806	Alexander Webster	27 Aug. 1801
F. Cockburn	3 Mar. 1804	J. Fitzgerald	11 Aug. 1804
C. Hawksbay	7 May 1807	M. F. A. Fresson	23 Nov. 1807
E. Purdon	27 Aug. 1807	W. Sampson	1 Dec. 1807
J. Ikershaw	29 Oct. 1807	Joseph von König	2 Dec. 1807
J. E. Bell	20 Jan. 1808	M. du Chatelet	3 Dec. 1807
J. D. Plancher	21 Jan. 1808	John P. Passley	5 Dec. 1807
Benjamin Rogers	12 May 1808	James Wilson	6 Dec. 1807
Alexander Campbell	15 May 1808	Henry Muller	8 Dec. 1807
		William Lucstow	9 Dec. 1807

M

Lieutenants (continued)—

Rank and Name.	Rank in Regiment.
F. Baron Eberstein	.. 10 Dec. 1807
D. C. Brown ..	.. 14 Jan. 1808
Colin Campbell ..	.. 3 Sept.1795
James G. Schmidt ..	.. 5 May 1808
Robert Mitchell ..	.. 22 Sept.1808
R. S. Redman..	.. 25 Feb. 1808
F. de Gilse ..	Adjt. 26 Sept.1809
Charles Steiby.. ..	.. 27 Sept.1809
J. H. Adair	.. 28 Sept.1809
John Carlos	.. 29 Sept.1809
F. Strobeck ..	Adjt. 30 Sept.1809
J. S. de Bernegg ..	.. 1 Oct. 1809
Isaac R. D'Arcy ..	.. 2 Oct. 1809
William Wynne ..	.. 3 Oct. 1809
Andrew Lachs..	Adjt. 4 Oct. 1809
John Joyce	.. 5 Oct. 1809
Daniel Faries	.. 6 Oct. 1809
James Lewis	.. 7 Oct. 1809
Jul. von Boeck ..	.. 9 Oct. 1809
J. Louis Barbaz ..	.. 10 Oct. 1809
—— de Bree ..	.. 11 Oct. 1809
Andrew Ellison ..	.. 12 Oct. 1809
R. B. Hislop ..	.. 29 Oct. 1809
Leo. de Froger ..	.. 30 Oct. 1809
William Gregory ..	.. 31 Oct. 1809
W. Morgenthal ..	S. 1 Nov. 1809
J. T. Allinson.. ..	.. 2 Nov. 1809
J. Pelt	.. 3 Nov. 1809
Matthew Furst ..	.. 4 Nov. 1809
James Fontane ..	.. 5 Nov. 1809
Richard Pasley ..	.. 6 Nov. 1809
George Robinson ..	.. 7 Nov. 1809
J. F. Crozier ..	.. 8 Nov. 1809
Anthony F. Evans..	.. 9 Nov. 1809
John Altenstein ..	.. 17 Feb. 1810
John Hearn ..	.. 18 Feb. 1810
Peter Kennedy ..	.. 19 Feb. 1810
Alexander Rule ..	.. 20 Feb. 1810
Thomas Sheridan ..	.. 22 Feb. 1810
Thomas Jack ..	.. 23 Feb. 1810
Thomas Smith ..	.. 24 Feb. 1810
Hector Downie ..	.. 25 Feb. 1810
M. De Ravarier ..	.. 26 Feb. 1810
E. Fitzgerald ..	.. 27 Feb. 1810
Robert Ellison ..	.. 28 Feb. 1810
George F. Stern ..	.. 1 Mar. 1810
John Mackay	.. 3 Mar. 1810
Benjamin Webster ..	4 Mar. 1810
Andrew Leitch ..	.. 5 Mar. 1810
Richard Gore ..	.. 6 Mar. 1810
Abraham Myers ..	.. 7 Mar. 1810
John Trewren ..	.. 8 Mar. 1810
E. F. Pitch	1 Feb. 1807
James Roberts ..	.. 24 May 1809
W. Goldsmith ..	.. 11 June 1810
M. Cottnam ..	.. 12 June 1810
Richard Hilliard ..	.. 13 June 1810
Sylvester O'Hehir ..	.. 14 June 1810
Stephen Major ..	.. 26 July 1810
John Blundell ..	.. 5 May 1808
J. B. Donnelly ..	.. 16 Aug. 1810
Peter Eason ..	.. 8 Oct. 1810
Thomas Marsh ..	.. 9 Oct. 1810
Stephen Price ..	.. 10 Oct. 1810
T. P. Conway ..	.. 11 Oct. 1810

Lieutenants (continued)—

Rank and Name.	Rank in Regiment.
John Couper ..	.. 12 Oct. 1810
J. J. Sargent ..	.. 13 Oct. 1810
Samuel Kerr ..	.. 14 Oct. 1810
William Rind..	.. 15 Oct. 1810
Michael Kent ..	.. 16 Oct. 1810
Samuel Sargent ..	17 Oct. 1810
M. M'Namara ..	.. 18 Oct. 1810

Ensigns—

Rank and Name.	Rank in Regiment.
V. S. Altenstein ..	.. 19 Jan. 1809
—— Erdberg.. ..	.. 29 Sept.1809
John Gowen	.. 9 Oct. 1809
Eugene Downing ..	.. 2 Nov. 1809
Thomas Webb ..	.. 3 Nov. 1809
Richard Saunders ..	.. 4 Nov. 1809
David Lecount ..	.. 5 Nov. 1809
Silvanus Johes ..	.. 9 Nov. 1809
T. M'Mahon ..	.. 15 Nov. 1809
—— Larbusch ..	.. 16 Nov. 1809
F. P. N. de Kruger	. 30 Nov. 1809
—— de Ingersleben	14 Dec. 1809
E. Burglnuagen ..	.. 24 Jan. 1810
A. P. de Borgh ..	.. 7 Mar. 1810
C. J. de Franciosi ..	.. 8 Mar. 1810
Andrew Virusseux ..	.. 22 Mar. 1810
John Taylor	.. 7 Dec. 1809
William Rafter ..	.. 22 Sept.1808
—— de Schanz ..	.. 16 May 1810
J. B. Gaff	.. 17 May 1810
L. V. Fleischhut ..	.. 11 June 1810
C. W. Bretthauer ..	.. 12 June 1810
R. H. L. Schloffer..	.. 13 June 1810
John Beaumont ..	.. 28 June 1810
Peter Broetz ..	.. 12 July 1810
A. F. de Breuney ..	.. 26 July 1810
Francis Allen ..	.. 16 Aug. 1810
Frederick Pictet ..	.. 8 Oct. 1810
D. Drummond ..	.. 9 Oct. 1810
John Brector ..	.. 11 Oct. 1810
Robert Atkinson ..	.. 12 Oct. 1810
J. Fleeson ..	.. 13 Oct. 1810
William Magee ..	.. 14 Oct. 1810
Henry Hudson ..	.. 16 Oct. 1810
W. H. Rose ..	.. 17 Oct. 1810
John Hargrove ..	.. 18 Oct. 1810
Joseph Fanreloth ..	.. 25 Oct. 1810

Paymasters—

Rank and Name.	Rank in Regiment.
Edward Hansler ..	.. 1 Dec. 1804
George Gilbert ..	.. 6 Feb. 1806
Patrick Heyns ..	.. 19 Jan. 1809
Henry Jackson ..	.. 12 Oct. 1809
G. M. Slade ..	.. 19 Oct. 1809
R. B. Fisher ..	.. 19 July 1810

Adjutants—

Rank and Name.	Rank in Regiment.
John Moore	.. 9 Aug. 1799
Rank in Army, Lieut.	22 Oct. 1800
Henry Dibbly	.. 5 Feb. 1800
Rank in Army, Lieut.	23 May 1804
W. Simpson	.. 23 May 1805
Rank in Army, Lieut.	1 Dec. 1807
F. de Gilse	.. 18 May 1806
Rank in Army, Lieut.	26 Sept.1809
F. Strobeck	.. 20 Nov. 1806
Rank in Army, Lieut.	30 Sept.1809
Andr. Lach..	.. 23 April 1807
Rank in Army, Lieut.	4 Oct. 1809

Rank and Name.	Rank in Regiment.
Quartermasters—	
James A. Kemmeter	.. 30 Dec. 1797
J. Chattoway ..	.. 3 July 1800
J Wilson ..	.. 25 May 1804
A. Brunerhofer	.. 25 Nov. 1807
H. Heartsooke	.. 25 Nov. 1808
—— Verbregge	.. 30 Mar. 1809
Surgeons –	
John Faries ..	.. 21 Dec. 1800
William Ireland	.. 29 June 1809
W. B. Morle ..	.. 2 Nov. 1809
J. Morris ..	.. 11 Jan. 1810
John Bennett ..	.. 15 May 1806
James du Moulin	.. 1 Feb. 1810
Assistant-Surgeons –	
Frederick Midike	.. 1 Mar. 1800
Charles Welsarg	.. 6 Feb. 1805
A. B. Ross ..	.. 10 Sep. 1807
Robin Ayton ..	.. 1 May 1806
L. W Whitestone	.. 28 Mar. 1809
Thomas Conelly	.. 8 June 1809
J. D. Hibbert ..	.. 12 Oct. 1809
J. H. Walker ..	.. 2 Nov. 1809
George M Bennett	.. 2 Nov. 1809
George Moodie	.. 26 April 1810
William Morrison	.. 19 July 1810
C. G. Berger ..	.. 18 Oct. 1810

Regimentals—Red facings blue, white lace, 2 blue stripes.

5th Rifle Battalion green.

Agents—Messrs. Greenwood, Cox, and Co., Craig's Court.

1811.

Six Battalions.

England Africa West Indies—Spain.

Colonel-in-Chief –	
H.R.H. the Duke of York, K.G., K.B. ..	.. 23 Aug. 1797
Rank in Army, Field-Marshal	.. 10 Feb. 1795
Cols-Commandant—	
T. Carleton	.. 6 Aug. 1794
Rank in Army, Gen. 25 Sept. 1803	
E. Morrison ..	1 Jan. 1805
Rank in Army, Lt.-Gen. 1 Jan. 1805	
N. C. Burton ..	3 Jan. 1806
Rank in Army, Lt.-Gen. 1 Jan. 1805	
Sir G. Prevost, Bart. ..	8 Sept. 1806
Rank in Army, Maj.-Gen. 1 Jan. 1805	
H. E. Phipps..	.. 25 Aug. 1807
Rank in Army, Lt.-Gen. 25 April 1808	
Ar. Whetham ..	7 Feb. 1811
Rank in Army, Maj.-Gen. 1 Jan. 1805	
Lieut-Colonels—	
J. A. Harris ..	16 Jan. 1788
Rank in Army, Lt.-Gen. 1 Jan. 1805	
G. W. Ramsay ..	30 Dec. 1797
Rank in Army, Col. 30 Oct. 1805	
F. Baron de Rottenburg 30 Dec. 1797	
Rank in Army, Maj.-Gen. 25 July 1810	

Rank and Name.	Rank in Regiment.
Lieut.-Colonels (continued)—	
J. Hope	.. 30 June 1804
Rank in Army, M-Gen. 25 July 1810	
Edw. Codd	.. 26 Oct. 1804
T. Austin.. ..	.. 20 June 1805
P. Anderson ..	.. 14 Jan. 1808
Rank in Army, 17 Oct. 1805	
F. Viscount Lake ..	.. 10 May 1808
Rank in Army, Col. 25 April 1808	
W. Dowdeswell ..	2 June 1808
Rank in Army, Lt.-Gen. 25 July 1810	
G. Mackie ..	.. 22 Dec. 1808
Wm. Williams ..	.. 15 Nov. 1809
James Lomax.. ..	.. 16 Nov. 1809
Anthony Wharton..	.. 16 Aug. 1810
Majors—	
F. St. Mart	.. 5 Jan. 1805
W. Marlton ..	.. 25 July 1805
W. Woodgate.. ..	.. 13 Aug. 1807
James Grout ..	.. 8 Nov. 1809
Rank in Army, 25 April 1808	
J. F. Fitzgerald ..	9 Nov. 1809
Rank in Army, Lt. Col. 25 July 1810	
John Gubliffe ..	15 Mar. 1810
Rank in Army, 25 April 1808	
Rob. Hazen	.. 14 June 1810
A. Rumpler	.. 16 Aug. 1810
Rank in Army, 25 July 1810	
A. Andrews	.. 17 Jan. 1811
C. D. H. Bouterie ..	2 Oct. 1811
Rank in Army, 25 July 1810	
Gustav. Brown ..	3 Oct. 1811
Rank in Army, 25 July 1810	
Captains—	
C. De Salaberry ..	.. 10 July 1799
W. Fraser	.. 25 July 1799
J. W. Aldred	.. 19 Nov. 1800
W. Batteley	.. 15 Mar. 1803
Rank in Army, Major 25 April 1808	
Edw. Norton ..	.. 24 June 1803
Jas. Bunting	.. 25 June 1803
L. de Mangon	.. 25 June 1803
P. Mauringe ..	.. 2 July 1803
Geo. Gran ..	.. 24 Nov. 1802
J. MacMahon.. ..	.. 20 Aug. 1803
Tho. Hames	.. 12 Nov. 1803
Cha. Vigny ..	.. 4 Mar. 1804
M. de Wendt.. ..	.. 7 Dec. 1804
J. Jordon.. ..	.. 28 Mar. 1805
Rank in Army, Maj. 25 April 1808	
H de Salve	.. 23 April 1805
C. Kinsinger ..	.. 24 April 1805
Lewis Inturn	.. 25 April 1805
Adam Kuen	.. 23 May 1805
A Livingstone ..	.. 8 Aug. 1805
J. Schoedie	.. 19 Sept. 1805
H Kennells	.. 13 July 1805
F. Anthorn	.. 3 Dec. 1805
P. Bassare ..	.. 4 Dec. 1805
J. H. Weld	.. 4 Dec. 1805
Ga. A. Reynauld ..	.. 11 Dec. 1806
J. Prevost	.. 2 Dec. 1806
C. Hinckleday.. ..	.. 7 May 1807
E. Purdon	.. 27 Aug. 1807
J. E. Bell..	.. 20 Jan. 1808
J. D. Plancher ..	.. 21 Jan. 1808

M 2

Captains (continued)—

Rank and Name.	Rank in Regiment.
Ben. Rogers	12 May 1808
Alex. Campbell	15 May 1808
A. Ligertwood	30 Mar. 1809
Rank in Army, Major 25 Oct. 1810	
C. H. Tyler	20 April 1809
C. du Sable	29 June 1809
Ant. Stamba	10 Oct. 1809
Henry Petrie	11 Oct. 1809
C. W. H. Koch	12 Oct. 1809
Philip Myer	23 Nov. 1809
C. Mackenzie	10 Jan. 1810
Rank in Army, 12 Dec. 1799	
G. H. Zulke	11 Jan. 1810
F. McCarthy	24 May 1810
Robert Kelly	16 Aug. 1810
John Moore	2 Jan. 1811
Anthony Suasso	3 Jan. 1811
Charles Shaw	10 Jan. 1811
C. Deary	27 Aug. 1804
L. Gibbons	25 Feb. 1804
Thos. Smith	23 Mar. 1807
Chas. Hastings	7 Mar. 1811
H. Fischbach	11 April 1811
Wm. Hay	2 May 1811
Rich. England	11 July 1811
H. B. Bence	15 Aug. 1811
Wm. Walther	18 Sept. 1811
E. Holmes	19 Sept. 1811
Rich. Philbin	15 Oct. 1811
Dan. Page	16 Oct. 1811
Han. P. Fra. Cust	17 Oct. 1811

Lieutenants—

Rank and Name.	Rank in Regiment.
Wm. Friess	8 Aug. 1800
G. F. Gibson	2 June 1803
Ev. Baring	7 Aug. 1804
R. H. Hughes	3 Mar. 1804
J. Tumback	21 May 1804
H. Dibbly	Adjt. 23 May 1804
John Watson	24 May 1804
Fred. Stitz	9 June 1804
John Blair	1 Oct. 1794
J. Franchini	8 Nov. 1804
A. C. Bowers	26 Oct. 1804
Fra. Beritz	16 Oct. 1805
Cha. Appelius	17 Oct. 1805
Val. Reichard	20 Nov. 1805
Cha. Deckner	23 Nov. 1805
Va. Klinkerfuss	24 Nov. 1805
E. A. Baron Eberstein	27 Nov. 1805
Geo. Germain	28 Nov. 1805
Fred. Duncker	21 Jan. 1806
J. F. Galbraith	23 Jan. 1806
John Correvont	4 Feb. 1806
Fred. Schriene	6 Feb. 1806
John Perry	12 Feb. 1806
H. Hoffman	30 Dec. 1797
Alex. Webster	27 Aug. 1803
J. Fitzgerald	11 Aug. 1804
M. F. A. Tresson	29 Nov. 1807
W. Simpson	1 Dec. 1807
Jos. von Konig	2 Dec. 1807
M. du Chatelet	3 Dec. 1807
John P. Passley	5 Dec. 1807
Henry Miller	8 Dec. 1807
Wm. Linstow	9 Dec. 1807

Lieutenants (continued)—

Rank and Name.	Rank in Regiment.
F. Baron Eberstein	10 Dec. 1807
D. C. Brown	14 Jan. 1808
Col. Campbell	3 Sept. 1795
Rob. Mitchell	22 Sept. 1808
R. S. Redman	25 Feb. 1808
F. de Gilse	26 Sept. 1809
Charles Steiby	27 Sept. 1809
J. Hein. Adair	28 Sept. 1809
John Carlos	29 Sept. 1809
F. Strobeck	Adjt. 30 Sept. 1809
J. S. de Bernegg	10 Oct. 1809
Isaac R. D'Arcy	2 Oct. 1809
Wm. Wynne	3 Oct. 1809
Aud. Lachs	Adjt. 4 Oct. 1809
John Joyce	5 Oct. 1809
James Lewis	7 Oct. 1809
Jul. von Boeck	9 Oct. 1809
J. Louis Barbaz	10 Oct. 1809
C. Chev. de Bree	11 Oct. 1809
Andrew Ellison	12 Oct. 1809
R. H. Hislop	29 Oct. 1809
Leo de Froger	30 Oct. 1809
W. Morgenthal	1 Nov. 1809
J. T. Allinson	2 Nov. 1809
J. Pelt	3 Nov. 1809
Matthew Furst	4 Nov. 1809
Jas. Fontane	5 Nov. 1809
Richard Pasley	6 Nov. 1809
Geo. Robinson	7 Nov. 1809
J. F. Crozier	8 Nov. 1809
An. F. Evans	9 Nov. 1809
John Altenstein	17 Feb. 1810
John Hearn	18 Feb. 1810
Peter Kennedy	19 Feb. 1810
Alex. Rule	Adjt. 20 Feb. 1810
Tho. Jack	23 Feb. 1810
Tho. Smith	24 Feb. 1810
Hector Downie	25 Feb. 1810
M. de Ravarier	26 Feb. 1810
F. Fitzgerald	27 Feb. 1810
R. Ellison	Adjt. 28 Feb. 1810
Geo. F. Stern	1 Mar. 1810
John Mackay	3 Mar. 1810
Benj. Webster	4 Mar. 1810
And. Leitch	5 Mar. 1810
E. F. Firch	1 Feb. 1807
W. Goldsmith	11 June 1810
Man. Cottman	12 June 1810
Rich. Hilliard	13 June 1810
Sylv. O'Hehir	14 June 1810
J. B. Donnelly	16 Aug. 1810
Peter Eason	8 Oct. 1810
Tho. Marsh	9 Oct. 1810
Stephen Price	10 Oct. 1810
T. P. Conway	11 Oct. 1810
J. J. Sargent	13 Oct. 1810
Samuel Kerr	14 Oct. 1810
William Rind	15 Oct. 1810
J. D. Kent	16 Oct. 1810
Sam. Sargent	17 Oct. 1810
M. M'Namara	18 Oct. 1810
Eug. Downing	24 Oct. 1810
Rich. Saunders	25 Oct. 1810
David Le Count	26 Oct. 1810
Ter. M'Mahon	28 Oct. 1810

Lieutenants (continued)—			Paymasters (continued)—		
Rank and Name.		*Rank in Regiment.*	*Rank and Name.*		*Rank in Regiment.*
F. de Lahrbusch	..	.. 29 Oct. 1810	G. M. Slade ..	..	.. 19 Oct. 1809
F. P. N. de Kruger		.. 30 Oct. 1810	R. B. Fisher ..	..	.. 19 July 1801
F. L. de Ingersleben		.. 31 Oct. 1810	*Adjutants—*		
M. D. Carr ..	..	1 Nov. 1810	Hen. Dibbly ..	..	5 Feb. 1800
Tho. Sowerby ..	..	5 Jan. 1809	*Rank in Army,* Lieut. 23 May 1804		
C. B. Alcock ..	..	6 Dec. 1810	F. Strobeck	..	.. 20 Nov. 1806
E. Burghaagen	..	.. 28 Mar. 1811	*Rank in Army,* Lieut. 30 Sept. 1809		
A. P. de Borgh	..	18 April 1811	And. Laebs	..	.. 23 April 1807
Edw. Smith	..	2 May 1811	*Rank in Army,* **Lieut.** 4 Oct. 1809		
Sam. Burges ..	..	9 Feb. 1809	Peter Broetz ..	..	.. 14 Mar. 1811
Arthur Mitchell	..	4 Dec. 1806	Robert Ellison	..	.. 28 Mar. 1811
Wm. Coleman..	..	15 Aug. 1811	Alex. Rule ..	..	.. 17 Oct. 1811
—— Erdberg ..	..	.., 30 Sept. 1811	*Quartermasters—*		
C. J. de Franciosi ..		1 Oct. 1811	J. A. Kemmeter ..		.. 30 Dec. 1797
Wm. Rafter ..	..	2 Oct. 1811	J. Chattoway ..	..	.. 3 July 1800
—— de Schanz	..	3 Oct. 1811	Jos. Wilson ..	..	.. 25 May 1804
J. B. Goff	..	4 Oct. 1811	A. Hennerhofer ..		.. 25 Nov. 1807
L. V. Fleisbrt..	..	5 Oct. 1811	H. Heartsmke ..		.. 25 Nov. 1808
C. W. Breitbauer ..		6 Oct. 1811	—— Verbregge	..	.. 30 Mar. 1809
R. H. L. Schlosser ..		7 Oct. 1811	*Surgeons—*		
John Beaumont	..	8 Oct. 1811	John Faries ..	..	.. 21 Dec. 1800
Pet. Broetz ..	..	9 Oct. 1811	Wm. Ireland ..	..	.. 29 June 1809
Francis Allen ..	..	10 Oct. 1811	W. B. Morle ..	..	.. 2 Nov. 1809
Ensigns—			Jos. Morris ..	..	.. 11 Jan. 1810
L. F. V. S. Altenstein	..	19 Jan. 1809	J. du Moulin ..	..	1 Feb. 1810
John Gowen	..	9 Oct. 1809	John Arthur, M.D.	..	5 Sept. 1811
D. Drummond..	..	9 Oct. 1810	*Assistant-Surgeons—*		
John Beetor	..	11 Oct. 1810	Chas. Welsarg. ..	..	6 Feb. 1805
Rob. Atkinson ..	..	12 Oct. 1810	Robin Axton ..	..	1 May 1806
Jas. Fleeson ..	..	13 Oct. 1810	L. W. Whitestone ..		.. 23 Mar. 1809
Henry Hudson	..	16 Oct. 1810	J. H. Walker ..	..	2 Nov. 1809
John Hargrave	..	18 Oct. 1810	Geo. M'Dermott ..		.. 30 Nov. 1809
Joseph Cross ..	..	26 Oct. 1810	Geo. Meade ..	..	.. 26 April 1810
Don Urquhart..	..	27 Oct. 1810	C. G. Berger ..	..	.. 18 Oct. 1810
Geo. Cochrane..	..	28 Oct. 1810	Fra. Murray ..	..	.. 31 Jan. 1811
E. Y. Le Mastre	..	31 Oct. 1810	Leb. Membdorff..	..	.. 14 Mar. 1811
D. Carmichael..	..	1 Nov. 1810	Alex. Melvin ..	..	.. 26 Sept. 1811
Wm. Taaffe ..	..	14 Feb. 1811	Francis King ..	..	.. 26 Sept. 1811
Chas. Fisher ..	..	20 Mar. 1811			
Hen. Hed	..	21 Mar. 1811	*Regimentals*—Red, facings blue, white		
Jas. Kent..	..	11 April 1811	lace, 2 blue stripes.		
I. W. Patterson	..	18 April 1811			
Henry Molloy..	..	25 April 1811	*Agents*—Messrs. Greenwood, Cox, and Co.,		
Jas. Beattie ..	..	29 Aug. 1811	Craig's Court.		
J. W. von Dallmann	..	21 Feb. 1811			
Chas. Machan..	..	26 Sept. 1811			
John Hanley ..	..	29 Sept. 1811			
Francis Lane ..	..	30 Sept. 1811			
A. B. Kutrus ..	..	1 Oct. 1811	**1812.**		
John Currie ..	..	2 Oct. 1811			
Rob. Mackenzie	..	3 Oct. 1811	*Six Battalions.*		
Wm. Brady ..	..	4 Oct. 1811			
C. N. Machan ..	..	5 Oct. 1811	Africa West India England Spain.		
H. Sutherland..	..	6 Oct. 1811	*Colonel-Chief—*		
John Hamilton	..	7 Oct. 1811	H R H the Duke of York,		
W. C. Bagnell..	..	8 Oct. 1811	K.G., K.B .. .. 23 Aug. 1797		
Jas. Lawless ..	..	10 Oct. 1811	*Rank in Army,* Field-Mar. 10 Feb. 1795		
Cuth. Fournesel	..	17 Oct. 1811	*Cols.-Commandant—*		
Wm. Battcley..	..	14 Nov. 1811	T. Carleton .. .. .. 6 Aug. 1794		
Fred. Baring ..	..	15 Nov. 1811	*Rank in Army,* Gen. 25 Sept. 1803		
Paymasters—			E. Morrison .. .. .. 1 Jan. 1805		
Edw. Hausler..	..	1 Dec. 1804	*Rank in Army,* Lt.-Gen. 1 Jan. 1805		
Geo. Gilbert ..	..	6 Feb. 1805	N. C. Barton .. .. .. 3 Jan. 1806		
Pat. Hevus ..	..	19 Jan. 1809	*Rank in Army,* Lt.-Gen. 1 Jan. 1805		
Henry Jackson	..	12 Oct. 1809	Sir G. Prevost, Bart. .. 3 Jan. 1788		
			Rank in Army, Lt.-Gen. 4 June 1811		

Rank and Name.	*Rank in Regiment.*
Cols.-Commandant (continued)—	
W. E. Phipps	25 Aug. 1807
Rank in Army, Lt.-Gen.	25 April 1808
A. Wetham	7 Feb. 1811
Rank in Army, Lt.-Gen.	4 June 1811
Lieut.-Colonels—	
J. A. Harris	16 Jan. 1788
Rank in Army, Lt.-Gen.	1 Jan. 1805
G. W. Ramsay	30 Dec. 1797
Rank in Army,Maj.-Gen.	4 June 1811
Fras. Baron de Rottenburg	30 Dec. 1797
Rank in Army, Maj.-Gen.	25 July 1810
J. Hope	30 June 1801
Rank in Army,Maj.-Gen.	25 July 1810
Edw. Codd	26 Oct. 1804
T. Austin..	20 June 1805
P. Anderson	14 Jan. 1808
Rank in Army,	17 Oct. 1805
F. Viscount Lake	10 May 1808
Rank in Army,Maj.-Gen.	4 June 1811
W. Dowdeswell	2 June 1808
Rank in Army, Lt.-Gen.	25 July 1810
G. Mackie	22 Dec. 1809
Wm. Williams	15 Nov. 1809
James Lomax	16 Nov. 1809
Ant. Wharton..	16 Aug. 1810
Majors—	
Francis St. Mart	5 Jan. 1805
W. Marlton	25 July 1805
W. Woodgate..	13 Aug. 1807
Rank in Army, Lt.-Col.	30 May 1811
James Grant	8 Nov. 1809
Rank in Army,	25 April 1808
J. F. Fitzgerald	9 Nov. 1809
Rank in Army, Lt.-Col.	25 July 1810
John Galiffe	15 Mar. 1810
Rank in Army,	25 April 1808
Rob. Hazen	14 June 1810
A. Rumpler	16 Aug. 1810
Rank in Army,	25 July 1810
A. Andrews	17 Jan. 1811
C. D. H. Bouverie.. ..	2 Oct. 1811
Rank in Army,	25 July 1810
Gustav. Brown	3 Oct. 1811
Rank in Army,	25 July 1810
Captains—	
C. de Salaberry	
Rank in Army, Major	4 June 1811
W. Fraser	
Rank in Army, Major	4 June 1811
J. W. Aldred	
W. Batteley	
Rank in Army, Major	25 April 1808
Edwd. Norton..	24 June 1803
Jas. Bunting	25 June 1803
C. L. de Mangon	25 June 1803
P. Maurriage	2 July 1803
T. MacMahon..	20 Aug. 1803
Thos. Hames..	12 Nov. 1803
Chas. Vigny	4 Mar. 1804
M. de Wendt	7 Dec. 1804
J. Jordan	28 Mar. 1805
Rank in Army, Major	25 April 1808
C. Kinsngen	25 April 1805
Rank in Army, Major	25 Oct. 1811
Lew. Inturn	25 April 1805
Captains (continued)—	
Adan Krien	23 May 1805
A. Livingstone	8 Aug. 1805
J. Schoedde	19 Sept. 1805
H. Rennells	13 July 1805
F. Inturn	3 Dec. 1805
P. Blassiere	4 Dec. 1805
J. A. Wolff	5 June 1806
Ga. Reynauld..	11 Dec. 1806
C. Hinckleday..	7 May 1807
E. Purdon	27 Aug. 1807
J. E. Bell..	20 Jan. 1808
J. D. Plancher	21 Jan. 1808
Ben. Rogers	12 May 1808
A. Ligertwood..	30 Mar. 1809
Rank in Army, Major	25 Oct. 1810
C. du Sable	29 June 1809
Ant. Stemba	10 Oct. 1809
Henry Petrie..	11 Oct. 1809
C. W. H. Koch	12 Oct. 1809
Philip Myer	23 Nov. 1809
C. Mackenzie	10 Jan. 1810
Rank in Army, Major	4 June 1811
G. H. Zulke	11 Jan. 1810
F. McCarthy	24 May 1810
Robert Kelly	16 Aug. 1810
John Moore	2 Jan. 1811
Charles Shaw	10 Jan. 1811
C. Drury	27 Aug. 1804
L. Gibbons	25 Feb. 1804
Thos. Smith	23 Mar. 1809
H. Fischbach	11 April 1811
Wm. Walther..	18 Sept. 1811
F. Holmes	19 Sept. 1811
Dan. Page	16 Oct. 1811
Hon. P. Fra. Cast	17 Oct. 1811
Jas. Marsden	14 May 1807
F. G. Goodwin	5 Dec. 1811
Thos. Dundas..	26 Dec. 1811
G. F. Gibson	9 Jan. 1812
A. W. Mackenzie	23 Jan. 1812
Ed. Baring	13 Feb. 1812
W. Tonkinson	12 Mar. 1812
Melv. Glenie	14 July 1808
Jas. Stopford	17 Feb. 1808
C. C. Bacon	4 Sept. 1795
Lieutenants—	
Wm. Friess	8 Aug. 1800
R. H. Hughes..	3 Mar. 1804
J. Trunbuck	21 May 1804
H. Dibbly	23 May 1804
John Watson	24 May 1804
Fred. Stitz	9 June 1804
John Blair	1 Oct. 1794
J. Franchini	8 Nov. 1804
A. C. Bowers	26 Oct. 1804
Fra. Beritz	10 Oct. 1805
Chas. Appelius	17 Oct. 1805
Val. Reichard..	20 Nov. 1805
Cha. Deckner	23 Nov. 1805
Va. Klinkerfuss	24 Oct. 1805
E. A. Baron Eberstein ..	27 Nov. 1805
Geo. Germann..	28 Nov. 1805
Fred. Duncker	21 Jan. 1806
J. F. Galbraith	23 Jan. 1806
John Correvont	4 Feb. 1806

Rank and Name.	Rank in Regiment.
Lieutenants (continued)—	
Fred. Schriene	6 Feb. 1806
John Perry	12 Feb. 1806
H. Hoffman	30 Dec. 1797
Alex. Webster	27 Aug. 1807
J. Fitzgerald	11 Aug. 1804
M. F. A. Tresson	29 Nov. 1807
W. Simpson	1 Dec. 1807
Jos. von Kong	2 Dec. 1807
M. du Chatelet	3 Dec. 1807
John P. Passley	5 Dec. 1807
Henry Muller	8 Dec. 1807
Wm. Linstow	9 Dec. 1807
F. Baron Eberstein	10 Dec. 1807
D. C. Brown	14 Jan. 1808
Col. Campbell	3 Sept. 1795
Rob. Mitchell	22 Sept. 1808
R. S. Redman	25 Feb. 1808
F. de Gline	26 Sept. 1809
Charles Steiby	27 Sept. 1809
J. Hein Adair	28 Sept. 1809
John Carlos	29 Sept. 1809
F. Strobeck	30 Sept. 1809
J. S. de Bernegg	1 Oct. 1809
Isaac R. D'Arcy	2 Oct. 1809
Wm. Wynne	3 Oct. 1809
And. Lachs	4 Oct. 1809
John Joyce	5 Oct. 1809
Jul. von Bock	9 Oct. 1809
Louis Barbaz	10 Oct. 1809
Chas. de Bree	11 Oct. 1809
Andrew Ellison	12 Oct. 1809
R. B. Bishop	29 Oct. 1809
Leo de Froger	30 Oct. 1809
W. Morgenthal	1 Nov. 1809
J. T. Atkinson	2 Nov. 1809
J. Pelt	3 Nov. 1809
Mathew Furst	4 Nov. 1809
Jas Fontane	5 Nov. 1809
Richard Pasley	6 Nov. 1809
Geo. Robinson	7 Nov. 1809
J. F. Crozier	8 Nov. 1809
An. F. Evans	9 Nov. 1809
John Hearn	18 Feb. 1810
Peter Kennedy	19 Feb. 1810
Alex. Rule	20 Feb. 1810
Thos. Jack	23 Feb. 1810
Thos. Smith	24 Feb. 1810
Hector Downie	25 Feb. 1810
M. de Baravier	26 Feb. 1810
E. Fitzgerald	27 Feb. 1810
Rob. Ellison	28 Feb. 1810
Geo. F. Stern	1 Mar. 1810
John Mackay	3 Mar. 1810
Benj. Welster	4 Mar. 1810
And. Leitch	5 Mar. 1810
E. F. Pirch	1 Feb. 1810
W. Goldsmith	11 June 1810
Man. Cottman	12 June 1810
Rich. Hubard	13 June 1810
Syly. O'Hehar	14 June 1810
J. B. Donnelly	16 Aug 1810
Peter Eason	8 Oct. 1810
Tho. Marsh	9 Oct. 1810
Stephen Price	10 Oct. 1810
T. P. Conway	11 Oct. 1810

Rank and Name.	Rank in Regiment.
Lieutenants (continued)—	
J. J. Sargent	13 Oct. 1810
Samuel Kerr	14 Oct. 1810
William Kind	15 Oct. 1810
J. D. Kent	16 Oct. 1810
Sam. Sergeant	17 Oct. 1810
M. M'Namara	18 Oct. 1810
Eug. Downing	24 Oct. 1810
Rich. Saunders	25 Oct. 1810
David Le Count	26 Oct. 1810
Ter. MacMahon	28 Oct. 1810
F. de Lahrbusch	29 Oct. 1810
F. P. N. de Kruger	30 Oct. 1810
F. L. de Ingersleben	31 Aug. 1810
Dawson Carr	1 Nov. 1810
C. H. Alcock	6 Dec. 1810
E. Burghagen	28 Mar. 1811
A. P. de Borgh	18 April 1811
Sam. Burges	9 Feb. 1809
Arthur Mitchell	14 Dec. 1806
Wm. Coleman	15 Aug. 1811
—— Erdberg	30 Sept. 1811
C. J. de Francitei	1 Oct. 1811
Wm. Rafter	2 Oct. 1811
—— de Schanz	3 Oct. 1811
J. H. Gaff	4 Oct. 1811
L. V. Fleischhut	5 Oct. 1811
C. W. Reetthauer	6 Oct. 1811
R. H. L. Schhower	7 Oct. 1811
John Beaumont	8 Oct. 1811
Pet. Broetz	9 Oct. 1811
Francis Allen	10 Oct. 1811
D. Drummond	19 Dec. 1811
S. Roepel	28 Feb. 1812
J. Humphreys	12 Mar. 1812
Sam. Nicholls	11 Aug. 1808
John Beevor	24 Mar. 1812
Rob. Atkinson	25 Mar. 1812
Jas. Fleeson	26 Mar. 1812
Henry Hudson	27 Mar. 1812
John Hargrave	28 Mar. 1812
Joseph Crow	29 Mar. 1812
Don. Urquhart	30 Mar. 1812
Geo. Cochrane	31 Mar. 1812
E. Y. Le Maitre	1 April 1812
D. Carmichael	2 April 1812
C. Marchington	7 May 1812
Wm. Taaffe	14 May 1812
Ensigns—	
I. E. V. S. Altenstem	19 Jan. 1809
Chas. Fisher	20 Mar. 1811
Hen. Heal	21 Mar. 1811
Jas. Kent	11 April 1811
J. W. Patterson	18 April 1811
Henry Molloy	25 April 1811
Jas. Beattie	29 Aug. 1811
J. W. von Dallmann	21 Feb. 1811
Chas. Maclean	26 Sept. 1811
John Hanley	29 Sept. 1811
A. B. Kairns	1 Oct. 1811
John Currie	2 Oct. 1811
Robt. Mackenzie	3 Oct. 1811
Wm. Brady	4 Oct. 1811
C. N. Maclean	5 Oct. 1811
H. Sutherland	6 Oct. 1811
John Hamilton	7 Oct. 1811

Rank and Name.	Rank in Regiment.
Ensigns (continued)—	
W. C. Bagnal	.. 8 Oct. 1811
Jas. Lawless	.. 10 Oct. 1811
C. Fourneret	.. 17 Oct. 1811
Wm. Batteley	.. 14 Nov. 1811
Fred. Baring	.. 15 Nov. 1811
Wm. Lupton	.. 28 Nov. 1811
Jeremy Jones	.. 9 May 1811
A. M. J. Durnford ..	.. 30 Jan. 1812
W. F. A. Gillfillan ..	.. 4 Mar. 1812
Wm. Handley	.. 25 Mar. 1812
Henry Blunt	.. 26 Mar. 1812
Jas. Rollo	.. 27 Mar. 1812
John Tarbock	.. 28 Mar. 1812
Rich. Ring	.. 29 Mar. 1812
Robt. Pannell	.. 30 Mar. 1812
C. B. Martin	.. 31 Mar. 1812
Hugh Dickson	.. 1 April 1812
R. B. Nettles	.. 2 April 1812
Gottl. Lerche	.. 14 May 1812

Paymasters—	
Edw. Hansler	.. 1 Dec. 1801
Geo. Gilbert	.. 6 Feb. 1806
Pat. Hevns	.. 19 Jan. 1809
Henry Jackson	.. 12 Oct. 1809
G. M. Slade	.. 19 Oct. 1809
R. B. Fisher	.. 19 July 1810

Adjutants—	
Hen. Dibbly	.. 5 Feb. 1800
Rank in Army, Lieut. 23 May 1804	
F. Strobeck	.. 20 Nov. 1806
Rank in Army, Lieut. 30 Sept. 1806	
And. Lochs	.. 23 April 1807
Rank in Army, Lieut. 4 Oct. 1809	
Peter Brootz	.. 14 Mar. 1811
Rank in Army, Lieut. 9 Oct. 1811	
Robt. Ellison	.. 28 Mar. 1811
Rank in Army, Lieut. 28 Feb. 1810	
Alex. Rule	.. 17 Oct. 1811
Rank in Army, Lieut. 20 Feb. 1810	

Quartermasters—	
J. A. Kemmeter ..	.. 30 Dec. 1797
J. Chattaway	.. 3 July 1800
Jas. Wilson	.. 25 May 1804
A. Hennerhofer ..	.. 25 Nov. 1807
—— Verbrugge ..	.. 30 Mar. 1809

Surgeons—	
John Faries	.. 21 Dec. 1800
Wm. Ireland	.. 29 June 1809
W. B. Morle	.. 2 Nov. 1809
Ja. du Moulin	.. 1 Feb. 1810
John Arthur, M.D. ..	.. 5 Sept. 1811

Assistant-Surgeons—	
Chas. Welsarg ..	.. 6 Feb. 1805
L. W. Whitestone ..	.. 23 Mar. 1806
J. H. Walker	.. 2 Nov. 1809
Geo. McDermott ..	.. 30 Nov. 1809
Geo. Meade	.. 26 April 1810
C. G. Berger	.. 18 Oct. 1810
Fra. Murray	.. 31 Jan. 1811
Leh. Menshoff	.. 14 Mar. 1811
Alex. Melvin	.. 26 Sept. 1811

Rank and Name.	Rank in Regiment.
Assistant-Surgeons (continued)—	
Francis King	.. 26 Sept. 1811
John C. Spry	.. 29 Aug. 1811

Regimentals—Red, facings blue, white
lace, 2 blue stripes.

5th Rifle Battalion, green

Agents—Messrs. Greenwood, Cox, and Co.,
Craig's Court.

1813.

Eight Battalions.

Africa—West Indies—Spain—France—
England.

Col.-in-Chief—	
H.R.H. Fred., Duke of	
York, K.G., K.B. ..	23 Aug. 1797
Rank in Army, Field-Mar. 10 Feb. 1795	

Cols.-Commandant—	
T. Carleton	.. 6 Aug. 1794
Rank in Army, Gen. 25 Sept. 1803	
N. C. Burton	.. 3 Jan. 1806
Rank in Army, Lt.-Gen. 1 Jan. 1805	
H. E. Phipps	.. 25 Aug. 1807
Rank in Army, Lt.-Gen. 25 April 1808	
J. Robinson	.. 2 Jan. 1813
Rank in Army, Lt.-Gen. 4 June 1811	
Hon. C. Hope	.. 15 Feb. 1813
Rank in Army, Lt.-Gen. 1 Jan. 1812	
Sir H. Clinton, K.B. ..	20 May 1813
Rank in Army, Maj.-Gen. 25 July 1810	
Sir G. Murray, K.B. ..	9 Aug. 1813
Rank in Army, Maj.-Gen. 1 Jan. 1812	
J. Kempt	.. 4 Nov. 1813
Rank in Army, Maj.-Gen. 1 Jan. 1812	

Lieut.-Colonels—	
J. A. Harris	.. 16 Jan. 1788
Rank in Army, Lt.-Gen. 1 Jan. 1805	
G. W. Ramsay	.. 30 Dec. 1797
Rank in Army, Maj.-Gen. 4 June 1811	
J. Hope	.. 30 June 1804
Rank in Army, Maj.-Gen. 25 July 1810	
Edward Codd	.. 26 Oct. 1804
Rank in Army, Col. 4 June 1813	
T. Austin	.. 20 June 1805
Rank in Army, Col. 4 June 1813	
P. Anderson	.. 11 Jan. 1808
Rank in Army, 17 Oct. 1805	
F. Viscount Lake	10 May 1808
Rank in Army, Maj.-Gen. 4 June 1811	
W. Dowdeswell	2 June 1808
Rank in Army, Lt.-Gen. 25 July 1810	
G. Mackie	.. 22 Dec. 1808
J. Lomax	.. 16 Nov. 1809
Ant. Wharton	.. 16 Aug. 1810
John Keane	.. 25 June 1812
Rank in Army, Col. 1 Jan. 1812	
H. John	.. 9 Aug. 1813
J. P. Hunt	.. 11 Nov. 1813
Rank in Army, 27 April 1812	

Majors—	
F. St. Mart	.. 5 June 1805
Rank in Army, Lt.-Col. 1 Jan. 1812	
W. Maclton	.. 25 July 1812
Rank in Army, Lt.-Col. 1 Jan. 1815	

Rank and Name.	Rank in Regiment.
Majors (continued)—	
W. Woodgate	13 Aug. 1807
Rank in Army, Lt.-Col.	30 May 1811
James Grant	8 Nov. 1809
Rank in Army,	25 April 1808
J. F. Fitzgerald ..	9 Nov. 1809
Rank in Army, Lt.-Col.	25 July 1810
John Galiffe	15 Mar. 1810
Rank in Army,	25 April 1818
A. Rumpler	16 Aug. 1810
Rank in Army,	25 July 1810
A. Andrews	17 Jan. 1811
C. D. H. Bouverie ..	20 Oct. 1811
Rank in Army,	25 July 1810
G. Brown	3 Oct. 1811
Rank in Army, Lt.-Col.	17 Aug. 1812
Hen. Wyndham ..	9 Aug. 1813
F. O. Tripp	10 Nov. 1813
H. Fitzgerald	11 Nov. 1813
C. de Salaberry ..	18 Nov. 1813
Rank in Army, Lt.-Col.	17 Aug. 1812
Captains—	
W. Fraser	25 July 1799
Rank in Army, Major	4 June 1811
J. W. Aldred ..	19 Nov. 1800
Rank in Army,	1 Jan. 1812
W. Batteley	15 Mar. 1803
Rank in Army, Major	25 April 1808
Edward Norton ..	24 June 1803
M. D. Mangin ..	25 June 1803
P. Mauriage	2 July 1803
J. MacMahon	20 Aug. 1803
Charles Vigny ..	4 Mar. 1804
M. de Wendt	7 Dec. 1804
J. Jordan	28 Mar. 1805
Rank in Army, Major	25 April 1808
C. Kissinger ..	24 April 1805
Rank in Army, Major	24 Oct. 1811
F. Inturn	24 April 1805
Lew. Inturn	25 April 1805
Adam Krien	23 May 1805
L. Schoedde	19 Sept. 1805
Rank in Army, Major	21 June 1813
H. Rennells	13 July 1805
P. Blassere	4 Dec. 1805
Jas. A. Wolff ..	5 June 1806
Go. Reymould ..	11 Dec. 1806
C. Hinckleslay.. ..	7 May 1807
E. Purdon	27 Aug. 1807
J. E. Bell	20 Jan. 1808
A. Ligertwood.. ..	30 Mar. 1809
Rank in Army, Major	25 Oct. 1809
C. du Sable	29 June 1809
Anthony Stanton ..	10 Oct. 1809
Henry Petre	11 Oct. 1809
C. W. H. Koch ..	12 Oct. 1809
Philip Myer	23 Nov. 1809
C. McKenzie	10 Jan. 1810
Rank in Army, Major	4 Jan. 1811
G. H. Zulke	11 Jan. 1810
F. M'Carthy	24 May 1810
Robert Kelly	16 Aug. 1810
John Moore	2 Jan. 1811
C. Drury	27 Aug. 1811
L. Gibbons	20 Feb. 1811
H. Fischbach	11 April 1811
Captains (continued)—	
F. Holmes	19 Sept. 1811
Dan. Page	16 Oct. 1811
G. F. Gibson	9 Jan. 1812
Ev. Baring	13 Feb. 1812
Melv. Glenie	14 July 1808
James Stopford ..	17 Feb. 1808
J. W. Harrison ..	15 Oct. 1807
Hon. E. S. Erskine	27 Dec. 1810
R. H. Hughes.. ..	27 Aug. 1812
J. Trombuck	28 Aug. 1812
R. A. Dalziel	24 Sept. 1812
Rank in Army, Col.	1 Jan. 1812
H. Dibbly	23 Dec. 1812
John Blair	21 Jan. 1813
J. Franchini	28 Jan. 1813
A. C. Bowers	11 Feb. 1813
A. A. Wood	4 Mar. 1813
W. H. Sewell	12 Mar. 1812
Jas. Johnson	10 June 1813
Fra. Bertz	1 Aug. 1813
Val. Reichard	2 Aug. 1813
Chas. Deckuer.. ..	3 Aug. 1813
E. A. Eberstein ..	4 Aug. 1813
J. Strongitharm ..	5 Aug. 1813
C. Ward	9 Aug. 1813
J. N. Nealson	10 Aug. 1813
A. E. de la Bourdonnaye	11 Aug. 1813
A. de Damas	12 Aug. 1813
P. F. Thorne	13 Aug. 1813
C. Barrington	14 Aug. 1813
W. Pearce	15 Aug. 1813
J. H. Edwards ..	16 Aug. 1813
A. E. D'Orfeuille ..	17 Aug. 1813
John Bagwell	18 Aug. 1813
J. B. Pym	4 Nov. 1813
C. Leslie	5 Nov. 1813
T. Power..	6 Nov. 1813
J. D. Weatherley ..	7 Nov. 1813
J. Carmichael	8 Nov. 1813
C. Campbell	9 Nov. 1813
E. Brandon	10 Nov. 1813
J. S. Lillie	11 Nov. 1813
R. Getlon	12 Nov. 1813
G. Ploian	13 Nov. 1813
Lieutenants—	
Wm. Knox	8 Aug. 1805
Geo. Germain.. ..	28 Nov. 1805
Fred. Duncker ..	21 Jan. 1806
J. F. Galbraith ..	23 Jan. 1806
John Corryvait ..	4 Feb. 1806
Fred. Schirmer ..	6 Feb. 1806
J. Fitzgerald	11 Aug. 1804
M. a Tresson ..	29 Nov. 1807
W. Simpson	1 Dec. 1807
Jas. von Kontz ..	2 Dec. 1807
M. du Chatelet ..	3 Dec. 1807
John P. Paisley ..	5 Dec. 1807
Henry Muller.. ..	8 Dec. 1807
Wm. Linstow	9 Dec. 1807
D. C. Brown	11 Jan. 1808
Col. Campbell.. ..	3 Sept. 1795
Rob't Mitchell ..	22 Sept. 1808
R. S. Redman	25 Feb. 1808
F. de Gilse	26 Sept. 1809

Lieutenants (continued)—

Rank and Name.	Rank in Regiment.
J. Hein, Adair	28 Sept. 1809
John Carlos	29 Sept. 1809
F. Strobeck	30 Sept. 1809
J. S. de Bernegg ..	1 Oct. 1809
Isaac R. D'Arcy ..	2 Oct. 1809
Wm. Wynne	3 Oct. 1809
Andrew Lachs	4 Oct. 1809
Jul. von Bocck ..	9 Oct. 1809
J. Louis Barbaz ..	10 Oct. 1809
And. Ellison	12 Oct. 1809
R. B. Bishop	29 Oct. 1809
Leo. de Froger.. ..	30 Oct. 1809
J. T. Allinson.. ..	2 Nov. 1809
Matthew Furst ..	4 Nov. 1809
Ja. Fontane	5 Nov. 1809
Richard Pasley ..	6 Nov. 1809
Geo. Robinson.. ..	7 Nov. 1809
An. F. Evans	9 Nov. 1809
John Hearn	18 Feb. 1810
Peter Kennedy ..	19 Feb. 1810
Alex. Rule	20 Feb. 1810
Thos. Jack	23 Feb. 1810
Thos. Smith	24 Feb. 1810
Hector Downie ..	25 Feb. 1810
M. de Ravarier ..	26 Feb. 1810
Robt. Ellison	28 Feb. 1810
Geo. F. Stern	1 Mar. 1810
And. Leitch	5 Mar. 1810
E. F. Pirch	1 Feb. 1807
W. Goldsmith.. ..	11 June 1810
M. Cottman	12 June 1810
Rich. Hilliard	13 June 1810
Sylv. O'Hehir	14 June 1810
J. B. Donnelly ..	16 Aug. 1810
Peter Eason	8 Oct. 1810
Tho. Marsh	9 Oct. 1810
Stephen Price	10 Oct. 1810
T. P. Conway	11 Oct. 1810
J. S. Sargent	13 Oct. 1810
Samuel Kerr	14 Oct. 1810
J. D. Kent	16 Oct. 1810
Samuel Sergeant ..	17 Oct. 1810
M. M'Namara	18 Oct. 1810
Eug. Downing.. ..	24 Oct. 1810
R. Saunders	25 Oct. 1810
David Le Count ..	26 Oct. 1810
Fer. M'Mahon.. ..	28 Oct. 1810
F. de Larbusch ..	29 Oct. 1810
F. P. N. de Kruger..	30 Oct. 1810
Dawson Carr	1 Nov. 1810
C. B. Alcock	6 Dec. 1810
E. Burghaagen ..	28 Mar. 1811
A. P. de Borgh ..	18 April 1811
Sam. Burges	9 Feb. 1809
Arthur Mitchell ..	4 Dec. 1806
Wm. Coleman.. ..	15 Aug. 1811
——— Erdberg.. ..	30 Sept. 1811
C. J. de Francisoi ..	1 Oct. 1811
W. Rafcer	2 Oct. 1811
——— de Schanz ..	3 Oct. 1811
J. B. Goff	1 Oct. 1811
L. V. Fleischbut ..	5 Oct. 1811
C. W. Bretthauer ..	6 Oct. 1811
R. H. L. Schlosser..	7 Oct. 1811
Francis Allen	10 Oct. 1811

Lieutenants (continued)—

Rank and Name.	Rank in Regiment.
D. Drummond	19 Dec. 1811
G. Roepel..	28 Feb. 1812
J. Humphries.. ..	12 Mar. 1812
John Beevor	24 Mar. 1812
Jas. Fleeson	26 Mar. 1812
Hen. Hudson	27 Mar. 1812
Jos. Crow..	29 Mar. 1812
John Urquhart	30 Mar. 1812
Geo. Cochrane.. ..	31 Mar. 1812
D. Carmichael	2 April 1812
Wm. Taaffe	14 May 1812
Hen. Heil	6 Aug. 1812
Jas. Kent	2 Sept. 1812
J. W. Patterson ..	3 Sept. 1812
Hen. Molloy	29 Oct. 1812
Jas. Beatty	19 Dec. 1812
Chas. Maclean.. ..	20 Dec. 1812
John Currie	22 Dec. 1812
Rob. Mackenzie ..	23 Dec. 1812
Wm. Brady	24 Dec. 1812
H. Sutherland.. ..	30 Dec. 1812
John Hamilton	31 Dec. 1812
Wm. C. Bagnall ..	14 Jan. 1813
Jas. Lawless	21 Jan. 1813
C. Fournent	6 Feb. 1813
Wm. Batteley.. ..	7 Feb. 1813
Fred. Baring	8 Feb. 1813
W. Lupton	9 Feb. 1813
Jeremy Jones	10 Feb. 1813
Matt. Moore	31 May 1810
Thos. Eccles	5 Mar. 1812
A. N. J. Durnford ..	5 May 1813
W. F. A. Gilfillan ..	6 May 1813
Bishop Straker	19 Dec. 1811
M. Hayes..	15 Oct. 1812
J. Moore	22 July 1813
John Torback	1 Aug. 1813
Rob. Pannell	2 Aug. 1813
C. B. Martin	3 Aug. 1813
Hugh Dickson.. ..	4 Aug. 1813
Rob. Nettles	5 Aug. 1813
Wm. Nixon	4 Feb. 1813
H. J. Russell	10 Aug. 1813
E. Hunter	11 Aug. 1813
R. Tighes..	12 Aug. 1813
John Frend	13 Aug. 1813
A. Mellis	14 Aug. 1813
Hen. Boldero	16 Aug. 1813
Gottl. Lerche.. ..	19 Aug. 1813
P. R. A. van Dyck ..	18 Aug. 1812
T. Andrews	8 Sept. 1812
J. Wallace	9 Sept. 1812
E. Worsley	11 Sept. 1812
A. Bromelhurst ..	15 Sept. 1812
W. Nagel..	16 Sept. 1812
E. Webb	2 Jan. 1811
L. A. von Battenberg ..	22 Oct. 1813
C. Ross	4 Nov. 1813
T. Acton	5 Nov. 1813
S. Tresseder	6 Nov. 1813
H. Gage	7 Nov. 1813
S. Nason	19 Sept. 1811
Aug. Kelly	18 Nov. 1813

Ensigns—

Rank and Name.	Rank in Regiment.
L. F. V. S. Altenstein ..	19 Jan. 1809

Rank and Name.	Rank in Regiment.
Ensigns (continued):—	
John Hanley	.. 29 Sept. 1811
Fred. Pictet	.. 25 June 1813
Jero. Cochran.. ..	.. 6 Aug. 1813
Joseph Stewart ..	.. 2 Sept. 1813
J. H. Crawford ..	.. 3 Sept. 1813
Lewis Clare	.. 10 Sept. 1813
R. A. Coates	.. 22 Oct. 1813
J. Armstrong	.. 29 Oct. 1813
Robert Hall	.. 19 Nov. 1813
A. Weiburg	.. 10 Dec. 1813
Tho. Wright	.. 18 Dec. 1813
Wm. Williams.. ..	.. 19 Dec. 1813
John Brown	.. 20 Dec. 1813
Benj. Clare	.. 21 Dec. 1813
Wm. Faweett	.. 22 Dec. 1813
H. Shewbridge.. ..	.. 23 Dec. 1812
Richard Ferzar ..	.. 24 Dec. 1812
Hon. A. Macdonald	.. 29 Dec. 1812
Wm. Scott	.. 30 Dec. 1812
Philip Vigoun ..	.. 31 Dec. 1812
H. M. Randall.. ..	.. 21 Jan. 1813
E. J. Bruce	.. 6 Feb. 1813
J. T. Hislop	.. 7 Feb. 1813
Thos. Lemmon ..	.. 8 Feb. 1813
Thos. Burton.. ..	.. 9 Feb. 1813
Wm. Donovan.. ..	.. 10 Feb. 1813
J. Lewis	.. 3 Mar. 1813
G. B. Symes	.. 5 May 1813
Henry Senior ..	.. 6 May 1813
Thomas Abell.. ..	.. 15 July 1813
—— Rutledge..	.. 1 Aug. 1813
Geo. Eberstein ..	.. 2 Aug. 1813
Alex Blossl	.. 3 Aug. 1813
Kerry Supple ..	.. 4 Aug. 1813
Hamilton Reed ..	.. 9 Aug. 1813
W. H. Barnes.. ..	.. 10 Aug. 1813
Chas. Harris	.. 11 Aug. 1813
C. H. Dehuston..	.. 12 Aug. 1813
Martin Burke ..	.. 13 Aug. 1813
S. M'Queen	.. 14 Aug. 1813
Ambrose Syong..	.. 15 Aug. 1813
R. P. Pack	.. 16 Aug. 1813
John Curtis	.. 17 Aug. 1813
Thos. Kent	.. 18 Aug. 1813
Peter Moore	.. 19 Aug. 1813
F. G. Bartlett ..	.. 20 Aug. 1813
J. F. Myers	.. 26 Aug. 1813
Jas. Reeser	.. 4 Nov. 1813
L. A. Rousseau ..	.. 5 Nov. 1813
Clifton Curtis.. ..	.. 6 Nov. 1813
Arthur Smith.. ..	.. 7 Nov. 1813
John Kelly	.. 8 Nov. 1813
Geo. Campbell ..	.. 9 Nov. 1813
Paymasters—	
Pat. Reyns	.. 19 Jan. 1809
G. M. Slade	.. 19 Oct. 1809
R. B. Fisher	.. 19 July 1810
Hen. Biggs	.. 22 Oct. 1812
Geo. Read	.. 6 May 1813
Henry Heartsonke ..	.. 7 May 1813
Adjutants—	
And. Lachs	.. 23 April 1807
Robert Ellison.. ..	.. 28 Mar. 1811
Alex Rule	.. 17 Oct. 1811
A. Weiburg	.. 10 Dec. 1812

Rank and Name.	Rank in Regiment.
Adjutants (continued)—	
J. Kent	.. 31 Dec. 1812
J. F. Myers	.. 26 Aug. 1813
Quartermasters—	
J. Chattoway	.. 3 July 1800
A. Hennerhofer ..	.. 25 Nov. 1807
—— Maxwell.. ..	.. 6 July 1812
Alex. Johnson.. ..	.. 24 Sept. 1812
—— Reckney.. ..	.. 31 Dec. 1812
Tho. Burrowes ..	.. 26 Aug. 1813
Surgeons—	
John Faries	.. 21 Dec. 1800
Wm. Ireland	.. 29 June 1809
W. B. Morle	.. 2 Nov. 1809
John Arthur, M.D..	.. 5 Sept. 1811
A. L. Lomsworth ..	.. 26 Sept. 1811
Jos. Abell	.. 15 July 1813
J. G. Hassell	.. 9 Sept. 1813
Assistant-Surgeons—	
J. B. Walker, M.D.	.. 2 Nov. 1809
Geo. M'Dermott ..	.. 30 Nov. 1809
C. G. Berger	.. 18 Oct. 1810
Fra. Murray	.. 31 Jan. 1811
Leh. Memlorff.. ..	.. 14 Mar. 1811
Alex Melvin	.. 26 Sept. 1811
Francis King	.. 26 Sept. 1811
Arthur Johnson ..	.. 28 May 1812
Chas. Denley	.. 4 Mar. 1813
Henry Keller	.. 28 Oct. 1813
P. Smith..	.. 11 Nov. 1813

Regimentals—Red, facings blue, white
lace, 2 blue stripes.

5th Rifle Battalion, green.

Agents—Messrs. Greenwood, Cox, and Co.,
Craig's Court.

1814.

Eight Battalions.

Africa   West Indies   France   Ireland—
England   Mediterranean   North
America   Portugal.

The following denote honorary distinction of individual officers:

K.G., Knight of the Garter.
G.C.B., Grand Cross of the Bath.
K.C.B., Knight Commander of the Bath.
† after name, Companion of the Bath.
K.T., Knight of the Thistle.
K.St.P., Knight of St. Patrick.
K.C., Knight of the Crescent.
◪ Cross.
◪◪ Cross with clasps.
Medals.
— Medals with clasps.
Officers having * prefixed to their
names have temporary rank only.

N.B.—Officers who have no date in the
column of rank in the Army take rank in
the Army by their regimental commissions.

Colonel-in-Chief.
H.R.H. Frederick, Duke
of York, K.G. .. .. 23 Aug. 1797
Rank in Army, Field-Mar. 10 Feb. 1795

Rank and Name.	Rank in Regiment.

Cols.-Commandant—

Thomas Carleton .. .. 6 Aug. 1794
  Rank in Army, Gen. 25 Sept. 1803
Napier Christie Burton.. 3 Jan. 1806
  Rank in Army, Lt.-Gen. 1 Jan. 1805
Hon. Edmund Phipps .. 25 Aug. 1807
  Rank in Army, Lt.-Gen. 25 April 1808
John Robinson .. .. 2 Jan. 1813
  Rank in Army, Lt.-Gen. 4 June 1811
Hon. Charles Hope .. 15 Feb. 1813
  Rank in Army, Lt.-Gen. 1 Jan. 1812
Sir Henry Clinton, K.B. 20 May 1813
  Rank in Army, Maj.-Gen. 25 July 1810
Sir George Murray, K.B. .. .. .. 9 Aug. 1813
  Rank in Army, Maj.-Gen. 1 Jan. 1812
James Kempt .. .. 4 Nov. 1813
  Rank in Army, Maj.-Gen. 1 Jan. 1812

Lieut.-Colonels—

John Adolphus Harris .. 16 Jan. 1788
  Rank in Army, Lt.-Gen. 1 Jan. 1805
George Wm. Ramsay .. 30 Dec. 1797
  Rank in Army, Maj.-Gen. 4 June 1811
John Hope.. .. .. 30 June 1804
  Rank in Army, Maj.-Gen. 25 July 1810
Edward Codd.. .. .. 26 Oct. 1804
  Rank in Army, Col. 4 June 1813
Thomas Austin .. .. 20 June 1805
  Rank in Army, Col. 4 June 1813
Paul Anderson .. .. 11 Jan. 1808
  Rank in Army, Col. 4 June 1813
Fra. Ger. Viscount Lake 10 May 1808
  Rank in Army, Maj.-Gen. 4 June 1811
Wm. Dowdeswell .. .. 2 June 1808
  Rank in Army, Lt.-Gen. 25 July 1810
George Mackie .. .. 22 Dec. 1808
James Lomax.. .. .. 16 Nov. 1809
Anthony Wharton.. .. 16 Aug. 1810
John Keane .. .. .. 25 June 1812
  Rank in Army, Col. 1 Jan. 1812
Henry John .. .. .. 9 Aug. 1813
John Philip Hunt .. 11 Nov. 1813
  Rank in Army, 27 April 1812

Majors—

Francis St. Mart .. .. 5 Jan. 1805
  Rank in Army, Lt.-Col. 1 Jan. 1812
William Marlton .. .. 25 July 1805
  Rank in Army, Lt.-Col. 1 Jan. 1812
William Woodgate .. 13 Aug. 1807
  Rank in Army, Lt.-Col. 30 May 1811
James Grout .. .. .. 8 Nov. 1809
  Rank in Army, Lt.-Col. 25 April 1808
John Foster Fitzgerald .. 9 Nov. 1809
  Rank in Army, Lt.-Col. 25 July 1810
John Galiffe .. .. .. 15 Mar. 1810
  Rank in Army, 28 April 1808
Anthony Rumpler .. .. 10 Aug. 1810
  Rank in Army, 23 July 1810
Alexander Andrews .. 17 Jan. 1811
Charles de la Houssaye Bouverie .. .. .. 25 Oct. 1811
  Rank in Army, 25 July 1810
Gustavus Brown .. 3 Oct. 1811
  Rank in Army, Lt.-Gen. 17 Aug. 1812
Henry Wynidum .. .. 9 Aug. 1813

Rank and Name.	Rank in Regiment.

Majors (continued)—

Ernest Otto Tripp.. .. 10 Nov. 1813
  Rank in Army, 14 April 1813
Henry Fitzgerald .. .. 11 Nov. 1813
Charles de Salaberry .. 18 Nov. 1813
  Rank in Army, Lt.-Col. 24 Sept. 1812

Captains—

William Fraser .. .. 25 July 1799
  Rank in Army, Major 4 June 1811
John William Aldred .. 19 Nov. 1800
  Rank in Army, Major 1 Jan. 1812
William Batteley .. .. 15 Mar. 1803
  Rank in Army, Major 25 April 1808
Edward Norton .. .. 24 June 1803
Lewis de Mangon .. .. 25 June 1803
Philip Mauriage .. .. 2 July 1803
John MacMahon .. .. 20 Aug. 1803
Charles Vigny.. .. .. 1 Nov. 1804
Michael de Wendt.. .. 7 Dec. 1804
Jacob Jordan.. .. .. 28 Mar. 1805
  Rank in Army, Major 25 April 1808
Charles Kinsinger .. .. 24 April 1805
  Rank in Army, Major 24 Oct. 1811
Frederick Inturn .. .. 24 April 1805
Lewis Inturn.. .. .. 24 April 1805
Adam Krien .. .. .. 23 May 1805
John Schaedde .. .. 19 Sept. 1805
  Rank in Army, Major 21 June 1813
Henry Rennells .. .. 2 Dec. 1805
  Rank in Army, 13 July 1803
Peter Blassiere .. .. 4 Dec. 1805
John Anthony Wolff .. 5 June 1806
Galenius Reynauld.. .. 11 Dec. 1806
Charles Hinckleday .. 7 May 1807
Edward Purdon .. .. 27 Aug. 1807
James Erskine Bell .. 20 Jan. 1808
Alexander Ligertwood .. 30 Mar. 1809
  Rank in Army, Major 25 Oct. 1810
Charles du Sable .. .. 29 June 1809
Anthony Stamba .. .. 10 Aug. 1809
Henry Petrie .. .. .. 11 Aug. 1809
C. W. H. Koch .. .. 12 Aug. 1809
Philip Myer .. .. .. 23 Nov. 1809
Charles Mackenzie.. .. 10 Jan. 1810
  Rank in Army, Major 4 June 1811
George Henry Zulke .. 11 Jan. 1810
Florence Macarthy .. 24 May 1810
Robert Kelly .. .. .. 16 Aug. 1810
John Moore .. .. .. 2 Jan. 1811
C. Drury .. .. 24 Jan. 1811
  Rank in Army, 27 Aug. 1804
Leonard Gibbins .. .. 14 Feb. 1811
  Rank in Army, 25 Feb. 1804
Henry Fischbach .. .. 11 April 1811
Francis Holmes .. .. 19 Sept. 1811
Daniel Page .. .. .. 16 Oct. 1811
George F. Gibson .. .. 9 Jan. 1812
Melville Glenie .. .. 26 Mar. 1812
  Rank in Army, 14 July 1808
James Stopford .. .. 9 April 1812
  Rank in Army, 17 Feb. 1808
J. W. Harrison .. .. 12 Aug. 1812
  Rank in Army, 15 Oct. 1807
Hon. E. Stuart Erskine.. 13 Aug. 1812
  Rank in Army, 27 Dec. 1810
Richard Henry Hughes.. 27 Aug. 1812

Rank and Name.	Rank in Regiment.
Captains (continued)—	
J. Trumbeck	28 Aug. 1812
Robert Alex. Dalziel ..	24 Sept. 1812
Rank in Army, Col. 1 Jan. 1812	
Henry Dibbly..	23 Dec. 1812
John Blair	24 Jan. 1813
John Franchini	28 Jan. 1813
Aubra Carteret Bowers..	11 Feb. 1813
Adam Alex. Wood.. ..	4 Mar. 1813
Wm. Henry Sewell.. ..	29 April 1813
Rank in Army, 12 April 1812	
James Johnston	10 June 1813
Francis Beritz	1 Aug. 1813
Valentine Reichard ..	2 Aug. 1813
Charles Drekner	3 Aug. 1813
Ern. A. Baron Eberstein.	4 Aug. 1813
John Strengitharm.. ..	5 Aug. 1813
Cuthbert Ward	9 Aug. 1813
J. M. Nealson..	10 Aug. 1813
Ed. de la Bourdonnaye..	11 Aug. 1813
Adolphus de Danas ..	12 Aug. 1813
Peregrine Fra. Thorne ..	12 Aug. 1813
Charles Barrington ..	14 Aug. 1813
Wm. Pearce	15 Aug. 1813
John Bautilion Edwards.	16 Aug. 1813
A. E. D'Orfeuille	17 Aug. 1813
John Bagwell	18 Aug. 1813
John Barton Pym	4 Nov. 1813
Charles Leslie..	5 Nov. 1813
Thomas Power	6 Nov. 1813
James Dent Weatherley.	7 Nov. 1813
John Carmichael	8 Nov. 1813
Colin Campbell	9 Nov. 1813
Richard Brunton	10 Nov. 1813
John S. Lilley..	11 Nov. 1813
Richard Gethin	12 Nov. 1813
George Phelan	14 Nov. 1813
Lieutenants—	
Wm. Price	8 Aug. 1831
George Germann	28 Nov. 1835
Frederick Hoecker.. ..	21 Jan. 1836
J. F. Galbraith	23 Jan. 1836
John Cotterand	4 Feb. 1836
Frederick Seurross .	6 Feb. 1836
John Fitzgerald	12 June 1807
Rank in Army, 11 Aug. 1836	
M. Francis A. Trevosa.	29 Nov. 1837
Wm. Simpson..	1 Dec. 1837
Joseph von Komg	2 Dec. 1837
Maximilian du Chatelet..	3 Dec. 1837
John Panton Passley ..	5 Dec. 1837
Henry Muller..	8 Dec. 1837
Wm. Linstow..	9 Dec. 1837
Dietrich Christ. Brown..	14 Jan. 1838
Colin Campbell	18 Feb. 1838
Rank in Army, 3 Sept. 1835	
Robert Mitchell	22 Sept. 1838
R. S. Redman..	14 June 1839
Rank in Army, 25 Feb. 1838	
Frederick A. Gilse.. ..	26 Sept. 1839
Johann Hein. Adair ..	28 Sept. 1839
John Carlos	29 Sept. 1839
Frederick Strobeck.. ..	30 Sept. 1839
John Sprecher de Bernegg	1 Oct. 1839
Isaac Raboteau d'Arcy ..	2 Oct. 1839
Wm. Wynne	3 Oct. 1839

Rank and Name.	Rank in Regiment.
Lieutenants (continued)—	
Andrew Lucks	4 Oct. 1809
Julius von Boeck	9 Oct. 1809
John Louis Barbaz ..	10 Oct. 1809
Andrew Ellison	12 Oct. 1809
R. B. Hislop	29 Oct. 1809
Leopold de Frager.. ..	30 Oct. 1809
J. T. Allinson	2 Nov. 1809
Mathew Furst..	4 Nov. 1809
Richard Pasley	6 Nov. 1809
George Robinson	7 Nov. 1809
Augustus F. Evans ..	9 Nov. 1809
John Bearn	18 Feb. 1810
Peter Kennedy	19 Feb. 1810
Alexander Rule	20 Feb. 1810
Thomas Jack	23 Feb. 1810
Thomas Smith	24 Feb. 1810
Hector Downie	25 Feb. 1810
Mayne de Ravanic ..	26 Feb. 1810
Robert Ellison	28 Feb. 1810
Geo. Frederick **Stern** ..	1 Mar. 1810
Andrew Leitch	5 Mar. 1810
Ernest Frederick Firch..	11 April 1810
Rank in Army, 1 Feb. 1807	
Wm. Goldsmith	11 June 1810
Maurice Coutman	12 June 1810
Richard Hilliard	15 June 1810
James Brown Donnelly..	16 Aug. 1810
Sylvester O'Hehir	14 June 1810
Peter Eason	8 Oct. 1810
Thomas Marsh	9 Oct. 1810
Stephen Price..	10 Oct. 1810
Thomas Percy Conway ..	11 Oct. 1810
Peter James Sargent ..	13 Oct. 1810
Samuel Kerr	14 Oct. 1810
Michael Kent	16 Oct. 1810
Samuel Sergeant	17 Oct. 1810
Michael McNamara ..	18 Oct. 1810
Eugene Downing	24 Oct. 1810
Richard Saunders	25 Oct. 1810
David Le Count	26 Oct. 1810
Terence MacMahon ..	28 Oct. 1810
Frederick de Lahrbusch.	29 Oct. 1810
Fred. P. N. de Kruger..	30 Oct. 1810
Dawson Carr	1 Nov. 1810
C. B. Alcock	6 Dec. 1810
Edward Burghaagen ..	28 Mar. 1811
A. P. de Bergh	18 April 1811
Samuel Burgess	10 July 1811
Rank in Army, 9 Feb. 1809	
Arthur Mitchell	11 July 1806
Rank in Army, 14 Sept. 1806	
William Coleman	15 Aug. 1811
— Erdberg..	30 Sept. 1811
Chs. Jos. de Franciosi ..	1 Oct. 1811
William Rutter	2 Oct. 1811
— de Schanz	3 Oct. 1811
James Briscoe Gall.. ..	4 Oct. 1811
Lieut. Valentine Herschbut	5 Oct. 1811
Carol. Wm. Brettlauer .	6 Oct. 1811
Rich. Henry L. Schlosser	7 Oct. 1811
Francis Allen	10 Oct. 1811
Donald Drummond ..	19 Dec. 1811
Govert Roepel..	28 Feb. 1812
John Humphreys	12 Mar. 1812
John Bector	24 Mar. 1812

Rank and Name.	Rank in Regiment.
Lieutenants (continued)—	
James Fleeson..	26 Mar. 1812
Henry Hudson	27 Mar. 1812
Joseph Crow	29 Mar. 1812
Donald Urquhart	30 Mar. 1812
George Cochrane	31 Mar. 1812
Dougald Carmichael	2 April 1812
William Taffe..	14 May 1812
Henry Heil	6 Aug. 1812
James Kent	2 Sept. 1812
John W. Patterson	3 Sept. 1812
Henry Molloy..	29 Oct. 1812
James Beatty..	19 Dec. 1812
Charles Machean	20 Dec. 1812
John Currie	22 Dec. 1812
Robert Mackenzie	23 Dec. 1812
William Brady	24 Dec. 1812
Hugh Sutherland	30 Dec. 1812
John Hamilton	31 Dec. 1812
W. Cuthbert Bagnall	14 Jan. 1813
James Lawless	21 Jan. 1813
Cuthbert Fourneret	5 Feb. 1813
Wm. Batteley..	7 Feb. 1813
Frederick Baring	8 Feb. 1813
William Lupton	9 Feb. 1813
Jeremy Jones..	10 Feb. 1813
Matthew Moore	11 Feb. 1813
A. M. Ls. Durnford..	5 May 1813
Rank in Army, 31 May 1813	
W. F. Anderson Gillillan,	6 May 1813
Bishop Straker	10 June 1813
Rank in Army, 19 Dec. 1811	
Mark Hayes	8 July 1813
Rank in Army, 15 Oct. 1812	
John Moore	22 July 1813
John Torbick ..	1 Aug. 1813
Robert Pannell	2 Aug. 1813
Christ. Bernard Martin..	3 Aug. 1813
Hugh Dickson..	4 Aug. 1813
Robert Nettles	5 Aug. 1813
Wm. Nixon	9 Aug. 1813
Rank in Army, 4 Feb. 1813	
Henry James Russell	10 Aug. 1813
Edward Hunter	11 Aug. 1813
Richard Tighes	12 Aug. 1813
John Freud	13 Aug. 1813
Adam Mallis ..	14 Aug. 1813
Henry Boldero	16 Aug. 1813
Gottlieb Lersche	19 Aug. 1813
Peter R. A. Van Dyck	2 Sept. 1813
Rank in Army, 18 Aug. 1812	
Thomas Andrews	8 Sept. 1813
James Wallace	9 Sept. 1813
Edward Worsley	14 Sept. 1813
Adolphus Brouckhurst	15 Sept. 1813
William Nagel..	16 Sept. 1813
Edward Webb..	24 Oct. 1813
Rank in Army, 2 Jan. 1811	
L. A. von Battenburg	22 Oct. 1813
Charles Ross	4 Nov. 1813
Samuel Tresidder	6 Nov. 1813
Hodgson Gage ..	7 Nov. 1813
Stephen Thomas Nason..	17 Nov. 1813
Rank in Army, 19 Sept. 1811	
Augustus Kelly	19 Nov. 1813

Rank and Name.	Rank in Regiment.
Ensigns—	
L. F. Vonstein Altenstein	19 Jan. 1809
John Hanley	29 Sept. 1811
Frederick Pictet	25 June 1812
Jerome Cochrane	6 Aug. 1812
Joseph Stewart	2 Sept. 1812
John Hay Crawford	3 Sept. 1812
Lewis Clare	10 Sept. 1812
Richard Aylmer Coats	22 Oct. 1812
John Armstrong	29 Oct. 1812
Robert Hall	19 Nov. 1812
Andrew Weiburg	10 Dec. 1812
Thomas Wright	18 Dec. 1812
William Williams	19 Dec. 1812
John Brown	20 Dec. 1812
Benjamin Clare	21 Dec. 1812
William Fawcett	22 Dec. 1812
Henry Shewbridge..	23 Dec. 1812
Richard Ferrar	24 Dec. 1812
Hon. Arch. Macdonald..	29 Dec. 1812
William Scott..	30 Dec. 1812
Philip Vignan..	31 Dec. 1812
Henry Morgan Randall..	21 Jan. 1813
Edward John Bruce	6 Feb. 1813
John Thomas Hislop	7 Feb. 1813
Thomas Lemmon	8 Feb. 1813
Thomas Burton	9 Feb. 1813
William Donovan	10 Feb. 1813
James Lewis	4 May 1813
Rank in Army, 3 Mar. 1813	
George Bowles Symes	5 May 1813
Henry Senior	6 May 1813
Thomas Abell..	15 July 1813
—— Ratledge..	1 Aug. 1813
George Eberstein	2 Aug. 1813
Alexander Black	3 Aug. 1813
Kerry Supple ..	4 Aug. 1813
Hamilton Reed	9 Aug. 1813
Wm. Henry Barnes	10 Aug. 1813
Charles Harris	11 Aug. 1813
Charles Henry Delamain	12 Aug. 1813
Martin Burke..	13 Aug. 1813
Simon M'Queen	14 Aug. 1813
Ambrose Sponge	15 Aug. 1813
Richard Percy Pack	16 Aug. 1813
John Curtis	17 Aug. 1813
Thomas Keal	18 Aug. 1813
Peter Moore	19 Aug. 1813
Frederick Geo. Bartlet	20 Aug. 1813
John Frederick Myers	26 Aug. 1813
Robert Roeser..	4 Nov. 1813
Lewis Alex. Rousseau	5 Nov. 1813
Clifton Curtis..	6 Nov. 1813
Arthur Smith ..	7 Nov. 1813
John Kelly	8 Nov. 1813
George Campbell	9 Nov. 1813
Paymasters—	
Patrick Heyns..	19 Jan. 1809
George Milner Slade	19 Oct. 1809
Richard Barnard Fisher	19 July 1810
Henry Biggs	22 Oct. 1812
George Read	6 May 1813
Henry Heartsoake ..	7 May 1813
Adjutants—	
Andrew Lachs	23 April 1807
Rank in Army, Lieut. 4 Oct. 1809	

Rank and Name.	Rank in Regiment.
Adjutants (continued)—	
Robert Ellison	**28 Mar.** 1810
Rank in Army, Lieut. 28 Feb. 1810	
Alexander Rule	17 Oct. 1810
Rank in Army, Lieut. 20 Feb. 1810	
Andrew Weiburg	10 Dec. 1812
Rank in Army, Ensign 10 Dec. 1812	
James Kent	31 Dec. 1812
Rank in Army, Lieut. 2 Sept. 1812	
John Frederick Myers	26 Aug. 1813
Rank in Army, Ensign 26 **Aug.** 1813
Quartermasters—	
Joseph Chattoway	3 July 1800
Augustus Hennerhofer	25 Nov. 1807
——— Maxwell	6 July 1812
Alexander Johnston	24 Sept. 1812
——— Herkney	31 Dec. 1812
Thomas Burrowes	26 Aug. 1813
Surgeons—	
John Faries	21 Dec. 1800
William Ireland	20 June 1808
William H. Morle	2 Nov. 1809
John Arthur	5 Sept. 1811
A. L. Lobsworth	28 May 1812
Rank in Army, 26 Sept. 1811	
Joseph Abel	9 Aug. 1813
Rank in Army, 15 July 1813	
J. O. Hassell	9 Sept. 1813
Assistant-Surgeons—	
John H. Walker	**2 Nov.** 1807
George M'Dermott	30 Nov. 1809
Christopher G. Berger	18 Oct. 1810
Francis Murray	31 Jan. 1811
Lebrecht Memhoff	14 Mar. 1811
Alexander **Melvin**	26 Sept. 1811
Francis King	26 Sept. 1811
Arthur Johnson	28 May 1812
Charles Dealey	4 Mar. 1813
Henry Keller	28 Oct. 1813
P. Smith	11 Nov. 1813

Regimentals—1st, 2nd, **3rd, 4th, 6th, 7th,** 8th Battalions, red, facings blue, lace silver, 2 blue stripes.

5th Rifle Battalion, green, facings scarlet.

Agents—Messrs. Greenwood, Cox, and Hammersley, Craig's Court.

1815.

Eight Battalions.

Africa— West Indies   Ireland   North America   Mediterranean.

Col.-in-Chief—
H.R.H. Frederick, Duke of York, K.G. 28 Aug. 1797
  Rank in Army, Field-Marshal 10 Feb. 1795
Cols.-Commandant—
Thos. Carleton 6 Aug. 1794
  Rank in Army, Gen. 25 Sept. 1803
Napier Christie Burton 3 Jan. 1805
  Rank in Army, Gen. 4 June 1814
Hon. Edmund Phipps 25 Aug. 1807
  Rank in Army, Lt.-Gen. 25 April 1808

Rank and Name.	Rank in Regiment.
Cols.-Commandant (continued)—	
John Robinson	2 Jan. 1813
Rank in Army, Lt.-Gen. 4 June 1814	
Hon. Charles Hope	15 Feb. 1813
Rank in Army, Lt.-Gen. 1 Jan. 1812	
Sir Henry Clinton, K.B.	20 Mar. 1813
Rank in Army, Lt.-Gen. 4 June 1814	
Sir George Murray, K.B.	**9 Aug.** 1813
Rank in Army, Maj.-Gen. 1 Jan. 1812	
James Kempt	**4 Nov.** 1813
Rank in Army, Maj.-Gen. 1 Jan. 1812	
Lieut.-Colonels—	
George William Ramsay	30 Dec. 1797
Rank in Army, Maj.-Gen. 4 June 1811	
Edward Gold	26 Oct. 1804
Rank in Army, Col. 4 June 1813	
Thomas Austin	20 June 1806
Rank in Army, Col. 4 June 1813	
Paul Anderson	14 Jan. 1808
Rank in Army, Col. 4 June 1813	
Fra. Ger. Viscount Lake	10 May 1808
Rank in Army, Maj.-Gen. 4 June 1811	
George Miskin	22 Dec. 1808
Rank in Army, Col. 4 June 1814	
James Jonas	16 Nov. 1809
Henry John	9 Aug. 1813
William MacRott	26 May 1814
Rank in Army, Col. 4 Jan. 1812	
Adolphus J. Dalrymple	4 June 1814
William Woodgate	16 June 1814
Rank in Army, 30 May 1811	
Majors—	
James Grant	8 Nov. 1809
Rank in Army, Lt.-Col. 4 June 1814	
J. Forster Fitzgerald	9 Nov. 1809
Rank in Army, Lt.-Col. 25 July 1810	
John Nixhile	15 Mar. 1810
Rank in Army, Lt.-Col. 3 May 1814	
Anthony Bonquer	16 Aug. 1810
Rank in Army, 25 July 1810	
Alexander Andrews	17 Jan. 1811
Charles de la Houssaye Bonrere	2 Oct. 1811
Rank in Army, Lt.-Col. 14 July 1814	
Gustavus Brown	3 Oct. 1811
Rank in Army, Lt.-Col. 17 Aug. 1812	
Ernest Otto Tripp	10 Nov. 1813
Rank in Army, 1 April 1813	
Henry Fitzgerald	11 Nov. 1813
Henry Tarleton	21 April 1814
Robert Barton	28 April 1814
Rank in Army, Col. 4 June 1813	
John William Aldred	26 May 1814
Rank in Army, 1 Jan. 1812	
William Battrley	11 Aug. 1814
Rank in Army, Lt.-Col. 4 June 1814	
Lewis de Mangon	8 Dec. 1814
Rank in Army, 4 June 1814	
Captains—	
Philip Maurrage	2 July 1803
Rank in Army, Major 4 June 1814	
John MacMahon	20 Aug. 1803
Rank in Army, Major 4 June 1814	

Captains (continued)—

Rank and Name.	Rank in Regiment.
Charles Vigny..	1 Nov. 1804
Rank in Army, Major	4 June 1814
Michael de Wendt.. ..	7 Dec. 1804
Rank in Army, Major	4 June 1814
Jacob Jordan	28 Mar. 1805
Rank in Army, Lt.-Col.	4 June 1814
Fredk. Imturn	24 April 1805
Lewis Inturn..	25 April 1805
Adam Krien	23 May 1805
John Schoedde	19 Sept. 1805
Rank in Army, Major	21 June 1813
Henry Rennells	2 Dec. 1805
Rank in Army, Major	4 June 1814
Peter Blassiere	4 Dec. 1805
John Anthony Wolff ..	5 June 1806
Galenius Reynauld.. ..	11 Dec. 1806
Charles Hinckleday ..	7 May 1807
Edward Purdon	27 Aug. 1807
Rank in Army, Major	12 April 1814
James Erskine Bell ..	20 Jan. 1808
Alexander Ligertwood ..	30 Mar. 1809
Rank in Army, Major	25 Oct. 1810
Charles du Sable	29 June 1809
Anthony Stamba	10 Oct. 1809
Henry Petric	11 Oct. 1809
C. W. H. Koch	12 Oct. 1809
Philip Myer	23 Nov. 1809
Charles Mackenzie	10 Jan. 1810
Rank in Army, Major	4 June 1811
Wm. Friess	24 May 1810
Robert Kelly	16 Aug. 1810
John Moore	2 Jan. 1811
Leonard Gibbons	14 Feb. 1811
Rank in Army, Major	4 June 1814
Francis Holmes	19 Sept. 1811
Daniel Page	16 Oct. 1811
George F. Gibson	9 Jan. 1812
Everard Baring	13 Feb. 1812
Melville Glenie	26 Mar. 1812
Rank in Army,	14 July 1808
John Wm. Harrison ..	12 Aug. 1812
Rank in Army,	15 Oct. 1807
Hon. Esme Stuart Erskine	13 Aug. 1812
Rank in Army,	27 Dec. 1810
Richard Henry Hughes..	27 Aug. 1812
J. Trunback	28 Aug. 1812
Henry Dibbly..	23 Dec. 1812
John Franchini	28 Jan. 1813
Aubrey Carteret Bowers	11 Feb. 1813
Adam Alexander Wood..	4 Mar. 1813
Wm. Henry Sewell ..	29 April 1813
Rank in Army, Major	3 Mar. 1814
Francis Beritz	1 Aug. 1813
Valentine Reichard ..	2 Aug. 1813
Charles Deckner	3 Aug. 1813
Ern. A. Baron Eberstein.	4 Aug. 1813
John Strongitharm.. ..	5 Aug. 1813
Cuthbert Ward	9 Aug. 1813
J. N. Nealson	10 Aug. 1813
Adolphus de Demas ..	12 Aug. 1813
Peregrine Fra. Thorne ..	13 Aug. 1813
Charles Barrington.. ..	14 Aug. 1813
William Pearce	15 Aug. 1813
A. E. D'Orfeuille	17 Aug. 1813
John Bagwell	18 Aug. 1813

Captains (continued)—

Rank and Name.	Rank in Regiment.
Charles Leslie..	5 Nov. 1813
Thomas Power	6 Nov. 1813
James Dent Weatherley .	7 Nov. 1813
John Carmichael	8 Nov. 1813
Colin Campbell	9 Nov. 1813
Richard Brunton	10 Nov. 1813
— John S. Lilly	11 Nov. 1813
Richael Gethin	12 Nov. 1813
George Phelan	13 Nov. 1813
William Wilkinson.. ..	16 Dec. 1813
Rank in Army,	2 Sept. 1813
George Warde Clarke ..	6 Jan. 1814
William Rafter	10 Feb. 1814
Roche Meade	17 Feb. 1814
John Hewett	14 April 1814
George Germain	19 April 1814
Frederick Duncker.. ..	20 April 1814
William Henry Taynton..	2 June 1814
Rank in Army, Major	4 June 1813
John Correront	27 July 1814
Charles Johnson	18 Aug. 1814
Thomas Maling	17 Nov. 1814
Rank in Army,	11 July 1805
Roderick M'Neill	1 Dec. 1814
Edward Wildman	7 Dec. 1814
John Hovenden	8 Dec. 1814
Lieutenants —	
Fredk. Schriene	6 Feb. 1806
M. Francis A. Tresson ..	29 Nov. 1807
William Simpson	1 Dec. 1807
Joseph von König	2 Dec. 1807
Maximilian du Chatelet..	3 Dec. 1807
John Pauton Passley ..	5 Dec. 1807
Henry Muller..	8 Dec. 1807
William Linstow	9 Dec. 1807
Colin Campbell	18 Feb. 1808
Rank in Army,	3 Sept. 1795
Robt. Mitchell	22 Sept. 1808
R. S. Redman..	14 June 1809
Rank in Army,	26 Feb. 1808
Frederick de Gilse	26 Sept. 1809
Johann Hein, Adair ..	28 Sept. 1809
John Carlos	29 Sept. 1809
Frederick Strubeck.. ..	30 Sept. 1809
Isa. Raboteau d'Arcy ..	2 Oct. 1809
William Wynne	3 Oct. 1809
Andrew Lachs	4 Oct. 1809
John Joyce	5 Oct. 1809
Julius von Boeck	9 Oct. 1809
Andrew Ellison	12 Oct. 1809
R. B. Hislop	29 Oct. 1809
Leopold de Froger.. ..	30 Oct. 1809
J. T. Allinson	2 Nov. 1809
Matthew Furst	4 Nov. 1809
James Fontaine	5 Nov. 1809
Richard Pasley	6 Nov. 1809
George Robinson	7 Nov. 1809
Augustine F. Evans ..	9 Nov. 1809
Charles Andrews	10 Nov. 1809
John Hearn	18 Feb. 1810
Peter Kennedy	19 Feb. 1810
Alex. Rule	20 Feb. 1810
Thomas Jack	23 Feb. 1810
Thomas Smith	24 Feb. 1810
Hector Downie	25 Feb. 1810

Rank and Name.	Rank in Regiment.
Lieutenants (continued)—	
Mayne de Bavarier.	26 Feb. 1810
Henry Baron Altenstein	28 Feb. 1810
Robert Ellison	28 Feb. 1810
George Frederick Stern.	1 Mar. 1810
Andrew Leitch	5 Mar. 1810
William Goldsmith	11 June 1810
Maurice Cottman	12 June 1810
Richard Hillard	13 June 1810
Sylvester O'Hehir	14 June 1810
James Brown Donnelly	16 Aug. 1810
Peter Eason	**8** Oct. 1810
Thomas Marsh	9 Oct. 1810
Stephen Price	10 Oct. 1810
John James Sargent	13 Oct. 1810
Samuel Kerr	14 Oct. 1810
James D. Kent	16 Oct. 1810
Samuel Sergeant	17 Oct. 1810
Michael M'Namara	18 Oct. 1810
Eugene Downing	24 Oct. 1810
Richard Saunders	25 Oct. 1810
David Le Count	26 Oct. 1810
Terence M'Mahon	28 Oct. 1810
Frederick de Lahrbusch	29 Oct. 1810
Fred. P. N. de Kruger	30 Oct. 1810
Dawson Carr	1 Nov. 1810
C. B. Alcock	6 Dec. **1810**
Edward Burghangen	28 Mar. 1811
A. P. de Burgh	18 April 1811
Samuel Burgess	10 July 1811
Rank in Army, 9 Feb. **1809**	
Arthur Mitchell	11 July 1811
Rank in Army, 4 Dec. **1806**	
William Colman	15 Aug. 1811
Cha. Jas. de Fauchier	4 Oct. 1811
— de Schanz	5 Oct. 1811
James Briscoe Goff	5 Oct. 1811
Lieu. Valentine Fleischbut	5 Oct. 1811
Christ. Wm. Bradhauer	6 Oct. 1811
Richard Henry Lewis Schlösser	7 Oct. 1811
Donald Drummond	13 Dec. 1811
Gavret Roepel	28 Feb. 1812
John Humphreys	12 Mar. 1812
James Fleeson	25 Mar. 1812
Henry Hudson	27 Mar. 1812
Joseph Crow	20 Mar. 1812
Donald Urquhart	30 Mar. 1812
George Cochrane	31 Mar. 1812
Dougald Carmichael	2 April 1812
William Taaffe	14 May 1812
Henry Holt	6 Aug. 1812
James Kent	2 Sept. 1812
John W. Patterson	3 Sept. 1812
Henry Molloy	29 Oct. 1812
James Beatti	19 Dec. 1812
Charles Maclean	20 Dec. 1812
John Currie	22 Dec. 1812
Robt. Muckenzie	23 Dec. 1812
Wm. Brady	24 Dec. 1812
Hugh Sutherland	30 Dec. 1812
W. Cuthbert Bagnall	11 Jan. 1813
James Lawless	24 Jan. 1813
Cuthbert Fourneret	6 Feb. 1813
Wm. Batteley	7 Feb. 1813
Frederick Baring	8 Feb. 1813

Rank and Name.	Rank in Regiment.
Lieutenants (continued)—	
Wm. Lupton	9 Feb. **1813**
Jeremy Jones	10 Feb. **1813**
Matthew Moore	11 Mar. **1813**
Rank in Army, 31 May **1810**	
A. M. Isaacson Burnford	5 May **1813**
W. F. Anderson Gilfillan	6 May **1813**
Mark Hayes	8 July **1813**
Rank in Army, 15 Oct. **1813**	
John Moore	22 July **1813**
Robt. Torbock	1 Aug. **1813**
Robt. Pannell	2 Aug. **1813**
Christ. Bernard Martin	3 Aug. **1813**
Hugh Dickson	4 Aug. **1813**
Robt. Nettles	5 Aug. **1813**
Wm. Nixon	9 Aug. **1813**
Rank in Army, 4 Feb. **1813**	
Henry James Russell	10 Aug. **1813**
Edward Hunter	11 Aug. **1813**
Richard Tighes	12 Aug. **1813**
John Freud	13 Aug. **1813**
Adam Mellis	14 Aug. **1813**
Gottlieb Lerche	19 Aug. **1813**
Peter R. A. Von Dyck	2 Sept. **1813**
Rank in Army, 18 Aug. **1812**	
James Wallace	9 Sept. **1813**
Edmund Wossler	14 Sept. **1813**
Adolphus Brockhurst	15 Sept. **1813**
Edward Webb	21 Oct. **1813**
Rank in Army, 2 Jan. **1811**	
L. A. von Battenburg	22 Oct. **1813**
Charles Ross	4 Nov. **1813**
Thomas Acton	5 Nov. **1813**
Samuel Tresedder	6 Nov. **1813**
Hudson Gage	7 Nov. **1813**
Stephen Thomas Nixon	17 Nov. **1813**
Rank in Army, 19 Sept. **1811**	
Augustus Reilly	18 Nov. **1813**
Edward Jones	2 Dec. **1813**
Harry Thomas Heath	9 Dec. **1813**
John Caldon	22 Dec. **1813**
Matthew Nixon	23 Dec. **1813**
Frederick Paget	22 Jan. **1814**
Jerome Cochrane	24 Jan. **1814**
Joseph Stewart	24 Jan. **1814**
John Hay Crawford	25 Jan. **1814**
Lewis Clare	26 Jan. **1814**
Richard Aylmer Coates	27 Jan. **1814**
P. Nugent	3 Mar. **1814**
Hugh Goldicutt	17 Mar. **1814**
J. Ed. Moreton Douglas	11 April **1814**
John Armstrong	19 April **1814**
Robt. Hall	20 April **1814**
Andrew Weyburg	21 April **1814**
Thos. Wright	22 April **1814**
Jas. Freeth	23 April **1814**
Richard Archdall	24 April **1814**
Ambrose Sponge	26 April **1814**
Jas. Ron Lewis Nealson	27 April **1814**
Rank in Army, 6 Jan. **1814**	
Frederick Klostes	19 May **1814**
Rank in Army, 21 Mar. **1805**	
Henry Matson	2 June **1814**
Samuel Ridd	11 Aug. **1814**
Rank in Army, 25 June **1805**	
Henry Perry	18 Aug. **1814**

N

Rank and Name.	Rank in Regiment.
Lieutenants (continued)—	
Thomas Beauclerk	8 Sept. 1814
Rank in Army, 30 Nov. 1809	
William Williams	9 Dec. 1814
John Brown	10 Dec. 1814
Benjamin Clare	11 Dec. 1814
Henry Shewbridge.. ..	12 Dec. 1814
Richard Farrar	13 Dec. 1814
William Scott..	14 Dec. 1814
Philip Vignau..	15 Dec. 1814
Ensigns—	
John Hanley	29 Sept. 1811
Hon. Arch. Macdonald ..	29 Dec. 1812
Henry Morgan Randall..	21 Jan. 1813
Edward John Bruce ..	6 Feb. 1813
John Thomas Hislop ..	7 Feb. 1813
Thomas Lemmon	8 Feb. 1818
Thomas Burton	9 Feb. 1813
Wm. Donovan	10 Feb. 1813
Jas. Lewis	4 May 1813
Rank in Army, 3 Mar. 1813	
Thomas Abell..	15 July 1813
George Eberstein	2 Aug. 1813
Alexander Blood	3 Aug. 1813
Kerry Supple	4 Aug. 1813
Hamilton Reed	9 Aug. 1813
William Henry Barnes ..	10 Aug. 1813
Charles Harris..	11 Aug. 1813
Martin Burke..	13 Aug. 1813
Simon M'Queen	14 Aug. 1813
Richard Percy Pack ..	16 Aug. 1813
John Curtis	17 Aug. 1813
Thomas Neal	18 Aug. 1813
Peter Moore	19 Aug. 1813
Frederick George Bartlett	20 Aug. 1813
John Frederick Myers ..	26 Aug. 1813
Clifton Curtis	6 Nov. 1813
Arthur Smith..	7 Nov. 1813
John Kelly	8 Nov. 1813
George Campbell	9 Nov. 1813
J. Gourville	2 Dec. 1813
George Prittie..	3 Dec. 1813
Alexander Paterson ..	4 Dec. 1813
Carl Wevel von Kruger ,	22 Jan. 1814
Christian Katzmann ..	23 Jan. 1814
Frederick Weiss	24 Jan. 1814
William Bruns	25 Jan. 1814
Charles Wilhelme	26 Jan. 1814
William Heurman	27 Jan. 1814
Richard Stapleton	19 April 1814
Wm. Slater	20 April 1814
Joseph Robinson	21 April 1814
Robt. Alex. Andrews ..	18 Aug. 1814
Daniel O'Brien	1 Sept. 1814
Wm. M. Collings	28 Sept. 1814
Rank in Army, 3 Mar. 1814	
Wm. Bletterman Caldwell	29 Sept. 1814
Walter Bernard	20 Oct. 1814
Edward Maguire	1 Dec. 1814
Chas. Osborn Cushman..	9 Dec. 1814
John Day	10 Dec. 1814
—— Smith	11 Dec. 1814
R. Newman	12 Dec. 1814
Donald M'Kay	13 Dec. 1814
Ernest Pollman	14 Dec. 1814

Rank and Name.	Rank in Regiment.
Ensigns (continued)—	
John Magennis	15 Dec. 1814
Michael Pack	16 Dec. 1814
Paymasters—	
Patrick Heyns	19 Jan. 1809
George Milner Slade ..	19 Oct. 1809
Richard Barnard Fisher .	19 July 1810
Henry Biggs	22 Oct. 1812
George Read	6 May 1813
Henry Heartsonke.. ..	7 May 1813
Cha. Corn. Sev. Worsley .	25 Nov. 1813
Richard Jellicoe	24 Feb. 1814
Adjutants—	
Andrew Lachs	23 April 1807
Rank in Army, Lieut. 4 Oct. 1809	
Robert Ellison	28 Mar. 1811
Rank in Army, Lieut. 28 Feb. 1810	
Alexander Rule	17 Oct. 1811
Rank in Army, Lieut. 20 Feb. 1810	
Andrew Weiburg	10 Dec. 1812
Rank in Army, Lieut. 21 April 1814	
James Kent	31 Dec. 1812
Rank in Army, Lieut. 2 Sept. 1812	
John Frederick Myers ..	26 Aug. 1813
Rank in Army, Ensign 26 Aug. 1813	
Samuel Tresidder	9 June 1814
Rank in Army, Lieut. 6 Nov. 1813	
John Curtis	1 Dec. 1814
Rank in Army, Ensign 17 Aug. 1813	
Quartermasters—	
Joseph Chattoway	1 July 1800
Augustus Hennerhofen ..	25 Nov. 1807
—— Maxwell..	6 July 1812
Alexander Johnston ..	24 Sept. 1812
Alexander Reckney ..	31 Dec. 1812
Thomas Burrows	26 Aug. 1813
George Wahl..	20 Jan. 1814
Thos. Adams	27 Jan. 1814
Surgeons—	
John Faries	21 Dec. 1800
William Ireland	29 June 1809
William B. Morle	2 Nov. 1809
John Arthur	5 Sept. 1811
A. L. Lainsworth	28 May 1812
Rank in Army, 26 Sept. 1811	
Joseph Abell	9 Aug. 1813
Rank in Army, 15 July 1813	
George Vermeulen	2 Dec. 1813
John Grey Hibbert ..	8 Dec. 1814
Rank in Army, 26 May 1814	
Assistant-Surgeons—	
John H. Walker	2 Nov. 1809
George M'Dermott ..	30 Nov. 1809
Francis Murray	31 Jan. 1811
Lebrecht Mendorff.. ..	14 Mar. 1811
Alexander Melvin	26 Sept. 1811
Arthur Johnson	28 May 1812
Charles Dealey	4 Mar. 1813
Peter Smith	11 Nov. 1813
William Stevenson.. ..	25 Nov. 1813
Charles Newcome	24 Feb. 1814
William Dawson	9 June 1814

Rank and Name.	Rank in Regiment.
Assistant-Surgeons (continued)—	
Alexander Spalding	6 Oct. 1814
Charles Simpson	8 Dec. 1814

Regimentals—Red, facings blue, white lace,
2 blue stripes.

5th Rifle Battalion, green, facings scarlet.

Agents—Messrs. Greenwood, Cox, **and**
Hammersley, Craig's Court.

1816.

Eight Battalions.

Africa—West Indies—North America—
Ireland—England—Mediterranean.

Col.-in-Chief—
H.R.H. Fred., Duke of
York, K.G., G.C.B. .. 23 Aug. 1797
Rank in Army, Field-Mar. 10 Feb. 1793

Cols.-Commandant—
Thomas Carleton .. .. 6 Aug. 1794
Rank in Army, **Gen.** 25 Sept. 1803
Napier Christie Burton.. 3 Jan. 1806
Rank in Army, Gen. 4 June 1814
Hon. Edmund Phipps .. 25 Aug. 1807
Rank in Army, Lt.-Gen. 25 April 1808
John Robinson .. .. 2 Jan. 1813
Rank in Army, Lt.-Gen. 4 June 1814
Hon. Charles Hope .. 15 Feb. 1813
Rank in Army, Lt.-Gen. 1 Jan. 1812
Sir Geo. Murray, G.C.B. 9 Aug. 1813
Rank in Army, Maj.-Gen. 1 Jan. 1812
Sir James Kempt, G.C.B. **4 Nov.** 1813
Rank in Army, Maj.-Gen. **1 Jan.** 1812
(?) Sir W. Pat. Acklund,
K.C.B. .. .. **9 Aug.** 1815
Rank in Army, Lt.-Gen. **4 June** 1814

Lieut.-Colonels—
Edward Codd .. .. 26 Oct. 1804
Rank in Army, **Col.** 4 June 1814
Thomas Austen .. .. 20 June 1807
Rank in Army, Col. 4 June 1813
Paul Anderson, C.B. .. 14 Jan. 1808
Rank in Army, Col. 4 June 1814
George Mackie, C.B. .. 22 Dec. 1808
Rank in Army, Col. 4 June 1814
James Loome .. .. 16 Nov. 1810
William Marlton .. .. 26 May 1811
Rank in Army, 1 Jan. 1812
William Woodgate, C.B. 16 June 1811
Rank in Army, 30 May 1811
Edward Walker .. .. 9 Feb. 1815
Rank in Army, 1 Oct. 1812
James Stopford .. .. 9 Mar. 1815

Majors—
John Forster Fitzgerald,
C.B. .. .. .. 9 Nov. 1809
Rank in Army, Lt.-Col. 25 July 1810
John Guliffe, C.B. .. 15 Mar. 1810
Rank in Army, Lt.-Col. 3 Mar. 1814
Anthony Rumpler .. .. 16 Aug. 1810
Rank in Army, 25 July 1810
Alexander Andrews .. 17 Jan. 1811

Rank and Name.	**Rank in Regiment.**
Majors (continued)—	
Ch. de **la** Houssaye	
Bouverie	2 Oct. **1811**
Rank in Army, Lt.-Col.	14 July **1814**
Ernest Otto Tripp ..	10 Nov. **1813**
Rank in Army, Lt.-Col.	20 April **1814**
Henry Fitzgerald ..	11 Nov. **1813**
Henry Tarleton	21 April **1814**
Robert Burton.. ..	28 April **1814**
Rank in Army, Col.	**4 June 1814**
John William Aldred ..	26 May **1814**
Rank in Army,	1 Jan. **1812**
William Batteley ..	11 Aug. **1814**
Rank in Army, Lt.-Col.	4 June **1814**
Lewis de Mangon ..	8 Dec. **1814**
Rank in Army,	4 June **1814**
Charles Hincksleday ..	9 Mar. **1815**
Philip Maurange ..	9 Aug. **1815**
Rank in Army,	4 June **1814**
John MacMahon ..	10 Aug. **1815**
Rank in Army,	4 June **1814**

Captains—	
Charles Vigny.. ..	1 Nov. 1804
Rank in Army, Major 4 June 1814	
Michael de Wendt ..	7 Dec. 1804
Rank in Army, Major 4 June 1814	
Jacob Jordan	28 Mar. 1805
Rank in Army, Lt.-Col. 4 June 1814	
Frederick Fretture ..	24 April 1805
Lewis Izatture.. ..	25 April 1805
Adam Knox	23 May 1805
John Scheuble	19 Sept. 1805
Rank in Army, Major 24 June 1813	
Henry Reinche ..	2 Dec. 1805
Rank in Army, Major 4 June 1814	
Galentus Reinsault..	11 Dec. 1806
Edward Purdon ..	27 Aug. 1807
Rank in Army, Major 12 April 1813	
James Erskine Bell ..	20 Jan. 1808
Charles du Sable ..	**29 June** 1808
Anthony Stanhur ..	**10 Oct.** 1809
Henry Petrie	**11 Oct.** 1809
C. W. H. Koch ..	**12 Oct.** 1809
Philip Myer	**23 Nov.** 1809
Charles Mackour ..	10 Jan. 1810
Rank in Army, Major 4 June 1814	
William Fyers	24 May 1810
Rank in Army, Major 4 June 1814	
Robert Kelly	16 Aug. 1810
Leonard Gibbons ..	14 Feb. 1811
Rank in Army, Major 4 June 1814	
Francis Holmes ..	19 Sept. 1811
Daniel Page	16 Oct. 1811
George F. Gibson ..	9 Jan. 1812
Everard Baring ..	13 Feb. 1812
Melville Glenie	26 Mar. 1812
Rank in Army, 14 July 1808	
Hon. Esme Stuart Erskine 13 Aug. 1812	
Rank in Army, Major 18 June 1815	
Richard Henry Hughes 27 Aug. 1812	
J. Tindock	28 Aug. 1812
Henry Dudly	23 Dec. 1812
John Franchini ..	28 Jan. 1813
Aubrey Carteret Bowers 11 Feb. 1813	
William Henry Sewell	20 April 1813
Rank in Army, Major 3 Mar. 1814	

N 2

Captains (continued)—

Rank and Name.	Rank in Regiment.
Francis Beritz	1 Aug. 1813
Ern. A. Baron Eberstein	4 Aug. 1813
John Strongitharm	5 Aug. 1813
J. N. Nealson	10 Aug. 1813
Adolphus de Damas ..	12 Aug. 1813
Peregrine Fra. Thorne ..	13 Aug. 1813
Charles Barrington.. ..	14 Aug. 1813
William Pearce	15 Aug. 1813
John Bagwell	18 Aug. 1813
Charles Leslie.. ..	5 Nov. 1813
Thomas Power ..	6 Nov. 1813
James Dent Weatherley .	7 Nov. 1813
Colin Campbell	9 Nov. 1813
Richard Brunton	10 Nov. 1813
John S. Lilly	11 Nov. 1813
Richard Geihen	12 Nov. 1813
George Phelan	13 Nov. 1813
William Wilkinson.. ..	16 Dec. 1813
Rank in Army, 2 Sept. 1813	
George Ward Clarke ..	6 Jan. 1814
William Rafter	10 Feb. 1814
Roche Meade	17 Feb. 1814
John Hewitt	14 Apr. 1814
George Germain	19 Feb. 1814
John Correvont	27 July 1814
Thomas Maling	17 Nov. 1814
Rank in Army, 11 July 1805	
John Hovenien	8 Dec. 1814
Frederick Schriene.. ..	22 Dec. 1814
Robert Mitchell	18 Jan. 1815
Charles O'Hegerty.. ..	23 Feb. 1815
Rank in Army, 16 Sept. 1813	
Francis Gomer	16 Mar. 1815
Rank in Army, Lt.-Col. 4 June 1814	
John Alexander Wilson..	19 April 1815
Rank in Army, 14 July 1814	
Lord John T. H. Somerset	18 May 1815
Rank in Army, Major 18 June 1815	
Stepney Rawson Stepney	1 June 1815
Rank in Army, 30 Mar. 1814	
John Burrell	2 June 1815
Rank in Army, 18 May 1815	
William James Rea ..	22 June 1815
William Bower	24 Aug. 1815
Rank in Army, 7 Oct. 1813	
John B. Brown	28 Aug. 1815
Rank in Army, 25 Aug. 1813	
Francis A. Tresson	29 Aug. 1815
William Simpson	30 Aug. 1815
John George Fitzgerald..	31 Aug. 1815
Richard Barrow	7 Sept. 1815
Rank in Army, 2 Jan. 1806	
Montgomery Cairnes ..	7 Sept. 1815
Andrew Leitch	27 Sept. 1815
Kewan Izod Leslie.. ..	18 Oct. 1815
Tristram Carey	19 Oct. 1815

Lieutenants—

Rank and Name.	Rank in Regiment.
Alexander Webster ..	7 May 1807
Rank in Army, 27 Aug. 1803	
Joseph von König	2 Dec. 1807
Maximilian du Chatelet..	3 Dec. 1807
John Panton Passley ..	5 Dec. 1807
Henry Müller	8 Dec. 1807
Colin Campbell	18 Feb. 1808
Rank in Army, 3 Sept. 1795	

Lieutenants (continued)—

Rank and Name.	Rank in Regiment.
R. S. Redman..	14 June 1809
Rank in Army, 26 Feb. 1808	
Johann Hein. Adair ..	28 Sept. 1809
John Carlos	29 Sept. 1809
Isaac Raboteau d'Arcy ..	2 Oct. 1809
William Wynne	3 Oct. 1809
Andrew Lachs..	4 Oct. 1809
John Joyce	5 Oct. 1809
Julius von Bock	9 Oct. 1809
Andrew Ellison	12 Oct. 1809
R. B. Hislop	29 Oct. 1809
Leopold de Froger.. ..	30 Oct. 1809
John Thomas Allinson ..	2 Nov. 1809
Matthew Furst	4 Nov. 1809
Richard Pasley	6 Nov. 1809
George Robinson	7 Nov. 1809
Augustine F. Evans ..	9 Nov. 1809
Henry Baron Altenstein	10 Nov. 1809
John Hearn	18 Feb. 1810
Peter Kennedy	19 Feb. 1810
Alexander Rule	20 Feb. 1810
Rank in Army, Adjutant	
Thomas Jack	23 Feb. 1810
Thomas Smith..	24 Feb. 1810
Hector Downie	25 Feb. 1810
Mayne de Ravarier.. ..	26 Feb. 1810
Robert Ellison	28 Feb. 1810
George Frederick Stern..	1 Mar. 1810
William Gouldsmith ..	11 June 1810
Maurice Cottman	12 June 1810
Richard Hilliard	13 June 1810
Sylvester O'Hehir	14 June 1810
James Brown Donnelly..	16 Aug. 1810
Peter Eason	8 Oct. 1810
Thomas Marsh	9 Oct. 1810
Stephen Price	10 Oct. 1810
John James Sargent ..	13 Oct. 1810
Samuel Kerr	14 Oct. 1810
James D. Kent	16 Oct. 1810
Samuel Sergeant	17 Oct. 1810
Michael M'Namara ..	18 Oct. 1810
Eugene Downing	24 Oct. 1810
Richard Saunders	25 Oct. 1810
David Le Count	26 Oct. 1810
Terence M'Mahon	28 Oct. 1810
Frederick de Lalrbusch	29 Oct. 1810
Frederick P. N. de Kruger	30 Oct. 1810
Dawson Carr	1 Nov. 1810
C. B. Alcock	6 Dec. 1810
Edward Burghangen ..	28 Mar. 1811
Samuel Burges	10 July 1811
Rank in Army, 9 Feb. 1809	
Arthur Mitchell	11 July 1811
Rank in Army, 4 Dec. 1806	
William Coleman	15 Aug. 1811
—— de Schanz	3 Oct. 1811
James Briscoe Gall ..	4 Oct. 1811
Lewis Valentine Fleischbut	5 Oct. 1811
Christ. Wm. Bretthauer..	6 Oct. 1811
Richard Heary Lew. Schlosser	7 Oct. 1811
Donald Drummond ..	19 Dec. 1811
James Fleeson..	26 Mar. 1812
Henry Hudson	27 Mar. 1812
Joseph Crow	29 Mar. 1812

Rank and Name.	Rank in Regiment.
Lieutenants (continued)—	
Donald Urquhart	30 Mar. 1812
George Cochrane	31 Mar. 1812
Dougald Carmichael	2 April 1812
William Taaffe	14 May 1812
Henry Hell	6 Aug. 1812
James Kent	2 Sept. 1812
John W. Patterson	3 Sept. 1812
James Beatty	19 Dec. 1812
Charles Maclean	20 Dec. 1812
John Currie	22 Dec. 1812
Robert Mackenzie	23 Dec. 1812
William Brady	24 Dec. 1812
Hugh Sutherland	30 Dec. 1812
James Lawless	21 Jan. 1813
Cuthbert Fourneret	6 Feb. 1813
William Battersby	7 Feb. 1813
Frederick Baring	8 Feb. 1813
William Lupton	9 Feb. 1813
Jeremy Jones	10 Feb. 1813
Matthew Moore	11 Mar. 1813
Rank in Army, 31 May 1850	
A. M. Fraser Dornford	5 May 1813
W. F. Anderson Gulliam	6 May 1813
Mark Hayes	8 July 1813
Rank in Army, 15 Oct. 1812	
John Moore	22 July 1813
Robert Pannell	2 Aug. 1813
Christ. Bernard Martin	3 Aug. 1813
Hugh Dickson	4 Aug. 1813
Robert Nettles	5 Aug. 1813
William Nixon	9 Aug. 1813
Rank in Army, 4 Feb. 1813	
Henry James Russell	10 Aug. 1813
Edward Hunter	11 Aug. 1813
Richard Tighes	12 Aug. 1813
John Freud	13 Aug. 1813
Adam Mellis	14 Aug. 1813
Gottlieb Lerche	19 Aug. 1813
Peter R. A. Van Dyck	2 Sept. 1813
Rank in Army, 18 Aug. 1812	
James Wallace	9 Sept. 1813
Edmond Worsley	14 Sept. 1813
Adolphus Broockhurst	15 Sept. 1813
Edward Webb	21 Oct. 1813
Rank in Army, 2 Jan. 1811	
L. A. von Battenburg	22 Oct. 1813
Charles Ross	4 Nov. 1813
Thomas Acton	5 Nov. 1813
Samuel Fraichler	6 Nov. 1813
Hodgson Gage	7 Nov. 1813
Stephen Thomas Nason	17 Nov. 1813
Rank in Army, 19 Sept. 1811	
Augustus Kelly	18 Nov. 1813
Edward Jones	2 Dec. 1813
Henry Thomas Heath	9 Dec. 1813
John Calden	22 Dec. 1813
Matthew Nixon	23 Dec. 1813
Frederick Pictet	22 Jan. 1814
Jerome Cochrane	23 Jan. 1814
Joseph Stewart	24 Jan. 1814
John Hay Crawford	25 Jan. 1814
Lewis Clare	26 Jan. 1814
Richard Aylmer Coates	27 Jan. 1814
P. Nugent	3 Mar. 1814
Hugh Goldcutt	17 Mar. 1814

Rank and Name.	Rank in Regiment.
Lieutenants (continued)—	
John Armstrong	19 April 1814
Robert Hall	20 April 1814
Andrew Weiburg	21 April 1814
Thomas Wright	22 April 1814
Richard Archdall	24 April 1814
Ambrose Sponge	26 April 1814
Jas. Ren. Lewis Nealson	27 April 1814
Rank in Army, 6 Jan. 1814	
Henry Matson	2 June 1814
Samuel Reid	11 Aug. 1814
Rank in Army, 25 June 1805	
Thomas Beauclerk	8 Sept. 1814
Rank in Army, 30 Nov. 1809	
William Williams	9 Dec. 1814
John Brown	10 Dec. 1814
Benjamin Clare	11 Dec. 1814
Henry Shewbridge	12 Dec. 1814
Richard Farrar	13 Dec. 1814
William Scott	14 Dec. 1814
Philip Vignan	15 Dec. 1814
Joseph Gutty	25 Dec. 1814
Rank in Army, 29 Oct. 1812	
J. D. Kane	25 Dec. 1814
John Styles Powell	12 Jan. 1815
John M'Causland	26 Jan. 1815
Rank in Army, 9 Sept. 1813	
James Tracie	31 Jan. 1815
Rank in Army, 18 Nov. 1813	
Charles Barr	3 Feb. 1815
Patrick Grant	16 Feb. 1815
George Bakewell	7 Mar. 1815
Rank in Army, 25 Nov. 1812	
Henry Morgan Randall	8 Mar. 1815
Edward John Bruce	9 Mar. 1815
Samuel Haughton	8 June 1815
Rank in Army, 26 Jan. 1815	
John Thomas Hislop	15 June 1815
Thomas Lennnon	28 June 1815
Thomas Burton	29 June 1815
William Donovan	6 July 1815
William Henry Sperling	10 Aug. 1815
Rank in Army, 4 May 1815	
Daniel White	28 Sept. 1815
James Lewis	12 Oct. 1815
William Steele	26 Oct. 1815
Rank in Army, 28 Sept. 1804	
Alexander Blood	9 Nov. 1815
W. D. Collingwood	23 Nov. 1815
Rank in Army, 8 Oct. 1812	
John Hunfield Taggart	30 Nov. 1815
Rank in Army, 5 Oct. 1815	
Ensigns—	
John Hanky	29 Sept. 1811
Hon. Arch. Macdonald	29 Dec. 1812
George Eberstein	2 Aug. 1813
Kerry Supple	4 Aug. 1813
Hamilton Reed	9 Aug. 1813
William Henry Barnes	10 Aug. 1813
Charles Harris	11 Aug. 1813
Martin Burke	13 Aug. 1813
Simon M'Queen	14 Aug. 1813
Richard Percy Pack	16 Aug. 1813
John Curtis	17 Aug. 1813
Thomas Neal	18 Aug. 1813
Frederick George Bartlett	20 Aug. 1813

Rank and Name.	Rank in Regiment.
Ensigns (continued)—	
John Frederick Myers	.. 26 Aug. 1813
Clifton Curtis ..	.. 6 Nov. 1813
Arthur Smith ..	.. 7 Nov. 1813
John Kelly ..	.. 8 Nov. 1813
George Campbell ..	.. 9 Nov. 1813
I. Gourville ..	.. 2 Dec. 1813
George Prittie ..	.. 3 Dec. 1813
Alexander Patterson ..	.. 4 Dec. 1813
Carl Nevel von Kruger ..	22 Jan. 1814
Christian Katzmann ..	.. 23 Jan. 1814
Frederick Weiss ..	.. 24 Jan. 1814
William Bruns ..	.. 25 Jan. 1814
Charles Wilhelme ..	.. 26 Jan. 1814
William Hearman ..	.. 27 Jan. 1814
Richard Stapleton ..	.. 19 April 1814
William Slater ..	.. 20 April 1814
Joseph Robinson ..	.. 21 April 1814
Robert Alex. Andrews ..	18 Aug. 1814
Daniel O'Brien ..	.. 1 Sept. 1814
William M. Collings ..	28 Sept. 1814
Rank in Army, 3 Mar. 1814	
Wm. Bletterman Caldwell 29 Sept. 1814	
Walter Bernard ..	.. 20 Oct. 1814
William Plunkett ..	.. 1 Nov. 1814
Chas. Osborn Bushman ..	9 Dec. 1814
John Day ..	.. 10 Dec. 1814
Charles Smith ..	.. 11 Dec. 1814
R. Newman ..	.. 12 Dec. 1814
Donald M'Kay ..	.. 13 Dec. 1814
Ernest Pollman ..	.. 14 Dec. 1814
John Magenis ..	.. 15 Dec. 1814
Michael Pack ..	.. 16 Dec. 1814
George Hopkins ..	.. 16 Feb. 1815
James Cates ..	.. 16 Mar. 1815
Charles James Munn ..	6 April 1815
Donald Mackay ..	.. 25 May 1815
Frederick Restus ..	.. 1 June 1815
Charles Henry Somerset ..	15 June 1815
Thomas Adams ..	.. 16 June 1815
James Imlach ..	.. 22 June 1815
Rank in Army, 27 Oct. 1814	
Henry Colclough ..	.. 28 June 1815
George Henry Douglas ..	29 June 1815
Adam Hallberg ..	.. 6 July 1815
Edward Forman ..	.. 31 Aug. 1815
Oliver Hutchinson ..	.. 12 Oct. 1815
Francis Moore ..	.. 19 Oct. 1815
—— Lavoine ..	.. 9 Nov. 1815
Richard Parker ..	.. 16 Nov. 1815
Paymasters—	
George Milner Slade ..	19 Oct. 1809
Richard Barnard Fisher ..	19 July 1810
Henry Biggs ..	.. 22 Oct. 1812
George Read ..	.. 6 May 1813
Henry Heartseake ..	.. 7 May 1813
Chas. Corn. Sey. Worsley	25 Nov. 1813
Richard Jellicoe ..	.. 24 Feb. 1814
Adjutants—	
Robert Ellison ..	.. 28 Mar. 1811
Alexander Rule ..	.. 17 Oct. 1811
Andrew Weiburg ..	.. 10 Dec. 1813
James Kent ..	.. 31 Dec. 1813
John Frederick Myers ..	26 Aug. 1813
John Curtis ..	.. 1 Dec. 1814

Rank and Name.	Rank in Regiment.
Adjutants (continued)—	
Thomas Adams ..	.. 16 June 1815
Richard Baker ..	.. 16 Nov. 1815
Quartermasters—	
W. Maxwell ..	.. 6 July 1812
Alexander Johnston ..	24 Sept. 1812
—— Beckney ..	.. 31 Dec. 1812
Thomas Burrowes ..	.. 26 Aug. 1813
George Waldt ..	.. 20 Jan. 1814
Daniel Housman ..	.. 17 Aug. 1814
John Keins ..	.. 6 April 1815
John Dodd ..	.. 16 June 1815
Surgeons—	
John Faries ..	.. 21 Dec. 1800
William B. Merle ..	.. 2 Nov. 1809
A. L. Loinsworth ..	.. 28 May 1812
Rank in Army, 26 Sept. 1811	
Joseph Abell ..	.. 9 Aug. 1813
Rank in Army, 15 July 1813	
George Vermoulen ..	.. 2 Dec. 1813
John Gray Hibbert ..	.. 8 Dec. 1814
Rank in Army, 26 May 1814	
John H. Walker ..	.. 22 Nov. 1815
George M'Dermott ..	.. 23 Nov. 1815
Assistant-Surgeons—	
Francis Murray ..	.. 31 Jan. 1811
Alexander Melvin ..	.. 26 Sept. 1811
Arthur Johnson ..	.. 28 May 1812
Charles Denley ..	.. 4 Mar. 1813
Peter Smith ..	.. 11 Nov. 1813
William Stevenson ..	.. 25 Nov. 1813
Charles Newcome ..	.. 24 Feb. 1814
William Dawson ..	.. 9 June 1814
Alexander Spalding ..	6 Oct. 1814
Charles Simpson ..	.. 8 Dec. 1815
Robert Dundas ..	.. 3 Aug. 1815
James Thompson ..	.. 24 Aug. 1815
Nathaniel Morgan ..	.. 28 Sept. 1815
Samuel Wylie ..	.. 9 Nov. 1815

Regimentals— Red, facings blue, white lace, 2 blue stripes.

5th Rifle Battalion, green, facings scarlet.

Dress changed this year—All battalions green, facings scarlet.

Agents Messrs. Greenwood, Cox, and Hammersley, Craig's Court.

1817.

Seven Battalions.

Africa—West Indies—North America— England—Mediterranean.

Col.-in-Chief—
H.R.H. Fred. Duke of
York, K.G., G.C.B., .. 23 Aug. 1797
Rank in Army, Field-Mar. 10 Feb. 1795

Col.-Commandants—
Thos. Carleton .. .. 6 Aug. 1794
Rank in Army, Gen. 25 Sept. 1803
Napier Christie Burton .. 3 Jan. 1806
Rank in Army, Gen. 4 June 1814
Hon. Edmund Phipps .. 25 Aug. 1807
Rank in Army, Lt.-Gen. 25 April 1808

Rank and Name.	Rank in Regiment.

Cols.-Commandant (continued)—

John Robinson	2 Jan. 1813
Rank in Army, Lt.-Gen.	4 June 1811
Hon. Charles Hope ..	15 Feb. 1813
Sir George Murray, G.C.B...	9 Aug. 1813
Rank in Army, Maj.-Gen.	1 Jan. 1812
Sir James Kempt, G.C.B...	4 Nov. 1813
Rank in Army, Maj.-Gen.	1 Jan. 1812

Lieut.-Colonels —

Edward Codd	26 Oct. 1804
Rank in Army, Col.	4 June 1813
Thos. Austin	20 June 1805
Rank in Army, Col.	4 June 1813
Paul Anderson † ..	14 Jan. 1808
Rank in Army, Col.	4 June 1813
George Mackie † ..	22 Dec. 1808
Rank in Army, Col.	4 June 1814
James Lomax	16 Nov. 1809
William Woodgate † .	16 June 1814
Rank in Army,	30 May 1811
James Stopford ..	9 Mar. 1815
Alex. Andrews	14 Dec. 1815

Majors—

John Foster Fitzgerald †	9 Nov. 1809
Rank in Army, Lt.-Col.	25 July 1810
John Galiffet	15 Mar. 1810
Rank in Army, Lt.-Col.	3 Mar. 1814
Anthony Rumpler ..	16 Aug. 1810
Rank in Army,	25 July 1810
Ch. de la Houssaye Bouverie	2 Oct. 1811
Rank in Army, Lt.-Col.	14 July 1814
Ernest Otto Tripp ..	10 Nov. 1813
Rank in Army, Lt.-Col.	20 April 1815
Henry Fitzgerald ..	11 Nov. 1813
Henry Tarleton ..	21 April 1814
John W. Aldred ..	26 May 1814
Rank in Army,	1 Jan. 1812
Wm. Batteley.. ..	11 Aug. 1814
Rank in Army, Lt.-Col.	4 June 1814
Charles Hinckleday	3 Mar. 1815
Philip Maurnge ..	3 Aug. 1815
Rank in Army,	4 June 1814
John MacMahon ..	10 Aug. 1815
Rank in Army,	4 June 1814
Charles Gardiner ..	14 Dec. 1815
Edward Fitzgerald..	14 July 1816

Captains—

Charles Vigny ..	1 Nov. 1804
Rank in Army, Major	4 June 1814
Jacob Jordan	28 Mar. 1805
Rank in Army, Lt.-Col.	4 June 1814
Frederick Imturn ..	24 April 1805
Lewis Imturn ..	25 April 1805
Adam Krien	23 May 1805
John Schoedde ..	19 Sept. 1805
Rank in Army, Major	21 June 1814
Henry Reunells ..	2 Dec. 1805
Rank in Army, Major	4 June 1814
Galanius Reynauld..	11 Dec. 1805
Edward Purdon ..	27 Aug. 1807
Rank in Army, Major	12 April 1814
James Erskine Bell	20 Jan. 1808

Rank and Name.	Rank in Regiment.

Captains (continued)—

Charles du Sable ..	29 June 1809
Anthony Stamba ..	10 Oct. 1809
Henry Petrie	11 Oct. 1809
Philip Mayer	23 Nov. 1809
Charles Mackenzie..	10 Jan. 1810
Rank in Army, Major	4 June 1811
Robert Kelly	16 Aug. 1810
Leonard Gibbons ..	14 Feb. 1811
Rank in Army, Major	4 June 1814
Francis Holmes ..	19 Sept. 1811
Daniel Page	16 Oct. 1811
George F. Gibson ..	9 Jan. 1812
Everard Baring ..	13 Feb. 1812
Melville Glenie ..	26 Mar. 1812
Rank in Army,	14 July 1808
J. Trumback	28 Aug. 1808
John Franchini ..	28 Jan. 1813
Aubrey Cartaret Bowers	11 Feb. 1813
William Henry Sewell ..	20 April 1813
Rank in Army, Major	8 Mar. 1814
Francis Beritze ..	1 Aug. 1813
Ernest A. Baron Eberstein	4 Aug. 1813
John Strongitharm ..	5 Aug. 1813
J. N. Neelson	10 Aug. 1813
Adolphus de Damas ..	12 Aug. 1813
Peregrine Francis Thorne	13 Aug. 1813
Charles Barrington..	14 Aug. 1813
William Pearce ..	15 Aug. 1813
Charles Leslie ..	5 Nov. 1813
Thos. Power	6 Nov. 1813
James Dent Westherley	7 Nov. 1813
Colin Campbell ..	9 Nov. 1813
Richard Brandon ..	10 Nov. 1813
John S. Lilly ..	11 Nov. 1813
Richard Gethin ..	12 Nov. 1813
George Phelan ..	13 Nov. 1813
William Wilkinson ..	16 Dec. 1813
Rank in Army,	2 Sept. 1813
George Ward Clarke ..	6 Jan. 1814
William Rafter ..	10 Feb. 1814
John Hewett	14 April 1814
John Correront ..	27 July 1814
Thos. Malung	17 Nov. 1814
Rank in Army,	11 July 1805
John Hovenden ..	8 Dec. 1814
Fredk. Schreene ..	22 Dec. 1814
Francis Gomer ..	16 Mar. 1815
Rank in Army, Lt.-Col.	4 June 1814
John Alexander Wilson..	19 April 1815
Rank in Army,	14 July 1814
Stepney Rawson Stepney	1 June 1815
Rank in Army,	30 Mar. 1814
John Barrell	2 June 1815
Rank in Army,	18 May 1815
Wm. Bower	24 Aug. 1815
Rank in Army,	7 Oct. 1813
John B. Brown ..	28 Aug. 1815
Rank in Army,	25 Aug. 1813
Alexander Webster ..	28 Aug. 1815
Francis A. Tresson ..	29 Aug. 1815
William Simpson ..	30 Aug. 1815
John George Fitzgerald	31 Aug. 1815
Montgomery Cairns ..	7 Sept. 1815
Andrew Leitch	27 Sept. 1815

Rank and Name.	Rank in Regiment.
Captains (continued)—	
[ED] Kewan Izod Leslie..	18 Oct. 1815
Tristram Carey	19 Oct. 1815
Christopher Williamson .	11 Jan. 1816
Rank in Army, Major 4 June 1814	
John le Breton	7 Mar. 1816
Lewis C. Appelius .. .	7 Nov. 1816
Rank in Army, 21 Dec. 1815	
Alexander Cuppage ..	8 Nov. 1816
Rank in Army, 28 Mar. 1816	
John George Green ..	27 Nov. 1816
Rank in Army, 31 May 18?0	
Richard Crompton . ..	28 Nov. 1816
Rank in Army, 6 June 1811	
Lieutenants—	
Joseph von König	2 Dec. 1807
John Panton Pasley ..	5 Dec. 1807
Henry Muller..	8 Dec. 1807
Colin Campbell	18 Feb. 1808
Rank in Army, 3 Sept. 1795	
R. S. Redman	14 June 1806
Rank in Army, 26 Feb. 1808	
Johann Hein. Adair ..	28 Sept. 1809
John Carlos	29 Sept. 1809
Isaac Rabateau d'Arcy ..	2 Oct. 1809
William Wynne	3 Oct. 1809
Andrew Lachs	4 Oct. 1809
John Joyce	5 Oct. 1809
Julius von Boeck.. ..	9 Oct. 1809
Andrew Ellison	12 Oct. 1809
R. B. Hislop	29 Oct. 1809
Leopold de Froger . ..	30 Oct. 1809
Matthew Frost	4 Nov. 1809
Richard Pasley	6 Nov. 1809
George Robinson	7 Nov. 1809
Augustine F. Evans ..	9 Nov. 1809
Henry Baron Altenstein.	10 Nov. 1809
John Hearn	18 Feb. 1810
Peter Kennedy	19 Feb. 1810
Alexander Rule	20 Feb. 1810
Thomas Jack	23 Feb. 1810
Thomas Smith..	24 Feb. 1810
Hector Downie.	25 Feb. 1810
Mayne de Bavarier.. ..	26 Feb. 1810
George Fred. Sterne ..	1 Mar. 1810
William Gouldsmith ..	11 June 1810
Maurice Cottman	12 June 1810
Richard Hilliard	13 June 1810
Sylvester O'Hehir	14 June 1810
Peter Eason	8 Oct. 1810
Thomas Marsh	9 Oct. 1810
Stephen Price	10 Oct. 1810
John James Sargent ..	13 Oct. 1810
Samuel Kerr	14 Oct. 1810
James D. Kent	16 Oct. 1810
Samuel Sergeant	17 Oct. 1810
Michael M'Namara.. ..	18 Oct. 1810
Eugene Downing	24 Oct. 1810
Richard Saunders	25 Oct. 1810
David Le Count	26 Oct. 1810
Terence M'Mahon	28 Oct. 1810
Frederick de Lahrbusch .	29 Oct. 1810
Dawson Carr	1 Nov. 1810
C. B. Meek	6 Dec. 1810
Samuel Burges	10 July 1811
Rank in Army, 9 Feb. 1809	

Rank and Name.	Rank in Regiment.
Lieutenants (continued)—	
Arthur Mitchell	11 July 1811
Rank in Army, 4 Dec. 1806	
William Coleman	15 Aug. 1811
— - de Schanz	3 Oct. 1811
James Briscoe Gaff ..	4 Oct. 1811
Donald Drummond ..	19 Dec. 1812
James Fleeson	26 Mar. 1812
Henry Hudson	27 Mar. 1812
Joseph Crow	29 Mar. 1812
Donald Urquhart	30 Mar. 1812
George Cochrane	31 Mar. 1812
Dougald Carmichael. ..	2 April 1812
William Taaffe	14 May 1812
Henry Heil	6 Aug. 1812
James Kent	2 Sept. 1812
John W. Patterson.. ..	3 Sept. 1812
James Beatty	19 Dec. 1812
Charles Maclean	20 Dec. 1812
John Currie	22 Dec. 1812
Robert Mackenzie ..	23 Dec. 1812
William Brady	24 Dec. 1812
Hugh Sutherland	30 Dec. 1812
James Lawless	21 Jan. 1813
Cuthbert Foueneret ..	6 Feb. 1813
William Battelcy	7 Feb. 1813
Fredk. Baring	8 Feb. 1813
Wm. Lupton	9 Feb. 1813
J. Jones	10 Feb. 1813
Matthew Moore	11 Mar. 1813
Rank in Army, 31 May 1810	
A. M. Isaacson Durnford	5 May 1813
W. F. Anderson Gilfillan	6 May 1813
Mark Hayes	8 July 1813
Rank in Army, 15 Oct. 1812	
John Moore	22 July 1813
Robert Pannell	2 Aug. 1813
Wm. Nixon	9 Aug. 1813
Rank in Army, 4 Feb. 1813	
Henry James Russell ..	10 Aug. 1813
Edward Hunter	11 Aug. 1813
Richard Tighe	12 Aug. 1813
John Freud	13 Aug. 1813
James Wallace	9 Sept. 1813
Edmund Worsley	14 Sept. 1813
Adolphus Bromckhurst ..	15 Sept. 1813
L. A. Battenburg	22 Oct. 1813
Charles Ross	4 Nov. 1813
Thos. Acton	5 Nov. 1813
Samuel Tresidder	6 Nov. 1813
Hodgson Gage..	7 Nov. 1813
Stephen Thomas Nason .	17 Nov. 1813
Rank in Army, 19 Sept. 1811	
Augustus Kelly	18 Nov. 1813
Edward Jones	2 Dec. 1813
Harry Thomas Heath ..	9 Dec. 1813
John Calder	22 Dec. 1813
Matthew Nixon	23 Dec. 1813
Fred. Pictet	22 Jan. 1814
Jerome Cochrane	23 Jan. 1814
Joseph Stewart	24 Jan. 1814
John Hay Crawford ..	25 Jan. 1814
Lewis Clare	26 Jan. 1814
Richard Aylmer Coates..	27 Jan. 1814
P. Nugent	3 Mar. 1814
Hugh Goldicutt	17 Mar. 1814

Rank and Name.	Rank in Regiment.
Lieutenants (continued)—	
John Armstrong	19 April 1814
Robert Hall	20 April 1814
J. Andrew Weiburg ..	21 April 1814
Thomas Wright	22 April 1814
Ambrose Sponge	26 April 1814
Henry Matson	2 June 1814
Samuel Ridd	11 Aug. 1814
Rank in Army, 25 June 1805	
Thomas Beauclerk	8 Sept. 1814
Rank in Army, 30 Nov. 1809	
William Williams	9 Dec. 1814
John Brown	10 Dec. 1814
Benjamin Clare	11 Dec. 1814
Henry Shewbridge ..	12 Dec. 1814
Richard Farrar	13 Dec. 1814
Wm. Scott	14 Dec. 1814
Philip Vignan	15 Dec. 1814
Joseph Gatty	25 Dec. 1814
Rank in Army, 20 Oct. 1812	
John Styles Powell ..	12 Jan. 1815
John M'Causland	26 Jan. 1815
Rank in Army, 9 Sept. 1813	
James Tracie	31 Jan. 1815
Rank in Army, 18 Nov. 1813	
Charles Barry	3 Feb. 1815
George Hakewill	7 Mar. 1815
Rank in Army, 24 Nov. 1812	
Henry Morgan Randall ..	8 Mar. 1815
Edward John Brice ..	9 Mar. 1815
Samuel Haggline	8 June 1815
Rank in Army, 26 Jan. 1815	
John Thomas Heslop ..	16 June 1815
Thomas Barton	22 June 1815
William Donovan	8 July 1815
William Henry Sperling	10 Aug. 1815
Rank in Army, 4 May 1815	
Daniel White	28 Sept. 1815
William Steele	20 Oct. 1815
Rank in Army, 28 Sept. 1809	
Alex. Blood	9 Nov. 1815
W. D. Collingwood ..	23 Nov. 1815
Rank in Army, 8 Oct. 1812	
John Harefield Taggart	20 Dec. 1815
Rank in Army, 5 Oct. 1815	
E. Kerry Supple	14 Feb. 1816
Hamilton Reed	15 Feb. 1816
James Creevy	29 Feb. 1816
Charles Steele	22 Feb. 1816
Thomas Gладstone 18 April 1816	
Rank in Army, 20 July 1815	
Charles Edward Turner	6 June 1816
Rank in Army, 12 Oct. 1815	
Charles Harris	12 June 1816
Martin Burke	13 June 1816
Joseph G. Wolseme ..	20 June 1816
Rank in Army, 26 July 1815	
William Prosser Symonds	1 Aug. 1816
Rank in Army, 2 July 1807	
Fred. Henry Perfect ..	29 Aug. 1816
Rank in Army, 26 April 1808	
Simon M'Queen	23 Oct. 1816
Anthony Donaghue ..	21 Nov. 1816
Rank in Army, 8 Oct. 1815	
Robert Kerr	28 Nov. 1816
Rank in Army, 25 May 1815	

Rank and Name.	Rank in Regiment.
Ensigns—	
Hon. Arch. Macdonald ..	29 Dec. 1812
Richard Percey Pack ..	16 Aug. 1813
John Curtis	17 Aug. 1813
Thomas Krule	18 Aug. 1813
Fred. George Bartlett ..	20 Aug. 1813
John Frederick Myers ..	26 Aug. 1813
Clifton Curtis	6 Nov. 1813
Arthur Smith	7 Nov. 1813
John Kelly	8 Nov. 1813
George Campbell	9 Nov. 1813
George Prettie	3 Dec. 1813
Alexander Paterson ..	4 Dec. 1813
Carl Wetzl von Kruger .	22 Jan. 1814
Christian Katzmann ..	23 Jan. 1814
Fred. Weiss	24 Jan. 1814
William Bruns	25 Jan. 1814
William Heurmann ..	27 Jan. 1814
Richard Stapleton ..	19 April 1814
William Slater	20 April 1814
Joseph Robinson	21 April 1814
Robert Alex. Andrews ..	18 Aug. 1814
Daniel O'Brien	1 Sept. 1814
Wm. M'Collings	28 Sept. 1814
Wm. Betterman Cold-	
well	29 Sept. 1814
Walter Bernard	20 Oct. 1814
William Plunkett	1 Nov. 1814
Ch. Osborn Roubacuse	9 Dec. 1814
John Day	10 Dec. 1814
Charles Smith	11 Dec. 1814
R. Newman	12 Dec. 1814
Donald M'Kay	13 Dec. 1814
John Maurice	15 Dec. 1814
George Hopkins	16 Feb. 1815
James Coles	16 Mar. 1815
Fred. Byrne	1 June 1815
Charles Henry Somerset	15 June 1815
Thomas Adams	16 June 1815
Henry Coldbough ..	28 June 1815
Edward Farman	31 Aug. 1815
Oliver Hutchinson ..	12 Oct. 1815
Francis Moore	19 Oct. 1815
—— Lavenu	9 Nov. 1815
Richard Packer	16 Nov. 1815
David Dixon	8 Dec. 1815
Charles Henry Cowper ..	21 Dec. 1815
Henry Johnson Cotter ..	18 Jan. 1816
George Gosselin	14 Feb. 1816
John Henry Burnall ..	15 Feb. 1816
John Tracie	25 April 1816
Rank in Army, 26 Oct. 1815	
—— Muller	1 May 1816
James Hamilton	2 May 1816
Wm. Pollock	9 May 1816
Rank in Army, 29 June 1815	
J. Alex. de Rottenburg ..	12 June 1816
Rank in Army, 19 Oct. 1815	
Peter Gordon	13 June 1816
Jacob Jordan	4 July 1816
Peter Donald Helme ..	29 Aug. 1816
Charles Laocke	17 Oct. 1816
Rank in Army, 15 June 1815	
Standish Bury Power ..	24 Oct. 1816
Robert Cole	21 Nov. 1816

Rank and Name.	Rank in Regiment.

Paymasters—

Richard Barnard Fisher	19 July 1810
Henry Biggs	22 Oct. 1812
George Read	6 May 1813
Henry Heartsoake	7 May 1813
Chas. Corn. Sey. Worsley	25 Nov. 1813
Richard Jellicoe	24 Feb. 1814

Adjutants—

Alexander Rule	17 Oct. 1811
J. Andrew Weiburg ..	10 Dec. 1812
Rank in Army, Lieut.	20 Feb. 1814
James Kent	31 Dec. 1812
Rank in Army, Lieut.	2 Sept. 1812
John Frank Myers.. ..	26 Aug. 1813
Rank in Army, Ensign	26 Aug. 1813
John Curtis	1 Dec. 1814
Rank in Army, Ensign	17 Aug. 1813
Thomas Adams	16 June 1815
Rank in Army, Ensign	16 June 1815
Richard Packer	16 Nov. 1815
Rank in Army, Ensign	16 Nov. 1815

Quartermasters—

W. Maxwell	6 July 1812
Alex. Johnston	24 Sept. 1812
—— Rickney..	31 Dec. 1812
Thomas Burrowes	26 Aug. 1813
George Wahlt	20 Jan. 1814
Daniel Hausman	17 Aug. 1814
John Keins	6 April 1815

Surgeons—

John Faries	21 Dec. 1800
Wm. B. Morle	2 Nov. 1809
A. L. Loinsworth	28 May 1812
Rank in Army,	26 Sept. 1811
Joseph Abell	9 Aug. 1813
Rank in Army,	15 July 1813
John Gray Hibbert . ..	8 Dec. 1814
Rank in Army,	26 May 1814
John H. Walker	22 Nov. 1815
George M'Dermott . ..	23 Nov. 1815

Assistant-Surgeons—

Francis Murray	31 Jan. 1811
Alex. Melvin	26 Sept. 1811
Arthur Johnston	28 May 1812
Charles Denley	4 Mar. 1813
Peter Smith	11 Nov. 1813
Wm. Stevenson	25 Nov. 1813
Alex. Spalding	6 Oct. 1814
Chas. Simpson	8 Dec. 1814
Robert Dundas	3 Aug. 1815
James Thompson	24 Aug. 1815
Samuel Wylie..	9 Nov. 1815
G. Wilkinson	28 Mar. 1816
Hubert Prendergast. ..	25 Aug. 1816
Rank in Army,	9 Nov. 1815
Thomas Robertson.. ..	7 Nov. 1816
Rank in Army,	31 Aug. 1815

Regimentals—Green, facings scarlet.

Agents—Messrs. Greenwood, Cox, and Hammersley, Craig's Court.

1817.

LIST OF OFFICERS OF 2ND BAT-
TALION PLACED ON HALF-PAY
ON REDUCTION OF 6TH AND 7TH
BATTALIONS, 1816–17.

Rank and Name.

Colonel T. Carleton.

Lieut.-Colonel E. Codd.

Major A. Rumpler.
  ,,   P. Mauriage.

Captain L. Inturn.
  ,,   L. Gibbons.
  ,,   F. Beritz.
  ,,   J. N. Nelson.
  ,,   C. Barrington.
  ,,   W. Pearce.
  ,,   T. Power.
  ,,   J. D. Weatherley.
  ,,   W. Rafter.
  ,,   J. A. Wilson.

Lieutenant R. S. Redman.
  ,,   J. H. Adair.
  ,,   J. Carlos.
  ,,   W. Wynne.
  ,,   J. Beurn.
  ,,   P. Kennedy.
  ,,   T. Jack.
  ,,   H. Downie.
  ,,   T. Marsh.
  ,,   W. Coleman.
  ,,   W. Traffe.
  ,,   C. Mackean.
  ,,   R. Mackenzie.
  ,,   F. Baring.
  ,,   W. Nixon.
  ,,   H. J. Russell.
  ,,   E. Hunter.
  ,,   R. Tighe.
  ,,   J. Frend.
  ,,   L. von Battenberg.
  ,,   R. A. Coates.
  ,,   T. Beauclerk.

Ensign B. Park.
  ,,   W. Weiss.
  ,,   W. Bruns.
  ,,   R. Stapleton.
  ,,   D. O'Brien.
  ,,   C. O. Bushman.
  ,,   C. Smith.
  ,,   G. Hopkins.

Paymaster G. Read.

Adjutant J. Curtis.

1818.

Six Battalions.

Africa—North America—West Indies—
England—Mediterranean.

	Rank in Regiment.
Col.-in-Chief—	
H.R.H. Frederick Duke	
of York, K.G., G.C.B. 23 Aug. 1797	
Rank in Army, Field-Mar. 10 Feb. 1795	
Cols.-Commandant—	
Napier, Christie Burton 3 Jan. 1806	
Rank in Army, Gen. 4 June 1814	
Hon. Edmund Phipps .. 25 Aug. 1807	
Rank in Army, Lt.-Gen. 25 April 1808	
John Robinson .. .. 2 Jan. 1813	
Rank in Army, Lt.-Gen. 4 June 1811	
Hon. Charles Hope .. 15 Feb. 1813	
Rank in Army, Lt.-Gen. 1 Jan. 1812	
⊗ ▦ Sir James Kempt,	
G.C.B. .. .. .. 4 Nov. 1813	
Rank in Army, Maj.-Gen. 1 Jan. 1812	
Lieut.-Colonels—	
Edward Cadd .. .. 26 Oct. 1804	
Rank in Army, Col. 4 June 1814	
⊗ George Mackie .. 22 Dec. 1808	
Rank in Army, Col. 4 June 1814	
James Lomax .. .. 16 Nov. 1809	
James Stopford .. .. 9 Mar. 1815	
Alexander Andrews .. 14 Dec. 1815	
Majors—	
⊗ John Foster Fitzgerald 9 Nov. 1809	
Rank in Army, Lt.-Col. 25 July 1810	
⊗ John Galiffe .. .. 15 Mar. 1810	
Rank in Army, Lt.-Col. 3 Mar. 1814	
Anthony Rampier .. 16 Aug. 1810	
Rank in Army, 25 July 1810	
C. de la Hogueye Bonene 2 Oct. 1811	
Rank in Army, Lt.-Col. 30 July 1810	
Henry Fitzgerald .. 11 Nov. 1813	
John Wm. Adlard .. 26 May 1814	
Rank in Army, 1 Jan. 1812	
Charles Hinckleday 9 Mar. 1815	
Philip Murriage .. 9 Aug. 1815	
Rank in Army, 4 June 1814	
John MacMahon .. 10 Aug. 1815	
Rank in Army, 4 June 1814	
Charles Gardner .. 14 Dec. 1815	
Captains—	
Jacob Jordan .. .. 28 Mar. 1805	
Rank in Army, Lt.-Col. 4 June 1814	
Fred. Latour .. 24 April 1805	
Lewis Latour .. .. 25 April 1805	
Adam Krien .. .. 23 May 1805	
John Schosilde .. 19 Sept. 1805	
Rank in Army, 24 June 1812	
Galenius Reynould .. 14 Dec. 1805	
Edward Purdon .. 27 Aug. 1807	
Rank in Army, Major 12 April 1814	
James Erskine Bell.. 29 Jan. 1808	
Charles du Sable .. 29 June 1809	
Anthony Stemba .. 10 Oct. 1809	
Henry Petrie.. .. 11 Oct. 1809	
Philip Mayer .. .. 23 Nov. 1809	
Charles Mackenzie.. 10 Jan. 1810	
Rank in Army, Major 4 June 1811	
Robert Kelly .. .. 16 Aug. 1810	

Rank and Name.	Rank in Regiment.
Captains (continued)—	
Leonard Gibbons .. .. 14 Feb. 1811	
Rank in Army, 4 June 1814	
Francis Holmes .. .. 19 Sept. 1811	
Daniel Page .. .. 16 Oct. 1811	
Melville Glenie .. .. 26 Mar. 1812	
Rank in Army, 14 July 1808	
J. Thrumbuck .. .. 28 Aug. 1812	
John Franchini .. .. 28 Jan. 1813	
Aubrey Carterel Bowers 11 Feb. 1813	
Wm. Henry Sewell .. 29 April 1813	
Rank in Army, Lt.-Col. 24 June 1817	
Francis Beritz .. .. 1 Aug. 1813	
Ern. A. Baron Eberstein 4 Aug. 1813	
John Strongitharm.. .. 5 Aug. 1813	
Adolphus de Bauras .. 12 Aug. 1813	
Charles Barrington.. .. 14 Aug. 1813	
William Pearce .. .. 15 Aug. 1813	
Charles Leslie.. .. .. 5 Nov. 1813	
⊙ Thomas Power .. .. 6 Nov. 1813	
James Dent Weatherley.. 7 Nov. 1813	
Colin Campbell .. .. 9 Nov. 1813	
Richard Brunton .. .. 10 Nov. 1813	
⊗ Sir John Scott Lillie, Bt. 11 Nov. 1813	
Rank in Army, Major 21 June 1817	
Richard Gethin .. .. 12 Nov. 1813	
George Phelan .. .. 13 Nov. 1813	
William Wilkinson.. .. 16 Dec. 1813	
Rank in Army, 2 Sept. 1813	
George Ward Clarke .. 6 Jan. 1814	
William Rafter .. .. 10 Feb. 1814	
John Hewett .. .. .. 14 April 1814	
John Correcont .. .. 27 July 1814	
Thomas Maling .. .. 17 Nov. 1814	
Rank in Army, 11 July 1805	
John Hovenden .. .. 8 Dec. 1814	
Robert Mitchell .. .. 18 Jan. 1815	
John Alex. Wilson.. .. 19 April 1815	
Rank in Army, 14 July 1814	
Stepney Rawson Stepney 1 June 1815	
Rank in Army, 30 Mar. 1814	
John Burrell .. .. .. 2 June 1815	
Rank in Army, 18 May 1815	
William Bower .. .. 24 Aug. 1815	
Rank in Army, 7 Oct. 1813	
John B. Browne .. .. 28 Aug. 1815	
Rank in Army, 25 Aug. 1815	
William Wynne .. .. 24 July 1817	
Lieutenants—	
John Panton Passley .. 5 Dec. 1807	
Henry Muller.. .. .. 8 Dec. 1807	
Colin Campbell .. .. 18 Feb. 1808	
Rank in Army, 3 Sept. 1795	
R. S. Redman.. .. .. 14 June 1809	
Rank in Army, 26 Feb. 1808	
Johann Hein. Adair .. 28 Sept. 1809	
John Carlos .. .. .. 29 Sept. 1809	
Isaac Raledeau d'Arcy .. 2 Oct. 1809	
Andrew Lachs.. .. .. 4 Oct. 1809	
Julius von Beeck .. .. 9 Oct. 1809	
Andrew Ellison .. .. 12 Oct. 1809	
R. E. Hislop .. .. .. 29 Oct. 1809	
Leopold de Froger .. .. 30 Oct. 1809	
Matthew Furst .. .. 1 Nov. 1809	
Richard Pasley .. .. 6 Nov. 1809	
George Robinson .. .. 7 Nov. 1809	

Lieutenants (continued)—

Rank and Name.	Rank in Regiment.
Augustine F. Evans	9 Nov. 1809
Henry Baron Altenstein.	10 Nov. 1809
John Hearn	18 Feb. 1810
Peter Kennedy	19 Feb. 1810
Thomas Jack	23 Feb. 1810
Thomas Smith..	24 Feb. 1810
M. de Ravarier	26 Feb. 1810
George Frederick Stern..	1 Mar. 1810
William Goldsmith ..	11 June 1810
Maurice Cottman	12 June 1810
Sylvester O'Hehir	14 June 1810
Peter Eason	8 Oct. 1810
Stephen Price	10 Oct. 1810
John James Sargent ..	13 Oct. 1810
Michael M'Namara ..	18 Oct. 1810
Eugene Downing	24 Oct. 1810
Richard Saunders	25 Oct. 1810
David Le Count	26 Oct. 1810
Frederick de Lahrbusch	29 Oct. 1810
Dawson Carr	1 Nov. 1810
Arthur Mitchell	11 July 1811
Rank in Army,	4 Dec. 1806
William Coleman	15 Aug. 1811
James Briscoe Gaff ..	4 Oct. 1811
James Fleeson	26 Nov. 1812
Henry Hudson	27 Nov. 1812
Joseph Crow	29 Nov. 1812
George Cochrane	31 Nov. 1212
Dougald Carmichael ..	2 April 1812
William Tauffe	14 May 1812
James Kent	2 Sept. 1812
John W. Patterson ..	3 Sept. 1812
James Beatty..	19 Dec. 1812
Charles Maclean	20 Dec. 1812
John Currie	22 Dec. 1812
William Brady	24 Dec. 1812
James Lawless	24 Jan. 1813
Cuthbert Fourneret ..	6 Feb. 1813
Frederick Baring	8 Feb. 1813
Jeremy Jones..	10 Feb. 1813
Matthew Moore	11 Mar. 1813
Rank in Army,	31 May 1810
A. M. Isaacson Durnford	5 May 1813
W. F. Anderson Gilfillan	6 May 1813
John Moore	22 July 1813
Robert Pannell	2 Aug. 1813
William Nixon	9 Aug. 1813
Rank in Army,	4 Feb. 1813
Henry James Russell ..	10 Aug. 1813
Edward Hunter	11 Aug. 1813
Richard Tighes	12 Aug. 1813
John Freud	13 Aug. 1813
Edward Worsley	14 Sept. 1813
Adolphus Brouckhurst ..	15 Sept. 1813
L. A. von Battenburg ..	22 Oct. 1813
Charles Ross	4 Nov. 1813
Thomas Acton	5 Nov. 1813
Samuel Tresidder	6 Nov. 1813
Hodgson Gage	7 Nov. 1813
Stephen Thomas Masson..	17 Nov. 1813
Rank in Army,	19 Sept. 1811
Edward Jones..	2 Dec. 1813
John Cubbon	22 Dec. 1813
Frederick Pictet	22 Jan. 1814
Jerome Cochrane	23 Jan. 1814

Lieutenants (continued)—

Rank and Name.	Rank in Regiment.
Joseph Stewart	24 Jan. 1814
John Hay Crawford ..	25 Jan. 1814
Lewis Clare	26 Jan. 1814
Richard Rylmer Coates..	27 Jan. 1814
P. Nugent	3 Mar. 1814
Hugh Goldicutt	17 Mar. 1814
John Armstrong	19 April 1814
Robert Hull	20 April 1814
J. Andrew Weiburg ..	21 April 1814
James Wright	22 April 1814
Ambrose Sponge	26 April 1814
Henry Matson	2 June 1814
Samuel Ridd	11 Aug. 1814
Rank in Army,	25 June 1805
Thomas Beauclerk ..	8 Sept. 1814
Rank in Army,	30 Nov. 1809
William Williams	9 Dec. 1814
John Brown	10 Dec. 1814
Benjamin Clare	11 Dec. 1814
Henry Shewbridge.. ..	12 Dec. 1814
Richard Ferror	13 Dec. 1814
Philip Vignan..	15 Dec. 1814
John Styles Powell ..	12 Jan. 1815
John McCausland	26 Jan. 1815
Rank in Army,	9 Sept. 1813
Charles Henry Somerset..	21 Aug. 1817
James Frade	25 Sept. 1817
Rank in Army,	18 Nov. 1813
William Steele	11 Dec. 1817
Rank in Army,	28 Sept. 1809

Ensigns—

Rank and Name.	Rank in Regiment.
Richard Percy Pack ..	16 Aug. 1813
Thomas Keal	18 Aug. 1813
Frederick George Bartlett	20 Aug. 1813
John Frederick Myer ..	26 Aug. 1813
Arthur Smith..	7 Nov. 1813
John Kelly	8 Nov. 1813
George Campbell	9 Nov. 1813
George Prettie	3 Dec. 1813
Alexander Paterson ..	4 Dec. 1813
Carel Wevel von Krüger	22 Jan. 1814
Christian Katzmann ..	23 Jan. 1814
Frederick Weiss	24 Jan. 1814
William Bruns	25 Jan. 1814
William Heurman	27 Jan. 1814
Richard Stapleton	19 April 1814
Joseph Robinson	21 April 1814
Robert Alex. Andrews ..	18 Aug. 1814
Daniel O'Brien	1 Sept. 1814
William Moore Collings..	28 Sept. 1814
Rank in Army,	3 Mar. 1814
Wm. Bletterman Caldwell	29 Sept. 1814
John Day	10 Dec. 1814
R. Newman	12 Dec. 1814
Donald M'Kay	13 Dec. 1814
John Maguire	15 Dec. 1814
George Hopkins	16 Feb. 1815
James Cates	16 Mar. 1815
Frederick Resins	1 June 1815
Thomas Adams	16 June 1815
Henry Colclough	28 June 1815
Edward Forman	31 Aug. 1815
Oliver Hutchinson	12 Oct. 1815
Francis Moore..	19 Oct. 1815
—— Lavione	9 Oct. 1815

Rank and Name.	Rank in Regiment.
Ensigns (continued)—	
Richard Packer	16 Nov. 1815
David Dixon	8 Dec. 1815
Charles Henry Couper ..	21 Dec. 1815
Henry Johnson Catler ..	18 Jan. 1816
George Gosselin	14 Feb. 1816
John Henry Burnall ..	15 Feb. 1816
William Pollock	9 May 1816
Rank in Army,	29 June 1815
J. Alex. de Rottenburg	12 June 1816
Rank in Army,	10 Oct. 1815
Jacob Jordan	27 Nov. 1817
Rank in Army,	4 July 1816
Paymasters—	
Henry Biggs	22 Oct. 1812
George Read	6 May 1813
Henry Heartsenke	7 May 1813
Chas. Corn. Sey. Worsley	25 Nov. 1813
Richard Jellicoe	24 Feb. 1814
Adjutants—	
J. Andrew Weiburg ..	10 Dec. 1812
Rank in Army, Lieut.	21 April 1814
John Fred. Myer	26 Aug. 1813
Rank in Army, Ensign	26 Aug. 1813
Thomas Adams	16 June 1815
Rank in Army, Ensign	16 June 1815
Richard Packer	16 Nov. 1815
Rank in Army, Ensign	16 Nov. 1815
Quartermasters—	
W. Maxwell	6 July 1812
Alexander Johnson ..	24 Sept. 1812
—— Rechney	31 Dec. 1812
Daniel Hausman	17 Aug. 1814
John Kieus	10 July 1817
Rank in Army,	6 April 1814
Surgeons—	
John Faries	24 Dec. 1800
William B. Morle ..	2 Nov. 1809
A. L. Leinsworth ..	28 May 1812
Rank in Army,	26 Sept. 1811
Joseph Abell	9 Aug 1813
Rank in Army,	15 July 1813
Martin Carthourt ..	20 Nov. 1817
Rank in Army,	27 April 1815
Assistant Surgeons—	
Francis Murray	31 Jan. 1811
Alexander Melvin ..	26 Sept. 1811
Arthur Johnston ..	28 May 1812
Charles Dealey	4 Mar. 1813
Peter Smith	11 Nov. 1813
William Stevenson ..	25 Nov. 1813
Charles Simpson	8 Dec 1814
Thomas Thompson ..	24 Aug 1815
Samuel Wylie	9 Nov 1815
Regimental Clothing, facings scarlet.	
Agents: Messrs. Greenwood, Cox and Hammersley, Craig's Court.	

1819.

Two Battalions.
2nd Rifle Battalion. 3rd Light Infantry.
Africa—North America—England.
Col.-in-Chief—
H.R.H. Fred., Duke of
York, K.G., G.C.B. .. 23 Aug. 1797
Rank in Army, Field-Mar. 10 Feb. 1795

Rank and Name.	Rank in Regiment.
Cols.-Commandant—	
Napier Christie Burton..	3 Jan. 1806
Rank in Army, Gen.	4 June 1814
Hon. Edmund Phipps ..	23 Aug. 1807
Rank in Army, Lt.-Gen.	25 Apr. 1808
Lieut.-Colonels—	
Edward Codd	26 Oct. 1804
Rank in Army, Col.	4 June 1813
George Mackie † ..	22 Dec. 1808
Rank in Army, Col.	4 June 1814
Majors—	
J. Forster Fitzgerald †	9 Nov. 1809
Rank in Army, Lt.-Col.	25 July 1810
John Galiffe †	15 Mar. 1810
Rank in Army, Lt.-Col.	3 Mar. 1814
Anthony Rampler	16 Aug. 1810
Rank in Army,	25 July 1810
C. de la Honsaye Bouverie	2 Oct. 1811
Rank in Army, Lt.-Col.	14 July 1814
Captains—	
Frederick Intarn	24 Apr. 1805
Lewis Intarn	25 Apr. 1805
Adam Krien	23 May 1805
John Schoedde	19 Sept. 1805
Rank in Army, Maj.	21 June 1812
Gabriue Reynauld.. ..	11 Dec. 1806
Edward Purdon	27 Aug. 1807
Rank in Army, Maj.	12 Apr. 1814
James Erskine Bell ..	20 Jan. 1808
Anthony Stamba	10 Oct. 1809
Henry Petrie	11 Oct. 1809
Charles Mackenzie.. ..	10 Jan. 1810
Rank in Army, Maj.	4 June 1811
Robert Kelly	16 Aug. 1810
Leonard Gibbons	14 Feb. 1811
Rank in Army, Maj.	4 June 1814
Francis Holmes	19 Sept. 1811
Melville Glenie	26 Mar. 1812
Rank in Army,	14 July 1808
John Franchud	28 Jan. 1813
Andrew Carteret Bowers.	11 Feb. 1813
William Henry Sewell ..	23 Apr. 1813
Rank in Army, Lt.-Col.	21 June 1817
Francis Beritz	1 Aug. 1813
John Strongtham	5 Aug. 1813
Adolphus de Dumas ..	12 Aug. 1813
Lieutenants—	
Henry Muller	8 Dec. 1807
Colin Campbell	18 Feb. 1808
Rank in Army,	3 Sept. 1795
R. S. Redman	14 June 1809
Rank in Army,	26 Feb. 1808
Johann Hein. Adair ..	28 Sept. 1809
John Carles	29 Sept. 1809
Isaac Ralsdom d'Arcy ..	2 Oct. 1809
Andrew Lardie	4 Oct. 1809
Julius von Baeck ..	9 Oct. 1809
Andrew Ellison	12 Oct. 1809
R. B. Hiskp	29 Oct. 1809
Leopold de Forger ..	30 Oct. 1809
Matthew Furst	4 Nov. 1809
Richard Pasley	6 Nov. 1809
George Robinson	7 Nov. 1809
Augustine F. Evans ..	9 Nov. 1809
Henry Baron Altenstein.	10 Nov. 1809
John Hearn	18 Feb. 1810

Rank and Name.	Rank in Regiment.
Lieutenants (continued)—	
Peter Kennedy	19 Feb. 1810
Thomas Jack	23 Feb. 1810
Thomas Smith	24 Feb. 1810
George Frederick Stern..	1 Mar. 1810
William Gouldsmith ..	11 June 1810
J. Andrew Weiburg ..	24 Apr. 1814
Richard Percy Pack ..	16 Aug. 1813
Thomas Keal	18 Aug. 1813
Frederick Geo. Bartlett..	20 Aug. 1813
John Frederick Myer ..	26 Aug. 1813
Arthur Smith	7 Nov. 1813
John Kelly	8 Nov. 1813
George Campbell	9 Nov. 1813
George Prettie	3 Dec. 1813
Alexander Paterson ..	4 Dec. 1813
Carl Wevel von Krüger .	22 Jan. 1814
Christian Katzmann ..	23 Jan. 1814
William Bruns	25 Jan. 1814
William Heurman	27 Jan. 1814
Richard Stapleton ..	19 Apr. 1814
Joseph Robinson	21 Apr. 1814
Robt. Alexander Andrews	18 Aug. 1814
Daniel O'Brien	1 Sept. 1814
William Moore Collings .	28 Sept. 1814
Rank in Army,	3 Mar. 1814
Wm. Bletterman Caldwell	29 Sept. 1814
Paymasters—	
Henry Biggs	22 Oct. 1812
Georg Read	6 May 1813
Adjutants—	
J. Andrew Weiburg ..	10 Dec. 1812
Rank in Army, Lieut.	24 Apr. 1814
John Frederick Myer ..	26 Aug. 1813
Rank in Army, Ensign	26 Aug. 1813
Quartermasters—	
Frederick Maxwell.. ..	6 July 1812
Alexander Johnston ..	24 Sept. 1812
Surgeons—	
John Faries	21 Dec. 1800
William B. Morle ..	2 Nov. 1809
Francis Murray	31 Jan. 1811
Alexander Melvin ..	26 Sept. 1811

Regimentals—Green, facings scarlet.

Agents—Messrs. Greenwood, Cox, and Hammersley, Craig's Court.

1820.

Two Battalions.

1st, or Rifle Battalion. 2nd, or Light Infantry.

North America.

Martinique— Peninsula.

Colonel-in-Chief—
H.R.H. Frederick, Duke
of York, K.G., G.C.B. 23 Aug. 1797
Rank in Army, Field-Mar. 10 Feb. 1795
Cols.-Commandant—
Napier Christie Burton.. 3 Jan. 1806
Rank in Army, Gen. 4 June 1814
Hon. Edmund Phipps .. 25 Aug. 1807
Rank in Army, Gen. 12 Aug. 1819
Edward Codd .. .. 26 Oct. 1804
Rank in Army, Maj.-Gen. 12 Aug. 1819

Rank and Name.	Rank in Regiment.
Lieut.-Colonels—	
George Mackie	15 Mar. 1808
Rank in Army, Col.	4 June 1814
Alexander Andrew.. ..	12 Aug. 1819
Rank in Army,	14 Dec. 1815
Majors—	
John Forster Fitzgerald	9 Nov. 1809
Rank in Army, Col.	12 Aug. 1819
John Galiffe	15 Mar. 1810
Rank in Army, Lt.-Col.	3 Mar. 1814
Anthony Rumpler	16 Aug. 1810
Rank in Army, Lt.-Col.	12 Aug. 1819
Henry Fitzgerald	11 Nov. 1813
Captains—	
Frederick Imturn	24 April 1805
Rank in Army, Maj.	12 Aug. 1819
Lewis Imturn..	25 April 1805
Rank in Army, Maj.	12 Aug. 1819
Adam Krien	23 May 1805
Rank in Army, Maj.	12 Aug. 1819
John Schoedde	19 Sept. 1805
Rank in Army, Maj.	21 June 1813
Galenius Reynauld.. ..	11 Dec. 1806
Rank in Army,	12 Aug. 1819
Edward Purdon	27 Aug. 1807
Rank in Army,	12 April 1814
Anthony Stanba	10 Oct. 1809
Henry Petrie	14 Oct. 1809
Charles Mackenzie ..	10 Jan. 1810
Rank in Army, Lt.-Col.	12 Aug. 1819
Robert Kelly	16 Aug. 1810
Francis Holmes	19 Sept. 1811
Melville Glenie	26 Mar. 1812
Rank in Army,	14 July 1808
Ignatius Franchini ..	28 Jan. 1813
Aubrey Carteret Bowers.	11 Feb. 1813
William Henry Sewell ..	29 April 1813
Rank in Army, Lt.-Col.	21 June 1817
Francis Beritz	1 Aug. 1813
John Strongitharm.. ..	5 Aug. 1813
Adolphus de Damas ..	12 Aug. 1813
Charles Barrington.. ..	14 Aug. 1813
William Pearce	4 Nov. 1819
Rank in Army,	15 Aug. 1813
Lieutenants—	
Henry Muller	8 Dec. 1807
Colin Campbell	18 Feb. 1808
Rank in Army,	3 Sept. 1795
R. S. Redman.. ..	14 June 1809
Rank in Army,	26 Feb. 1808
Johann Hem. Adair ..	28 Sept. 1809
John Carlos	29 Sept. 1809
Isaac Robateau d'Arcy ..	2 Oct. 1809
Andrew Lochs.. ..	4 Oct. 1809
Julius von Boeck ..	9 Oct. 1809
Andrew Ellison	12 Oct. 1809
R. B. Bishop	29 Oct. 1809
Leopold de Forger.. ..	30 Oct. 1809
Matthew Furst	4 Nov. 1809
Richard Pasley	6 Nov. 1809
Augustus F. Evans ..	9 Nov. 1809
Henry Baron Altenstein	10 Nov. 1809
John Hearn	18 Feb. 1810
Peter Kennedy	19 Feb. 1810
George Frederick Stern..	1 Mar. 1810

Rank and Name.	Rank in Regiment.

Lieutenants (continued)—
Maurice Cottman	12 June 1810
J. Andrew Weiburg ..	21 April 1814
Silvester O'Hehir	3 Nov. 1810
Rank in Army, 14 June 1810	
Peter Eason	4 Jan. 1819
Rank in Army, 8 Oct. 1810	
Ambrose Sponge	2 Dec. 1810
Rank in Army, 26 April 1814	

Ensigns—
Richard Percy Pack ..	16 Aug. 1813
Thomas Keal	18 Aug. 1813
Frederick George Bartlett	20 Aug. 1813
Arthur Smith	7 Nov. 1813
John Kelly	8 Nov. 1813
Alexander Paterson ..	4 Dec. 1813
Carl Wetzel von Kruger	22 Jan. 1814
Christian Katzmann ..	23 Jan. 1814
William Heurman ..	27 Jan. 1814
Richard Stapleton ..	19 April 1814
Joseph Robinson ..	21 Jan. 1814
Robert Alexander Andrews	18 Aug. 1814
Daniel O'Brien	1 Sept. 1814
William Moore Collings	28 Sept. 1814
Rank in Army, 3 Mar 1814	
Wm. Bletterman Caldwell	28 Sept. 1814
John Day	10 Dec. 1814
Thomas Adams	6 May 1819
Rank in Army, 16 June 1815	
David Dixon	4 Nov 1819
Rank in Army, 8 Dec. 1815	
William Slater	16 Dec. 1819
Rank in Army, 20 April 1815	

Paymasters—
| Henry Biggs .. .. .. | 22 Oct. 1812 |
| George Read .. .. | 6 May 1819 |

Adjutants—
J. Andrew Weiburg ..	10 Dec. 1812
Rank in Army, Lieut. 21 April 1814	
Thomas Adams	6 May 1819
Rank in Army, Ensign 16 June 1815	

Quartermasters—
| W. Maxwell .. .. .. | 6 July 1812 |
| Alexander Johnston .. | 24 Sept. 1812 |

Surgeons—
| John Furies .. .. | 21 Dec. 1800 |
| William B. Morle .. .. | 2 Nov. 1809 |

Assistant-Surgeons—
Alexander Melvin	26 Sept. 1811
Charles A. Simpson ..	3 June 1819
Rank in Army, 8 Dec. 1814	

Regimentals—Green, facings scarlet.

Agents—Messrs Greenwood, Cox, and Hammersley, Craig's Court.

1821.

Two Battalions.

1st Rifle Battalion. 2nd Light Infantry.

North America.

Martinique—Peninsula.

Col.-in-Chief—
H.R.H. Fred., Duke of	
York, K.G., G.C.B. ..	23 Aug 1797
Rank in Army, Field Mar. 10 Feb 1793	

Rank and Name.	Rank in Regiment.

Cols.-Commanding—
Napier Christie Burton ..	3 Jan. 1806
Rank in Army, Gen. 4 June 1814	
Hon. Edmund Phipps ..	25 Aug. 1807
Rank in Army, Gen. 12 Aug. 1819	

Lieut.-Colonels—
Edward Codd	26 Oct. 1804
Rank in Army, Maj.-Gen. 12 Aug. 1819	
⊙ George Mackie † ..	22 Dec. 1808
Rank in Army, Col. 4 June 1814	
Alexander Andrews	12 Aug. 1819
Rank in Army, 14 Dec. 1815	

Majors—
◼ John Forster Fitz-	
gerald †	9 Nov. 1809
Rank in Army, Col. 12 Aug. 1819	
◼ John Galiffe †	15 Mar. 1810
Rank in Army, Lt.-Col. 30 Nov. 1814	
Anthony Rumpler ..	16 Aug. 1810
Rank in Army, Lt.-Col. 12 Aug. 1819	
Henry Fitzgerald	11 Nov. 1813

Captains—
Frederick Inturn	24 April 1805
Rank in Army, Major 12 Aug. 1819	
Lewis Inturn	25 April 1805
Rank in Army, Major 12 Aug. 1819	
Adam Krien	23 May 1805
Rank in Army, Major 12 Aug. 1819	
◯ John Schwable	19 Sept. 1805
Rank in Army, Major 21 June 1813	
Edward Purdon	27 Aug. 1807
Rank in Army, Major 12 April 1814	
Anthony Stamba	10 Oct. 1809
Henry Petrie	11 Oct. 1809
Charles Mackenzie	10 Jan. 1810
Rank in Army, Lt.-Col. 12 Aug. 1819	
Robert Kelly	16 Aug. 1810
Francis Holmes	19 Sept. 1811
Melville Glenie	26 Mar. 1812
Rank in Army, 14 July 1808	
Ignatius Franchini ..	28 Jan. 1813
William Henry Snell ..	29 April 1813
Rank in Army, Lt.-Col. 21 June 1817	
Francis Beretz	1 Aug. 1813
John Strongitharm	5 Aug. 1813
Adolphus de Damas ..	12 Aug. 1813
Charles Barrington	14 Aug. 1813
William Pearce	4 Nov. 1813
Rank in Army, 15 Aug. 1813	
Henry Muller	18 May 1820
Charles Leslie	6 July 1820
Rank in Army, 5 Nov. 1813	

Lieutenants—
Colin Campbell	18 Feb. 1808
Rank in Army, 3 Sept. 1795	
R. S. Redman	14 June 1809
Rank in Army, 26 Feb. 1808	
Johann Henr. Adair ..	28 Sept. 1809
John Carb	29 Sept. 1809
Andrew Lachs	4 Oct. 1809
Julius von Beeck	9 Oct. 1809
Andrew Ellison	12 Oct. 1809
R. B. Bishop	21 Oct. 1809
Leopold de Forger ..	30 Oct. 1809
Matthew Furst	4 Nov. 1809
Richard Pasley	6 Nov. 1809

Rank and Name.	Rank in Regiment.

Lieutenants (continued)—

Augustine F. Evans .. 9 Nov. 1809
Henry Baron Altenstein 10 Nov. 1809
John Hearn .. .. .. 18 Feb. 1810
Peter Kennedy .. .. 19 Feb. 1810
Maurice Cottman .. .. 12 June 1810
J. Andrew Weiburg .. 21 April 1814
Peter Eason .. .. .. 4 Nov. 1819
    Rank in Army, 8 Oct. 1810
Ambrose Sponge .. .. 2 Dec. 1819
    Rank in Army, 26 April 1814
Charles Chichester .. .. 16 Mar. 1820
    Rank in Army, 4 Nov. 1812
Richard Percy Pack .. 12 April 1820
Thomas Keal .. .. .. 13 April 1820
Frederick George Bartlett 18 May 1820

Ensigns—

Arthur Smith.. .. .. 7 Nov. 1813
John Kelly .. .. .. 8 Nov. 1813
Alexander Paterson .. 4 Dec. 1813
Carl Wevel von Kruger 22 Jan. 1814
Christian Heurman .. 27 Jan. 1814
Richard Stapleton .. .. 19 April 1814
Joseph Robinson .. .. 21 April 1814
Robt. Alex. Andrews .. 18 Aug. 1815
Daniel O'Brien .. .. 1 Sept. 1814
William Moor Collings .. 28 Sept. 1814
    Rank in Army, 3 Mar. 1814
W. Bletterman Caldwell 29 Sept. 1814
John Day.. .. .. .. 10 Dec. 1814
Thomas Adams .. .. 6 May 1819
    Rank in Army, 16 June 1815
David Dixon .. .. .. 4 Nov. 1819
    Rank in Army, 8 Dec. 1815
William Slater .. .. 16 Dec. 1819
    Rank in Army, 20 April 1814
John O'Gorman .. .. 12 April 1820
    Rank in Army, 29 April 1813
James Sweeney .. .. 11 May 1820
    Rank in Army, 9 Sept. 1813
Henry James Gmn.. .. 15 June 1820
    Rank in Army, 15 July 1813

Paymasters—

Henry Biggs .. .. 22 Oct. 1812
George Read .. .. 6 May 1813

Adjutants—

J. Andrew Weiburg .. 16 Dec. 1812
    Rank in Army, Lieut. 21 April 1814
Thomas Adams .. .. 6 May 1813
    Rank in Army, Ensign 16 June 1815

Quartermasters—

W. Maxwell .. .. .. 6 July 1812
John Kiens .. .. .. 28 Sept. 1820
    Rank in Army, 6 April 1815

Surgeons—

John Faries .. .. .. 21 Dec. 1800
W. B. Morle .. .. .. 2 Nov. 1809

Assistant-Surgeons—

Alexander Melvin .. .. 26 Sept. 1811
Peter Smith .. .. .. 25 May 1820
    Rank in Army, 11 Nov. 1813

Regimentals—Green, facings scarlet.

Agents—Messrs. Greenwood, Cox, and Hammersley, Craig's Court.

1822.

Two Battalions.

1st Rifle Battalion, 2nd Light Infantry.

North America, Bermuda.
Roleia, Vimiera, Martinique, Talavera, Fuentes d'Onor, Ciudad Rodrigo, Badajoz, Salamanca, Vittoria, Nivelle, Orthes, Toulouse, Peninsula.

Rank and Name.	Rank in Regiment.

Col.-in-Chief—

H.R.H. Fred., Duke of
    York, K.G., G.C.B. .. 23 Aug. 1797
    Rank in Army, Field-Mar. 10 Feb. 1795

Cols.-Commanding—

Napier Christie Burton.. 3 Jan. 1806
    Rank in Army, Gen. 4 June 1814
Hon. Edmund Phipps .. 25 Aug. 1807
    Rank in Army, Gen. 12 Aug. 1819

Lieut.-Colonels—

Edward Codd .. .. .. 26 Oct. 1804
    Rank in Army, Maj.-Gen. 12 Aug. 1819
◯ George Mackie † .. 22 Dec. 1808
    Rank in Army, Col. 4 June 1814
◯ Alexander Andrews.. 12 Aug. 1819
    Rank in Army, 14 Dec. 1815

Majors—

☒ John Forster Fitz-
    gerald † .. .. .. 9 Nov. 1809
    Rank in Army, Col. 12 Aug. 1819
☒ John Galiffe † .. .. 15 Mar. 1810
    Rank in Army, Lt.-Col. 3 Mar. 1814
Anthony Rumpler .. .. 16 Aug. 1810
    Rank in Army, Lt.-Col. 12 Aug. 1819
Henry Fitzgerald .. .. 11 Nov. 1813

Captains—

Frederick Imturn .. .. 24 April 1805
    Rank in Army, Major 12 Aug. 1819
Lewis Imturn .. .. .. 25 April 1805
    Rank in Army, Major 12 Aug. 1817
Adam Krien .. .. .. 23 May 1805
    Rank in Army, Major 12 Aug. 1819
◯ John Schoedde .. .. 19 Sept. 1805
    Rank in Army, Major 24 June 1813
Edward Purdon .. .. 27 Aug. 1807
    Rank in Army, Major 12 April 1814
Anthony Stamba .. .. 10 Oct. 1809
Charles Mackenzie .. .. 10 Jan. 1810
    Rank in Army, Lt.-Col. 12 Aug. 1819
Robert Kelly .. .. .. 16 Aug. 1810
Francis Holmes .. .. 19 Sept. 1811
Melville Glenie .. .. 25 Mar. 1812
    Rank in Army, 14 July 1808
Ignatius Franchini.. .. 28 Jan. 1813
Francis Beritz .. .. 1 Aug. 1813
John Strongitharm.. .. 5 Aug. 1813
Adolphus de Damas .. 12 Aug. 1813
Charles Barrington.. .. 14 Aug. 1813
William Pearce .. .. 4 Nov. 1819
    Rank in Army, 15 Aug. 1813
Henry Muller .. .. .. 18 May 1820
Charles Leslie.. .. .. 6 July 1820
    Rank in Army, 5 Nov. 1813

Lieutenants—

Colin Campbell .. .. 18 Feb. 1808
    Rank in Army, 3 Sept. 1795

Rank and Name.	Rank in Regiment.
Lieutenants (continued)—	
R. S. Redman	.. 14 June 1809
Rank in Army,	26 Feb. 1808
Johann Hein. Adair ..	28 Sept. 1809
John Carlos	29 Sept. 1809
Julius von Boeck ..	9 Oct. 1809
Andrew Ellison ..	.. 12 Oct. 1809
B. B. Heslop	.. 29 Oct. 1809
Leopold de Forger..	30 Oct. 1809
Matthew Furst	.. 4 Nov. 1809
Richard Pasley ..	6 Nov. 1809
Augustine F. Evans ..	9 Nov. 1809
Henry Baron Altenstein..	10 Nov. 1809
John Hearn	.. 18 Feb. 1810
Peter Kennedy ..	.. 19 Feb. 1810
Maurice Cottman ..	.. 12 June 1810
J. Andrew Weiburg ..	21 April 1814
Peter Eason	.. 4 Nov. 1819
Rank in Army,	8 Oct. 1810
Ambrose Sponge	2 Dec. 1819
Rank in Army,	26 April 1814
Charles Chichester..	16 Mar. 1820
Rank in Army,	4 Nov. 1812
Richard Perry Pack ..	12 April 1820
Thomas Keal	.. 13 April 1820
Ensigns—	
Arthur Smith.. ..	.. 7 Nov. 1813
John Kelly	.. 8 Nov. 1813
Alexander Paterson ..	4 Dec. 1813
Carl Wewel von Kruger..	22 Jan. 1814
Christian Katzman ..	.. 23 Jan 1814
William Herriman ..	.. 27 Jan. 1814
Richard Stapleton ..	19 April 1814
Joseph Robinson ..	.. 21 April 1814
Robt. Alexander Andrews	18 Aug 1814
William Moore Collings	28 Aug 1814
Rank in Army,	3 Mar 1814
Daniel O'Brien ..	1 Sept. 1814
Wm. Biesterman Caldwell	20 Sept. 1814
John Day	10 Dec. 1814
Thomas Adams ..	6 May 1819
Rank in Army,	16 June 1815
David Dixon	4 Nov. 1819
Rank in Army,	8 Dec. 1815
William Slater	16 Dec. 1819
Rank in Army,	20 April 1814
John O'Gorman	12 April 1820
Rank in Army,	29 April 1813
Paymasters—	
Henry Biggs	22 Oct. 1812
George Read	6 May 1813
Adjutants—	
J. Andrew Weiburg ..	10 Dec. 1812
Rank in Army, Lieut.	21 April 1814
Thomas Adams ..	6 May 1819
Rank in Army, Ensign	16 June 1815
Quartermasters—	
W. Maxwell	6 July 1812
John Krens	28 Sept. 1820
Rank in Army,	6 April 1815
Surgeons—	
John Faries	21 Dec. 1800
William B. Morle	2 Nov. 1820

Rank and Name.	Rank in Regiment.
Assistant-Surgeons—	
Alexander Melvin	26 Sept. 1811
Peter Smith	25 May 1820
Rank in Army, 11 Nov. 1813	

*Regimentals—*Green, facings scarlet.

*Agents—*Messrs. Greenwood, Cox, and Hammersley, Craig's Court.

1823.

Two Battalions.

1st Rifle Battalion—2nd Light Infantry.

North America—Newfoundland—Bermuda.

Roleia, Vimiera, Martinique, Talavera, Fuentes d'Onor, Ciudad Rodrigo, Badajoz, Salamanca, Vittoria, Nivelle, Orthes, Toulouse, Peninsula.

Col.-in-Chief—
H.R.H. Fredk., Duke of York, K.G., G.C.B.
G.C.H. .. .. .. 23 Aug. 1797
Rank in Army, Field-Mar. 10 Feb. 1795

Cols.-Commandant—
Napier Christie Burton.. 3 Jan. 1806
Rank in Army, Gen. 4 June 1814
Hon. Edmund Phipps.. 25 Aug. 1807
Rank in Army, Gen. 12 Aug. 1819

Lieut.-Colonels—
Edward Codd .. 26 Oct. 1804
Rank in Army, Maj.-Gen. 12 Aug. 1819
George Mackay.. .. 22 Dec. 1816
Rank in Army, Col. 4 June 1814
Alexander Andrews .. 12 Aug. 1819
Rank in Army, 13 Dec. 1815

Majors—
◗ John Forster Fitzgerald 9 Nov. 1809
Rank in Army, Col. 12 Aug. 1819
◗ John Guliffe .. .. 15 Mar. 1810
Rank in Army, Lt.-Col. 3 Mar. 1814
Anthony Rumpler .. .. 16 Aug. 1810
Rank in Army, Lt.-Col. 12 Aug. 1819

Captains—
Frederick Imturn .. .. 24 April 1805
Rank in Army, Major 12 Aug. 1819
Lewis Imturn .. .. 25 April 1805
Rank in Army, Major 12 Aug. 1819
Adam Knen .. .. .. 23 May 1805
Rank in Army, Major 12 Aug. 1819
John Schoedde .. .. 19 Sept. 1805
Rank in Army, Major 21 June 1813
Edward Purdon .. .. 27 Aug. 1807
Rank in Army, Major 12 April 1814
Anthony Stamba .. .. 10 Oct. 1809
Charles Mackenzie .. 10 Jan. 1810
Rank in Army, Lt.-Col. 12 Aug. 1819
Robert Kelly .. .. .. 16 Aug. 1810
Melville Glenie .. .. 26 Mar. 1812
Rank in Army, 13 July 1808
Ignatius Fratchini.. .. 28 Jan. 1813
Francis Beritz.. .. 1 Aug. 1813
John Strongitharm .. 5 Aug. 1813
Adolphus de Dunas .. 12 Aug. 1813

H

Rank and Name.	Rank in Regiment.

Captains (continued)—

Charles Barrington	.. 14 Aug. 1813
William Pearce ..	.. 4 Nov. 1819
Rank in Army, 15 Aug. 1813	
Henry Muller.. ..	.. 18 May 1820
Charles Leslie ..	.. 6 July 1820
Rank in Army, 5 Nov. 1813	

Lieutenants—

Colin Campbell ..	.. 18 Feb. 1808
Rank in Army, 3 Sept. 1795	
Johann Hein. Adair	.. 28 Sept. 1809
John Carlos ..	.. 29 Sept. 1809
Julius von Boeck ..	.. 9 Oct. 1809
Andrew Ellison ..	.. 12 Oct. 1809
R. Braddyll Heslop ..	29 Oct. 1809
Matthew Furst ..	.. 4 Nov. 1809
Richard Pasley ..	.. 6 Nov. 1809
Augustine F. Evans ..	9 Nov. 1809
Henry Baron Altenstein	10 Nov. 1809
Peter Kennedy ..	.. 19 Feb. 1810
Maurice Cottman ..	.. 12 June 1810
J. Andrew Weiburg ..	21 April 1811
Peter Eason	.. 4 Nov. 1819
Rank in Army, 8 Oct. 1810	
Ambrose Sponge ..	.. 2 Dec. 1819
Rank in Army, 26 April 1811	
Charles Chichester ..	16 Mar. 1820
Rank in Army, 4 Nov. 1812	
Richard Percy Pack ..	12 April 1820
Thomas Keal.. ..	.. 13 April 1820
Frederick George Bartlett	18 May 1820
Thomas Stopford ..	.. 24 July 1822
Rank in Army, 11 Mar. 1813	
Hon. George Hervey ..	25 July 1822
Rank in Army, 24 Oct. 1821	

Ensigns—

Arthur Smith	.. 7 Nov. 1813
John Kelly	.. 8 Nov. 1813
Alexander Paterson ..	4 Dec. 1813
Carl Mevel von Krüger ..	22 Jan. 1814
Richard Stapleton ..	.. 19 April 1814
Joseph Robinson ..	.. 21 April 1814
Robert Alex. Andrews ..	18 Aug. 1814
Daniel O'Brien ..	.. 1 Sept. 1814
Wm. Moore Collings ..	28 Sept. 1814
Rank in Army, 3 Mar. 1814	
Wm. Bletterman Caldwell	29 Sept. 1814
John Day	.. 10 Dec. 1814
David Dixon	.. 4 Nov. 1819
Rank in Army, 8 Dec. 1815	
William Slater.. ..	.. 6 Dec. 1819
Rank in Army, 20 April 1814	
John O'Gorman ..	.. 12 April 1820
Rank in Army, 29 April 1813	
James Sweeny ..	.. 11 May 1820
Rank in Army, 9 Sept. 1813	
Joseph Alex. Wolff ..	25 Dec. 1821
Giles Vandeleur Creagh	4 July 1822
Rank in Army, 2nd Lt. 6 Jan. 1820	

Paymasters—

Henry Biggs	.. 22 Oct. 1812
George Read	.. 6 May 1813

Adjutants—

J. Andrew Weiburg ..	19 Dec. 1812
Rank in Army, Lt. 21 April 1814	

Rank and Name.	Rank in Regiment.

Adjutants (continued)—

Joseph Alex. Wolff ..	25 Dec. 1821
Rank in Army, Ensign 25 Dec. 1821	

Quartermasters—

A. Maxwell	.. 6 July 1812
John Kiens	.. 28 Sept. 1820
Rank in Army, 6 April 1815	

Surgeons—

John Faries	.. 21 Dec. 1800
John Glasco	.. 19 Sept. 1822
Rank in Army, 8 Feb. 1816	

Assistant-Surgeons—

Alexander Melvin ..	.. 26 Sept. 1811
Peter Smith	.. 25 May 1820
Rank in Army, 11 Nov. 1813	

Regimentals—Green.

Agents—Messrs. Greenwood, Cox, and Hammersley.

1824.

THE 60TH, OR THE DUKE OF YORK'S OWN RIFLE CORPS.

Two Battalions.

1st Rifle Battalion.   2nd Light Infantry.

England — West Indies — North America — Newfoundland — Bermuda.

Rolica, Vimiera, Martinique, Talavera, Fuentes d'Onor, Ciudad Rodrigo, Badajoz, Salamanca, Vittoria, Nivelle, Orthes, Toulouse, Peninsula.

Col.-in-Chief—

H.R.H. Fred., Duke of York, K.G., G.C.B., G.C.H...	23 Aug. 1797
Rank in Army, Field-Mar.	

Cols.-Commandant—

N. J. Burton	.. 3 Jan. 1806
Rank in Army, Gen.	
Hon. E. Phipps	23 Aug. 1807
Rank in Army, Gen.	

Lieut.-Colonels—

E. Codd	.. 26 Oct. 1804
Rank in Army, Maj.-Gen.	
G. Mackie †	.. 22 Dec. 1808
Rank in Army, Col.	
Thos. Bunbury	5 Feb. 1824

Majors—

John Galiffe †	15 Mar. 1810
Rank in Army, Lt.-Col.	
A. Rampler	.. 16 Aug. 1810
Rank in Army, Lt.-Col.	
Hen. Fitzgerald	11 Nov. 1813
Fred. Inturn	.. 9 Oct. 1823

Captains—

L. Inturn	.. 25 April 1805
Rank in Army, Major	
A. Krien	23 May 1805
Rank in Army, Major	
J. Schoedde	.. 23 May 1819
Rank in Army, Major	
A. Stamba	.. 10 Oct. 1809
C. Mackenzie	.. 12 Dec. 1799
Rank in Army, Lt.-Col.	

Rank and Name.	Rank in Regiment.
Captains (continued)—	
Robert Kelly	16 Aug. **1810**
Melv. Glenie	14 July 1808
J. Franchini	28 Jan. 1813
Fra. Beritz	1 Aug. 1813
J. Strongitharm ..	5 Aug. 1813
A. de Damas	12 Aug. 1813
C. Barrington.. ..	14 Aug. 1813
Wm. Pearce	15 Aug. 1813
Charles Leslie.. ..	5 Nov. 1813
Henry Muller.. ..	18 May 1820
J. Hein. Adair.. ..	8 Jan. 1824
Lieutenants—	
John Carlos	29 Sept. 1809
Jul. von Boeck ..	9 Oct. 1809
Andrew Ellison ..	12 Oct. 1809
R. Bradylt Heslop..	29 Oct. 1809
Matthew Furst ..	4 Nov. 1809
Richard Pasley ..	6 Nov. 1809
Hon. F. Evans ..	9 Nov. 1809
H. B. Altenstein ..	10 Nov. 1809
Peter Kennedy ..	19 Feb. 1810
M. Cottman	12 June 1810
J. A. Weiburg.. ..	21 April 1814
Peter Eason	8 Oct. 1810
Amb. Sponge	26 April 1814
C. Chichester	4 Nov. 1812
Thos. Keal	13 April 1820
F. G. Bartlett.. ..	18 May 1820
Hon. G. Hervey ..	24 Oct. 1821
Herbert Cornwall ..	19 Oct. 1820
G. F. Greaves.. ..	18 Jan. 1815
Ensigns—	
Arthur Smith.. ..	7 Nov. 1813
John Kelly	4 Dec. 1813
C. W. von Kruger ..	22 Jan. 1814
R. Stapelton	19 April 1814
J. Robinson.. ..	21 April 1814
D. O'Brien	1 Sept. 1814
D. Dixon..	8 Dec. 1815
J. O'Gorman	29 April 1814
Jas. Sweeney	9 Sept. 1815
J. A. Wolff	25 Dec. 1821
Fra. Coghlan	25 Sept. 1824
George Fothergill ..	25 Sept. 1817
C. Binstead	2 May 1816
—— Nesbitt	27 Mar. 1824
Paymasters—	
Henry Biggs	22 Oct. 1812
George Rend	6 May 1813
Adjutants—	
J. A. Weiburg.. ..	10 Dec. 1812
Rank in Army, Lieut.	
J. A. Wolff	25 Dec. 1821
Rank in Army, Ensign	
Quartermasters—	
P. Maxwell	6 July 1812
John Kiero	6 April 1815
Surgeons—	
John Glasco	8 Feb. 1816
Alexander Melvin ..	10 Dec. 1823
Assistant Surgeons—	
Peter Smith	11 Nov. 1813

Regimentals—Green, facings scarlet.

Agents—Messrs. Greenwood and Co.

From July to December 1824.

60TH, THE DUKE OF YORK'S OWN RIFLE CORPS.

North America—Newfoundland—Bermuda—England—West Indies.

Celer et Audax.

Roleia, Vimiera, Martinique, Talavera, Fuentes d'Onor, Ciudad Rodrigo, Badajoz, Salamanca, Vittoria, Nivelle, Orthes, Toulouse, Peninsula.

Rank and Name.	Rank in Regiment.
Col.-in-Chief—	
H.R.H. Fred., Duke of York, K.G., G.C.B., G.C.H.	23 Aug. 1797
Rank in Army, Field.-Mar.	
Cols.-Commandant—	
N. C. Burton.. ..	3 Jan. 1806
Rank in Army, Gen.	
Hon. E. Phipps ..	25 Aug. 1807
Rank in Army, Gen.	
Lieut.-Colonels—	
E. Codd	26 Oct. 1804
Rank in Army, Maj.-Gen.	
G. Mackie †	22 Dec. 1808
Rank in Army, Col.	
Thos. Bunbury ..	5 Feb. 1824
Majors—	
John Galiffe † ..	15 Mar. 1810
Rank in Army, Lt.-Col.	
A. Rumpler	16 Aug. 1810
Rank in Army, Lt.-Col.	
Henry Fitzgerald ..	11 Nov. 1813
Fred. Imturn	9 Oct. 1823
Captains—	
L. Imturn	25 April 1805
Rank in Army, Major	
A. Krien	23 May 1805
Rank in Army, Major	
J. S. Hoedde	19 Sept. 1805
Rank in Army, Major	
A. Stambo	10 Oct. 1809
C. Mackenzie	12 Dec. 1809
Rank in Army, Lt.-Col.	
Robert Kelly	10 Aug. 1810
Melv. Glenie	14 July 1808
J. Franchini	28 Jan. 1813
Fra. Beritz	1 Aug. 1813
J. Strongitharm ..	5 Aug. 1813
A. de Damas	12 Aug. 1813
C. Barrington.. ..	14 Aug. 1813
W. Pearce	15 Aug. 1813
C. Leslie	5 Nov. 1813
J. Hein. Adair ..	8 Jan. 1824
H. H. Manners ..	9 Sept. 1819
First Lieutenants—	
John Carlos	29 Sept. 1809
Jul. von Boeck ..	9 Oct. 1809
Andrew Ellison ..	12 Oct. 1809
R. Bradyll Heslop ..	29 Oct. 1809
Matthew Furst ..	4 Nov. 1809
Richard Pasley ..	6 Nov. 1809
A. F. Evans	9 Nov. 1809
H. Baron Altenstein ..	10 Nov. 1809
Peter Kennedy ..	19 Feb. 1810
J. H. Weiburg ..	21 April 1814

Rank and Name.	Rank in Regiment
First Lieutenants (continued)—	
Peter Eason	8 Oct. 1810
Amb. Sponge	26 April 1814
C. Chichester	4 Nov. 1812
Thos. Keal..	13 April 1820
Hon. G. Hervey	24 Oct. 1821
G. F. Greves	18 Jan. 1821
F. R. P. Tempest	30 Nov. 1820
Thos. Wood	12 June 1823
Second Lieutenants—	
Arthur Smith	7 Nov. 1813
John Kelly	8 Nov. 1813
R. Stapleton	19 April 1814
J. Robinson	21 April 1814
D. O'Brien	1 Sept. 1814
D. Dixon	8 Dec. 1815
J. O'Gorman	29 April 1813
Jas. Sweeny	9 Sept. 1813
J. H. Wolff	25 Dec. 1821
Fra. Coghlan	25 Sept. 1823
G. Fothergill	25 Sept 1817
C. Binstead	2 May 1816
C. L. Nesbitt	27 Mar. 1824
J. Liddell..	19 Aug. 1824
George Pigott..	1 Mar. 1821
Rank in Army, Ensign	
George Brockman	21 Oct. 1824
Paymasters—	
Henry Baggs	22 Oct. 1812
George Read	6 May 1813
Adjutants—	
J. A. Weiburg..	10 Dec. 1812
Rank in Army, Lieut.	
J. A. Wolff	25 Dec. 1821
Rank in Army, Ensign	
Quartermasters—	
W. Maxwell	6 July 1812
John Kien	6 April 1815
Surgeons—	
John Glasco	8 Feb. 1816
Alexander Melvin	10 Dec. 1823
Assistant-Surgeons	
Peter Smith	11 Nov. 1813

Regimentals—Green.

Agents—Messrs. Greenwood, Cox, and
Hammersley, Craig's Court.

1825.

Two Battalions.

England—West Indies.

Color of Indus.

Roleia, Vimiera, Martinique, Talavera, Fuentes d'Onor, Albuhera, Ciudad Rodrigo, Badajoz, Salamanca, Vittoria, Pyrenees, Nivelle, Nive, Orthes, Toulouse, Peninsula.

Colonel-in-Chief—

H.R.H. Fred., Duke of York, K.G., G.C.B., G.C.H.	23 Aug. 1797
Rank in Army, Field-Mar.	
Cols.-Commandant—	
N. C. Barton	3 Jan. 1806
Rank in Army, Gen.	

Rank and Name.	Rank in Regiment.
Cols.-Commandant (continued)—	
Hon. E. Phipps	25 Aug. 1807
Rank in Army, General	
Lieut.-Colonels—	
E. Codd	26 Oct. 1804
Rank in Army, Maj.-Gen.	
George Mackie†	22 Dec. 1808
Rank in Army, Maj.-Gen.	
Thos. Bunbury	5 Feb. 1824
John Galiffe†	18 June 1825
Majors—	
A. Rumpler	16 Aug. 1810
Rank in Army, Lt.-Col.	
H. Fitzgerald	11 Nov. 1813
J. H. Schoedde	20 Jan. 1825
L. Inturn	18 June 1825
Captains—	
An. Stamba	10 Oct. 1809
C. Mackenzie	12 Dec. 1799
Rank in Army, Lt.-Col.	
Robt. Kelly	16 Aug. 1810
Melvin Glenie..	3 July 1808
Rank in Army, Major	
J. Franchini	28 Jan. 1813
J. Strongitharm	5 Aug. 1813
Wm. Pearce	15 Aug. 1813
Chas. Leslie	5 Nov. 1813
J. Hein. Adair	8 Jan. 1824
H. H. Manners	28 Sept. 1814
Ambrose Sponge	18 Nov. 1824
C. Chichester	23 Dec. 1824
Andrew Ellison	20 Jan. 1825
J. Baxter Carlos	7 April 1825
Jas. Goldstrup..	25 Nov. 1821
Thos. Keal	19 May 1825
Hon. G. Hervey	2 June 1825
J. C. S. Slyfield	26 May 1825
R. Bradalyll Heslop ..	18 June 1825
First Lieutenants —	
Matthew Furst	4 Nov. 1809
Richard Pasley	6 Nov. 1809
An. F. Evans	9 Nov. 1809
Peter Kennedy	19 Feb. 1810
Peter Eason	8 Oct. 1810
G. F. Greaves..	18 Jan. 1815
T. R. P. Tempest	30 Nov. 1820
Jos. Robinson	18 Nov. 1824
John Campbell	1 April 1813
David Dixon	23 Dec. 1824
George Fothergill	20 Jan. 1825
Rich. Stapleton	7 April 1825
Daniel O'Brien	8 April 1825
Ed. C. Smith	10 Feb. 1825
J. Murphy	11 April 1825
Melvin Dalyell	19 May 1825
John Temple	21 Oct. 1824
C. L. Nesbitt	2 June 1825
George Pigott	23 June 1825
T. C. Hamill	5 April 1825
F. Coghlan	12 Oct. 1825
J. Liddell..	13 Oct. 1825
Second Lieutenants—	
John F. Evans	18 Nov. 1824
J. S. Wallord	19 Nov. 1824
W. B. Neynoe..	20 Dec. 1824
Fra. Marlion	20 Dec. 1824

Rank and Name.	Rank in Regiment.
Second Lieutenants (continued)—	
D. Fitzgerald	23 **Dec. 1824**
J. Archer..	21 **Aug. 1815**
Rank in Army, Ensign	
George Mason..	20 Jan. 1825
R. Gibbons	18 Nov. 1824
Rank in Army, Ensign	
J. O'Meara	7 Oct. **1813**
Rank in Army, Ensign	
T. Havelock	27 Sept. **1815**
Rank in Army, Ensign	
Auchmuty Tucker	10 April 1815
T. N. Bruere	11 April 1815
C. H. Spence	20 April 1815
Alex. Grierson	9 Jan. 1815
C. O'Donoghue	10 Jan. 1815
H. S. Brown	23 Jan. 1815
S. E. Goodman	7 July 1815
Lewis J. Hay	12 **May** 1815
Rank in Army, Ensign	
Paymaster—	
Henry Briggs	22 Oct. 1812
Adjutants—	
J. Liddell	19 Aug. 1824
Rank in Army, Lieut.	
F. Coghlan	28 July 1825
Rank in Army, Lieut.	
Quartermasters—	
Wm. Maxwell..	6 July 1812
A. Mitchell	17 Feb. 1825
Rank in Army, Lieut. 4 Dec. 1808	
Surgeons—	
John Glasco	8 Feb. 1816
Alexander Melvin	10 Dec. 1823
Assistant-Surgeons—	
Peter Smith	11 Nov. 1813
P. Lamond	27 May 1821

Regimentals—Green, facings scarlet.

Agents—Messrs. Greenwood, Cox, and Hammersley, Craig's Court.

1826.

Two Battalions.

England—West Indies.

Roleia, Vimiera, Martinique, Talavera, Fuentes d'Onor, Albuhera, Ciudad Rodrigo, Badajoz, Salamanca, Vittoria, Pyrenees, Nivelle, Nive, Orthes, Toulouse, Peninsula.

Col.-in-Chief	
H.R.H. Fred., Duke of York, K.G., G.C.B., G.C.H.	23 Aug. 1797
Rank in Army, Field-Mar. 10 Feb. 1795	
Cols.-Commandant	
Napier Christie Burton ..	3 Jun. 1806
Rank in Army, Gen. .. 4 June 1814	
Hon. Edmund Phipps ..	25 Aug 1807
Rank in Army, Gen. .. 12 Aug 1819	
Lieut.-Colonels	
Thomas Bunbury ..	5 Feb. 1824
Rank in Army, 5 Feb. 1824	
Henry Fitzgerald ..	25 Dec. 1825

Rank and Name.	Rank in Regiment.
Majors—	
Anthony Rumpler.. ..	16 Aug. 1810
Rank in Army, Lt.-Col. 12 Aug. 1819	
② James Holmes Schoedde 20 Jan. 1825	
Rank in Army, 21 June 1813	
William Pearce	25 Dec. 1825
Henry Herbert Manners	25 Dec. 1825
Captains—	
Anthony Stamba	10 Oct. 1809
Charles Mackenzie	10 Jan. 1810
Rank in Army, Lt.-Col. 12 Aug. 1819	
Robert Kelly	16 Aug. 1810
Melville Glenie	26 Mar. 1812
Rank in Army, Major 27 May 1825	
Ignatius Franchini.. ..	28 Jan. 1813
John Strangitharm ..	5 Aug. 1813
Charles Leslie	17 May 1820
Rank in Army, 5 Nov. 1813	
Johann Hein. Adair ..	8 Jan. 1824
Ambrose Sponge	18 Nov. 1824
Charles Chichester	23 Dec. 1824
Andrew Sillson	20 Jan. 1825
John Baxter Chifos ..	7 April 1825
James Goldstrap	9 April 1825
Hon. George Hervey ..	2 June 1825
R. Bradshyll Heslop ..	18 June 1825
Jos. Slav. Chol. Slyfield . 24 June 1825	
Rank in Army, 26 May 1825	
George Fred. Greaves ..	25 Dec. 1825
Thomas Rich. Finnie	
Tempest	25 Dec. 1825
John Campbell	26 Dec. 1825
First Lieutenants—	
Matthew Furst	4 Nov. 1809
Richard Pasley	6 Nov. 1809
Augustine F. Evans ..	9 Nov. 1809
Peter Kennedy	19 Feb. 1810
Peter Eason	4 Nov. 1810
Rank in Army, 8 Oct. 1810	
Joseph Robinson	18 Nov. 1824
David Dixon	23 Dec. 1824
George Fothergill	20 Jan. 1825
Richard Stapleton ..	7 April 1825
Edm. Carrington Smith.. 10 April 1825	
Rank in Army, 10 Feb. 1825	
② James Murphy	11 April 1825
Melville Dalzell	12 May 1825
Cosby Lewis Nesbitt ..	2 June 1825
George Pigott	23 June 1825
Thos. Cochrane Hammill 24 Sept. 1825	
Rank in Army, 5 April 1810	
Francis Coghlan	12 Oct. 1825
John Liddell	13 Oct. 1825
John Thomas Evans ..	1 Dec. 1825
John Sutton Wilford ..	25 Dec. 1825
Wm. Bridges Neynoe ..	25 Dec. 1825
Francis Marlton	26 Dec. 1825
David Fitzgerald	28 Jan. 1826
Second Lieutenants—	
John Archer	6 Jan. 1825
Rank in Army, Ensign 31 Aug. 1815	
Richard Gibbons	25 Jan. 1825
Rank in Army, Ens. 18 Nov. 1824	
John O'Meara	8 April 1825
Rank in Army, Ensign 7 Oct. 1813	

Rank and Name.	Rank in Regiment.

Second Lieutenants (continued)—
Thomas Havelock .. .. 10 April 1825
  Rank in Army, Ensign 27 Sept. 1815
Auchmuty Tucker .. .. 10 April 1825
Thomas Neale Bruere .. 11 April 1825
Charles H. Spence .. .. 20 April 1825
Alex. Grierson .. .. 9 June 1825
Charles O'Donoghue .. 10 June 1825
Henry Sabine Browne .. 23 June 1825
Lewis James Hay .. .. 6 Oct. 1825
  Rank in Army, Ensign 12 May 1825
Edward Chambers .. .. 1 Dec. 1825
Wm. Anderson .. .. 14 Dec. 1825
John Wm. Cross .. .. 21 Dec. 1825
James Bell .. .. .. 25 Dec. 1825
Charles Henry Churchill 26 Dec. 1825
Richard Lonquet Orlebar 27 Dec. 1825
Jonathan Greetham .. 5 Jan. 1826
Paymaster—
Henry Biggs .. .. .. 22 Oct. 1812
Adjutants—
John Liddell .. .. .. 19 Aug. 1824
  Rank in Army, 1st Lt. 13 Oct. 1825
Francis Coghlan .. .. 28 July 1825
  Rank in Army, 1st Lt.12 Oct. 1825
Quartermasters—
Wm. Maxwell.. .. .. 6 July 1812
Arthur Mitchell .. .. 17 Feb. 1825
  Rank in Army, Lieut. 4 Dec. 1806
Surgeons—
John Glasco .. .. .. 19 Sept. 1822
  Rank in Army, 8 Feb. 1816
Alexander Melvin .. .. 10 Dec. 1823
Assistant-Surgeons—
Peter Smith .. .. .. 25 May 1820
  Rank in Army, 11 Nov. 1813
Peter Lamond, M.D. .. 27 May 1824
Wm. Scott M'Crodie .. 12 Jan. 1826

Regimentals—Green, facings red.

Agents—Messrs. Greenwood, Cox, and Hammersley, Craig's Court.

1827.
Two Battalions.
Portugal—West Indies.

Celer et Audax.

Roleia, Vimiera, Martinique, Talavera, Fuentes d'Onor, Albuhera, Ciudad Rodrigo, Badajoz, Salamanca, Vittoria, Pyrenees, Nivelle, Nive, Orthes, Toulouse, Peninsula.
Col.-in-Chief—
H.R.H. A. F., Duke of Cambridge, K.G., G.C.B., G.C.H. .. .. 22 Jan. 1827
  Rank in Army, Field-Mar.
Cols.-Commandant—
Napier Christie Burton.. 3 Jan. 1806
  Rank in Army, Gen. 4 June 1814
Hon. Edmund Phipps .. 25 Aug. 1807
  Rank in Army, Gen. 12 Aug. 1819
Lieut.-Colonels—
Thomas Bunbury .. .. 5 Feb. 1821
  Rank in Army, 5 July 1821

Rank and Name.	Rank in Regiment.

Lieut.-Colonels (continued)—
Henry Fitzgerald .. .. 2 Sept. 1825
Majors—
J. Holmes Schoedde.. 20 Jan. 1825
  Rank in Army, 21 June 1813
Hon. H. Aug. Fred. Ellis 25 May 1826
  Rank in Army, 12 Nov. 1825
Charles Chichester.. .. 29 Aug. 1826
Charles Shee .. .. .. 26 Oct. 1826
  Rank in Army, 20 May 1826
Captains—
Charles Mackenzie .. .. 10 Jan. 1810
  Rank in Army, Lt.-Col. 12 Aug. 1819
Robt. Kelly .. .. .. 16 Aug. 1810
Melville Glenie .. .. 26 Mar. 1812
  Rank in Army, Major 27 May 1825
Ignatius Franchini.. .. 28 Jan. 1813
John Strongitharm.. .. 5 Aug. 1813
Charles Leslie .. .. .. 17 May 1820
  Rank in Army, 6 Nov. 1813
Johann Hein. Adair .. 8 Jan. 1824
Ambrose Sponge .. .. 18 Nov. 1824
Andrew Ellison .. .. 20 Jan. 1825
John Baxter Carlos .. 7 April 1825
James Goldstrap .. .. 9 April 1825
  Rank in Army, 25 Nov. 1821
Lord George Hervey .. 2 June 1825
R. Braddyll Heslop .. 18 June 1825
Jos. Slav. Slad. Slyfield .. 21 July 1825
  Rank in Army, 26 May 1825
Thomas Rich. Plumbe Tempest .. .. .. 25 Dec. 1825
John Campbell .. .. 26 Dec. 1825
Hon. H. Montagu Upton 2 Feb. 1826
  Rank in Army, 19 Nov. 1825
John Rich. Broadhead .. 12 Oct. 1826
  Rank in Army, 23 July 1825
C. Berkeley Berkeley .. 26 Oct. 1826
  Rank in Army, 3 Dec. 1825
First Lieutenants—
Matthew Furst .. .. 4 Nov. 1809
Richard Pasley .. .. 6 Nov. 1809
Augustine F. Evans .. 9 Nov. 1809
Peter Kennedy .. .. 19 Feb. 1810
Peter Eason .. .. .. 4 Nov. 1810
  Rank in Army, 8 Oct. 1810
Joseph Robinson .. .. 18 Nov. 1824
David Dixon .. .. .. 23 Dec. 1824
Richard Stapleton.. .. 7 April 1825
James Murphy.. .. 11 April 1825
Cosby Lewis Nesbitt .. 2 June 1825
George Pigott.. .. .. 23 June 1825
Thos. Cochrane Hammill 24 Sept. 1825
  Rank in Army, 5 April 1810
Francis Coghlan .. .. 12 Oct. 1825
John Liddell .. .. .. 13 Oct. 1825
John Sutton Wilford .. 25 Dec. 1825
W. Brydges Neynoe .. 25 Dec. 1825
Francis Mariton .. .. 26 Dec. 1825
David Fitzgerald .. .. 28 Jan. 1826
Richard Gibbons .. .. 8 April 1826
Henry Croly .. .. 7 Sept. 1826
  Rank in Army, 10 June 1813
Chas. Howe Spence .. 28 Sept. 1826
John Archer .. .. .. 6 Jan. 1825
  Rank in Army, Ensign 31 Aug. 1815

Rank and Name.	Rank in Regiment.
Second Lieutenants—	
Thomas Havelock	10 April 1825
Rank in Army, Ensign 27 Sept. 1815	
Thos. Neale Bruere..	11 April 1825
Charles O'Donoghue ..	10 June 1825
William Anderson	14 Dec. 1825
John W Cross	21 Dec. 1825
Chas. Henry Churchill ..	26 Dec. 1825
Richard Lonquet Orlebar	27 Dec. 1825
Jonathan Greetham ..	5 Jan. 1826
Edward Welch Eversley	2 Feb. 1826
George Bulman	8 April 1826
John Reynolds Peyton ..	9 April 1826
William Rakes Faber ..	10 April 1826
Charles Orgell Leman ..	12 April 1826
John Baily Sergeant ..	13 July 1826
Robert Atkins..	24 Aug. 1826
St. George Cronie	27 Sept. 1826
Rank in Army, Ensign 8 June 1826	
Martin Edward Haworth	28 Sept. 1826
Wm. Joshua Iremonger .	18 Oct. 1826
Thos. Morris	23 Nov. 1826
Paymasters—	
Henry Biggs	22 Oct. 1812
Edward Cozen	9 Feb. 1826
Rank in Army, Capt. 8 April 1825	
Adjutants—	
John Liddell	19 Aug. 1824
Rank in Army, 1st Lt. 13 Oct. 1825	
Francis Coghlan	28 July 1825
Rank in Army, 1st Lt. 12 Oct. 1825	
Quartermasters—	
Arthur Mitchell	17 Feb. 1825
Rank in Army, Lieut. 4 Dec. 1806	
Jonathan Booth	4 May 1826
Surgeons—	
Alex Melvin..	19 Dec. 1823
Francis Leigh, M.D. ..	12 Oct. 1826
Rank in Army, 9 Sept. 1813	
Assistant-Surgeons—	
Peter Smith	25 May 1820
Rank in Army, 11 Nov. 1813	
Peter Lauquoil, M.D. ..	27 May 1824
Wm. Scott M'Crodie ..	12 Jan. 1826

Regimentals—Green, facings scarlet.

Agents—Messrs. Greenwood, Cox, and Hammersley, Craig's Court.

1828.

Two Battalions.

Portugal—Ireland—West Indies.

Celer et Audax.

Rolcia, Vimiera, Martinique, Talavera, Fuentes d'Onor, Albuhera, Ciudad Rodrigo, Badajoz, Salamanca, Vittoria, Pyrenees, Nivelle, Nive, Orthes, Toulouse, Peninsula.

Col.-in-Chief —
H.R.H. A. F., Duke of Cambridge, K.G., G.C.B, G.C.H .. .. 22 Jan. 1827
Rank in Army, Field-Mar.

Rank and Name.	Rank in Regiment.
Cols.-Commandant—	
N. C. Burton	3 Jan. 1806
Rank in Army, Gen.	
Hon. E. Phipps, M.P. ..	26 Aug. 1807
Rank in Army, Gen.	
Lieut.-Colonels—	
T. Bunbury	6 Feb. 1824
H. Fitzgerald	2 Sept. 1825
Majors—	
J. H. Schoedde	20 June 1825
Hon.Aug. Fred. Ellis, M.P.	25 May 1826
C. Chichester	29 Aug. 1826
Charles Shee	26 Oct. 1826
Captains—	
Robert Kelly	16 Aug. 1810
M. Glenie	4 July 1808
Rank in Army, Major	
J. Strongitharm	6 Aug. 1808
Charles Leslie..	5 Nov. 1808
J Hem. Adair	8 Jan. 1824
Aub. Spenge	18 Nov. 1824
And. Ellison	20 Jan. 1825
J. Baxter Carlos	7 April 1825
J. Goldstrap	25 Nov. 1825
T. R. P. Tempest	25 Dec. 1825
John Campbell	26 Dec. 1825
Hon. O. Upton	12 Dec. 1826
W. Trevelyan.. ..	19 Sep. 1826
C. Ramsden	8 April 1826
C. Markham	29 Aug. 1826
George Brown.. ..	26 April 1827
Arthur, Marquis of Douro	8 May 1828
Hon. G Vaughan ..	29 Aug. 1826
First Lieutenants—	
M. Furst	4 Nov. 1809
Richard Pasley	6 Nov. 1809
Peter Eason	8 Oct. 1810
Jas. Robinson..	18 Nov. 1824
G. J. Nesbitt	2 June 1825
George Figost	23 June 1825
J. S. Wifford	25 Dec. 1825
Wm. B. Neynoe	25 Dec. 1825
Fred. Marston	26 Dec. 1825
D. Fitzgerald	28 Jan. 1826
Richard Gibbons ..	8 April 1826
Henry Cody	10 June 1813
C. L. Spence	28 Sept. 1826
R. W. Crocker.. ..	1 Jan. 1826
William Knox.. ..	20 Mar. 1827
W Anderson	15 Nov. 1827
J. Archer..	23 Jan. 1828
John Wm. Cross	24 Jan. 1828
C. H. Churchill	27 Mar. 1828
W T Gunn	18 Oct. 1827
Second Lieutenants—	
T N. Bruere	11 April 1825
Richard L. Orlebar ..	27 Dec. 1825
G. Greetham	5 Jan. 1826
E. W. Eversley	2 Feb. 1826
Geo. Bulman	8 April 1826
John R Payton	9 April 1826
C. O. Leman	12 April 1826
Robert Atkins.. ..	24 Aug. 1826
M. E. Haworth	28 Sept. 1826
W. J. Iremonger	29 Oct. 1826
J. St. J. Munro	29 Mar. 1827

Rank and Name.	Rank in Regiment.
Second Lieutenants (continued)—	
H. Bingham	.. 30 April 1827
S. Brel-ford	.. 25 Aug. 1827
Alfred Mundey ..	.. 1 Nov. 1827
S. P. Plumer	.. 15 Nov. 1827
Thos. Bunbury ..	.. 23 Jan. 1828
F. Jessop..	.. 24 Oct. 1827
W. H. Fitzgerald ..	.. 17 Jan. 1828
Rank in Army, Ensign	
T. Townsend	.. 24 Jan. 1828
Lord E. Thynne ..	.. 27 Mar. 1828
Hon. T. D. G. Dillon ..	31 July 1828
Rank in Army, Ensign	
W. E. T. Corbett ..	.. 24 Nov. 1828
R. C. Bingham ..	.. 25 Nov. 1828
Paymasters—	
Henry Biggs	.. 22 Oct. 1812
Edward Coxen.. ..	.. 9 Feb. 1826
Rank in Army, Capt.	8 April 1825
Adjutants—	
S. Brel-ford	.. 25 Aug. 1827
Rank in Army, 2nd. Lt.	
T. Townsend	.. 24 Jan. 1828
Rank in Army, 2nd. Lt.	
Quartermasters—	
John Booth	.. 4 May 1826
John Ottley	.. 30 July 1800
Surgeons—	
Alex. Melvin	.. 10 Dec. 1823
F. Leigh, M.D. ..	.. 9 Sept. 1813
Assistant-Surgeons—	
Peter Smith	.. 11 Nov. 1813
P. Lamond, M.D. ..	.. 27 May 1824
W. S. McCredie ..	.. 12 Jan. 1826

Regimentals—Green, facings scarlet.

Agents—Messrs. Greenwood, Cox, and Hammersley, Craig's Court.

1829.
Two Battalions.
Ireland—West Indies.
Celer et Audax.

Roleia, Vimiera, Martinique, Talavera, Fuentes d'Onor, Albuhera, Ciudad Rodrigo, Badajoz, Salamanca, Vittoria, Pyrenees, Nivelle, Nive, Orthes, Toulouse, Peninsula.

Col.-in-Chief—
H.R.H. A. F., Duke of Cambridge, K.G.,
G.C.B., G.C.H. .. .. 22 Jan. 1827
Rank in Army, Field-Mar. 26 Nov. 1813
Cols.-Commandant—
Napier Christie Burton.. 3 Jan. 1806
Rank in Army, Gen. 4 June 1814
Hon. Edmund Phipps .. 25 Aug. 1807
Rank in Army, Gen. 12 Aug. 1819
Lieut.-Colonels—
Thomas Bunbury .. .. 5 Feb. 1824
Rank in Army, 5 Jan. 1821
Hon. Henry Augt. Fred.
Ellis .. .. 18 Dec. 1828
Majors—
J. Holmes Schoedde .. 20 Jan. 1825
Rank in Army, 21 June 1813

Rank and Name.	Rank in Regiment
Majors (continued)—	
Charles Chichester.. ..	29 Aug. 1826
Charles Shee	.. 26 Oct. 1826
Rank in Army, 20 May 1826	
Charles Leslie.. ..	.. 18 Dec. 1828
Captains—	
Melville Glenie ..	.. 26 Mar. 1812
Rank in Army, Major 27 Mar. 1825	
John Strongitharm ..	5 Aug. 1813
Johann Hein. Adair ..	8 Jan. 1824
Ambrose Sponge ..	.. 18 Nov. 1824
Andrew Ellison ..	.. 20 Jan. 1825
John Buxter Carlos ..	7 April 1825
James Goldstrap	9 April 1825
Rank in Army, 25 Nov. 1825	
Lord George Hervey ..	2 June 1825
Jos. Clav. Shule Slyfield..	21 July 1828
Rank in Army, 26 May 1825	
Thos. R. Plumbe Tempest	25 Dec. 1825
John Campbell	26 Dec. 1825
Hon. George Upton ..	13 Feb. 1827
Rank in Army, 12 Dec. 1826	
Walter Trevelyan ..	5 April 1827
Rank in Army, 19 Sept. 1826	
Charles Ramsden ..	.. 12 April 1827
Rank in Army, 8 April 1826	
Charles Markham ..	.. 7 June 1827
Rank in Army, 29 Aug. 1826	
George Browne ..	.. 25 Oct. 1827
Rank in Army, 26 April 1827	
Arthur, Marq. of Douro .	24 July 1828
Rank in Army, 8 May 1828	
Hon. George Vaughan ..	21 Nov. 1828
Rank in Army, 29 Aug. 1826	
Cosby Lewis Nesbitt ..	18 Dec. 1828
Hon. Geo. Augt. Spencer	15 Jan. 1829
Rank in Army, 19 Dec. 1826	
First Lieutenants—	
Matthew Furst ..	.. 4 Nov. 1809
Richard Pasley ..	.. 6 Nov. 1809
Peter Eason	.. 4 Nov. 1810
Rank in Army, 8 Oct. 1810	
Joseph Robinson ..	.. 18 Nov. 1824
George Pigott.. ..	.. 23 June 1825
John Sutton Wilford ..	25 Dec. 1825
Wm. Brydges Neynoe ..	25 Dec. 1825
Francis Marlton ..	.. 26 Dec. 1825
David Fitzgerald ..	.. 28 Jan. 1826
Richard Gibbons ..	.. 8 April 1826
Henry Croly	.. 7 Sept. 1826
Rank in Army, 10 June 1813	
Charles Howe Spence ..	28 Sept. 1826
Rich. William Crocker ..	29 April 1827
Rank in Army, 1 Jan. 1826	
William Knox.. ..	.. 12 July 1827
Rank in Army, 20 Mar. 1827	
William Anderson ..	.. 15 Nov. 1827
John Archer	.. 23 Jan. 1828
John Wm. Cross ..	.. 24 Jan. 1828
Chas. Henry Churchill ..	27 Mar. 1828
William Townsend Gunn	3 July 1828
Rank in Army, 18 Oct. 1827	
Second Lieutenants—	
Thomas Neale Bruere ..	11 April 1825
Rich. Lonquet Orlebar ..	27 Dec. 1825
Jonathan Greetham ..	5 Jan. 1826

Rank and Name.	Rank in Regiment.
Second Lieutenants (continued)—	
Edw. Welch Eversley	2 Feb. 1826
George Bulman	8 April 1826
John Reynolds Peyton	9 April 1826
Charles Orgell Leman	12 April 1826
Robert Atkins	24 Aug. 1826
Martin Edw. Haworth	28 Sept. 1826
James St. John Munro	29 Mar. 1827
Henry Bingham	30 April 1827
Samuel Brelsford	25 Aug. 1827
Alfred Mundy	1 Nov 1827
Spencer Perceval Plumer	15 Nov. 1827
Francis Jessop	23 Jan. 1828
Rank in Army, 24 Oct. 1827	
Thomas Bunbury	23 Jan. 1828
Thomas Townsend	24 Jan. 1828
Wm. Henry Fitzgerald	30 Jan. 1828
Rank in Army, 17 Jan. 1828	
Lord Edward Thynne	27 Mar. 1828
Hon. Theodore Dominick	
Geoffrey Dillon	28 Aug. 1828
Rank in Army, **Ensign** 31 July 1828	
William Edwin **Thomp.**	
Corbett	24 Nov. 1828
Richard Clavell Bingham 25 Nov. 1828	
Paymasters—	
Henry Biggs	22 Oct. **1812**
Edward Cosen	9 Feb. 1826
Rank in Army, Capt. 8 April 1825	
Adjutants—	
Samuel Brelsford	25 Aug. 1827
Rank in Army, 2nd Lt. 25 Aug. 1827	
Thomas Townsend	24 Jan. 1828
Rank in Army, 2nd Lt. 24 Jan. 1828	
Quartermasters—	
Jonathan Booth	4 May 1826
John Ottley	20 Mar. 1828
Rank in Army, 30 July 1830	
Surgeons—	
Alexander Melvin	10 Dec. 1823
Francis Leigh, M.D.	12 Oct. 1826
Rank in Army, 9 Sept. 1813	
Assistant-Surgeons—	
Peter Smith	25 May 1820
Rank in Army, 11 Nov. 1813	
Peter Lamond, M.D.	27 May 1824
Wm. Scott M'Credie	12 Jan. 1826
Regimentals—Green, facings scarlet.	
Agents—Messrs. Greenwood, Cox, and Hammersley, Craig's Court.	

1830.

Two Battalions.

Ireland—Mediterranean—England.

Celer et Audax.

Roleia, Vimiera, Martinique, Talavera, Fuentes d'Onor, Albuhera, Ciudad Rodrigo, Badajoz, Salamanca, Vittoria, Pyrenees, Nivelle, Nive, Orthes, Toulouse, Peninsula.

Col.-in-Chief—
H.R.H. A. F., Duke of Cambridge, K.G.,
G.C.B., G.C.H. ... 22 Jan. 1827
Rank in Army, Field-Mar. 26 Nov. 1813

Rank and Name.	Rank in Regiment.
Cols.-Commandant—	
Napier Christie Burton	3 Jan. 1806
Rank in Army, Gen. 4 June 1814	
Hon. Edmund Phipps	23 Aug. 1807
Rank in Army, Gen. 12 Aug. 1819	
Lieut.-Colonels—	
Thomas Bunbury	5 Feb. **1824**
Rank in Army, 5 July **1821**	
Hon. Aug. Fred. Ellis, M.P. 18 Dec. **1828**	
Majors—	
Charles Chichester	29 Aug. 1826
Charles Shee	26 Oct. 1826
Rank in Army, 20 May 1826	
Charles Leslie	18 Dec. 1828
Hon. Charles Grey	23 April 1829
Rank in Army, 19 Feb. **1828**	
Captains—	
Melville Glenie	26 Mar. 1812
Rank in Army, Major 27 May 1825	
John Strongitharm	5 Aug. 1813
Johann Hen. Adair	8 Jan. 1824
Ambrose Spange	18 Nov 1824
Andrew Ellison	20 Jan. 1825
John Baxter Carlos	7 April 1825
James Goldstrap	9 April 1825
Rank in Army, 25 Nov. 1821	
Jos. Clav. Slad. Slyfield	21 July 1825
Rank in Army, 26 May 1825	
Thomas Rich. Plumbe	
Tenquest	25 Dec. 1825
John Campbell	26 Dec. 1825
Hon. George Upton	13 Feb. 1827
Rank in Army, 12 Dec. 1826	
Walter Trevelyan	5 April 1827
Rank in Army, 29 Sept. 1826	
Charles Ramsden	12 April 1827
Rank in Army, 8 April 1826	
Charles Markham	7 June 1827
Rank in Army, 29 Aug. 1826	
George Browne	25 Oct. 1827
Rank in Army, 26 April 1827	
Arthur, Marq. of Douro, 24 July 1828	
Rank in Army, 8 May 1828	
Hon. George Vaughan	21 Nov. 1828
Rank in Army, 29 Aug. 1826	
Cosby Lewis Nesbitt	18 Dec. 1828
Hon. George Aug. Spencer 15 Jan. 1829	
Rank in Army, 19 Dec. 1826	
George Pigott	20 Mar. 1829
First Lieutenants—	
Matthew Forst	4 Nov. 1809
Richard Pooley	6 Nov. 1809
Peter Eason	4 Nov. 1819
Rank in Army, 8 Oct. 1810	
Joseph Robinson	18 Nov. 1824
John Sutton Wilford	25 Dec. 1825
Francis Marlton	26 Dec. 1825
David Fitzgerald	28 Jan. 1826
Richard Gibbons	8 April 1826
Charles Howe Spence	21 Sept. 1826
Richard William Crocker 29 April 1827	
Rank in Army, 1 Jan. 1826	
William Knox	12 July 1827
Rank in Army, 20 Mar. 1827	
William Anderson	15 Nov. 1827
John William Cross	24 Jan. 1828

Rank and Name.   Rank in Regiment.

First Lieutenants (continued)—

Charles Henry Churchill	27 Mar. 1828	
William Townsend Gunn	3 July 1828	
	Rank in Army, 18 Oct. 1827	
Frederick Francis Lewis		
Dayrolles	5 Feb. 1829	
	Rank in Army, 21 Nov. 1828	
Edward Welch Eversley	20 Mar. 1829	
Thomas Neale Bruere	14 May 1829	
George Armstrong.. ..	15 May 1829	
	Rank in Army, 8 May 1828	
Alexander Visc. Fincastle	9 July 1829	
	Rank in Army, 14 Aug. 1827	

Second Lieutenants—

Jonathan Greetham	5 Jan. 1826	
George Bulman	8 April 1826	
John Reynolds Peyton	9 April 1826	
Charles Orgell Leman	12 April 1826	
Robt. Atkins	24 Aug. 1826	
Martin Edward Haworth	28 Sept. 1826	
James St. John Munro ..	29 Mar. 1827	
Henry Bingham	30 April 1827	
Samuel Brelsford	25 Aug. 1827	
Alfred Mundy..	1 Nov. 1827	
Spencer Perceval Plumer.	15 Nov. 1827	
Francis Jessop..	23 Jan. 1828	
	Rank in Army, 24 Oct. 1827	
Thomas Bunbury	23 Jan. 1828	
Thomas Townsend	24 Jan. 1828	
Wm. Henry Fitzgerald ..	30 Jan. 1828	
	Rank in Army, Ensign 17 Jan. 1828	
Hon. Theodore Dominick		
Geoffrey Dillon	28 Aug. 1828	
	Rank in Army, Ensign 31 July 1828	
William Edwin Thomp.		
Corbett..	24 Nov. 1828	
Richard Clavell Bingham	25 Nov. 1828	
Wm. Fanshawe Bedford.	18 Dec. 1828	
Hon. Henry Lyttleton		
Powys..	2 April 1829	
Henry Wm. Ellis	14 May 1829	
Hon. George Byng.. ..	25 June 1829	

Paymasters—

Henry Higgs	22 Oct. 1812	
⚔ Edward Coxen ..	9 Feb. 1826	
	Rank in Army, Capt. 8 April 1825	

Adjutants—

⚔ Samuel Brelsford ..	25 Aug. 1827	
	Rank in Army, 2nd Lt. 25 Aug. 1827	
Thomas Townsend	24 Jan. 1828	
	Rank in Army, 2nd Lt. 24 Jan. 1828	

Quartermasters—

Jonathan Booth	4 May 1826	
John Ottley	20 Mar. 1826	
	Rank in Army, 30 July 1800	

Surgeons—

Alexander Melvin	10 Dec. 1823	
Francis Leigh, M.D. ..	12 Oct. 1826	
	Rank in Army, 9 Sept. 1813	

Assistant-Surgeons—

Peter Smith	25 May 1820	
	Rank in Army, 11 Nov. 1813	
Peter Lamond, M.D. ..	27 May 1824	

Regimentals—Green, facings scarlet.

Agents—Messrs. Greenwood, Cox, and Hammersley, Craig's Court.

1831.

Two Battalions.

Mediterranean—England—Ireland.

Celer et Audax.

Roleia, Vimiera, Martinique, Talavera, Fuentes d'Onor, Albuhera, Ciudad Rodrigo, Badajoz, Salamanca, Vittoria, Pyrenees, Nivelle, Nive, Orthes, Toulouse, Peninsula.

Rank and Name.   Rank in Regiment.

Col.-in-Chief—

H.R.H. A. F., Duke of		
Cambridge, K.G., G.C.B.,		
G.C.H..	22 Jan. 1827	
	Rank in Army, Field-Mar. 26 Nov. 1813	

Cols.-Commandant—

Napier Christie Burton..	3 Jan. 1806	
	Rank in Army, Gen. 4 June 1814	
Hon. Edmund Phipps ..	25 Aug. 1807	
	Rank in Army, Gen. 12 Aug. 1819	

Lieut.-Colonels—

Joseph Bunbury	5 Feb. 1824	
	Rank in Army, 5 July 1821	
Hon. Aug. Fred. Ellis, M.P.	18 Dec. 1828	

Majors—

Charles Chichester.. ..	29 Aug. 1826	
Charles Shee	26 Oct. 1826	
	Rank in Army, 20 May 1826	
Charles Leslie..	18 Dec. 1828	
Hon. Charles Grey.. ..	23 April 1829	
	Rank in Army, 19 Feb. 1828	

Captains—

Melville Glenie	26 Mar. 1812	
	Rank in Army, Major 27 May 1825	
John Strongitharm.. ..	5 Aug. 1813	
Johann Hein. Adair ..	8 Jan. 1824	
Ambrose Spongs	18 Nov. 1824	
Andrew Ellison	20 Jan. 1825	
John Baxter Carles ..	7 April 1825	
James Gold-trap	9 April 1825	
	Rank in Army, 25 Nov. 1821	
Jos. Clav. Shad. Slyfield..	21 July 1825	
	Rank in Army, 26 May 1825	
Thomas Rich. Plumbe		
Tempest	25 Dec. 1825	
Walter Trevelyan	5 April 1827	
	Rank in Army, 19 Sept. 1826	
Charles Ramsden	12 April 1827	
	Rank in Army, 8 April 1826	
—— Markham	7 June 1827	
	Rank in Army, 29 Aug. 1826	
George Browne	25 Oct. 1827	
	Rank in Army, 26 April 1827	
Hon. George Vaughan..	28 Nov. 1828	
	Rank in Army, 29 Aug. 1826	
Cosby Lewis Nesbitt ..	18 Dec. 1828	
Edward Bagott	8 June 1830	
	Rank in Army, 8 Nov. 1827	
Hon. George Spencer ..	15 Jan. 1829	
	Rank in Army, 19 Dec. 1826	
George Pigott	20 Mar. 1829	
Hon. Francis Petre ..	10 Sept. 1830	
	Rank in Army, 21 Feb. 1828	
John Sutton Wilford ..	2 Nov. 1830	

Rank and Name.	Rank in Regiment.
First Lieutenants—	
Richard Pasley	6 Nov. 1809
Peter Eason	4 Nov. 1819
Rank in Army,	8 Oct. 1810
Joseph Robinson ..	18 Nov. 1824
Francis Marlton ..	26 Dec. 1825
David Fitzgerald ..	28 Jan. 1826
Richard Gibbons ..	8 April 1826
Charles Howe Spence	28 Sept. 1826
William Knox	10 July 1827
Rank in Army,	20 Mar. 1827
William Anderson ..	15 Nov. 1827
John Wm. Cross ..	24 Jan. 1828
Charles Henry Churchill	27 Mar. 1828
Wm. Townsend Gunn	3 July 1828
Rank in Army,	18 Oct. 1827
Frederick Francis Lewis	
Dayrolles	5 Feb. 1829
Rank in Army,	21 Nov. 1827
Edward Welch Eversley	20 Mar. 1829
George Armstrong ..	15 May 1829
Rank in Army,	8 May 1828
Alexander Visc. Fincastle	9 July 1829
Rank in Army,	14 Aug. 1827
Richard Jefferson Eaton	11 June 1830
Rank in Army,	8 June 1830
Robert Bayly	31 Aug. 1830
Rank in Army,	3 Dec. 1829
George Bulman	1 Nov. 1830
John Reynolds Peyton	2 Nov. 1830
Peter Slingsby Fitzgerald	26 Nov. 1830
Rank in Army, Lieut.	17 Oct. 1826
Second Lieutenants—	
Charles Orgell Leman ..	12 April 1826
Robert Atkins	24 Aug. 1826
Martin Edward Haworth	28 Sept. 1826
James St. John Munro ..	29 Mar. 1827
Henry Bingham	30 April 1827
Samuel Brisford ..	25 Aug. 1827
Alfred Mundy ..	1 Nov. 1827
Spencer Perceval Phipps	15 Nov. 1827
Francis Jessop	23 Jan. 1828
Rank in Army,	24 Oct. 1827
Thomas Bunbury ..	23 Jan. 1828
—— Townsend	24 Jan. 1828
Wm. Henry Fitzgerald ..	30 Jan. 1828
Rank in Army, Ensign	17 Jun. 1828
Hon. Theodore Dominick	
Geoffrey Dillon	28 Aug. 1828
Rank in Army, Ensign	31 July 1828
Wm. Edwin T. Corbett..	24 Nov. 1828
Richard Clavell Bingham	25 Nov. 1828
Wm. Fanshawe Bedford	18 Dec. 1828
Hon. H. Lyttleton Powys	2 April 1829
Henry Wm. Ellis	14 May 1829
Hon. George Byng.. ..	25 June 1829
Arthur A. T. Cunynghame	2 Nov. 1830
Robert Aldridge	26 Nov. 1830
Rank in Army,	9 July 1830
Paymasters—	
Henry Biggs	22 Oct. 1812
Edward Coxen ..	9 Feb. 1826
Rank in Army, Capt.	8 April 1825
Adjutants—	
Thomas Townsend ..	24 Jan. 1828
Rank in Army, 2nd Lt.	24 Jan. 1828

Rank and Name.	Rank in Regiment.
Adjutants (continued)—	
George Bulman	15 June 1830
Rank in Army, 1st Lt.	1 Nov. 1830
Quartermasters—	
Jonathan Booth	4 May 1826
John Ottley	20 Mar. 1828
Rank in Army,	30 July 1800
Surgeons—	
Alexander Melvin	10 Dec. 1823
Francis Leigh, M.D. ..	12 Oct. 1826
Rank in Army,	9 Sept. 1813
Assistant-Surgeons—	
Peter Smith	25 May 1820
Rank in Army,	11 Nov. 1813
Peter Lamond, M.D. ..	27 May 1824
Wm. Scott M'Credie ..	28 Sept. 1830
Rank in Army,	12 Jan. 1826

Regimentals—Green, facings scarlet.

Agents—Messrs. Greenwood, Cox, and **Co.**, Craig's Court.

1832.

Two Battalions.

Mediterranean—Ireland.

Color of Medal.

Roleia, Vimiera, Martinique, Talavera, Fuentes d'Onor, Albuhera, Ciudad Rodrigo, Badajoz, Salamanca, Vittoria, Pyrenees, Nivelle, Nive, Orthes, Toulouse, Peninsula.

Col.-in-Chief—
H.R.H. A. F., Duke of Cambridge, K.G., G.C.B., G.C.H. .. .. 22 Jan. 1827
Rank in Army, Field-Mar. 26 Nov. 1813

Cols.-Commandant—
Napier Christie Burton.. 3 Jan. 1806
Rank in Army, Gen. 4 June 1814
Hon. Edmund Phipps .. 25 Aug. 1807
Rank in Army, Gen. 12 Aug. 1819

Lieut.-Colonels—
Thomas Bunbury .. .. 5 Feb. 1824
Rank in Army, 5 July 1821
Hon. Aug. Fred. Ellis, M.P. 18 Dec. 1828

Majors—
Charles Leslie .. .. .. 18 Dec. 1828
J. Clavell Sladdon Slyfield 12 April 1821
Thos. Richard Plumbe
Tempest .. .. .. 12 July 1831
James Badham Thornhill 13 July 1831

Captains—
Melville Glenie .. .. 26 Mar. 1812
Rank in Army, Major 27 May 1825
John Strongitharm.. .. 5 Aug. 1813
Johann Hein. Adair .. 8 Jan. 1824
Ambrose Spooge .. .. 18 Nov. 1824
Andrew Ellison .. .. 20 Jan. 1825
John Baxter Carlos .. 7 April 1825
James Goldstrap .. .. 9 April 1825
Rank in Army, 25 Nov. 1824

Rank and Name.	Rank in Regiment.

Captains (continued)—

Walter Trevelyan .. ..   5 April 1827
    Rank in Army, 19 Sept. 1826
Charles Markham .. ..   7 June 1827
    Rank in Army, 29 Aug. 1826
George Browne .. ..   25 Oct. 1827
    Rank in Army, 26 April 1827
Hon. George Vaughan ..   21 Nov. 1828
    Rank in Army, 29 Aug. 1826
Cosby Lewis Nesbitt ..   18 Dec. 1828
Hon. Geo. Aug. Spencer   15 Jan. 1829
    Rank in Army, 19 Dec. 1826
George Pigott.. .. ..   20 Mar. 1829
Edward Bagott .. ..   8 June 1830
    Rank in Army, 8 Nov. 1827
John Sutton Wilford ..   2 Nov. 1830
Francis Marlton .. ..   12 April 1831
David Fitzgerald .. ..   12 July 1831
Clement Johnson .. ..   9 Aug. 1831
    Rank in Army, 30 July 1829
George Young.. .. ..   4 Oct. 1831
    Rank in Army, Major 22 July 1830

First Lieutenants—

Richard Pasley .. ..   6 Nov. 1809
Peter Eason .. .. ..   4 Nov. 1819
    Rank in Army, 8 Oct. 1810
Joseph Robinson .. ..   18 Nov. 1824
Richard Gibbons .. ..   8 April 1826
Charles Howe Spence ..   28 Sept. 1826
William Knox.. .. ..   12 July 1827
    Rank in Army, 20 Mar. 1827
William Anderson .. ..   15 Nov. 1827
John Wm. Cross .. ..   24 Jan. 1828
Charles Henry Churchill   27 Mar. 1828
Wm. Townsend Ginn ..   3 July 1828
    Rank in Army, 18 Oct. 1827
Frederick Fran. Lewis
Daytolles .. .. ..   5 Feb. 1829
    Rank in Army, 21 Nov. 1828
Edward Welch Eversley   20 Mar. 1829
George Armstrong.. ..   15 May 1829
    Rank in Army, 8 May 1828
Alexander Visc. Fincastle   9 July 1829
    Rank in Army, 14 Aug. 1827
Richard Jefferson Eaton   11 June 1830
    Rank in Army, 8 June 1830
Robert Bayly .. .. ..   31 Aug. 1830
    Rank in Army, 3 Dec. 1829
George Bulman .. ..   1 Nov. 1830
John Reynolds Peyton ..   2 Nov. 1830
Peter Slingsby Fitzgerald   26 Nov. 1830
    Rank in Army, 17 Oct. 1826
Charles Orgell Leman ..   12 April 1831
Robert Atkins.. .. ..   12 July 1831

Second Lieutenants—

Martin Edward Haworth   28 Sept. 1826
James St. John Munro ..   29 Mar. 1827
Henry Bingham .. ..   30 April 1827
Samuel Brelsford   25 Aug. 1827
Alfred Mundy.. .. ..   1 Nov. 1827
Francis Jessop .. ..   23 Jan. 1828
    Rank in Army, 23 Oct. 1827
Thomas Banbury .. ..   23 Jan. 1828
Thomas Townsend.. ..   24 Jan. 1828
Wm. Henry Fitzgerald ..   24 Jan. 1828
    Rank in Army, Ensign 17 Jan. 1828

Rank and Name.	Rank in Regiment.

Second Lieutenants (continued)—

Hon. Theodore Dominick
Geoffrey Dillon .. ..   28 Aug. 1828
    Rank in Army, Ensign 31 July 1828
Wm. Edwin T. Corbett..   24 Nov. 1828
Richard Clavell Bingham   25 Nov. 1828
Wm. Fanshawe Bedford   18 Dec. 1828
Hon. H. Lyttleton Powys   2 April 1829
Henry Wm. Ellis .. ..   14 May 1829
Arthur Aug. Thurlow
Cunynghame .. ..   2 Nov. 1830
Robert Aldridge .. ..   26 Nov. 1830
    Rank in Army, 9 July 1830
Richard Byrd Levett ..   12 April 1831
Johann Armie Morris ..   12 July 1831
Sir Broderick Harkewell,
Bart. .. ..   1 Nov. 1831
Reginald Wilton Mac-
donald .. ..   18 Nov. 1831

Paymasters—

Henry Biggs .. .. ..   22 Oct. 1812
Edward Coxen ..   9 Feb. 1826
    Rank in Army, Capt. 8 April 1825

Adjutants—

Thomas Townsend .. ..   24 Jan. 1828
    Rank in Army, 2nd Lt. 24 Jan. 1828
George Bulman .. ..   15 June 1830
    Rank in Army, 1st Lt. 1 Nov. 1830

Quartermasters—

Jonathan Booth .. ..   4 May 1826
John Ottley .. .. ..   20 Mar. 1828
    Rank in Army, 30 July 1800

Surgeons—

Alexander Melvin .. ..   10 Dec. 1823
Francis Leigh, M.D. ..   12 Oct. 1826
    Rank in Army, 9 Sept. 1813

Assistant-Surgeons—

Peter Laimond, M.D. ..   27 May 1824
William Scott M. Credie   28 Sept. 1830
    Rank in Army, 12 Jan. 1826
Richard Swift.. .. ..   22 Mar. 1831
    Rank in Army, 19 Aug. 1813

Regimentals—Green, facings scarlet.

Agents—Messrs. Greenwood, Cox, and
Hammersley, Craig's Court.

1833.

Two Battalions.

Mediterranean—Ireland.

Celer et Audax.

Roleia, Vimiera, Martinique, Talavera,
Fuentes d'Onor, Albuhera, Ciudad
Rodrigo, Badajoz, Salamanca, Vittoria,
Pyrenees, Nivelle, Nive, Orthes, Tou-
louse, Peninsula.

Col.-in-Chief—

H.R.H. A. F., Duke of
Cambridge, K.G.,G.C.B.,
G.C.H. .. .. ..   22 Jan. 1827
    Rank in Army, Field-Mar.

Col.-Commandant—

N. C. Burton .. .. ..   5 Feb. 1824
    Rank in Army, Gen.

Rank and Name.	Rank in Regiment.
Cols.-Commandant (continued)—	
Hon. E. Phipps ... 25 Aug. 1807	
Rank in Army, Gen.	
Lieut.-Colonels—	
T. Bunbury ... ... 5 Feb. 1824	
Hon. Aug. F. **Ellis, M.P.** 18 Dec. 1828	
Majors—	
J. C. S. Slyfield ... 12 April 1831	
T. R. P. Tempest ... 12 July 1831	
W. Trevelyan ... 28 Dec. 1833	
Charles Markham ... 31 May 1833	
Captains—	
M. Glenie ... 4 July 1808	
Rank in Army, Major	
J. Strengitharm ... 5 Aug. 1813	
J. Hein. Adair ... 8 Jan. 1823	
Ambrose Spenge ... 18 Nov. 1824	
C. L. Nesbitt ... 18 Dec. 1828	
Hon. G. Spencer ... 19 Dec. 1826	
George Pigott ... 20 Mar. 1829	
Edward Bagott ... 8 Nov. 1827	
J. S. Wilford ... 2 Nov. 1830	
D. Fitzgerald ... 12 July 1831	
Clemence Johnson ... 30 July 1829	
Richard Pasley ... 16 Mar. 1832	
G. A. Malcolm ... 30 Dec. 1831	
Oliver de Lancey ... 3 May 1831	
Randal Rumblier ... 14 Aug. 1827	
R. Gibbons ... 9 Aug. 1832	
William Knox ... 14 Dec. 1832	
F. W. Hamilton ... 4 Jan. 1831	
Peter Esson ... 21 Jan. 1833	
T. Combie ... 18 May 1832	
First Lieutenants—	
Joseph Robinson ... 18 Nov 1824	
C. Howe Spence ... 28 Sept 1826	
J. W. Eversley ... 20 Mar. 1826	
R. Jefferson Eaton ... 8 June 1830	
Robert Bayly ... 3 Dec. 1829	
George Hillman ... 1 Nov. 1830	
G. O. Lamont ... 12 April 1831	
Robert Atkins ... 12 July 1831	
M. E. Haworth ... 16 Mar. 1832	
J. St. J. Munro ... 9 Aug. 1832	
H. Bingham ... 28 Sept. 1832	
H. D. H. Murray ... 9 Nov. 1830	
W. H. Westgate ... 11 Oct. 1831	
F. Jessop ... 14 Dec. 1832	
T. Bunbury ... 28 Dec. 1832	
John Jones ... 2 Dec. 1831	
J. Fordyce ... 11 May 1832	
W. H. Fitzgerald ... 31 May 1833	
Thomas Wright ... 4 Dec. 1832	
T. Townsend ... 20 Jan. 1833	
Hon. T. D. G. Dillon ... 21 Jan. 1833	
W. F. Belford ... 28 Jan. 1833	
Second Lieutenants—	
Hon. H. I. Powys ... 2 April 1829	
H. W. Ellis ... 14 May 1829	
A. A. T. Cunyghame ... 2 Nov. 1830	
Robert Aldridge ... 9 July 1830	
R. Byrd Levett ... 12 April 1831	
J. P. O'Neil Power ... 27 Jan. 1832	

Rank and Name.	Rank in Regiment.
Second Lieutenants (continued)—	
C. H. Courtenay ... 9 Mar. 1832	
Rank in Army, **Ensign**	
S. J. L. Nicoll ... 27 April 1832	
R. Buckner ... 4 May 1832	
J. K. Mackenzie ... 16 Dec. 1831	
T. Guy Gisborn ... 9 Aug. 1832	
Wm. Geo. Rose ... 28 Sept. 1832	
Chas. Wm. Jebb ... 12 Oct. 1832	
Miles Banthwayte Weston 14 Dec. 1832	
Ross Mahon ... 14 Dec. 1832	
Wm. Fred. Hill Rook ... 28 Dec. 1832	
R. T. Brandling ... 31 May 1833	
Lord G. Loftus ... 22 June 1833	
S. G. Bunbury ... 28 June 1833	
H. Maitland ... 26 July 1833	
Paymasters—	
Henry Riggs ... 22 Oct. 1812	
Edward Coxen ... 9 Feb. 1826	
Rank in Army, Capt. 8 April 1825	
Adjutants—	
T. Townsend ... 24 Jan. 1828	
Rank in Army, 1st Lt.	
Tho. Wright ... 14 June 1833	
Rank in Army, 1st Lt.	
Quartermasters—	
Jon. Booth ... 4 May 1826	
John Ottley ... 13 July 1800	
Surgeons—	
Alexander Melvin ... 10 Dec. 1823	
F. Leigh, M.D. ... 9 Sept. 1813	
Assistant-Surgeons—	
P. Lamond, M.D. ... 27 May 1824	
Rich. Swift ... 19 Aug. 1813	
William Odell ... 9 Nov. 1830	

Regimentals—Green, facings scarlet.

Agents Messrs. Greenwood, Cox and Hammersley, Craig's Court.

1834.

Two Battalions.

Mediterranean—Ireland.

Celer et Audax.

Roleia, Vimiera, Martinique, Talavera, Fuentes d'Onor, Albuhera, Ciudad Rodrigo, Badajoz, Salamanca, Vittoria, Pyrenees, Nivelle, Nive, Orthes, Toulouse, Peninsula.

Colonel-in-Chief—
H R H. A. F. Duke of Cambridge, K G.,G C.B., G C M G., G C H ... 22 Jan. 1827
Rank in Army, Field-Mar. 26 Nov. 1813
Cols.-Commandant—
Napier Christie Burton.. 3 Jan. 1806
Rank in Army, Gen. 4 June 1814
Hon. Edmund Phipps .. 25 Aug. 1807
Rank in Army, Gen. 12 Aug. 1819

Rank and Name.	Rank in Regiment.
Lieut.-Colonels—	
Thomas Bunbury	5 Feb. 1824
Rank in Army,	5 July 1821
Hon. Augustus Frederick	
Ellis, M.P.	18 Dec. 1828
Majors—	
J. Clavell Sladdon Slyfield	12 April 1831
Thomas Richard Plumbe	
Tempest	12 July 1831
Walter Trevelyan	28 Dec. 1832
Charles Markham	31 May 1833
Captains—	
Melville Glenie	26 Mar. 1812
Rank in Army, Major	27 May 1825
John Strongitharm.. ..	5 Aug. 1813
Johann Hein. Adair ..	8 Jan. 1824
Ambrose Sponge ..	18 Nov. 1824
Cosby Lewis Nesbitt ..	18 Dec. 1828
Hon. George Augustus	
Spencer	15 Jan. 1829
Rank in Army,	19 Dec. 1826
George Pigott..	20 Mar. 1829
Edward Bagott	8 June 1830
Rank in Army,	8 Nov. 1827
John Sutton Wilford ..	2 Nov. 1830
David Fitzgerald	12 July 1831
Clement Johnson	9 Aug. 1831
Rank in Army,	30 July 1829
Richard Pasley	16 Mar. 1832
George Alex. Malcolm ..	20 April 1832
Rank in Army,	30 Dec. 1831
Oliver De Lancey	25 May 1832
Rank in Army,	3 May 1831
Randal Rumblier	13 July 1832
Rank in Army,	14 Aug. 1827
Richard Gibbons	9 Aug. 1832
William Knox..	14 Dec. 1832
Fred. Wm. Hamilton ..	15 Feb. 1833
Rank in Army,	4 Jan. 1831
Thomas Crombie	25 July 1833
Rank in Army,	18 May 1832
Samuel Ives Sutton.. ..	27 Dec. 1833
Rank in Army,	11 June 1830
First Lieutenants—	
Joseph Robinson	18 Nov. 1824
Charles Howe Spence ..	28 Sept. 1826
Edward Welch Eversley	20 May 1829
Richard Jefferson Eaton..	11 June 1830
Rank in Army,	8 June 1830
Robert Bayly	31 Aug. 1830
Rank in Army,	3 Dec. 1829
George Bulman	1 Nov. 1830
Charles Orgell Leman ..	12 April 1831
Robert Atkins..	12 July 1831
Martin Edward Haworth	16 Mar. 1832
James St. John Munro ..	9 Aug. 1832
Henry Bingham	28 Sept. 1832
How. David Hen. Murray	23 Nov. 1832
Rank in Army,	9 Nov. 1830
Wm. Harding Westgate	13 Dec. 1832
Rank in Army,	14 Oct. 1831
Francis Jessop..	14 Dec. 1832
Thomas Bunbury	28 Dec. 1832
John Jones	4 Jan. 1833
Rank in Army,	2 Dec. 1831

Rank and Name.	Rank in Regiment.
First Lieutenants (continued)—	
John Fordyce	1 Feb. 1833
Wm. Henry Fitzgerald ..	31 May 1833
Thomas Wright	14 June 1833
Rank in Army,	4 Dec. 1832
Thomas Townsend.. ..	20 June 1833
Hon. Theodore Dominick	
Geoffrey Dillon	21 June 1833
William Fanshawe Bedford	28 June 1833
Second Lieutenants—	
Hon. H. Lyttleton Powys	2 April 1829
Henry William Ellis ..	14 May 1829
Arthur Augustus Thurlow	
Cunynghame	2 Nov. 1830
Robert Aldridge	26 Nov. 1830
Rank in Army,	9 July 1830
Richard Byrd Levett ..	12 April 1831
Joseph Jas. O'Neil Power	27 Jan. 1832
George Henry Courtenay	7 April 1832
Rank in Army, Ensign	9 Mar. 1832
Samuel John Luke Nicoll	27 April 1832
Richard Buckner	4 May 1832
Joseph Kenneth Mackenzie	8 June 1832
Rank in Army,	16 Dec. 1831
Thomas Guy Gisborne ..	9 Aug. 1832
William George Roser ..	9 Aug. 1832
Charles William Jebb ..	12 Oct. 1832
Miles Branthwayte Weston	14 Dec. 1832
Ross Mahon	14 Dec. 1832
W. Frederick Hill Rook	28 Dec. 1832
Ralph Thos. Brandling ..	31 May 1833
Lord George Loftus ..	22 June 1833
Stonehouse Geo. Bunbury	28 June 1833
Henry Maitland	26 July 1833
Paymasters—	
Henry Briggs	22 Oct. 1812
Edward Coxen ..	9 Feb. 1826
Rank in Army, Capt.	8 April 1825
Adjutants—	
Thomas Townsend ..	24 Jan. 1824
Rank in Army, 1st Lt.	20 June 1833
Thomas Wright	14 June 1833
Rank in Army, 1st Lt.	4 Dec. 1832
Quartermasters—	
Jonathan Booth	4 May 1826
John Ottley	29 Mar. 1828
Rank in Army,	30 July 1800
Surgeons—	
Alexander Melvin	10 Dec. 1823
Francis Leigh, M.D. ..	12 Oct. 1826
Rank in Army,	9 Sept. 1813
Assistant-Surgeons—	
Peter Lamond, M.D. ..	27 May 1824
Richard Smith	22 Mar. 1831
Rank in Army,	19 Aug. 1813
William Odell..	12 July 1833
Rank in Army,	9 Nov. 1830

Regimentals—Green, facings scarlet.

Agents—Messrs. Greenwood, Cox, and Hammersley, Craig's Court.

1835.

Two Battalions.

Mediterranean—Ireland.

Coler et Audax.

Roleia, Vimiera, Martinique, Talavera, Fuentes d'Onor, Albuhera, Ciudad Rodrigo, Badajoz, Salamanca, Vittoria, Pyrenees, Nivelle, Nive, Orthes, Toulouse, Peninsula.

Rank and Name.	Rank in Regiment.
Col.-in-Chief—	
H.R.H. A. F., Duke of Cambridge, K.G., G.C.B., G.C.M.G., G.C.H.	22 Jan. 1827
Rank in Army, Field-Mar.	26 Nov. 1813
Cols.-Commandant—	
Hon. Edmund Phipps	25 Aug. 1807
Rank in Army, Gen.	12 Aug. 1819
Sir John Macleod, K.C.B.	7 Jan. 1835
Rank in Army, Maj.-Gen.	27 May 1825
Lieut.-Colonels—	
Thomas Bunbury, K.H.	5 Feb. 1824
Rank in Army,	5 July 1821
Hon. Augustus F. Ellis, M.P.	18 Dec. 1828
Majors—	
J. Clavell Slaidon Slyfield	12 April 1831
Thomas Rich. Plumbe Tempest	12 July 1831
Walter Trevelyan	28 Dec. 1832
Charles Markham	31 May 1833
Captains—	
Melville Glenie	26 Mar. 1812
Rank in Army, Major	27 May 1825
John Strongitharm	5 Aug. 1813
Johann Hein. Arbar	8 Jan. 1824
Ambrose Sponge	18 Nov. 1824
Cosby Lewis Nesbitt	18 Dec. 1828
Hon. Geo. Augustus Spencer	15 Jan. 1829
Rank in Army,	19 Dec. 1826
Edward Bagott	8 June 1830
Rank in Army,	8 Nov. 1827
John Sutton Wilford	2 Nov. 1830
David Fitzgerald	12 July 1831
Clement Johnson	9 Aug. 1831
Rank in Army,	30 July 1829
Richard Pasley	16 Mar. 1832
Geo. Alexander Malcolm	20 April 1832
Rank in Army,	30 Dec. 1831
Oliver de Lancey	25 May 1832
Rank in Army,	3 May 1831
Randal Rumblier	13 July 1832
Rank in Army,	14 Aug. 1827
Richard Gibbons	9 Aug. 1832
Wm. Knox	14 Dec. 1832
Fredk. William Hamilton	15 Mar. 1833
Rank in Army,	4 Jan. 1831
Thos. Crombie	26 July 1833
Rank in Army,	18 May 1832
Samuel Ives Sutton	27 Dec. 1833
Rank in Army,	11 June 1830
Freeman Murray	11 July 1834
Rank in Army,	21 Dec. 1832

Rank and Name.	Rank in Regiment.
First Lieutenants—	
Joseph Robinson	18 Nov. 1824
Chas. Home Spence	28 Sept. 1826
Edwd. Welch Eversley	20 Mar. 1829
Rich. Jefferson Eaton	11 June 1830
Rank in Army,	8 June 1830
Robt. Bayly	31 Aug. 1830
Rank in Army,	3 Dec. 1829
George Bulman	1 Nov. 1830
Charles Orgell Leman	12 April 1831
Robert Atkins	12 July 1831
Martin Edward Haworth	16 Mar. 1832
James St. John Munro	9 Aug. 1832
Henry Bingham	28 Sept. 1832
Hon. David Henry Murray	23 Nov. 1832
Rank in Army,	9 Nov. 1830
Wm. Harding Woodgate	13 Dec. 1832
Rank in Army,	11 Oct. 1831
Thomas Bunbury	28 Dec. 1832
John Jones	4 Jan. 1833
Rank in Army,	2 Dec. 1831
Wm. Henry Fitzgerald	31 May 1833
Thomas Wright	14 June 1833
Rank in Army,	4 Dec. 1832
Thomas Townsend	20 June 1833
Hon. Theo. Dominick G. Dillon	21 June 1833
Wm. Fanshawe Belford	28 June 1833
Hon. Hen. Lyttleton Powys	19 Sept. 1834
James MacCarthy	31 Oct. 1834
Rank in Army,	8 Oct. 1827
Second Lieutenants—	
Henry William Ellis	14 May 1829
Arthur Aug. Thurlow Cunninghame	2 Nov. 1830
Robert Aldridge	26 Nov. 1830
Rank in Army,	9 July 1830
Rich. Byrd Levett	12 April 1831
Joseph James O'Neil Power	27 Jan. 1832
Geo. Henry Courtenay	7 April 1832
Rank in Army, Ensign	9 Mar. 1832
John Kenneth Mackenzie	8 June 1832
Rank in Army,	16 Dec. 1831
Thomas Guy Gisborne	9 Aug. 1832
Wm. George Row	28 Sept. 1832
Charles Wm. Jebb	12 Oct. 1832
Miles Branthwayte Weston	14 Dec. 1832
Ross Mahon	14 Dec. 1832
Ralph Thos. Brandling	31 May 1833
Stonehouse Geo. Bunbury	28 June 1833
Henry Maitland	26 July 1833
Hudson Lowe	7 Feb. 1833
Rank in Army, Ensign	17 Jan. 1834
John Steven Robinson	11 April 1833
Thomas Butler	9 May 1833
Edw. John Vesey Brown	12 Sept. 1833
Webbe Butler	19 Sept. 1833
Paymasters—	
Henry Biggs	22 Oct. 1812
Edward Coxen	9 Feb. 1826
Rank in Army, Capt.	8 April 1825
Adjutants—	
Thomas Townsend	24 Jan. 1828
Rank in Army, 1st Lieut.	20 June 1833

Rank and Name.	Rank in Regiment.

Adjutants (continued)—
Thomas Wright .. .. 14 June 1833
Rank in Army, 1st Lieut. 4 Dec. 1832

Quartermasters—
Jonathan Booth .. .. 4 May 1826
John Ottley .. .. .. 20 Mar. 1828
    Rank in Army, 30 July 1800

Surgeons—
Francis Leigh, M.D. .. 12 Oct. 1826
    Rank in Army, 9 Sept. 1813
Hugh Fraser .. .. .. 30 Dec. 1834

Assistant-Surgeons—
Peter Lamond, M.D. .. 27 May 1821
William Odell .. .. .. 12 July 1833
    Rank in Army, 9 Nov. 1830
Alexander Leigh, M.D... 15 Aug. 1834

Regimentals—Green, facings scarlet.

Agents—Messrs. Cox and Co., Craig's Court.

1836.

Two Battalions.

Mediterranean.

Celer et Audax.

Roleia, Vimiera, Martinique, Talavera, Fuentes d'Onor, Albuhera, Ciudad Rodrigo, Badajoz, Salamanca, Vittoria, Pyrenees, Nivelle, Nive, Orthes, Toulouse, Peninsula.

Col.-in-Chief —
H.R.H. A. F., Duke of Cambridge, K.G.,G.C.B., G.C.M.G., G.C.H. .. 22 Jan. 1827
Rank in Army, Field-Mar. 26 Nov. 1813

Cols.-Commandant—
Hon. Edmund Phipps .. 25 Aug. 1807
    Rank in Army, 12 Aug. 1819
Sir John Maclean, K.C.B. 7 Jan. 1835
    Rank in Army, Maj.-Gen. 27 May 1825

Lieut.-Colonels—
Hon. Augustus Fred. Ellis 18 Dec. 1828
Hon. Henry Ric.Molyneux 24 April 1835
    Rank in Army, 9 April 1829

Majors—
J. Chavell Shaddon Slyfield 12 April 1831
Thomas Rich. Plumbe
  Tempest .. .. .. 12 July 1831
Walter Trevelyan .. .. 28 Dec. 1832
Charles Markham .. .. 31 May 1833

Captains—
Melville Glenie .. .. 26 Mar. 1812
    Rank in Army, Major 27 May 1825
Ambrose Sponge .. .. 18 Nov. 1824
Cosby Lewis Nesbitt .. 18 Dec. 1828
Hon. George Aug. Spencer 15 Jan. 1829
    Rank in Army, 19 Dec. 1826
Edward Bagott .. .. 8 June 1830
    Rank in Army, 8 Nov. 1827
John Sutton Wilford .. 2 Nov. 1830
David Fitzgerald .. .. 12 July 1831
Clement Johnson .. .. 9 Aug. 1831
    Rank in Army, 30 July 1829
Richard Pasley .. .. 16 Mar. 1832

Rank and Name.	Rank in Regiment.

Captains (continued)—
Randal Rumblier .. .. 13 July 1832
    Rank in Army, 14 Aug. 1827
Richard Gibbons .. .. 9 Aug. 1832
William Knox.. .. .. 14 Dec. 1832
Fred. William Hamilton. 15 Mar. 1833
    Rank in Army, 4 Jan. 1831
Thomas Crombie .. .. 26 July 1833
    Rank in Army, 18 May 1832
Samuel Ives Sutton.. .. 27 Dec. 1833
    Rank in Army, 11 June 1830
Freeman Murray .. .. 11 July 1834
    Rank in Army, 21 Dec. 1832
George Bulman .. .. 29 May 1835
Patrick Colin Campbell .. 17 July 1835
    Rank in Army, 8 April 1826
Charles Orgell Leman .. 4 Sept. 1835
Edward C. Giffard.. .. 18 Dec. 1835
    Rank in Army, 9 Oct. 1835

First Lieutenants—
Joseph Robinson .. .. 18 Nov. 1824
Charles Home Spence .. 28 Sept. 1826
Edward Welch Eversley . 20 Mar. 1829
Robert Atkins.. .. .. 12 July 1831
Martin Edward Haworth 16 Mar. 1832
James St. John Munro.. 9 Aug. 1832
Henry Bingham .. .. 28 Sept. 1832
Thomas Bunbury .. .. 28 Dec. 1832
John Jones .. .. .. 4 Jan. 1833
    Rank in Army, 2 Dec. 1831
William Henry Fitzgerald 31 May 1833
Thomas Wright .. .. 14 June 1833
    Rank in Army, 4 Dec. 1832
Thomas Townsend .. .. 20 June 1833
Hon. Theo. Dominick Geff.
Dillon .. .. 21 June 1833
Wm. Fanshawe Bedford 28 June 1833
Hon. H. Lyttleton Powys 19 Sept. 1834
Henry William Ellis .. 17 April 1835
Arthur Aug. Thurlow
  Cunynghame .. .. 22 May 1835
Robert Aldridge .. .. 29 May 1835
Walling Everard .. .. 3 July 1835
    Rank in Army, 15 May 1835
Richard Byrd Levett .. 4 Sept. 1835
Joseph Jas. O'Neil Power 5 Sept. 1835
Richard Maxwell .. .. 9 Oct. 1835
    Rank in Army, 8 Feb. 1833

Second Lieutenants—
George Henry Courtenay 7 April 1832
    Rank in Army, Ensign 9 Mar. 1832
John Kenneth Mackenzie 8 June 1832
    Rank in Army, 16 Dec. 1831
Thos. Guy Gisborne .. 9 Aug. 1832
Wm. George Rose .. .. 28 Sept. 1832
Chas. Wm. Jebb .. .. 12 Oct. 1832
Miles Branthwayte Weston 14 Dec. 1832
Sir Ross Manon, Bart. .. 14 Dec. 1832
Ralph Thos. Brandling .. 31 May 1833
Stonehouse Geo. Bunbury 28 June 1833
Henry Maitland .. .. 26 July 1833
Hudson Lowe .. .. .. 7 Feb. 1834
    Rank in Army, Ensign 17 Jan. 1834
John Stephen Robinson.. 11 April 1834
Thomas Butler .. .. 9 May 1834
Edwd. John Vesey Brown 12 Sept. 1834

Rank and Name.	Rank in Regiment.
Second Lieutenants (continued)—	
Webbe Butler	19 Sept. **1834**
Thomas Mitchell	27 Feb. **1834**
Constantine Edw. Phipps	17 April **1834**
Henry Robt. Beresford ..	22 May **1834**
Henry Halbech ..	29 May **1834**
Hon. John Edmund Hovel	
Thurlow	4 Sept. **1834**
Richard Ingram Dausey..	5 Sept. **1834**
Paymasters—	
Edward Coxen.. ..	9 Feb. **1826**
Rank in Army, Captain	8 April **1825**
Henry Edwd. O'Dell ..	10 July **1835**
Rank in Army, Captain	9 Jan. **1822**
Adjutants—	
Thomas Townsend ..	24 Jan. **1828**
Rank in Army, 1st Lt.	20 June **1833**
Thomas Mitchell	27 Feb. **1835**
Rank in Army, 2nd Lt.	27 Feb. **1835**
Quartermasters—	
Jonathan Booth	4 May **1826**
John Brennan.. ..	18 Sept. **1835**
Rank in Army, Ensign	5 Sept. **1835**
Surgeons—	
Francis Leigh, **M.D.** ..	12 Oct. **1826**
Rank in Army,	9 Sept. **1813**
Hugh Fraser..	30 Dec. **1834**
Assistant-Surgeons—	
Peter Lamond, M.D. ..	27 May **1824**
Alex. Leigh, M.D. ..	15 Aug. **1834**
David Maurice, **M.D.** ..	29 May **1835**
George Ferguson ..	30 Oct. **1835**
Rank in Army,	12 June **1828**

Regimentals—Green, facings scarlet.

Agents—Messrs. Cox and Co., Craig's
Court.

1837.

Two Battalions.

Mediterranean.

Celer et Audax.

Roleia, Vimiera, Martinique, Talavera, Fuentes d'Onor, Albuhera, Ciudad Rodrigo, Badajoz, Salamanca, Vittoria, Pyrenees, Nivelle, Nive, Orthes, Toulouse, Peninsula.

Col.-in-Chief—
H.R.H. A. F., Duke of
Cambridge, K.G., G.C.B.,
G.C.M.G., G.C.H. .. 22 Jan. **1827**
Rank in Army, Field-Mar. 26 Nov **1813**
Cols.-Commandant—
Hon. Edmund Phipps .. 25 Aug. **1807**
Rank in Army, Gen. 12 Aug. **1819**
Sir John Maclean,
K.C.B.. .. .. .. 7 Jan. **1835**
Rank in Army, Maj.-Gen. 27 May **1825**
Lieut.-Colonels—
Hon. Augustus Frederick
Ellis .. .. .. 18 Dec. **1828**
Hon. Henry Richard
Molyneux .. .. 24 Apr. **1835**
Rank in Army, Bt.-Col. 9 Apr. **1829**

Rank and Name.	Rank in Regiment.
Majors—	
J. Clavell Shaddon Slyfield	12 Apr. **1831**
T. Rich. Plumbe Tempest	12 July **1831**
Walter Trevelyan	28 Dec. **1832**
Charles Markham	31 May **1833**
Captains—	
Melville Glenie	26 Mar. **1812**
Rank in Army, Major	27 May **1825**
Ambrose Sponge	18 Nov. **1824**
Cosby Lewis Nesbitt ..	18 Dec. **1828**
Hon. George Aug. Spencer	15 Jan. **1829**
Rank in Army,	19 Dec. **1826**
Edward Bagot..	8 June **1830**
Rank in Army,	8 Nov. **1827**
John Sutton Wilford ..	2 Nov. **1830**
David Fitzgerald	12 July **1831**
Clement Johnson	9 Aug. **1831**
Rank in Army,	30 July **1831**
Richard Pasley	16 Mar. **1832**
Randal Rumley	13 July **1832**
Rank in Army,	14 Aug. **1827**
Richard Gibbens	9 Aug. **1832**
Fred. William Hamilton	15 Mar. **1833**
Rank in Army,	4 Jan. **1831**
Thomas Crombie	26 July **1833**
Rank in Army,	18 May **1832**
Samuel Ives Sutton ..	27 Dec. **1833**
Rank in Army,	11 June **1830**
Freeman Murray	11 July **1834**
Rank in Army,	21 Dec. **1832**
George Bulman	29 May **1835**
Patrick Colin Campbell..	17 July **1835**
Rank in Army,	8 April **1826**
Charles Orgell Lennon ..	4 Sept. **1835**
Edward C. Gifford ..	18 Dec. **1835**
Rank in Army,	9 Oct. **1835**
Robert Atkins..	16 Sept. **1836**
First Lieutenants—	
Joseph Robinson	18 Nov. **1824**
Charles Howe Spence ..	28 Sept. **1826**
Martin Edward Haworth	16 Mar. **1832**
James St. John Munro ..	9 Aug. **1832**
Henry Bingham	28 Sept. **1832**
Thomas Bradbury	28 Dec. **1832**
John Jones	4 Jan. **1833**
Rank in Army,	2 Dec. **1831**
Wm. Henry Fitzgerald ..	31 May **1833**
Thomas Townsend	20 June **1833**
Hon. Theo. Dominick	
Geoffrey Dillon	21 June **1833**
Wm. Fanshawe Bedford	28 June **1833**
Hon Hon Lyttleton Powys	19 Sept. **1834**
Henry Wm Ellis	17 Apr. **1835**
Arthur Aug. Thurlow	
Cunynghame	22 May **1835**
Robert Aldridge	29 May **1835**
Walling Everard	3 July **1835**
Rank in Army,	15 May **1835**
Richard Byrd Levett ..	4 Sept. **1835**
Richard Maxwell	9 Oct. **1835**
Rank in Army,	6 Feb. **1833**
Francis Roger Palmer ..	26 Feb. **1836**
Rank in Army,	21 Apr. **1835**
George Henry Courtenay	8 Apr. **1836**
John Kenneth Mackenzie	16 Sept. **1836**
Thomas Guy Gisborne	21 Oct. **1836**

F

Rank and Name.	Rank in Regiment.
Second Lieutenants—	
William George Rose ..	28 Sept. 1832
Charles William Jebb ..	12 Oct. 1832
Miles Branthwayte Weston	14 Dec. 1832
Sir Ross Mahon, Bart. ..	14 Dec. 1832
Stonehouse Geo. Bunbury	28 June 1833
John Stephen Robinson..	11 Apr. 1834
Thomas Butler	9 May 1834
Edwd. John Vesey Brown	12 Sept. 1834
Webbe Butler	19 Sept. 1834
Thos. Mitchell..	27 Feb. 1835
Hen. Robert Beresford ..	22 May 1835
Henry Holbech	29 May 1835
Hon. Jn. Edm. T. Hovel	4 Sept. 1835
Richard Ingram Dansey..	5 Sept. 1835
Charles Stewart Cochrane	8 Apr. 1836
Wm. Mark Lockwood ..	22 July 1836
Hon. Cornwallis Maude..	16 Sept. 1836
John Henry Ellis Ridley	23 Sept. 1836
Charles Sedley Burdett..	21 Oct. 1836
Thos. Price	2 Dec. 1836

Paymasters—

Edward Coxen.. .. 9 Feb. 1826
Rank in Army, Capt. 8 Apr. 1825
Henry Edward O'Dell .. 10 July 1835
Rank in Army, Capt. 9 Jan. 1822

Adjutants—

Thomas Townsend.. .. 24 Jan. 1828
Rank in Army, 1st Lt. 20 June 1833
Thomas Mitchell .. .. 27 Feb. 1835
Rank in Army, 2nd Lt. 27 Feb. 1835

Quartermasters—

Jonathan Booth .. .. 4 May 1826
John Brannan.. .. 18 Sept. 1835
Rank in Army, Ensign 5 Sept. 1835

Surgeons—

Francis Leigh, M.D. .. 12 Oct. 1826
Rank in Army, 9 Sept. 1813
Hugh Fraser .. .. .. 30 Dec. 1834

Assistant-Surgeons—

Peter Lamond, M.D. .. 27 May 1824
Alexander Leigh, M.D... 15 Aug. 1834
David Maurice, M.D. .. 29 May 1835
George Ferguson .. .. 30 Oct. 1835
Rank in Army, 12 June 1828

*Regimentals—*Green, facings scarlet.
*Agents—*Messrs. Cox and Co., Craig's Court.

1838.

Two Battalions.
Mediterranean.
Color et Audax.
Roleia, Vimiera, Martinique, Talavera, Fuentes de Onor, Albuhera, Ciudad Rodrigo, Badajoz, Salamanca, Vittoria, Pyrenees, Nivelle, Nive, Orthes, Toulouse, Peninsula.
Col.-in-Chief—
H.R.H. A. F., Duke of Cambridge, K.G., G.C.B., G.C.M.G., G.C.H. .. 22 Jan. 1827
Rank in Army, Field-Mar. 26 Nov. 1813

Rank and Name.	Rank in Regiment.
Cols.-Commandant—	

Sir John Maclean, K.C.B... .. .. .. 7 Jan. 1835
Rank in Army, Maj.-Gen. 27 May 1825
Hon. Patrick Stuart .. 26 Sept. 1837
Rank in Army, Lt.-Gen. 10 Jan. 1837

Lieut.-Colonels—

Hon. Augustus Frederick Ellis .. .. .. 18 Dec. 1828
Hon. Henry Richard Molyneux .. .. 24 April 1835
Rank in Army, 9 April 1829

Majors—

John Clavell Sladdon Slyfield, K.H. .. .. .. 12 April 1831
Thos. Rich. Plumbe Tempest .. .. .. 12 July 1831
Walter Trevelyan .. .. 28 Dec. 1832
Charles Markham .. .. 31 May 1833

Captains—

Melville Glenie .. .. 26 Mar. 1812
Rank in Army, Major 27 May 1825
Ambrose Sponge .. .. 18 Nov. 1824
Crosby Lewis Nesbitt .. 18 Dec. 1828
Hon. George Augustus Spencer .. .. .. 15 Jan. 1829
Rank in Army, 19 Dec. 1826
Edward Bagot.. .. .. 8 June 1830
John Sullivan Wilford .. 2 Nov. 1830
David Fitzgerald .. .. 12 July 1831
Richard Pasley .. .. 16 Mar. 1832
Randal Rumley .. .. 13 July 1832
Rank in Army, 14 Aug. 1827
Richard Gibbons .. .. 9 Aug. 1832
Fra. William Hamilton.. 15 Mar. 1833
Rank in Army, 4 Jan. 1831
Thomas Crombie .. .. 26 July 1833
Rank in Army, 18 May 1832
Freeman Murray .. .. 11 July 1834
Rank in Army, 21 Dec. 1832
George Bulman .. .. 29 May 1835
Charles Orgell Leman .. 4 Sept. 1835
Edward Carter Giffard.. 18 Dec. 1835
Rank in Army, 9 Oct. 1835
Robert Atkins.. .. .. 16 Sept. 1836
George Stewart .. .. 21 April 1837
Rank in Army, 8 July 1836
Harrington Trevelyan .. 14 July 1837
Rank in Army, 7 April 1837
James St. John Munro .. 17 Nov. 1837

First Lieutenants—

Joseph Robinson .. .. 18 Nov. 1824
Charles Howe Spence .. 28 Sept. 1826
Henry Bingham .. .. 28 Sept. 1832
Thomas Bunbury .. .. 28 Dec. 1832
John Jones .. .. .. 4 Jan. 1833
Rank in Army, 2 Dec. 1831
Wm. Henry Fitzgerald .. 31 May 1833
Thomas Townsend.. .. 20 June 1833
Hon. Theodore Dominick
Geoffrey Dillon .. .. 21 June 1833

Rank and Name.	Rank in Regiment.

First Lieutenants (continued)—

Wm. Fanshawe Bedford .. 28 June 1833
Hon. Henry Lyttleton
  Powys .. .. 19 Sept. 1834
Henry Wm. Ellis .. .. 17 April 1835
Arthur Aug. **Thurlow**
  Cunyngham .. .. 22 May 1835
Robert Aldridge .. .. 29 May 1835
Walling Everard .. .. 3 July 1835
  Rank in Army, 15 May 1835
Richard Byrd Levett .. 4 Sept. 1835
Richard Maxwell .. .. 9 Oct. 1835
  Rank in Army, 8 Feb. 1833
Francis Roger Palmer .. 26 Feb. 1836
  Rank in Army, 23 April 1835
George Henry Courtenay 8 April 1836
John Kenneth Mackenzie 16 Sept. 1836
Wm. George Rose .. .. 27 Oct. 1837
Charles Wm. Jebb .. .. 17 Nov. 1837
M. Branthwayte Weston 8 Dec. 1837

Second Lieutenants—

Sir **Ross** Mahon, Bart... 14 Dec. 1832
Stonehouse Geo. Bunbury 28 June 1833
John Stephen Robinson .. 11 April 1834
Edw. John Vesey Brown 12 Sept. 1834
Webbe Butler.. .. .. 19 Sept. 1834
Thomas Mitchell .. .. 27 Feb. 1835
Henry Robert Beresford 22 May 1835
Henry Holbech .. .. 29 May 1835
Hon. John Edmund **Hovel**
  Thurlow .. .. .. 4 Sept. 1835
Richard Ingram Dansey . 5 Sept. 1835
Charles Stewart Cochrane 8 April 1836
William Mark Lockwood 22 July 1836
Hon. Cornwallis Maude.. 16 Sept. 1836
John Henry Ellis Bailey 23 Sept. 1836
Charles Sedley Burdett.. 21 Oct. 1836
Thomas Price .. .. .. 2 Dec. 1836
Wm. Lewis Grant.. .. 7 April 1837
George Allan Hicks .. 27 Oct. 1837
John Borlase Maxwell.. 17 Nov. 1837
Thomas **Bateson** .. .. 8 Dec. 1837

Paymasters—

Edward Coxen.. .. 9 Feb. 1826
  Rank in Army, Capt. 8 April 1825
Henry Edward O'Dell .. 10 July 1835
  Rank in Army, Capt. 9 Jan. 1822

Adjutants—

Thomas Townsend.. .. 24 Jan. 1828
  Rank in Army, 1st Lt. 20 June 1833
Thomas Mitchell .. .. 27 Feb. 1835
  Rank in Army, 2nd Lt. 27 Feb. 1835

Quartermasters -

Jonathan Booth .. .. 4 May 1826
John Brannan .. .. 18 Sept. 1835
  Rank in Army, Ensign 5 Sept. 1835

Surgeons—

Francis Leigh, M D .. 12 Oct. 1826
  Rank in Army, 2 Sept. 1813
Hugh Fraser .. .. .. 30 Dec. 1834

Assistant-Surgeons -

Peter Lamond, M D. .. 27 May 1824
Alexander Leigh, M.D. .. 15 Aug. 1834

Rank and Name.	Rank in Regiment.

Assistant-Surgeons (continued)—

David Maurice, M.D. .. 29 May 1835
George Ferguson .. .. 30 Oct. 1835
  Rank in Army, 12 June 1828

Regimentals—Green, facings scarlet.

Agents—Messrs. Cox and Co., Craig's
  Court.

1839.

Two Battalions.

Mediterranean.

Celer et Audax.

Roleia, Vimiera, Martinique, Talavera,
Fuentes d'Onor, Albuhera, Ciudad Rodrigo, Badajoz, Salamanca, Vittoria,
Pyrenees, Nivelle, Nive, Orthes, Toulouse, Peninsula.

Col.-in-Chief—

H.R.H. A. F., Duke of
  Cambridge, K.G ,G.C.B.,
  G.C.M.G., O.C.H. .. 22 Jan. 1827
  Rank in Army, Field-Mar. 26 Nov. 1813

Cols.-Commandant—

Sir John Maclean,
  K.C.B. .. .. .. 7 Jan. 1835
  Rank in Army, Lt.-Gen. 28 June 1838
Hon. Patrick Stuart .. 26 Sept. 1837
  Rank in Army, Lt.-Gen. 10 Jan. 1837

Lieut.-Colonels—

Hon. Augustus Frederick
  Ellis .. .. 18 Dec. 1828
Hon. Henry Richard
  Molyneux .. .. 24 April 1835
  Rank in Army, 9 April 1829

Majors—

J. Clavell Sheldon Slyfield,
  K.H... .. .. .. 12 April 1831
Walter Trevelyan .. .. 28 Dec. 1832
Charles Markham .. .. 31 May 1833
Wemyss Thos. Cockburn, 6 July 1838
  Rank in Army, 25 Nov. 1828

Captains—

Melville Glenie .. .. 26 Mar. 1812
  Rank in Army, Bt.-Maj. 27 May 1825
Ambrose Sponge .. .. 18 Nov. 1824
  Rank in Army, Major 28 June 1838
Cosby Lewis Nesbitt .. 18 Dec. 1828
Hon. George Augustus
  Spencer .. .. .. 15 Jan. 1829
  Rank in Army, 19 Dec. 1825
Edward Bayne .. .. 8 June 1830
  Rank in Army, 8 Nov. 1827
John Sutton Watford .. 2 Nov. 1830
David Fitzgerald .. .. 12 July 1831
Richard Pasley .. .. 16 Mar. 1832
Ratclif Rumley .. .. 13 July 1832
  Rank in Army, 14 Aug. 1827
Richard Gibbons .. .. 9 Aug. 1832
Fred. Wm. Hamilton .. 15 Mar. 1833
  Rank in Army, 1 Jan. 1831
Thomas Crombie .. .. 26 July 1833
  Rank in Army, 18 May 1832

P 2

Rank and Name.	Rank in Regiment.

Captains (continued)—

Freeman Murray .. .. 11 July 1834
   Rank in Army, 21 Dec. 1832
George Bulman .. .. 9 May 1835
Charles Orgell Lemon .. 4 Sept. 1835
Edward Carter Giffard .. 18 Dec. 1835
   Rank in Army, 9 Oct. 1835
Robert Atkins.. .. .. 16 Sept. 1836
George Stewart .. .. 21 April 1837
   Rank in Army, 8 July 1836
Harrington Trevelyan .. 14 July 1837
   Rank in Army, 7 April 1837
James St. John Munro .. 17 Nov. 1837

First Lieutenants—

Joseph Robinson .. .. 18 Nov. 1824
Charles Howe Spencer .. 28 Sept. 1826
Henry Bingham .. .. 28 Sept. 1832
Thomas Bunbury .. .. 28 Dec. 1832
John Jones .. .. .. 4 Jan. 1833
   Rank in Army, 2 Dec. 1831
Wm. Henry Fitzgerald .. 31 May 1833
Thomas Townsend.. .. 20 June 1833
Hon. Theo. Dominick
  Geoffrey Dillon .. .. 21 June 1833
Wm. Fanshawe Bedford 28 June 1833
Hon. Henry Lyttleton
  Powys .. .. 19 Sept. 1834
Henry Wm. Ellis .. .. 17 April 1835
Arthur Aug. Thurlow
  Cunynghame .. .. 22 May 1835
Robert Aldridge .. .. 29 May 1835
Walling Everard .. .. 3 July 1835
   Rank in Army, 15 May 1835
Richard Byrd Levett .. 4 Sept. 1835
Richard Maxwell .. .. 9 Oct. 1835
   Rank in Army, 8 Feb. 1833
Francis Roger Palmer .. 26 Feb. 1836
   Rank in Army, 24 April 1835
George Henry Courtenay 8 April 1836
John Kenneth Mackenzie 16 Sept. 1836
Charles Wm. Jebb.. .. 17 Nov. 1837
Sir Ross Mahon, Bart. .. 23 Nov. 1838
Stonehouse Geo. Bunbury 25 Dec. 1838

Second Lieutenants—

John Stephen Robinson.. 11 April 1834
Edwd. John Vesey Brown 12 Sept. 1834
Webbe Butler.. .. .. 19 Sept. 1834
Thomas Mitchell .. .. 27 Feb. 1835
Henry Robt. Beresford .. 22 May 1835
Henry Holbech .. .. 29 May 1835
Hon. Edm. John Hovel
  Thurlow .. .. .. 4 Sept. 1835
Richard Ingram Dansey .. 5 Sept. 1835
Wm. Markwood .. .. 22 July 1836
Hon. Cornwallis Maude.. 16 Sept. 1836
John Hen. Ellis Ridley.. 23 Sept. 1836
Charles Sedley Burdett.. 21 Oct. 1836
Thomas Price.. .. .. 2 Dec. 1836
William Lewis Grant .. 7 April 1837
Geo. Allan Hicks .. .. 27 Oct. 1837
John Burlase Maunsell .. 17 Nov. 1837
Thomas Bateson .. .. 8 Dec. 1837
James Douglas .. .. 17 Aug. 1838
Hon. Adrian Hope.. .. 23 Nov. 1838
C. W. Hamilton Sotheby. 25 Dec. 1838

Rank and Name.	Rank in Regiment.

Paymasters—

Edwd. Coxen .. .. 9 Feb. 1826
   Rank in Army, Capt. 8 April 1825
Henry Edwd. Odell .. 10 July 1835
   Rank in Army, Capt. 9 June 1822

Adjutants—

Thomas Townsend.. .. 24 June 1828
   Rank in Army, 1st Lt. 20 June 1833
Thomas Mitchell .. .. 27 Feb. 1835
   Rank in Army, 2nd Lt. 27 Feb. 1835

Quartermasters—

John Brannan.. .. 18 Sept. 1835
   Rank in Army, Ensign 5 Sept. 1835
Allan Waterhouse .. .. 27 July 1838

Surgeons—

Francis Leigh, M.D. .. 12 Oct. 1826
   Rank in Army, 9 Sept. 1813
Hugh Fraser .. .. .. 30 Dec. 1834

Assistant-Surgeons—

Peter Lamond, M.D. .. 27 May 1824
Alexr. Leigh, M.D. .. 15 Aug. 1834
David Maurice, M.D. .. 29 May 1835
George Ferguson .. .. 30 Oct. 1835
   Rank in Army, 12 June 1822

Regimentals—Green, facings scarlet.

Agents—Messrs. Cox and Co., Craig's
Court.

1840.

Two Battalions.

Mediterranean—England.

Celer et Audax.

Rolcia, Vimiera, Martinique, Talavera,
Fuentes d'Onor, Albuhera, Ciudad
Rodrigo, Badajoz, Salamanca, Vittoria,
Pyrenees, Nivelle, Nive, Orthes, Tou-
louse, Peninsula.

Col.-in-Chief—

H.R.H. A. F., Duke of Cambridge,
K.G., G.C.B., G.C.M.G., G.C.H.,22 Jan.,
1827.
  Rank in Army, Field-Mar., 26 Nov. 1813

Cols.-Commandant—

Sir John Maclean, K.C.B.—Ensign, 30
April, 1794 ; Lieut., 1 May, 1794 ;
Captain, 15 June, 1797; Major, 2
August, 1804 ; Lieut.-Colonel, 9 June,
1808 ; Colonel, 14 June, 1814 ; Major-
General, 27 May, 1815 ; Lieut.-General,
28 June, 1838 ; Colonel, 60th Rifles, 7
Jan., 1835.
Hon. Patrick Stuart—Cornet and
Sub-Lieutenant, 26 Sept., 1793 ; Lieu-
tenant, 6 June, 1794 ; Captain, 12 April,
1796 ; Major, 1 Feb., 1803 ; Lieut.-
Colonel, 25 Sept., 1806 ; Colonel, 4
June, 1814 ; Major-Gen., 19 July, 1824 ;
Lieut.-Gen., 10 Jan., 1837 ; Colonel,
60th Rifles, 26 Sept., 1837.

Lieut.-Colonels—

Hon. Aug. Fred. Ellis—Cornet, 10
April, 1817 ; Lieutenant, 17 Dec.,
1818 ; Captain, 21 Oct., 1824 ; Major

Lieut.-Colonels (continued)—

12 Nov., 1825 ; Lieut.-Col., **18 Dec.,** 1828.

Hon. Henry Richard Molyneux—Ensign, 22 May, 1817 ; Lieutenant, 24 Oct. 1821 ; Captain, 9 May, 1823 ; Major, 24 Aug., 1826 ; Lieut.-Col., 9 April, 1829.

Majors—

J. Clavel Staddon Slyfield, K.H.—Ensign, 15 Oct., 1812 ; Lieutenant, 30 Mar. 1814 ; Captain, 26 May, 1825 ; Major, 12 April, 1831.

Walter Trevelyan—2nd Lieutenant, 18 Nov.,1817; Lieutenant, 20 Sept. 1825; Captain, 19 Sept., 1826 ; Major, 28 Dec., 1832.

Charles Markham—Cornet, 28 June, 1821 ; Lieutenant, 23 June, 1825 ; Captain, 29 Aug., 1826 ; Major, 31 May, 1833.

Wemyss Thos. Cockburne—Cornet, 22 May, 1817 ; Lieutenant, 10 Dec., 1818 ; Captain, 26 Dec., 1822 ; Major, 25 Nov., 1828.

Captains—	Rank and Name.	Rank in Regiment.
Melville Glenie	..	4 July 1808
Rank in Army, Bt.-Maj	27 May	1825
Ambrose Spooge	18 Nov.	1824
Rank in Army, Bt.-Maj	28 June	1838
Cosby Lewis Nesbitt	..	18 Dec. 1828
Hon. Aug. G. Spencer	..	19 Dec. 1826
Edward Bagot	..	8 Nov. 1827
John Sutton Wilford	..	2 Nov. 1830
David Fitzgerald	..	12 July 1831
Randal Rumley	..	14 Aug. 1832
Richard Gibbons	..	9 Aug. 1832
Fred. Wm. Hamilton	..	4 Jan. 1831
Thos. Crombie	..	18 May 1832
Freeman Murray	..	29 May 1835
George Buhman	..	29 May 1835
Chas. Orgell Leman	..	4 Sept. 1835
Edward Carter Giffard	..	9 Oct. 1835
Robert Atkins	..	16 Sept. 1836
George Stewart	..	8 July 1836
Harrington Trevelyan	..	7 April 1837
James St. John Munro	..	17 Nov. 1837
John Temple	..	28 Jan. 1826

First Lieutenants—		
Charles Howe Spence	..	28 Sept. 1826
Henry Bingham	..	28 Sept. 1832
Thomas Bunbury	..	28 Sept. 1832
John Jones	..	2 Dec. 1831
Thomas Townsend	..	20 June 1833
Hon. Theo. D. G. Dillon	24 June 1833
Wm. Fanshawe Belford	28 June 1834
Hon. H. Lyttleton Powys	19 Sept. 1834
Henry Wm. Ellis	..	17 April 1835
A. A. T. Cunynghame	..	22 May 1835
Robert Aldridge	..	29 May 1835
Walling Everard	..	15 May 1835
Rich. Byrd Levett	..	4 Sept. 1835
Rich. Maxwell	..	8 Feb. 1833
Fra. Roger Palmer	..	24 April 1835
Geo. Hen. Courtenay	..	8 April 1836

Rank and Name.		Rank in Regiment.
First Lieutenants (continued)—		
J. Kenneth Mackenzie	..	16 Sept. 1836
Charles Wm. Jebb	..	17 Nov. 1837
Sir Ross Mahon, Bart.	..	23 Nov. 1838
Wm. Stamer O'Grady	..	31 Oct. 1834
John Stephen Robinson	..	19 Oct. 1839

Second Lieutenants—		
Edw. J. Vesey Brown	..	12 Sept. 1834
Webbe Butler	..	19 Sept. 1834
Thomas Mitchell	..	27 Feb. 1835
Henry R. Beresford	..	22 May 1835
Henry Holbech	..	30 May 1835
Hon. J. E. H. Thurlow	..	4 Sept. 1835
R. Ingram Dansey	..	5 Sept. 1835
Wm. Monk Wood	..	22 July 1836
Hon. Cornwallis Maude	..	16 Sept. 1836
John H. E. Ridley	..	23 Sept. 1836
Cha. Sedley Burdett	..	21 Oct. 1836
Wm. Lewis Grant	..	7 April 1837
George Allan Hicks	..	27 Oct. 1837
Thomas Batesman	..	8 Dec. 1837
James Douglas	..	17 Aug. 1838
Hon. Adrian Hope	..	23 Nov. 1838
Chas. W. H. Sotheby	..	25 Dec. 1838
Hon. A. C. L. Fitzroy	17 May 1839
Hon. Ellis R. Plunkett	..	20 July 1839
Rich. F. Waldo Sibthorp	20 Sept. 1839
John Breedon	..	19 Oct. 1839

Paymasters—

☒ Edward Cozen, 9 Feb. 1826 ; 2nd Lieutenant, 5 April, 1820 ; Lieutenant, 28 June, 1810 ; Captain, 8 April, 1825.

Wm. Henry FitzGerald, 20 Sept., 1839 ; Ensign, 17 Jan., 1828 ; Lieutenant, 31 May, 1833.

Adjutants—

Thomas Townsend, 1st Lieut., 24 Jan., 1828.

Thomas Mitchell, 2nd Lieut., 27 Feb., 1835.

Quartermasters—

☒ John Brennan, 18 Sept., 1835 ; Ensign, 5 Sept., 1835.

Allen Waterhouse, 27 July, 1838.

Surgeons—

Hugh Fraser, 30 Oct., 1834 ; Assistant-Surgeon, 26 July, 1815.

Peter Lamond, M.D., 7 June, 1839 ; Assistant-Surgeon, 27 May, 1824 ; Hospital Assistant, 16 June, 1815.

Assistant-Surgeons—

David Maurice, M.D., 29 May, 1835. George Ferguson, 12 June, 1828 ; Hospital Assistant, 8 Nov., 1826.

Johnstone Thomas Richardson, M.D., 1 Feb., 1839.

Joshua Paynter, 11 Jan., 1839.

Regimentals—Green, facings scarlet.

Agents Messrs. Cox and Co.

Irish Agent Sir E. R. Borough, Bart., Craig's Court.

1841.

Two Battalions.

England—Mediterranean—West Indies.

Celer et Audax.

Rolica, Vimiera, Martinique, Talavera, Fuentes d'Onor, Albuhera, Ciudad Rodrigo, Badajoz, Salamanca, Vittoria, Pyrenees, Nivelle, Nive, Orthes, Toulouse, Peninsula.

Col.-in-Chief—

H.R.H. A. F., Duke of Cambridge, K.G.,G.C.B., G.C.M.G.,G.C.H.,22Jan., 1827.

Rank in Army, Field-Mar. 26 Nov. 1813

Cols.-Commandant

Sir John Maclean, K.C.B.—Ensign, 30 April, 1794; Lieut., 1 May, 1794; Captain, 15 June, 1797; Major, 2 Aug., 1804; Lieut.-Col., 9 June, 1808; Col. 4 June, 1814; Major-Gen., 27 May, 1825; Lieut.-Gen., 28 June, 1838; Col. 60th Rifles, 7 Jan., 1835.

Hon. Patrick Stuart—Cornet and Sub-Lieutenant, 26 Sept. 1793; Lieutenant, 6 June, 1794; Captain, 12 April, 1796; Major, 1 Feb., 1803; Lieut.-Col. 25 Sept., 1806; Colonel, 4 June, 1814; Major-Gen., 19 July, 1821; Lieutenant-Gen., 10 Jan.1837; Colonel 60th Rifles, 26 Sept. 1837.

Lieut.-Colonels—

Hon.Aug.Fred.Ellis—Cornet,10 April, 1817; Lieut. 17 Dec. 1818; Captain, 24 Oct. 1821; Major, 12 Nov. 1825; Lieut.-Colonel, 18 Dec. 1828.

Hon. Hen. Rich. Molyneux—Ensign, 22 May, 1817; Lieut., 24 Oct., 1821; Captain, 9 May, 1823; Major, 29 Aug. 1826; Lieut.-Colonel, 9 April, 1829.

Majors—

J. Clavell Shaddon Slyfield, K.H.—Ensign, 15 Oct. 1812; Lieut., 30 Mar., 1814; Captain, 26 May, 1825; Major, 12 April, 1831.

Walter Trevelyan—2nd Lt., 18 Nov. 1817; Lieut., 25 Sept., 1825; Captain, 19 Sept. 1826; Major, 28 Dec., 1832.

Charles Markham—Cornet, 28 June, 1821; Lieut., 13 June, 1825; Captain, 29 Aug. 1826; Major, 31 May, 1833.

Wemyss Thos. Cockburn—22 May, 1817; Lieut., 10 Dec., 1818; Captain, 26 Dec., 1822; Major, 25 Nov. 1828.

Captains —

Rank and Name.	Rank in Regiment.
Melville Glenie	4 July 1808
Rank in Army, Bt.-Maj.27 May 1825	
Ambrose Sponge	18 Nov. 1821
Rank in Army, Bt.-Maj. 28 June 1838	
Cosby Lewis Nesbitt ..	18 Dec. 1824
Hon. G. Aug. Spencer ..	19 Dec. 1825
Edward Bagot..	8 Nov. 1827
John Sutton Wilford ..	2 Nov. 1830
David Fitzgerald	12 July 1831
Randal Rumley	14 Aug. 1827

Rank and Name.	Rank in Regiment.
Captains (continued)—	
Richard Gibbons	7 Aug. 1832
Fred. Wm. Hamilton ..	4 Jan. 1831
Thomas Crombie	18 May 1832
Freeman Murray	21 Dec. 1832
Edward Carter Giffard ..	9 Oct. 1835
Robert Atkins..	16 Sept.1836
George Stewart	8 July 1836
Harrington Trevelyan ..	7 April 1837
James St. John Munro ..	17 Nov. 1837
John Temple	28 Jan. 1826
Robt. Spread Grady ..	10 Jan. 1840
Joseph Robinson	7 June 1839
First Lieutenants—	
Chas. Howe Spence ..	28 Sept. 1826
Henry Bingham	28 Sept. 1832
John Jones	2 Dec. 1831
Thomas Townsend.. ..	20 June 1833
Hon.Theo. D. G.Dillon..	21 June 1833
Wm. Fanshawe Bedford	28 June 1833
Hon. H. Lyttleton Fowys	19 Sept. 1824
Henry Wm. Ellis	17 April 1835
A. A. T. Cunynghame ..	22 May 1835
Robt. Aldridge	29 May 1835
Walling Everard	15 May 1835
Rich. Byrd Levett.. ..	4 Sept. 1835
Fra. Roger Palmer.. ..	24 April 1835
Geo. Hen. Courtenay ..	8 April 1836
J. K. Mackenzie	16 Sept. 1836
Chas. Wm. Jebb	17 Nov. 1837
Sir Ross Mahon, Bart. ..	23 Nov. 1838
Wm. Stauer O'Grady ..	31 Oct. 1834
John Stephen Robinson..	19 Oct. 1839
Edw. Missenden Love ..	17 Aug. 1838
Webbe Butler	15 Dec. 1840
Second Lieutenants -	
Edw. J. Vesey Brown ..	12 Sept. 1834
Thomas Mitchell	27 Feb. 1835
Hon. R. Beresford.. ..	22 May 1835
Henry Holbech	22 May 1835
Hon.J. E. H. Thurlow..	4 Sept. 1835
Wm. Mark Wood	22 July 1836
Chas. Sedley Burdett ..	21 Oct. 1836
James Douglas	17 Aug. 1838
Hon. Adrian Hope.. ..	23 Nov. 1838
Chas. W. H. Sotheby ..	25 Dec. 1838
Hon. A. C. L. Fitzroy ..	17 May 1839
Rich. F. Waldo Sibthorp	20 Sept. 1839
John Breedon..	19 Oct. 1839
Dudl. Wilmot Carleton..	10 April 1840
Aug. Rich. Saunders ..	12 June 1840
Wm. Greufell	3 July 1840
Thos. Somers Armstrong	28 July 1840
Ashton Mosley	28 Aug. 1840
Hen. Friend Kennedy ..	11 Sept. 1840
Fred. Marcus Callaghan..	9 Oct. 1840
Henry Robinson	15 Dec. 1840
Paymasters—	

[C] Edward Coxen, 9 Feb., 1826; 2nd Lieut., 5 April, 1804; Lieut., 28 June, 1840; Captain, 8 April, 1825.

Wm. Henry Fitzgerald, 20 Sept., 1839; Ensign, 17 Jan., 1828; Lieut., 31 May, 1838.

Adjutants-

T.Townsend, 1st.Lieut., 24 Jan., 1828

Adjutants (continued)—
  Thomas Mitchell, 2nd Lieut., 27 Feb.,
  1835.
Quartermasters—
  Wm. John Brannan, 18 Sept., 1835 ;
  Ensign, 5 Sept., 1835.
  Allan Waterhouse, 27 July, 1838.
Surgeons—
  Hugh Fraser, 30 Dec., 1834 ; Assist.-
  Surgeon, 26 Jan., 1815 ; Hospital-Assist-
  ant, 10 May, 1813.
  Thos. Hall, 29 May, 1840 ; Assistant-
  Surgeon, 30 June, 1825 ; Hospital-
  Assistant, 19 May, 1815.
Assistant-Surgeons—
  David Maurice, M.D., 29 May, 1835.
  Geo. Ferguson, 12 June, 1828 ; Hos-
  pital-Assistant, 8 Nov. 1826.
  Johnstone Thomson Richardson, M.D.,
  1 Feb., 1839.

Regimentals—Green, facings scarlet.

Agents—Messrs. Cox and Co.

Irish Agents—Sir E. R. Borough, Bart. ;
  Armit and Co.

1842.

Two Battalions.

England—West Indies.

Color of Audax.

Rolein, Vimiera, Martinique, Talavera,
Fuentes d'Onor, Albuhera, Cindad
Rodrigo, Badajoz, Salamanca, Vit-
toria, Pyrenees, Nivelle, Nive, Orthes,
Toulouse, Peninsula.

Col.-in-Chief—
  H.R.H. A. F., Duke of Cambridge,
  K.G.,G.C.B.,G.C.M.G., G.C.H., 22 Jan.,
  1827.
  Rank in Army, Field-Mar., 26 Nov. 1813.
Cols.-Commandant—
  Sir John Maclean, K.C.B.—Ensign,
  30 April, 1794 ; Lieut., 1 May, 1794 ;
  Captain, 15 June, 1797 ; Major, 2 Aug.,
  1804 ; Lieut.-Colonel, 9 June, 1808 ;
  Colonel, 4 June, 1814 ; Major-Gen., 27
  May, 1825 ; Lieut.-Gen., 28 June, 1838 ;
  Colonel 46th Rifles, 7 Jan., 1835.
  Hon. Patrick Stuart—Cornet and Sub-
  Lieut., 26 Sept., 1793 ; Lieut., 6 June,
  1794 ; Captain, 12 April, 1796 ; Major,
  1 Feb., 1803 ; Lieut.-Col., 25 Sept., 1808 ;
  Colonel, 4 June, 1814 ; Major-Gen., 19
  July, 1821 ; Lieut.-Gen., 10 Jan., 1837 ;
  Colonel 69th Rifles, 26 Sept., 1847.
Lieut.-Colonels—
  Walter Trevelyan—2nd Lieut., 18 Nov.,
  1817 ; Lieut., 25 Sept., 1825 ; Captain,
  19 Sept., 1826 ; Major, 28 Dec., 1832 ;
  Lieut.-Colonel, 10 Aug., 1841.
  Charles Markham—Cornet, 28 June,
  1821 ; Lieut., 23 June, 1825 ; Captain,
  29 Aug., 1826 ; Major, 31 May, 1833 ;
  Lieut.-Colonel, 17 Aug., 1841.

Majors—
  Wemyss Thos. Cockburn—Cornet, 22
  May, 1817 ; Lieut., 10 Dec., 1818 ;
  Capt., 26 Dec., 1822 ; Major, 25 Nov.,
  1828 ; Brevet Lieut.-Col., 23 Nov., 1841.
  Cosby Lewis Nesbitt—2nd Lieut., 27
  Mar., 1824 ; Lieut., 2 June, 1825 ;
  Capt., 18 Dec., 1829 ; Major, 10 Aug.,
  1841.
  Hon. George Augustus Spencer—2nd
  Lieut., 12 Feb., 1824 ; Lieut., 16 June,
  1825 ; Captain, 19 Dec., 1826 ; Major,
  17 Aug., 1841.
  Thomas Crombie—Ensign, 12 Aug.,
  1824 ; Lieut., 8 April, 1826 ; Captain,
  18 May, 1832 ; Major, 16 Nov., 1841.

Rank and Name.	*Rank in Regiment.*
Captains—	
Edward Bagot.. ..	8 Nov. 1827
Rank in Army, Bt.-Maj.	23 Nov. 1841
John Sutton Wilford ..	2 Nov. 1830
Randal Rumley ..	14 Aug. 1827
Rank in Army, Bt.-Maj.	23 Nov. 1841
Freeman Murray	21 Dec. 1832
Edward Carter Giffard ..	9 Oct. 1835
Harrington Trevelyan ..	7 Apr. 1837
James St. John Munro ..	17 Nov. 1837
John Temple	28 Jan. 1826
Rank in Army, Bt.-Maj.	23 Nov. 1841
Robert Spread Grady ..	10 Jan. 1840
Joseph Robinson ..	7 June 1839
Charles Howe Spence ..	24 May 1841
Henry Bingham	25 June 1841
John Jones	16 July 1841
Wm. Fanshawe Bedford	23 July 1841
Thomas Townsend ..	10 Aug. 1841
Andrew Carden ..	30 Dec. 1841
Robert Aldridge ..	24 Sept. 1841
Hon. H. Lyttleton Powys	17 Aug. 1841
Walling Everard ..	16 Nov. 1841
George Isaac Austin ..	26 June 1835
First Lieutenants—	
Fras. Roger Palmer.. ..	24 Apr. 1835
Geo. Henry Courtenay ..	8 Apr. 1836
J. K. Mackenzie, D. Adj.	16 Sept. 1836
Sir Ross Mahon, Bart. ..	23 Nov. 1838
Edwd. Missenden Love..	17 Aug. 1838
Webbe Butler.. ..	15 Dec. 1840
Thomas Mitchell ..	29 Dec. 1840
Hon. Robert Beresford ..	5 Jan. 1841
Henry Holbech ..	4 Mar. 1841
Hon. J. E. H. Thurlow ..	19 Mar. 1841
William Mark Wood ..	24 May 1841
Charles Scilley Burslett ..	25 June 1841
James Douglas ..	16 July 1841
Hon. Adrian Hope	23 April 1841
Chas. Wm. H. Sotheby ..	17 Aug. 1841
R. F. Waldo Sibthorp ..	10 Sept. 1841
John Brereton	24 Sept. 1841
Augustus R. Saunders ..	14 Oct. 1841
William Grenfell ..	14 Oct. 1841
T. Somers Armstrong ..	16 Nov. 1841
Douglas Jones.. ..	26 Nov. 1841
Second Lieutenants—	
Ashton Mosley	28 Aug. 1840
Henry Friend Kennedy	11 Sept. 1840

Rank and Name.	Rank in Regiment.

Second Lieutenants (continued)—

Fred. Marcus Callaghan	9 Oct. 1840
Henry Robinson	15 Dec. 1840
George Clapcott	29 Dec. 1840
Dudley Loftus Magan ..	5 Jan. 1841
Geo. Waldegrave Bligh	12 Mar. 1841
Godfrey Rhodes	19 Mar. 1841
Stephen Kenny	8 June 1841
Gibbes Rigaud	11 June 1841
Edw. Fitzger. Campbell..	2 July 1841
Eustace Henry Rose ..	16 July 1841
Peter Burton Rose.. ..	23 July 1841
William Roche	17 Aug. 1841
Wm. Percival Salmon ..	27 Aug. 1841
James Fraser..	10 Sept. 1841
Richard O'Connor	23 Sept. 1841
George Vavasour	24 Sept. 1841
Edward Coxen	14 Oct. 1841
Edw. Rowland Forman	15 Oct. 1841
Edmund Bellairs	16 Nov. 1841

Paymasters—

Edward Coxen, 9 Feb. 1826—2nd Lieut., 28 June, 1810; Captain, 8 April, 1825.

Wm. Henry Fitzgerald, 20 Sept. 1839 —Ensign, 17 Jan. 1828; Lieut.,31 May, 1833.

Adjutants—

T. Mitchell, 1st Lieut., 27 Feb., 1835.

Richard O'Connor, 2nd Lieut., 23 Sept., 1841.

Quartermasters—

John Brannan, 18 Sept., 1835 —Ensign, 5 Sept., 1835.

Allan Waterhouse, 27 July, 1835.

Surgeons—

Hugh Fraser, 30 Dec.,1834—Assistant-Surg., 26 Jan., 1815; Hospital-Assist., 10 May, 1843.

Thos. Hall, 29 May,1840—Assistant-Surg., 30 June, 1825; Hospital-Assist., 19 May, 1845.

Assistant-Surgeons—

David Maurice, M.D., 29 May, 1835.

Johnstone Thompson Richardson, M.D., 1 Feb., 1839.

Thomas Cowan, M.D., 17 Sept., 1841.

Regimentals—Green, facings scarlet.

Agents—Messrs. Cox and Co.; Irish Agent, Sir E. R. Borough, Bart.; Armit and Co.

1843.

Two Battalions.

England—Ireland—West Indies.

Color et Aulax.

Roleia, Vimiera, Martinique. Talavera, Fuentes d'Onor, Albuhera, Ciudad Rodrigo, Badajoz, Salamanca, Vittoria, Pyrenees, Nivelle, Nive, Orthes, Toulouse, Peninsula.

Col.-in-Chief—

H.R.H. A. F., Duke of Cambridge, K.G.,G.C.B.,G.C.M.G.,G.C.H.,22 Jan., 1827.

Rank in Army, Field-Mar., 26 Nov. 1813.

Cols.-Commandant—

Hon.Patrick Stuart—Cornet and Sub.-Lieut., 26 Sept., 1793; Lieut., 6 June, 1794; Captain, 12 April,1796; Major, 1 Feb., 1803; Lieut.-Colonel, 25 Sept., 1806; Colonel, 4 June, 1814; Major-Gen., 19 July, 1821; Lieut.-Gen., 10 Jan., 1837; Colonel 60th Rifles, 26 Sept., 1837.

Sir Wm.Gabriel Davy, C.B.,K.C.H.—Ensign, March, 1797; Lieut., 22 May, 1797; Captain, 1 Jan., 1802; Major, 5 Feb., 1807; Lieut.-Col., 28 Dec., 1809; Colonel, 12 Aug., 1819; Major-Gen., 22 July, 1830; Lieut.-Gen., 23 Nov., 1841; Colonel,60th Rifles, 2 Nov., 1842.

Lieut.-Colonels—

Walter Trevelyan—2nd Lieut.,18Nov., 1817; Lieut., 25 Sept. 1825; Captain, 19 Sept., 1826; Major, 28 Dec., 1832; Lieut.-Col., 10 Aug., 1841.

Wemyss Thomas Cockburn—Cornet, 22 May, 1817; Lieut., 10 Dec., 1818; Captain, 26 Dec., 1822; Major, 25 Nov., 1828; Brevet Lieut.-Col., 23 Nov., 1841; Lieut.-Col., 23 April, 1842.

Majors—

Cosby Lewis Nesbitt—2nd Lieut., 27 March, 1824; Lieut., 2 June, 1825; Captain, 18 Dec., 1828; Major, 10 Aug., 1841.

Hon. Augustus Spencer—2nd Lieut., 12 Feb., 1824; Lieut., 16 June, 1825; Captain, 19 Dec., 1826; Major, 17 Aug., 1841.

Thomas Crombie—Ensign, 12 August, 1824; Lieut., 8 April, 1826; Captain, 18 May, 1832; Major, 16 Nov., 1841.

John Sutton Wilford—2nd Lieut., 19 Nov., 1824; Lieut., 25 Dec., 1825; Captain, 2 Nov., 1830; Major, 23 April, 1842.

Rank and Name.	Rank in Regiment.

Captains—

Randal Rumley	14 Aug. 1827
Rank in Army, Bt.-Maj.	23 Nov. 1841
Freeman Murray	21 Dec. 1832
Edward Carter Giffard ..	9 Oct. 1835
Harrington Trevelyan ..	7 Nov. 1837
James St. John Munro ..	17 Nov. 1837
John Temple	28 Jan. 1826
Rank in Army, Bt.-Maj.	23 Nov. 1826
Robert Spread Grady ..	10 Jan. 1840
Joseph Robinson	7 June 1839
Chas. Howe Spence ..	24 May 1841
Henry Bingham	25 June 1841
John Jones	16 July 1841
Wm. Fanshawe Bedford	23 July 1841
Thomas Townsend.. ..	10 Aug. 1841
Andrew Carden	30 Dec. 1840
Robt. Aldridge	24 Sept. 1841
Hon. H. Lyttleton Powys	17 Aug. 1841
Walling Everard	16 Nov. 1841
Fra. Roger Palmer.. ..	11 Mar. 1842
John K. Mackenzie ..	23 April 1842
Edward Missenden Love	20 Dec. 1842

Rank and Name.	Rank in Regiment.
First Lieutenants—	
Webbe Butler ..	15 Dec. 1840
Thomas Mitchell ..	29 Dec. 1840
Henry Holbech ..	4 Mar. 1841
Hon. J. E. H. Thurlow..	19 Mar. 1841
William Mark Wood ..	24 May 1841
James Douglas ..	16 July 1841
Hon. Adrian Hope..	23 April 1841
Chas. Wm. H. Sotheby..	17 Aug. 1841
Rich. F. Waldo Sibthorp	10 Sept. 1841
John Breedon ..	24 Sept. 1841
Aug. Richards Saunders	14 Oct. 1841
Wm. Grenfell ..	14 Oct. 1841
Thos. Somers Armstrong.	16 Nov. 1841
Douglas Jones.. ..	26 Nov. 1841
Charles Napier North ..	28 Dec. 1838
John Wingfield Fraser ..	19 July 1839
John Francis Jones ..	12 April 1839
Ashton Moseley ..	11 Mar. 1842
Henry Friend Kennedy	7 April 1842
Fred. Marcus Callaghan	23 April 1842
Henry Robinson ..	20 Dec. 1842
Second Lieutenants—	
Geo. Clapcott . ..	29 Dec. 1840
Geo. Waldegrave Bligh..	12 Mar. 1841
Godfrey Rhodes ..	19 Mar. 1841
Stephen Kemp ..	8 June 1841
Gibbes Rigaud ..	11 June 1841
Edw. Fitzgerald Campbell	2 July 1841
Eustace Henry Rose ..	16 July 1841
Peter Barton Rose ..	23 July 1841
William Roche ..	17 Aug. 1841
Wm. Percival Salmon ..	27 Aug. 1841
James Fraser	10 Sept. 1841
Richard O'Connor..	23 Sept. 1841
Geo. Vavasour ..	24 Sept. 1841
Edward Coxen.. ..	14 Oct. 1841
Ed. Rowland Forman ..	15 Oct. 1841
Henry Saunders ..	31 Dec. 1841
Henry Lawrie Bruyeres..	11 Mar. 1842
William Parker ..	20 May 1842
John Washington ..	17 June 1842
William Ferguson Laing	
Mason..	16 Aug. 1842
John Bailie	20 Dec. 1842

Paymasters—

☒ Edward Coxen, 9 Feb., 1826; 2nd Lieut., 5 April, 1825; Lieut., 28 June, 1810; Captain, 8 April, 1825.

William Henry Fitzgerald, 20 Sept., 1839; Ensign, 17 Jan., 1828; Lieut., 31 May, 1833.

Adjutants—

Thomas Mitchell, 1st Lieut., 27 Feb., 1835.

Richard O'Connor, 2nd Lieut., 23 Sept., 1841.

Quartermasters—

☒ John Brannan, 18 Sept., 1835; Ensign, 5 Sept., 1835.

Thomas Berry, 29 March, 1842.

Surgeons—

Hugh Fraser, 30 Dec. 1844; Assistant-Surgeon, 26 Jan., 1815; Hospital-Assist., 10 May, 1815.

Thomas Hall, 29 May, 1840; Assistant-

Surgeons (continued.)—

Surgeon, 30 June, 1825; Hospital-Assist. 19 May, 1815.

Assistant-Surgeons—

David Maurice, M.D., 29 May, 1835.

Johnstone Thomson Richardson, M.D., 1 Feb., 1839.

Thomas Cowan, M.D., 17 Sept., 1841.

Regimentals—Green, facings scarlet.

Agents—Messrs. Cox and Co.

Irish Agents—Sir E. R. Boroughs, Bart.; Armit and Co.

1844.

Two Battalions.

Ireland—West Indies—North America.

Celer et Audax.

Roleia, Vimiera, Martinique, Talavera, Fuentes d'Onor, Albuhera, Ciudad Rodrigo, Badajoz, Salamanca, Vittoria, Pyrenees, Nivelle, Nive, Orthes, Toulouse, Peninsula.

Col.-in-Chief—

H.R.H. A. F., Duke of Cambridge, K.G., G.C.B., G.C.M.G., G.C.H., 22 Jan., 1827.

Rank in Army, Field-Mar., 26 Nov. 1813.

Cols.-Commandant—

Sir Wm. Gabriel Davy, C.B., K.C.H. —Ensign, March, 1797; Lieutenant, 22 May, 1797; Captain, 1 Jan., 1802; Major, 5 Feb., 1807; Lieut.-Colonel, 28 Dec., 1809; Colonel, 12 Aug., 1819; Major-Gen., 22 July, 1830; Lieutenant-Gen., 23 Nov., 1841; Colonel 60th, 2 Nov., 1842.

Sir Wm. Cornwallis Eustace, C.B., K.C.H.—Lieutenant, 27 Feb., 1781; Captain, 24 Dec., 1802; Major, 17 Mar., 1808; Lieut.-Colonel, 23 Aug., 1810; Colonel, 12 Aug., 1813; Major-General, 22 July, 1830; Lieut.-Gen., 23 Nov., 1841; Colonel, 60th Rifles, 7 April, 1843.

Lieut.-Colonels—

Walter Trevelyan, 2nd Lieut., 18 Nov., 1817; Lieut., 25 Sept., 1825; Captain, 19 Sept., 1826; Major, 28 Dec., 1842; Lieut.-Colonel, 10 Aug., 1844.

Wemyss Thomas Cockburn—Cornet, 22 May, 1817; Lieutenant, 10 Dec., 1818; Captain, 26 Nov., 1822; Major, 25 Nov., 1828; Brevet Lieut.-Colonel, 23 Nov., 1841; Lieut.-Colonel, 23 April, 1842.

Majors—

Cosby Lewis Nesbitt, 2nd Lieut., 27 March, 1824; Lieutenant, 2 June, 1825; Captain, 18 Dec., 1828; Major, 10 Aug., 1841.

Hon Geo. Augustus Spencer, 2nd Lieut., 12 Feb., 1824; Lieutenant, 16 June, 1825; Captain, 19 Dec., 1826; Major, 17 Aug., 1841.

Majors (continued)—

Thomas Crombie—Ensign, 12 Aug., 1824; Lieutenant, 8 April, 1828; Capt., 18 May, 1832; Major, 16 Nov., 1841.

John Sutton Wilford—2nd Lieutenant, 19 Nov., 1824; Lieutenant, 25 Dec., 1825; Captain, 2 Nov., 1830; Major, 23 April, 1842.

Rank and Name.		*Rank in Regiment.*

Captains—

Randal Rumley .. .. 14 Aug. 1827
   Rank in Army, Bt.-Maj. 23 Nov. 1841
Freeman Murray .. 21 Dec. 1832
Edward Carter Giffard .. 9 Oct. 1835
Harrington Trevelyan .. 7 April 1837
James St. John Munro .. 17 Nov. 1837
John Temple .. .. .. 28 Jan. 1826
   Rank in Army, Bt.-Maj. 23 Nov. 1841
Joseph Robinson .. .. 7 June 1839
Chas. Howe Spence .. 27 May 1841
Henry Bingham .. 25 June 1841
John Jones .. .. .. 16 July 1841
Wm. Fanshawe Bedford 23 July 1841
Thomas Townsend .. .. 10 Aug. 1841
Andrew Carden .. 30 Dec. 1840
Robert Aldridge .. .. 24 Sept. 1841
Hon. H. Lyttleton Powys 17 Aug. 1841
Walling Everard .. 16 Nov. 1841
Fra. Roger Palmer.. .. 11 Mar. 1842
John Kean Mackenzie .. 23 April 1842
Edward Missenden Love 20 Dec. 1842
James Thomas .. .. 7 Aug. 1842

First Lieutenants—

Webbe Butler .. .. 15 Dec. 1840
Thomas Mitchell .. 29 Dec. 1840
Henry Holbech .. .. 4 Mar. 1841
Hon. J. E. H. Thurlow.. 19 Mar. 1841
Wm. Mark Wood .. .. 24 May 1841
James Douglas .. 16 July 1841
Hon. Adrian Hope.. .. 23 April 1841
Chas. Wm. H. Sotheby.. 17 Aug. 1841
Rich. F. Waldo Sibthorp 19 Sept. 1841
Aug. Richard Saunders.. 14 Oct. 1841
Wm. Grenfell .. 14 Oct. 1841
Thos. Somers Armstrong 16 Nov. 1841
Douglas Jones .. .. 26 Nov. 1841
Charles Napier North .. 28 Dec. 1838
John Wingfield S. Fraser 19 July 1839
John Francis Jones,. .. 12 April 1839
Ashton Moseley .. 11 Mar. 1842
Henry Friend Kennedy.. 7 April 1842
Fred. Marcus Callaghan.. 24 April 1842
Henry Robinson .. .. 20 Dec. 1842
George Clapcott .. .. 31 Mar. 1843

Second Lieutenants—

Geo. Waldegrave Bligh.. 12 Mar. 1841
Godfrey Rhodes .. .. 19 Mar. 1841
Stephen Kenny .. 8 June 1841
Gibbs Rigaud .. .. 11 June 1841
Edw. Fitzgerald Campbell 2 July 1841
Eustace Henry Rose .. 16 July 1841
Peter Burton Roe .. 23 July 1841
Wm. Roche .. .. 17 Aug. 1841
Wm. Percival Salmon .. 27 Aug. 1841
James Fraser .. .. 10 Sept. 1841
George Vavasour .. 21 Sept. 1841
Edward Coxen .. 14 Oct. 1841

Rank and Name.	*Rank in Regiment.*

Second Lieutenants (continued)—

Edw. Rowland Forman.. 15 Oct. 1841
Henry Saunders .. .. 31 Dec. 1841
Henry Lawrie Bruyeres.. 11 Mar. 1842
Wm. Biddulph Parker .. 20 May 1842
John Warburton .. .. 17 June 1842
W. Ferguson Laing Mason 16 Aug. 1842
John Bailie .. .. .. 20 Dec. 1842
Randle Joseph Fielden.. 31 Mar. 1843
Geo. Bingham Jennings 21 July 1843

Paymasters—

Edward Coxen, 9 Feb., 1826; 2nd Lieutenant, 5 April, 1809; Lieutenant, 28 June, 1810; Captain, 8 April, 1825.

William Henry Fitzgerald, 20 Sept., 1839; Ensign, 17 Jan., 1828; Lieut., 31 May, 1833.

Adjutants—

Thomas Mitchell, 1st Lieut., 27 Feb., 1835.

Stephen Kenny, 2nd Lieut., 9 May, 1843.

Quartermasters—

John Brannan, 18 Sept., 1835; Ensign, 5 Sept., 1835.

Thomas Berry, 29 March, 1842.

Surgeons—

Charles Robert Boyes, M.D., 2 July, 1841; Assistant - Surgeon, 22 Nov., 1827; Hospital-Assist., 17 Aug., 1826.

Augustus Henry Cowen, 2 July, 1841; Assist.-Surgeon, 29 July, 1839; Hospital-Assist., 2 Nov., 1826.

Assistant-Surgeons—

David Maurice, M.D., 29 May, 1835.

Johnstone Thomson Richardson,M.D., 1 Feb., 1839.

Thomas Cowan, M.D., 17 Sept., 1841.

Regimentals—Green, facings scarlet.

Agents—Messrs. Cox and Co.

1845.

Two Battalions.

Ireland—India—North America.

Celer et Audax.

Roleia, Vimiera, Martinique, Talavera, Fuentes d'Onor, Albuhera, Ciudad Rodrigo, Badajoz, Salamanca, Vittoria, Pyrenees, Nivelle, Nive, Orthes, Toulouse, Peninsula.

Col.-in-Chief—

H.R.H. A. F., Duke of Cambridge, K.G.,G.C.B., G.C.M.G., G.C.H.,22 Jan., 1827.

   Rank in Army, Field-Mar., 26 Nov. 1813.

Cols.-Commandant—

Sir Wm. Gabriel Davy, C.B., K.C.H., — Ensign, March 1797; Lieut., 22 May, 1797; Captain, 1 Jan. 1802; Major, 5 Feb. 1807; Lieut.-Colonel, 28 Dec. 1809; Colonel, 12 Aug. 1819; Major-Gen., 22 July, 1830; Lieut.-Gen., 23 Nov. 1841; Col. 60th Rifles, 2 Nov. 1842.

Cols.-Commandant (continued)—

Sir Wm. Cornwallis Eustace, **C.B.**, K.C.H.—Lieut., 27 Sept., 1783 ; Capt., 24 Dec., 1802 ; Major, 17 March, 1808 ; Lieut.-Colonel, 23 Aug., 1810 ; Colonel, 12 August, 1819 ; Major-Gen., 22 July, 1830 ; Lieut.-General, 23 Nov., 1841 ; Colonel, 60th Rifles, 1 April, 1843.

Lieut.-Colonels—

Hon. Henry Dundas, C.B.—Ensign and Lieut., 18 Nov. 1819 ; Captain, 1 April, 1824 ; Major, 11 July, 1826 ; Lieut.-Col., 3 Dec., 1829 ; Colonel, 23 Nov. 1841.

Cosby Lewis Nesbitt—2nd Lieut., 27 March, 1824 ; Lieut., 2 June, 1825 ; Captain, 18 Dec., 1828 ; Major, 10 Aug., 1841 ; Lieut.-Colonel, 26 July, 1844.

Hon. Geo. Augustus Spencer—Ensign, 12 Feb., 1824 ; Lieut., 16 June, 1825 ; Captain, 19 Dec., 1826 ; Major, 17 Aug., 1841 ; Lieut.-Col., 20 Dec., 1844.

Majors—

Thomas Crombie—Ensign, 12 Aug., 1824 ; Lieut., 8 April, 1826 ; Captain, 18 May, 1832 ; Major, 16 Nov., 1841.

Randal Rumley—Cornet, 30 Dec., 1824 ; Lieut., 8 Oct., 1825 ; Captain, 14 Aug., 1827 ; Brevet Major, 23 Nov., 1841 ; Major, 26 July, 1844.

Freeman Murray—Ensign, **24 Feb.**, 1825 ; Lieut., 8 April, 1826 ; **Captain**, 21 Dec., 1832 ; Major, 20 Aug., **1844.**

Edward Carter Gifford—Ensign, **23** Nov., 1825 ; Lieut., 8 Feb., 1831 ; Capt., 9 Oct., 1835 ; Major, 20 Dec., **1844.**

Rank and Name.   Rank in Regiment.

Captains—

Harrington **Trevelyan** .. 7 April 1837
James St. John **Munro** .. 17 Nov. 1837
John Temple .. .. 28 Jan. 1826
Rank in Army, Bt.-Maj. 23 Nov. 1841
Joseph Robinson .. .. 7 June 1839
Charles Rowe Spence .. 24 May 1841
Henry Bingham .. .. 25 June 1841
John Jones .. .. .. 16 July 1841
Wm. Eanshawe Bedford 23 July 1841
Hon. H. Lyttleton **Powys** 17 Aug. 1841
Andrew Cawdon .. .. 30 Dec. 1840
Walbog Everard .. .. 16 Nov. 1841
Francis Roger Palmer .. 11 Mar. 1842
John Kenn. MacKenzie .. 23 April 1842
Edward Massendon Love 20 Dec. 1842
Henry Helfsch .. .. 25 June 1844
Webbe Butler .. .. 26 July 1844
Hon. J. E. H. Thurlow .. 2 Aug. 1844
Wm. Mark Wood .. .. 20 Aug. 1844
James Douglas .. .. 29 Sept. 1844
Hon. Adrian Hope .. .. 20 Dec. 1844

First Lieutenants—

Thomas Mitchell .. .. 29 Dec. 1840
Charles W. H. Sotheby .. 17 Aug. 1841
R. F. Waldo Sibthorp .. 10 Sept. 1841
Aug. Richard Saunders .. 14 Oct. 1841
William Grenfell .. .. 14 Oct. 1841
Thos. Somers Armstrong 16 Nov. 1841
Douglas Jones .. .. 26 Nov. 1841

Rank and Name.   Rank in Regiment.

First Lieutenants (continued)—

Charles Napier North .. 28 Dec. 1838
J. Wingfield S. Fraser .. 19 July 1839
John Francis Jones .. 12 April 1839
Ashton Moseley .. .. 11 Mar. 1842
Henry Friend Kennedy.. 7 April 1842
F. Marcus Callaghan .. 23 April **1842**
Henry Robinson .. .. 20 Dec. **1842**
George Clapcott .. .. 31 Mar. **1843**
Godfrey Rhodes .. .. 25 June 1844
Warren W. Johnson .. 29 Mar 1842
G. Waldegrave Bligh .. 26 July 1844
Stephen Kenny .. .. 26 July 1844
Gibbes Rigaud .. .. 26 July 1844
E. Fitzgerald Campbell.. 26 July 1844
Eustace Henry Rose .. 26 July 1844
Peter Horton Roe .. .. 26 July 1844
W. Percival Salmon .. 26 July 1844
James Fraser .. .. 26 July 1844
George Vavasour .. .. 26 July 1844
E. Uniacke Coxen .. .. 26 July 1844
Henry Saunders .. 26 July 1844
Henry Laurie Bruyeres .. 19 Aug. 1844
W. Biddulph Parker .. 20 Aug. 1844
John Warburton .. .. 30 Sept. 1844
W. F. Laing Mason .. 20 Dec. **1844**

Second Lieutenants—

John Bathe .. .. .. 20 Dec. 1842
Bardle Joseph Fielden .. 31 Mar. 1843
George Bingham Jennings 21 July 1843
Henry Edward Warren.. 5 Jan. 1844
John Thomas Eustace .. 25 June 1844
Garnett Warburton .. 5 July 1844
Abercrombie Robinson .. 26 July 1844
Arthur England Johnson 26 July 1844
Francis Dawson .. .. 26 July 1844
Hunter B. Farndon .. 27 July 1844
Frederick Arthur St. John 28 July 1844
Lyon Conway Travers .. 29 July 1844
John Prevost Battersby .. 30 July 1844
John Lambert E. Baynes 31 July 1844
Bernard Ward .. .. 1 Aug. 1844
Herbert Henry Vaughan 2 Aug. 1844
Richard Wm. Aldworth 19 Aug. 1844
John Henry Payne .. 20 Aug. 1844
Herman Ernest Galton.. 20 Dec. 1844

Paymasters—

Edward Coxen, 9 Feb. 1826—2nd Lieut., 5 April, 1809 ; Lieut., 28 June, 1810 ; Captain, 8 April, 1825.

Wm. Henry Fitzgerald, 20 Sept. 1839 - Ensign, 17 Jan., 1828 ; Lieut., 31 May, 1833.

Adjutants—

Stephen Kenny, 1st Lieut., 9 May, 1843.

Douglas Jones, 1st Lieut., 5 July, 1844.

Quartermasters—

John Brannan, 18 Sept., 1835—Ensign, 5 Sept. 1835.

Thomas Berry, 29 March, 1842.

Surgeons—

Charles Robert Boyes, M.D., 2 July, 1841 Assistant-Surgeon, 22 Nov., 1827 ; Hospital-Assistant, 17 Aug. 1826.

Surgeons (continued)—
Augustus Henry Cowen, 2 July, 1841
—Assistant-Surgeon, 29 July, 1830 ;
Hospital-Assistant, 2 Nov., 1826.

Assistant-Surgeons—
David Maurice, M.D., 29 May, 1835.
J. T. Richardson, M.D., 1 Feb., 1839.
Thomas Cowan, M.D., 17 Sept., 1841.
Wm. Joseph Macfarlane,16 Feb.,1844.
F. John Folliott Payne, 31 May, 1844.

Regimentals—Green, facings scarlet.

Agents—Messrs. Cox and Co,

1846.

Two Battalions.

India—North America.

Celer et Audax.

Roleia, Vimiera, Martinique, Talavera,
Fuentes d'Onor, Albuhera, Ciudad
Rodrigo, Badajoz, Salamanca, Vittoria,
Pyrenees, Nivelle, Nive, Orthes, Tou-
louse, Peninsula.

Col.-in-Chief—
H.R.H. A. F., Duke of Cambridge,
K.G., G.C.B., G.C.M.G., G.C.H., 22
Jan., 1827.
Rank in Army, Field-Mar., 26 Nov. 1813.

Cols.-Commandant—
Sir Wm. Gabriel Davy, C.B., K.C.H.—
Ensign, March, 1797 ; Lieutenant, 22
May, 1797 ; Captain, 1 Jan., 1802;
Major, 5 Feb., 1807; Lieut.-Colonel,
28 Dec., 1809 ; Colonel, 12 Aug., 1819;
Major-General, 22 July, 1830 ; Lieut.-
General, 23 Nov., 1841 ; Colonel, 60th
Rifles, 2 Nov. 1842.
Sir William Cornwallis Eustace, C.B.,
K.C.H.—Lieutenant, 27 Sept., 1783 ;
Captain, 24 Dec., 1802 ; Major, 17
March, 1808 ; Lieut.-Colonel, 23 Aug.,
1810 ; Colonel, 12 Aug., 1819 ; Major-
General, 22 July, 1830 ; Lieut.-General,
23 Nov., 1841 ; Colonel, 60th Rifles,
7 April, 1843.

Lieut.-Colonels—
Hon. Henry Dundas,C.B.— Ensign and
Lieutenant, 18 Nov., 1819 ; Captain,
1 April, 1825 ; Lieut.-Colonel, 3 Dec., 1829 ; Colonel,
23 Nov., 1841.
Cosby Lewis Nesbitt—2nd Lieutenant,
27 March, 1821 ; Lieutenant, 2 June,
1825 ; Captain, 18 Dec., 1828 ; Major,
10 Aug., 1841 ; Lieut.-Colonel, 26 July,
1843.
Joseph Bradshaw—Ensign, 12 May,
1825 ; Lieutenant, 12 Dec., 1826 ; Captain, 2 Dec., 1831 ; Major, 9 Dec., 1836;
Lieut.-Colonel, 27 Aug., 1844.

Majors—
Thos. Crombie—Ensign,12 Aug.,1824;
Lieutenant, 8 April, 1826 ; Captain, 18
May, 1832 ; Major, 16 Nov., 1841.

Majors (continued)—
Freeman Murray—Ensign, 24 Feb.,
1825 ; Lieutenant, 8 April, 1826 ; Capt.,
21 Dec., 1832 ; Major, 20 Aug., 1844.
Edward Carter Giffard—Ensign, 23
Nov., 1826 ; Lieutenant, 8 Feb., 1831 ;
Captain, 9 Oct., 1835 ; Major, 20 Dec.,
1844.
Maurice Griffin Dennis—Ensign, 9
May, 1826 ; Lieutenant, 5 July, 1827 ;
Captain, 15 Dec., 1837 ; Major, 2 May,
1845.

Rank and Name.	Rank in Regiment.
Captains—	
Jas. Harrington Trevelyan	7 April 1837
Jas. St. John Munro	17 Nov. 1837
John Temple	28 Jan. 1826
Rank in Army, Bt. Maj. 23 Nov. 1841	
Joseph Robinson	7 June 1839
Chas. Howe Spence	29 May 1841
Henry Bingham	25 June 1841
John Jones	16 July 1841
Wm. Fanshawe Bedford	23 July 1841
Hon. H. Lyttleton Powys	17 Aug. 1841
Andrew Carden	30 Dec. 1840
Walling Everard	16 Nov. 1841
Fm. Roger Palmer	11 Mar. 1842
John Keau. Mackenzie	23 April 1842
Edwd. Missenden Love	29 Dec. 1842
Henry Holbech	25 June 1844
Webbe Butler	26 July 1844
James Douglas	20 Sept. 1844
Hon. Adrian Hope	29 Dec. 1844
Henry John Darell	12 Jan. 1844
Geo. de Rottenburg	13 July 1832
Rank in Army, Bt. Maj. 31 Dec. 1841	
First Lieutenants—	
Thos. Mitchell	29 Dec. 1840
Chas. Wm. H. Sotheby	17 Aug. 1841
Rich. F. Waldo Sibthorp	10 Sept. 1841
Wm. Grenfell	13 Oct. 1841
Thos. Somers Armstrong	16 Nov. 1841
Douglas Jones	26 Nov. 1841
Chas. Napier North	28 Dec. 1838
John Wingfield S. Fraser	19 July 1839
John Francis Jones	12 April 1839
Ashton Moseley	11 Mar. 1842
Henry Friend Kennedy	7 April 1842
F. Marcus Callaghan	23 April 1842
Henry Robinson	29 Dec. 1842
Geo. Chapcott	31 Mar. 1843
Godfrey Rhodes	25 June 1844
Warner West. Johnson	29 Mar. 1842
Geo. Waldegrave Bligh	26 July 1844
Stephen Kenny	26 July 1844
Gibbes Rigaud	26 July 1844
Edwd. Fitzger. Campbell	26 July 1844
Eustace Henry Rhodes	26 July 1844
Peter Barton Roe	26 July 1844
Wm. Percival Salmon	26 July 1844
James Fraser	26 July 1844
John Warburton	29 Sept. 1844
Wm. Hutchinson	26 April 1844
Randle Joseph Feilden	25 Feb. 1845
Dunbar Douglas Muter	17 Jan. 1845
Henry Francis Williams	20 Dec. 1844

Rank and Name.	Rank in Regiment.

First Lieutenants (continued)—
John Arch. MacQueen ..   6 June 1845
C. Alex. Boswell Gordon. 13 June 1845
John Maguire ..   ..   ..   4 July 1845

Second Lieutenants—
Henry Edwd. Warren ..   5 Jan. 1844
John Thos. Eustace   .. 25 June 1844
Garnett Warburton   ..   5 July 1844
Abercrombie Robinson .. 26 July 1844
Arthur England Johnson 26 July 1844
Francis Dawson   ..   .. 26 July 1844
Hunter Richardson Farn-
den   ..   .. **27 July** 1844
Fredk. Arthur St. John.. **28 July** 1844
Lyon Conway Travers .. **29 July** 1844
John Prevost Battersby.. **30 July** 1844
John Lambert Edward
Baynes ..   ..   .. **31 July** 1844
Bernard Ward..   ..   **1 Aug.** 1844
Herbert Henry Vaughan   **2 Aug.** 1844
Richard Wm. Aldworth **19 Aug.** 1844
John Henry Payne..   .. **20 Aug.** 1844
Herman Ernest Galton.. **20 Dec.** 1844
Clinton F. B. Dawkins .. **31 Dec.** 1844
Vincent Tongue   ..   **14 Feb.** 1845
Rich. Harcourt Robinson **25 Feb.** 1845
Arthur Chas. Greville ..   4 April 1845

Paymasters—
  Edward Coxen, 9 Feb., 1826; 2nd
Lieutenant, 5th April, 1809; Lieute-
nant, 28 June, 1810; Captain, 8 April,
1825.
  Wm. Henry Fitzgerald, 26 Sept., 1839
—Ensign, 17 Jan., 1828; Lieutenant,
31 May, 1833.

Adjutants—
  Stephen Kenny, 1st Lieut., 9 May,
1843
  Douglas Jones, 1st Lieut., 5 July,
1844.

Quartermasters—
  John Freeman, 18 Sept., 1835—
Ensign, 5 Sept., 1835.
  Thomas Berry, 23 March, 1842.

Surgeons—
  Chas. Robt. Boyes, M.D., 2 July, 1841
—Assistant-Surgeon, 22 Nov., 1827;
Hospital Assistant, 17 Aug., 1826.
  Augustus Hen. Cowen, 2 July, 1841—
Assistant-Surgeon, 29 July, 1830; Hos-
pital Assistant, 2 Nov., 1826.

Assistant-Surgeons—
  Johnstone Thomson Richardson, M.D.,
1 Feb., 1839.
  Thomas Cowan, M.D., 17 Dec., 1841
  Wm Joseph Macfarlane, 16 Feb., 1844
  Fredk. John Folbott Payne, 31 May,
1844.
  Edwd. Scott Docker, 29 Dec., 1840.

Regimentals Green, facings scarlet

  Agents Messrs Cox and Co.

1847.

Two Battalions.

India—North America—**England.**

Celer et Audax.

Rolica, Vimiera, Martinique, Talavera,
Fuentes d'Onor, Albuhera, Ciudad
Rodrigo, Badajoz, Salamanca, Vittoria,
Pyrenees, Nivelle, Nive, Orthes, Tou-
louse, Peninsula.

Col.-in-Chief—
  Field-Marshal H.R.H. A. **F., Duke of**
Cambridge, 22 Jan., 1827.

Cols. Commandant—
  Sir Wm. Gabriel Davy, C.B., K.C.H.—
Ensign, March, 1797; Lieut., 22 May,
1797; Capt., 1 Jan. 1802; Major, 5 Feb.,
1807; Lieut.-Col., 28 Dec., 1809; **Col.**,
12 Aug., 1819; Major-General, 22 **July,**
1830; Lieut.-General, 23 Nov. **1841;**
Colonel, 60th Rifles, 2 Nov., 1842.
  Sir Wm. Cornwallis Eustace, C.B.,
K.C.H.—Lieut., 27 Sept., 1783; Captain, 24 Dec., 1802; Major, 17 March,
1806; Lieut.-Colonel, 24 Aug., 1810;
Colonel, 12 August, 1819; Major-Gen.,
22 July, 1830; Lieut.-General, 23 Nov.,
1841; Colonel, 60th Rifles, 7 April, 1843.

Lieut.-Colonels—
  Hon. Henry Dundas, C.B.—Ensign
and Lieutenant, 18 Nov., 1819; Captain,
1 April, 1824; Major, 11 July, 1826;
Lieut.-Colonel, 3 Dec., 1829; Colonel,
23 Nov., 1841.
  Cosby Lewis Nesbitt—2nd Lieutenant,
27 March, 1821; Lieutenant, 2 June,
1825; Captain, 18 Dec., 1828; Major,
10 Aug., 1841; Lieut.-Colonel, 26 July,
1844.
  Joseph Bradshaw—Ensign, 12 May,
1825; Lieutenant, 12 Dec., 1826; Captain, 2 Dec., 1831; Major, 9 Dec., 1830;
Lieut.-Col., 27 Aug., 1841.

Majors—
  Thomas Crombie—Ensign, 12 Aug.,
1821; Lieutenant, 8 April, 1826; Captain, 18 May, 1832; Major, 16 Nov.,
1841.
  Freeman Murray—Ensign, 24 Feb.,
1825; Lieutenant, 8 April, 1826; Captain, 24 Dec., 1832; Major, 20 Aug.,
1844.
  Edward Carter Giffard—Ensign, 23
Nov., 1826; Lieutenant, 8 Feb., 1831;
Captain, 9 Oct., 1835; Major, 20 Dec.,
1844.
  Maurice Griffin Dennis—Ensign, 9
May, 1826; Lieutenant, 5 July, 1827;
Captain, 15 Dec., 1837; Major, 2 May,
1845

Rank and Name.	Rank in Regiment.

Captains—
Jas. Harrington Trevelyan   7 April 1837
John Temple ..   ..   .. 28 Jan. 1826
  Rank in Army, Bt. Maj. 23 Nov. 1841
Joseph Robinson   ..   ..   7 June 1829

Rank and Name.	Rank in Regiment.
Captains (continued)—	
Charles Howe Spence	.. 24 May 1841
Henry Bingham ..	.. 25 June 1841
John Jones	.. 16 July 1841
Wm. Fanshawe Bedford	23 July 1841
Hon. H. Lyttleton Powys	17 Aug. 1841
Walling Everard ..	.. 16 Nov. 1841
Fra. Roger Palmer..	.. 11 Mar. 1842
John Kenn. Mackenzie	.. 23 April 1842
Edwd. Missenden Love..	20 Dec. 1842
Henry Holbech ..	.. 25 June 1844
Webbe Butler. ..	.. 26 July 1844
James Douglas ..	.. 29 Sept. 1844
Henry John Darell..	.. 12 Jan. 1844
Hon. Adrian Hope..	.. 20 Dec. 1844
Geo. Pleydell Mansel	.. 28 July 1845
C. W. Hamilton Sotheby	14 Aug. 1841
First Lieutenants—	
Thos. Mitchell.. ..	.. 29 Dec. 1840
Rich. F. Waldo Sibthorp	10 Sept. 1841
Wm. Greufell.. ..	.. 14 Oct. 1841
Thos. Somers Armstrong	16 Nov. 1841
Douglas Jones ..	.. 26 Nov. 1841
Chas. Napier North	.. 28 Dec. 1838
John Francis Jones	.. 12 April 1839
Ashton Moseley ..	.. 11 Mar. 1842
Henry Friend Kennedy..	7 April 1842
George Clapcott ..	.. 31 Mar. 1843
Godfrey Rhodes ..	.. 25 June 1841
Warner Westen. Johnson	29 Mar. 1842
Geo. Waldegrave Bligh..	26 July 1844
Stephen Kenny ..	.. 26 July 1844
Gibbes Rigaud ..	.. 26 July 1844
Edw. Fitzgerald Campbell	26 July 1844
Eustace Henry Rose ..	26 July 1844
Peter Burton Roe ..	.. 26 July 1844
Wm. Percival Salmon ..	26 July 1844
James Fraser	.. 26 July 1844
John Warburton ..	.. 20 Sept. 1844
Wm. Hutchinson ..	.. 29 April 1844
Randal Joseph Feilden ..	25 Feb. 1845
Dunbar Douglas Muter..	17 Jan. 1845
Henry Francis Williams	20 Dec. 1845
John Archibald MacQueen	6 June 1845
Charles Alex. Boswell Gordon	.. 13 June 1845
John Maguire.. ..	.. 4 July 1843
Henry Edward Warren..	30 Dec. 1845
Alfred Fitzgerald ..	13 Feb. 1846
Garnett Warburton ..	31 July 1846
George Abercrombie Robinson	.. 14 Aug. 1846
Second Lieutenants—	
Francis Dawson ..	.. 26 July 1844
Hunter Richardson Farnden	27 July 1844
Fredk. Arthur St. John..	28 July 1844
Lyon Conway Travers ..	29 July 1844
John Prevost Battersby..	30 July 1844
John Lambert Edward Baynes..	31 July 1844
Bernard Ward.. ..	1 Aug. 1844
Herbert Henry Vaughan	2 Aug. 1844
R. Wm. Aldworth ..	.. 19 Aug. 1844
John Henry Payne..	.. 20 Aug. 1844
Herman Ernest Galton ..	20 Dec. 1844

Rank and Name.	Rank in Regiment.
Lieutenants (continued)—	
Clinton F. Berens Dawkins	31 Dec. 1844
Vincent Tongue ..	.. 14 Feb. 1845
Richd. Harcourt Robinson	25 Feb. 1845
Arthur Charles Greville..	4 April 1845
Robert Wilmot Brooke..	30 Dec. 1845
Richard Freer.. ..	.. 22 May 1846
Franc. Charters Fletcher	31 July 1846
Edward Bowles ..	.. 11 Aug. 1846
Charles Wm. Earl..	.. 24 Dec. 1846
Paymasters—	
☒ Edwd. Coxen, 9 Feb., 1826—2nd Lieutenant, 5 April, 1809; Lieutenant, 28 June, 1810; Captain, 8 April, 1825.	
W. Henry Fitzgerald, 20 Sept., 1839—Ensign, 17 Jan., 1828; Lieutenant, 31 May, 1833.	
Adjutants—	
Stephen Kenny, 1st Lieut., 9 May, 1843.	
Douglas Jones, 1st Lieut., 5 July, 1844.	
Quartermasters—	
☒ John Brannan, 18 Sept., 1835—Ensign, 5 Sept., 1835.	
Thomas Berry, 29 March, 1842.	
Surgeons—	
Charles Robert Boyes, M.D., 2 July, 1841; Assistant-Surgeon, 27 Nov., 1827; Hospital Assistant, 17 August, 1826.	
Augustus Henry Cowen, 2 July, 1841; Assistant-Surgeon, 29 July, 1830; Hospital Assistant, 2 Nov., 1826.	
Assistant-Surgeons—	
Johnstone Thomson Richardson, M.D., 1 Feb., 1839.	
Thomas Cowan, M.D., 17 Sept., 1841.	
Wm. Jos. Macfarlane, 16 Feb., 1844.	
Fred. J. Folliott Payne, 31 May, 1844.	
Edward Scott Docker, 29 Dec., 1840.	
Regimentals—Green, facings scarlet.	
Agents—Messrs. Cox and Co.	

1848.

Two Battalions.

India—England—Ireland.

Color et Audax.

Roleia, Vimiera, Martinique, Talavera, Fuentes d'Onor, Albuhera, Ciudad Rodrigo, Badajoz, Salamanca, Vittoria, Pyrenees, Nivelle, Nive, Orthes, Toulouse, Peninsula.

Col.-in-Chief—

H.R.H. A. F., Duke of Cambridge, K.G., G.C.B., G.C.M.G., G.C.H., 22 Jan., 1827.

Rank in Army, Field-Mar., 26 Nov. 1813.

Cols.-Commanding—

Sir William Gabriel Davy, C.B., K.C.H.—Ensign, March 1797; Lieut., 22 May, 1797; Captain, 1 Jan., 1802; Major, 5 Feb. 1807; Lieut.-Colonel, 28 Dec. 1809; Colonel, 12 Aug. 1819; Major-Gen., 22

Cols.-Commanding (continued)—

July, 1830; Lieut.-Gen., 23 Nov., 1841; Colonel, 60th Rifles, 2 Nov., 1842.

Sir Wm. Cornwallis Eustace, C.B., K.C.H.—Lieut., 27 Sept. 1783; Captain, 24 Dec., 1802; Major, 17 March, 1808; Lieut.-Colonel, 23 Aug., 1810; Colonel, 12 Aug., 1819; Major-Gen., 22 July, 1830; Lieut.-Gen., 23 Nov., 1841; Colonel 60th Rifles, 7 April, 1843.

Lieut.-Colonels—

Hon. Henry Dundas, C.B.—Ensign and Lieut., 10 Nov., 1819; Captain, 1 April, 1824; Major, 11 July, 1826; Lieut.-Colonel, 3 Dec., 1829; Colonel, 23 Nov., 1841.

Cosby Lewis Nesbitt—2nd Lieut., 27 March, 1824; Lieut., 2 June, 1825; Captain, 18 Dec., 1828; Major, 10 Aug., 1841; Lieut.-Colonel, 26 July, 1844.

Joseph Bradshaw—Ensign, 12 May, 1825; Lieut., 12 Dec., 1826; Captain, 2 Dec., 1831; Major, 9 Dec., 1836; Lieut.-Colonel, 27 Aug., 1841.

Majors—

Thomas Crombie—Ensign, 12 Aug., 1824; Lieut., 8 April, 1826; Captain, 18 May, 1832; Major, 16 Nov., 1841.

Maurice Griffin Dennis—Ensign, 9 Mar., 1826; Lieut., 5 July, 1827; Capt. 15 Dec., 1837; Major, 2 May, 1845.

John Gordon—Ensign, 14 June, 1827; Lieut., 5 April, 1831; Captain, 5 April, 1833; Major, 15 Dec., 1840.

J. Harrington Trevelyan—Ensign, 16 April, 1829; Lieut., 23 Aug., 1832; Captain, 7 April, 1837; Major, 5 March, 1847.

Rank and Name	Rank in Regiment.
Captains—	
John Temple	28 Jan. 1826
Rank in Army, Bt. Maj. 23 Nov., 1841	
Joseph Robinson	7 June 1839
Charles Howe Spence ..	24 May 1841
Henry Bingham ..	25 June 1841
John Jones	16 July 1841
Wm. Fanshawe Bedford	23 July 1841
Hon. H. Lyttleton Powys	17 Aug. 1841
Andrew Carden ..	30 Dec., 1840
Francis Roger Palmer ..	11 Mar. 1842
John Kean Mackenzie ..	23 April 1842
Henry Bullock	25 June 1844
Webbe Butler	26 July 1844
James Douglas ..	20 Sept., 1844
Hon. Adrian Hope ..	20 Dec. 1844
Henry John Davell ..	12 Jan. 1844
Geo. Pleydell Mansell ..	28 July 1843
C. W. Hamilton Sotheby	14 Aug 1846
Wm. James Yonge ..	10 July 1846
R. F. Waldo Sibthorp ..	5 Mar. 1847
William Greufell	22 June 1847
First Lieutenants—	
Douglas Jones	26 Nov., 1841
Charles Napier North ..	28 Dec. 1841
John Francis Jones ..	12 April 1842
Ashton Moseley	11 Mar. 1842
Henry Friend Kennedy ..	7 April 1842

Rank and Name.	Rank in *Regiment.*
First Lieutenants (continued)—	
George Clapcott	31 **Mar. 1843**
Godfrey Rhodes ..	23 **June 1844**
Warner West Johnson ..	29 **Mar. 1842**
G. Wablegrave Bligh ..	26 **July 1844**
Stephen Kenny	26 **July 1844**
Gibbes Rigaud	26 **July 1844**
E. Fitzgerald Campbell ..	26 **July 1844**
Eustace Henry Rose ..	26 **July 1844**
Peter Burton Roe ..	26 **July 1844**
Wm. Percival Salmon ..	26 **July 1844**
James Fraser	26 **July 1844**
John Warburton ..	20 **Sept. 1844**
William Hutchinson ..	26 **April 1844**
Randle Joseph Feilden ..	25 **Feb. 1845**
Dunbar Douglas Maber ..	17 **Jan. 1845**
Henry Francis Williams ..	20 **Dec. 1844**
John Arch. MacQueen ..	6 **June 1845**
C. Alex. Boswell Gordon	13 **June 1845**
John Maguire	4 **July 1843**
Henry Edward Warren ..	30 **Dec. 1845**
Alfred Fitzgerald	13 **Feb. 1846**
A. H. Hastead Mercer ..	1 **Nov. 1842**
Fred. Arthur St. John ..	5 **Mar. 1847**
Francis Andrews ..	19 **Dec. 1845**
Francis Dawson ..	7 **June 1847**
Lyon Conway Travers ..	22 **June 1847**
Wm. Henry Stirling ..	31 **Mar. 1846**
Second Lieutenants—	
H. Richardson Farmiloe ..	27 **July 1844**
John Prevost Battersby ..	30 **July 1844**
J. Lambert Edw. Boyne..	31 **July 1844**
Bernard Ward	1 **Aug. 1844**
Herbert Henry **Vaughan**	2 **Aug. 1844**
John Henry Payne ..	20 **Aug. 1844**
Herman Ernest Gadlon ..	20 **Dec. 1844**
Vincent Fonque ..	14 **Feb. 1845**
R. Harcourt Robinson ..	25 **Feb. 1845**
Arthur Charles Greville..	4 **April 1845**
Robert Walmot Brooke ..	30 **Dec. 1845**
Richard Freer	22 **May 1846**
Francis C. **Fletcher** ..	31 **July 1846**
Edward **Bowles** ..	14 **Aug. 1846**
Charles Wm. **Earle** ..	24 **Dec. 1846**
Robt. J. E. **Robertson** ..	5 **Mar. 1847**
Thomas **Nicholson** ..	22 **June 1847**
George **Clarke**	1 **Aug. 1846**
William **Muir**	22 **Oct. 1847**
John Du Cane	5 **Nov. 1847**
Paymasters —	

E4 Edward Coxen, 9 Feb., 1826—2nd Lieut., 5 April, 1809; Lieut., 28 June, 1810; Captain, 8 April, 1825.

W. Henry Fitzgerald, 20 Sept., 1832; Ensign, 17 Jan. 1828; Lieut., 31 May, 1833.

Adjutants—

Stephen Kenny, 1st Lieut., 9 May, 1843.

Douglas Jones, 1st Lieut., 5 July, 1844.

Quarter-masters—

Thomas Berry, 29 Mar., 1842.

Richard Power, 28 Mar., 1847.

Surgeons—

Charles Robert Boyes, M.D., 2 July, 1841; Assistant-Surgeon, 22 Nov., 1827; Hospital Surgeon, 17 Aug., 1826.

Assistant-Surgeons—
Thomas Cowan, M.D., 17 Sept., 1841.
Wm.Joseph Macfarlane,16 Feb., 1844.
F. John Folliott Payne, 31 May, 1844.
E. E.Hare O'Brien, M.D.,13 Dec.,1844.

Regimentals - Green, facings scarlet.

Agents—Messrs. Cox and Co.

1849.

Two Battalions.

India—Ireland.

Celer et Audax.

Roleia, Vimiera, Martinique, Talavera, Fuentes d'Onor, Albuhera, Ciudad Rodrigo, Badajoz, Salamanca, Vittoria, Pyrenees, Nivelle, Nive, Orthes, Toulouse, Peninsula.

Col.-in-Chief—
Field-Marshal H.R.H. A. F., Duke of Cambridge, 22 Jan., 1827.

Cols.-Commandant—
Sir William Gabriel Davy, C.B., K.C.H.—Ensign, March, 1797; Lieut., 22 May, 1797; Captain, 1 Jan., 1802; Major, 5 Feb. 1807; Lieut.-Colonel, 28 Dec., 1809; Colonel, 12 Aug., 1819; Major-Gen., 22 July, 1830; Lieut.-Gen., 23 Nov. 1841; Colonel, 60th Rifles, 2 Nov. 1842.
Sir Wm. Cornwallis Eustace, C.B., K.C.H.—Lieut., 27 Sept. 1783; Capt., 24 Dec., 1802; Major, 17 March, 1808; Lieut.-Colonel, 23 Aug., 1810; Colonel, 12 Aug., 1819; Major-Gen., 22 July, 1830; Lieut.-General, 23 Nov. 1841; Colonel, 60th Rifles, 7 April, 1843.

Lieut.-Colonels—
Hon. Henry Dundas, C.B.—Ensign and Lieut., 18 Nov., 1819; Captain, 1 April, 1824; Major, 11 July, 1826; Lieut.-Colonel, 3 Dec., 1829; Colonel, 23 Nov. 1841.
Cosby Lewis Nesbitt—2nd Lieut., 27 March, 1824; Lieut., 2 June, 1825; Captain, 18 Dec., 1828; Major, 10 Aug., 1841; Lieut.-Colonel, 26 July, 1844.
Joseph Bradshaw—Ensign, 12 May, 1825; Lieut., 12 Dec., 1826; Captain, 2 Dec., 1831; Major, 9 Dec., 1836; Lieut.-Colonel, 27 Aug., 1844.

Majors—
Maurice Griffin Dennis—Ensign, 9 May, 1826; Lieut., 5 July, 1827; Capt., 15 Dec., 1847; Major, 2 May, 1845.
John Gordon—Ensign, 14 June, 1827; Lieut., 5 April, 1841; Captain, 5 April, 1833; Major, 15 Dec., 1840.
John Temple—2nd Lieut., 14 May, 1818; Lieut., 21 Oct., 1824; Captain, 28 Jan., 1826; Brevet Major, 23 Nov., 1841; Major, 28 Jan., 1848.

Majors (continued)—
Charles Howe Spence—2nd Lieut., 20 April, 1825; Lieut., 28 Sept., 1826; Captain, 24 May, 1841; Major, 20 Oct., 1848.

Rank and Name.	*Rank in Regiment.*
Captains—	
Joseph Robinson	7 June 1839
Henry Bingham	25 June 1841
John Jones	16 July 1841
Wm. Fanshawe Bedford	23 July 1841
Hon. H. Lyttleton Powys	17 Aug. 1841
Andrew Carden	30 Dec. 1840
Francis Roger Palmer	11 Mar. 1842
John Kenn. Mackenzie	23 April 1842
Henry Holbech	25 June 1844
Webbe Butler	26 July 1844
James Douglas	20 Sept. 1844
Hon. Adrian Hope	20 Dec. 1844
Henry John Darell	12 Jan. 1844
C. W. Hamilton Sotheby	14 Aug. 1846
Wm. James Yongc	10 July 1846
R. F. Waldo Sibthorp	5 Mar. 1847
William Grenfell	22 June 1847
Douglas Jones	28 Jan. 1848
Ashton Moseley	25 Feb. 1848
H. Friend Kennedy	20 Oct. 1848
First Lieutenants—	
Charles Napier North	28 Dec. 1838
John Francis Jones	12 April 1839
George Clapcott	31 Mar. 1843
Godfrey Rhodes	25 June 1844
G. Waldegrave Bligh	26 July 1844
Stephen Remy	26 July 1844
Gibbes Rigaud	26 July 1844
E. Fitzgerald Campbell	26 July 1844
Eustace Henry Rose	26 July 1844
Peter Burton Roe	26 July 1844
Wm. Percival Salmon	26 July 1844
James Fraser	26 July 1844
John Warburton	20 Sept. 1844
Wm. Hutchinson	26 April 1844
Randle Joseph Feilden	25 Feb. 1845
Dunbar Douglas Muter	17 Jan. 1845
Henry Francis Williams	20 Dec. 1844
John Arch. MacQueen	6 June 1845
C. Alex. Boswell Gordon	13 June 1845
John Maguire	4 July 1845
Henry Edward Warren	30 Dec. 1845
Alfred Fitzgerald	13 Feb. 1846
A. H. Hastead Mercer	1 Nov. 1842
Fred. Arthur St. John	5 Mar. 1847
Francis Andrews	19 Dec. 1847
Francis Dawson	7 June 1843
Lyon Conway Travers	22 June 1847
John Prevost Battersby	28 Jan. 1848
J. Lambert E. Boynes	25 Feb. 1848
Bernard Ward	5 May 1848
John Henry Payne	12 Sept. 1848
H. Anthony O'Molony	10 Mar. 1847
Second Lieutenants—	
H. Richardson Farnden	27 July 1844
Vincent Tongue	11 Feb. 1845
R. Harcourt Robinson	25 Feb. 1845
Arthur Charles Greville	4 April 1845
Robert Wilmot Brooke	30 Dec. 1845
Richard Freer	22 May 1846

Rank and Name.   Rank in Regiment.
Second Lieutenants (continued)—

Francis Charteris Fletcher 31 July **1846**
Edward Bowles .. .. 14 Aug. **1846**
Charles Wm. Earle .. 24 Sept. **1846**
R. J. E. Robertson.. .. 5 Mar. **1847**
Thomas Nicholson .. .. 22 June **1847**
George Clarke .. .. 1 Aug. **1846**
William Mure.. .. .. 22 Oct. **1847**
John Du Cane .. .. 5 Nov. **1847**
C. W. Pownall Lillingston 28 Jan. **1848**
Conyngham Jones .. .. 25 Feb. **1848**
William Tedlie .. .. 5 May **1848**
B. Viney Douglas **Smith** 12 Sept **1848**
H. James Robertson .. 20 Oct. **1848**
Henry Cockburn .. .. 10 Nov. **1848**

Paymasters—

Edward Coxen, 9 Feb. **1826—2nd** Lieut., 5 April, 1823; Lieut., **28 June,** 1810; Captain, 8 April, 1825.

W. Henry Fitzgerald, 24 Sept., 1832 —Ensign, 17 Jan., 1828, Lieut., 31 May, 1833.

Adjutants—

Stephen Kenny, 1st Lieut. **9 May 1843**
E. F. Campbell, 1st Lieut **12 May 1848**

Quartermasters

Thomas Berry. .. .. **29 Mar. 1842**
Richard Power .. .. **28 May 1847**

Surgeons—

Charles Redd. Boyes, M.D. 2 July, 1841; Assistant-Surgeon, 22 Nov., 1827; Hospital Assistant, 17 Aug., 1826

Augustus Henry Cowen, 2 July, 1844; Assistant-Surgeon, 20 July, 1830; Hospital Assistant, 2 Nov. 1826.

Assistant-Surgeons

Thomas Cowan, M.D. .. 17 Sept 1841
W. Joseph Macfarlane .. 16 Feb. 1844
F. J. Follott Payne .. 31 May 1844
G. A. F. Shelton, M.B... 3 Jan. 1845

Regimentals Green, facings scarlet.
Agents—Messrs. Cox and Co.
Irish Agents— Sir E. R. Borough, Bart.; Armit and Co.

1850.

Two Ball Crosses.

India Ireland.

Color et Audax.

Rolea, Vimiera, Martinique, Talavera, Fuentes d'Onor, Albuhera, Ciudad Rodrigo, Badajoz, Salamanca, Vittoria, Pyrenees, Nivelle, Nive, Orthes, Toulouse, Peninsula.

Col.-in-Chief

H.R.H. A. F., Duke of Cambridge, K.G., G.C.B., G.C.M.G., G.C.H., 22 Jan., 1827.
Rank in Army, Field-Mar. 26 Nov. 1843
Cols.-Commanding

Sir Wm. Gabriel Davy, C.B., K.C.H. —Ensign, March, 1777; Lieut., 22

Cols.-Commanding (continued)—

May, 1797; Captain, 1 Jan., **1802**; Major, 5 Feb., 1807; Lieut.-Colonel, 28 Dec., 1809; Colonel, 12 Aug., 1819; Major-Gen., 22 July, 1830; Lieut.-Gen., 23 Nov., 1841; Colonel 60th Rifles, 2 Nov., 1842.

Sir William Cornwallis Eustace, **C.B.,** K.C.H.—Lieut., 27 Sept., 1783; Capt. 24 Dec., 1802; Major, 17 March, 1808; Lieut.-Col., 28 Aug., 1810; Colonel, 12 Aug., 1819; Major-Gen., 22 July, 1830; Lieut.-Gen., 23 Nov., 1841; Colonel 60th Rifles, **7** April, 1843.

Lieut. Colonels—

Hon. Sir Henry Dundas, K.C.B.— Ensign and Lieut., 18 Nov., 1819; Captain, 1 April, 1824; Major, 11 July, 1826; Lieut.-Colonel, **3** Dec., 1828; Colonel, 23 Nov., 1841.

Cecil Lewis Nesbitt, 2nd **Lieut., 27** March, 1824; Lieut., 2 June, **1825;** Captain, 18 Dec., 1828; Major, 10 **Aug.,** 1841; Lieut.-Col., 26 July, 1844.

Joseph Bradshaw, C.B.—Ensign, 12 May, 1825; Lieut., 12 Dec., 1826; Captain, 2 Dec., 1831; Major, 9 Dec., 1836; Lieut.-Col., 27 **Aug.,** 1841.

Majors—

Maurice Griffin Dennis—Ensign, **9** May, 1826; Lieut., **5** July, 1827; Capt., 15 Dec., 1837; Major, 2 May, 1845; Brevet Lieut.-Colonel, 7 June, 1849.

Charles Hawe Spencer, 2nd Lieut., 20 April, 1825; Lieut., 28 Sept., 1826; Captain, 24 May, 1831; Major, 20 Oct., 1848.

J. Jones—2nd Lieut., 12 June, 1828; Lieut., 2 Dec., 1831; Capt., 16 July, 1841; Major, 20 July, 1849.

Wm. Fanshawe Bedford—2nd Lieut., 18 Dec., 1828; Lieut., 28 June, 1833; Captain, 23 July, 1841; Major, 12 Oct., 1849.

Rank and Name.   Rank in Regiment.
Captains

Henry Bingham .. .. 25 June 1841
Hon. H. Lyttleton Powys 17 Aug. 1841
Andrew Carden .. .. 30 Dec. 1840
Francis Roger Palmer .. 11 Mar. 1842
John Kennedy Mackenzie 23 April 1842
Webbe Butler.. .. 26 July 1844
James Douglas .. .. 20 Sept. 1844
Hon. Adrian Hope.. .. 20 Dec. 1844
Henry John Davell.. .. 12 Jan. 1844
C. W. Hamilton Sotheby 14 Aug. 1846
Wm. James Yorge.. .. 10 July 1846
R. F. Waldo-Sethorp .. 5 Mar. 1847
William Grenfell .. .. 12 June 1847
Douglas Jones .. .. 28 Jan. 1848
Ashton Moseley .. .. 25 Feb. 1848
Henry Friend Kennedy.. 20 Oct. 1848
Charles Napier North .. 28 Dec. 1848
John Francis Jones .. 26 Aug. 1849
Geo. Waldegrave High.. 12 Oct. 1849
Alex. Crie Meik .. .. 20 May 1847

Rank and Name.	Rank in Regiment.

First Lieutenants—

George Clapcott .. .. 31 Mar. 1843
Stephen Kenny .. .. 26 July 1844
Gibbes Rigaud .. .. 26 July 1844
Sir E. Fitzgerald Camp-
　bell, Bart. .. .. .. 26 July 1844
Eustace Henry Rose .. 26 July 1844
Peter Burton Roe .. .. 26 July 1844
Wm. Percival Salmon .. 26 July 1844
James Fraser .. .. .. 26 July 1844
John Warburton .. .. 20 Sept. 1844
Wm. Hutchinson .. .. 26 April 1844
Randle Joseph Feilden .. 25 Feb. 1845
Dunbar Douglas Muter .. 17 Jan. 1845
Henry Francis Williams. 20 Dec. 1844
John Archibald McQueen 6 June 1845
Ch. Alex. Boswell Gordon 13 June 1845
John Maguire.. .. .. 4 July 1845
Henry Edward Warren . 30 Dec. 1845
Alfred Fitzgerald .. .. 13 Feb. 1846
Arthur Hill Hastead
　Mercer.. .. .. .. 1 Nov. 1842
Fred. Arthur St. John .. 5 Mar. 1847
Francis Andrews .. .. 19 Dec. 1845
Francis Dawson .. .. 7 June 1847
Lyon Conway Travers .. 22 June 1847
John Prevost Battersby 28 June 1848
John Lambert Edward
　Baynes.. .. .. .. 25 Feb. 1847
Bernard Ward .. .. 5 May 1848
H. Anthony O. Malony .. 10 Mar. 1837
Vincent Tongue .. .. 28 Dec. 1848
Rich. Harcourt Robinson 20 July 1849
Arthur Charles Greville . 26 Aug. 1849
Robert Wilmot Brooke .. 12 Oct. 1849
Richard Freer.. .. .. 13 Dec. 1849

Second Lieutenants—

Francis Charteris Fletcher 31 July 1846
Edward Bowles .. .. 14 Aug. 1846
Charles William Earle .. 24 Dec. 1846
Robert J. E. Robinson .. 5 Mar. 1847
Thomas Nicholson .. .. 22 June 1847
George Clarke.. .. .. 1 Aug. 1846
William Murr.. .. .. 22 Oct. 1847
John Du Cane .. .. 5 Nov. 1847
Chas. Wm. Pownall Lil-
　lingston .. .. .. 28 Jan. 1848
Conyngham Jones .. .. 25 Feb. 1848
William Teulie .. .. 5 May 1848
Bryan Viney Douglas
　Smith .. .. .. 12 Sept. 1848
Henry James Robertson. 20 Oct. 1848
Henry Cockburn .. .. 10 Nov. 1848
Geo. Bliss MacQueen .. 9 Mar. 1849
Hugh Parker Montgomery 24 Aug. 1849
Francis FitzPatrick .. 11 Sept. 1849
Henry Semple.. .. .. 19 Oct. 1849
Rowley Willis Hinxman . 23 Nov. 1849

Paymasters—

Edward Coxen, 9 Feb., 1826 – 2nd
Lieut., 5 April, 1809; Lieut., 28 June,
1810; Captain, 8 April, 1825.
W. Henry Fitzgerald, 20 Sept., 1839;
Ensign, 17 January, 1828; Lieut., 31
May, 1833.

Rank and Name.	Rank in Regiment.

Adjutants—

Stephen Kenny,1st Lieut. 9 May 1843
John Maguire, 1st Lieut. 2 June 1849

Quartermasters—

Thomas Berry .. .. 29 Mar. 1842
Richard Power .. .. 28 May 1847

Surgeons—

Charles R. Boyes, M.D., 2 July, 1841;
Assistant-Surgeon. 22 Nov., 1827; Hos-
pital Assistant, 17 Aug., 1826.
Augustus Henry Cowen, 2 July, 1841;
Assistant - Surgeon, 29 July, 1830;
Hospital Assistant, 2 Nov., 1826.

Assistant-Surgeons—

William Joseph Macfar-
　lane .. .. 16 Feb. 1844
Frederick John Folliott
　Payne .. .. .. 31 May 1844
Geo. Augustus Frederick
　Shelton, M.B. .. .. 3 Jan. 1845
Nesbitt Heffernan, M.D., 11 Jan. 1841

*Regimentals—*Green, facings scarlet.

*Agents—*Messrs. Cox and Co.

*Irish Agents—*Sir E. R. Borough, Bart. ;
Armit and Co.

1851.

Two Battalions.

India—Ireland—Africa.

Celer et Audax.

Rolcia, Vimiera, Martinique, Talavera,
Fuentes d'Onor, Albuhera, Ciudad
Rodrigo, Badajoz, Salamanca, Vittoria,
Pyrenees, Nivelle, Nive, Orthes, Tou-
louse, Peninsula.

Colonel-in-Chief—

Field-Marshal H.R.H. Francis Albert
Augustus Charles Emanuel, Duke of
Saxony, Prince of Saxe Coburg and
Gotha, K.G., K.T., K.P., G.C.B.,
G.C.M.G., 15 Aug., 1850.

Cols.-Commandant—

Sir Wm. Gabriel Davy, G.B., K.C.H.
—Ensign, March, 1797 ; Lieutenant, 22
May, 1797 ; Captain, 1 Jan., 1802 ;
Major, 5 Feb., 1807 ; Lieut.-Colonel, 28
Dec., 1809 ; Colonel, 12 Aug., 1819 ;
Major-Gen., 22 July, 1830 ; Lieut.-
Gen., 23 Nov., 1841 ; Colonel, 60th
Rifles, 2 Nov., 1842.
Sir Wm. Cornwallis Eustace, C.B.,
K.C.H.—Lieutenant, 27 Sept., 1783 ;
Captain, 24 Dec., 1802 ; Major, 17
Mar., 1808 ; Lieut.-Col., 23 Aug., 1810 ;
Colonel, 12 Aug., 1819 ; Major-Gen.,
22 July, 1830 ; Lieut.-Gen., 23 Nov.,
1841 ; Colonel, 60th Rifles, 7 April,
1843.

Lieut.-Colonels—

Hon. Sir Henry Dundas, K.C.B.—
Ensign and Lieut., 18 Nov., 1819 ; Capt.,
1 April, 1824 ; Major, 11 July, 1826 ;

Lieut.-Colonels (continued)—

Lieut.-Colonel, 3 Dec., 1829 ; Colonel, 23 Nov., 1841.

Cosby Lewis Nesbitt—2nd Lieutenant, 27 March, 1824 ; Lieutenant, 2 June, 1825 ; Captain, 18 Dec., 1828 ; Major, 10 Aug., 1841 ; Lieut.-Colonel, 26 July, 1844.

Joseph Bradshaw, C.B.—Ensign, 12 May, 1825 ; Lieutenant, 12 Dec., 1826 ; Captain, 2 Dec., 1821 ; Major, 9 Dec., 1836 ; Lieut.-Colonel, 27 Aug., 1841.

Majors—

Maurice Griffin Dennis—Ensign, 9 May,1826 ; Lieut. 5 July, 1827 ; Captain, 15 Dec., 1837 ; Major, 2 May, 1845 ; Brevet Colonel, 7 June, 1849.

Charles Howe Spence—2nd Lieut., 20 April, 1825 ; Lieutenant, 28 Sept., 1826 ; Captain, 24 May, 1841 ; Major, 20 Oct., 1848.

John Jones—2nd Lieutenant, 12 June, 1828 ; Lieutenant, 2 Dec., 1831 ; Captain, 16 July, 1841 ; Major, 20 July, 1849.

W. Fanshawe E. Bedford—2nd Lieut. 18 Dec., 1828 ; Lieutenant, 28 June, 1833 ; Captain, 23 July, 1841 ; Major. 12 Oct., 1849.

Rank and Name.	*Rank in Regiment.*
Captains—	
Henry Bingham	25 June 1841
Hon. H. Lyttleton Powys	17 Aug. 1841
Fra. Roger Palmer.. ..	11 Mar. 1842
John Kenn. Mackenzie..	28 April 1842
Webbe Butler..	26 July 1844
James Douglas	20 Sept. 1844
Hon. Adrian Hope.. ..	20 Dec. 1844
Henry John Darell ..	12 Jan. 1844
C. W. Hamilton Sotheby	14 Aug. 1846
William James Youge ..	10 July 1846
R. F. Waldo Sibthorp ..	5 Mar. 1847
Douglas Jones..	28 Jan. 1848
Ashton Mosley..	25 Feb. 1848
Henry Friend Kennedy..	20 Oct. 1848
Charles Napier North ..	28 Dec. 1848
John Francis Jones ..	26 Aug. 1849
Geo. Waldegrave Bligh..	12 Oct. 1849
Alexander Croe Mcik ..	29 May 1849
Gibbes Rigaud..	16 Aug. 1850
Sir E. F. Campbell, Bart.	27 Dec. 1850
First Lieutenants—	
George Chapcoat	31 Mar. 1843
Stephen Kenny	26 July 1843
Eustace Henry Rose ..	26 July 1843
Peter Burton Roe	26 July 1843
Wm. Percival Salmon ..	26 July 1843
James Fraser	26 July 1843
John Warburton	20 Sept. 1843
Wm. Hutchinson	26 April 1843
Randle Joseph Feilden ..	25 Feb. 1845
Dunbar Douglas Muter ..	17 Jan. 1845
Henry Francis Williams..	20 Dec. 1845
John Arch. MacQueen ..	6 June 1845
Ch. Alex. Boswell Genlon	13 June 1845
John Maguire..	4 July 1845
Henry Edward Warren..	30 Dec. 1845

Rank and Name.	*Rank in Regiment.*
First Lieutenants (continued)—	
Alfred Fitzgerald	13 **Feb. 1846**
Arthur Hill **Hastead** Mercer	1 Nov. 1842
Fred Arthur St. John ..	5 Mar. 1847
Francis Andrews	19 Dec. 1845
Francis Dawson	7 June 1847
Lyon Conway Travers ..	22 June 1847
John Prevost Battersby..	28 Jan. 1848
John Lambert Edward Baynes..	25 **Feb. 1848**
Bernard Ward	5 **May 1848** .
Vincent Tongue	28 **Dec. 1848**
Richard Harcourt **Robin**son	20 July 1849
Arthur Charles Greville..	26 Aug. 1849
Robert Wilmot Brooke ..	12 Oct. 1849
Richard Freer..	13 Dec. 1849
Francis Charteris Fletcher	16 Aug. 1850
Edward Bowles	16 Aug. 1850
K. J. Eustace Robertson..	27 Dec. 1850
Second Lieutenants—	
Charles Wm. Earle.. ..	24 Dec. 1846
Thomas Nicholson	22 June 1847
George Clark	1 Aug. 1846
William Mure..	22 Oct. 1847
John Du Cane	5 Nov. 1847
Conyngham Jones	25 Feb. 1848
Wm. Tedlie	5 May 1848
B. V. Douglas Samwell Vernon..	12 Sept. 1848
Henry James Robertson..	20 Oct. 1848
Henry Cockburn	10 Nov. 1848
George Illus MacQueen..	9 Mar. 1849
Hugh Parker Montgomery	21 Aug. 1849
Francis Fitzpatrick.. ..	11 Sept. 1849
Henry Semple..	19 Oct. 1849
Rowley Willis Hinxman..	23 Nov. 1849
Tristram Squire Richardson	18 Jan. 1850
Hon G. Barrington Legge	18 Jan. 1850
Charles Cholmeley Hale..	15 Feb. 1850
Henry Mitchell Jones ..	10 April 1849

Paymasters—

Edward Cozen, 9 Feb., 1826 - 2nd Lieutenant, 5 April, 1809 ; Lieutenant, 28 June, 1810 ; Captain, 8 April, 1825.

W. Henry Fitzgerald, 20 Sept., 1839 Ensign, 17 Jan., 1828 ; Lieutenant, 31 May, 1833.

Adjutants—		
Stephen Kenny, 1st Lieut.	9 May 1843
J. Maguire, 1st Lieut. ..	2 June 1849

Quartermasters—

| Thomas Berry .. .. | 29 Mar. 1842 |
| Richard Power .. .. | 28 May 1847 |

Surgeons—

Charles Robert Boyes, M.D., 2 July, 1841 ; Assistant-Surgeon, 22 Nov. 1827 ; Hospital-Assistant, 17 Aug., 1826.

Thomas Alexander, 30 May, 1845 ; Assistant-Surgeon, 10 Oct., 1834.

Assistant-Surgeons—

W. Joseph Macfarlane, 16 Feb., 1844

Q 2

Assistant-Surgeons (continued)—
Frederick J. Follhott Payne, 31 May, 1844.
G. Aug. Fred. Shelton, M.B., 3 Jan., 1845.
N. Hefferman, M.D., 11 June, 1841.

Regimentals—Green, facings scarlet.

Agent—Sir John Kirkland.

Irish Agents—Sir E. R. Borough, Bart.; Armit and Co.

1852.

Two Battalions.

India—Africa.

Celer et Audax.

Roleia, Vimiera, Martinique, Talavera, Fuentes d'Onor, Albuhera, Ciudad Rodrigo, Badajoz, Salamanca, Vittoria, Pyrenees, Nivelle, Nive, Orthes, Toulouse, Peninsula.

Col.-in-Chief—
Field Marshal H.R.H. Francis Albert Augustus Chas. Emanuel, Duke of Saxony, Prince of Saxe Coburg and Gotha, K.G., K.T., K.P., G.C.B., G.C.M.G., 15 Aug. 1850.

Cols.-Commandant—
Sir Wm. Gabriel Davy, C.B., K.C.H., —Ensign, March, 1797; Lieut., 22 May, 1797; Captain, 1 Jan., 1802; Major, 5 Feb., 1807; Lieut.-Colonel, 28 Dec., 1809; Colonel, 12 Aug., 1819; Major-Gen.,22July,1830; Lieut.-Gen., 23 Nov., 1841; Colonel, 60th Rifles, 2 Nov., 1842.
Sir Wm. Cornwallis Eustace, C.B., K.C.H.—Lieut., 27 Sept., 1783; Capt., 24 Dec., 1802; Major, 17 March, 1808; Lieut.-Colonel, 23 Aug., 1810; Colonel, 12 Aug., 1819; Major-Gen., 22 July, 1830; Lieut.-General, 23 Nov. 1841; Colonel, 60th Rifles, 7 April, 1843.

Lieut.-Colonels—
Henry Viscount Melville, K.C.B.—Ensign and Lieut., 8 Nov. 1819; Capt., 1 April, 1821; Major, 11 July, 1826; Lieut.-Colonel, 3 Dec., 1829; Colonel, 23 Nov. 1841.
Cosby Lewis Nesbitt—2nd Lieut., 27 March, 1824; Lieut., 2 June, 1825; Captain, 18 Dec., 1828; Major, 10 Aug., 1841; Lieut.-Colonel, 26 July, 1844.

Majors—
Maurice Griffin Dennis—Ensign, 9 May, 1826; Lieut., 5 July, 1827; Capt., 15 Dec., 1837; Major, 2 May, 1845; Brevet Lieut.-Colonel, 7 June, 1849.
Charles Howe Spence—2nd Lieut., 20 April, 1825; Lieut., 28 Sept., 1826; Captain, 24 May, 1841; Major, 20 Oct., 1848.
John James—Ensign, 12 June, 1828; Lieut., 2 Dec., 1841; Captain, 16 July, 1844; Major, 20 July, 1849.

Majors (continued)—
Wm. Fanshawe Bedford—2nd Lieut., 18 Dec., 1828; Lieut., 28 June, 1833; Captain, 23 July, 1841; Major, 12 Oct., 1849.

	Rank and Name.	Rank in Regiment.
Captains—		
	Henry Bingham	25 June 1841
	Hon. H. Lyttleton Powys	17 Aug. 1841
	F. Roger Palmer	11 Mar. 1842
	John Kenn. Mackenzie	23 April 1842
	Webbe Butler	26 July 1844
	James Douglas	20 Sept. 1844
	Hon. Adrian Hope	20 Dec. 1844
	Henry John Darell	12 Jan. 1844
	C. W. Hamilton Sotheby	14 Aug. 1846
	Wm. James Yonge	10 July 1846
	R. F. Waldo Sibthorp	5 May 1847
	Douglas Jones	28 Jan. 1848
	Ashton Moseley	25 Feb. 1848
	H. Friend Kennedy	20 Oct. 1848
	Charles Napier North	28 Dec. 1848
	G. Waldegrave Bligh	12 Oct. 1849
	Gibbes Rigaud	16 Aug. 1850
	Sir E. F. Campbell, Bart.	27 Dec. 1850
	Eustace Henry Rose	28 Feb. 1851
	Peter Burton Roe	17 June 1851
First Lieutenants—		
	George Clapcott	31 Mar. 1843
	Stephen Kenny	26 July 1844
	Wm. Percival Salmon	26 July 1844
	James Fraser	26 July 1844
	Wm. Hutchinson	26 April 1844
	Randle James Feilden	25 Feb. 1845
	Dunbar Douglas Muter	17 Jan. 1845
	H. Francis Williams	20 Dec. 1844
	J. Archibald MacQueen	6 June 1845
	C. A. Boswell Gordon	13 June 1845
	John Maguire	4 July 1843
	Henry Edward Warren	30 Dec. 1845
	Alfred Fitzgerald	13 Feb. 1846
	Fred. Arthur St. John	5 Mar. 1847
	Francis Andrews	19 Dec. 1845
	Francis Dawson	7 June 1847
	Lyon Conway Travers	22 June 1847
	J. Prevost Battersby	28 Jan. 1848
	John Lambert E. Baynes	24 Feb. 1848
	Bernard Ward	5 May 1848
	Vincent Tongue	28 Dec. 1848
	R. H. Robinson	20 July 1849
	Arthur Charles Greville	26 Aug. 1849
	Robert Wilmot Brooke	12 Oct. 1849
	Richard Freer	13 Dec. 1849
	F. Charteris Fletcher	16 Aug. 1850
	Edward Bowles	16 Aug. 1850
	R. J. Eustace Robertson	27 Dec. 1850
	Charles Wm. Earle	28 Feb. 1851
	C. H. K. Holloway	1 Oct. 1847
	Thomas Nicholson	17 June 1851
	William Mure	11 July 1851
Second Lieutenants—		
	George Clarke	1 Aug. 1846
	John Du Cane	5 Nov. 1847
	Conyngham Jones	25 Feb. 1848
	William Trollie	5 May 1848
	H. James Robertson	20 Oct. 1848
	Henry Cockburn	10 Nov. 1848

Rank and Name.	Rank in Regiment.
Second Lieutenants (continued)—	
G. Bliss MacQueen	.. 9 Mar. 1849
H. Parker Montgomery	.. 27 Aug. 1849
Francis Fitzpatrick	.. 11 Sept. 1849
Henry Semple	.. 19 Oct. 1849
R. Willes Hjaxman	.. 23 Nov 1849
T. Squire Richardson	.. 18 Jan. 1850
H. Mitchell James	.. 10 Apr. 1849
Wm. Waller Fox	.. 14 Feb. 1851
C. D. Cuningham Ellis	.. 17 Jan. 1851
Winchester H. Jones	.. 15 May 1851
Atholl C. J. Liddell	.. 16 May 1851
Charles Williamson	.. 11 July 1851
Arthur Hood G Gregory	19 Aug. 1851
Francis S. Travers	.. 20 Aug. 1851

Paymasters—
Edward Coxen, 9 Feb., 1826.—2nd Lieut., 5 April, 1809; Lieut., 28 June, 1810; Captain, 8 April, 1825.
Wm. H. Fitzgerald, 26 Sept., 1839 —Ensign, 17 Jan., 1828; Lieut., 31 May, 1835.

Adjutants—
Stephen Kenny, 1st Lieut. 9 May 1843
John Maguire, 1st Lieut. 2 June 1849

Quartermasters—
Thomas Berry .. .. 29 Mar. 1842
Richard Power .. .. 28 May 1847

Surgeons—
Charles Robt. Bayes, M.D., 2 July, 1841; Assistant-Surgeon, 22 Nov., 1827; Hospital Assistant, 17 Aug. 1826.
Thomas Alexander, 30 May, 1845; Assistant-Surgeon, 10 Oct., 1834.

Assistant-Surgeons—
W. Joseph Macfarlane .. 16 Feb. 1844
F. J. Folliott Payne .. 31 May 1844
Geo. A. F. Shelton, M.B. 3 Jan. 1845
Brinsley Nicolson, M.D. 25 Sept. 1846
David Ogilby Hoile, M D, 14 Oct. 1851

Regimentals—Green, facings scarlet.

Agent—Sir John **Kirkland.**

Irish Agents—Sir E. R. Borough, Bart., Armit and Co.

1853.

Two Battalions.

India Africa.

Celer et Audax.

Rolcia, Vimiera, Martinique, Talavera, Fuentes d'Onor, Albuhera, Ciudad Rodrigo, Badajoz, Salamanca, Vittoria, Pyrenees, Nivelle, Nive, Orthes, Toulouse, Peninsula.

Col.-in-Chief
General Viscount Beresford, G.C.B., G.C.H., 23 Sept., 1852.

Cols.-Commandant
Sir Wm. Gabriel Davy, C.B., K C H — Ensign, March 1797; Lieut., 22 May, 1797; Captain, 1 Jan., 1802; Major, 5

Cols.-Commandant (continued)—
Feb., 1807; Lieut.-Colonel, 28 Dec., 1809; Colonel, 12 Aug. 1819; Major-Gen., 22 July, 1830; Lieut.-Gen., 23 Nov., 1841; Colonel, 60th Rifles, 2 Nov. 1812.

Sir Wm. Cornwallis Eustace C.B., K.C.H.—Lieut., 27 Sept. 1783; Capt., 24 Dec., 1802; Major, 17 March, 1808; Lieut.-Colonel, 23 Aug., 1810; Colonel, 12 Aug. 1819; Major-Gen., 22 July, 1830; Lieut.-General, 23 Nov., 1841; Colonel, 60th Rifles, 7 April, 1843.

Lieut.-Colonels—
Henry Viscount Melville, K.C.B.—Ensign and Lieut., 18 Nov. 1819; Capt. 1 April, 1824; Major, 11 July, 1826; Lieut.-Colonel, 3 Dec., 1829; Colonel, 23 Nov. 1841.
Cosby Lewis **Nesbitt**—2nd Lieut., 27 March, 1824; **Lieut.,** 2 June, 1825; Captain, 18 Dec., 1828; Major, 10 Aug. 1841; Lieut.-Colonel, 26 July, 1844.
Maurice Griffin Dennis—Ensign, 9 May, 1826; Lieut., 5 July, 1827; Capt., 15 Dec., 1837; Major, 2 May, 1845; Brevet Lieut.-Colonel, 7 June, 1849; Lieut. Colonel, 19 Oct., 1851.

Majors—
Charles Howe Spence—2nd Lieut., 29 **April,** 1825; Lieut., 28 Sept., 1826; **Captain,** 24 May, 1841; Major, 20 Oct., 1848.
John Jones—Ensign, 12 June, 1828; **Lieut.,** 2 Dec., 1831; Captain, 16 July, 1841; Major, 20 July, 1849.
Wm. Fanshawe Bedford—2nd Lieut., 18 Dec., 1828; Lieut., 28 June, 1833; **Captain,** 23 July, 1841; Major, 12 Oct., 1849.
H. Bingham—2nd Lieut., 30 April, 1827; Lieut., 28 Sept., 1832; Captain, 25 June, 1841; Major, 19 Oct., 1851.

Rank and Name.	Rank in Regiment.
Captains—	
Hon. H. Lyttleton Powys	17 Aug. 1841
F. Roger Palmer	.. 11 Mar. 1842
J. Kenn Mackenzie	.. 23 April 1842
Webbe Butler	.. 26 July 1844
James Douglas	.. 20 Sept. 1844
Hon. Adrian Hope	.. 20 Dec. 1844
Henry John Darell	.. 12 Jan. 1845
C. W. Hamilton Sotheby	14 Aug. 1846
R. F. Waldo Sibthorp	.. 5 Mar. 1847
Douglas Jones	.. 28 Jan. 1848
Henry Friend Kennedy	.. 20 Oct. 1848
Charles Napier North	.. 28 Dec. 1848
G Wahlegrave High	.. 12 Oct. 1849
Gildas Rigaud	.. 16 Aug. 1850
Sir E. F. Campbell, Bart.	27 Dec. 1850
Eustace Henry Rose	.. 28 Feb. 1851
Peter Burton Rose	.. 17 June 1851
George Chapcott	.. 19 Oct. 1851
Wm. Percival Salmon	.. 13 April 1852
First Lieutenants—	
Stephen Kenny	.. 26 July 1844
James Fraser	.. .. 26 July 1844

Rank and Name.	Rank in Regiment.

First Lieutenants (continued)—

Wm. Hutchinson	26 April 1844
Randle James Feilden	25 Feb. 1845
Dunbar Douglas Muter..	17 Jan. 1845
Henry Francis Williams..	20 Dec. 1844
John Arch. MacQueen	6 June 1845
C. Alex. Boswell Gordon	13 June 1845
John Maguire	4 July 1843
Henry Edward Warren..	30 Dec. 1845
Alfred Fitzgerald	13 Feb. 1846
F. Arthur St. John	5 Mar. 1847
Francis Andrews	19 Dec. 1845
Francis Dawson	7 June 1847
Lyon Conway Travers	22 June 1847
J. Prevost Battersby	28 Jan. 1848
J. Lambert E. Baynes ..	24 Feb. 1848
Bernard Ward	5 May 1848
Vincent Tongue	28 Dec. 1848
R. Harcourt Robinson	20 July 1849
Arthur C. Greville..	26 Aug. 1849
Robert Wilmot Brooke..	12 Oct. 1849
Richard Freer	13 Dec. 1849
F. Charteris Fletcher	16 Aug. 1850
Edward Bowles	16 Aug. 1850
R. J. Eustace Robertson..	27 Dec. 1850
Charles William Earle	28 Feb. 1851
C. H. Elphin. Holloway..	1 Oct. 1847
Thomas Nicholson ..	17 June 1851
Wm. Mure	11 July 1851
John Du Cane	19 Oct. 1851
William Tedlie	13 April 1852

Second Lieutenants—

Conyngham Jones ..	25 Feb. 1848
H James Robertson	20 Oct. 1848
Henry Cockburn	10 Nov. 1848
G. Bliss MacQueen..	9 Mar. 1849
H. Parker Montgomery..	21 Aug. 1849
Francis Fitzpatrick	11 Sept. 1849
Henry Semple..	19 Oct. 1849
Rowley W. Hinxman	23 Nov. 1849
Tristram S. Richardson..	18 Jan. 1850
Henry Mitchell James	10 April 1850
William Walter Fox	14 Feb. 1851
C. D. Cuningham Ellis ..	17 Jan. 1851
Atholl C. J. Liddell	16 May 1851
Charles Williamson	11 July 1851
Arthur H. G. Gregory ..	19 Aug. 1851
Francis Stewart Travers..	20 Aug. 1851
Wm. Aug. Dean Pitt	22 April 1852
Wykeham L. Pemberton	23 April 1852
Henry Pardoe Eaton	11 June 1852
James H. Aug. Stewart ..	17 Aug. 1852

Paymasters—

Edward Coxen, 9 Feb., 1826—2nd Lieut., 5 April, 1809; Lieut., 28 June, 1810; Captain, 8 April, 1825.

Wm. Henry Fitzgerald, 20 Sept., 1839—Ensign, 17 Jan., 1828; Lieut., 31 May, 1833.

Adjutants—

Stephen Kenny, 1st Lieut. 9 May 1843
John Maguire, 1st Lieut. 2 June 1849

Quartermasters—

Thomas Berry..	29 Mar. 1842
Richard Power	28 May 1847

Rank and Name.	Rank in Regiment.

Surgeons—

Charles Robert Boynes, M.D., 2 July, 1841; Assistant-Surgeon, 22 Nov. 1827; Hospital Assistant, 17 Aug. 1826.

Thomas Alexander, 30 May, 1845; Assistant-Surgeon, 10 Oct. 1834.

Assistant-Surgeons—

Wm. J. Macfarlane	16 Feb. 1844
G. A. F. Shelton, M.B...	3 Jan. 1845
Brinsley Nicholson, M.D.	25 Sept. 1846
David Ogilvy Hoile, M.D.	14 Oct. 1851
James Crenar ..	3 Sept. 1847

Regimental—Green, facings scarlet.

Agent—Sir John Kirkland.

Irish Agents—Sir E. R. Borough, Bart.; Armit and Co.

1854.

Two Battalions.

India—Africa.

Celer et Audax.

Rolcia, Vimiera, Martinique, Talavera, Fuentes d'Onor, Albuhera, Ciudad Rodrigo, Badajoz, Salamanca, Vittoria, Pyrenees, Nivelle, Nive, Orthes, Toulouse, Peninsula, Punjaub, Mooltan, Goojerat.

Col.-in-Chief—

General Viscount Beresford, G.C.B., G.C.H., 23 Sept. 1852.

Cols.-Commandant—

Sir Wm. Gabriel Davy, C.B., K.C.H. Ensign, March, 1797; Lieut., 22 May, 1797; Captain, 1 Jan., 1802; Major, 5 Feb., 1807; Lieut.-Colonel, 28 Dec., 1809; Colonel, 12 Aug., 1819; Major-Gen., 22 July, 1830; Lieut.-Gen., 23 Nov., 1841; Colonel, 60th Rifles, 2 Nov., 1842.

Sir Wm. Cornwallis Eustace, C.B., K.C.H.—Lieut., 27 Sept., 1783; Capt., 24 Dec., 1802; Major, 17 March, 1808; Lieut.-Colonel, 23 Aug., 1810; Colonel, 12 Aug., 1819; Major-Gen., 22 July, 1830; Lieut.-General, 23 Nov., 1841; Colonel, 60th Rifles, 7 April, 1813.

Lieut.-Colonels—

Henry Viscount Melville, K.C.B.—Ensign and Lieut., 18 Nov., 1819; Capt., 1 April, 1824; Major, 11 July, 1826; Lieut.-Colonel, 3 Dec., 1829; Colonel, 23 Nov., 1841.

Maurice Griffin Dennis—Ensign, 9 May, 1826; Lieut., 5 July, 1827; Capt., 15 Dec., 1837; Major, 2 May, 1845; Brevet Lieut.-Col., 7 June, 1849; Lieut.-Colonel, 19 Oct., 1851.

Charles Howe Spence—2nd Lieut., 20 April, 1825; Lieut., 28 Sept., 1826; Captain, 24 May, 1844; Major, 20 Oct., 1848; Lieut.-Colonel, 2 Oct., 1853.

Majors—

Wm. Fanshawe Bedford—2nd Lieut., 18 Dec., 1828 ; Lieut., 28 June, 1833 ; Captain, 23 July, 1841 ; Major, 12 Oct., 1849 ; Brevet Lieut.-Col., 28 May, 1853.

Henry Bingham—2nd Lieut., 30 April, 1827; Lieut., 28 Sept., 1832 ; Captain, 25 June, 1841 ; Major, 19 Oct., 1851.

Hon. Henry Lyttleton Powys—2nd Lieut., 2 April, 1829 ; Lieut., 19 Sept., 1834 ; Captain, 17 Aug., **1841** ; Major, 23 Dec., 1853.

Rank and Name.	Rank in Regiment.
Captains—	
F. Roger **Palmer** ..	.. 11 Mar. **1842**
J. Kean. **Mackenzie** ..	.. 23 April **1842**
Webbe Butler.. ..	.. 26 July **1844**
James Douglas ..	.. 20 Sept. **1844**
Hon. Adrian Hope ..	.. 20 Dec. **1844**
Henry John Darell..	.. 12 Jan. **1844**
Rank in Army, Bt. Maj. 28 May **1853**	
C. W. H. Sotheby ..	.. 14 Aug. **1846**
Wm. James Yonge ..	.. 10 July **1846**
H. Friend Kennedy ..	.. 20 Oct. **1848**
Charles Napier North	.. 28 Dec. **1848**
G. Waldegrave High	.. 12 Oct. **1849**
Gibbes Rigaud ..	.. 16 Aug. **1850**
Sir E. F. Campbell, Bart.	27 Dec. **1850**
Peter Burton Rowe	.. 17 June **1851**
George Clayoott ..	.. 19 Oct. **1851**
Wm. Percival Salmon	.. 13 April **1852**
James Fraser	.. 7 Jan. **1853**
F. Charles **Annesley** ..	.. 26 Dec. **1853**
Stephen Keatty ..	.. 15 Mar. **1853**
Wm. Hutchinson ..	.. 15 Mar. **1853**
Thomas Biggs	.. 8 April **1853**
Randle J. Feilden ..	.. 23 Dec. **1853**
First Lieutenants—	
Dunbar D. Muter ..	.. 17 Jan. **1845**
Henry Francis Williams..	20 Dec. **1844**
C. A. B. Gordon ..	.. 13 June **1845**
John Maguire	.. 4 July **1845**
Henry Edward Warren ..	30 Dec. **1845**
Alfred Fitzgerald ..	.. 13 Feb. **1846**
Fred. Arthur St. John ..	5 Mar. **1847**
Francis Andrews ..	.. 13 Dec. **1845**
Francis Dawson ..	.. 22 June **1847**
John Prevost Battersby..	28 Jan. **1848**
J. Lambert F. Baynes ..	25 Feb. **1848**
Bernard Edward Ward..	5 May **1848**
Vincent Tongue ..	.. 28 Dec. **1848**
R. **Harcourt** Robinson ..	20 July **1849**
R. Wilmot Brooke ..	.. 12 Oct. **1849**
Richard Freer ..	.. 13 Dec. **1849**
F. Charteris Fletcher ..	16 Aug. **1850**
Edward Bowles ..	.. 16 Aug. **1850**
R. J. Eustace Robertson	27 Dec. **1850**
Charles Wm. Earle..	.. 28 Feb. **1851**
William Mure.. ..	.. 11 July **1851**
William Tedlie ..	.. 13 April **1852**
Conyngham Jones ..	.. 21 Oct. **1852**
H. J. Robertson ..	.. 7 Jan. **1853**
Henry Cockburn ..	.. 20 Sept. **1853**
H. P. Montgomery ..	.. 16 Dec. **1853**
G. C. Henry Waters ..	18 Mar. **1853**
Henry Semple.. ..	.. 23 Dec. **1853**
G. Bliss MacQueen ..	28 Oct. **1853**

Rank and Name.	Rank in Regiment.
Second Lieutenants—	
Francis Fitzpatrick.. ..	19 Oct. **1849**
Rowley W. Hinxman ..	23 Nov. **1849**
Tristram S. Richardson..	18 Jan. **1850**
Henry Mitchell James ..	10 April **1849**
Wm. Waller Fox	14 Feb. **1851**
C. David C. Ellis ..	17 Jan. **1851**
Atholl C. J. Liddell ..	16 May **1851**
Charles Williamson ..	11 July **1851**
Francis Stewart Travers..	20 Aug. **1851**
Wm. Aug. Dean Pitt ..	22 April **1852**
Wykeham L. Pemberton	23 April **1852**
Henry Pardoe Eaton ..	11 June **1852**
J. Henry Aug. Stewart ..	17 Aug. **1852**
William Cubitt	15 Oct. **1852**
Fra. Dundas Farquharson	18 Feb. **1853**
John James Phillips ..	27 May **1853**
H. K. Edwards Hope ..	20 Sept. **1853**
J. S. Davenport M'Gill ..	16 Dec. **1853**

Paymasters—

Edward Coten, 9 Feb. **1826**—2nd Lieut., 5 April, 1809 ; Lieut., 28 June, 1819 ; Captain, 8 April, 1825.

Edward Rawlings Hannam, 15 July, 1853—Ensign, 4 July, 1815 ; Lieut., 3 April, 1846.

Adjutants—

John Maguire, 1st Lieut. 2 June **1840**
Richd. Harcourt Robinson 1st Lieut. .. .. .. 15 July **1853**

Quartermasters—

Thomas Berry .. .. 29 Mar, **1842**
Luke Fitz Gibbon .. .. 15 Oct. **1847**

Surgeons—

Charles Robert Boyes, M.D., 2 July, 1844 ; Assistant Surgeon, 22 Nov., 1827 ; Hospital Assistant, 17 Aug., 1826.

Henry James Schooles, M.D., 1 Oct., 1847 ; Assistant Surgeon, 28 June, 1839.

Assistant Surgeons—

W. J. Macfarlane .. 16 Feb. **1844**
O. A. F. Shelton, M.B. .. 3 Jan. **1849**
B. Nicholson, M.D... 25 Sept. **1846**
David Ogilvy Hoile, M.D. 14 Oct. **1851**
James Crerar .. .. 3 Sept. **1847**

Regimentals—Green, facings scarlet.

Agent—Sir John Kirkland.

Irish Agents—Sir E. R. Borough, Bart. ; Armit and Co.

1855.

Three Battalions.

India—Africa—Ireland.

Celer et Audax.

Roleia, Vimiera, Martinique, Talavera, Fuentes d'Onor, Albuhera, Ciudad Rodrigo, Badajoz, Salamanca, Vittoria, Pyrenees, Nivelle, Nive, Orthes, Toulouse, Peninsula, Punjaub, Mooltan, Goojerat.

Col.-in-Chief—

General Viscount Gough, G.C.B., 28 January, 1854.

Cols. Commandant—

Sir Wm. Gabriel Davy, C.B., K.C.H.—Ensign, March, 1797; Lieut., 22 May, 1797; Captain, 1 Jan., 1802; Major, 5 Feb., 1807; Lieut.-Col., 28 Dec., 1809; Colonel, 12 Aug., 1819; Major-Gen., 22 July, 1830; Lieut.-Gen., 23 Nov., 1841; General, 20 June, 1854; Colonel, 60th Rifles, 2 Nov., 1842.

Sir Wm. Cornwallis Eustace, C.B., K.C.H.—Lieut. 27 Sept., 1783; Captain, 24 Dec., 1802; Major, 17 March, 1808; Lieut.-Colonel, 23 Aug., 1810; Colonel, 12 Aug., 1819; Major-Gen., 22 July, 1830; Lieut.-Gen., 23 Nov., 1841; General, 20 June, 1854; Colonel, 60th Rifles, 7 April, 1813.

Lieut.-Colonels—

Maurice Griffin Dennis—Ensign, 9 May, 1826; Lieut., 5 July, 1827; Capt., 15 Dec., 1837; Major, 2 May, 1845; Brevet Lieut.-Colonel, 7 June, 1849; Lieut.-Colonel, 19 Oct., 1851; Colonel, 28 Nov., 1854.

Charles Howe Spence—2nd Lieut., 20 April, 1825; Lieut., 28 Sept. 1826; Captain, 24 May, 1841; Major, 29 Oct., 1848; Lieut.-Colonel, 2 Oct., 1853.

John Jones—Ensign, 12 June, 1828; Lieut., 2 Dec., 1831; Captain, 16 July, 1841; Major, 20 July, 1849; Lieut.-Colonel, 20 June, 1854.

Majors—

Wm. Fanshawe Bedford—2nd Lieut., 18 Dec., 1828; Lieut., 28 June, 1833; Captain, 22 July, 1841; Major, 12 Oct., 1849; Brevet Lieut.-Colonel, 28 May, 1853.

Henry Bingham—2nd Lieut., 30 April, 1827; Lieut., 28 Sept., 1832; Captain, 25 June, 1841; Major, 19 Oct., 1851.

Hon. Henry Lyttleton Powys 2nd Lieut., 2 April, 1829; Lieut., 19 Sept., 1834; Captain, 17 Aug., 1841; Major, 2 Oct., 1853.

Francis Roger Palmer— 2nd Lieut., 15 March, 1833; Lieut., 24 April, 1835; Captain, 11 March, 1842; Major, 20 June, 1854.

Rank and Name.	Rank in Regiment.
Captains—	
J. Kenn. Mackenzie	.. 23 April 1842
Rank in Army, Bt. Maj. 20 June 1841	
Webbe Butler ..	.. 26 July 1841
James Douglas ..	.. 20 Sept. 1841
Hon. A. Hope ..	.. 20 Dec. 1841
Rank in Army, Bt. Maj. 28 May 1853	
Henry John Darell..	.. 12 Jan. 1844
Rank in Army, Bt. Maj. 12 Dec. 1854	
Wm. James Yonge..	.. 10 July 1846
H. Friend Kennedy	.. 20 Oct. 1848
Charles Napier North	.. 28 Dec. 1848
G. Wahlegrave Bligh	.. 12 Oct. 1849
Gibbes Rigaud ..	.. 16 Aug. 1850
Sir E. C. Campbell, Bart. 27 Dec. 1850	
Peter Barton Roe ..	.. 17 June 1851
George Clapcott ..	.. 19 Oct. 1851

Rank and Name.	Rank in Regiment.
Captains (continued)—	
Wm. Perceval Salmon	.. 13 April 1852
James Fraser	.. 7 Jan. 1853
Wm. Hutchinson ..	.. 15 Mar. 1853
Thomas Biggs.. ..	.. 8 April 1853
Randle J. Feilden ..	.. 23 Dec. 1853
H. Francis Williams	.. 3 Mar. 1854
Dunbar Douglas Muter..	31 May 1854
C. A. Boswell Gordon ..	6 June 1854
John Maguire	20 June 1854
Henry Edward Warren..	4 Aug. 1854
John Robert Wilton ..	14 July 1854
First Lieutenants—	
Alfred Fitzgerald ..	.. 13 Feb. 1846
F. Arthur St. John	.. 5 Mar. 1847
Francis Andrews ..	.. 19 Dec. 1845
Francis Dawson ..	.. 22 June 1847
John Prevost Battersby ..	28 Jan. 1848
J. Lambert E. Baynes ..	24 Feb. 1848
Bernard E. Ward ..	.. 5 May 1848
Vincent Tongue ..	.. 28 Dec. 1848
R. Harcourt Robinson ..	20 July 1849
Robt. Wilmot Brooke ..	12 Oct. 1849
Richard Freer	13 Dec. 1849
Francis Charteris Fletcher	16 Aug. 1850
Edward Bowles ..	.. 16 Aug. 1850
R. J. E. Robertson ..	.. 27 Dec. 1850
Charles William Earle ..	28 Feb. 1851
William Tedlie ..	.. 13 April 1852
Conyngham Jones ..	.. 21 Oct. 1852
Henry James Robertson..	7 Jan. 1853
Henry Cockburn ..	.. 23 June 1853
George Bliss MacQueen..	2 Oct. 1853
Hugh P. Montgomery ..	28 Oct. 1853
Geo. Chas. Henry Waters	18 Mar. 1853
Henry Semple ..	.. 16 Dec. 1853
Rowley W. Hinxman ..	3 Mar. 1854
Randolph R. Adderley ..	10 Mar. 1854
Francis Fitzpatrick ..	31 May 1854
Tristram S. Richardson..	6 June 1854
Wm. Waller Fox	6 June 1854
C. D. Cuningham Ellis ..	20 June 1854
Athol C. J. Liddell ..	20 June 1854
Charles Williamson ..	11 Aug. 1854
Francis Stewart Travers..	18 Aug. 1854
Wm. Augustus Denn Pitt	18 Aug. 1854
Wykeham L. Pemberton	25 Aug. 1854
Second Lieutenants—	
Henry Pardoe Eaton	.. 11 June 1852
William Cubitt ..	.. 15 Oct. 1852
Fra. Dundas Farquharson	18 Feb. 1853
John James Phillips ..	27 May 1853
J. S. Davenport M'Gill..	16 Dec. 1853
James Durham Dundas..	3 Mar. 1854
James Hare	17 Mar. 1854
Ensigns—	
Herbert Geo. Deedes ..	11 Aug. 1854
John d'Olier George ..	23 Aug. 1854
Llewellyn E. Traherne ..	24 Aug. 1854
James Joseph Collins ..	25 Aug. 1854
D. G. N. Watts-Russell..	29 Sept. 1854
Arthur Wm. Knox-Gore	8 Dec. 1854
James Arthur Morrah ..	8 Sept. 1854
Hon. Richard P. Vereker	29 Dec. 1854
Paymasters—	
Edward Coxen, 9 Feb., 1826—2nd	

Rank and Name.   *Rank in Regiment.*

Paymasters (continued) —
Lieut., 3 April, 1836; Lieut., 28 June, 1810; Captain, 8 April, 1825.
Edward Rawlings Hannan, **15 July,** 1855—Ensign, 4 July, 1846; **Lieut., 3** April, 1846.

Adjutants —
Richard Harcourt Robinson,1st Lieut., 15 July, 1853.
Francis Dawson, 1st Lieut., **18 Aug.,** 1854.

Quartermasters —
Luke FitzGibbon .. .. **15 Oct. 1857**
George Charles Kelly .. **20 Oct. 1854**

Surgeons —
Charles Robert Boyes, M.D., **2 July,** 1841; Assistant-Surgeon, 22 Nov. 1827; Hospital Assistant, 17 Aug., 1826.
Henry James Schooles, M.D., 1 Oct., 1847—Assistant-Surgeon, **28 June, 1839.**

Assistant-Surgeons —
W. Joseph Macfarlane .. **16 Feb. 1844**
Brinsley Nicholson, M.D. **25 Sept. 1846**
David Ogilvy Hole, M.D. **11 Oct. 1851**
James Crerar .. .. .. **3 Sept. 1847**
A. Graham Young.. .. **5 May 1854**

Regimentals —Green, **facings scarlet.**

Agents—Messrs. Charles R. and Walter McGregor.

Irish Agents—Sir E. R. Borough, Bart.; Armit and Co.

1856.

Three Battalions.

India —Africa — Ireland.

Celer et Audax.

Roleia, Vimiera, Martinique, Talavera, Fuentes d'Onor, Albuhera, Ciudad Rodrigo, Badajoz, Salamanca, Vittoria, Pyrenees, Nivelle, Nive, Orthes, Toulouse, Peninsula, Punjaub, Mooltan, Goojerat.

Col.-in-Chief —
General Viscount Gough, G.C.B., 28 January, 1854.

Cols.-Commandant —
Sir W. Gabriel Davy, C.B., K.C.H. Ensign, March, 1797; Lieutenant, 22 May, 1797; Captain, 1 Jan., 1802; Major, 5 Feb. 1807; Lieut.-Colonel, 28 Dec., 1809; Colonel, 12 Aug. 1819; Major-General, 22 July, 1830; Lieut.-General, 23 Nov., 1841; General, 20 June, 1854; Colonel, 60th Rifles, 2 Nov. 1842.
Thomas Bunbury, K.H. Ensign, 25 March, 1804; Lieutenant, 23 Dec., 1804; Captain, 3 Nov., 1808; Major, 14 April, 1814; Lieut.-Colonel, 5 July, 1821; Colonel, 10 Jan. 1837; Major-General, 9 Nov., 1846; Lieut.-General, 20 June, 1854; Colonel, 60th Rifles, 9 Feb., 1855.

Lieut.-Colonels —
Maurice Griffin Dennis—Ensign, 9 May, **1826**; Lieutenant, 5 July, 1827; Captain, 15 Dec., 1837; Major, 2 May, 1845; Brevet Lieut.-Colonel, 7 June, 1849; Lieut. Colonel, 19 Oct., 1854; Colonel, 28 Nov., 1854.
Charles Howe Spence—2nd **Lieut.,** 20 April, 1825; Lieutenant, 28 **Sept.,** 1826; Captain, 24 May, 1841; **Major,** 20 Oct., 1848; Lieut.-Colonel, **2 Oct.,** 1853.
John Jones—Ensign, 12 June, 1828; Lieutenant, **2** Dec., 1831; Captain, 16 July, 1841; Major, 20 July, 1849; Lieut.-Colonel, 20 June, 1854.
Wm. Fanshawe Bedford —2nd Lieut., 18 Dec., 1828; Lieutenant, 28 June, 1833; Captain, 23 July, 1841; Major, 12 Oct., 1849; Brevet Lieut.-Colonel, 28 May, 1853; Lieut.-Colonel, 23 March, 1855.

Majors —
Henry Bingham—2nd **Lieutenant,** 30 April, 1827; Lieutenant, 28 Sept., 1832; Captain, 25 June, 1841; **Major,** 19 Oct., 1854.
Francis Roger Palmer—Ensign, 15 March, 1833; Lieutenant, 24 April, 1835; Captain, 11 March, **1842;** Major, 20 June, 1854.
Webbe Butler—2nd Lieutenant, 19 Sept., 1831; Lieutenant, 15 Dec., 1840; Captain, 20 July, 1843; **Major, 23** March, 1855.
James Douglas—2nd Lieutenant, 17 Aug., 1838; Lieutenant, 16 July, 1841; Captain, 20 Sept., 1844; Major, 23 March, 1855.
Hon. A. Hope—2nd Lieutenant, 23 Nov., 1838; Lieutenant, 23 April, 1841; Captain, 20 Dec. 1844; Brevet Major, 28 May, 1853; Brevet Lieut.-Colonel, 12 Dec. 1854; Major, 23 March, 1855.
Henry Friend Kennedy—2nd Lieutenant, 11 Sept., 1840; Lieut., 7 April, 1842; Captain, 20 Oct., 1848; Major, 17 Aug., 1855.

Rank and Name.   *Rank in Regiment.*

Captains —
Wm. James Yonge.. .. .. 10 July 1846
Charles Napier North .. 28 Dec. 1848
G. Waldegrave Bligh .. 12 Oct. 1849
Gibbes Rigaud .. .. .. 16 Aug. 1850
Sir E. F. Campbell, Bt... 27 Dec. 1850
Peter Burton Roe .. .. 17 June 1851
George Clapcott .. .. 19 Oct. 1851
James Fraser .. .. .. 7 Jan. 1853
William Hutchinson .. 15 Mar. 1853
Thomas Biggs.. .. .. 8 April 1853
Randle J. Feilden .. .. 23 Dec. 1853
Hen. Francis Williams .. 3 Mar. 1854
Dunbar Douglas Muter., 31 May 1854
C. A. Boswell Gordon .. 6 June 1854
John Maguire .. .. .. 20 June 1854
Hon. Edward Warren .. 1 Aug. 1854
John Robert Wilton .. 11 July 1854

Rank and Name.	Rank in Regiment.

Captains (continued)—

Alfred J. Fitzgerald. ..	23 Mar. 1855
Fred. Arthur St. John ..	23 Mar. 1855
Francis Andrews	23 Mar. 1855
Francis Dawson	23 Mar. 1855
John Provost Battersby .	23 Mar. 1855
J. Lambert Edw. Baynes	23 Mar. 1855
Bernard Edw. Ward ..	23 Mar. 1855
Rank in Army, Bt. Maj.	20 July 1855
Vincent Tongue	23 Mar. 1855
R. Harcourt Robinson ..	23 Mar. 1855
Robert Wilmot Brooke ..	23 Mar. 1855
Richard Freer..	23 Mar. 1855
Fran. Charteris Fletcher.	23 Mar. 1855
Edward Bowles	23 Mar. 1855
R. J. E. Robertson ..	23 Mar. 1855
Hen. James Robertson ..	29 June 1855
Hugh P. Montgomery ..	17 Aug. 1855
Wm. Waller Fox	31 Aug. 1855
C. D. Cuningham Ellis .	21 Dec. 1855
Hon. Atholl C. J. Liddell	21 Dec. 1855

Lieutenants—

Wm. Tedlie	13 April 1852
Conyngham Jones	21 Oct. 1852
Henry Cockburn	23 June 1853
George Bliss MacQueen..	2 Oct. 1853
George Ch. Henry Waters	18 Mar. 1853
Henry Semple..	16 Dec. 1853
Rowley Willis Hinxman..	3 Mar. 1854
Trist. Squire Richardson.	6 June 1854
Charles Williamson ..	11 Aug. 1854
Francis Stewart Travers .	18 Aug. 1854
William Aug. Dean Pitt .	18 Aug. 1854
Wykeham Leigh Pemberton	25 Aug. 1854
Henry Pardoe Eaton ..	23 Mar. 1855
William Cubitt	23 Mar. 1855
Fra. Dundas Farquharson	23 Mar. 1855
John James Phillips. ..	23 Mar. 1855
J.Shuter Davenport M'Gill	23 Mar. 1855
James Durham Dundas..	23 Mar. 1855
James Hare	23 Mar. 1855
Herbert George Deedes.	25 Mar. 1855
John d'Olier George ..	23 Mar. 1855
Llewellyn Edw. Traherne	23 Mar. 1855
James Joseph Collins ..	23 Mar. 1855
Dan. G. N. Watts-Russell	23 Mar. 1855
Anthony Carlisle	22 Sept. 1854
John Hedley	4 April 1854
Arthur Wm. Knox-Gore	11 May 1855
James Arthur Morrah ..	11 May 1855
Hon. R. Prendergast Vereker	11 May 1855
John Steel	27 June 1854
Francis Vernon Northey .	27 July 1855
Philip Julian Curtis ..	31 Aug. 1855
Wm. F. Carleton	17 Aug. 1855
John Baptiste Shackle ..	23 Oct. 1855
James Forbes	23 Oct. 1855
Robert Morris Hazen ..	23 Oct. 1855
Chas. James Phillipps ..	23 Oct. 1855
Geo. French Stehelin ..	26 Oct. 1855
Edward Cockburn Allen .	26 Oct. 1855
Burnet Bell Forsyth ..	25 Oct. 1855
Cromer Ashburnham ..	26 Oct. 1855
Geo. Kennedy Shaw ..	26 Oct. 1855

Rank and Name.	Rank in Regiment.

Ensigns—

Augustus Morgan	21 April 1855
Kennett Gregg Henderson	23 April 1855
W. Brindley Scott Conyers	24 April 1855
G. C. Kelly	1 May 1855
Fred Austin	8 May 1855
Edward Campbell Ainslie	9 May 1855
J.Sturgeon Hamilton Algar	10 May 1855
E. Robt. King-Harman..	11 May 1855
Chas. Yarworth Jones ..	25 May 1855
Matthew Tilford	31 May 1855
Joseph John Bradshaw ..	1 June 1855
Fred. Simon A. Orchard..	8 June 1855
James Kiero Watson ..	20 July 1855
Chas. Chris. Willoughby	20 July 1855
Jenico Preston	14 Sept. 1855
Robert John Hickman ..	20 Oct. 1855
Thomas Monsell Warren.	21 Oct. 1855
George Hatchell	22 Oct. 1855
John Owen Young.. ..	23 Oct. 1855
John Malcolm Sewell ..	25 Oct. 1855
Joseph Wigg	26 Oct. 1855
Arthur Tufnell	9 Nov. 1855
Richard F. Jennings ..	23 Nov. 1855
Frank Sadlier Brereton..	14 Dec. 1855
Wm. Henry Napier ..	21 Dec. 1855

Paymasters—

Ⓔ Edward Coxen, 9 Feb., 1826—2nd Lieutenant, 5 April, 1809; Lieut., 28 June, 1810; Captain, 8 April, 1825.

Francis Fitzpatrick, 2 March, 1855—Ensign, 19 Oct., 1849; Lieutenant, 31 May, 1854.

Frederick Thomas Patterson, 19 June, 1855.

Adjutants—

James Forbes, Lieut. ..	5 April 1855
Geo. Chas. Kelly, Ensign	1 May 1855
Matthew Tilford, Ensign.	9 Oct. 1855

Quartermasters—

Luke Fitzgibbon	15 Oct. 1847
Hugh Campbell	23 Mar. 1855
William Hunter	13 July 1855

Surgeons—

Henry Schooles, M.D., 1 Oct., 1847; Assistant-Surgeon, 28 June, 1839.

John Harry Kerr Innis,11 March,1853; Assistant-Surgeon, 8 April, 1842.

Deodatus Wm. Eaton, 11 May,1855; Assistant-Surgeon, 24 Oct., 1845.

Assistant-Surgeons—

Brinsley Nicholson, M.D.	25 Sept. 1846
Frd. Ogilvy Hoile, M.D..	14 Oct. 1851
A. Graham Young.. ..	5 May 1854
John Mathew Biddle ..	3 June 1853
Thomas John Murphy ..	28 April 1854
James Macartney	6 Oct. 1854
Arthur Stretton	1 Sept. 1854

Regimentals—Green, facings scarlet.

Agents—Messrs. Chas. R. and Walter McGregor.

Irish Agents—Sir E. R. Borough, Bart.; Armit and Co.

1857.

Three Battalions.

India—Africa—Ireland.

Celer et Audax.

Roleia, Vimiera, Martinique, Talavera, Fuentes d'Onor, Albuhera, Ciudad Rodrigo, Badajoz, Salamanca, Vittoria, Pyrenees, Nivelle, Nive, Orthes, Toulouse, Peninsula, Punjaub, Mooltan, Goojerat.

Col.-in-Chief—

General Viscount Gough, K.P.,G.C.B., 28 January, 1854.

Cols. Commandant—

Thomas Bunbury, K.H.—Ensign, 26 March, 1804; Lieut., 24 Dec., 1804; Captain, 3 Nov., 1808; Major, 14 April, 1814; Lieut.-Colonel, 5 July, 1821; Colonel, 10 Jan., 1837; Major-Gen., 9 Nov., 1846; Lieut.-Gen., 20 June, 1854; Colonel, 60th Rifles, 9 Feb., 1855.

Sir Wm. George Moore, K.C.B.—Ensign, 18 April, 1811; Lieut., 10 Sept., 1812; Captain, 14 April, 1814; Major, 21 Jan., 1819; Lieut.-Colonel, 12 Jan., 1821; Colonel, 28 June, 1838; Major-Gen., 11 Nov., 1851; Lieut.-Gen., 5 June, 1855; Colonel, 60th Rifles, 20 January, 1856.

Lieut.-Colonels—

Maurice Griffin Dennis—Ensign, 9 May, 1826; Lieut., 5 July, 1827; Capt., 15 Dec., 1837; Major, 2 May, 1845; Brevet Lieut.-Colonel, 7 June, 1849; Lieut.-Colonel, 10 Oct., 1851; Colonel, 28 November, 1854.

Charles Howe Spence—2nd Lieut., 29 April, 1825; Lieut., 28 Sept., 1826; Captain, 24 May, 1841; Major, 20 Oct., 1848; Lieut.-Colonel, 2 October, 1853; Colonel, 2 October, 1856.

John Jones—Ensign, 12 June, 1829; Lieut., 2 Dec., 1831; Captain, 16 July, 1841; Major, 20 July, 1849; Lieut.-Colonel, 23 June, 1854.

Wm. Fanshawe Bedford—2nd Lieut. 18 Dec., 1828; Lieut., 28 June, 1833; Captain, 23 July, 1841; Major, 12 Oct., 1849; Brevet Lieut.-Colonel, 28 May, 1853; Lieut.-Colonel, 23 March, 1855.

Majors—

Henry Bingham—2nd Lieut., 30 April, 1827; Lieut., 28 Sept., 1832; Captain, 25 June, 1841; Major, 19 Oct., 1851.

Francis Roger Palmer—Ensign, 15 March, 1833; Lieut., 24 April, 1845; Captain, 11 March, 1842; Major, 20 June, 1854.

Webbe Butler—2nd Lieut., 19 Sept., 1834; Lieut., 15 Dec., 1840; Captain, 26 July, 1844; Major, 23 March, 1855.

James Douglas—2nd Lieut., 17 Aug., 1838; Lieut., 16 July, 1841; Captain, 20 Sept., 1844; Major, 23 March, 1855.

Majors (continued)—

Henry Friend Kennedy—2nd Lieut., 11 Sept., 1840; Lieut., 7 April, 1842; Captain, 20 Oct., 1848; Major, 17 Aug., 1855.

Wm. James Yonge—Ensign, 27 July, 1826; Lieut., 17 May, 1827; Captain, 10 July, 1846; Major, 25 Jan., 1856.

Captains—	*Rank and Name.*	*Rank in Regiment.*
Charles Napier North	..	28 Dec. 1848
G. Wallegrave Bligh	..	12 Oct. 1849
Gibbes Rigaud	..	16 Aug. 1850
Sir E. F. Campbell, Bart.	..	27 Dec. 1850
Peter Burton Roe	.. ..	17 June 1851
James Fraser	..	7 Jan. 1853
Wm. Hutchinson	..	15 Mar. 1853
Thomas Biggs	.. ..	8 April 1853
Randle J. Feilden	..	26 Dec. 1853
Hon. Francis Williams	..	3 Mar. 1854
Dunbar Douglas Muter	..	31 May 1854
C. A. Boswell Gordon	..	6 June 1854
Rank in Army, Bt. Maj.		6 June 1856
John Maguire	..	20 June 1854
Hon. Edward Warren	..	4 Aug. 1854
John Robert Wilton	..	14 July 1854
Alfred J. Fitzgerald	..	23 Mar. 1855
Fred. Arthur St. John	..	23 Mar. 1855
Francis Andrews	..	23 Mar. 1855
Francis Dawson	..	23 Mar. 1855
J. Prevost Battersby	..	23 Mar. 1855
J. Lambert E. Baynes	..	23 Mar. 1855
Bernard F. Ward	..	23 Mar. 1855
Rank in Army, Bt. Maj.		20 July 1855
Vincent Tongue	..	23 Mar. 1855
R. Harcourt Robinson	..	23 Mar. 1855
Robt. Walmol Brooke	..	23 Mar. 1855
F. Charteris Fletcher	..	23 Mar. 1855
Edward Bowles	..	23 Mar. 1855
R. J. Kruger Robertson	..	23 Mar. 1855
Hon. James Robertson	..	20 June 1855
Hugh P. Montgomery	..	17 Aug. 1855
Wm. Waller Fox	..	31 Aug. 1855
C. D. Cunningham	..	14 Dec. 1855
Hon. Atholl C. J. Liddell		21 Dec. 1855
William Tedlie	..	25 Jan. 1856
Wm. Douglas Philips	..	7 April 1854
Conyngham Jones	..	6 May 1856

Lieutenants—

Henry Cockburn	..	23 June 1853
G. Bliss MacQueen	..	2 Oct. 1853
G. C. Henry Waters	..	18 Mar. 1853
Henry Semple	..	16 Dec. 1853
Rowley Wallis Huxman		3 Mar. 1854
Tristram S. Richardson	..	6 June 1854
Charles Williamson	..	11 Aug. 1854
Fran. Stewart Travers	..	18 Aug. 1854
Wykeham I. Penderton	25 Aug. 1854	
Henry Parloe Eaton	..	23 Mar. 1855
William Cubitt	..	23 Mar. 1855
F. D. Farquharson	..	23 Mar. 1855
John James Philips	..	23 Mar. 1855
J. S. Devonport M'Gill	..	23 Mar. 1855
James Durham Dundas	..	23 Mar. 1855
James Hare	..	23 Mar. 1855
Herbert Geo. Beeles	..	23 Mar. 1855
John d'Olier George	..	23 Mar. 1855

Rank and Name.	Rank in Regiment.

Lieutenants (continued)—

Llewellyn E. Traherne	23 Mar. 1855
James Joseph Collins	23 Mar. 1855
D. G. N. Watts-Russell	23 Mar. 1855
Anthony Carlisle	22 Sept. 1854
Arthur W. Knox-Gore	11 May 1855
James Arthur Morrah	11 May 1855
Hon. R. P. Vereker	11 May 1855
John Steel	27 June 1854
F. Vernon Northey	27 July 1855
Philip Julian Curtis	31 Aug. 1855
Wm. F. Carleton	17 Aug. 1855
John Baptist Shackle	23 Oct. 1855
James Forbes	23 Oct. 1855
Robt. Morris Hazen	23 Oct. 1855
Charles James Phillipps	23 Oct. 1855
Geo. French Stehelin	26 Oct. 1855
Edw. Cockburn Allen	26 Oct. 1855
Burnet Bell Forsyth	26 Oct. 1855
Cromer Ashburnham	26 Oct. 1855
George Kennedy Shaw	26 Oct. 1855
Augustus Morgan	25 Jan. 1856
K. Gregg Henderson	6 May 1856
Frederick Austin	9 May 1856
Edward Campbell Ainslie	9 May 1856
J. S. Hamilton Agar	9 May 1856
E. R. King Harman	9 May 1856
Joseph John Bradshaw	9 May 1856
N. Fitzgerald Uniacke	7 Mar. 1856
Wm. Brindley S. Conyers	19 Sept. 1856

Ensigns—

G. C. Kelly	1 May 1855
Charles Yarworth Jones	25 May 1855
Matthew Tilford	31 May 1855
F. Simon A. Orchard	8 June 1855
James Kiero Watson	20 July 1855
Charles C. Willoughby	20 July 1855
Jenico Preston	14 Sept. 1855
Robt. John Hickman	20 Oct. 1855
George Hatchell	22 Oct. 1855
John Owen Young	23 Oct. 1855
John Malcolm Sewell	25 Oct. 1855
Joseph Wigg	26 Oct. 1855
Arthur Tufnell	9 Nov. 1855
Richard F. Jennings	23 Nov. 1855
F. Sadlier Brereton	14 Dec. 1855
Wm. Henry Napier	21 Dec. 1855
Wm. Greer Turle	1 Feb. 1856
Cary Hampton Borrer	8 Feb. 1856
Henry Stephen Hodge	29 Feb. 1856
Alfred Lewis	14 Mar. 1856
James Walker King	8 July 1856
Ashley H. Woodgate	
George H. Mackenzie	9 May 1856
R. Jephson Verschoyle	10 May 1856
Stanley Mortimer	14 May 1856
Wm. J. Evered Poole	15 May 1856
Alfred S. Heathcote	16 May 1856
Newton Jones Pauli	27 May 1856

Instructor of Musketry—

| Captain Francis Dawson | 20 June 1856 |

Paymasters—

Edward Coxen, 9 Feb., 1826—2nd Lieut., 5 April, 1806; Lieut., 28 June, 1816; Captain, 8 April, 1825.

Rank and Name.	Rank in Regiment.

Paymasters (continued)—

Francis Fitzpatrick, 2 March, 1855—Ensign, 19 Oct., 1849; Lieut., 31 May, 1854.

Frederick Thomas Patterson, 16 June, 1855.

Adjutants—

James Forbes, Lieut.	5 April 1855
George C. Kelly, Ensign	1 May 1855
Matthew Tilford, Ensign	9 Oct. 1855

Quartermasters—

Luke FitzGibbon	15 Oct. 1847
Hugh Campbell	23 Mar. 1855
Wm. Hunter	13 July 1855

Surgeons—

Henry James Schooles, M.D., 1 Oct., 1847; Assistant-Surgeon, 28 June, 1833.

John Harry Kerr Innis, 11 March, 1853; Assistant-Surgeon, 8 April, 1842.

Deodatus W. Eaton, 11 May, 1855; Assistant-Surgeon, 28 Oct., 1845.

Assistant Surgeons—

Brinsley Nicholson, M.D.	25 Sept. 1846
David Ogilvy Hoile, M.D.	14 Oct. 1851
A. Graham Young	5 May 1854
John Mathew Biddle	3 June 1853
Thos. John Murphy	28 April 1854
James Macartney	6 Oct. 1854
Arthur Stretton	1 Sept. 1854

Regimentals—Green, facings scarlet.

Agents—Messrs. Charles R. and Walter McGregor.

Irish Agents—Messrs. Cane and Sons.

1858.

Four Battalions.

Africa—India—England.

Celer et Audax.

Rolcia, Vimiera, Martinique, Talavera, Fuentes d'Onor, Albuhera, Ciudad Rodrigo, Badajoz, Salamanca, Vittoria, Pyrenees, Nivelle, Nive, Orthes, Toulouse, Peninsula, Punjaub, Mooltan, Goojerat.

Col.-in-Chief—

General Hugh Viscount Gough, K.P., G.C.B., 21 Jan., 1854.

Cols.-Commandant—

Sir William George Moore, K.C.B., — Ensign, 18 April, 1811; Lieutenant, 10 Sept. 1812; Captain, 14 April, 1814; Major, 21 Jan., 1819; Lieut.-Colonel, 12 Jan., 1824; Colonel, 28 June, 1838; Major-General, 11 Nov., 1851; Colonel, 60th Rifles, 26 Jan., 1856.

Joseph Paterson - Ensign, 17 May, 1799; Lieut., 7 Feb., 1801; Captain, 23 Oct., 1806; Major, 29 Sept., 1814; Lieut.-Colonel, 31 Dec., 1825; Colonel, 28 June, 1838; Major-General, 11 Nov., 1851; Col.-Commandant, 60th Rifles, 14 April, 1857.

Lieut.-Colonels—

Maurice Griffin Dennis—Ensign, 9 May, 1826; Lieutenant, 5 July, 1827; Captain, 15 Dec., 1837; Major, 2 May, 1845; Brevet Lieut.-Colonel, 7 June, 1849; Lieut.-Colonel, 19 **Oct., 1851**; Colonel, 28 Nov., 1854.

Charles Howe Spence—2nd **Lieutenant**, 20 April, 1825; Lieutenant, 28 Sept., 1826; Captain, 24 May, 1841; Major, 20 Oct., 1848; Lieut.-Colonel, 2 Oct., 1853; Colonel, 2 Oct., 1856.

John Jones—Ensign, 12 June, 1828; Lieutenant, 2 Dec., 1831; Captain, 16 July, 1841; Major, 20 July, 1849; Lieut.-Colonel, 20 June, 1854.

William Fanshawe Bedford—**2nd** Lieutenant, 18 Dec., 1828; Lieutenant, 28 June, 1833; Captain, 23 July, 1841; Major, 12 **Oct.**, 1849; Brevet Lieut.-Colonel, 28 May, 1853; Lieut.-Colonel, 23 March, 1855.

Henry Bingham—2nd Lieutenant, 30 April, 1827; Lieutenant, 28 Sept., 1833; Captain, 23 June, 1841; Major, 19 Oct., 1851; Lieut.-Col., 19 June, 1857.

Edward John Vesey Brown—2nd Lieutenant, 12 Sept., 1834; Lieutenant, 29 Dec., 1840; Captain, 6 Nov., 1846; Brevet Major, 12 Dec., 1854; Major, 23 March, 1855; Lieut.-Colonel, 27 May, 1856.

Majors—

Francis Roger Palmer—Ensign, 15 March, 1833; Lieutenant, 24 April, 1835; Captain, 11 March, 1842; **Major**, 20 June, 1854.

Webbe Butler—2nd Lieutenant, 19 Sept., 1834; Lieutenant, 16 July, 1841; Captain, 20 Sept., 1844; **Major**, 23 March, 1855.

James Douglas—2nd Lieutenant, 17 Aug., 1838; Lieutenant, 16 July, 1841; Captain, 20 Sept., 1844; Major, 23 March, 1855.

Hon. Friend Kennely—**2nd Lieutenant**, 11 Sept., 1840; Lieutenant, 7 **April, 1842**; Captain, 20 Oct., 1848; **Major**, 17 Aug., 1855.

William James Yonge—Ensign, 27 July, 1826; Lieutenant, 17 May, 1827; **Captain, 10 July, 1846**; Major, 25 Jan., 1856.

Charles Napier North Ensign, 20 May, 1836; Lieutenant, 28 Dec., 1838; Captain, 28 Dec., 1848; Major, 19 June, 1857.

William Prettyman—Ensign, 8 May, 1840; Lieutenant, 5 Aug., 1842; Captain, 11 Sept., 1849; Brevet Major, 2 Nov., 1855; Major, 9 Sept., 1856; Brevet Lieut.-Colonel, 26 Dec., 1856.

Robert B. Hawley Ensign, 28 Aug., 1838; Lieutenant, 31 Dec., 1838; Captain, 10 Jan., 1857; Brevet Major, 2 Nov., 1855; Major, 5 Sept., 1856.

Rank and Name.		Rank in Regiment.
Captains—		
G. Waldegrave **Bligh**	..	**12 Oct. 1849**
Gibbes Rigaud	.. ..	**16 Aug. 1850**
Sir E. F. Campbell, **Bart.**		**27 Dec. 1850**
Peter Burton Roe	.. ..	**17 June 1851**
James Fraser	.. .. ..	**7 Jan. 1853**
Thomas Biggs..	.. ..	**8 April 1853**
Randle J. Feilden	..	**23 Dec.** 1853
Hon. Francis Williams	..	**3 Mar.** 1854
Dunbar Douglas Muter..		**31 May 1854**
C. H. Boswell Gordon	..	**6 June 1854**
Rank in Army, Bt. Maj.		**6 June 1856**
John Maguire..	..	**20 June 1854**
Hon. Edward Warren	..	**4 Aug. 1854**
John C. A. Wilton..	..	**14 July 1854**
Alfred J. Fitzgerald	..	**23 Mar. 1855**
Francis Dawson	.. ..	**23 Mar. 1855**
John Prevost Battersby ..		**23 Mar. 1855**
J. Lambert Edw. Baynes		**23 Mar. 1855**
Bernard Edward Ward..		**23 Mar. 1855**
Rank in Army, Bt. Maj.		**20 July 1855**
Vincent Tongue	..	**23 Mar. 1855**
R. Harcourt Robinson	..	**23 Mar. 1855**
Robert Wilmot Brooke..		**23 Mar. 1855**
Fran. Charteris Fletcher..		**23 Mar. 1855**
Edward Bowles	..	**23 Mar. 1855**
R. J. Eust. Robertson	..	**23 Mar. 1855**
Hugh P. Montgomery	..	**17 Aug. 1855**
C. D. C. Ellis..	..	**14 Dec. 1855**
Hon. Atholl C. J. Liddell		**21 Dec. 1855**
William Tedlie	.. ..	**25 Jan. 1856**
Wm. Douglas Philips	..	**7 April 1854**
Conyngham Jones ..	..	**6 May 1856**
O. Ch. Henry Waters	..	**1 May 1857**
C. H. Spencer Churchill..		**4 Aug. 1854**
Rank in Army, Bt. Maj.		**2 Nov. 1855**
Henry Cockburn	.. ..	**31 May 1857**
G. Biss MacQueen ..		**19 June 1857**
Hon. John Colborne	..	**1 Feb. 1856**
Henry Semple ..	..	**25 May 1857**
Edmund Holden Stewart		**28 Dec. 1855**
Edward Aug. Stotherd ..		**8 Jan. 1856**
Wm. James Holes .	..	**18 Jan. 1856**
William Paterson ..		**25 Mar. 1856**
Robert Crowe..	.. ..	**15 April 1856**
Wm. Spicer Cookworthy,		**22 Aug. 1856**
Thomas Aldridge ..		**4 Sept. 1857**
Charles Williamson	..	**16 Oct. 1857**
Lieutenants—		
Rowley Wills Hinxman..		**3 Mar. 1854**
Francis Stewart Travers .		**18 Aug. 1854**
Wykeham L. Pemberton		**25 Aug. 1854**
Henry Pardoe Eaton ..		**23 Mar. 1855**
F. Dundas Farquharson..		**23 Mar. 1855**
John James Phillips	..	**23 Mar. 1855**
J. S. Davenport M'Gill..		**23 Mar. 1855**
James Durham Dundas .		**23 Mar. 1855**
James Hare ..	..	**23 Mar. 1855**
Herbert George Deedes..		**23 Mar. 1855**
John d'Urber George	..	**23 Mar. 1855**
Llewellyn Ed. Traherne		**23 Mar. 1855**
James Joseph Collins	..	**23 Mar. 1855**
D. G. N. Watt-Russell ..		**23 Mar. 1855**
Anthony Carlisle	..	**22 Sept. 1854**
Arthur Wm. Knox-Gore		**11 May 1855**
James Arthur Morrah ..		**11 May 1855**

Rank and Name.	Rank in Regiment.
Lieutenants (continued)—	
Hon. R. P. Vereker .	.. 11 May 1855
John Steel	.. 27 June 1854
F. Vernon Northey .	.. 27 July 1855
Wm. F. Carleton ..	.. 17 Aug. 1855
Philip Julian Curtis	.. 31 Aug. 1855
John Baptist Shackle	.. 23 Oct. 1855
James Forbes	.. 23 Oct. 1855
Robert Morris Hazen	.. 23 Oct. 1855
G. French Stehelin .	.. 26 Oct. 1855
Edw. Cockburn Allen	.. 26 Oct. 1855
Burnet Bell Forsyth	.. 26 Oct. 1855
Cromer Ashburnham .	.. 26 Oct. 1855
G. Kennedy Shaw .	.. 26 Oct. 1855
Augustus Morgan ..	.. 25 Jan. 1856
Kennett G. Henderson	6 May 1856
Fred. Austin	.. 9 May 1856
Edward Campbell Ainslie	9 May 1856
J. S. Hamilton Algar	.. 9 May 1856
Ed. Robt. King-Harman	9 May 1856
Joseph John Bradshaw ..	9 May 1856
N. Fitzgerald Uniacke ..	7 May 1856
G. C. Kelly	.. 16 Nov. 1856
Charles Yarworth Jones .	16 Nov. 1855
Matthew Tilford ..	.. 17 Mar. 1857
Fred. Simon A. Orchard.	17 Mar. 1857
James Kiero Watson ..	1 May 1857
Chas. Chris. Willoughby.	31 May 1857
James Preston.	19 June 1857
Robert John Hickman ..	25 Aug. 1857
John Owen Young .	.. 25 Aug. 1857
Henry Brackenbury ..	25 June 1850
Wm. Norcott Manners ..	23 Oct. 1855
Fred. H. Anson Hamilton	16 Nov. 1855
Henry Robert Milligan ..	23 Nov. 1855
Wm. M. Miller Fortescue	25 Jan. 1856
Edward Wm. Denne ..	26 Feb. 1856
Alex. Thomas Ewens ..	26 Feb. 1856
George Hatchell ..	.. 27 Sept. 1857
John Malcolm Sewell ..	23 Oct. 1857
Ensigns—	
Joseph Wigg	.. 26 Oct. 1855
Arthur Tufnell ..	.. 9 Nov. 1855
Richard F. Jennings ..	23 Nov. 1855
Frank Sadlier Brereton ..	14 Dec. 1855
Wm. Greer Turle	1 Feb. 1856
Carey Hampton Borrer ..	8 Feb. 1856
Henry Stephen Hodges..	29 Feb. 1856
Alfred Lewis	.. 14 Mar. 1856
G. Henry Mackenzie ..	9 May 1856
Stanley Mortimer ..	.. 14 May 1856
Wm. John Evered Poole	15 May 1856
Alfred Spencer Heathcote	16 May 1856
Newton Jones Pauli ..	27 Mar. 1856
James Walker King ..	8 July 1856
Ashley Henry Woodgate	19 Sept. 1856
Fred. Augustus Campbell	5 Dec. 1856
Wm. Henry Moseley ..	1 May 1857
G. Hewitt Trotman . ..	12 May 1857
W. Lewis Kinloch Ogilvy	18 June 1857
Hugh Saint O. Barton ..	19 June 1857
W. Keith Murray	25 Aug. 1857
Eaton Stannard Steward.	26 Aug. 1857
Henry Richard Treeve ..	27 Aug. 1857
Richard Albert Massy ..	28 Aug. 1857

Rank and Name.	Rank in Regiment.
Ensigns (continued)—	
Joseph Henry Cowan ..	7 Dec. 1855
James Davis Billam ..	27 Feb. 1856
Latham C. Brownrigg ..	28 Feb. 1856
Julius Lovell	24 Feb. 1857
Richard Russell Gubbins	19 June 1857
Charles Henry Cox . ..	26 Dec. 1856
W. Langford Sainsbury .	25 Aug. 1857
J. Barrett L. Nevinson..	24 July 1857
Henry John Barker ..	14 Aug. 1857
R. F. W. de B. Barry ..	30 Oct. 1857
Henry Brodrick	27 Nov. 1857
J. East. Hunter Peyton..	18 Dec. 1857
Instructor of Musketry—	
Lieutenant James Kiero Watson,	
1 Aug., 1857.	
Ensign Frank Sadlier Brereton, 28	
Aug., 1857.	
Paymasters—	
Francis Fitzpatrick, 2 March, 1855—	
Ensign, 19 Oct., 1849; Lieutenant, 31	
May, 1854.	
Frederick Thomas Patterson, 10 June,	
1855.	
John Henry Chads, 29 May, 1857—	
Ensign, 9 Jan., 1844; Lieutenant, 12	
May, 1844; Captain, 15 Jan., 1856.	
George Fred. Lamert, 6 Oct., 1857.	
Adjutants—	
James Forbes, Lieut. ..	5 April 1855
G. Ch. Kelly, Lieut. ..	1 May 1855
Matthew Tilford, Lieut.	9 Oct. 1855
Alex. Thos. Ewens, Lieut.	4 Sept. 1857
Quartermasters—	
Lake Fitzgibbon ..	.. 15 Oct. 1857
Hugh Campbell ..	.. 23 Mar. 1855
William Hunter ..	.. 13 July 1855
Thomas Walker ..	.. 10 Mar. 1848
Surgeons—	
Henry James Schooles, M.D., 1 Oct.,	
1847; Assistant-Surgeon, 28 June, 1839.	
John Harry Kerr Innis, 11 March,	
1833; Assistant-Surgeon, 8 April, 1842.	
George Waterloo Pennington Spar-	
row, 6 July, 1855; Assistant-Surgeon,	
25 Sept., 1845.	
John Riggs Miller Lewis, M.D.,	
7 Dec., 1856—Assistant-Surgeon, 11	
Feb., 1848.	
Assistant-Surgeons—	
David Ogilvy Hoile, M.D.	14 Oct. 1851
A. Graham Young.. ..	5 May 1854
Thos. John Murphy ..	28 April 1854
James Macartney	6 Oct. 1854
Arthur Stretton	1 Sept. 1854
Ebenezer J. Hatchell ..	15 Jan. 1856
Robt. Owen Hayden ..	15 Sept. 1857
Fred. William Wade ..	15 Sept. 1857
William Silver Oliver ..	15 Sept. 1857
Regimentals—Green, facings scarlet.	
Agents—Messrs. Charles R. and Walter	
McGregor.	

1859.

Four Battalions.

India—England.

Color of Ausbar.

Roleia, Vimiera, Martinique, Talavera,
Fuentes d'Onor, Albuhera, Ciudad
Rodrigo, Badajoz, Salamanca, Vittoria,
Pyrenees, Nivelle, Nive, Orthes, Tou-
louse, Peninsula, Punjaub, Mooltan,
Goojerat.

Col.-in-Chief—

General Hugh, Viscount Gough, K.P.,
G.C.B., 21 January, 1854.

Cols.-Commandant—

☒ Sir Wm. George Moore, K.C.B.—
Ensign, 18 April, 1811; Lieut., 10 Sept.,
1812; Captain, 14 April, 1814; Major,
21 Jan., 1819; Lieut.-Colonel, 12 Jan.,
1824; Colonel, 28 June, 1838; Major-
Gen., 11 Nov., 1851; Lieut.-Gen., 5
June, 1855; Colonel, 60th Rifles, 26
January, 1856.

Joseph Paterson—Ensign, 17 May,
1799; Lieut., 7 Feb., 1801; Captain,
23 Oct., 1806; Major, 23 Sept., 1814;
Lieut.-Colonel, 31 Dec., 1825; Colonel,
28 June, 1838; Major-Gen., 11 Nov.,
1851; Lieut.-Gen., 26 August, 1858;
Colonel-Com., 60th Rifles, 14 April, 1857.

Lieut.-Colonels—

Maurice Griffin Dennis—Ensign, 9
May, 1826; Lieutenant, 5 July, 1827;
Captain, 15 Dec., 1837; Major, 2 May,
1845; Brevet Lieut.-Colonel, 7 June,
1849; Lieut.-Colonel, 19 Oct., 1851;
Colonel, 28 November, 1854.

Sir John Jones, K.C.B.—Ensign, 12
June, 1828; Lieut., 2 Dec., 1831; Capt.,
16 July, 1841; Major, 20 July, 1849;
Lieut.-Colonel, 20 June, 1854; Colonel,
19 January, 1858.

Wm. Fanshawe Bedford—2nd Lieut.,
18 Dec., 1828; Lieut., 28 June, 1833;
Captain, 23 July, 1841; Major, 12 Oct.,
1849; Brevet Lieut.-Colonel, 28 Nov.,
1854; Colonel, 28 Nov., 1854; Lieut.-
Colonel, 23 March, 1855.

Henry Bingham—2nd Lieut., 30 April,
1827; Lieut., 28 Sept., 1832; Captain,
25 June, 1841; Major, 19 Oct., 1854;
Lieut.-Colonel, 19 June, 1857.

Edward John Vesey Brown—2nd
Lieut., 12 Sept., 1834; Lieut., 29 Dec.,
1840; Captain, 6 Nov., 1846; Brevet
Major, 12 Dec., 1854; Major, 23 March,
1855; Lieut.-Colonel, 27 May, 1856.

Francis Roger Palmer, C.B.—Ensign,
15 March, 1833; Lieut., 24 April, 1835;
Captain, 11 March, 1842; Major, 20
June, 1854; Lieut.-Colonel, 22 June,
1858.

Webbe Butler—2nd Lieut., 19 Sept.,
1834; Lieut., 15 Dec., 1840; Captain,
26 July, 1844; Major, 23 March, 1855;
Lieut.-Colonel, 9 Sept., 1858.

Majors—

Henry Friend Kennedy—2nd Lieut.,
11 Sept. 1840; Lieut., 7 April, 1842;
Captain, 20 Oct., 1848; Major, 17 Aug.,
1855.

Wm. James Yonge—Ensign, 27 July,
1826; Lieut., 17 May, 1827; Captain,
10 July, 1846; Major, 25 Jan., 1856.

Charles Napier North—Ensign, 20
May, 1836; Lieut., 28 Dec., 1838;
Captain, 28 Dec., 1848; Major, 19 June,
1857; Brevet Lieut.-Col., 20 July, 1858.

W. Prettiman—Ensign, 8 May, 1840;
Lieut., 5 Aug., 1842; Captain, 11 Sept.,
1849; Brevet Major, 2 Nov., 1855;
Major, 9 Sept., 1856; Brevet Lieut.-
Colonel, 28 December, 1856.

Robt. B. Hawley—Ensign, 28 Aug.,
1838; Lieut., 31 Dec., 1839; Captain,
10 Jan., 1847; Brevet Major, 2 Nov.,
1855; Major, 5 Sept., 1856.

Geo. Wahlegrave Bligh—2nd Lieut.,
12 March, 1841; Lieut., 26 July, 1844;
Capt. 12 Oct., 1849; Major, 24 April, 1858.

Gibbes Rigaud—2nd Lieut., 11 June,
1841; Lieut., 26 July, 1844; Captain,
16 Aug., 1850; Major, 22 June, 1858.

Sir Edward Fitzgerald Campbell,
Bart.—2nd Lieut., 2 July, 1844; Lieut.,
30 July, 1844; Captain, 27 Dec., 1850;
Brevet Major, 19 Jan., 1858; Major, 9
September, 1858.

Last and Same.   **Rank in Regiment.**

Captains—

Peter Burton Roe	17 June 1851
James Fraser	7 Jan. 1853
Thomas Biggs	8 April 1853
Randle J. Feilden	23 Dec. 1853
Henry Francis Williams ..	3 Mar. 1854
Rank in Army, Bt. Maj.	19 Jan. 1858
D. D. Muter	31 May 1854
U.C. ..	20 July 1858
Rank in Army, Bt. Maj.	19 Jan. 1858
C. A. Boswell Gordon ..	6 June 1854
Rank in Army, Bt Maj.	6 June 1856
John Maguire	20 June 1854
Rank in Army, Bt. Maj	20 July 1858
Henry Edward Warren ..	4 Aug. 1854
John Robert Welton ..	11 July 1854
Rank in Army, Bt. Maj.	19 Jan. 1858
Alfred J. Fitzgerald ..	23 Mar. 1855
Francis Dawson	23 Mar. 1855
John Prevost Battersby..	23 Mar. 1855
J. Lambert Edw. Baynes	23 Mar. 1855
Bernard Edward Ward ..	23 Mar. 1855
Rank in Army, Bt. Maj.	20 July 1855
Vincent Tongue	23 Mar. 1855
R. Harcourt Robinson ..	23 Mar. 1855
Robert Wilmot Brooke ..	23 Mar. 1855
Francis Charteris Fletcher	23 Mar. 1855
Edward Bowles	23 Mar. 1855
R. J. Eustace Robertson	23 Mar. 1855
Hugh P. Montgomery ..	17 Aug. 1855
C. D. C. Ellis	14 Dec. 1855
Hon. Atholl C. J. Liddell	21 Dec. 1855
William Tedlie	25 Jan. 1856
Rank in Army, Bt. Maj.	20 July 1858

Rank and Name.	Rank in Regiment.
Captains (continued)—	
Wm. Douglas Philips	7 April 1854
Conyngham Jones	6 May 1856
George C. Henry Waters	1 May 1857
C. H. Spencer Churchill.	4 Aug. 1854
Rank in Army, Bt. Maj.	2 Nov. 1855
George Bliss MacQueen.	10 June 1857
Hon. John Colborne	1 Feb. 1856
Henry Semple	25 May 1857
Edward Aug. Stotherd	8 Jan. 1856
William James Hales	18 Jan. 1856
Robert Crowe	15 April 1856
W. Spicer Cookworthy	22 Aug. 1856
Charles Williamson.	16 Oct. 1857
Rowley Willes Hinxman.	15 Jan. 1858
Francis Stewart Travers.	15 Jan. 1858
Wykeham P. Pemberton	23 Mar. 1858
Henry Pardoe Eaton	23 April 1858
F. Dundas Farquharson.	24 April 1858
John James Phillips	14 May 1858
J. S. Davenport M'Gill.	14 May 1858
James Durham Dundas.	22 June 1858
Herbert George Deedes.	2 July 1858
John d'Olier George	2 July 1858
James Hare	9 Sept. 1858
Lieutenants—	
Llewellyn E. Traherne	23 Mar. 1855
James Joseph Collins	23 Mar. 1855
D. G. N. Watt-Russell.	23 Mar. 1855
Anthony Carlisle	22 Sept. 1854
Arthur W. Knox-Gore	11 May 1855
James Arthur Morrah	11 May 1855
Hon. R. P. Vereker	11 May 1855
John Steel	27 June 1854
Francis Vernon Northey	27 July 1855
Wm. F. Carleton	17 Aug. 1855
Philip Julian Curtis	31 Aug. 1855
James Forbes	23 Oct. 1855
Robert Morris Hazen	23 Oct. 1855
Geo. Ffrench Stebelin	26 Oct. 1855
Edw. Cockburn Allen	26 Oct. 1855
Burnet Bell Forsyth	26 Oct. 1855
Cromer Ashburnham	26 Oct. 1855
George Kennedy Shaw	26 Oct. 1855
Augustus Morgan	25 Jan. 1856
Kennett G. Henderson	6 May 1856
Frederick Austin	9 May 1856
Edw. Campbell Ainslie	9 May 1856
Jas. S. Hamilton Algar	9 May 1856
E. Robt. King-Harman.	9 May 1856
Joseph John Bradshaw	9 May 1856
N. Fitzgerald Unineke	7 May 1856
G. C. Kelly	16 Nov. 1856
Charles Yarworth Jones.	16 Nov. 1856
Matthew Tilford	17 Mar. 1857
Fred. Simon A. Orchard	17 Mar. 1857
James Kiero Watson	1 May 1857
C. Christoph. Willoughby	31 May 1857
Jenico Preston	19 June 1857
Robert John Hickman	25 Aug. 1857
John Owen Young	25 Aug. 1857
Wm. Norcott Manners	23 Oct. 1855
Fred. H. Anson Hamilton	16 Nov. 1855
Harry Robert Milligan	23 Nov. 1855
W. M. Miller Fortescue.	25 Jan. 1856
Alex. Thomas Ewens	26 July 1856

Rank and Name.	Rank in Regiment.
Lieutenants (continued)—	
George Hatchell	27 Sept. 1857
Joseph Wigg	27 Sept. 1857
Arthur Tufnell	15 Jan. 1858
Richard Francis Jennings	15 Jan. 1858
Frank. Sadler Brereton.	13 Feb. 1858
Wm. Greer Turle	23 May 1858
Cary Hampton Borrer	23 April 1858
Henry Stephen Hodges.	24 April 1858
Alfred Lewis	21 May 1858
George Henry Mackenzie	21 May 1858
Stanley Mortimer	21 May 1858
Wm. John Evered Poole	21 May 1858
Newton Jones Pauli	4 June 1858
Ashley Hen. Woodgate.	15 June 1858
Wm. Henry Moseley	15 June 1858
W. L. Kinloch Ogilvy	15 June 1858
Alfred Spence Heathcote	22 June 1858
James Walker King	8 July 1858
Fred. Aug. Campbell	9 Sept. 1858
Hugh St. George Barton	9 Nov. 1858
Ensigns—	
Geo. Hewitt Trotman	12 May 1857
Wm. Keith Murray	25 Aug. 1857
Eaton Stannard Steward	26 Aug. 1857
Henry Richard Treeve	27 Aug. 1857
Richard Albert Massy	28 Aug. 1857
Letham C. Brownrigg	28 Feb. 1856
Julius Lovell	24 Feb. 1857
Richard Russell Gubbins	19 June 1857
Charles Henry Cox	26 Dec. 1856
Walter L. Sainsbury	25 Aug. 1857
John Barrett L. Nevinson	24 July 1857
Henry John Barker	14 Aug. 1857
R. Fitz-Wm. de B. Barry	30 Oct. 1857
Henry Brodrick	27 Nov. 1857
John East Hunter Peyton	18 Dec. 1857
Pearce O'Brien Butler	2 Feb. 1858
Julius Tottenham	5 Feb. 1858
Reginald H. Beadon	6 Feb. 1858
George D. Anderson	26 Mar. 1858
John Wm. Marshall	27 Mar. 1858
Richard Meade	28 Mar. 1858
Chas. Bateman Prust	29 Mar. 1858
Harcourt James Lees	30 Mar. 1858
Pennyman W. Worsley	31 Mar. 1858
Astley Fellowes Terry	1 April 1858
John Gustavus Crosbie	23 April 1858
Nesbit W. Wallace	26 Mar. 1858
Charles Gosling	14 May 1858
Marcus Wm. O'Rorke	25 April 1858
Arthur Morris	21 May 1858
Alexander Borthwick	22 May 1858
Redvers Henry Buller	23 May 1858
Henry M. Pryor	25 June 1858
John T. U. Coxen	25 June 1858
John Alexander Hudson	13 July 1858
G. E. G. Foster Pigott	14 July 1858
Charles Pierson Cramer	24 Aug. 1858
Edward Digby O'Rorke.	31 Aug. 1858
John Charles Mariette	15 Oct. 1858
John Miller	9 Nov. 1858
Paymasters—	
Francis Fitzpatrick, 2 March, 1855	
—Ensign, 19 Oct., 1849; Lieut., 31 May, 1854.	

Rank and Name.	Rank in Regiment.

Paymasters (continued)—
Frederick Thomas Patterson, **19 June**, 1855.
John Henry Chads, **29 May, 1857**—Ensign, 9 Jan., 1841; Lieut., 12 May, 1844; Captain, 15 Jan., 1856.
George Fred. Lamert, 6 Oct., **1857**.

Adjutants—
James Forbes, Lieut. .. 5 April 1855
Geo. Chas. Kelly, Lieut. .. 1 May 1855
Matthew Tilford, Lieut. .. 9 Oct. 1855
Alex. Thos. Ewens, Lieut. 4 Sept. 1857

Instructors of Musketry—
Jas. Kiero Watson, Lieut. 1 Aug. 1857
Frank S. Brereton .. 28 Aug. 1857
Wm. N. Manners, Lieut. 22 Mar. 1858

Quartermasters—
Luke Fitzgibbon .. .. 15 Oct. 1847
William Hunter .. .. 13 July 1855
Thomas Walker .. .. 10 Mar. 1848
Robert Duncan .. .. 13 Aug. 1858

Surgeons—
Henry James Schooles, M.D., 1 Oct., 1847; Assistant-Surgeon, 28 June, 1839.
John Harry Kerr Innes, C.B., 11 March, 1853; Assist.-Surgeon, 8 April, 1842.
Geo. Waterloo Pennington **Sparrow**, 6 July, 1855; Assistant-Surgeon, 25 September, 1846.
John Riggs Miller Lewis, **M.D.**, 7 Dec., 1855; Assist.-Surgeon, 4 Sept., 1857.

Assistant-Surgeons—
A. Graham Young .. .. 5 May 1854
Thomas John Murphy .. 28 April 1854
James Macartney .. .. 6 Oct. 1854
Ebenezer J. Hatchell .. 15 Jan. 1857
Robt. Owen Hayden .. 15 Sept. 1857
Frederick Wm. Wade .. 15 Sept. 1857
Wm. Silver Oliver, M.D. 15 Sept. 1857
Seth Sam .. .. .. 9 Nov. 1857
James Doran, M.D. .. 9 Nov. 1857
John Alexander Laush .. 22 June 1858

Regimentals—Green, facings scarlet.

Agents—Sir C. R. McGregor, Bart., and Walter McGregor, Esq.

1860.
Four Battalions.
India—China—England—Ireland.
Celer et Audax.

Rolcia, Vimiera, Martinique, Talavera, Fuentes d'Onor, Albuhera, Ciudad Rodrigo, Budajoz, Salamanca, Vittoria, Pyrenees, Nivelle, Nive, Orthes, Toulouse, Peninsula, Punjaub, Mooltan, Goojerat.

Col.-in-Chief—
General Hugh Viscount Gough, K.P., G.C.B., 21 Jan., 1854.

Cols.-Commandant—
Sir William Geo. Moore, K.C.B.—Ensign, 18 April, 1811; Lieutenant,

Cols.-Commandant (continued)—
10 Sept., 1812; Captain, 14 April, 1814; Major, 21 Jan., 1819; Lieut.-Colonel, 12 Jan., 1824; Colonel, 28 June, 1838; Major-General, 11 Nov., 1851; Lieut.-General, 5 June, 1855; Colonel, 60th Rifles, 26 Jan., 1856.
Joseph Paterson—Ensign, 17 May, 1799; Lieutenant, 7 Feb., 1801; Captain, 23 Oct., 1806; Major, 29 Sept., 1814; Lieut.-Colonel, 31 Dec., 1825; Colonel, 28 June, 1838; Major-General, 11 Nov., 1851; Lieut.-General, 26 Aug., 1858; Col.-Commandant, 60th Rifles, 14 April, 1857.

Lieut.-Colonels—
Maurice Griffin Dennis, C.B.—Ensign, 9 May, 1826; Lieutenant, 5 July, 1827; Captain, 15 Dec., 1837; Major, 2 May, 1845; Brevet Lieut.-Colonel 7 June, 1849; Lieut.-Colonel, 19 Oct., 1851; Colonel, 28 Nov., 1854.
Sir John Jones, K.C.B.—Ensign, 12 June 1828; Lieutenant, 2 Dec., 1831; Captain, 16 July, 1841; Major, 20 July, 1849; Lieut.-Colonel, 20 June, 1854; Colonel, 19 Jan., 1858.
William Fanshawe Bedford—2nd Lieutenant, 18 Dec., 1828; Lieutenant, 28 June, 1833; Captain, 23 July, 1841; Major, 12 Oct., 1849; Brevet Lieut.-Colonel, 28 May, 1853; Colonel, 28 Nov., 1854; Lieut.-Colonel, 23 March, 1855.
Henry Bingham—2nd Lieutenant, 30 April, 1827; Lieutenant, 28 Sept., 1832; Captain, 25 June, 1841; Major, 19 Oct., 1851; Lieut.-Colonel, 19 June, 1857.
Francis Roger Palmer, C.B.—Ensign, 15 March, 1839; Lieutenant, 24 April, 1845; Captain, 11 March, 1842; Major, 20 June, 1851; Lieut.-Colonel, 22 June, 1858.
Webbe Butler—2nd Lieutenant, 19 Sept., 1834; Lieutenant, 15 Dec., 1840; Captain, 26 July, 1844; Major, 23 March, 1855; Lieut.-Colonel, 9 Sept., 1858.
William Prettyman—Ensign, 8 May, 1840; Lieutenant, 5 Aug., 1842; Captain, 11 Sept., 1849; Brevet Major, 2 Nov., 1855; Major, 9 Sept., 1856; Brevet Lieut.-Colonel, 26 Dec., 1856; Lieut.-Colonel, 29 April, 1859.

Majors—
Henry Friend Kennedy—2nd Lieutenant, 11 Sept., 1840; Lieutenant, 7 April, 1842; Captain, 20 Oct., 1848; Major 17 Aug., 1855.
Charles Napier North—Ensign, 29 May, 1846; Lieutenant, 28 Dec., 1838; Captain, 28 Dec., 1848; Major, 19 June, 1857; Brevet Lieut.-Colonel, 20 July, 1858.
Robert B. Hawley—Ensign, 28 Aug.,

R

Majors (continued)—
1838; Lieutenant, 31 Dec., 1839; Captain, 10 Jan., 1857; Brevet Major, 2 Nov., 1855; Major, 5 Sept., 1856.

George Waldegrave Bligh—2nd Lieutenant, 12 March, 1841; Lieutenant, 26 July, 1844; Captain, 12 Oct., 1849; Major, 24 April, 1858.

Gibbes Rignaud—2nd Lieutenant, 11 June, 1841; Lieutenant, 26 July, 1844; Captain, 16 Aug., 1850; Major, 22 June, 1858.

Sir Edward Fitzgerald Campbell, Bart.—2nd Lieutenant, 2 July, 1841; Lieutenant, 26 July, 1844; Captain, 27 Dec., 1850; Brevet Major, 19 Jan., 1858; Major, 9 Sept., 1858.

Peter Burton Roe —2nd Lieutenant, 23 July, 1841; Lieutenant, 26 July, 1844; Captain, 17 June, 1851; Major, 20 April, 1859.

James Fraser—2nd Lieutenant, 10 Sept., 1841; Lieutenant, 26 July, 1844; Captain, 7 Jan., 1853; Major, 18 Oct., 1859.

Rank and Name.	Rank in Regiment.
Captains—	
Thomas Biggs	8 April 1853
Randle J. Feilden	23 Dec. 1853
Henry Francis Williams .	3 Mar. 1854
Rank in Army, Bt. Maj. 19 Jan. 1858	
D. D. Muter	31 May 1854
Rank in Army, Bt. Maj. 19 Jan. 1858	
C. A. Boswell Gordon ..	6 June 1854
Rank in Army, Bt. Maj. 6 June 1856	
John Maguire	20 June 1854
Rank in Army, Bt. Maj. 20 July 1858	
Henry Edward Warren..	4 Aug. 1854
John Robert Wilton ..	4 July 1854
Rank in Army, Bt. Maj. 19 Jan. 1858	
Alfred J. Fitzgerald ..	23 Mar. 1856
Francis Dawson	23 Mar. 1856
John Prevost Battersby..	23 Mar. 1856
J. Lambert Ed. Baynes..	23 Mar. 1856
Bernard Ed. Ward . ..	23 Mar. 1856
Rank in Army, Bt. Maj. 20 July 1855	
Vincent Tongue	23 Mar. 1856
R. Harcourt Robinson ..	23 Mar. 1856
Robert Wilmot Brooke..	23 Mar. 1856
Fran. Charteris Fletcher .	23 Mar. 1856
Edward Bowles	23 Mar. 1856
R. J. East. Robertson ..	23 Mar. 1856
Hugh P. Montgomery ..	17 Aug. 1855
C. D. C. Ellis	14 Dec. 1855
Hon. Atholl C. J. Liddell	21 Dec. 1855
William Teillie . ..	25 Jan. 1856
Rank in Army, Bt. Maj. 20 July 1858	
Conyngham Jones	6 May 1856
Rank in Army, Bt. Maj. 26 April 1859	
G. C. Henry Waters ..	1 May 1857
C. H. Spence Churchill ..	4 Aug. 1854
Rank in Army, Bt. Maj. 2 Nov. 1855	
George Bliss Marqueen..	19 June 1857
Hon. John Colborne ..	1 Feb. 1856
Henry Semple..	25 May 1857
Edward Aug. Stothead ..	8 Jan. 1856

Rank and Name.	Rank in Regiment.
Captains (continued)—	
Robert Crowe	15 April 1856
Wm. Spicer Cookworthy.	22 Aug. 1856
Charles Williamson ..	16 Oct. 1857
Rowley Willis Hinxman..	15 Jan. 1858
Francis Stewart Travers .	15 Jan. 1858
Wykeham L. Pemberton.	23 Mar. 1858
Henry Pardoe Eaton ..	23 April 1858
John James Phillips ..	14 May 1858
F. Dundas Farquharson..	24 April 1858
James Durham Dundas..	22 June 1858
Herbert G. Deedes.. ..	2 July 1858
John d'Olier George ..	2 July 1858
James Hare	9 Sept. 1858
John Joseph Collins ..	19 July 1859
John W. Medhurst . ..	4 April 1856
J. H. Lawrence Archer..	12 Feb. 1858
D. G. N. Watts-Russell..	29 Nov. 1859
Arthur W. Knox-Gore ..	16 Dec. 1859

Lieutenants—	
Llewellyn Edm. Traherne	23 Mar. 1855
Anthony Carlisle	22 Sept. 1854
J. Arthur Morrah	11 May 1855
Hon. R. P. Vereker ..	11 May 1855
Francis Vernon Northey	27 July 1855
Philip Julian Curtis ..	3 Aug. 1855
Wm. F. Carleton	17 Aug. 1855
James Forbes	23 Oct. 1855
Robert Morris Hazen ..	23 Oct. 1855
G. French Stehelin.. ..	26 Oct. 1855
Burnet Bell Forsyth ..	26 Oct. 1855
Cromer Ashburnham ..	26 Oct. 1855
G. Kennedy Shaw	26 Oct. 1855
Augustus Morgan	25 Jan. 1856
Kennett Gregg Henderson	6 May 1856
Fred. Austin	9 May 1856
Ed. Campbell Ainslie ..	9 May 1856
J. S. Hamilton Algar ..	9 May 1856
Joseph John Bradshaw..	9 May 1856
N. Fitzgerald Unineke ..	7 Mar. 1856
G. C. Kelly	16 Nov. 1856
Matthew Tilford	17 Mar. 1857
Fred. Simon A. Orchard .	17 Mar. 1857
James Kiero Watson ..	1 May 1857
Ch. Chris. Willoughby..	31 May 1857
Jenico Preston	19 June 1857
Robert John Hickman ..	25 Aug. 1857
John Owen Young.. ..	25 Aug. 1857
Wm. Norcott Manners..	23 Oct. 1855
Fred. H. Anson Hamilton	16 Nov. 1855
Harry Robert Milligan ..	23 Nov. 1855
W. M. Miller Fortescue.	25 Jan. 1856
George Hatchell	27 Sept. 1857
Arthur Tufnell	15 Jan. 1858
Richard Fred. Jennings..	15 Jan. 1858
Frank Sadlier Brereton..	13 Feb. 1858
Wm. Greer Turle	23 Mar. 1858
Cary Hampton Barrer ..	23 April 1858
Henry Stephen Hodges..	24 April 1858
Alfred Lewis	21 May 1858
G. Henry Mackenzie ..	21 May 1858
Stanley Mortimer	21 May 1858
Wm. John Evered Poole	21 May 1858
Newton Jones Pauli ..	4 June 1858

Rank and Name.	Rank in Regiment.

Lieutenants (continued)—

Ashley Henry Woodgate.	15 June 1858
Wm. Henry Moseley ..	15 June 1858
W. Lewis Kinloch Ogilvy	15 June 1858
Alfred Spencer Heathcote	22 June 1858
James Walker King ..	8 July 1858
Fred. Aug. Campbell ..	9 Sept. 1858
Hugh St. Geo. Barton ..	9 Nov. 1858
Geo. Hewitt Trotman ..	13 Aug. 1859
Rich. Albert Massy ..	16 Aug. 1859
Julius Lovell	30 Sept. 1859
Rich. Russell Gubbins ..	7 Oct. 1859
Charles Henry Cox . ..	4 Nov. 1859
W. Langford Sainsbury..	16 Dec. 1859
J. Barret L. Nevinson ..	16 Dec. 1859

Ensigns—

Eaton Stannard **Steward.**	26 Aug. 1857
Henry Richard Treeve ..	27 Aug. 1857
Latham C. Brownrigg ..	28 Feb. 1856
Henry John Barker ..	14 Aug. 1857
R. Fitzwilliam de B. Barry	30 Oct. 1857
Henry Brodrick ..	27 Nov. 1857
J. Eust. Hunter Peyton .	18 Dec. 1857
Pierce O'Brien Butler ..	2 Feb. 1858
Julius Tottenham ..	5 Feb. 1858
Reginald H. Bewdon ..	6 Feb. 1858
George D. Anderson ..	26 Mar. 1858
John Wm. Marshall ..	27 Mar. 1858
Richard Meade ..	28 Mar. 1858
Charles Bateman Praut ..	29 Mar. 1858
Harcourt James Lees ..	30 Mar. 1858
P. White Worsley ..	31 Mar. 1858
Astley Fellowes Terry ..	1 April 1858
John Geo. Crosbie ..	23 April 1858
N. Willoughby Wallace .	26 Mar. 1858
Ch. Gosling ..	14 May 1858
M. Wm. O'Rorke ..	25 April 1858
Arthur Morris ..	21 May 1858
Alex. Borthwick ..	22 May 1858
Red. Henry Butler.. ..	23 May 1858
Henry M. Pryor ..	25 June 1858
O. Ed. G. Foster Pigott .	14 July 1858
Ch. Pierson Cramer ..	24 Aug. 1858
Ed. Digby O'Rorke ..	31 Aug. 1858
Johann Ch. Mariette ..	15 Oct. 1858
John Miller	9 Nov. 1858
Courtenay Forbes Terry .	8 April 1859
Han. W. Court Pepys ..	14 June 1859
Francis Wm. Robyns ..	22 July 1859
Francis W. Greenfell ..	5 Aug. 1859
B. Henry Davidson ..	5 Aug. 1859
John Wm. Rhodes.. ..	7 Oct. 1859
Andrew Vere O'Brien ..	18 Oct. 1859
R. F. D. St. Andrew St. John	15 Nov. 1859
John Ed. P. Barlow ..	16 Dec. 1859
Ch. Lewis **C. de Robeck** .	22 Oct. 1859

Paymasters—

Francis Fitzpatrick, 2 March, 1855;
Ensign, 19 Oct., 1844; Lieut., 31 May, 1854.

Fred. Thomas Patterson, 19 June, 1855;
John Henry Chads, 29 May, 1857;
Ensign, 9 Jan., 1841; Lieut., 12 May, 1844; Captain, 15 Jan., 1856.

Edward Charles Grant, 28 Dec., 1855.

Rank and Name.	Rank in Regiment.

Adjutants—

James Forbes, Lieut. ..	5 April 1855
George Ch. Kelly, Lieut..	1 May 1855
M. Tilford, Lieut.	9 Oct. 1855
L. C. Brownrigg, Ensign.	18 Jan. 1859

Instructors of Musketry—

J. Kiero Watson, Lieut...	6 Aug. 1857
F. S. Brereton, Lieut. ..	28 Aug. 1857
Wm. N. Manners ..	22 Mar. 1858

Quartermasters—

Luke Fitzgibbon	15 Oct. 1847
William Hunter	13 July 1855
Thomas Walker	10 Mar. 1848
Robert Duncan	13 Aug. 1858

Surgeons—

Henry James Schooles, M.D., Assistant-Surgeon, 28 June, 1839; Surgeon, 1 Oct., 1847; Surgeon-Major, 22 July, 1859.

George Waterloo Pennington Sparrow, 6 July, 1855; Assistant-Surgeon, 25 Sept., 1846.

Edward William Young, M.D., 8 Dec., 1854; Assistant-Surgeon, 7 Aug., 1850.

James Crowe, 6 April, 1855; Assistant-Surgeon, 3 Sept., 1847.

Assistant-Surgeons—

A. Graham Young.. ..	5 May 1854
Thomas John Murphy ..	28 April 1854
James Macarthey	6 Oct. 1854
Ebenezer J. Hatcheld ..	15 Jan. 1856
Robt. Owen Hayden ..	15 Sept. 1857
Frederick Wm. Wade ..	15 Sept. 1857
Wm. Silver Oliver, M.D.	15 Sept. 1857
Seth Sam...	9 Nov. 1857
J. Doran, M.D.	9 Nov. 1857
John Alex. Lamb	22 June 1858
Alex. C. M'Intosh ..	12 June 1859

Regimentals.—Green, facings scarlet.

Agents.—Sir C. R. M'Gregor, Bart., and Walter McGregor, Esq.

1861.

Four Battalions.

India China England Ireland Canada.

Color of Facings.

Roleia, Vimiera, Martinique, Talavera, Fuentes d'Onor, Albuhera, Ciudad Rodrigo, Badajoz, Salamanca, Vittoria, Pyrenees, Nivelle, Nive, Orthes, Toulouse, Peninsula, Punjaub, Mooltan, Goojerat.

Colonel in Chief.

General Hugh Viscount Gough, K.P., G.C.B., 21 Jan., 1854.

Colonel Commandant.

Sir William George Moore, K.C.B. — Ensign, 18 April, 1811; Lieut., 10

R 2

Cols.-Commandant (continued)—

Sept. 1812 ; Captain, 14 April, 1814 ; Major, 21 Jan., 1819 ; Lieut.-Colonel, 12 Jan. 1824 ; Colonel, 28 June, 1838 ; Major-Gen., 11 Nov. 1851 ; Lieut.-Gen., 5 June, 1855 ; Colonel, 60th Rifles, 26 Jan. 1856.

Joseph Paterson—Ensign. 17 May, 1799 ; Lieut., 7 Feb, 1801 ; Captain, 23 Oct., 1806 ; Major, 29 Sept., 1814 ; Lieut.-Colonel, 31 Dec., 1825 ; Colonel, 28 June, 1838 ; Major-Gen., 11 Nov., 1851 ; Lieut.-General, 26 Aug. 1858 ; Col.-Commandant, 60th Rifles, 14 April, 1857.

Lieut.-Colonels—

Sir John Jones, K.C.B.—Ensign, 12 June, 1828 ; Lieut., 2 Dec., 1834 ; Capt. 16 July, 1841 ; Major, 20 July, 1849 ; Lieut.-Colonel, 20 June, 1851 ; Colonel, 19 Jan., 1858.

Henry Bingham—2nd Lieut.,30 April, 1827 ; Lieut., 28 Sept., 1832 ; Captain, 25 June, 1841 ; Major, 19 Oct. 1851 ; Lieut.-Colonel, 19 June, 1857.

Francis Rogers Palmer, C.B. Ensign. 15 March, 1833 ; Lieut., 24 April, 1835 ; Captain, 11 March, 1842 ; Major, 20 June, 1854 ; Lieut.-Colonel, 22 June, 1858.

Webbe Butler—2nd Lieut., 19 Sept., 1844 ; Lieut., 15 Dec., 1840 ; Captain, 26 July, 1844 ; Major, 23 March, 1855 ; Lieut.-Colonel, 9 Sept., 1858.

Robert B. Hawley—Ensign, 28 Aug., 1838 ; Lieut., 31 Dec., 1839 ; Captain, 10 Jan., 1851 ; Bt. Major, 2 Nov., 1855 ; Major, 5 Sept., 1856 ; Lieut.-Colonel, 18 May, 1860.

Peter Burton Roe—2nd Lieut., 23 July, 1841 ; Lieut., 26 July, 1844 ; Captain, 17 June, 1851 ; Major, 29 April, 1859 ; Lieut.-Colonel, 18 Sept., 1860.

Majors—

Henry Friend Kennedy—2nd Lieut., 11 Sept., 1840 ; Lieut., 7 April, 1842 ; Captain, 20 Oct., 1848 ; Major, 17 Aug., 1855.

Charles Napier North—Ensign, 20 May, 1836 ; Lieut., 28 Dec., 1838 ; Capt. 28 Dec., 1848 ; Major, 19 June, 1857 ; Brevet Lieut.-Colonel, 20 July, 1858.

Gibbes Rigaud—2nd Lieut., 14 June, 1844 ; Lieut., 26 July, 1844 ; Captain, 16 Aug. 1850 ; Major, 22 June, 1858.

Sir Edward Fitzgerald Campbell, Bt.—2nd Lieut., 2 July, 1841 ; Lieut., 26 July, 1844 ; Captain, 16 Aug., 1850 ; Bt. Major, 19 Jan., 1858 ; Major, 9 Sept., 1858 ; Bt. Lieut.-Colonel, 23 Oct., 1860.

James Fraser—2nd Lieut., 10 Sept., 1844 ; Lieut., 26 July, 1844 ; Captain, 7 Jan., 1853 ; Major, 18 Oct., 1859 ; Randle Joseph Feilden—2nd Lieut.,

Majors (continued)—

31 March, 1843 ; Lieut., 25 Feb., 1845 ; Captain, 23 Dec., 1853 ; Major, 18 May, 1860.

Dunbar Douglas Muter—Ensign, 14 14 April, 1843 ; Lieut., 17 Jan., 1845 ; Captain, 31 May, 1854 ; Brevet Major, 19 Jan., 1858 ; Brevet Lieut.-Colonel, 20 July, 1858 ; Major, 19 July, 1860.

Charles Alex. Boswell Gordon—Ensign, 21 April, 1843 ; Lieut., 13 June, 1845 ; Captain, 6 June, 1854 ; Brevet Major, 6 June, 1856 ; Major, 18 Sept., 1860.

	Rank and Name.	Rank in Regiment.
Captains—		
	Thomas Biggs..	8 April 1853
	Hen. Francis Williams ..	3 Mar. 1854
	Rank in Army, Bt. Maj. 19 Jan. 1858	
	John Maguire..	20 June 1854
	Rank in Army, Bt. Maj. 20 July 1858	
	Henry Edward Warren..	4 Aug. 1854
	John Robert Wilton ..	14 July 1854
	Rank in Army, Bt. Maj. 19 Jan. 1858	
	Alfred J. Fitzgerald ..	23 Mar. 1855
	Francis Dawson	23 Mar. 1855
	John Prevost Battersby..	23 Mar. 1855
	Bernard Edw. Ward ..	23 Mar. 1855
	Rank in Army, Bt. Maj. 20 July 1855	
	Vincent Tongue	23 Mar. 1855
	R. Harcourt Robinson ..	23 Mar. 1855
	Robt. Wilmot Brooke ..	23 Mar. 1855
	Fran. Charteris Fletcher .	23 Mar. 1855
	Edward Bowles	23 Mar. 1855
	R. J. East. Robertson ..	23 Mar. 1855
	Hugh P. Montgomery ..	17 Aug. 1855
	Chas. D. Cunningham Ellis	14 Dec. 1855
	Rank in Army, Bt. Maj. 23 Oct. 1860	
	Hon. Atholl C. J. Liddell	21 Dec. 1855
	William Tedlie	25 Jan. 1856
	Rank in Army, Bt. Maj. 20 July 1858	
	Conyngham Jones ..	6 May 1856
	Rank in Army, Bt. Maj. 26 April 1859	
	C. H. Spen. Churchill ..	4 Aug. 1854
	Rank in Army, Bt. Maj. 2 Nov. 1855	
	Hon. John Colborne ..	1 Feb. 1856
	Henry Semple.. ..	25 May 1857
	Edward Aug. Stotherd ..	8 Jan. 1856
	Robert Crowe	15 April 1856
	Wm. Spicer Cookworthy.	22 Aug. 1856
	Charles Williamson ..	16 Oct. 1857
	Rowley Willis Hinxman..	15 Jan. 1858
	Francis Stewart Travers..	15 Jan. 1858
	Wykeham L. Pemberton.	23 Mar. 1858
	Henry Pardoe Eaton ..	23 April 1858
	Fra. Dundas Farquharson	24 April 1858
	John James Phillips ..	14 May 1858
	James Durham Dundas..	22 June 1858
	Herbert George Deedes..	2 July 1858
	Rank in Army, Bt. Maj. 25 Sept. 1860	
	John d'Olier George ..	2 July 1858
	James Hare	9 Sept. 1858
	John Wm. Medhurst ..	4 April 1856
	James Joseph Collins ..	19 July 1859
	Jos. Hy. Lawrence Archer	12 Feb. 1858
	D. G. N. Watts-Russell..	29 Feb. 1859
	Arthur Wm. Knox-Gore	16 Dec. 1859

Rank and Name.	Rank in Regiment.
Captains (continued)—	
Anthony Carlisle	9 Mar. 1860
Francis Vernon Northey .	18 May 1860
Philip Julian Curtis ..	10 July 1860
William F. Carleton ..	18 Sept. 1860
Joseph Cheese..	1 Feb. 1856
Percy Chaplin	15 Nov. 1859
Lieutenants—	
James Arthur Morrsh ..	11 May 1855
Hon. R. P. Vereker.. ..	11 May 1855
James Forbes	23 Oct. 1855
Robert Morris Hazen ..	23 Oct. 1855
Geo. French Stehehn ..	26 Oct. 1855
Burnet Bell Fereth ..	26 Oct. 1855
Cromer Ashburnham ..	26 Oct. 1855
Geo. Kennedy Shaw ..	26 Oct. 1855
Augustus Morgan	25 Jan. 1856
Kennett Gregg Henderson	6 May 1856
Fred. Austin	9 May 1856
Edw. Campbell Ainslie ..	9 May 1856
Jas. S. Hamilton Algar..	9 May 1856
Joseph John Bradshaw ..	9 May 1856
Norman Fitzgerald Uniacke	7 Mar. 1856
G. C. Kelly	16 Nov. 1856
Matthew Tilford	17 Mar. 1857
Fred. Simon A. Orchard	17 Mar. 1857
James Kiero Watson ..	1 May 1857
C. Christopher Willoughby	31 Mar. 1857
Robt. John Hickman ..	25 Aug. 1857
John Owen Young ..	25 Aug. 1857
Wm. Norcott Manners ..	23 Oct. 1857
Fred. H. Anson Hamilton	16 Nov. 1857
Harry Robt. Milligan ..	23 Nov. 1857
George Hatchell ..	27 Sept. 1857
Arthur Tuffnell ..	15 Jan. 1858
Richard Fras. Jennings ..	15 Jan. 1858
Frank Sadleir Brereton	13 Feb. 1858
William Greer Tario ..	23 Mar. 1858
Cary Hampton Borrer ..	23 April 1858
Alfred Lewis	21 May 1858
Geo. Henry Mackenzie ..	21 May 1858
Stanley Mortimer ..	21 May 1858
Wm. John Everest Poole	21 May 1858
Neaton James Pauli ..	4 June 1858
Ashley Henry Woodgate	15 June 1858
Wm. Henry Mossley ..	15 June 1858
Wm. Lewis Kinloch Ogilvy	15 June 1858
C. C. A. Spencer Heathcote	22 June 1858
Fred. Augustus Campbell	3 Sept. 1858
Hugo Saint George Barton	2 Nov. 1858
George Hewitt Tindman..	18 Aug. 1859
Richard Albert Maen ..	16 Aug. 1859
Richard Russell Robbins	7 Oct. 1859
Charles Henry Cox.. ..	4 Nov. 1859
John Barrett L. Nevinson	16 Dec. 1859
Henry Richard Treeve ..	2 Mar. 1860
Latham C. Brownrigg ..	9 Mar. 1860
R. Fitzwilliam de B Barry	5 May 1860
John East Hunter Peyton	11 Sept. 1860
Julius Tottenham	11 Sept. 1860
Reginald B. Bendon ..	11 Sept. 1860
John William Marshall ..	11 Sept. 1860
Richard Meade	11 Sept. 1860
Harcourt James Lees	11 Sept. 1860

Rank and Name.	Rank in Regiment.
Lieutenants (continued)—	
Pennyman White Worsley	11 Sept. 1860
Astley Fellowes Terry ..	18 Sept. 1860
John Gustavus Crosbie ..	26 Oct. 1860
Ensigns—	
Charles Bateman Prust ..	29 Mar. 1858
Pierce O'Brien Butler ..	2 Feb. 1858
George D. Anderson ..	26 Mar. 1858
N. Willoughby Wallace..	26 Mar. 1858
Charles Gosling	14 May 1858
Marcus Wm. O'Rorke ..	25 April 1858
Arthur Morris..	21 May 1858
Alexander Borthwick ..	22 May 1858
Redvers Henry Buller ..	23 May 1858
Henry M. Pryor	25 June 1858
G. E. G. Foster Pigott ..	14 July 1858
Charles Pierson Cramer..	24 Aug. 1858
Edward Digby O'Rorke..	31 Aug. 1858
John Charles Mariette ..	15 Oct. 1858
John Miller	9 Nov. 1858
Courtenay Forbes Terry..	8 April 1859
Hon. W. Courtenay Pepys	14 June 1859
Francis Wm. Robins ..	22 July 1859
Francis Wallace Grenfell	6 Aug. 1859
Barnard Henry Davidson	16 Aug. 1859
John Willtam Rhodes ..	7 Oct. 1859
Aubrey Vere O'Brien ..	18 Oct. 1859
R. F. St. Andrew St. John	15 Nov. 1859
John Edw. Pratt Barlow	16 Dec. 1859
Charles Louis C. de Robeck	22 Oct. 1859
T. Wentworth M.Edmunds	6 Jan. 1860
Clifford Fortescue Borrer	20 April 1860
Cecil Henry Paulet.. ..	31 July 1860
Charles Gilbert Fryer ..	14 Aug. 1860
Fred. Edward Lonsdale..	4 Sept. 1860
Edward Burr	11 Sept. 1860
Arthur Richard Lees ..	12 Sept. 1860
R. Dalrymple Elphinstone	18 Sept. 1860
Cecil John Shepherd ..	19 Sept. 1860
Thomas Henry Duncombe	20 Sept. 1860
Francis Semwen Blunt ..	21 Sept. 1860
Henry James Daubuz ..	22 Sept. 1860
William Warren	12 Oct. 1860
Charles Gathorne Hardy	26 Oct. 1860
George Thomas Whitaker	24 Dec. 1860

Paymasters—

Francis Fitzpatrick, 2 March, 1855—Ensign, 19 Oct., 1849; Lieut., 31 May, 1851; Hon. Captain, 1 Jan. 1860.

Frederick Thomas Patterson, 19 June, 1855

John Henry Clads, 29 May, 1857—Ensign, 9 Jan., 1844; Lieut., 12 May, 1848; Captain, 15 Jan. 1858.

Edward Charles Grant, 28 Dec., 1855.

Adjutants—

James Forbes, Lieut. ..	5 April 1855
George C. Kelly, Lieut...	1 May 1855
L. C. Brown, Lieut. ..	18 Jan. 1859
J. S. Hamilton Algar ..	7 Feb. 1860

Instructors of Musketry—

F. S. Brereton, 2nd Lieut.—	28 Aug. 1857
Wm. N. Manners, Lieut...	22 Mar. 1858

Rank and Name.   Rank in Regiment.

Instructors of Musketry (continued)—

P. W. Worsley, Lieut... 15 Feb. 1860
W. G. Turlo   ..   .. 21 Aug. 1860

Quartermasters—

Luke Fitzgibbon ..   .. 15 Oct. 1847
William Hunter ..   .. 13 July 1855
Thomas Walker ..   .. 10 Mar. 1848
Robert Duncan ..   .. 13 Aug. 1858

Surgeons—

Henry James Schooles, M.D., Assist.-
Surgeon, 28 June, 1839 ; Surgeon, 1 Oct.
1847 ; Surgeon-Major, 22 July, 1859.
Geo. Waterloo Pennington Sparrow,
M.D., 6 July, 1855 ; Assistant-Surgeon,
25 Sept., 1846.
Edward Wm. Young, M.D., 8 Dec.,
1854 ; Assistant-Surgeon, 7 Aug., 1846.
James Crerar, 6 April, 1855 ; Assist.-
Surgeon, 3 Sept., 1847.

Assistant-Surgeons—

A. Graham Young ..   .. 5 May 1854
James Macartney ..   .. 6 Oct. 1854
Ebenezer John Hatchell.. 15 Jan. 1856
Robert Owen Hayden   .. 15 Sept. 1857
Frederick Wm. Wade   .. 15 Sept. 1857
Wm. Silver Oliver, M.D. 15 Sept. 1857
Seth Sam.. .. ..   .. 9 Nov. 1857
James Doran, M.D..   .. 9 Nov. 1857
John Alexander Lamb .. 22 June 1858
Alex. Campbell McTavish 12 Jan. 1859

Regimentals—Green, facings scarlet.

Agents   Sir C. R. McGregor, Bart., and
Walter McGregor, Esq.

1862.

Four Battalions.

England—India—Burmah—Canada.

Celer et Audax.

Roleia, Vimiera, Martinique, Talavera,
Fuentes d'Onor, Albuhera, Ciudad
Rodrigo, Badajoz, Salamanca, Vittoria,
Pyrenees, Nivelle, Nive, Orthes, Tou-
louse, Peninsula, Punjaub, Mooltan,
Goojerat.

Col.-in-Chief—

General Hugh Viscount Gough, K.P.,
G.C.B., 28th Jan., 1854.

Cols.-Commandant—

[symbol] Sir Wm. George Moore, K.C.B.—
Ensign, 18 April, 1811 ; Lieut., 10 Sept.,
1812 ; Captain, 11 April, 1814 ; Major,
21 Jan., 1819 ; Lieut.-Colonel, 12 Jan.,
1821 ; Colonel, 28 June, 1838 ; Major-
Gen., 11 Nov., 1851 ; Lieut.-Gen., 5
June, 1855 ; Colonel, 60th Rifles, 26
Jan., 1856.

Cols.-Commandant (continued)—

Joseph Paterson—Ensign, 17 May,
1799 ; Lieut., 7 Feb., 1801 ; Captain,
23 Oct., 1806 ; Major, 29 Sept., 1814 ;
Lieut.-Colonel, 31 Dec., 1825 ; Colonel,
28 June, 1838 ; Major-Gen., 11 Nov.,
1851 ; Lieut.-General, 26 Aug., 1858 ;
Col.-Comm., 60th Rifles, 14 April, 1857.

Lieut.-Colonels—

Henry Bingham—2nd Lieut., 30 April,
1827 ; Lieut., 28 Sept., 1832 ; Captain,
25 June, 1841 ; Major, 19 Oct., 1851 ;
Lieut.-Colonel, 19 June, 1857.
Francis Roger Palmer, C.B.—Ensign,
15 March, 1833 ; Lieut., 24 April, 1835 ;
Captain, 11 March, 1842 ; Major, 20
June, 1854 ; Lieut.-Col., 22 June, 1858.
Webbe Butler—2nd Lieut., 19 Sept.,
1834 ; Lieut., 15 Dec., 1840 ; Captain,
26 July, 1844 ; Major, 23 March, 1855 ;
Lieut.-Colonel, 9 Sept., 1858.
Robert P. Hawley—Ensign, 28 Aug.,
1838 ; Lieut., 31 Dec., 1839 ; Captain,
10 Jan., 1851 ; Brevet Major, 2 Nov.,
1855 ; Major, 5 Sept., 1856 ; Lieut.-
Col., 18 May, 1860.
Peter Burton Roe—2nd Lieut., 23
July, 1841 ; Lieut., 26 July, 1844 ;
Captain, 17 June, 1851 ; Major, 29
April, 1859 ; Lieut.-Col., 18 Sept., 1860.

Majors—

Henry Friend Kennedy—2nd Lieut.,
11 Sept., 1840 ; Lieut., 7 April, 1842 ;
Captain, 20 Oct., 1848 ; Major, 17 Aug.,
1855.
Charles Napier North—Ensign, 20
May, 1836 ; Lieut., 28 Dec., 1838 ;
Captain, 28 Dec., 1848 ; Major, 19 June,
1857 ; Brevet Lieut.-Col., 24 March, 1858.
Gibbes Rigaud—2nd Lieut., 11 June,
1841 ; Lieut., 26 July, 1844 ; Captain,
16 Aug., 1850 ; Major, 22 June, 1858 ;
Brevet Lieut.-Col., 15 Feb., 1861.
Sir Edward Fitzgerald Campbell,
Bart.— 2nd Lieut., 2 July, 1841 ; Lieut.,
26 July, 1844 ; Captain, 27 Dec., 1850 ;
Brevet Major, 19 Jan., 1858 ; Major,
9 Sept., 1858 ; Brevet Lieut.-Col., 23
Oct., 1860.
James Fraser—2nd Lieut., 10 Sept.,
1841 ; Lieut., 26 July, 1844 ; Captain,
7 Jan., 1853 ; Major, 18 Oct., 1859.
Randle Joseph Feilden—2nd Lieut.,
31 March, 1843 ; Lieut., 25 Feb., 1845 ;
Captain, 23 Dec., 1853 ; Major, 18 May,
1860.
Dunbar Douglas Muter—Ensign, 14
April, 1843 ; Lieut., 17 Jan., 1845 ;
Captain, 31 May, 1854 ; Brevet Major,
19 Jan., 1858 ; Brevet Lieut.-Col., 20
July, 1858 ; Major, 10 July, 1860.
Charles Alex. Boswell Gordon—Ensign, 21 April, 1843 ; Lieut., 13 June,
1845 ; Capt. 6 June, 1854 ; Bt. Major,
6 June, 1856 ; Major, 18 Sept., 1860.

Rank and Name.	Rank in Regiment.	Rank and Name.	Rank in Regiment.
Captains—		*Lieutenants* (continued)—	
Thomas Biggs	8 April 1853	Kennett Gregg Henderson	6 May 1856
Hon. Francis Williams	3 Mar. 1854	Fred Austin	9 May 1856
Rank in Army, Bt. Maj.	19 Jan. 1858	Edward Campbell Ainslie	9 May 1856
John Maguire	20 June 1854	Jas. S. Hamilton Algar	9 May 1856
Rank in Army, Bt. Maj.	20 July 1858	Norman Fitzgerald Uniacke	7 Mar. 1856
Hon. Edward Warren	4 Aug. 1854	O. C. Kelly	**16 Nov. 1856**
Alfred J. Fitzgerald	23 Mar. 1855	Matthew Tilford	**17 Mar. 1857**
Francis Dawson	23 Mar. 1855	James Kiero Watson	**1 Mar. 1857**
John Prevost Battersby	23 Mar. 1855	C. Christ. Willoughby	**31 May 1857**
Bernard Edwd. Ward	23 Mar. 1855	Robt. John Hickman	**25 Aug. 1857**
Rank in Army, Bt. Maj.	20 July 1855	John Owen Young	**25 Aug. 1857**
Vincent Tongue	23 Mar. 1855	Wm. Norcott Manners	**23 Oct. 1855**
Robt. Wilmot Brooke	23 Mar. 1855	Fred. H. Anson Hamilton	16 Nov. 1855
Rank in Army, Bt. Maj.	15 Feb. 1861	Harry Robt. Milligan	23 Nov. 1855
Francis Charteris Fletcher	23 Mar. 1855	George Hatchell	27 Sept. 1857
Edward Bowles	23 Mar. 1855	Arthur Tufnell	15 Jan. 1858
R. J. Eust. Robinson	23 Mar. 1855	Rich. Francis Jennings	15 Jan. 1858
Hugh P. Montgomery	17 Aug. 1855	Frank Sadlier Brereton	13 Feb. 1858
C. D. Cunningham Ellis	14 Dec. 1855	Wm. Greer Turle	23 Mar. 1858
Rank in Army, Bt. Maj.	23 Oct. 1860	Carr Hampton Boyer	23 April 1858
Hon. Atholl C. J. Liddell	24 Dec. 1855	Alfred Lewis	**21 May 1858**
Wm. Tedlie	25 Jan. 1856	Stanley Mortimer	21 May 1858
Rank in Army, Bt. Maj.	20 July 1858	Wm. J. Everest Pyle	21 May 1858
Conyngham Jones	6 May 1856	Newton James Paoli	4 June 1858
Rank in Army, Bt. Maj.	20 April 1858	Ashley Hen. Woodgate	16 June 1858
C. H. Spen. Churchill	4 Aug. 1856	Wm. Henry Mockler	**15 June 1858**
Rank in Army, Bt. Maj.	2 Nov. 1857	W. Lowry Knight Nights	15 June 1858
Hon. John Colborne	4 Feb. 1856	& C. Alf. Spen. Heathcote	22 June 1858
Henry Semple	25 Aug. 1857	Fred. Augustus Campbell	9 Sept. 1858
Edwd. Aug. Motherel	8 Jan. 1857	Hugh St. George Barton	9 Nov. 1858
Wm. Spicer Cookworthy	22 Aug. 1857	George Hewitt Trotman	13 Aug. 1859
Chas. Williamson	16 Oct. 1857	Richard Albert Massy	16 Aug. 1859
Rowley Wells Ringwood	15 Jan. 1858	Richard Russell Giddings	7 Oct. 1859
Francis Stewart Travers	15 Jan. 1858	Charles Henry Cox	4 Nov. 1859
Wykham Leith Pemberton	20 Mar. 1858	John B. E. Newbison	16 Dec. 1859
Hen. Pardoe Eaton	23 April 1858	Henry Richard Travers	2 Mar. 1860
F. Dawkins Farquharson	24 April 1858	Tarlton C. Trowerscott	9 Mar. 1860
John James Phillips	14 May 1858	E. Trevallion de B. Barry	9 Mar. 1860
James Durham Dundas	22 June 1858	John Fred. Hunter Dorton	5 May 1860
Herbert John Deedes	2 July 1858	Julius Tottenham	11 Sept. 1860
Rank in Army, Bt. Maj.	25 Sept. 1860	Reginald H. Gosden	11 Sept. 1860
John d'Olier George	2 July 1858	John Wm. Marshall	11 Sept. 1860
James Hare	9 Sept. 1858	Richard Meade	11 Sept. 1860
John Wm. Medhurst	4 April 1858	Harcourt Jas. Lees	11 Sept. 1860
James Joseph Collins	9 July 1858	Pennyman White Worsley	11 Sept. 1860
Jas. Hen. Lawrence Archer	12 Feb. 1858	Astley Fellowes Terry	11 Sept. 1860
D. G. N. Watts-Russell	29 Nov. 1858	John Gustavus Crosbie	18 Sept. 1860
Arthur Wm. Kincaid Gore	16 Dec. 1858	Charles Bates at Prust	26 Oct. 1860
Anthony Carlisle	9 Mar. 1860	N. Willoughby Wallner	4 Jan. 1861
Francis Vernon Northey	18 May 1860	Charles Gosling	15 Jan. 1861
Philip John Curtis	10 July 1860	Marcus Wm. O'Rorke	16 April 1861
Wm. E. Carleton	18 Sept. 1860	Charles F. Fuller	3 Feb. 1860
Joseph Chorley	1 Feb. 1860	Arthur Morris	1 June 1861
Percy Chaplin	15 Nov. 1859	Percy O'Brien Butler	17 Sept. 1861
Robt. Morris Hazen	4 Jan. 1861		
Harriet Bell Forsyth	15 Jan. 1861	*Ensigns—*	
& C. Nathaniel Burdon	20 Nov. 1860	George D. Anderson	26 Mar. 1858
		Alexander Best-wick	22 May 1858
Lieutenants—		Beavers Henry Bailey	24 May 1858
James Arthur Morrah	11 May 1855	Henry M. Pryor	25 June 1858
Hon. R. P. Verekers	11 May 1855	G. J. J. Graham F. Pigott	14 July 1858
James Forbes	23 Oct. 1855	Chas. Pierson Crozier	21 Aug. 1858
Geo. French Nicholas	26 Oct. 1855	Edwd. Digby O'Rorke	31 Aug. 1858
Conner Ashburnham	26 Oct. 1855	Jas. Miller	9 Nov. 1858
Augustus Morgan	25 Jan. 1856	Courtenay Forbes-Terry	8 April 1859

Rank and Name.	Rank in Regiment.

Ensigns (continued)—

Hon. W. Courtenay Pepys 14 June 1859
Francis Wm. Robins .. 22 July 1859
Francis Wallace Grenfell 5 Aug. 1859
Barnard Henry Davidson 16 Aug. 1859
John Wm. Rhodes.. .. 7 Oct. 1859
Aubrey Vere O'Brien .. 18 Oct. 1859
Rich. F. St. Andrew St.
    John .. .. .. 15 Nov. 1859
John Edwd. Pratt Barlow 16 Dec. 1859
Chas. Louis C. de Robeck 22 Oct. 1859
T. W. M. Edmunds .. 6 Jan. 1860
Clifford Fortescue Borrer 20 April 1860
Hon. Ralph Abercromby 15 June 1860
Cecil Henry Paulet.. .. 31 July 1860
Chas. Gilbert Fryer .. 14 Aug. 1860
Fred. Edward Lonsdale.. 4 Sept. 1860
Edward Burr .. .. .. 11 Sept. 1860
Arthur Richard Lees .. 12 Sept. 1860
R. Dalrymple Elphinstone 18 Sept. 1860
Cecil John Shephard .. 19 Sept. 1860
Francis Seawen Blunt .. 21 Sept. 1860
Henry James Daubuz .. 22 Sept. 1860
Wm. Warren .. .. .. 12 Oct. 1860
Charles Gathorne Hardy 26 Oct. 1860
Geo. Thos. Whitaker .. 21 Dec. 1860
George Carpenter .. .. 4 Jan. 1860
R. Collingwood Robinson 6 Jan. 1860
J. Lance McLean Farmer 16 April 1861
E. Walter Horne Crofton 6 June 1861
Dennis Bingham .. .. 17 Aug. 1861
John Henry Gambleton.. 27 Sept. 1861
Chas. Mosley Turner .. 3 Dec. 1861

Paymasters—

Francis Fitzpatrick, 2 March, 1855
Ensign, 19 Oct., 1849 ; Lieut., 31 May,
1854 ; Honorary Captain, 1 Jan., 1860.
Fred. Thos. Patterson, 19 June,1855—
Honorary Captain, 19 June, 1860.
John Henry Chads, 29 May, 1857—
Ensign, 9 Jan., 1841 ; Lieut., 12 May,
1841 ; Captain, 15 Jan., 1856.
Edwd. Chas. Grant, 28 Dec., 1855—
Honorary Captain, 28 Dec., 1860.

Adjutants—

James Forbes, Lieut. .. 5 April 1855
Geo. Chas. Kelly, Lieut.. 1 May 1855
Lath. Coldington Brown-
    rigg, Lieut. .. .. .. 18 Jan. 1859
James Arthur Morrah,
    Lieut. 22 Sept.1860

Instructors of Musketry—

F. Sadler Brereton, Lieut. 28 Aug. 1857
Wm. N. Manners, Lieut. 22 Mar. 1858
P. H. Worsley, Lieut. .. 15 Feb. 1860
W. G. Turle, Lieut. .. 21 Aug. 1860

Quartermasters—

Wm. Hunter .. .. .. 13 July 1855
Thos. Walker .. .. .. 10 Mar. 1848
Robert Duncan .. .. 13 Aug. 1858
Richard Storey .. .. 14 June 1861

Surgeons—

George Waterloo Pennington Sparrow,

Rank and Name.	Rank in Regiment.

Surgeons (continued)—

M.D., 6 July, 1855 ; Assist.-Surgeon,
25 Sept., 1846.
Edwd. Wm. Young, M.D., 8 Dec.,
1854 ; Assist.-Surgeon, 7 Aug. 1846.
James Crerar, 6 April, 1855 ; Assist.-
Surgeon, 3 Sept., 1847.
John Philips Cunningham, M.D., 11
March, 1859 ; Assist.-Surgeon, 13 April,
1852.

Assistant-Surgeons—

A. Graham Young.. .. 5 May 1854
Jas. Macartney .. .. 6 Oct. 1854
Ebenezer John Hatchell . 15 Jan. 1856
Robert Owen Hayden .. 15 Sept.1857
Fredk. Wm. Wade.. .. 15 Sept.1857
Wm. Silver Oliver, M.D. 15 Sept.1857
James Doran, M.D... .. 9 Nov. 1857

Regimentals—Green, facings scarlet.

Agents—Sir C. R. McGregor, Bart., and
    Walter McGregor, Esq.

1863.

Four Battalions.

England—Burmah—Canada.

Celer et Audax.

Roleia, Vimiera, Martinique, Talavera,
Fuentes d'Onor, Albuhera, Ciudad
Rodrigo, Badajoz, Salamanca, Vittoria,
Pyrenees, Nivelle, Nive, Orthes, Tou-
louse, Peninsula, Punjaub, Mooltan,
Goojerat, Taku Forts, Pekin.

Col.-in-Chief—

Field-Marshal Hugh Viscount Gough,
K.P., G.C.B., 28 Jan., 1854.

Cols.-Commandant—

Joseph Paterson—Ensign, 17 May,
1799 ; Lieutenant, 7 Feb., 1801 ; Captain, 23 Oct., 1806 ; Major, 29 Sept.,
1811 ; Lieut.-Colonel, 31 Dec., 1825 ;
Colonel, 28 June, 1838 ; Major-General,
11 Nov., 1851 ; Lieut.-General, 26 Aug.,
1858 ; Colonel Commanding, 60th Rifles,
14 April, 1854.
Hon. George Fred. Upton, C.B.—
Ensign, 24 April, 1823 ; Lieutenant,
29 Oct., 1825 ; Captain, 12 Dec., 1826 ;
Major, 16 June, 1837 ; Lieut.-Colonel,
16 April, 1841 ; Colonel, 11 Nov. 1851 ;
Major-General, 26 Oct., 1858 ; Colonel-
Commandant, 60th Rifles, 24 Oct., 1862.

Lieut.-Colonels—

Henry Bingham—2nd Lieutenant,
30 April, 1827 ; Lieutenant, 28 Sept.,
1832 ; Capt., 25 June, 1841 ; Major,
19 Oct., 1851 ; Lieut.-Colonel, 19 June,
1857 ; Colonel, 2 Feb., 1862.
Francis Roger Palmer, C.B.—Ensign,
15 Mar., 1833 ; Lieutenant, 24 April,

Lieut.-Colonels (continued)—
1835; Captain, 11 March, 1842; Major,
20 June, 1854; Lieut.-Colonel, 22 June,
1858.

Webbe Butler—2nd Lieutenant, 19
Sept., 1834; Lieutenant, 15 Dec., 1840;
Captain, 26 July, 1844; Major, 23
March, 1855; Lieut.-Col., 9 Sept., 1858.

Robert B. Hawley—Ensign, 28 Aug.,
1838; Lieutenant, 31 Dec., 1839; Capt.,
10 Jan., 1851; Brevet Major, 2 Nov.
1855; Major, 5 Sept., 1856; Lieut.-
Colonel, 18 May, 1860.

Peter Burton Roe—2nd Lieutenant,
23 July, 1841; Lieutenant, 26 July
1844; Captain, 17 June, 1851; Major,
29 April, 1859; Lieut.-Colonel, 18
Sept., 1860.

Majors—
Henry Friend Kennedy—2nd Lieutenant, 11 Sept., 1840; Lieut., 7 April,
1842; Captain, 20 Oct., 1848; Major,
17 Aug., 1855.

Charles Napier North—Ensign, 20
May, 1836; Lieutenant, 28 Dec., 1838;
Captain, 28 Dec., 1848; Major, 49 June,
1857; Brevet Lieut.-Colonel, 23 March,
1858.

Gibbes Rigaud—2nd Lieutenant, 11
June, 1841; Lieutenant, 26 July, 1844;
Captain, 16 Aug., 1851; Major, 22
June, 1858; Brevet Lieut.-Colonel, 15
Feb., 1861.

Sir Edward Fitzgerald Campbell,
Bart.—2nd Lieutenant, 2 July, 1841;
Lieutenant, 26 July, 1844; Capt. 27
Dec., 1850; Brevet Major, 19 Jan.,
1858; Major, 9 Sept., 1858; Brevet
Lieut.-Colonel, 23 Oct., 1860.

James Fraser—2nd Lieutenant, 10
Sept., 1841; Lieutenant, 26 July, 1844;
Captain, 7 Jan., 1853; Major, 18 Oct.,
1858.

Randle Joseph Feilden—2nd Lieutenant, 31 March, 1843; Lieutenant,
25 Feb., 1846; Captain 23 Dec., 1853;
Major, 18 May, 1861.

Charles Alex. Roswell Gordon—En-
sign, 21 April, 1843; Lieutenant, 13
June, 1845; Captain, 6 June, 1851;
Brevet Major, 9 June, 1856; Major, 18
Sept., 1860.

Henry Christopher Marriott—Ensign,
5 Sept., 1843; Lieutenant, 19 June,
1846; Captain, 2 Feb., 1852; Brevet
Major, 26 April, 1859; Major, 16 Nov.,
1860.

Rank and Name.	Rank in Regiment.
Captains—	
Thomas Riggs	8 April 1853
Henry Francis Williams ..	3 Mar. 1854
Rank in Army, Bt. Maj. 19 Jan. 1858	
John Maguire	20 June 1854
Rank in Army, Bt. Maj. 20 July 1858	
Henry Edward Warren..	4 Aug. 1854
Alfred J. Fitzgerald ..	23 Mar. 1855

Rank and Name.	Rank in Regiment.
Captains (continued)—	
Francis Dawson	23 Mar. 1855
John Prevost Battersby..	23 Mar. 1855
Bernard Edward Ward..	23 Mar. 1855
Rank in Army, Bt. Maj. 20 July 1855	
Vincent Tongue ..	23 Mar. 1855
Robert Wilmot Brooke..	23 Mar. 1855
Rank in Army, Bt. Maj. 15 Feb. 1861	
Francis Charteris Fletcher 23 Mar. 1855	
Edward Bowles ..	23 Mar. 1855
R. J. Eustace Robertson	23 Mar. 1855
Hugh P. Montgomery ..	17 Aug. 1855
Chas D. Cunningham Ellis 14 Dec. 1855	
Rank in Army, Bt. Maj. 23 Oct. 1860	
Hon. Atholl C. J. Liddell 21 Dec. 1855	
William Tedlie	25 Jan. 1856
Rank in Army, Bt. Maj. 20 July 1858	
Conyngham Jones ..	6 May 1856
Rank in Army, Bt. Maj. 26 April 1859	
C. H. Spencer Churchill ..	4 Aug. 1854
Rank in Army, Bt. Maj. 2 Nov. 1855	
Hon. John Colborne ..	1 Feb. 1856
Henry Semple ..	25 Aug. 1857
Edw. Aug. Stafford	8 Jan. 1856
Wm. Spicer Cookworthy	22 Aug. 1856
Charles Williamson	16 Oct. 1857
Rowley Wills Hinxman..	15 Jan. 1858
Francis Stewart Travers	23 Mar. 1858
Wickham L. Pemberton	23 Mar. 1858
Henry Purdon Eaton	23 April 1858
F. Dundas Farquharson..	24 April 1858
John James Phillips	14 May 1858
James Durham Dundas.	22 July 1858
Herbert George Dowles..	2 July 1858
Rank in Army, Bt. Maj. 25 Sept. 1860	
John Arthur George ..	2 July 1858
James Hare	9 Sept. 1858
James Joseph Collins	19 July 1859
Jas Hy Lawrence Archer	12 Feb. 1858
D. G. Nev. Watts-Russell	29 Nov. 1859
Anthony Carlisle ..	9 Mar. 1860
Francis Vernon Northey..	18 May 1860
Philip Julian Curtis ..	10 July 1860
Wm. F. Carleton	18 Sept. 1860
Joseph Cheese.. ..	1 Feb. 1856
Percy Chaplin.. ..	15 Nov. 1859
Robt Morris Hazen ..	4 Jan. 1861
Barnet Bell Forsyth ..	15 Jan. 1861
Nathaniel Burslem.. ..	20 Nov. 1860
Geo Redd Stewart Black	14 Feb. 1860
E Gambier Elliot Atherley	6 Nov. 1860
Lieutenants—	
James Arthur Morrah ..	11 May 1855
Hon. R. P. Verelier ..	11 May 1855
James Forbes	23 Oct. 1855
Geo. French Stehelin ..	26 Oct. 1855
Cromer Ashburnham ..	26 Oct. 1855
Augustus Morgan ..	25 Jan. 1856
Kenneth Gregg Henderson	4 Jan. 1861
Fred Austin	15 Jan. 1861
Edw. Campbell Airshe..	9 May 1856
Jas S. Hamilton Algar..	9 May 1856
G. C. Kelly	9 May 1856
Matthew Tilford	17 Mar. 1857
James Kiero Watson ..	1 May 1857

Rank and Name.	Rank in Regiment.
Lieutenants (continued)—	
Chas. Chris. Willoughby .	31 May 1857
Robt. John Hickman ..	25 Aug. 1857
John Owen Young.. ..	25 Aug. 1857
Wm. Norcott Manners..	23 Oct. 1855
Fred. H. Anson Hamilton	16 Nov. 1855
Harry Robt. Milligan ..	23 Nov. 1855
George Hutchell	27 Sept. 1857
Arthur Tuffnell	16 Jan. 1858
Richard Francis Jennings	15 Jan. 1858
Frank Sadlier Brereton..	13 Feb. 1858
Wm. Greer Turle	23 Mar. 1858
Cary Hampton Borrer ..	23 April 1858
Alfred Lewis	21 May 1858
Stanley Mortimer	21 May 1858
Wm. John E. Poole ..	21 May 1858
Newton Jones Pauli ..	4 June 1858
Ashley Henry Woodgate.	15 June 1858
Wm. Henry Moseley ..	15 June 1858
W. L. K. Ogilvy	15 June 1858
U.C., A. S. Heathcote ..	22 June 1858
F. A. Campbell	9 Sept. 1858
H. St. George Barton ..	9 Nov. 1858
G. H. Trotman	13 Aug. 1859
R. A. Massy	16 Aug. 1859
Chas. Henry Cox	4 Nov. 1859
L. C. Brownrigg, Adj. ..	9 Mar. 1860
R. Fitzwilliam de B. Barry	9 Mar. 1860
J. E. H. Peyton	5 May 1860
Julius Tottenham	11 Sept. 1860
R. H. Beadon..	11 Sept. 1860
J. W. Marshall	11 Sept. 1860
Richard Meade	11 Sept. 1860
Harcourt James Lees ..	11 Sept. 1860
Pennyman White Worsley	11 Sept. 1860
Astley Fellows Terry ..	11 Sept. 1860
John Gustavus Crosbie..	11 Sept. 1860
Charles Bateman Prust .	26 Oct. 1860
N. Willoughby Wallace..	4 Jan. 1861
Chas. Gosling	15 Jan. 1861
Marcus Wm. O'Rorke ..	16 April 1861
Chas. F. Faber	3 Feb. 1860
Arthur Morris..	4 June 1861
Pierce O'Brien Butler ..	17 Sept. 1861
Ellis Houlton Ward ..	20 Nov. 1861
Alex. Borthwick	8 Aug. 1862
Chas. Matt. Calderon ..	26 Oct. 1860
Redvers Henry Buller ..	9 Dec. 1862
Ensigns—	
Geo. D. Anderson	26 Mar. 1858
G. Edw. Graham Foster Pigott	11 July 1858
Chas. Pierson Cramer ..	24 Aug. 1858
Edw. Digby O'Rorke ..	31 Aug. 1858
John Miller	9 Nov. 1858
Courtenay Forbes Terry .	8 April 1859
Hon. W. Courtenay Pepys	14 June 1859
Fran. Wm. Robins ..	22 July 1859
Fran. Wallace Grenfell..	5 Aug. 1859
Barnard Henry Davidson	16 Aug. 1859
John Wm. Rhodes.. ..	7 Oct. 1859
Aubrey Vere O'Brien ..	18 Oct. 1859
R. F. St. Andrew St.John	15 Nov. 1859
John Ed. Pratt Barlow..	16 Dec. 1859
Chas. Louis C. de Robeck	22 Oct. 1859

Rank and Name.	Rank in Regiment.
Ensigns (continued)—	
T.WentworthM.Edmunds	6 Jan. 1860
Clifford Fortescue Borrer	20 April 1860
Hon. Ralph Abercromby.	15 June 1860
Cecil Henry Paulet ..	31 July 1860
Chas. Gilbert Fryer ..	14 Aug. 1860
Fred. Ed. Lonsdale ..	4 Sept. 1860
Ed. Burr..	11 Sept. 1860
R. Dalrymple Elphinstone	18 Sept. 1860
Cecil John Shepherd ..	19 Sept. 1860
Francis Scawen Blunt ..	21 Sept. 1860
Henry James Daubuz ..	22 Sept. 1860
Wm. Warren	19 Oct. 1860
Chas. Gathorne Hardy ..	26 Oct. 1860
Geo. Thos. Whitaker ..	21 Dec. 1860
Geo. Carpenter	4 Jan. 1860
R. Collingwood Robinson	6 Jan. 1860
G. L. McLean Farmer ..	16 April 1861
Ed. Walter Home Crofton	4 June 1861
Dennis Bingham	17 Aug. 1861
John Henry Gumbleton .	27 Sept. 1861
Charles Mosley Turner ..	3 Dec. 1861
C. Horatio G. Powys-Keck	4 Mar. 1862
J. Talbot Darnley Crosbie	8 Aug. 1862
Herbert Fitzroy Eaton ..	25 Mar. 1862
Francis Henry Baillie ..	9 Dec. 1862

Paymasters—

Francis Fitzpatrick, 2 Mar. 1855—Ensign, 19 Oct., 1849; Lieutenant, 31 May, 1854; Hon. Captain, 1 Jan., 1860.

Fred. Thos. Patterson, 19 June, 1855 —Hon. Captain, 19 June, 1860.

Edw. Chas. Grant, 28 Dec. 1855— Hon. Captain, 28 Dec., 1860.

Robert Champion Streatfield, 8 June, 1858—Ensign, 12 Aug., 1859; Lieut., 26 Oct., 1855.

Adjutants—

James Forbes, Lieut. ..	5 April 1855
Geo. C. Kelly, Lieut. ..	1 May 1855
L. Codd.Brownrigg, Lieut.	18 Jan. 1859
James A. Morrah, Lieut.	22 Sept. 1860

Instructors of Musketry—

F. S. Brereton, Lieut. ..	28 Aug. 1857
Wm. N. Manners	22 Mar. 1858
P. W. Worsley	15 Feb. 1860
W. G. Turle	21 Aug. 1860

Quartermasters—

Wm. Hunter	13 July 1855
Robt. Duncan..	13 Aug. 1858
Rich. Storey	4 June 1861
Thomas Jarvis..	2 Dec. 1862

Surgeons—

Geo. Waterloo Pennington Sparrow, M.D., 6 July, 1855; Assistant-Surgeon, 25 Sept., 1846.

Edward William Young, M.D., 8 Dec., 1854; Assistant-Surgeon, 7 Aug., 1846.

James Creear, 6 April, 1855; Assistant-Surgeon, 3 Sept., 1847.

Rank and Name. **Rank in Regiment.**

Surgeons (continued):—
John Phillips Cunningham, M.D., 11 March, 1859; Assistant-Surgeon, 13 April, 1852.

Assistant-Surgeons—
A. Graham Young . . . . 5 May 1854
Ebenezer John Hatchell . 15 Jan. 1856
Robt. Owen Hayden .. 15 Sept. 1857
Frederick Wm. Wade .. 28 Sept. 1857
Wm. Silver Oliver, M.D. 15 Sept. 1857
Alex. Campbell McTavish 12 Jan. 1859

Regimentals—Green, facings scarlet.

Agents—Sir C. R. McGregor, Bart., and Walter McGregor, Esq.

1864.

Four Battalions.

England—Burmah—Canada.

Color of Andes.

Roleia, Vimiera, Martinique, Talavera, Fuentes d'Onor, Albuhera, Ciudad Rodrigo, Badajoz, Salamanca, Vittoria Pyrenees, Nivelle, Nive, Orthes, Toulouse, Peninsula, Punjaub, Mooltan, Goojerat, Taku Forts, Pekin, Delhi.

Col.-in-Chief—
Field-Marshal Hugh Viscount **Gough,** K.P., G.C.B., 28 January, 1854.

Cols.-Commandant—
Geo. Frederick Vincount Templetown, C.B.—Ensign, 24 April, 1823; Lieut. 29 Oct., 1823; Captain, 12 Dec., 1826; Major, 16 June, 1857; Lieut.-Colonel, 16 April, 1841; Colonel, 11 Nov. 1851; Major-Gen. 20 Oct., 1858; Colonel Com. 60th Rifles 24 Oct., 1862.

Henry Viscount Melville, K.C.B.—Ensign and Lieut. 18 Nov. 1810; Capt. 1 April, 1824; Major, 11 July, 1826; Lieut.-Colonel, 3 Dec., 1829; Colonel 28 Nov., 1841; Major-Gen. 20 June, 1854; Lieut.-Gen. 5 May, 1859; Col.-Com. 60th Rifles 4 April, 1863.

Lieut.-Colonels—
Henry Bingham **2nd Lieut.**, 30 April, 1827; Lieut., 28 Sept., 1832; Captain, 25 June, 1841; Major, 19 Oct. 1851; Lieut.-Colonel, 19 June, 1857; Colonel, 2 Feb., 1862.

Francis Roger Palmer, C.B.—Ensign, 15 March, 1833; Lieut., 24 April 1835; Captain, 11 March, 1842; Major, 20 June, 1851; Lieut.-Colonel, 22 June, 1858; Colonel 8 August, 1860.

Wentworth Butler **2nd Lieut.**, 19 Sept., 1839; Lieut., 15 Dec., 1840; Captain, 26 July, 1847; Major, 23 March, 1855; Lieut.-Colonel, 9 Sept., 1858.

Robert B. Bowles—Ensign, 28 Aug., 1838; Lieut., 31 Dec., 1839; Captain,

Lieut.-Colonels (continued)—
10 Jan., 1851; Brevet Major, 2 Nov., 1855; Major, 5 Sept., 1856; Lieut.-Colonel, 18 May, 1860.

Peter Burton Roe—2nd Lieut., 23 July, 1841; Lieut., 26 July, 1844; Captain, 17 June, 1851; Major, 20 April, 1859; Lieut.-Colonel, 18 Sept., 1862.

Majors—
Henry Friend Kennedy—2nd Lieut., 11 Sept. 1840; Lieut., 7 April, 1842; Captain, 20 Oct., 1848; Major, 17 Aug., 1855.

Charles Napier North—Ensign, 20 May, 1836; Lieut., 28 Dec., 1838; Captain, 28 Dec., 1838; Major, 19 June, 1857; Brevet Lieut.-Colonel, 24 March, 1858.

Gibbes Rigaud, 2nd Lieut., 11 June, 1841; Lieut., 26 July, 1844; Captain, 16 Aug., 1850; Major, 22 June, 1858; Brevet Lieut.-Colonel, 15 Feb., 1861.

Sir Edward Fitzgerald Campbell, Bart.—2nd **Lieut.**, 2 July, 1841; Lieut., 26 July, 1844; Captain, 27 Dec., 1850; Brevet Major, 12 Jan. 1858; Major, 9 Sept., 1858; Brevet Lieut.-Colonel, 23 October, 1860.

Randle Joseph **Feilden**— **2nd Lieut.**, 31 March, 1843; **Lieut., 25 Feb., 1845;** Captain, 23 Dec., **1853; Major, 18 May,** 1860.

Charles Alexander Boswell Gordon—Ensign, 21 April, 1843; Lieut., 13 June, 1845; Captain, 6 June, 1851; Brevet Major, 6 June, 1856; Major, 18 Sept., 1860.

Henry Christopher Marriott—Ensign, 5 Sept., 1843; Lieut., 19 June, 1846; Captain, 2 Feb., 1849; Brevet-Major, 20 April, 1856; Major, 16 Nov., 1860.

Thomas Inges—Ensign, 2 Oct. 1840; **Lieut., 15** Nov., 1843; Captain, 8 April, **1853;** Major, 22 May, 1863.

Rank and Name. *Rank in Regiment.*

Captains—
Henry Francis Williams.. 3 Mar. 1854
Rank in Army, Bt. Maj. 19 Jan. 1858
John Maguire.. .. .. 20 June 1854
Rank in Army, Bt. Maj. 20 July 1858
Henry Edward Warren.. 4 Aug. 1854
Alfred J. Fitzgerald .. 23 Mar. 1855
John Prevost Battersby.. 23 Mar. 1855
Bernard Edward Ward .. 23 Mar. 1855
Rank in Army, Bt. Maj. 20 July 1855
Vincent Tongue .. .. 23 Mar. 1855
Robt. Walmot Brooke .. 23 Mar. 1855
Rank in Army, Bt. Maj. 15 Feb. 1861
Edward Bowles .. .. 23 Mar. 1855
R. J. Eustace Robertson 23 Mar. 1855
Hugh P. Montgomery .. 17 Aug. 1855
Chas. D. Cunningham Ellis 14 Dec. 1855
Rank in Army, Bt. Maj. 23 Oct. 1860
Hen. Athol C. J. Liddell 21 Dec. 1855
William Tedlie .. .. 25 Jan. 1856
Rank in Army, Bt. Maj. 20 July 1858

Rank and Name.	Rank in Regiment.
Captains (continued)—	
Conyngham Jones	6 May 1856
Rank in Army, Bt. Maj.	26 April 1859
C. H. Spencer Churchill..	4 Aug. 1854
Rank in Army, Bt. Maj.	2 Nov. 1855
Hon. John Colborne ..	1 Feb. 1856
Henry Semple..	25 Aug. 1857
Charles Williamson.. ..	16 Oct. 1857
Rowley Willes Hinxman	15 Jan. 1858
Francis Stewart Travers..	15 Jan. 1858
Wykeham L. Pemberton	23 Mar. 1858
Henry Pardoe Eaton ..	23 April 1858
Fra. Dundas Farquharson	24 April 1858
John James Phillips ..	14 May 1858
James Durham Dundas ..	22 June 1858
Herbert George Deedes..	2 July 1858
Rank in Army, Bt. Maj.	25 Sept. 1860
John d'Oher George ..	2 July 1858
James Hare	9 Sept. 1858
James Joseph Collins ..	19 July 1859
James H. L. Archer ..	12 Feb. 1858
D. G. N. Watts-Russell..	29 Nov. 1859
Anthony Carlisle	9 Mar. 1860
Francis Vernon Northey	18 May 1860
Philip Julian Curtis ..	10 July 1860
Wm. F. Carleton	18 Sept. 1860
Joseph Cheese..	1 Feb. 1856
Percy Chaplin..	15 Nov. 1859
Barnet Bell Forsyth ..	15 Jan. 1861
U. C. Nathaniel Bursdem	20 Nov. 1860
Geo. Robt. Stewart Black	11 Feb. 1860
Edw. Gambier E. Atherley	6 Nov. 1860
Cramer Ashburnham ..	23 Jan. 1863
James Arthur Morrah ..	28 April 1863
Hon. R. P. Vereker ..	7 May 1863
Kenneth Gregg Henderson	30 June 1863
Wm. Henry Irving ..	23 June 1863
Augustus Morgan	17 Nov. 1863
Lieutenants —	
Fred. Austin	9 May 1856
Edward C. Ainslie.. ..	9 May 1856
James S. H. Algar	9 May 1856
G. C. Kelly	16 Nov. 1856
Matthew Tilford	17 Mar. 1857
James Kiero Watson ..	1 May 1857
Chas. Chris. Willoughby	31 May 1857
Robt. John Hinxman ..	25 Aug. 1857
John C. Young	25 Aug. 1857
Wm. Norcott Manners ..	23 Oct. 1855
F. H. Anson Hamilton ..	16 Nov. 1855
Henry Robt. Milligan ..	23 Nov. 1855
George Hatchell	27 Sept. 1857
Arthur Tufnell	15 Jan. 1858
Rich. Francis Jennings..	15 Jan. 1858
Frank Sadlier Brereton ..	13 Feb. 1858
Wm. Greer Turle	23 Mar. 1858
Cary Hampton Borrer ..	20 April 1858
Alfred Lewis	21 May 1858
Stanley Mortimer	21 May 1858
Wm. John E. Poole ..	21 May 1858
Newton Jones Pauli ..	4 June 1858
Ashley Henry Woodgate	15 June 1858
Wm. Henry Moseley ..	15 June 1858
Wm. Lewis K. Ogilvy ..	15 June 1858
Fred. Aug. Campbell ..	9 Sept. 1858
Hugh St. George Barton	9 Nov. 1858

Rank and Name.	Rank in Regiment.
Lieutenants (continued)—	
Geo. Hewitt Trotman ..	13 Aug. 1859
Charles Henry Cox.. ..	4 Nov. 1859
Latham C. Brownrigg ..	9 Mar. 1860
R. Fitzwilliam de B. Barry	9 Mar. 1860
Reginald H. Beadon ..	11 Sept. 1860
John Wm. Marshall ..	11 Sept. 1860
Richard Meade	11 Sept. 1860
Pennyman W. Worsley..	11 Sept. 1860
Ashley Fellowes Terry ..	11 Sept. 1860
John Gustavus Crosbie..	18 Sept. 1860
Chas. Bateman Prust ..	26 Oct. 1860
N. Willoughby Wallace..	4 Jan. 1861
Charles Gosling	15 Jan. 1861
Maurice Wm. O'Rorke ..	16 April 1861
Charles F. Faber ..	3 Feb. 1860
Arthur Morris..	4 June 1861
Pierce O'Brien Butler ..	17 Sept. 1861
Ellis Houlton Ward ..	20 Nov. 1860
Alex. Borthwick	8 Aug. 1862
Chas. Matthew Calderon	26 Oct. 1860
Redvers Henry Buller ..	9 Dec. 1862
Daniel Moodie..	7 Feb. 1856
Chas. Pierson Cramer ..	21 April 1863
Edw. Digby O'Rorke ..	28 April 1863
John Miller	7 May 1863
Courtenay Forbes Terry..	22 May 1863
Hon. Walter C. Pepys ..	23 June 1863
Francis Wm. Robins ..	30 June 1863
James Henry H. Croft ..	31 Mar. 1863
Francis W. Grenfell ..	21 July 1863
Bernard Henry Davidson	11 Aug. 1863
John Wm. Rhodes.. ..	8 Sept. 1863
Aubrey Vere O'Brien ..	8 Sept. 1863
R. F. St. Andrew St. John	17 Nov. 1853
Ensigns —	
John E. P. Barlow.. ..	16 Dec. 1859
Chas. L. C. de Robeck ..	22 Oct. 1859
T. Went. M. Edmunds ..	6 Jan. 1860
Clifford Fortescue Borrer	20 April 1860
Hon. Ralph Abercromby	15 June 1860
Cecil Henry Paulet ..	31 July 1860
Charles Gilbert Fryer ..	14 Aug. 1860
Fred. Edw. Lonsdale ..	4 Sept. 1860
Robert D. Elphinstone ..	18 Sept. 1860
Cecil John Shephard ..	19 Sept. 1860
Wm. Warren	12 Oct. 1860
C. Gathorne Hardy ..	26 Oct. 1860
Geo. Thos. Whitaker ..	21 Dec. 1860
George Carpenter	4 Jan. 1860
Rich. C. Robinson.. ..	6 Jan. 1860
G. D. McLean Farmer ..	16 April 1861
Edw. W. H. Crofton ..	4 June 1861
Dennis Bingham	17 Aug. 1861
Geo. Hen. Gumbleton ..	27 Sept. 1861
C. Moseley Turner.. ..	3 Dec. 1861
C. H. G. Powys-Keck ..	4 Mar. 1862
John Talbot D. Crosbie..	8 Aug. 1862
Herbert F. Eaton	25 Mar. 1862
Francis H. Bailie	9 Dec. 1862
Jonathan W. B. Parish..	23 Jan. 1863
Walter Cowan..	13 Feb. 1863
Jerold Henry Talbot ..	29 May 1863
F. C. Blenkinsopp Coulson	12 June 1863
Henry Donald Browne ..	13 June 1863
Edmund Lennox Fraser..	23 June 1863

Rank and Name.	Rank in Regiment.

Ensigns (continued)—

Henry R. P. Lindesay .. .. 24 June 1863
John B. Stradling .. .. 30 June 1863
Hen. A. F. F. Coventry.. 21 July 1863
Francis Alex. Gordon .. 22 July 1863
Wm. Robert Green .. .. 11 Aug. 1863
Lewis Bradford .. .. 8 Sept. 1863
Frederick Vining .. .. 9 Sept 1863
Wm. Tilden .. .. .. 2 Oct. 1863
Rowland Willis .. .. 3 Oct. 1863
Hon. Henry S. Dormer.. 17 Nov. 1863

Paymasters—

Francis Fitzpatrick, 2 Mar., 1855—
Ensign, 19 Oct., 1849; Lieut., 31 May,
1854; Hon. Captain, 1 Jan., 1860.
Fred. Thos. Paterson, 19 June, 1855—
Hon. Captain, 19 June, 1863.
Edw. Charles Grant, 28 Dec., 1855—
Hon. Captain, 28 Dec., 1860.
Robt. Champion Streatfield, 8 June,
1858—Ensign, 12 Aug., 1853; Lieut.,
26 Oct., 1855; Hon. Captain, 8 June,
1863.

Adjutants—

G. C. Kelly, Lieut.. .. .. 1 May 1855
L. C. Browurigg, Lieut.. 18 June 1863
W. H. Moseley, Lieut... 13 June 1863
Astley F. Terry, Lieut... 23 June 1863

Instructors of Musketry—

F. S. Brereton, Lieut. .. 28 Aug. 1857
W. N. Manners, Lieut... 22 Mar. 1858
P. W. Worsley, Lieut... 15 Feb. 1859
W. G. Turbe, Lieut. .. 21 Aug. 1859

Quartermasters—

Wm. Hunter .. .. .. 13 July 1855
Robt. Duncan.. .. .. 13 Aug. 1858
Thos. Jarvis .. .. .. 2 Dec. 1862
John Cole .. .. .. 20 Mar. 1858
Cornet, 21 Feb. 1856

Surgeons—

Edw. W. Young, M.D., 8 Dec., 1854;
Assistant-Surgeon, 7 Aug., 1846.
John P. Cunningham, M.D., 11 March,
1859; Assistant-Surgeon, 13 April, 1852.
Richard S. Fitzgibbon, 22 July, 1856;
Assistant-Surgeon, 10 Jan., 1851.
Richard C. Todd, 3 Nov., 1857;
Assistant-Surgeon, 24 Sept., 1850.

Assistant-Surgeons—

A. Graham Young.. .. 5 May 1854
Ebenezer J. Hatchell .. 15 Jan., 1856
Robt. Owen Hayden .. 15 Sept. 1857
Frederick Wm. Wale .. 28 Sept. 1857
Wm. S. Oliver, M.D. .. 15 Sept. 1857
Alex. C. McTavish .. .. 12 Jan. 1859

Regimentals: Green, facings scarlet.

Agents—Sir C. R. McGregor, Bart., and
W. McGregor, Esq.

1865.

Four Battalions.

Ireland—England—Burmah—India—
Canada.

Celer et Audax.

Roleia, Vimiera, Martinique, Talavera,
Fuentes d'Onor, Albuhera, Ciudad
Rodrigo, Badajoz, Salamanca, Vittoria,
Pyrenees, Nivelle, Nive, Orthes, Tou-
louse, Peninsula, Punjaub, Mooltan,
Goojerat, Taku Forts, Pekin, Delhi.

Col.-in-Chief—

Field-Marshal Hugh Viscount Gough,
K.P., G.C.B., 28 Jan., 1854.

Cols.-Commandant—

Geo. Fred. Viscount Templetown, C.B.
— Ensign, 24 April, 1823; Lieutenant,
29 Oct., 1825; Captain, 12 Dec., 1826;
Major, 16 June, 1837; Lieut.-Colonel,
16 April 1841; Colonel, 11 Nov., 1851;
Major-Gen., 26 Oct., 1858; Col.-Com-
mandant, 60th Rifles, 24 Oct., 1862.
Henry Viscount Melville, K.C.B.—
Ensign and Lieut., 28 Nov., 1819; Capt.,
1 April, 1824; Major, 11 July, 1826;
Lieut.-Colonel, 3 Dec., 1829; Colonel,
28 Nov., 1841; Major-Gen., 20 June,
1854; Lieut.-Gen., 5 May, 1860; Col.-
Commandant, 60th Rifles, 1 April, 1863.

Lieut.-Colonels—

Henry Bingham 2nd Lieut., 30
April, 1827; Lieut., 28 Sept., 1832;
Capt., 25 June, 1841; Major, 19 Oct.,
1851; Lieut.-Colonel, 19 June, 1857;
Colonel, 2 Feb., 1862.
Francis Roger Palmer, C.B.—Ensign,
15 Mar., 1833; Lieut., 24 April, 1835;
Capt., 11 Mar., 1842; Major, 20 June,
1851; Lieut.-Colonel, 22 June, 1858;
Colonel, 22 June, 1863.
Robert H. Hawley—Ensign, 28 Aug.,
1838; Lieut., 31 Dec., 1839; Capt., 10
Jan., 1851; Brevet Major, 2 Nov., 1855;
Major, 5 Sept., 1856; Lieut.-Colonel, 18
May, 1860.
Peter Burton Roe—2nd Lieut., 23
July, 1841; Lieut., 26 July, 1844; Capt.,
17 June, 1851; Major, 29 April, 1859;
Lieut.-Colonel, 18 Sept., 1861.
Randle Joseph Feilden—2nd Lieut.,
31 March 1843; Lieut., 25 Feb., 1845;
Capt., 28 Dec., 1851; Major, 18 May,
1860; Lieut.-Colonel, 1 March, 1864.

Majors—

Henry Friend Kennedy—2nd Lieut.,
11 Sept., 1840; Lieut., 7 April, 1842;
Capt., 29 Oct., 1848; Major, 17 Aug.,
1855; Brevet Lieut.-Col., 7 Jan., 1854.
Charles Napier North—Ensign, 20
May, 1836; Lieut., 28 Dec., 1838;
Capt., 28 Dec., 1848; Major, 19 June,
1857; Brevet Lieut.-Col., 24 Mar., 1858.
Gibbes Rigaud—2nd Lieut., 11 June,
1841; Lieut., 26 July, 1844; Capt., 16

Majors (continued)—

Aug., 1859; Major, 22 June, 1858;
Brevet Lieut.-Colonel, 15 Feb., 1861.

Sir Edw. Fitzgerald Campbell, Bart.—
2nd Lieut., 2 July, 1841; Lieut., 26
July, 1844; Captain, 27 Dec., 1850;
Brevet Major, 19 Jan., 1858; Major,
9 Sept., 1858; Brevet Lieut.-Colonel,
23 Oct., 1860.

Charles Alex. Boswell Gordon—
Ensign, 21 April, 1843; Lieutenant, 13
June, 1845; Captain, 6 June, 1851;
Brevet Major, 6 June, 1856; Major,
18 Sept., 1860.

Henry Christopher Marriott—Ensign,
5 Sept., 1843; Lieut., 19 June, 1846;
Captain, 2 Feb., 1849; Brevet Major,
26 April, 1859; Major, 16 Nov., 1860.

Thomas Biggs—Ensign, 2 Oct., 1840;
Lieut., 15 Nov., 1843; Capt., 8 April,
1853; Major, 22 May, 1863.

Henry Edw. Warren—2nd Lieut., 5
Jan., 1844; Lieut., 30 Dec., 1845;
Captain, 4 Aug., 1854; Major, 1 Mar.,
1864.

Henry Francis Williams—Ensign, 19
May, 1843; Lieutenant, 20 Dec., 1844;
Captain, 30 March, 1854; Brevet Major,
19 Jan., 1858; Brevet Lieut.-Colonel,
4 Aug., 1861; Major, 28 Oct., 1864.

	Rank and Name.	Rank in Regiment.
Captains—		
John Maguire	..	29 June 1854
Rank in Army {	Bt. Maj.	29 July 1858
	Bt. Lt.-Col.	5 Aug. 1864
Alfred John Fitzgerald ..		23 Mar. 1855
John Prevost Battersby..		23 Mar. 1855
Bernard Edw. Ward	..	23 Mar. 1855
Rank in Army {	Bt. Maj.	29 July 1855
	Bt. Lt.-Col.	5 Jan. 1864
Vincent Tongue	..	23 Mar. 1855
Robert Wilmot Brooke ..		23 Mar. 1855
Rank in Army, Bt. Maj.		15 Feb. 1861
Edward Bowles ..		23 Mar. 1855
R. J. Eust. Robertson ..		23 Mar. 1855
Hugh P. Montgomery ..		17 Aug. 1855
Ch. D. Cunningham Ellis		14 Dec. 1855
Rank in Army, Bt. Maj.		23 Oct. 1860
William Teddie	..	25 Jan. 1856
Rank in Army, Bt. Maj.		20 July 1858
Conyngham Jones ..	..	6 May 1856
Rank in Army, Bt. Maj.		26 April 1859
C. H. Spencer Churchill .		4 Aug. 1854
Rank in Army, Bt. Maj.		2 Nov. 1855
Hon. John Colborne	..	1 Feb. 1856
Henry Semple	..	25 Aug. 1857
Charles Williamson	..	16 Oct. 1857
Rowley Willes Hinxman.		15 Jan. 1858
Rank in Army, Bt. Maj.		19 Jan. 1864
Francis Stewart Travers .		15 Jan. 1858
W. Leigh Pemberton ..		23 Mar. 1858
Fra. Dundas Farquharson		24 April 1858
John James Philips	..	14 May 1858
James Durham Dundas..		22 June 1858
Herbert George Deedes..		2 July 1858
Rank in Army, Bt. Maj.		25 Sept. 1860
John d'Olier George	..	2 July 1858

	Rank and Name.	Rank in Regiment.
Captains (continued)—		
James Joseph Collins	..	19 July 1859
D. G. NevilleWatts-Russell		29 Nov. 1859
Anthony Carlisle ..	..	9 Mar. 1860
Francis Vernon Northey		18 May 1860
Philip Justian Curtis	..	10 July 1860
Wm. Fred. Carleton	..	18 Sept. 1860
Percy Chaplin..	..	15 Nov. 1859
Burnet Bell Forsyth	..	15 Jan. 1861
Geo. Robt. Stewart Black		14 Feb. 1860
Cromer Ashburnham	..	23 Jan. 1863
James Arthur Morrah	..	28 April 1863
Hon. R. P. Vereker	..	7 May 1863
Kennett Gregg Henderson		30 June 1863
Wm. Henry Iviny..	..	23 June 1863
Augustus Morgan ..	..	17 Nov. 1863
Frederick Austin ..	..	19 Jan. 1864
Edw. Campbell Ainslie ..		1 Mar. 1864
Jas. S. Hamilton Algar..		17 May 1864
Henry Taylor ..	..	12 Feb. 1858
Chas. Chris. Willoughby .		18 Oct. 1864
George Charles Kelly ..		28 Oct. 1864
Robert John Hickman ..		28 Oct. 1864
F. H. Anson Hamilton ..		4 Nov. 1864
Harry Robert Milligan ..		22 Nov. 1864
Lieutenants—		
Matthew Tilford ..	..	17 Mar. 1857
James Kirco Watson ..		1 May 1857
John Owen Young..	..	25 Aug. 1857
Wm. Norcott Manners ..		23 Oct. 1855
George Hatchell	..	27 Sept. 1857
Arthur Tuffnell	..	15 Jan. 1858
Richard Fra. Jennings ..		15 Jan. 1858
Frank Sadlier Brereton ..		13 Feb. 1858
William Gayer Turle ..		23 Mar. 1858
Cary Hampton Borrer ..		23 April 1858
Alfred Lewis ..	..	21 May 1858
Stanley Mortimer ..	..	21 May 1858
Wm. John Everel Poole .		21 May 1858
Newton Jones Pauli ..		4 June 1858
Ashley Henry Woodgate .		15 June 1858
William Henry Moseley .		15 June 1858
W. Lewis Kinloch Ogilvy		15 June 1858
Fred. Augustus Campbell		9 Sept. 1858
Hugh St. George Burton .		9 Nov. 1858
George Hewitt Trotman .		13 Aug. 1859
Latham C. Brownrigg ..		9 Mar. 1860
Robt. Fitzm. de B. Barry		9 Mar. 1860
Reginald H. Bendon ..		11 Sept. 1860
John Wm. Marshall ..		11 Sept. 1860
Richard Meade ..	..	11 Sept. 1860
Pennyman White Worsley		11 Sept. 1860
Astley Fellowes Terry ..		11 Sept 1860
John Gustavus Crosbie..		18 Sept. 1860
Charles Bateman Prust ..		26 Oct. 1860
Nesbit Will. Wallace ..		4 Jan. 1861
Charles Gosling ..	..	15 Jan. 1861
Marcus William O'Rorke		16 Oct. 1860
Charles F. Faber ..	..	3 Feb. 1860
Arthur Morris..	..	4 June 1861
Pierce O'Brien Butler ..		17 Sept. 1861
Ellis Houlton Ward ..		20 Nov. 1861
Alexander Borthwick ..		8 Aug. 1862
Chas. Matthew Calderon .		26 Oct. 1860
R. H. Buller	..	9 Dec. 1862

Rank and Name.	Rank in Regiment.

Lieutenants (continued)—

Daniel Moodie	7 Feb. 1856
Charles Pierson Cramer ..	21 April 1863
Edward Digby O'Rorke..	28 April 1863
Courtenay Forbes Terry ..	22 May 1863
Hon. W. Courtenay Pepys	23 June 1863
Francis William Robins .	30 June 1863
Jas. Hy. Herbert Croft ..	31 Mar. 1863
Francis Wallace Grenfell.	21 July 1863
Bernard Henry Davidson	11 Aug. 1863
John William Rhodes ..	8 Sept. 1863
Aubrey Vere O'Brien ..	8 Sept. 1863
R. F. St. Andrew St. John	17 Nov. 1863
John Edw. Pratt Barlow .	19 Jan. 1864
Chas. Louis C. de Robeck	1 Mar. 1864
T. Wentwth. M. Edmunds	17 May 1864
Clifford Fortescue Borrer.	28 June 1864
Hon. Ralph Abercromby	3 Aug. 1864
Charles Gilbert Fryer	18 Oct. 1864
R. Dalrymple Elphinstone	28 Oct. 1864
Cecil John Shepherd ..	5 Nov. 1864
William Warren	22 Nov. 1864
Philip Julius H. **A. Barne**	12 June 1865

Ensigns—

Chas. Gathorne Hardy ..	26 Oct. 1860
Geo. Thomas Whitaker .	21 Dec. 1860
George Carpenter ..	4 Jan. 1860
R. Collingwood Robinson	6 Jan. 1860
C. Lance. McLean Farmer	16 April 1861
Edw. Walt. Home Crofton	4 June 1861
Lewis Bingham ..	17 Aug. 1861
John Henry Gambleton ..	27 Sept. 1861
Charles Moure Turner ..	3 Dec. 1861
Chas. H. G. Powys-Keck .	4 Mar. 1862
J. Talbot Dursley Crosbie .	8 Aug. 1862
Herbert Fitzroy Eaton ..	25 Mar. 1862
Francis Henry Baillie ..	9 Dec. 1862
J. Walker Bernhard Parish	23 Jan. 1863
Walter Cowan	13 Feb. 1863
F. C. Blenkinsopp Coulson	12 June 1863
Henry Donald Brown ..	13 June 1863
Ed. Lomax Fraser ..	23 June 1863
H. R. P. Lindesay ..	23 June 1863
John Barfoot Streatling ..	30 June 1863
Hy. A. F. F. Coventry ..	21 July 1863
Francis Alex. Gordon ..	22 July 1863
William Robert Green ..	11 Aug. 1863
Lewis Bradford	8 Sept. 1863
Frederick Young	9 Sept. 1863
William Tibbon	2 Oct. 1863
Rowland Willis	3 Oct. 1863
Hon. Hy. Edw. Barnes .	17 Nov. 1863
Hy. Blackwood Macduff	16 Feb. 1864
Thos. Ambrose Warwick .	1 Mar. 1864
Hon. Aug. Wm. C. Ellis.	5 April 1864
Benjamin Sweet	9 Feb. 1864
O. George Parker	11 June 1864
Ambrose H. Bircham ..	28 June 1864
J. Seymour Wynne Finch	12 July 1864
Edw. Collins Wood	18 Oct. 1864
H. A. Houlton Ward ..	28 Oct. 1864
Cecil Ralph Howard ..	29 Oct. 1864
Thos. B. Powys-Keck ..	9 Dec. 1864

Paymasters

Francis Fitzpatrick, 2 Mar., 1855—

Rank and Name.	Rank in Regiment.

Paymasters (continued)—

2nd Lieut., 19 Oct., 1849; Lieut., 31 May, 1854; Hon. Captain, 1 Jan., 1860.

Edw. Charles Grant, 28 Dec., 1855—Hon. Captain, 28 Dec., 1860.

Robert Champion Streatfield, 8 June, 1858—Ensign, 12 Aug., 1853; Lieut., 26 Oct., 1855; Hon. Captain, 8 June, 1863.

W. Banbury, 22 Nov., 1864—Quartermaster, 8 July, 1851.

Adjutants—

L. C. Brownrigg, Lieut...	18 Jan. 1850
W. H. Moseley, Lieut. ..	13 June 1863
M. F. Terry, Lieut. ..	23 June 1863
N. W. Wallace, Lieut. ..	28 Oct. 1864

Instructors of Musketry—

Frank Sadlier Brereton ..	28 Aug. 1857
Wm. N. Manners ..	22 Mar. 1858
F. W. Worsley, Lieut ..	15 Feb. 1860
W. G. Turle, Lieut. ..	21 Aug. 1860

Quartermasters—

Wm. Hunter	13 July 1855
Robt. Dawson	13 Aug. 1858
Thomas Jarvis.. ..	2 Dec. 1862
John Cole	26 Mar. 1858
	Cornet, 21 Feb. 1856

Surgeons—

Edw. W. Young, M.D., 8 Dec., 1854; Assistant-Surgeon, 7 Aug., 1846.

John Philips Cunningham, M.D., 11 March, 1859; Assistant-Surgeon, 13 April, 1852.

Rich. Edw. Fitzgibbon, 22 July, 1856; Assistant-Surgeon, 10 Jan., 1851.

Rich. Cooper Todd, 3 Nov., 1857; Assistant-Surgeon, 24 Sept., 1850.

Assistant-Surgeons—

Adam Graham Young ..	5 May 1854
Robt. Owen Hayden ..	15 Sept. 1857
Frederick Wm. Wade ..	28 Sept. 1857
Wm. Silver Oliver, M.D.	15 Sept. 1857
Geo. Allan Hutton.. ..	23 June 1854

Regimentals—Green, facings scarlet.

Agents Sir C. R. McGregor, Bart., and Walter McGregor, Esq.

1866.

Four Battalions.

Ireland Mediterranean England Indies Canada.

Celer et Audax.

Roleia, Vimiera, Martinique, Talavera, Fuentes d'Onor, Albuhera, Ciudad Rodrigo Badajoz, Salamanca, Vittoria, Pyrenees, Nivelle, Nive, Orthes, Toulouse, Peninsula, Punjaub, Mooltan, Goojerat, Taku Forts, Pekin, Delhi.

Colonel-in-Chief

Field-Marshal Hugh Viscount Gough, K.P., K.C.B., 28 Jan., 1854.

Cols.-Commandant

George Fred. Viscount Templetown,

Cols.-Commandant (continued)

C.B.—Ensign, 24 April, 1823; Lieut., 29 Oct., 1825; Captain, 12 Dec., 1826; Major, 16 June, 1837; Lieut.-Colonel, 16 April 1841; Colonel, 11 Nov., 1851; Major-General, 26 Oct., 1858; Lieut.-General, 9 Mar., 1865; Col.-Commanding, 60th Rifles 24 Oct., 1862

Henry Viscount Melville, G.C.B.— Ensign and Lieut., 18 Nov., 1819; Captain, 1 April, 1824; Major, 11 July, 1826; Lieut.-Colonel, 3 Dec., 1829; Colonel, 28 Nov., 1841; Major-General, 20 June, 1854; Lieut.-General, 5 May, 1860; Col.-Commanding 60th Rifles, 1 April, 1863.

Lieut.-Colonels—

Francis Roger Palmer, C.B.—Ensign, 15 March, 1833; Lieut., 24 April, 1835; Captain, 11 March, 1842; Major, 20 June, 1854; Lieut.-Colonel, 22 June, 1858; Colonel, 22 June, 1863.

Robert B. Hawley Ensign, 28 Aug., 1838; Lieut., 31 Dec., 1839; Captain, 10 Jan., 1851; Brevet Major, 2 Nov., 1855; Major, 5 Sept., 1856; Lieut.-Colonel, 18 May, 1860; Colonel, 18 May, 1865.

Peter Burton Roe, 2nd Lieut., 23 July, 1841; Lieut., 26 July, 1844; Captain, 17 June, 1851; Major, 29 April, 1859; Lieut.-Colonel, 18 Sept., 1860; Colonel, 18 Sept., 1865.

Randle Joseph Feilden, 2nd Lieut., 31 March, 1843; Lieut., 25 Feb., 1845; Captain, 23 Dec., 1853; Major, 18 May, 1860; Lieut.-Colonel, 1 March, 1864.

Majors—

Henry Friend Kennedy, 2nd Lieut., 11 Sept., 1840; Lieut., 7 April, 1842; Captain, 20 Oct., 1848; Major, 17 Aug., 1855; Brevet Lieut.-Colonel, 7 Jan., 1854.

Charles Napier North—Ensign, 20 May, 1846; Lieut., 28 Dec., 1858; Captain, 28 Dec., 1848; Major, 19 June, 1857; Brevet Lieut.-Colonel, 24 March, 1858; Colonel, 30 March, 1865.

Gibbes Rigaud, 2nd Lieut., 11 June, 1841; Lieut., 26 July, 1844; Captain, 16 Aug., 1850; Major, 22 June, 1858; Brevet Lieut.-Colonel, 15 Feb., 1861.

Sir Edward Fitzgerald Campbell, Bart.—2nd Lieut., 2 July, 1841; Lieut., 26 July, 1844; Captain, 27 Dec., 1850; Brevet Major, 19 Jan., 1858; Major, 9 Sept., 1858; Brevet Lieut.-Colonel, 23 Oct., 1860.

Charles Alex. Boswell Gordon— Ensign, 21 April, 1843; Lieut., 13 June, 1845; Captain, 6 June, 1851; Brevet Major, 6 June, 1856; Major, 18 Sept., 1860.

Thomas Biggs—Ensign, 2 Oct., 1840; Lieut., 15 Nov., 1843; Captain, 8 April, 1853; Major, 22 May, 1863.

Majors (continued)—

Henry Edw. Warren—2nd Lieut., 5 Jan., 1844; Lieut., 30 Dec., 1845; Capt., 4 Aug., 1854; Major, 1 March, 1864.

Henry Francis Williams—Ensign, 19 May, 1843; Lieut., 20 Dec., 1844; Captain, 3 March, 1854; Brevet Major, 19 Jan., 1858; Brevet Lieut.-Colonel, 4 Aug., 1864; Major, 28 Oct., 1864.

Alfred John Fitzgerald—Ensign, 8 Nov., 1842; Lieut., 13 Feb., 1846; Captain, 23 March, 1855; Major, 24 Jan., 1865.

	Rank and Name.	Rank in Regiment.

Captains—

Name		Rank in Regiment
John Maguire		2 June 1854
Rank in Army {	Bt. Maj.	20 July 1858
	Lt.-Col.	5 Aug. 1864
John Prevost Battersby		23 Mar. 1855
Bernard Ed. Ward		23 Mar. 1855
Rank in Army {	Bt. Maj.	23 Mar. 1855
	Bt. Lt.-Col.	5 Jan. 1864
Vincent Tongue		23 Mar. 1855
Robt. Wilmot Brooke		23 Mar. 1855
Rank in Army,	Bt. Maj.	15 Feb. 1861
Edw. Bowles		23 Mar. 1855
R. J. East. Robertson		23 Mar. 1855
Hugh P. Montgomery		17 Aug. 1855
Ch. D. C. Ellis		14 Dec. 1855
Rank in Army,	Bt. Maj.	23 Oct. 1860
Wm. Tedlie		25 Jan. 1856
Rank in Army,	Bt. Maj.	20 July 1858
Conyngham Jones		6 May 1856
Rank in Army,	Bt. Maj.	26 April 1859
C. H. Spencer Churchill		4 Aug. 1854
Rank in Army,	Bt. Maj.	2 Nov. 1855
Henry Semple		25 Aug. 1857
Ch. Williamson		16 Oct. 1851
Rowley Willis Hinxman		15 Jan. 1858
Rank in Army,	Bt. Maj.	19 Jan. 1864
Fr. Stewart Travers		15 Jan. 1858
W. Leigh Pemberton		23 Mar. 1858
Fr. Dundas-Farquharson		24 April 1858
John J. Phillips		14 May 1858
J. Durham Dundas		22 July 1858
Herbert Geo. Deedes		2 July 1858
Rank in Army,	Bt. Maj.	25 Sept. 1860
John d'Olier George		2 July 1858
J. Joseph Collins		19 July 1859
D. G. N. Watts-Russell		29 Nov. 1859
Anthony Carlisle		9 Mar. 1860
Fr. Vernon Northey		18 May 1860
Philip Julian Curtis		10 July 1860
Wm. Fred. Carleton		18 Sept. 1860
Geo. Robt. Stewart Black		14 Feb. 1860
Cramer Ashburnham		23 Jan. 1863
J. Arthur Morrah		28 April 1863
Kennett G. Henderson		30 June 1863
Wm. Henry Ivimy		23 June 1863
Augustus Morgan		17 Nov. 1863
Ed. Campbell Ainslie		1 Mar. 1864
J. S. Hamilton Algar		17 May 1864
Henry Taylor		12 Feb. 1858
George Ch. Kelly		6 Oct. 1864
Ch. Chris. Willoughby		18 Oct. 1864
Matthew Tilford		28 Oct. 1864
Robt. John Hickman		28 Oct. 1864

Rank and Name.	Rank in Regiment.	Rank and Name.	Rank in Regiment.
Captains (continued)—		*Lieutenants (continued)—*	
F. H. Anson Hamilton	4 Nov. 1864	Ch. Moseley Turner	10 Oct. 1865
H. Robert Milligan	22 Nov. 1864	Ch. H. A. Powys-Keck	1 Dec. 1865
George Hatchell	23 Jan. 1865	John T. D. Crosbie	1 Dec. 1865
J. Kiero Watson	1 May 1865		
Wm. Gerard Byron	3 Jan. 1865	*Ensigns—*	
Rich. Fr. Jennings	1 Dec. 1865	Herbert Fitzroy Eaton	25 Mar. 1862
Oare Hampton Borrer	15 Dec. 1865	Fr. Henry Baillie	9 Dec. 1862
Lieutenants—		Jas. W. Bernhard Parish	23 Jan. 1863
John Owen Young	25 Aug. 1857	Walter Cowan	13 Feb. 1863
Wm. Norcott Manners	23 Oct. 1855	F. C. Blenkinsopp Coulson	12 June 1863
Arthur Tufnell	15 Jan. 1858	Henry Donald Browne	13 June 1863
Wm. Greer Turle	23 Mar. 1858	Fras. Lennox Fraser	23 June 1863
Alfred Lewis	21 May 1858	H. E. P. Lindesay	24 June 1863
Stanley Mortimer	21 May 1858	John Bartlett Strodling	30 June 1863
Wm. J. Everest Poole	21 May 1858	H. A. Fred. F. Coventry	21 June 1863
Newton Jones Paull	4 June 1858	Fr. Alex. Gordon	22 July 1863
Ashley Henry Woodgate	15 June 1858	Lewis Bradford	8 Sept. 1863
Wm. Henry Moseley	15 June 1858	Wm. Tilden	2 Oct. 1863
Wm. L. Kincoch Ogilvy	15 June 1858	Rowland Willis	3 Oct. 1863
Fred. Augustus Campbell	9 Sept. 1858	Hon. Hen. Edw. Borrer	17 Nov. 1863
Hugh St. George Barton	9 Nov. 1858	Henry Blackwood Machin	16 Feb. 1864
Geo. Hewett Treatman	13 Aug. 1859	Benjamin Frend	9 Feb. 1864
Latham C. Browning	9 Mar. 1860	Odeur George Parker	14 June 1864
Robt. F. de B. Barry	9 Mar. 1860	Ambrose H. Birdeaus	28 June 1864
Reg. H. Bendon	11 Sept. 1860	J. Fessenue W. Finch	12 July 1864
John Wm. Marshall	11 Sept. 1860	H. Affleck Hoult Ward	28 Oct. 1864
Rich. Meade	11 Sept. 1860	Cecil Ralph Howard	29 Oct. 1864
P. White Worsley	11 Sept. 1860	Thos. B. Powys-Keck	9 Dec. 1864
Astley Fellowes Terry	11 Sept. 1860	Thos. N. Dick-Lauder	30 Dec. 1864
John Oak Crosbie	18 Sept. 1860	Percy A. J. H. Johnstone	31 Dec. 1864
Ch. Bateman Prust	26 Oct. 1860	A. F. H. Matchell-Innes	23 Jan. 1865
Nesbit W. Wallace	4 Jan. 1861	J. Pick Conyngham	31 Jan. 1865
Ch. Gosling	15 Jan. 1861	Crawford Lewis Allan	7 Feb. 1865
M. Wm. O'Rorke	16 April 1861	Wm. Forster	7 Mar. 1865
Arthur Morris	4 June 1861	Arthur Popes	11 April 1865
Pierce O'Brien Butler	17 Sept. 1861	Wm. Mitchell-Innes	2 May 1865
Ellis Houlton Ward	20 Nov. 1861	Robt. Croslock Brown	26 May 1865
Alex. Borthwick	8 Aug. 1862	Wm. Fr. C. Wigram	18 July 1865
Ch. M. Calderon	29 Oct. 1862	Hen. Philip Mars Welby	22 Sept. 1865
Redvers Henry Buller	9 Dec. 1862	J. N. Blackwood Price	10 Oct. 1865
Ch. Pierson Cramer	21 April 1863	F. John Adalbert Wood	10 Nov. 1865
Courtenay Forbes Terry	22 May 1863	Ch. Hallid Smith	1 Dec. 1865
Hon. W. Courtenay Pepys	23 June 1863	Henry Saville Marsham	2 Dec. 1865
Fr. Wm. Robins	30 June 1863	Thos. Sydenham Clarke	3 Dec. 1865
J. H. Herbert Croft	3 Mar. 1863	Algernon St. Maur	8 Dec. 1865
Fr. Well. Grenfell	24 July 1863	*Paymasters—*	
John Wm. Rhodes	8 Sept. 1863	Francis FitzPatrick, 2 March, 1855—	
Aubrey Vere Clifton	8 Sept. 1863	2nd Lieut., 19 Oct., 1849; Lieut., 31	
R. F. St. Andrew St. John	17 Nov. 1863	May, 1854; Hon. Major, 2 March, 1865.	
John Edw. P. Barlow	13 Jan. 1864	Edw. Ch. Grant, 25 Dec., 1855 Hon.	
Ch. Lewis C. de Roheck	1 Mar. 1864	Capt., 28 Dec., 1860.	
Clifford Fortescue Borrer	28 June 1864	Robert C. Streatfield, 8 June, 1858	
Hon. Ralph Abercromby	3 Aug. 1864	Ensign, 12 Aug., 1853; Lieut., 26 Oct.,	
Ch. Gilbert Fraser	6 Oct. 1864	1855; Hon. Capt., 8 June, 1863.	
Cecil John Shepherd	4 Nov. 1864	Wm. Banbury, 22 Nov., 1854	
Wm. Warren	22 Nov. 1864	Quartermaster, 8 July, 1854.	
P. Julius H. A. Barne	12 June 1864	*Adjutants—*	
Ch. Gathorne Hardy	30 Dec. 1864	L. C. Browning, Lieut. 18 Jan. 1859	
Geo. Thos. Whitaker	24 Jan. 1865	W. H. Moseley, Lieut. 13 June 1865	
George Carpenter	31 Jan. 1865	Nesbit W. Wallace, Lieut. 28 Oct. 1864	
R. Collingwood Robinson	7 Feb. 1865	*Instructors of Musketry—*	
C. L. McLean Farmer	7 Mar. 1865	W. N. Manners, Lieut. 22 Mar. 1858	
Edw. W. Home Crofton	2 May 1865	P. W. Worsley, Lieut. 15 Feb. 1860	
Denis Bingham	26 May 1865	A. V. O'Brien, Lieut. 21 June 1865	
John Henry Gumbleton	22 Sept. 1865	Clifford F. Borrer	7 Dec. 1865

S

Rank and Name.	Rank in Regiment.
Quartermasters—	
Wm. Hunter	13 July 1855
Robert Duncan	13 Aug. 1858
Thos. Jarvis	2 Dec. 1862
John Cole	26 Mar. 1858
	Cornet, 21 Feb. 1856

Surgeons—

Edw. Wm. Young, M.D., 8 Dec., 1854; Assist.-Surgeon, 7 Aug., 1846.

John Ph. Cunningham, M.D., 11 March, 1859; Assist.-Surgeon, 13 April, 1852.

Rd. Coope Todd, 3 Nov., 1857; Assist.-Surgeon, 24 Sept., 1820.

Adam Graham Young, 20 June, 1865; Assist.-Surgeon, 5 May, 1854.

Assistant-Surgeons—

Robt. Owen Hayden	.. 15 Sept. 1857
Fredk. Wm. Wade..	.. 28 Sept. 1857
Wm. S. Oliver, M.D.	.. 15 Sept. 1857
Alex. Comb. M'Tavish	.. 12 Jan. 1859
Geo. A. Hutton ..	.. 23 June 1854

Regimentals—Green, facings scarlet.

Agents—Sir C.R. McGregor, Bart., and Co.

1867.

Four Battalions.

Mediterranean—Canada—Ireland—India.

Celer et Audax.

Roleia, Vimiera, Martinique, Talavera, Fuentes d'Onor, Albuhera, Ciudad Rodrigo, Badajoz, Salamanca, Vittoria, Pyrenees, Nivelle, Nive, Orthes, Toulouse, Peninsula, Punjaub, Mooltan, Goojerat, Taku Forts, Pekin, Delhi.

Col.-in-Chief—

Field-Marshal Hugh Viscount Gough, K.P., G.C.B., G.C.S.I., 28 Jan., 1854.

Cols.-Commandant—

Geo. Fred. Viscount Templetown, C.B.—Ensign, 24 April, 1823; Lieutenant, 29 Oct., 1825; Captain, 12 Dec., 1826; Major, 16 June, 1837; Lieut.-Colonel, 16 April, 1841; Colonel, 11 Nov., 1851; Major-General, 26 Oct., 1858; Lieut.-General, 9 March, 1865; Col.-Com. 60th Rifles, 24 Oct., 1862.

Henry Viscount Melville, G.C.B.— Ensign and Lieutenant, 18 Nov., 1819; Captain, 1 April, 1824; Major, 11 July, 1826; Lieut.-Colonel, 3 Dec., 1829; Colonel, 28 Nov., 1841; Major-General, 20 June, 1854; Lieut.-General, 5 Nov., 1860; Col.-Commandant 60th Rifles, 1 April, 1863.

Lieut.-Colonels—

Francis Roger Palmer, C.B.—Ensign, 15 March, 1883; Lieutenant, 24 April, 1835; Captain, 11 March, 1842; Major, 20 June, 1854; Lieut.-Colonel, 22 June, 1858; Colonel, 22nd June, 1863.

Robert B. Hawley—Ensign, 28 Aug.,

Lieut.-Colonels (continued)—

1838; Lieutenant, 31 Dec., 1839; Captain, 10 Jan., 1851; Brevet Major, 2 Nov., 1855; Major, 5 Sept., 1856; Lieut.-Colonel, 18 May, 1860; Colonel, 18 May, 1865.

Peter Burton Roe—2nd Lieutenant, 23 July, 1841; Lieutenant, 26 July, 1844; Captain, 17 June, 1851; Major, 29 April, 1859; Lieut.-Colonel, 18 Sept., 1860; Colonel, 18 Sept., 1865.

Randle Joseph Feilden—2nd Lieut., 31 March, 1843; Lieutenant, 25 Feb., 1845; Captain, 23 Dec., 1853; Major, 18 May, 1860; Lieut.-Colonel, 1 Mar., 1864.

Majors—

Henry Friend Kennedy—2nd Lieut., 11 Sept., 1840; Lieutenant, 7 April, 1842; Captain, 20 Oct., 1848; Major, 17 Aug., 1855; Brevet Lieut.-Colonel, 7 Jan., 1864.

Charles Napier North—Ensign, 20 May, 1836; Lieutenant, 28 Dec., 1838; Captain, 28 Dec., 1848; Major, 19 June, 1857; Brevet Lieut.-Colonel, 24 March, 1858; Colonel, 30 March, 1865.

Gibbes Rignud—2nd Lieutenant, 11 June, 1841; Lieutenant, 26 July, 1844; Captain, 16 Aug., 1850; Major, 22 June, 1858; Brevet Lieut.-Col., 15 Feb., 1861.

Sir Edw. FitzgeraldCampbell, Bart.— 2nd Lieutenant, 2 July, 1841; Lieutenant, 26 July, 1844; Captain, 27 Dec., 1850; Brevet Major, 19 Jan., 1858; Major, 9 Sept., 1858; Brevet Lieut.-Colonel, 23 Oct., 1860.

Charles Alex. Boswell Gordon— Ensign, 21 April, 1843; Lieutenant, 13 June, 1845; Captain, 6 June, 1854; Brevet Major, 6 June, 1856; Major, 18 Sept., 1860.

Thomas Biggs—Ensign, 2 Oct., 1840; Lieutenant, 15 Nov., 1843; Captain, 8 April, 1853; Major, 22 May, 1863.

Henry Francis Williams—Ensign, 19 May, 1843; Lieutenant, 20 Dec., 1844; Captain, 3 March, 1854; Brevet Major, 19 Jan., 1858; Brevet Lieut.-Colonel, 4 Aug., 1861; Major, 28 Oct., 1864.

Alfred John Fitzgerald—Ensign, 8 Nov., 1842; Lieutenant, 13 Feb., 1846; Captain, 23 Mar., 1855; Major, 24 Jan., 1865.

Edward Thomas Wickham—Ensign, 19 Aug., 1842; Lieutenant, 26 July, 1844; Captain, 13 Feb., 1852; Brevet Major, 30 Nov., 1860; Major, 1 April, 1866.

Rank and Name.	Rank in Regiment.
Captains:	
John Prevost Battersby ..	23 Mar. 1854
Bernard Edward Ward..	23 Mar. 1855
Rank in Army {	Bt. Maj. 20 July 1855 Lt.-Col. 5 Jan. 1864
Robert Wilmot Brooke ..	23 Mar. 1855
Rank in Army, Bt. Maj. 15 Feb. 1861	

Rank and Name.	Rank in Regiment.

Captains (continued)—

Edward Bowles ..	23 Mar. 1855
R. J. Hurst Robertson ..	23 Mar. 1855
Hugh P. Montgomery ..	17 Aug. 1856
Charles D. C. Ellis..	14 Dec. 1855
Rank in Army, Bt. Maj.	23 Oct. 1860
William Tedlie ..	25 Jan. 1856
Rank in Army, Bt. Maj.	20 July 1858
Conyngham Jones	6 May 1856
Rank in Army, Bt. Maj.	26 April 1859
Henry Semple.. ..	25 Aug. 1857
Charles Williamson ..	16 Oct. 1857
Rowley Wilics Hinxman..	15 Jan. 1858
Rank in Army, Bt. Maj.	13 Jan. 1861
Francis Stewart Travers	15 Jan. 1858
Wykeham L. Pemberton	23 Mar. 1858
Fra. Dundas Farquharson	24 April 1858
John James Philips ..	14 May 1858
James Durham Dundas ..	22 June 1858
Herbert George Davies ..	2 July 1858
Rank in Army, Bt. Maj.	25 Sept. 1860
James Joseph Collins ..	19 July 1859
D. G. N. Watts-Russell..	29 Nov. 1859
Anthony Carlisle	9 Mar. 1860
Francis Vernon Northey..	18 May 1860
William Fred. Carleton..	18 Sept. 1860
George R. S. Black	14 Feb. 1861
Cromer Ashburnham ..	23 Jan. 1862
James Arthur Morrah ..	28 April 1862
Kennett Gregg Henderson	30 June 1862
Edward Campbell Anstie	1 Mar. 1863
James S. Hamilton Algar	17 May 1863
Henry Taylor..	12 Feb. 1864
George Charles Kells ..	6 Aug. 1864
C. C. Willoughby	18 Aug. 1864
Matthew Tillard	28 Oct. 1864
Robert John Hickman ..	28 Oct. 1864
Fred. H. Amos Hamilton	4 Nov. 1864
Harry Robert Milligan..	22 Nov. 1864
George Hatchell	23 Jan. 1865
James Kiero Watson ..	1 May 1865
William Gerard Byron ..	3 Jan. 1865
Richard Francis Jennings	1 Dec. 1865
Cary Hampton Borrer ..	1 Dec. 1865
Stanley Mortimer	30 Mar. 1866
Wm. John Everard Poole	3 April 1866
Newton Jones Pash ..	2 June 1866
W. Lewis Kirkcoldbright	11 Dec. 1866
Fred. Augustus Campbell	11 Dec. 1866

Lieutenants—

John Owen Young ..	25 Aug. 1857
Wm. Nopsott Meinertz..	23 Oct. 1857
Arthur Tarbell	15 Jan. 1858
William Green Loris ..	24 Mar. 1858
William Henry Mawley..	15 June 1858
Hugh St. George Barton	9 Nov. 1858
George Hewitt Freeman..	13 Aug. 1859
Latham C. Browning ..	9 Mar. 1860
R. Fitzw. de Barry Barry	9 Mar. 1860
Reginald H. Beadon ..	11 Sept. 1860
John William Marshall..	11 Sept. 1860
Pennyman W. Worsley..	11 Sept. 1860
Astley Fellowes Terry ..	11 Sept. 1860
John Gustavus Crosbie ..	18 Sept. 1860

Rank and Name.	Rank in Regiment.

Lieutenants (continued)—

Charles Bateman Prust..	26 Oct. 1860
N. Willoughby Wallace..	4 Jan. 1861
Charles Gosling	15 Jan. 1861
Marcus William O'Rorke	16 April 1861
Arthur Morris	4 June 1861
Pierce O'Brien Butler ..	17 Sept. 1861
Ellis Houlton Wood ..	20 Nov. 1861
Alexander Borthwick ..	8 Aug. 1862
Chas. Matthew Calderon.	26 Oct. 1860
Redvers Henry Buller ..	9 Dec. 1862
Charles Pierson Cramer..	21 April 1863
Courtenay Forbes Terry..	22 May 1863
Frances William Robins.	13 June 1863
James Henry Herb. Croft	31 Mar. 1863
Francis Wallace Grenfell	21 July 1863
Aubrey Vere O'Brien ..	8 Sept. 1863
R. F. St. Andrew St. John	17 Nov. 1863
Chas. Lewis C. de Robeck	1 Mar. 1864
Hon. Ralph Abercromby.	3 Aug. 1864
Charles Gilbert Fryer ..	6 Oct. 1864
William Warren	22 Nov. 1864
Philip J. H. A. Barne ..	12 June 1863
George Thomas Whitaker	23 Jan. 1865
George Carpenter	30 Jan. 1865
Roderick C. Robinson ..	7 Feb. 1865
Geo. L. McLean Farmer..	7 Mar. 1865
Edward W. H. Croston..	2 May 1865
Denis Bingham	26 May 1865
Charles Moseley Turner.	10 May 1865
Chas. M. G. Powys-Keck	1 Dec. 1865
John T. D. Crosbie.. ..	1 Dec. 1865
Herbert Kears Eaton ..	20 Feb. 1867
Francis Henry Budlie ..	30 Mar. 1866
J. Walter Barnard Parish	3 April 1866
Walter Cowan	3 April 1866
F. C. Blenkinsopp Coulson	26 June 1866
Henry Duvald Brown ..	14 Aug. 1866
Edmund Lamont Fraser..	21 Aug. 1866
Reginald Chabner	21 Feb. 1865
Harry R. P. Lindesay ..	2 Oct. 1866
Henry A. F. F. Coventry	27 Nov. 1866
Francis Alex Gordon ..	11 Dec. 1866
William Tebbs	11 Dec. 1866

Ensigns—

John Bartlett Stradling..	30 June 1863
Lewis Bradford	8 Sept. 1863
Henry B. MacColl.. ..	16 Feb. 1864
Benjamin Frend	9 Feb. 1864
Orlonr George Parker ..	14 June 1864
Aub. Humphry Bircham	28 June 1864
J. Seymour Wynne-Finch	12 July 1864
H. A. H. Ward	25 Oct. 1864
Cecil Ralph Howard ..	29 Oct. 1864
L. Bascke Powys-Keck..	9 Dec. 1864
Thos. North Dick Lauder	30 Dec. 1864
Percy A. J. H. Johnstone	31 Dec. 1864
A. F. H. Mitchell-Innes..	24 Jan. 1865
James Dick Cunningham	31 Jan. 1865
Crawford L. Mann ..	7 Feb. 1865
William Foster	7 Mar. 1865
Arthur Pepys	11 April 1865
William Mitchell-Innes..	2 May 1865
Robert Crookes Davies..	26 May 1865
W. Francis C. Wigston..	18 July 1865

s 2

Rank and Name.	Rank in Regiment.

Ensigns (continued)—

Henry P. M. Wylie .. 22 Sept. 1865
J. N. Blackwood-Price .. 10 Oct. 1865
Francis J. A. Wood .. 10 Nov. 1865
Charles Holled Smith .. 1 Dec. 1865
Henry Saville Marsham.. 2 Dec. 1865
Thos. Sydenham Clarke.. 3 Dec. 1865
Algernon St. Maur.. .. 8 Dec. 1865
Ernest Ferdinand Ires .. 5 Jan. 1866
Francis Grenfell Doyle .. 28 Feb. 1866
Ernest Hovell Thurlow.. 3 April 1866
John Aubrey Williams .. 30 Mar. 1866
Albert Augustus Phipps. 8 May 1866
Hon. Keith Turnour .. 2 Oct. 1866
Allayne Beaumont Legard 9 Nov. 1866
William Walter Dundas . 9 Nov. 1866
John Henry Burstall .. 11 Dec. 1866
Harry Paul Burnard .. 12 Dec. 1866
C. Champion de Crespigny 13 Dec. 1866

Paymasters—

Francis FitzPatrick, 2 March, 1855—
2nd Lieutenant, 19 Oct., 1849; Lieut.,
31 May, 1854; Hon. Major, 2 Mar., 1865.
Edward Chas. Grant, 28 Dec., 1855—
Hon. Captain, 28 Dec., 1860.
Robt. Champion Streatfield, 18 June,
1858—Ensign, 12 Aug., 1853; Lieut., 26
Oct., 1855; Hon. Captain, 8 June, 1863.
William Banbury, 22 Nov., 1861—
Quartermaster, 8 July, 1851.

Adjutants—

Latham C. Brownrigg, Lt. 18 Jan. 1859
Nesbit W. Wallace, Lieut. 28 Oct. 1864
R. F. de Barry Barry, Lt. 18 Nov. 1865
C. P. Cramer, Lieut. .. 2 Nov. 1866

Instructor of Musketry

W. N. Manners, Lieut. .. 22 Mar. 1858
A. V. O'Brien, Lieut. .. 21 June 1865
W. Warren, Lieut.. .. 27 July 1866
G. T. Whitaker, Lieut. .. 26 Sept. 1866

Quartermasters—

Robert Duncan .. .. 13 Aug. 1858
Thomas Jarvis .. .. 2 Dec. 1862
John Cole .. .. 26 Mar. 1858
         Cornet, 21 Feb. 1856
John Toale .. .. 13 Feb. 1866

Surgeons—

Edward William Young, M.D.,
Assistant-Surgeon, 7 Aug., 1846; Surgeon, 8 Dec., 1854; Surgeon-Major, 7
Aug., 1866.
John P. Cunningham, M.D., 11 Mar.,
1859; Assistant-Surgeon, 13 April, 1852.
Richard Cooper Todd, 3 Nov., 1857,
Assistant-Surgeon, 24 Sept., 1850.
Adam Graham Young, 2 June, 1865;
Assistant-Surgeon, 5 May, 1854.

Assistant-Surgeons—

Robt. Owen Hayden .. 15 Sept. 1857
Frederick W. Wade .. 28 Sept. 1857

Assistant-Surgeons (continued)—

W. Silver Oliver, M.D. .. 15 Sept. 1857
Alex. Campbell M'Tavish 12 Jan. 1859
Philip Lefeuvre Kilroy .. 2 Oct. 1865

Regimentals—Green, facings scarlet.

Agents—Sir C. R. McGregor, Bart., and Co.

Irish Agents—Messrs. Cane and Sons.

1868.

Four Battalions.

Canada—India.

Celer et Audax.

Roleia, Vimiera, Martinique, Talavera,
Fuentes d'Onor, Albuhera, Ciudad
Rodrigo, Badajoz, Salamanca, Vittoria,
Pyrenees, Nivelle, Nive, Orthes, Toulouse, Peninsula, Punjaub, Mooltan,
Goojerat, Taku Forts, Pekin, Delhi.

Colonel-in-Chief—

Field-Marshal Hugh Viscount Gough,
K.P., G.C.B., G.C.S.I., 28 Jan., 1854.

Cols.-Commandant

Geo. Fred. Viscount Templetown,
C.B. - Ensign, 24 April, 1823; Lieut.,
29 Oct., 1825; Captain, 12 Dec., 1826;
Major, 16 June, 1837; Lieut.-Colonel,
16 April, 1841; Colonel, 11 Nov., 1851;
Major-Gen., 26 Oct., 1858; Lieut.-Gen.,
9 Mar., 1865; Col.-Comm. 60th Rifles,
21 Oct., 1862.
Henry Viscount Melville, G.C.B.,—
Ensign and Lieut., 18 Nov., 1819; Capt.,
1 April, 1824; Major, 11 July, 1826;
Lieut.-Col., 3 Dec., 1829; Colonel, 28
Nov., 1841; Major-Gen., 20 June, 1854;
Lieut.-Gen., 5 May, 1860; Col.-Comm.
60th Rifles, 1 April, 1863.

Lieut.-Colonels—

Francis Roger Palmer, C.B.—Ensign,
15 Mar., 1833; Lieut., 24 April, 1835;
Capt., 11 Mar., 1842; Major, 29 June,
1854; Lieut.-Col., 22 June, 1858; Col.,
22 June, 1865.
Robert B. Hawley—Ensign, 28 Aug.,
1848; Lieut., 31 Dec., 1849; Captain,
10 Jan., 1851; Brevet Major, 2 Nov.,
1855; Major, 5 Sept., 1856; Lieut.-
Col., 18 May, 1860; Col., 18 May, 1865.
Peter Burton Roe—2nd Lieut., 23
July, 1841; Lieut., 26 July, 1844;
Captain, 17 June, 1851; Major, 29
April, 1859; Lieut.-Col., 18 Sept., 1860;
Col., 18 Sept., 1865.
Randle Joseph Feilden—2nd Lieut.,
31 Mar., 1843; Lieut., 25 Feb., 1845;
Captain, 23 Dec., 1853; Major, 18 May,
1860; Lieut.-Col., 1 March, 1864.

Majors—

Henry Friend Kennedy—2nd Lieut., 11 Sept., 1840; Lieut., 7 April, 1842; Capt., 20 Oct., 1858; Major, 17 Aug., 1855; Brevet Lieut.-Col., 7 Jan., 1864.

Gibbes Rignaud—2nd Lieut., **11 June**, 1841; Lieut., 26 July, 1844; **Captain**, 16 Aug., 1850; Major, 22 June, **1858**; Brevet Lieut.-Col., 15 Feb., 1861.

Sir Edwd. Fitzgerald Campbell, Bart.—2nd Lieut., 2 July, 1841; Lieut., 26 July, 1844; Captain, 27 Dec., 1850; Brevet Major, 19 Jan., 1858; Major, 9 Sept., 1858; Brevet Lieut.-Col., 23 Oct., 1860; Colonel, 12 Jan., 1867.

Chas. Alex. Roswell Gordon, Ensign, 21 April, 1843; Lieut., 13 June, 1845; Captain, 6 June, 1854; Brevet Major, 6 June, 1856; Major, 18 Sept. 1860.

Henry Francis Williams, Ensign, 19 May, 1843; Lieut., 28 Dec., 1844; Captain, 3 March, 1854; Brevet Major, 19 Jan., 1858; Brevet Lieut.-Col., 4 Aug., 1864; Major, 28 Oct., 1864.

Alfred John Fitzgerald, Ensign, 8 Nov., 1842; Lieut., 15 Feb., 1846; Capt., 23 Mar., 1855; Major, 24 Jan., 1865.

Edwd. Thos. Wickham, Ensign, 19 Aug., 1842; Lieut., 26 July, 1844; Captain, 13 Feb., 1852; Brevet Major, 30 Nov., 1860; Major, 1 April, 1866.

John Prevost Battersby—2nd Lieut., 30 July, 1844; Lieut., 28 Jan., 1848; Captain, 23 March, 1855; Major, 26 Feb., 1867.

Bernard Edwd. Ward—2nd Lieut., 1 Aug., 1844; Lieut., 5 May, 1848; Captain, 23 March, 1855; Brevet Major, 30 July, 1865; Brevet Lieut.-Colonel, **5 Jan.**, 1864; Major, 8 March, 1867.

Rank and Name.	*Rank in Regiment.*
Captains—	
Robt. Wilmot Brooke	23 Mar 1855
Rank in Army, Bt. Maj 15 Feb 1861	
Edward Bowles	23 Mar 1855
R. J. Enst. Robertson	23 Mar 1855
Hugh P. Montgomery	17 Aug 1855
Chas. D. C. Ellis	14 Dec 1855
Rank in Army, Bt. Maj 23 Oct 1861	
Wm. Tedlie	25 Jan 1856
Rank in Army, Bt. Maj 20 July 1858	
Henry Semple	25 Aug 1857
Chas. Williamson	16 Oct 1857
Rowley W. Hinxman	15 Jan 1858
Rank in Army, Bt Maj 19 Jan 1864	
Wykeham L. Pemberton	24 Mar 1858
Francis D. Farquharson	24 April 1858
John James Phillips	14 May 1858
James Durham Dundas	22 June 1858
Herbert George Deedes	2 July 1858
Rank in Army, Bt. Maj 25 Sept 1860	
James Joseph Collins	19 July 1859
D. G. Nev. Watts-Russell	20 Nov 1859
Anthony Carlisle	9 Mar 1860
Francis V. Northey	18 May 1860
Wm. Fred. Carleton	18 Sept 1860

Rank and Name.	*Rank in Regiment.*
Captains (continued)—	
Geo. R. S. Black	14 Feb. 1860
Cromer Ashburnham	23 Jan. 1860
Kennett Gregg Henderson	30 June 1863
Edwd. Campbell Ainslie	1 Mar. 1864
J. S. H. Algar	17 May 1864
Henry Taylor	12 Feb. 1858
Geo. Chas. Kelly	6 Oct. 1864
Chas. C. Willoughby	18 Oct. 1864
Matthew Tilford	28 Oct. 1864
Fred. H. Anson Hamilton	4 Nov. 1864
Henry R. Milligan	22 Nov. 1864
George Hatchell	24 Jan. 1865
Jas. Kiero Watson	1 May 1865
Wm. Gerard Byron	3 Jan. 1865
Rich. Francis Jennings	1 Dec. 1865
Stanley Mortimer	30 Mar. 1866
Wm. John E. Poole	3 April 1866
Newton J. Pauli	5 June 1866
Wm. L. K. Ogilvy	11 Dec. 1866
Fred. Aug. Campbell	11 Dec. 1866
Wm. Henry Moseley	27 Feb. 1867
Hugh St. Geo. Barton	8 Mar. 1867
R. Fitz W. de Barry Barry	15 Mar. 1867
John Owen Young	6 July 1867
Wm. Norcott Manners	17 Sept. 1867
Reginald H. Headon	16 Oct. 1867
Arthur Tufnell	23 Oct. 1867
Pennyman W. Worsley	6 Nov. 1867
John Charley	14 Aug. 1867
Astley F. Terry	8 Dec. 1867
Lieutenants	
Wm. Grier Turle	23 Mar. 1858
Geo. Hewitt Trotman	13 Aug. 1859
Latham C. Browning	9 Mar. 1860
John Gustavus Crosbie	18 Sept. 1860
Charles Bateman Prust	26 Oct. 1860
Nesbit W. Wallace	4 Jan. 1861
Charles Gosling	15 Jan. 1861
Marcus Wm. O'Rorke	16 April 1861
Arthur Morris	4 June 1861
Pierce O'Brien Butler	17 Sept. 1861
Ellis Houlton Ward	20 Nov. 1861
Alex. Borthwick	8 Aug. 1862
Chas. Matthew Calderon	26 Oct. 1862
Rodney Henry Biller	9 Dec. 1862
Chas. Pierson Cramer	21 April 1863
Courtenay Forbes Terry	22 May 1863
Francis Wm. Kelson	30 June 1863
Jas. Henry Herbert Croft	31 Mar. 1864
Francis Wallace Grenfell	21 July 1864
Aubrey Vere O'Brien	8 Sept. 1864
Chas. Lewis C. de Roback	1 Mar. 1864
Hon. Ralph Abercromby	3 Aug. 1864
Chas. Gilbert Fryer	6 Oct. 1864
Wm. Warren	22 Nov. 1864
Philip Julius H. A. Barne	12 June 1863
Geo. Hon. Whitaker	24 Jan. 1865
George Carpenter	31 Jan. 1865
Ed. Collingwood Robinson	7 Feb. 1865
G. L. Milman Farmer	7 Mar. 1865
Edwd. W. H. Crofton	2 May 1865
Denis Bingham	26 May 1865
Chas. Mowbray Turner	10 Oct. 1865
Chas. H. G. Powys-Keck	1 Dec. 1865
John T. D. Crosbie	1 Dec. 1865

Rank and Name.	Rank in Regiment.
Lieutenants (continued)—	
Herbert Fitz-Roy Eaton..	20 Feb. 1866
Francis Henry Baillie ..	30 Mar. 1866
J. W. B. Parish ..	3 April 1866
Walter Cowan.. ..	3 April 1866
Edk. C. B. Coulson.. ..	26 June 1866
Henry Donald Browne ..	14 Aug. 1866
Edmund Lomax Fraser ..	21 Aug. 1866
Reginald Chalmer	21 Feb. 1865
Henry R. P. Lindesay ..	2 Oct. 1866
Henry A. F. F. Coventry ..	27 Nov. 1866
Francis Alex. Gordon ..	11 Dec. 1866
Wm. Tilden	11 Dec. 1866
John Bartlett Stradling..	11 Jan. 1867
Henry Blackwood MacCall	19 Feb. 1867
Benjamin Frend	27 Feb. 1867
Orfeur George Parker ..	6 Mar. 1867
Ambrose H. Bircham ..	8 Mar. 1867
J. Seymour Wynne-Finch	15 Mar. 1867
Lewis Bradford	6 July 1867
H. A. H. Ward	7 Aug. 1867
Cecil Ralph Howard ..	7 Aug. 1867
Thos. Bancho Powys-Keck	17 Sept. 1867
Sir T. N. Dick-Lauder, Bt.	16 Oct. 1867
Percy A. J. H. Johnstone	6 Nov. 1867
Alex. F. H. Mitchell-Innes	20 Nov. 1867
James Dick Cunyngham..	18 Dec. 1867
Crawford Lewin Allan ..	25 Dec. 1867
Ensigns—	
William Foster	7 Mar. 1865
Arthur Pepys	11 April 1865
Wm. Mitchell-Innes ..	2 May 1865
Robt. Cradock Davies ..	26 May 1865
W. F. Chalmers Wigston .	18 July 1865
Henry Philip Miles Wylie	22 Sept. 1865
Jas. N. Blackwood-Price	10 Oct. 1865
Fra. John Adelbert Wood	10 Nov. 1865
Charles Holled Smith ..	1 Dec. 1865
Henry Saville Marsham..	2 Dec. 1865
Thos. Sydenham Clarke..	3 Dec. 1865
Algernon St. Maur ..	8 Dec. 1865
Ernest Ferdinand Ives ..	5 Jan. 1866
Francis Greville Doyle ..	20 Feb. 1866
Ernest Hovell Thurlow ..	3 April 1866
John Aubrey Williams ..	30 Mar. 1866
Albert Augustus Phipps .	8 May 1866
Hon. Keith Turnour ..	2 Oct. 1866
Allayne Beaumont Legard	9 Nov. 1866
William Walter Dundas..	9 Nov. 1866
John Henry Burstall ..	11 Dec. 1866
Harry Paul Burrard ..	12 Dec. 1866
Claude Cham. de Crespigny	13 Dec. 1866
Ernest William Jones ..	11 Jan. 1867
George Percy Gilbert ..	27 Feb. 1867
Arthur Greville Bagot ..	6 Mar. 1867
Henry S. Hutton Riddell	8 Mar. 1867
J. H. Fitzherbert Jackson	15 Mar. 1867
Herbert J. Hope-Edwardes	6 July 1867
Fiennes B. N. Dickinson .	8 Aug. 1867
Edwd. Thos. Hen. Hutton	9 Aug. 1867
Fulbert Wright Archer ..	10 Aug. 1867
Horace Walpole	11 Aug. 1867
Charles Michel	12 Oct. 1867
Shatto Robert Elwes ..	16 Oct. 1867
Arthur James Brander ..	6 Nov. 1867
Harry Wills Sandford ..	9 Nov. 1867

Rank and Name.	Rank in Regiment.
Ensigns (continued)—	
H. E. W. Fetherstonhaugh	18 Dec. 1867
Francis Moore Ward ..	25 Dec. 1867
Paymasters—	
Francis FitzPatrick, 2 Mar., 1855—	
2nd Lieut., 19 Oct., 1849; Lieut., 31	
May, 1854; Hon. Major, 2 March, 1865.	
Edward Chas. Grant, 28 Dec., 1855—	
Hon. Capt., 28 Dec., 1860.	
Robt. Champion Streatfield, 8 June,	
1858—Ensign, 12 Aug., 1853; Lieut.	
26 Oct., 1855; Hon. Capt., 8 June, 1863.	
W. Banbury, 22 Nov. 1864—Quarter-	
master, 8 July, 1851.	
Adjutants—	
Lat. C. Brownrigg, Lieut. 18 Jan. 1859	
Nesbit W. Wallasy, Lieut. 28 Oct. 1864	
C. P. Cramer, Lieut. .. 2 Nov. 1866	
A. Bircham, Lieut... .. 8 June 1867	
Instructors of Musketry—	
A. V. O'Brien, Lieut. .. 21 June 1865	
W. Warren, Lieut... .. 27 July 1866	
G. T. Whitaker, Lieut. .. 26 Sept. 1866	
Quartermasters—	
Thomas Jarvis .. .. 2 Dec. 1862	
John Toole .. .. .. 13 Feb. 1866	
Wm. Holmes .. .. .. 17 April 1867	
Wm. Fitzllenry .. .. 6 July 1867	
Surgeons—	
Edward Wm. Young, M.D., Assist.-	
Sur., 7 Aug. 1846; Surgeon, 8 Dec.,	
1854; Surg.-Maj., 7 Aug., 1866.	
John Phillips Cunningham, M.D.,	
Assist.-Surg., 13 April, 1852; Surgeon,	
11 Mar., 1859.	
Adam A. Young, Assist.-Surg., 5	
May, 1854; Surgeon, 20 June, 1865.	
Wm. Wilson Mills, Assist.-Surg., 28	
Mar., 1854; Surgeon, 28 June, 1864.	
Assistant-Surgeons—	
Robert Owen Hayden .. 15 Sept. 1857	
Fredk. Wm. Wade.. .. 28 Sept. 1857	
Wm. Silver Oliver, M.D. 15 Sept. 1857	
Alex. Campbell M'Tavish 12 Jan. 1859	
Philip Lefeuvre Kilroy .. 2 Oct. 1865	
W. Morton Harman, M.B. 2 Oct. 1866	
Regimentals—Green, facings scarlet.	
Agents—Sir C. R. McGregor, Bart., and Co.	

1869.

Four Battalions.

Canada India England.

Celer et Audax.

Roleia, Vimiera, Martinique, Talavera, Fuentes d'Onor, Albuhera, Ciudad Rodrigo, Badajoz, Salamanca, Vittoria, Pyrenees, Nivelle, Nive, Orthes, Toulouse, Peninsula, Punjaub, Mooltan, Goojerat, Taku Forts, Pekin, Delhi.

Col. in Chief—

Field-Marshal Hugh Viscount Gough, K.P., G.C.B., G.C.S.I., 28 Jan., 1854.

Cols.-Commandant—

George Fredk. Viscount Templetown,

Col.-Commandant (continued)—
C.B.—Ensign, 24 April, 1823; Lieut., 29 Oct., 1825; Captain, 12 Dec., 1826; Major, 16 June, 1837; Lieut.-Colonel, 16 April, 1841; Colonel, 11 Nov., 1851; Major-Gen., 26 Oct., 1858; Lieut.-Gen., 9 March, 1865; Colonel-Com. 60th Rifles, 24 Oct., 1862.

Henry Viscount Melville, G.C.B.—Ensign and Lieut., 18 Nov., 1819; Capt., 1 April, 1824; Major, 11 July, 1826; Lieut.-Colonel, 3 Dec., 1829; Colonel, 28 Nov., 1841; Major-Gen. 20 June, 1854; Lieut.-General, 5 May, 1860; General, 1 Jan., 1868; Colonel-Com. 60th Rifles, 1 April, 1863.

Lieut.-Colonels—
Francis Roger Palmer, C.B.—Ensign, 15 March, 1833; Lieut., 24 April, 1835; Captain, 11 March, 1842; Major, 29 June, 1854; Lieut.-Colonel, 22 June, 1858; Colonel, 22 June, 1863.

Robert B. Hawley—Ensign, 28 Aug., 1838; Lieut., 31 Dec., 1839; Captain, 10 Jan., 1851; Brevet Major, 2 Nov., 1855; Major, 5 Sept., 1856; Lieut.-Colonel, 18 May, 1860; Colonel, 18 May, 1865.

Peter Burton Roe—2nd Lieut., 23 July, 1841; Lieut., 26 July, 1844; Captain, 17 June, 1851; Major, 29 April, 1859; Lieut.-Colonel, 18 Sept., 1860; Colonel, 18 Sept., 1865.

Randle Joseph Feilden—2nd Lieut., 31 March, 1843; Lieut., 25 Feb., 1845; Captain, 23 Dec., 1853; Major, 18 May, 1859; Lieut.-Colonel, 1 March, 1864.

Majors—
Henry Friend Kennedy—2nd Lieut., 11 Sept., 1840; Lieut., 7 April, 1842; Captain, 29 Oct., 1848; Major, 17 Aug., 1855; Brevet Lieut.-Colonel, 7 Jan., 1864.

Gibbes Rigaud—2nd Lieut., 11 June, 1841; Lieut. 26 July, 1844; Captain, 16 Aug., 1852; Major, 22 June, 1858; Brevet Lieut.-Colonel, 15 Feb., 1861; Colonel, 22 April, 1868.

Sir Edw. Fitz-Gerald Campbell, Bart.—2nd Lieut., 2 July, 1841; Lieut., 26 July, 1844; Captain, 27 Dec., 1850; Brevet Major, 19 Jan., 1858; Major, 9 Sept., 1858; Brevet Lieut.-Colonel, 23 Oct., 1860; Colonel, 12 Jan., 1867.

Chas. Alex. Boswell Goslen—Ensign, 21 April, 1843; Lieut., 13 June, 1845; Captain, 6 June, 1854; Brevet Major, 6 June, 1856; Major, 18 Sept., 1858; Brevet Lieut.-Colonel, 1 Jan., 1868.

Henry Francis Williams—Ensign, 19 May, 1843; Lieut., 20 Dec., 1844; Capt., 3 March, 1854; Brevet Major, 19 Jan., 1858; Brevet Lieut.-Colonel, 4 Aug., 1864; Major, 28 Oct., 1864.

Alfred John Fitz-Gerald—Ensign, 8 Nov., 1842; Lieut., 13 Feb., 1846;

Lieut.-Colonels **(continued)**—
Captain, 23 **March, 1855**; **Major, 24** Jan., 1865.

Ed. Thos. Wickham—Ensign, 10 Aug., 1842; Lieut., 26 July, 1844; Captain, 13 Feb., 1852; Brevet Major, 30 Nov., 1860; Major, 1 April, 1865.

John Prevost Battersby—2nd **Lieut.,** 30 July, 1844; Lieut., 21 Jan., **1841**; Captain, 23 March, 1855; Major, **26** Feb., 1867.

Bernard Edw. Ward—2nd Lieut., **1** Aug., 1844; Lieut., 5 May, 1848; Capt., 23 March, 1855; Brevet Major, 29 July, 1855; Brevet Lieut.-Colonel, 5 Jan., 1864; Major, 1 March, 1867.

Robt. Wilmot Brooke—2nd Lieut., **30** Dec., 1845; Lieut., 12 Oct., 1848; Captain, 23 March, 1855; Brevet Major, 15 Feb., 1861; Major, 10 April, 1869.

	Rank and Name.	Rank in Regiment.

Captains—

Name	Rank in Regiment
Edward Bowles	23 Mar. 1855
B. J. Eastwe Robertson	23 Mar. 1855
Hugh P. Montgomery	25 June 1856
Wm. Teshe	25 June 1855
Rank in Army, Bt. Maj.	20 July 1858
Henry Semple	25 Aug. 1857
Charles Williamson	16 Oct. 1857
Rowley Willes Hinxman	15 Jan. 1858
Rank in Army, Bt. Maj.	19 Jan. 1864
Wykeham L. Pemberton	23 Mar. 1858
Francis D. Farquharson	24 April 1858
Jas. Durham Dundas	22 June 1858
Herbert George Deedes	2 July 1858
Rank in Army, Bt. Maj.	8 Sept. 1859
Jas. Joseph Collins	19 July 1859
D. G. N. Watts-Russell	29 Nov. 1859
Anthony Carlisle	9 Mar. 1860
Francis V. Northey	18 Mar. 1860
Wm. F. Carleton	18 Sept. 1860
Geo. R. Stewart Black	14 Feb. 1860
Cromer Ashburnham	23 Jan. 1863
Kennett G. Henderson	30 June 1863
Edw. Campbell Ainslie	1 Mar. 1864
Jas. S. Hamilton Algar	17 May 1864
Henry Taylor	12 Feb. 1858
Geo. Charles Kelly	6 Oct. 1864
Chas. C. Willoughby	18 Oct. 1864
Matthew Tilford	28 Oct. 1864
Fred. H. Anson Hamilton	4 Nov. 1864
Harry R. Milligan	22 Nov. 1864
George Hatchell	24 Jan. 1865
Jas. Kirte Watson	1 May 1865
Wm. Gerard Byron	3 Jan. 1865
Richard F. Jentings	1 Dec. 1865
Stanley Mortimer	30 Mar. 1866
Wm. J. S. Poole	3 April 1866
Newton J. Pauli	5 June 1866
Wm. Lewis K. Ogilvy	11 Dec. 1866
Fred. A. Campbell	11 Dec. 1866
Wm. Henry Moseley	27 Feb. 1867
Hugh St. Geo. Barton	8 Mar. 1867
R. Fitzwm. de U. Barry	15 Mar. 1867
John Owen Young	6 July 1867
Wm. N. Manners	17 Sept. 1867
Reynold H. Bendon	16 Oct. 1867

Rank and Name.	Rank in Regiment.
Captains (continued)—	
Arthur Tufnell	23 Oct. 1867
P. White Worsley	6 Nov. 1867
John Charley	14 Aug. 1867
Astley F. Terry	8 Dec. 1867
John G. Crosbie	20 May 1868
John Richard Crane	21 Oct. 1862
Charles B. Prust	28 Oct. 1868
Lieutenants—	
Geo. Hewitt Trotman	15 Aug. 1859
Latham C. Brownrigg	9 Mar. 1860
Nesbit W. Wallace	4 Jan. 1861
Maurice Wm. O'Rorke	16 April 1861
Arthur Morris	4 June 1861
Ellis Houlton Ward	20 Nov. 1861
Alexander Borthwick	8 Aug. 1862
Charles Matthew Calderon	26 Oct. 1862
Redvers Henry Buller	9 Dec. 1862
Chas. Pierson Cramer	21 April 1863
Courtenay Forbes Terry	22 May 1863
Francis Wm. Robins	30 June 1863
Jas. Henry H. Croft	31 Mar. 1863
Francis W. Grenfell	21 July 1863
Aubrey Vere O'Brien	8 Sept. 1863
Chas. L. C. de Robeck	1 Mar. 1864
Hon. Ralph Abercromby	3 Aug. 1864
Chas. Gilbert Fryer	6 Oct. 1864
Wm. Warren	22 Nov. 1864
Philip Julius H. A. Barne	12 June 1863
Geo. Thos. Whitaker	24 Jan. 1865
George Carpenter	31 Jan. 1865
Richard C. Robinson	7 Feb. 1865
G. L. M'Lean Farmer	7 Mar. 1865
Edw. W. Home Crofton	2 May 1865
Dennis Bingham	26 May 1865
Chas. H. G. Powys-Keck	1 Dec. 1865
John Talbot D. Crosbie	1 Dec. 1865
Herbert FitzRoy Eaton	28 Feb. 1866
Francis Henry Baillie	30 Mar. 1866
John Walker B. Parish	3 April 1866
Walter Cowan	3 April 1866
Frederick C. B. Coulson	26 June 1866
Henry Donald Browne	14 Aug. 1866
Edmund Lomax Fraser	21 Aug. 1866
Reginald Chalmer	21 Feb. 1865
Henry Rich. P. Lindesay	2 Oct. 1866
Hen. A. Fred. F. Coventry	27 Nov. 1866
William Tilden	11 Dec. 1866
John Bartlett Stradling	11 Jan. 1867
Hen. Blackwood MacCall	19 Feb. 1867
Benjamin Freul	27 Feb. 1867
Orfeur George Parker	6 Mar. 1867
Ambrose A. Bircham	8 Mar. 1867
J. Seymour Wynne-Finch	15 Mar. 1867
Lewis Bradford	6 July 1867
Henry A. Houlton Ward	7 Aug. 1867
Cecil Ralph Howard	7 Aug. 1867
Thos. B. Powys-Keck	17 Sept. 1867
Sir T. N. Dick-Lauder, Bt.	16 Oct. 1867
Percy A. J. H. Johnstone	6 Nov. 1867
A. F. H. Mitchell-Innes	20 Nov. 1867
Crawford Lewin Allan	25 Dec. 1867
William Forster	9 April 1868
Arthur Pepys	10 April 1868
Wm. Mitchell-Innes	13 June 1868
R. M. Cradock Davies	30 June 1868

Rank and Name.	Rank in Regiment.
Lieutenants (continued)—	
Wm. Fms. C. Wigston	24 Sept. 1868
Alex. Rawson Boddam	20 July 1867
Henry Philip M. Wylie	28 Oct. 1868
Ensigns—	
Jas. N. Blackwood-Price	10 Oct. 1865
Frederick J. A. Wood	10 Nov. 1865
Charles Holled Smith	1 Dec. 1865
Henry Savill Marsham	2 Dec. 1865
Thos. Sydenham Clarke	3 Dec. 1865
Algernon St. Maur	8 Dec. 1865
Ernest Ferdinand Ives	5 Jan. 1866
Francis Granville Doyle	20 Feb. 1866
Ernest Hovell Thurlow	5 April 1866
John Aubrey Williams	30 Mar. 1866
Albert Augustus Phipps	8 May 1866
Hon. Keith Turnour	9 Nov. 1866
Allayne B. Legard	9 Nov. 1866
Wm. Walter Dundas	9 Nov. 1866
John Henry Burstall	11 Dec. 1866
Henry Paul Burnard	12 Dec. 1866
Sir C. C. de Crespigny, Bt.	13 Dec. 1866
Ernest Wm. Jones	11 Jan. 1867
George Percy Gilbert	27 Feb. 1867
Arthur Greville Bagot	6 Mar. 1867
Henry S. Hutton Riddell	8 Mar. 1867
J. H. Fitzherbert Jackson	15 Mar. 1867
Herbert J. Hope-Edwardes	6 July 1867
Fiennes B. N. Dickenson	8 Aug. 1867
Edw. Thos. H. Hutton	9 Aug. 1867
Fulbert W. Archer	10 Aug. 1867
Homer Walpole	11 Aug. 1867
Charles Mitchell	12 Oct. 1867
Shuflo E. Elwes	16 Oct. 1867
Arthur Jas. Brander	6 Nov. 1867
Harry Willis Sandford	9 Nov. 1867
Hy. E. W. Fetherstonhaugh	18 Dec. 1867
Francis M. Ward	25 Dec. 1867
Chas. R. B. Thorne	25 Dec. 1867
Charles Hope	8 Jan. 1868
R. S. R. Fetherstonhaugh	25 Sept. 1867
Godfrey Astell	13 June 1868
Humphrey D. P. Okeden	2 Sept. 1868
Edw. Rhys. Wingfield	28 Oct. 1868
Edward St. Maur	18 Nov. 1868
Paymasters—	

Francis FitzPatrick, 2 March, 1855—2nd Lieut., 19 Oct., 1849; Lieut., 31 March, 1854; Hon. Major, 2 March, 1855.

Edward C. Grant, 28 Dec. 1855—Hon. Captain, 28 Dec. 1860.

Robt. C. Streatfield, 8 June, 1858—Ensign, 12 Aug., 1853; Lieut., 26 Oct., 1855; Hon. Major, 12 Aug., 1868.

W. Banbury, 22 Nov. 1864—Quartermaster, 8 July, 1851.

Adjutants—

L. C. Brownrigg, Lieut.	18 Jan. 1859
N. W. Wallace, Lieut.	28 Oct. 1864
C. B. Cramer, Lieut.	2 Nov. 1866
A. H. Bircham, Lieut.	8 June 1867

Instructors of Musketry—

A. V. O'Brien, Lieut.	21 June 1865
W. Warren, Lieut.	27 July 1866

Rank and Name.   *Rank in Regiment.*

Instructors of Musketry (continued)—
G. T. Whitaker, Lieut. .. 26 Sept. 1866
A. Borthwick, Lieut. .. 12 Dec. 1867

Quartermasters—
Thomas Jarvis.. .. .. 2 Dec. 1862
John Toole .. .. .. 13 Feb. 1866
Wm. Holmes .. .. .. 17 April 1867
Wm. FitzHenry .. .. 6 July 1867

Surgeons—
Edward W. Young, M.D., Assistant-Surgeon, 7 Aug., 1846; Surgeon, 8 Dec., 1854; Surgeon-Major, 7 Aug 1866.
Adam G. Young, Assistant-Surgeon, 6 May 1854; Surgeon, 20 June, 1865.
Wm. W. Mills, Assistant-Surgeon, 28 March, 1854; Surgeon, 28 June, 1864.
Wm. MacNamara, M.D., Assistant-Surgeon, 6 Oct., 1853; Surgeon, 16 March, 1867.

Assistant-Surgeons—
Robert C. Hayden .. 15 Sept. 1857
Fred. W. Wade .. .. 28 Sept. 1857
Wm. Silver Oliver, M.D.. 15 Sept 1857
Alex. C. M'Tavish .. .. 12 Jan. 1859
Philip L. Kilroy .. .. 2 Oct. 1865
Wm. M. Harmon M.B... 2 Oct. 1866

Regimentals—Green, facings scarlet.

Agents—Sir C. R. McGregor, Bart., and Co.

1870.

Four Battalions.

Canada — England — India.

Celer et Audax.

Badera, Vimiera, Martinique, **Talavera**, Fuentes d'Onor, Albuhera, Ciudad Rodrigo, Badajoz, Salamanca, **Vittoria**, Pyrenees, Nivelle, Orthes, Nive, Toulouse, Peninsula, Punjaub, **Mooltan**, Goojerat, Taku Forts, Pekin, **Delhi**.

Colonel-in-Chief—
Field-Marshal H.R.H. the Duke of Cambridge, K.G., K.P., G.C.B., G.C.M.G., 3 March, 1869.

Cols.-Commandant—
George Fred. Viscount **Templetown**, K.C.B. Ensign, 24 April, 1823; Lieut., 20 Oct., 1825; Capt., 12 Dec., 1826; Major, 16 June, 1847; Lieut.-Colonel, 16 April, 1841; Colonel, 11 Nov., 1851; Major-Gen., 28 Oct., 1858; Lieut.-Gen., 9 March, 1865; Col.-Commandant 60th Rifles 24 Oct., 1862.
Henry Viscount Melville, G.C.B. Ensign and Lieut., 18 Nov., 1819; Capt., 1 April, 1824; Major, 11 July, 1826; Lieut.-Colonel, 3 Dec., 1829; Colonel, 28 Nov., 1841; Major-Gen., 20 June, 1854; Lieut.-Gen., 5 May, 1860; General, 1 Jan., 1868; Col. Com. 60th Rifles, 1 April, 1864.

Lieut.-Colonels—
Francis Roger Palmer, C.B. Ensign, 15 March, 1833, Lieut., 24 April 1835;

Lieut.-Colonels (continued)—
Capt., 11 March, 1842; Major, 20 June, 1854; Lieut.-Col., 22 June, 1858; Col., 22 June, **1863**.
Robt. B. Hawley—Ensign, **28 Aug.**, 1838; Lieut., 31 Dec., 1839; **Capt.**, 10 Jan., 1851; Brevet Major, **2 Nov.**, 1855; Major, 5 Sept., 1856; Lieut.-Colonel, 18 May, 1860; Colonel, 18 May, 1865.
Peter Burton Roe—2nd Lieut., 23 July, 1841; Lieut., 26 July, 1844; Captain, 17 June, 1851; Major, 29 April, 1859; Lieut.-Col., 18 Sept., 1860; Colonel, 18 Sept., 1863.
Randle Joseph Feilden—2nd Lieut., 31 March 1843; Lieut., 25 Feb., 1845; Captain, 23 Dec., 1853; Major, 18 May, 1859; Lieut.-Col., 4 March, 1864; Colonel, 4 March, 1869.

Majors—
Henry Fred. **Kennedy**—2nd Lieut., 11 Sept., 1839; Lieut., 7 April, 1842; Captain, 20 Oct., 1848; Major, 17 Aug., 1855; Brevet Lieut.-Colonel, 7 Jan., 1864.
Gibbes Rigaud—2nd Lieut., 11 June, 1841; Lieut., 26 July, 1844; Captain, 16 Aug., 1851; Major, 22 June, 1858; Brevet Lieut.-Colonel, 15 Feb., 1861; Colonel, 22 April, 1868.
Sir Edward Fitzgerald **Campbell, Bart.**—2nd Lieut., 2 July, 1841; Lieut., 26 July, 1844; Captain, 27 Dec., 1850; Brevet Major, 19 Jan., 1858; Brevet Lieut.-Colonel, 23 Oct., 1860; Colonel, 12 Jan., 1867.
Charles Alexander Rowell Gordon—Ensign, 21 April, 1843; Lieut., 13 June, 1845; Captain, 6 June, 1854; Brevet Major, 6 June, 1856; Major, 18 Sept., 1860; Brevet Lieut.-Colonel, 1 Jan., 1868.
Henry Francis Williams—Ensign, 19 May, 1843; Lieut., 20 Dec., 1844; Captain, 3 March, 1854; Brevet Major, 19 Jan., 1858; Brevet Lieut.-Colonel, 1 Aug., 1864; Major, 28 Oct., 1864.
Alfred John Fitzgerald—Ensign, 8 Nov., 1842; Lieut., 13 Feb., 1846; Captain, 23 March, 1855; Major, 24 Jan., 1865.
John Prevost Battersby—2nd Lieut., 30 July, 1844; Lieut., 28 Jan., 1848; Captain, 24 March, 1855; Major, 26 Feb., 1867.
Edward Bowles—2nd Lieut., 14 Aug., 1846; Lieut., 16 Aug., 1850; Captain, 23 March, 1855; Major, 11 Jan., 1869.
Robert Jameson Eustace Robertson—2nd Lieut., 5 March, 1847; Lieut., 27 Dec., 1850; Captain, 23 March, 1855; Major, 29 May, 1869.
Hugh P. Montgomery—2nd Lieut., 21 Aug., 1849; Lieut., 28 Oct., 1853;

Majors (continued)—
Captain, 17 Aug., 1855; Major, 10 Nov., 1868.

Rank and Name.	Rank in Regiment.
Captains—	
William Tedlie	25 Jan. 1856
Rank in Army { Bt. Maj.	20 July 1858
Lt.-Col.	25 Mar. 1869
Henry Semple..	25 Aug. 1857
Charles Williamson ..	16 Oct. 1857
Rowley Willes Hinxman.	15 Jan. 1858
Rank in Army, Bt. Maj.	19 Jan. 1864
Wykeham L. Pemberton .	23 Mar. 1858
Fr. Dundas Farquharson .	24 April 1858
J. Durham Dundas ..	22 June 1858
Herbert Geo. Deedes ..	2 July 1858
Rank in Army, Bt. Maj.	25 Sept. 1860
James Joseph Collins ..	19 July 1859
D.G. Neville Watts-Russell	29 Nov. 1859
Anthony Carlisle	9 Mar. 1860
Francis V. Northey ..	18 May 1860
Wm. Fred. Carleton ..	18 Sept. 1860
Geo. Robt. Stewart Black	14 Feb. 1860
Cromer Ashburnham ..	23 Jan. 1863
Kennett Gregg Henderson	30 June 1863
Edw. Campbell Ainslie ..	1 Mar. 1864
J. S. Hamilton Afgar ..	17 May 1864
Geo. Charles Kelly.. ..	6 Oct. 1864
Ch. Chris. Willoughby ..	18 Oct. 1864
Matthew Tilford	28 Oct. 1864
F. H. Anson Hamilton ..	4 Nov. 1864
Harry Robt. Milligan ..	22 Nov. 1864
George Hatchell	24 Jan. 1865
James Kiero Watson ..	1 May 1865
Wm. Gerard Byron ..	3 Jan. 1865
Rd. Francis Jennings ..	1 Dec. 1865
Stanley Mortimer	30 Mar. 1866
Wm. J. Evered Poole ..	3 April 1866
Newton John Pauli ..	5 June 1866
Wm. L. Kinloch Ogilvy..	11 Dec. 1866
Hugh St. George Barton .	8 Mar. 1867
Robert F. de B. Barry ..	15 Mar. 1867
John Owen Young.. ..	6 July 1867
Wm. N. Manners	17 Sept. 1867
Reginald H. Bendon ..	16 Oct. 1867
Arthur Tufnell	23 Oct. 1867
Pennyman W. Worsley ..	6 Nov. 1867
John Charley	14 Aug. 1867
Astley Fellowes Terry ..	8 Dec. 1867
John Gustavus Crosbie..	20 May 1868
John Richard Crane ..	21 Oct. 1862
Geo. Hewitt Trotman ..	11 Jan. 1869
Nesbit W. Wallace.. ..	23 Jan. 1869
Marcus Wm. O'Rorke ..	24 April 1869
Arthur Morris..	24 April 1869
Ellis Houlton Ward ..	29 May 1869
Alex. Borthwick	10 Nov. 1869
Lieutenants—	
L. Codd. Brownrigg ..	9 Mar. 1860
Chas. M. Calderon.. ..	26 Oct. 1860
R. Henry Buller	9 Dec. 1862
Chas. Pierson Cramer ..	21 April 1863
C. Forbes Terry	22 May 1863
Fr. Wm. Robins	30 June 1863
James H. Herbert Croft .	31 Mar. 1863
Fr. Wallace Grenfell ..	21 July 1863
Aubrey Vere O'Brien ..	8 Sept. 1863

Rank and Name.	Rank in Regiment.
Lieutenants (continued)—	
Ch. L. C. de Robeck ..	1 Mar. 1864
Ch. G. Fryer	6 Oct. 1864
William Warren	22 Nov. 1864
P. J. H. A. Barne	12 June 1863
Geo. Thomas Whitaker..	24 Jan. 1865
George Carpenter	31 Jan. 1865
R. Collingwood Robinson	7 Feb. 1865
G. L. M'Lean Farmer ..	1 Mar. 1865
Edw. W. Home Crofton .	2 May 1865
Denis Bingham	26 May 1865
John T. D. Crosbie.. ..	1 Dec. 1865
Francis Henry Baillie ..	30 Mar. 1866
Walter Cowan..	3 April 1866
Fred. C. B. Coulson ..	26 June 1866
Henry Donald Browne ..	14 Aug. 1866
Edm. Lomax Fraser ..	21 Aug. 1866
Reginald Chalmer	21 Feb. 1865
Henry R. P. Landesay ..	2 Oct. 1866
H. A. Fred. F. Coventry	27 Nov. 1866
William Tilden	11 Dec. 1866
John B. Stradling	11 Jan. 1867
Henry B. MacCaul	19 Feb. 1867
Benjamin Frend	27 Feb. 1867
Orfeur Geo. Parker . ..	6 Mar. 1867
Amb. Humph. Birchom..	8 Mar. 1867
J. S. Wynne-Finch ..	15 Mar. 1867
Lewis Bedford..	6 July 1867
Henry A. Houlton Ward .	7 Aug. 1867
Cecil Ralph Howard ..	7 Aug. 1867
Thos. B. Powys-Keck ..	17 Sept. 1867
P. A. J. Hope Johnstone	6 Nov. 1867
A. F. H. Mitchell-Innes .	20 Nov. 1867
Crawford Lewin Allan ..	25 Dec. 1867
William Forster	9 April 1868
Arthur Pepys	10 April 1868
Wm. Mitchell-Innes ..	13 June 1868
Robert Cradock Davis ..	30 June 1868
W. F. Chalmers Wigston.	24 Sept. 1868
Alex. Rawson Boddam ..	20 Jan. 1867
H. Philip Miles Wylie ..	28 Oct. 1868
J. N. Blackwood-Price ..	11 Jan. 1869
Fr. John Adelbert Wood.	23 Jan. 1869
Charles Holled Smith ..	3 Feb. 1869
H. Savill Marsham	17 Feb. 1869
Thos. Sydenham Clarke .	24 April 1869
Algernon St. Maur	24 April 1869
Fr. Grenville Doyle . ..	29 May 1869
Ernest Hovell Thurlow..	29 May 1869
John Aubrey Williams ..	10 Nov. 1869
Ensigns—	
Albert Aug. Phipps ..	8 May 1866
Hon. Keith Turnour ..	2 Oct. 1866
A. Beaumont Legard ..	9 Nov. 1866
Wm. Walter Dundas ..	9 Nov. 1866
John Henry Burstall ..	11 Dec. 1866
Harry Paul Burnard ..	12 Dec. 1866
Sir C. C. de Crespigny, Bt.	13 Dec. 1866
Ernest Wm. Jones.. ..	11 Jan. 1867
George P. Gilbert	27 Feb. 1867
Arthur Greville Bagot ..	6 Mar. 1867
Henry S. Hutton Ruddell	8 Mar. 1867
H. J. Hope-Edwardes ..	6 July 1867
F. B. Newton Dickenson	8 Aug. 1867
Edw. T. Henry Hutton..	9 Aug. 1867
F. Wright Archer	10 Aug. 1867

Rank and Name.   **Rank in Regiment.**

Ensigns (continued)—

Horace Walpole .. .. 11 Aug. 1867
Charles Mitchell .. .. 12 Aug. 1867
Shafto Robert Elmes .. 16 Oct. 1867
Arthur James Brander .. 8 Nov. 1867
Harry Willes Sanford . 9 Nov. 1867
H. E. W. Fetherstonhaugh 18 Dec. 1867
Francis Moore Ward .. 25 Dec. 1867
Ch. R. B. Thorne .. .. 25 Dec. 1867
Charles Hope .. .. **8** Jan. 1868
R. S. R. Fetherstonhaugh 25 Sept. 1867
Godfrey Astell .. .. 13 June 1868
H. David P. Okeden .. 6 Sept. 1868
Edw. Rhys. Wingfield .. 28 Oct. 1868
Edw. St. Maur .. .. 18 Nov. 1868
N. Edw. de B. Fenwick. 24 **Jan.** 1869
Walter Henry Holbech.. 14 **Oct.** 1868
Wm. Sturrock Anderson . 3 **Feb.** 1869
Fred. A. Beauclerk. .. 14 **April** 1869
Clement Wm. Archer .. 15 **April** 1869
Henry Allfrey.. .. .. 19 **May** 1869
C. Stapleton Cotton .. 10 **Nov.** 1869

Paymasters—

Francis FitzPatrick—2 March, 1855;
2nd Lieut., 19 Oct., 1852; Lieut., 31
May, 1854; Hon. Major, 2 March, 1865.
Edward Charles Grant—28 Dec.,
1855; Hon. Capt., 28 Dec., 1869.
Robert Champ Streatfeild—8 June,
1838; Ensign, 12 Aug., 1853; Lieut.,
26 Oct., 1855; Hon. Maj., 12 Aug., 1868.
William Banbury—22 Nov., 1864;
Quartermaster, 8 July, 1854.

Adjutants—

L. C. Brownrigg, **Lieut.**. 18 **Jan.** 1859
A. H. Bircham, Lieut. .. **8 June** 1867
H. S. Marsham, Lieut.. .. 17 **Nov.** 1868
Reginald Chalmers, Lieut. 10 **Nov.** 1867

Instructors of Musketry—

A. V. O'Brien, Lieut. .. 21 June 1865
W. Warren, Lieut. .. .. 27 July 1866
A. Borthwick, Lieut. .. 12 Dec. 1867
F. H. Baillie, Lieut. .. 16 Mar. 1868

Quartermasters—

Thomas Jarvis .. .. .. 2 Dec. 1862
John Toole .. .. .. 13 Feb. 1863
Wm. Holmes .. .. 17 April 1867
Wm. FitzHenry .. .. 6 July 1867

Surgeons—

Edward William **Young**, M.D.
Assistant Surgeon, 7 Aug., 1846;
Surgeon, 8 Dec. 1854; Surgeon-Major,
7 Aug. 1866.
Adam Graham **Young**, Assistant
Surgeon, 5 May, 1854; Surgeon, 20
June, 1865.
William McNamara, M.D., Assistant Surgeon, 6 Oct., 1854; Surgeon,
16 March, 1867.
Arthur Edwin Temple Longhurst,
M.D., Assistant-Surgeon, 27 Oct.,
1854; Surgeon, 1 May, 1867.

Assistant Surgeons—

F. Wm. Wade.. .. .. 28 Sept. 1857
W. Silver Oliver, M.D.. 15 Sept. 1857
A. Campbell M'Tavish .. 12 Jan. 1859

Rank and Name.   *Rank in Regiment.*

Assistant-Surgeons (continued)—

Philip Lefeuvre Kilroy .. 2 Oct. 1865
W. M. Harman, M.B. .. 2 Oct. 1866
J. Patrick Rooney .. .. 31 Mar. 1866

Regimentals—Green, facings scarlet.

Agents—Messrs. Cox and Co.

1871.

Four Battalions.

Canada—England—India.

Celer et Audax.

Roleia, Vimiera, Martinique, Talavera,
Fuentes d'Onor, Albuhera, Ciudad
Rodrigo, Badajoz, Salamanca, Vittoria,
Pyrenees, Nivelle, Nive, Orthes, Toulouse, Peninsula, Punjaub, Mooltan,
Goojerat, Taku Forts, Pekin, Delhi.

Col.-in-Chief—

Field-Marshal **H.R.H. the Duke of
Cambridge, K.G., K.P., G.C.B.,**
G.C.M.G., 3 March, **1869.**

Cols.-Commandant—

G. Frid. Viscount Templetown, K.C.B.
—Ensign, 24 Apr. 1823; Lieut., 29 Oct.,
1825; Captain, 12 Dec., 1826; Major,
16 June, 1837; Lieut.-Colonel, 16 Apr.,
1841; Colonel, 11 Nov., 1851; Major-
Gen., 26 Oct., **1858**; Lieut.-General, 9
March, 1865; **Col.-Commanding** 60th
Rifles, 24 Oct. **1862.**

Hen. Viscount Melville, G.C.B.—
Ensign and Lieut., 18 Nov., 1819; Capt.,
1 Apr.,1824; Major, 11 July, 1826; Lt.-
Colonel, 3 Dec., 1829; Colonel, 28 Nov.,
1841; Major-Gen., 20 June, 1854; Lt.-
General, 5 May, 1860; General, 1 Jan.,
1868; Col.-Com. 60th Rifles, 1 Apr.,**1863.**

Lieut.-Colonels—

Francis Roger Palmer, C.B.—Ensign,
15 March, 1833; Lieut., 24 April, 1835;
Captain, 11 March, 1842; Major, 20
June, 1851; Lieut.-Colonel, 22 June,
1858; Colonel, 22 June, 1863.

Robt. H. Hawley—Ensign, **28 Aug.,**
1838; Lieut., 31 Dec., 1853; Captain,
to Jan., 1851; Brevet Major, 2 Nov.,
1855; Major, 5 Sept., 1856; Lieut.-
Col., 18 May, 1860; Col. 18 May, 1865.

Peter Burton Roe, 2nd Lieut., **23**
July, 1841; Lieut., 26 July, 1844;
Captain, 17 June, 1851; Major, 29 April,
1859; Lieut.-Colonel, 18 Sept., 1860;
Colonel, 18 Sept. 1865.

Randle Joseph Feilden, C.M.G.—
2nd Lieut., 31 March, 1843; Lieut.,
25 Feb., 1845; Captain, 23 Dec., 1853;
Major, 18 May, 1860; Lieut.-Colonel, 1
March, 1864; Colonel, 1 March, 1869.

Henry Freind Kennedy, 2nd Lieut.,
11 June, 1841; Lieut., 7 April, 1842;
Captain, 20 Oct., 1848; Major, 22 June,
1858; Brevet Lieut.-Colonel, 7 Jan.,
1864; Lieut.-Colonel, 22 Nov., 1869.

Majors—

Gibbes Rigaud—2nd Lieut., 11 June, 1841; Lieut., 26 July, 1844; Captain, 16 Aug., 1850; Major, 11 June, 1858; Brevet Lieut.-Colonel, 15 Feb., 1861; Colonel, 11 April, 1868.

Chas. Alexander Boswell Gordon— Ensign, 11 April, 1843; Lieut., 13 June, 1845; Captain, 6 June, 1854; Brevet Major, 6 June, 1856; Major, 18 Sept., 1860; Brevet Lt.-Colonel, 1 Jan., 1868.

Henry Francis Williams— Ensign, 19 May, 1843; Lieut., 10 Dec., 1844; Captain, 3 March, 1854; Brevet Major, 19 Jan., 1858; Brevet Lieut.-Colonel, 4 Aug., 1864; Major, 18 Oct., 1864.

Alfred John Fitzgerald—Ensign, 8 Nov., 1844; Lieut., 13 Feb., 1846; Capt. 13 March, 1855; Major, 14 Jan., 1865.

Edw. Bowles—2nd Lieut., 14 Aug., 1846; Lieut., 16 Aug., 1850; Captain, 23 March, 1855; Major, 11 Jan., 1869.

Robt. Jameson Eustace Robertson— 2nd Lieut., 5 March, 1847; Lieut., 27 Dec., 1850; Captain, 23 March, 1855; Major, 29 May, 1869.

Hugh P. Montgomery—2nd Lieut., 24 Aug., 1849; Lieut., 28 Oct., 1853; Capt., 17 Aug., 1855; Major, 10 Nov., 1869.

William Tedlie —2nd Lieut., 5 May, 1848; Lieut., 13 April, 1852; Captain, 25 Jan., 1856; Brevet Major, 29 July, 1858; Brevet Lieut.-Colonel, 25 March, 1869; Major, 9 April, 1870.

Rank and Name.	Rank in Regiment.
Captains —	
Henry Semple..	25 Aug. 1857
Chas. Williamson	16 Oct. 1857
Rowley Willes Hinxman	15 Jan. 1858
Rank in Army, Bt. Maj.	19 Jan. 1864
Wyk. Leigh Pemberton..	24 Mar. 1858
Fra. Dundas Farquharson	24 April 1858
James Durham Dundas..	22 June 1858
Rank in Army, Bt. Maj.	12 Nov. 1859
Herbert Geo. Deedes ..	2 July 1858
Rank in Army, Bt. Maj.	25 Sept. 1860
James Joseph Collins ..	19 July 1859
Anthony Carlisle	9 Mar. 1860
Francis V. Northey.. ..	18 May 1860
Rank in Army, Bt. Maj.	12 Nov. 1870
Wm. Fred. Carleton ..	18 Sept. 1860
Cramer Ashburnham ..	24 Jan. 1863
Kennett G. Henderson..	18 June 1863
Edw. Campbell Amelie..	1 May 1864
James S. Hamilton Algar	17 May 1864
Geo. Charles Kelly.. ..	6 Oct. 1864
Chas. Chris. Willoughby	18 April 1864
Fred. H. Anson Hamilton	4 Nov. 1864
Harry Robert Milligan ..	22 May 1864
George Hatchell	24 July 1865
James Kiero Watson ..	1 May 1865
Wm. Gerard Byron ..	3 Jan. 1865
Stanley Mortimer	30 Mar. 1866
Wm. John Everol Poole	3 April 1866
Newton Jones Paul ..	5 June 1866
Wm. Lewis Kinloch Ogilvy	14 Dec. 1866
Hugh St. George Barton	8 Mar. 1867

Rank and Name.	Rank in Regiment.
Captains (continued)—	
R. Fitzwilliam de B. Barry	15 Mar. 1867
John Owen Young.. ..	6 July 1867
Wm. Norcott Manners ..	17 Sept. 1867
Reginald H. Beadon ..	16 Oct. 1867
Arthur Tufnell	23 Oct. 1867
John Charley	14 Aug. 1867
Astley Fellowes Terry ..	8 Dec. 1867
John Gustavus Crosbie..	1 May 1868
John Rich Crane	21 Oct. 1862
Geo. Hewitt Trotman ..	11 Jan. 1869
Nesbit Willoughby Wallace	23 Jan. 1869
Marcus Wm. O'Rorke ..	24 April 1869
Arthur Morris..	24 April 1869
Ellis Houlton Ward ..	29 May 1869
Alexander Borthwick ..	10 Nov. 1869
Chas. Matthew Calderon.	9 Feb. 1870
Redvers Henry Buller ..	28 May 1870
Chas. Pierson Cramer ..	28 May 1870
Lieutenants—	
Latham C. Browxrigg ..	9 Mar. 1860
Courtenay Forbes Terry..	22 May 1863
Francis Wm. Robins ..	30 June 1863
James Hen. Herbt. Croft	31 Mar. 1863
Fran. Wallace Grenfell ..	21 July 1863
Aubrey Vere O'Brien ..	8 Sept. 1863
Chas. L. Cons. de Robeck	1 Mar. 1864
Chas. Gilbert Fryer ..	6 Oct. 1864
William Warren	22 Nov. 1864
Philip Julius H. A. Barne	12 June 1863
Geo. Thos. Whitaker ..	24 Jan. 1865
George Carpenter	31 Jan. 1865
Rich.Collingwood Robinson	7 Feb. 1865
G. Lau. M'Lean Farmer .	7 Mar. 1865
E. Walter Home Crofton	2 May 1865
Denis Bingham	26 May 1865
John T. Darnley Crosbie	1 Dec. 1865
Francis Henry Baillie ..	30 Mar. 1866
Walter Cowan..	3 April 1866
Fred. C. Glen. Coulson ..	26 June 1866
Henry Donald Browne ..	14 Aug. 1866
Edmund Lomax Fraser..	21 Aug. 1866
Reginald Chalmer	24 Feb. 1865
Henry R. Pons. Lindesay	2 Oct. 1866
Henry A. Fred. F. Coventry	27 Nov. 1866
William Tilden	11 Dec. 1866
John B. Sterling	11 Jan. 1867
Henry Blackwood MacCall	19 Feb. 1867
Benjamin Freud	27 Feb. 1867
Orfeur Geo. Parker ..	6 Mar. 1867
Amb. Humph. Bircham..	8 Mar. 1867
John S. Wynne-Finch ..	8 Mar. 1867
Henry A. Houlton Ward	7 Aug. 1867
Hon. Cecil R. Howard ..	7 Aug. 1867
Percy A.J.Hope Johnstone	6 Nov. 1867
Alex. F. H. Mitchell-Innes	20 Nov. 1867
Crawford Lewin Allan ..	25 Dec. 1867
William Forster	9 April 1868
Arthur Pepys	10 April 1868
Wm. Mitchell-Innes ..	13 June 1868
Robt. Cradock Davis ..	30 June 1868
Alex. R. B. Whetham ..	20 July 1867
Henry Philip Miles Wylie	28 Oct. 1868
James N. Blackwood-Price	14 Jan. 1869
Fran.John Adelbert Wood	23 Jan. 1869
Chas. H. Bel. Smith ..	3 Feb. 1869

Rank and Name.	Rank in Regiment.
Lieutenants (continued)—	
Henry Savill Marsham	17 Feb. 1869
Thos. Sydenham Clarke	24 April 1869
Fran. Grenville Doyle	29 May 1869
Ernest Hovell Thurlow	29 May 1869
John Aubrey Williams	10 Nov. 1869
Albert Aug. Phipps	5 Jan. 1870
Hon. Keith Turnour	9 Feb. 1870
Allayne Beaumont Legard	28 Mar. 1870
Wm. Walter Dundas	28 May 1870
John Henry Burstall	28 May 1870
Harry Paul Burrard	24 Sept. 1870
Arthur Greville Bagot	14 Dec. 1870
Ensigns—	
Geo. Percy Gilbert	27 Feb. 1867
Hon. S. Hutton Ruddell	8 Mar. 1867
H. James Hope-Edwardes	6 July 1867
Fiennes D. Newton Dickens	8 Aug. 1867
Edw. Thos. Henry Hutton	9 Aug. 1867
Fulbert Wright Archer	10 Aug. 1867
Horace Walpole	11 Aug. 1867
Charles Michell	12 Oct. 1867
Arthur James Brander	6 Nov. 1867
Harry Wills Stamford	9 Nov. 1867
Henry E. W. Fetherstonhaugh	18 Dec. 1867
Francis Moore Ward	25 Dec. 1867
Chas. R. B. Thorne	25 Dec. 1867
Charles Hope	8 Jan. 1868
R. S. R. Fetherstonhaugh	25 Sept. 1867
Godfrey Astell	13 June 1868
Humphrey D. P. Okeden	2 Sept. 1868
Edw. Rhys Wingfield	28 Oct. 1868
Edw. St. Maur	18 Nov. 1868
Nicholas E. de B. Fenwick	23 Jan. 1869
Walter Henry Halford	13 Oct. 1868
Wm. Starrock Anderson	3 Feb. 1869
Fred. Amelius Saunders	24 Apr. 1869
Clement Wm. Archer	25 Apr. 1869
Henry Alfrey	29 May 1869
Corbet Stapleton Corbet	10 Nov. 1869
Henry Lowth Farmer	9 Apr. 1870
Robert Henley	28 May 1870
Arthur G. Addey Martin	24 Sept. 1870
Paymasters—	
Francis FitzPatrick, 2 March, 1855; 2nd Lieut., 19 Oct. 1843; Lieut., 31 May, 1854; Hon. Major, 2 March, 1855	
Edw. Charles Graut, 28 Dec., 1855	
Hon. Captain, 28 Dec., 1855	
Robt. C. Streatfield, 8 June, 1858— Ensign, 12 Aug., 1853; Lieut., 26 Oct., 1855; Hon. Major, 12 Aug., 1858	
William Banbury, 2 Nov., 1864— Quartermaster, 8 July, 1851; Hon. Captain, 22 Nov., 1869	
Adjutants—	
L. C. Brownrigg, Lieut.	18 Jan. 1870
A. H. Bircham, Lieut.	8 June 1867
H. S. Marsham, Lieut.	17 Nov. 1869
Reginald Chalmer, Lieut.	10 Nov. 1869
Instructors of Musketry	
A. V. O'Brien, Lieut.	21 June 1865
W. Warren, Lieut.	27 July 1866
F. H. Baillie, Lieut.	16 Mar. 1869
C. G. Fryer, Lieut.	2 Feb. 1870

Rank and Name.	Rank in Regiment.
Quartermasters—	
Thomas Jarvis	2 Dec. 1852
John Toole	13 Feb. 1866
William Holmes	17 Apr. 1867
William FitzHenry	6 July 1867
Surgeons—	

Edw. Wm. Young, M.D., Assistant-Surgeon, 7 Aug. 1840; Surgeon, 8 Dec., 1854; Surgeon-Major, 7 Aug., 1866.

Adam Graham Young, Assistant-Surgeon, 5 May, 1854; Surgeon, 20 June, 1865.

Wm. Macnamara, M.D., Assistant-Surgeon, 6 Oct., 1854; Surgeon, 16 March, 1867.

Arthur Edwin Temple Longhurst, M.D., Assistant-Surgeon, 27 Oct., 1854; Surgeon, 1 May, 1867.

Assistant-Surgeons—

Fred. William Wade	28 Sept. 1857
Wm. Silver Oliver, M.D.	15 Sept. 1857
Alex. Campbell M'Tavish	12 Jan. 1859
Philip Lefeuvre Kilroy	2 Oct. 1865
W. Morton Harman, M.B.	2 Oct. 1866
James Patrick Rooney	31 Mar. 1866

Regimentals Green, facings scarlet.

Agents Messrs. Cox and Co.

1872.

Four Battalions.

Canada India Aden England.

Color et Audax.

Rolica, Vimiera, Martinique, Talavera, Fuentes d'Onor, Albuhera, Ciudad Rodrigo, Badajoz, Salamanca, Vittoria, Pyrenees, Nivelle, Nive, Orthes, Toulouse, Peninsula, Punjaub, Mooltan, Goojerat, Taku Forts, Pekin, Delhi.

Col.-in-Chief—

Field-Marshal H.R.H. the Duke of Cambridge, K.G., K.P., G.C.B., G.C.M.G., 3 Nov., 1869.

Cols. Commandant

Geo. Fred. Viscount Templetown, K.C.B. Ensign, 24 April, 1823; Lieut., 23 Oct., 1825; Capt., 12 Dec., 1826; Major, 16 June, 1847; Lieut.-Col., 16 April, 1841; Colonel, 11 Nov., 1851; Major-Gen. 26 Oct., 1858; Lieut.-Gen., 8 Mar. 1865; Col.-Com. 60th Rifles, 24 Oct., 1862

Henry Viscount Melville, G.C.B. Ensign and Lieut., 18 Nov., 1819; Capt., 1 Apr., 1824; Major, 11 July, 1826; Lt.-Col., 3 Dec. 1829; Col., 28 Nov., 1841; Major-Gen., 20 June, 1854; Lt.-Gen., 5 May, 1860; General, 1 Jan., 1868; Col.-Commandant 60th Rifles, 1 Apr., 1863.

Lieut.-Colonels—

Francis Roger Palmer, C.B. Ensign, 15 March, 1833; Lieut., 24 April, 1835; Capt., 11 Mar., 1842; Major, 20 June 1854; Lieut.-Col., 22 June, 1858; Col. 22 June, 1863

Lieut.-Colonels (continued)—

Robt. B. Hawley—Ensign, 28 Aug., 1838 ; Lieut., 31 Dec., 1839 ; Capt., 10 Jun., 1851 ; Bt. Major, 2 Nov., 1855 ; Major, 5 Sept., 1856 ; Lieut.-Col., 18 May, 1860 ; Colonel, 18 May, 1865.

Peter Burton Roe—2nd Lieut., 23 July, 1841 ; Lieut., 26 July, 1844 ; Capt., 17 June, 1851 ; Major, 29 April, 1859 ; Lieut.-Col., 18 Sept., 1860 ; Col., 18 May, 1865.

Henry Friend Kennedy—2nd Lieut., 11 Sept., 1840 ; Lieut., 7 April, 1842 ; Capt., 20 Oct., 1848 ; Major, 17 Aug., 1855 ; Brevet Lieut.-Col., 7 Jan., 1864 ; Lieut.-Col., 22 Nov., 1865.

Chas. Alex. Boswell Gordon—Ensign, 21 April, 1843 ; Lieut., 13 June, 1845 ; Capt., 6 June, 1851 ; Brevet-Major, 6 June, 1856 ; Major, 8 Sept., 1860 ; Brev. Lieut.-Col., 1 Jan., 1868 ; Lieut.-Col., 9 Aug., 1871.

Majors—

Gibbes Rigaud—2nd Lieut., 11 June, 1841 ; Lieut., 26 July, 1844 ; Capt., 16 Aug.,1850; Major, 22 June, 1858 ; Brev. Lieut.-Col., 15 Feb. 1861 ; Colonel, 22 April, 1868.

Henry Francis Williams—Ensign, 19 May, 1843 ; Lieut., 20 Dec., 1844 ; Capt., 3 Mar., 1854 ; Brevet Major, 19 Jan., 1858 ; Brevet Lieut.-Col., 15 Feb., 1861 ; Colonel, 22 April, 1868.

Alfred John Fitzgerald—Ensign, 8 Nov., 1842 ; Lieut., 13 Feb., 1846 ; Capt., 23 Mar., 1855 ; Major, 24 Jan., 1865.

Robt. Jameson Eustace Robertson—2nd Lieut., 5 Mar., 1847 ; Lieut., 27 Dec., 1850 ; Capt., 23 Mar.,1855 ; Major, 29 May, 1869.

Hugh P. Montgomery—2nd Lieut., 21 Aug., 1849 ; Lieut., 28 Oct., 1853 ; Capt., 17 August, 1855 ; Major, 10 Nov., 1869.

Wm. Tedlie—2nd Lieut., 5 May, 1848 ; Lieut., 13 April, 1852 ; Captain, 25 Jan., 1856 ; Brevet Major, 20 July, 1858 ; Brevet Lieut.-Col., 25 Mar., 1869 ; Major, 9 April, 1870.

Charles Williamson—2nd Lieut., 11 July, 1851 ; Lieut., 11 Aug., 1854 ; Capt., 16 Oct., 1857 ; Major, 9 Aug., 1871.

Wykeham Leigh Pemberton—2nd Lieut., 23 April, 1852 ; Lieut., 25 Aug., 1854 ; Captain, 23 Mar., 1858 ; Major, 28 Oct., 1871.

Rank and Name.	*Rank in Regiment.*
Captains	
Henry Semple..	25 Aug. 1857
Rowley Willis Hinxman..	15 Jan. 1858
Rank in Army, Bt. Maj.	19 Jan. 1864
Francis D. Farquharson..	24 April 1858
James Durham Dundas ..	22 June 1858
Rank in Army, Bt. Maj.	12 Nov. 1870
Herbert George Deedes..	2 July 1858
Rank in Army { Bt. Maj. 25 Sept. 1860	
{ Lt.-Col. 30 July 1871	

Rank and Name.	*Rank in Regiment.*
Captains (continued)—	
James Joseph Collins ..	19 July 1859
Anthony Carlisle	9 Mar. 1860
Francis Vernon Northey .	18 May 1860
Rank in Army, Bt. Maj.	12 Nov. 1870
William Fred. Carleton ..	18 Sept. 1860
Cromer Ashburnham ..	23 Jan. 1863
Kennett Gregg Henderson	30 June 1863
Edw. Campbell Ainslie ..	1 Mar. 1864
Jas. S. Hamilton Algar ..	17 May 1864
George Charles Kelly ..	6 Oct. 1864
Chas. Chris. Willoughby..	18 Oct. 1864
Fred. H. A. Hamilton ..	4 Nov. 1864
Harry Robt. Milligan ..	22 Nov. 1864
George Hatchell	24 Jan. 1865
James Kiero Watson ..	1 May 1865
William Gerard Byron ..	3 Jan. 1865
Wm. John Evered Poole	3 April 1866
Newton Jones Pauli ..	5 June 1866
Wm. Lewis K. Ogilvy ..	11 Dec. 1866
Hugh St. George Barton..	8 Mar. 1867
Robt. Fitz W. de B. Barry	15 Mar. 1867
John Owen Young.. ..	6 July 1867
Wm. Norcott Manners ..	17 Sept. 1867
Reginald H. Bendon ..	16 Oct. 1867
Arthur Tufnell	23 Oct. 1867
John Charley	14 Aug. 1867
Astley Fellowes Terry ..	8 Dec. 1867
John Gustavus Crosbie ..	20 May 1868
John Richard Crane ..	21 Oct. 1862
George Hewitt Trotman..	11 Jan. 1869
Nesbit W. Wallace ..	23 Jan. 1869
Arthur Morris..	24 April 1869
Ellis Houlton Ward ..	29 May 1869
Alexander Borthwick ..	10 Nov. 1869
Chas. Matthew Calderon .	9 Feb. 1870
Redvers Henry Buller ..	28 May 1870
Charles Pierson Cramer ..	28 May 1870
Courtenay Forbes Terry ..	4 Jan. 1871
Latham C. Brownrigg ..	20 April 1871
Jas. Hen. Herbert Croft ..	9 Aug. 1871
Francis Wallace Grenfell	28 Oct. 1871
Lieutenants—	
Francis Wm. Robins ..	30 June 1863
Aubrey Vere O'Brien ..	8 Sept. 1863
Chas. L. C. de Roheck ..	1 Mar. 1864
Charles Gilbert Fryer ..	6 Oct. 1864
Wm. Warren	22 Nov. 1864
Philip J. H. A. Barne ..	12 June 1863
Geo. Thos. Whitaker ..	3 Jan. 1865
George Carpenter	31 Jan. 1865
Richard C. Robinson ..	7 Feb. 1865
Geo. L. M'Lean Farmer..	7 Mar. 1865
Edward W. H. Crofton..	2 May 1865
Denis Bingham	26 May 1865
John Talbot D. Crosbie..	1 Dec. 1865
Francis Henry Baillie ..	30 Mar. 1866
Walter Cowan	3 April 1866
F. C. Blenkinsopp Coulson	26 June 1866
Henry Donald Browne ..	14 Aug. 1866
Edmund Lomax Fraser..	21 Aug. 1866
Reginald Chalmer	21 Feb. 1865
H. Ed. Ponsonby Lindesay	21 Oct. 1866
H. A. F. Ferguson Coventry	27 Nov. 1866
William Tilden	11 Dec. 1866
John Bartlett Stradling..	11 Jan. 1867

Rank and Name.	Rank in Regiment.
Lieutenants (continued)—	
Henry Blackwood MacCall	19 Feb. 1867
Benjamin Frend	27 Feb. 1867
Orfeur Geo. Parker. . ..	6 Mar. 1867
A. Humphreys Bircham .	8 Mar. 1867
J. Seymour Wynne-Finch	15 Mar. 1867
Henry A. Houlton Ward.	7 Aug. 1867
Hon. Cecil Ralph Howard	7 Aug. 1867
P. A. J. Hope Johnstone	6 Nov. 1867
A. F. H. Mitchell-Innes .	20 Nov. 1867
Crawford Lewin Allan ..	25 **Dec.** 1867
William Forster	9 April 1868
Arthur Pegrs	10 April 1868
Robt. Cradock Davies ..	30 June 1868
A. R. Boddam Wetham..	20 July 1867
Henry Philip Miles Wylie	28 Oct. 1868
J. N. Blackwood-Price .	11 **Jan.** 1869
Fra. John Adelbert Wood	23 **Jan.** 1869
Charles Holled Smith ..	3 **Feb.** 1869
Henry Saville Marsham..	17 **Feb.** 1869
Thomas Sydenham Clarke	24 **April** 1869
Ernest Howell Thurlow ..	29 **May** 1869
John Aubrey Williams ..	10 **Nov.** 1869
Albert Augustus Phipps..	5 **Jan.** 1870
Hon. Keith Turnour ..	9 **Feb.** 1870
Allayne Beaumont Legard	28 **Mar.** 1870
John Henry Burnall ..	28 **May** 1870
Arthur Greville Bagot ..	14 **Dec.** 1870
Henry S. Button Riddell	4 **Jan.** 1871
H. J. Hope-Edwardes ..	22 **Mar.** 1871
Thomas Prince Lloyd ..	29 **Nov.** 1871
F. B. Newton Dickenson.	12 **July** 1871
Ed. Thos. Henry Hutton.	9 **Aug.** 1871
Folbert Wright Archer ..	9 **Aug.** 1871
Horace Walpole	28 **Oct.** 1871
Charles Mitchell	1 **Nov.** 1871
Arthur James Brander ..	1 **Nov.** 1871
Harry Willis Sandford ..	1 **Nov.** 1871
D. E. W. Fetherstonhaugh	1 **Nov.** 1871
Francis Moore Ward ..	1 **Nov.** 1871
Charles Radley B. Thorne	1 **Nov.** 1871
Charles Hope	1 **Nov.** 1871
R. S. R. Fetherstonhaugh	1 **Nov.** 1871
Godfrey Axtell. . ..	1 **Nov.** 1871
Humphrey D. P. Olivier .	1 **Nov.** 1871
N. E. de B. Fenwick ..	1 **Nov.** 1871
Walter Henry Holbech ..	1 **Nov.** 1871
Wm. Starnock Anderson .	1 **Nov.** 1871
Fredk Amelius Heathcote	1 **Nov.** 1871
Clement Wm. Archer ..	1 **Nov.** 1871
Henry Allfrey.. ..	1 **Nov.** 1871
Corbet Stapleton Cotton..	1 **Nov.** 1871
Henry Lowth Farmer ..	1 **Nov.** 1871
Robert Henley.. ..	1 **Nov.** 1871
Arthur G. Addey Martin.	1 **Nov.** 1871
Arthur Cyprian Kindley..	1 **Nov.** 1871
Mordaunt Charles Boyle .	1 **Nov.** 1871
Paymasters—	

Francis FitzPatrick, 2 March, 1855,
2nd Lieutenant, 19 Oct., 1849 ; Lieutenant, 31 May, 1854 ; Hon. Major, 2
March, 1865.

Edward Charles Grant, 28 Dec., 1855
—Hon. Major, 28 Dec., 1870.

Robt. Champion Streatfield, 8 June,
1858, Ensign, 12 Aug., 1853 ; Lieu-

Rank and Name.	Rank in Regiment.
Paymasters (continued)—	

tenant, 26 Oct., 1855 ; Hon. **Major,** 12
Aug., 1868.

Charles Harrison Hignett. 10 May,
1871—Ensign, 28 July, 1863 ; Lieutenant, 7 Nov., 1868.

Adjutants—

Henry Saville Marsham..	17 Nov. 1869
Reginald Chalmer	10 Nov. 1869
Ambrose H. Bircham ..	8 June 1867
Henry Donald Browne ..	17 May 1871

Military Instructors—

Chas. Gilbert Fryer ..	2 Feb. 1870
W. Warren	27 July 1866
R. W. H. Crofton	3 Jan. 1871
F. H. Baillie	15 Mar. 1869

Quartermasters—

Thomas Jarvis..	2 Dec. 1862
John Toole	13 Feb. 1866
William Holmes	17 April 1867
William Fazlleury ..	6 July 1867

Surgeons—

Edwd. Wm. Young, M.D., Assistant-Surgeon, 7 Aug., 1846 ; Surgeon, 8 Dec.,
1854 ; Surgeon-Major, 7 Aug., 1866.

Adam Graham Young, Assistant-Surgeon, 5 May, 1854 ; Surgeon, 30
June, 1865.

Wm. Macnamara, M.D., Assist-Surg.,
6 Oct., 1854 ; Surgeon, 16 March, 1867.

Arthur Edwin Temple Longhurst,
M.D., Assistant-Surgeon, 27 Oct., 1854 ;
Surgeon, 1 May, 1867.

Assistant-Surgeons—

Fredk. Wm. Wade.. ..	28 Sept. 1857
Wm Silver Oliver, M.D..	15 Sept. 1857
Alex. Campbell M'Tavish	12 Jan. 1859
Philip Lefeuvre Kilroy..	2 Oct. 1865
W. Morton Harmon, M.B.	2 Oct. 1866
James Patrick Rooney ..	31 Mar. 1866

Regimentals Green, facings scarlet.

Agents Messrs. Cox and Co.

1873.

Four Battalions.

Canada India England.

Colours Authd.

R. I. a. Vimiera, Martinique, Talavera,
Fuentes d'Onor, Albuhera, Ciudad
Rodrigo, Badajoz, Salamanca, Vittoria,
Pyrenees, Nivelle, Nive, Orthes, Toulouse, Peninsula, Punjaub, Mooltan,
Goojerat, Taku Forts, Pekin, Delhi.

Colonel-in-Chief

Field Marshal H.R.H. the Duke of
Cambridge, K.G., K.P., G.C.B.,
G.C.M.G., 3 March, 1868.

Cols.-Commandant—

George Fred. Viscount Templetown, K.C.B.—Ensign, 24 April, 1823; Lieut., 29 Oct., 1825; Captain, 12 Dec., 1826; Major, 16 June, 1837; Lieut.-Colonel, 16 April, 1844; Colonel, 11 Nov., 1851; Major-Gen., 26 Oct., 1858; Lieut.-Gen., 9 March, 1865; Colonel-Com. 60th Rifles, 24 Oct., 1862.

Henry Viscount Melville, G.C.B.—Ensign and Lieut., 18 Nov., 1819; Captain, 1 April, 1824; Major, 11 July, 1826; Lieut.-Colonel, 3 Dec., 1829; Colonel, 28 Nov., 1841; Major-Gen., 20 June, 1854; Lieut.-Gen., 5 May, 1860; General, 1 Jan., 1868; Colonel-Com. 60th Rifles, 1 April, 1863.

Lieut.-Cols.—

Robert B. Hawley—Ensign, 28 Aug., 1838; Lieut., 31 Dec., 1839; Captain, 10 Jan., 1851; Brevet Major, 2 Nov. 1855; Major, 5 Sept., 1856; Lieut.-Colonel, 18 May, 1860; Colonel, 18 May, 1865.

Peter Burton Roe—2nd Lieut., 23 July, 1841; Lieut., 26 July, 1841; Captain, 17 June, 1851; Major, 23 April, 1859; Lieut.-Colonel, 18 Sept., 1860; Colonel, 18 Sept., 1865.

Charles Alexander Boswell Gordon Ensign, 21 April, 1843; Lieut., 13 June, 1845; Captain, 6 June, 1854; Brevet Major, 6 June, 1856; Major, 18 Sept., 1860; Brevet Lieut.-Colonel, 1 Jan., 1868; Lieut.-Colonel, 9 Aug., 1871.

Gibbes Rignaud—2nd Lieut., 11 June, 1841; Lieut., 26 July, 1841; Captain, 16 Aug., 1850; Major, 22 June, 1858; Brevet Lieut.-Colonel, 15 Feb., 1861; Colonel, 22 April, 1868; Lieut.-Colonel, 24 April, 1872.

Majors —

Henry Francis Williams—Ensign, 19 May, 1843; Lieut., 29 Dec., 1844; Captain, 3 March, 1854; Brevet Major, 19 Jan., 1858; Brevet Lieut. Colonel, 4 Aug., 1864; Major, 28 Oct., 1864; Colonel, 18 April, 1871.

Alfred John Fitzgerald—Ensign, 8 Nov., 1842; Lieut., 13 Feb., 1846; Captain, 23 March, 1855; Major, 24 January, 1865.

Robert Jameson Eustace Robertson—2nd Lieut., 5 March, 1847; Lieut., 27 Dec., 1850; Captain, 23 March, 1855; Major, 29 May, 1862.

Hugh Park Montgomery—2nd Lieut., 24 Aug., 1849; Lieut., 28 Oct., 1853; Captain, 17 Aug., 1855; Major, 10 November, 1869.

William Teslie—2nd Lieut., 5 May, 1848; Lieut., 13 April, 1852; Captain, 25 Jan., 1856; Brevet Major, 20 July, 1858; Brevet Lieut.-Colonel, 25 March, 1869; Major, 9 April, 1870.

Majors (continued)—

Charles Williamson—2nd Lieut., 11 July, 1851; Lieut., 11 Aug., 1854; Capt., 16 Oct., 1857; Maj., 9 Aug., 1871.

Wykeham Leigh Pemberton—2nd Lieut., 23 April, 1852; Lieut., 25 Aug., 1854; Captain, 23 March, 1858; Major, 28 October, 1871.

Rowley Willes Hinxman—Ensign, 23 Nov., 1849; Lieut., 3 March, 1854; Captain, 15 Jan., 1858; Brevet Major, 19 Jan., 1864; Major, 24 April, 1872.

Rank and Name.	Rank in Regiment.

Captains

Francis D. Farquharson..	24 April 1858
James Durham Dundas..	22 June 1858
Rank in Army, Bt. Maj.	12 Nov. 1870
H. G. Deedes, Assist. Adj.-General, Rawal Pindee, Division, Bengal.. ..	2 July 1858
Rank in { Bt. Maj.	25 Sept. 1860
Army { Bt. Lt.-Col.	30 July 1871
James Joseph Collins ..	19 July 1859
Anthony Carlisle	9 Mar. 1860
Francis Vernon Northey	18 May 1860
Rank in Army, Bt. Maj.	12 Nov. 1870
Wm. Fred. Carleton ..	18 Sept. 1860
Cromer Ashburnham ..	23 Jan. 1863
Kennett Gregg Henderson	30 June 1863
Edw. Campbell Ainslie..	1 Mar. 1864
Jas. S. Hamilton Algar ..	17 May 1864
George Charles Kelly ..	6 Oct. 1864
Chas. Chris. Willoughby..	18 Oct. 1864
Fredk. H. A. Hamilton..	4 Nov. 1864
Harry Robt. Milligan ..	22 Nov. 1864
George Hatchell	24 Jan. 1865
James Kiero Watson ..	1 May 1865
Wm. Gerard Byron ..	3 Jan. 1865
Wm. John Everel Poole, Brig. Major, Aldershot	3 April 1866
Newton Jones Pauli ..	5 June 1866
Wm. L. Kinloch Ogilvy, Brig. Major, Colchester	11 Dec. 1866
Hugh St. Geo. Barton ..	8 Mar. 1867
John Owen Young.. ..	6 July 1867
Wm. Norcott Manners ..	17 Sept. 1867
Reginald H. Beadon ..	16 Oct. 1867
Arthur Tufnell, A.P.C. to Sir E. H. Greathead ..	23 Oct. 1867
John Charley	14 Aug. 1867
Astley Fellowes Terry ..	8 Dec. 1867
John Gustavus Crosbie ..	20 May 1868
George Hewitt Trotman..	11 Jan. 1869
Nesbit W. Wallace ..	23 Jan. 1869
Arthur Morris	24 April 1869
Ellis Houlton Ward ..	29 May 1869
Chas. Matthew Calderon.	9 Feb. 1870
Redvers Henry Buller, at Staff College	28 May 1870
Chas. Pierson Cramer ..	28 May 1870
Latham C. Brownrigg ..	20 April 1871
Jas. Hen. Herbert Croft..	9 Aug. 1871
Francis Wallace Grenfell	28 Oct. 1871
Alex. A. Airlie Kinloch, D.A.A.G., for Musketry, Rawal Pindee	8 May 1870

Rank and Name.	Rank in Regiment.
Captains (continued) —	
Aubrey Yere O'Brien	24 April 1872
C. Louis Constantine de Robeck, Aide-de-Camp to Governor General of India	24 April 1872
Lieutenants —	
Chas. Gilbert Fryer	6 Oct. 1864
William Warren	22 Nov. 1864
Philip Julius H. **A. Barne**	12 June 1863
Geo. Thos. Whitaker	24 Jan. 1865
George Carpenter	31 Jan. 1865
Richard C. Robinson	7 Feb. 1865
Geo. L. M'Lean Farmer, Aide-de-Camp to the Lt.-Governor of Bengal	7 Mar. 1865
Edw. W. H. Crofton	2 May 1865
Denis Bingham	26 May 1865
John Talbot D. Crosbie	1 Dec. 1865
Francis Henry Baillie	30 Mar. 1866
Walter Cowan	3 April 1866
F. C. B. Coulson, Aide-de-Camp to the Governor General of Canada	26 June 1866
Henry Donald Browne	14 Aug. 1866
Edmund Lomax Fraser	23 Feb. 1865
Reginald Chalmer	21 Feb. 1865
Hon. Richard P. Lindesay	2 Oct. 1866
Hon. A. F. F. Coventry	27 Nov. 1866
William Tilden	11 Dec. 1866
Henry B. MacCall	19 Feb. 1867
Benjamin Freed	27 Feb. 1867
Ambrose H. Bircham	8 Mar. 1867
John S. W. Finch, extra Aide-de-Camp to Lord Lieut. of Ireland	15 Mar. 1867
Hon. Affleck B. Ward	7 Aug. 1867
Hon. Cecil R. Howard	7 Aug. 1867
P. A. J. Hope-Johnstone	6 Nov. 1867
Alex. F. M. Oliver	20 Nov. 1867
Crawford Lewin Allan	25 Dec. 1867
William Forster	9 April 1868
Arthur Pepys	10 April 1868
Robt. Cradock **Davies**	24 June 1868
Alex. R. B. Whetham	20 July 1867
Hon. Philip M. Wolfe	28 Oct. 1868
Jas. **Nugent** B. Price	11 Jan. 1869
Francis John A. Wessel	23 Jan. 1869
Chas. Hollist Smith	3 Feb. 1869
Henry Saville Marsham	17 Feb. 1869
Thos. Sydenham Clarke	24 April 1869
Ernest Hovell Thurlow	29 May 1869
John Aubrey Williams	10 Nov. 1869
Albert Augustus Phipps	5 Jan. 1870
Hon. Keith Turnour	9 Feb. 1870
John Henry Burstall	28 May 1870
Arthur Greville Baget	14 Dec. 1870
Henry S. H. Riddell	4 Jan. 1871
Herbert J. Hope-Edwardes	22 Mar. 1871
Thomas Prince Lloyd	29 Nov. 1864
Fiennes B. N. Dickenson	12 July 1871
Edw. Thos. H. Hatton	9 Aug. 1871
Fulbert Wright Archer	9 Aug. 1871
Horace Walpole	27 Oct. 1871
John Dowling Bowden	30 Nov. 1871
Charles Michell	28 Oct. 1871

Rank and Name.	Rank in Regiment.
Lieutenants (continued) —	
Arthur Jas. Brander	28 Oct. 1871
H. E. W. Fetherstonhaugh	28 Oct. 1871
Francis Moore Ward	28 Oct. 1871
Chas. Radley B. Thorne..	28 Oct. 1871
Chas. Hope (Interpreter)	28 Oct. 1871
R. S. R. Fetherstonhaugh	28 Oct. 1871
Godfrey Astell	28 Oct. 1871
Humphrey D. P. Okeden	28 Oct. 1871
Nicholas E. de B. Fenwick	28 Oct. 1871
Walter Henry Holbech..	28 Oct. 1871
William S. Anderson	28 Oct. 1871
Fred. Amelius Beauclerk	28 Oct. 1871
Clement Wm. Archer	28 Oct. 1871
Henry Allfrey..	28 Oct. 1871
Corbet Stapleton Cotton..	28 Oct. 1871
Henry Lowth Farmer	28 Oct. 1871
Robert Henley	28 Oct. 1871
Arthur G. A. Martin	28 Oct. 1871
Mordaunt C. Boyle..	28 Oct. 1871
Sub-Lieutenants	
Horatio R. Mends	30 Dec. 1871
Montagu C. B. F. Walker	6 Mar. 1872
Arthur Powys Vaughan..	29 May 1872
Geoffrey G. Grimwood	24 July 1872
Henry Vere	5 Oct. 1872

Paymasters

Francis FitzPatrick, 2 March, 1855
2nd Lieut., 19 Oct., 1849; Lieut., 31
May, 1854; Hon. Major, 2 March, 1865.

Edward Chas. Grant, 28 Dec., 1855—
Hon. Major, 28 Dec. 1870.

Charles Harrison Hignett, 10 May,
1871; Ensign, 28 July, 1863; Lieut.,
7 November, 1868.

Adjutants —

Henry D. Browne	17 May 1871
Ambrose H. Bircham	8 June 1867
Reginald Chalmer	10 Nov. 1869
Henry S. Marsham	17 Nov. 1869

Instructors of Musketry

Charles G. Fryer	2 Feb. 1870
William Warren	27 July 1866
Edw. W. H. Crofton	3 Jan. 1871
Francis H. Baillie	16 Mar. 1869

Quartermasters

Henry Jarvis	2 Dec. 1862
John Eade	14 Feb. 1866
Wellam Holmes	17 April 1867
Wellam FitzHenry	6 July 1867

Surgeons

Edward Wm. Young, M.D.; Assistant-
Surgeon, 7 Aug. 1856; Surgeon, 8 Dec.,
1864; Surgeon-Major, 7 Aug. 1866.

Alfred Graham Young; Assistant-
Surgeon, 5 May, 1864; Surgeon, 29
June 1865.

Wm. Mackinnon, M.D.; Assistant-
Surgeon, 6 Oct. 1864; Surgeon, 16
March, 1867.

Arthur Edwin Temple Longhurst,
M.D.; Assistant-Surgeon, 27 Oct. 1854;
Surgeon, 4 May, 1867.

Rank and Name.   *Rank in Regiment.*

Assistant-Surgeons—

Alex. C. M'Tavish ..   .. 12 Jan. 1859
Philip L. Kilroy ..   .. 2 Oct. 1862
Wm. H. Harman, M.B...   2 Oct. 1866
Jas. Patrick Rooney   .. 31 Mar. 1866
Wm. Godfrey Martelli .. 31 Mar. 1866

Regimentals — Green, facings scarlet.

Agents—Messrs. Cox and Co.

1874.

Four Battalions.

Canada—England—India—Ireland.

Celer et Audax.

Rolein, Vimiera, Martinique, Talavera, Fuentes d'Onor, Albuhera, Ciudad Rodrigo, Badajoz, Salamanca, Vittoria, Pyrenees, Nivelle, Nive, Orthes, Toulouse, Peninsula, Punjaub, Mooltan, Goojerat, Taku Forts, Pekin, Delhi.

Col.-in-Chief—

Field-Marshal H.R.H. the Duke of Cambridge, K.G., K.P., G.C.B., G.C.M.G., 3 March, 1869.

Cols.-Commandant—

George Fred. Viscount Templetown, K.C.B.— Ensign, 24 April, 1823; Lieut., 29 Oct., 1825 ; Captain, 12 Dec., 1826 ; Major, 16 June, 1837 ; Lieut.-Colonel, 16 April, 1841 ; Colonel, 11 Nov., 1851 ; Major-Gen., 26 Oct., 1858 ; Lieut.-General, 9 March, 1865 ; General, 6 April, 1863 ; Col.-Commandant, 60th Rifles, 24 Oct., 1862.

Henry Viscount Melville, G.C.B.— Ensign and Lieut., 18 March, 1819 ; Captain, 1 April, 1824 ; Major, 11 July, 1826 ; Lieut.-Col., 3 Dec., 1829 ; Col., 28 Nov., 1841 ; Major-Gen., 20 June, 1854 ; Lieut.-General, 5 May, 1860 ; General, 1 Jan., 1868 ; Col.-Comm., 60th Rifles, 1 April, 1863.

Lieut.-Colonels—

Peter Burton Roe 2nd Lieut., 23 July, 1811 ; Lieut., 26 July, 1844 ; Captain, 17 June, 1851 ; Major, 29 April, 1859 ; Lieut.-Colonel, 18 Sept., 1860 ; Colonel, 18 Sept., 1865.

Charles Alexander Boswell Gordon— Ensign, 21 April, 1843 ; Lieut., 13 June, 1845 ; Captain, 6 June, 1851 ; Brevet Major, 6 June, 1856 ; Major, 18 Sept., 1860 ; Brevet Lieut.-Colonel, 1 Jan., 1868 ; Lieut.-Colonel, 9 Aug., 1871.

Hugh Parker Montgomery — 2nd Lieut., 21 Aug., 1849 ; Lieut., 28 Oct., 1853; Captain, 17 Aug., 1855 ; Major, 10 Nov., 1869 ; Lieut.-Colonel, 13 Aug., 1873.

Charles Williamson 2nd Lieut., 11 July, 1851 ; Lieut., 11 Aug., 1854 ;

Lieut.-Colonels (continued)—

Captain, 16 Oct., 1857 ; Major, 9 Aug., 1871 ; Lieut.-Colonel, 18 Oct., 1873.

Majors—

Wykeham Leigh Pemberton—2nd Lieut., 23 April, 1852 ; Lieut., 25 Aug., 1854 ; Captain, 26 March, 1858 ; Major, 28 Oct., 1871.

Rowley Willes Hinxman—2nd Lieut., 23 Nov., 1849 ; Lieut., 3 March, 1854 ; Captain, 15 Jan., 1858 ; Brevet Major, 19 Jan., 1864 ; Major, 24 April, 1872.

Francis Dundas Farquharson—2nd Lieut., 18 Feb., 1853 ; Lieut., 23 March, 1855 ; Captain, 24 April, 1858 ; Brevet Major, 5 July, 1872 ; Major, 1 Feb., 1873.

James Durham Dundas—2nd Lieut., 3 March, 1854 ; Lieut., 23 March, 1855 ; Captain, 22 June, 1858 ; Brevet Major, 12 Nov., 1870 ; Major, 1 April, 1873.

Herbert George Deedes—Assistant Adjutant-General, Rawul Pindee, Bengal ; Ensign, 11 Aug., 1851 ; Lieut., 23 March, 1855 ; Captain, 2 July, 1858 ; Brevet Major, 25 Sept., 1860 ; Brevet Lieut.-Colonel, 30 July, 1871 ; Major, 5 July, 1873.

James Joseph Collins—Ensign, 25 Aug., 1854 ; Lieut., 23 March, 1855 ; Captain, 19 July, 1859 ; Brevet Major, 5 July, 1872 ; Major, 5 July, 1873.

Francis Vernon Northey— Ensign, 22 March, 1855 ; Lieut., 27 July, 1855 ; Captain, 18 May, 1860 ; Brevet Major, 12 Nov., 1870 ; Major, 5 July, 1873.

William Frederick Carleton—Ensign, 30 March, 1855 ; Lieut., 17 Aug., 1855; Captain, 18 Sept., 1860 ; Brevet Major, 23 May, 1873 ; Major, 13 Aug., 1873.

Cromer Ashburnham — Ensign, 20 April, 1855 ; Lieut., 26 Oct., 1855 ; Captain, 23 Jan., 1863 ; Major, 18 Oct., 1873.

Rank and Name.   *Rank in Regiment.*

Captains—

Kennett Gregg Henderson 30 June 1863
J. S. Hamilton Algar .. 17 May 1864
George Charles Kelly .. 6 Oct. 1864
Fred. H. A. Hamilton .. 4 Nov. 1864
Harry Robert Milligan .. 22 Nov. 1864
George Hatchell .. .. 24 Jan. 1865
James Kiero Watson .. 7 May 1865
Wm. Gerard Byron .. 3 Jan. 1865
W. J. Evered Poole.. 3 April 1866
Newton Jones Pauli .. 3 June 1866
Wm. L. Kinloch Ogilvy . 11 Dec. 1866
Hugh St. G. Barton .. 8 Mar. 1867
Reginald H. Beadon .. 16 Oct. 1867
Arthur Tufnell .. .. 23 Oct. 1867
John Charley .. .. .. 14 Aug. 1867
Astley Fellowes Terry .. 8 Dec. 1867
John Gustavus Crosbie .. 20 May 1868
George Hewitt Trotman . 11 Jan. 1869
Nesbit Willoughby Wallace 23 Jan. 1869
Arthur Morris.. .. .. 24 April 1869

Rank and Name.	Rank in Regiment.
Captains (continued)—	
Chas. Matthew Calderon.	9 Feb. 1870
Redvers Henry Buller ..	28 May 1870
Ch. Pierson Cramer ..	28 May 1870
Latham Codd. Browning	20 April 1871
J. Henry H. Crofts	9 April 1871
Francis Wallace Grenfell	28 Oct. 1871
Alex. A. Airlie Kinloch.	8 May 1870
Aubrey Vere O'Brien ..	24 April 1872
C. L. Const. de Robeck ..	24 April 1872
Chas. Gilbert Fryer ..	2 Jan. 1873
William Warren	1 Feb. 1873
P. J. H. Ascough Barne	12 Feb. 1873
George Thos. Whitaker..	26 Feb. 1873
George Carpenter	30 April 1873
R. Collingwood Robinson	28 May 1873
Geo. L. M'Lean Farmer..	5 July 1873
Edw. W. Home Crofton	5 July 1873
Denis Bingham	5 July 1873
J. T. Darnley Crosbie ..	13 Aug. 1873
Francis H. Baillie.. ..	18 Oct. 1873
Lieutenants—	
Walter Cowan.. ..	3 April 1866
F. Chas. Bleu Coulson ..	26 June 1866
Henry Donald Browne .	14 Aug. 1866
Edmund Lennox Fraser..	21 Aug 1866
Reginald Chaloner .	24 Feb 1865
H. R. Ponsonby Lindesay	2 Oct 1866
H. A. Fred. F. Coventry	27 Nov. 1866
William Tilden ..	11 Dec. 1866
H. Blackwood MacColl ..	19 Feb. 1867
Benjamin Fiend	27 Feb. 1867
Amb. Humph. Buchanan..	8 Mar. 1867
J. S. Wynne-Finch ..	15 Mar. 1867
H. A. Houlton Ward ..	7 Aug. 1867
Hon. Cecil Ralph Howard	7 Aug. 1867
P. A. J. Hope-Johnstone	6 Nov. 1867
A. F. H. Mitchell-Innes	20 Nov. 1867
Crawford Lewin Allan ..	25 Dec. 1867
William Forster ..	9 April 1868
Arthur Pepys ..	10 April 1868
Robt. Crosbeck Davies ..	30 June 1868
H. Ph. Miles Wylie ..	28 Oct. 1868
James N. H. Price ..	11 Jan. 1869
Fr John A. Wood ..	23 Jan. 1869
Ch. Hollol Smith ..	3 Feb. 1869
H. Saville Marsham ..	17 Feb. 1869
Thos Sydenham Clarke..	24 April 1869
Ernest H. Thornton ..	29 Mar 1869
J. Aubrey Williams ..	10 Nov. 1869
Albert Aug. Capps ..	5 Jan. 1870
Hon. Keith Turnour ..	9 Feb. 1870
John Henry Barstall ..	28 May 1870
Arthur Greville Bagot ..	14 Dec. 1870
H. S. H. Riddell ..	4 Jan. 1871
Herbert J Hope-Edwardes	22 Mar 1871
Thos. Prince Lloyd ..	29 Nov. 1871
F. B. Newton Dickenson	12 July 1871
Ed. Thos. Henry Hutton	9 Aug 1871
Fulbert Wright Archer	9 Aug 1871
Horace Walpole ..	27 Oct. 1871
John Dowling Howden	30 Nov 1871
Charles Michell ..	28 Oct 1871
Arthur James Brander	28 Oct 1871
H. E. W. Fetherstonhaugh	28 Oct. 1871

Rank and Name.	Rank in Regiment.
Lieutenants (continued)—	
Francis Moore Ward ..	28 Oct. 1871
Ch. R. Brittain Thorne..	28 Oct. 1871
Charles Hope	28 Oct. 1871
R. S. R. Fetherstonhaugh	28 Oct. 1871
Godfrey Astell	28 Oct. 1871
Humph. D. P. Okeden ..	28 Oct. 1871
N. E. de Berner Fenwick	28 Oct. 1871
Walter Henry Holbech..	28 Oct. 1871
Wm. Sturton Anderson..	28 Oct. 1871
Fred. A. Beauclerk.. ..	28 Oct. 1871
Henry Allfrey	28 Oct. 1871
C. Stapleton Cotton ..	28 Oct. 1871
H. Louth Farmer.. ..	28 Oct. 1871
Robert Henley	28 Oct. 1871
Arthur Geo. A. Martin..	28 Oct. 1871
Montague Chas. Bayle ..	28 Oct. 1871
Horatio Reginald Mends	30 Dec. 1871
Sub-Lieutenants—	
Mont. A. D. H. F. Walker.	6 Mar. 1872
Arthur Pelham Vaughan .	29 May 1872
Geoff. Greaves Grinwood	24 July 1872
Henry Very	5 Oct. 1872
E. Obert H. Wilkinson..	9 Aug. 1873
Hon. A. H. F. Greville..	9 Aug. 1873
Herbert Rich. Lovett ..	9 Aug. 1873
Geo. Greville Moore ..	21 Sept. 1872
Basil T. G. Montgomery	5 Oct. 1872
Robert Story	12 Nov. 1873
Eugene A. Sanford.. ..	12 Nov. 1873
R. C. Dighton Wilson ..	26 Mar. 1873

Paymasters—

Francis FitzPatrick, 2 March, 1855 2nd Lieut, 19 Oct, 1843; Lieut., 31 May, 1851; Hon. Major, 2 March, 1865.

Edward Chas. Grant, 28 Dec., 1855 Hon. Major, 28 Dec. 1870.

Charles Harrison Hignett, 10 May, 1871 Ensign, 28 July, 1863; Lieut., 7 Nov., 1868.

Adjutants—

A. G. Bagot	29 July 1874
E. T. Hutton	10 June 1874
H. S. Marsham	17 Nov. 1869
T. S. Clarke	6 Nov. 1873

Instructors of Musketry—

William Tilden	1 Nov. 1873
H. James Hope-Edwardes	16 June 1874
A. G. H. Martin ..	10 June 1874
P. A. J. Hope-Johnstone.	19 May 1873

Quartermasters—

F. Jarvis	2 Dec. 1862
John Toole	13 Feb. 1865
Wm. Hollows ..	17 April 1867
Wm. Litchfield ..	6 July 1867

Medical Officers—

Adam Graham Young, Surgeon-Major, Assistant-Surgeon, 5 May, 1854; Surgeon, 23 June, 1865.

Wm. Mactaggart, M.D., Surgeon-Major; Assistant-Surgeon, 6 Oct., 1854; Surgeon, 16 March 1867.

T 2

Medical Officers (continued)—

Arthur Edward Temple Longhurst, M.D., Surgeon-Maj.; Assistant-Surgeon, 27 Oct., 1854; Surgeon, 1 May, 1867. Wm. Silver Oliver, M.D., Surgeon-Major; Surgeon, 3 Feb., 1872.

Regimentals—Green, facings scarlet.

Agents—Messrs. Cox and Co.

Irish Agents—Sir E. Borough, Bt., and Co.

1875.

Four Battalions.

Canada—India—England—Ireland.

Celer et Audax.

Rolcia, Vimiera, Martinique, Talavera, Fuentes d'Onor, Albuhera, Ciudad Rodrigo, Badajoz, Salamanca, Vittoria, Pyrenees, Nivelle, Nive, Orthes, Toulouse, Peninsula, Punjaub, Mooltan, Goojerat, Taku Forts, Pekin, Delhi.

Col.-in-Chief—

Field Marshal H.R.H. the Duke of Cambridge, K.G., K.P., G.C.B., G.C.M.G., 3 March, 1869.

Cols.-Commandant

George Fred., Viscount Templetown, K.C.B. Ensign, 24 April, 1823; Lieut., 29 Oct., 1825; Captain, 12 Dec., 1826; Major, 16 June, 1837; Lieut.-Colonel, 16 April, 1841; Colonel, 11 Nov., 1851; Major-Gen., 26 Oct., 1858; Lieut.-Gen., 9 March, 1865; General, 6 April, 1873; Col. Com., 60th Rifles, 24 Oct., 1862.

Henry Viscount Melville, G.C.B.—Ensign and Lieut., 18 Nov., 1819; Capt., 1 April, 1824; Major, 11 July, 1826; Lieut.-Colonel, 3 Dec., 1829; Colonel, 28 Nov., 1841; Major-Gen., 20 June, 1854; Lieut.-Gen., 5 May, 1860; Gen., 1 Jan., 1868; Col.-Commandant, 60th Rifles, 1 April 1863.

Lieut.-Colonels—

Peter Barton Roe—2nd Lieut., 23 July, 1811; Lieut., 26 July, 1811; Captain, 17 June, 1851; Major, 29 April, 1859; Lieut.-Colonel, 18 Sept., 1860; Colonel, 18 Sept., 1865.

Charles Alex. Boswell Gordon—Ensign, 24 April, 1813; Lieut., 13 June 1845; Captain, 6 June, 1854; Brevet Major, 6 June, 1856; Major, 18 Sept., 1860; Brevet Lieut.-Colonel, 1 Jan., 1868; Lieut.-Colonel, 9 Aug., 1871.

Hugh Parker Montgomery—2nd Lieut., 24 Aug., 1849; Lieut., 28 Oct., 1853; Captain, 17 Aug., 1855; Major, 10 Nov., 1869; Lieut.-Colonel, 13 Aug., 1873.

Charles Williamson—2nd Lieut., 11 July, 1851; Lieut., 11 Aug., 1854; Captain, 16 Oct., 1857; Major, 9 Aug., 1871; Lieut.-Colonel, 18 Oct., 1873.

Majors—

Wykeham Leigh Pemberton—2nd Lieut., 23 April, 1852; Lieut., 25 Aug., 1854; Captain, 23 March, 1858; Major 28 Oct., 1871.

Rowley Willes Hinxman—Assistant Adjutant-General, Lahore Division, Bengal—2nd Lieut., 23 Nov., 1849; Lieut., 3 Mar., 1854; Captain, 15 Jan., 1858; Brevet Major, 19 Jan., 1864; Major, 24 April, 1872; Brevet Lieut.-Colonel, 7 Jan., 1874.

Francis Dundas Farquharson—2nd Lieut., 18 Feb., 1853; Lieut., 23 Mar., 1855; Captain, 24 April, 1858; Brevet Major, 5 July, 1872; Major, 1 Feb. 1873.

James Durham Dundas—2nd Lieut., 3 Mar., 1854; Lieut., 23 Mar., 1855; Captain, 22 June, 1858; Brevet Major, 12 Nov., 1870; Major, 1 April, 1873.

Herbert George Deedes, Private Secretary to the Secretary of State for War—Ensign, 11 Aug., 1854; Lieut., 23 March, 1855; Captain, 2 July, 1858; Brevet Major, 25 Sept., 1860; Brevet Lieut.-Colonel, 30 July, 1871; Major, 5 July, 1873.

James Joseph Collins—Ensign, 25 Aug., 1854; Lieut., 23 March, 1855; Captain, 19 July, 1859; Brevet Major, 5 July, 1872; Major, 5 July, 1873.

Francis Vernon Northey—Ensign, 22 March, 1855; Lieut., 27 July, 1855; Captain, 18 May, 1860; Brevet Major, 12 Nov., 1870; Major, 5 July, 1873.

William Fred. Carleton—Ensign, 30 March, 1855; Lieut., 17 Aug., 1855; Captain, 18 Sept., 1860; Brevet Major, 23 May, 1873; Major, 13 Aug., 1873.

Cromer Ashburnham—Ensign, 20 April, 1855; Lieut., 26 Oct., 1855; Captain, 23 Jan., 1863; Major, 18 Oct., 1873.

Kennett Gregg Henderson—Ensign, 23 April, 1855; Lieut., 6 May, 1856; Captain, 30 June, 1863; Major, 27 Mar., 1874.

Captains

	Rank and Name.	Rank in Regiment.
James Sturgeon Hamilton Algar	.. ..	17 May 1864
Geo. Chas. Kelly	.. ..	6 Oct. 1864
Fredk. Hardinge Anson Hamilton	.. .. ..	4 Nov. 1864
Harry Robert Milligan	..	22 Nov. 1864
Geo. Hatchell, Brigade Major, Chatham	..	24 Jan. 1865
James Kiero Watson	..	1 May 1865
William Gerard Byron	..	3 Jan. 1865
William John E. Poole, Adjutant, 4th Middlesex Rifle Volunteers	..	3 April 1866
Newton Jones Pauli	..	5 June 1866
W. L. K. Ogilvy, Adjutant 1st Adm. Batt., Aberdeen Volunteers	.. ..	11 Dec. 1866
Hugh St. Geo. Barton	..	8 Mar. 1867

Rank and Name.	Rank in Regiment.
Captains (continued) —	
Reginald H. Beadon ..	16 Oct. 1867
Arthur Tufnell	23 Oct. 1867
John Charley	14 Aug. 1867
A. F. Terry, Adjutant 5th Adm. Batt., Cheshire Rifle Volunteers ..	8 Dec. 1867
John Gustavus Crosbie ..	20 May 1868
George Hewitt Trotman..	11 Jan. 1869
Nesbit Willoughby Wallace	23 Jan. 1869
Arthur Morris	24 April 1869
Chas. Matthew Caldiron	9 Feb. 1870
R. H. Buller, C.B., Deputy Assist. Adj. General ..	28 May 1870
Rank in Army, Bt. Major	1 Apr. 1874
Charles Pierson Cramer .	28 May 1870
Latham Coddington Brownrigg	30 April 1871
Jas. Hen. Herbert Croft .	9 Aug. 1871
F. W. Grenfell, A.D.C. to Sir A. Cunynghame .	28 Oct. 1871
Alex. Angus Airlie Kinloch, D.A.A. General for Musketry, Rawal Pindee	8 May 1870
Aubrey Vere O'Brien, Adj., Clare Militia	24 April 1872
Chas. Lewis Constantine de Boissl . ..	24 April 1872
Chas. Gilbert Fryer ..	2 Jan. 1873
William Warron ..	1 Feb. 1873
Philip Julius H. A. Baron	12 Feb. 1873
George Thos. Whitaker..	26 Feb. 1873
George Carpenter ..	30 April 1873
Richard Collingwood Robinson	28 May 1873
Geo. L. M'Lean Farmer, A.D.C. to the Gov-Gen. of India	5 July 1873
Edward Walter Home Crofton..	5 July 1873
Denis Baughan	5 July 1873
John T. D. Crosbie, A.D.C. to Brigadier - General Herbert	13 Aug 1873
Walter Cowan.. ..	12 Nov. 1873
Henry Donald Browne ..	27 Mar. 1873
Edmund Lomax Fraser..	1 April 1874
Reginald Chalmer	2 April 1874
Hen. R. Ponsonby Lindesay	19 Sept. 1874
Lieutenants	
William Tibben ..	11 Dec. 1866
Hen. Blackwood MacCull	19 Feb. 1867
Benjamin Freud	27 Feb. 1867
Aub. Humphrys Burcham	8 Mar. 1867
J. Seymour Wynne-Finch, A.D.C. to Sir H. de Bathe	15 Mar. 1867
H. Adlock Boulton Ward	7 Aug. 1867
Hen. Cecil Ralph Howard	7 Aug. 1867
Percy Alex. John Hope-Johnstone	6 Nov. 1867
Alex. Ferdinand Henry Mitchell Innes ..	20 Nov. 1867
Crawford Lewin Allan .	25 Dec. 1867
William Forster ..	9 April 1868

Rank and Name.	Rank in Regiment.
Lieutenants (continued) —	
Arthur Pepys	10 April 1868
Robt. Cradock Davies .	30 June 1868
Hen. Philip Miles Wylie.	28 Oct. 1868
James Nugent Blackwood-Price	11 Jan. 1869
Francis J. Adelbert Wood	23 Jan. 1869
Chas. Hellet Smith ..	3 Feb. 1869
Henry Savile Marsham..	17 Feb. 1869
Thos. Sydenham Clarke..	24 Apr. 1869
Ernest Hovel Thurlow ..	29 May 1869
John Aubrey Williams ..	10 Nov. 1869
Albert Augustus Clopps.	5 Jan. 1870
Hon. Keith Turnour ..	9 Feb. 1870
John Henry Burstall ..	28 May 1870
Arthur O. Bagot	14 Dec. 1870
Henry Somerville Hutton Riddell..	4 Jan. 1871
Herbert James Hope-Edwardes	22 Mar. 1871
Thomas Prince Lloyd ..	29 Nov. 1864
Fiennes Boughton Newton Dickenson	12 July 1871
Edwd. Thos. Hen. Hutton	9 Aug. 1871
Fulbert Wright Archer .	9 Aug. 1871
Horace Walpole	27 Oct. 1871
John Docking Howden..	30 Nov. 1871
Charles Michell	28 Oct. 1871
Arthur James Braunder .	28 Oct. 1871
Hen. Ernest Wm. Fetherstonhaugh	28 Oct. 1871
Francis Moore Ward ..	28 Oct. 1871
Charles Radley Brittain Thorne	28 Oct. 1871
Charles Hope	28 Oct. 1871
Richard Steele Rupert Fetherstonhaugh ..	28 Oct. 1871
Godfrey Astell	28 Oct. 1871
Humphrey David Parry Okeden	28 Oct. 1871
Nicholas Edward de Berner Fenwick	28 Oct. 1871
Walter Henry Hollech..	28 Oct. 1871
Wm. Sturrock Anderson.	28 Oct. 1871
Fred. Amelius Beauclerk	28 Oct. 1871
Henry Allfrey.. ..	28 Oct. 1871
Corbet Stapleton Cotton	28 Oct. 1871
Henry Lowth Farmer ..	28 Oct. 1871
Robert Henley	28 Oct. 1871
Arthur George A. Martin	28 Oct. 1871
Mordaunt Charles Boyle	28 Oct. 1871
Horatio Reginald Meade	30 Dec. 1871
Montagu C. B. F. Walker	6 Mar. 1872
Arthur Powys Vaughan.	29 May 1872
Geoffry Grimwood Grimwood	24 July 1872
Henry Vere	5 Oct. 1872
Robt. Chas. D. Wilson .	19 Oct. 1872
J. Herbert Carteret Carey	12 Nov. 1873
Lionel Wm. Herbert ..	2 Dec. 1874
Sub-Lieutenants	
Edward Obert Hincey Wilkinson	2 Aug. 1873
Hon. Moore Henry F. Greville	9 Aug. 1873
Hubert Richard Lovett..	9 Aug. 1873

Rank and Name.   *Rank in Regiment.*

Sub-Lieutenants (continued)—

George Greville Moore .. 21 Sept. 1872
Basil Temple G. Mont-
gomery.. .. .. .. 6 Oct. 1872
Robert Story .. .. .. 12 Nov. 1873
Eugene Ayshford Sanford 12 Nov. 1873
Robert Erskine Wade C.
Crawford .. .. .. 7 Jan. 1874
Grenville Hylton Wells.. 28 Feb. 1874
Guy Theophilus Campbell 28 Feb. 1874
Fredk. Savill Marshum .. 15 Jan. 1873
Charles Baldwyn Childe
Pemberton .. .. .. 28 Feb. 1874
Robt. Henry Gunning .. 26 Mar. 1873
George Vere Boyle.. .. 18 Mar. 1874

Paymasters—

Francis FitzPatrick, 2 March, 1855—
2nd Lieut., 10 Oct., 1849; Lieut., 31
May, 1854; Hon. Major, 2 Mar., 1865.
Edw. Charles Grant, 28 Dec., 1855 —
Hon. Major, 28 Dec., 1870.
William Fred. Nixon, 8 Jan., 1841—
Ensign, 3 Aug., 1830; Lieut., 22 Jan.,
1836; Hon. Major, 1 Jan., 1860.

Adjutants—

A. G. Bagot .. .. .. 29 July 1874
E. T. Hutton .. .. .. 10 June 1874
H. S. Marshum .. .. 17 Nov. 1869
T. S. Clarke .. .. .. 6 Nov. 1873

Instructors of Musketry—

William Tilden .. .. 1 Nov. 1873
H. James Hope-Edwardes 16 June 1873
A. G. H. Martin .. .. 10 June 1874
P. A. J. Hope-Johnstone 19 May 1873

Quartermasters —

John Toole .. .. .. 13 Feb. 1866
William Holmes .. .. 17 April 1867
William FitzHenry .. 6 July 1867
William Robinson .. .. 12 Aug. 1874

Medical Officers ·

Adam Graham Young, Surgeon-Maj.;
Surgeon, 29 June, 1865.
William Macnamara, M.D., Surgeon-
Major; Surgeon, 16 Mar., 1867.
Arthur Edwin Temple Longhurst,
M.D., Surg. Maj.; Surgeon, 1 May, 1867.
William Silver Oliver, M.D., Surgeon
Major; Surgeon, 3 Feb., 1873.

Regimentals- Green, facings scarlet.

Agents— Messrs. Cox and Co.

Irish Agents— Sir E. Borough, Bt., and Co.

1876.

Four Battalions.

Canada— India— England— Ireland.

Celer et Audax.

Rolein, Vimiera, Martinique, Talavera,
Fuentes d'Onor, Albuhera, Ciudad
Rodrigo, Badajoz, Salamanca, Vittoria,
Pyrenees, Nivelle, Nive, Orthes, Tou-
louse, Peninsula, Punjaub, Mooltan,
Goojerat, Taku Forts, Pekin, Delhi.

Col.-in-Chief—

Field-Marshal H.R.H. the Duke of
Cambridge, K.G., K.P., G.C.B.,
G.C.M.G., 3 March, 1869.

Cols.-Commandant—

George Fred., Viscount Templetown,
K.C.B.—Ensign, 24 April, 1823; Lieut.,
29 Oct., 1825; Captain, 12 Dec., 1826;
Major, 16 June, 1837; Lieut.-Colonel,
16 April, 1841; Colonel, 11 Nov., 1851;
Major-General, 26 Oct., 1858; Lieut.-
General, 9 March, 1865; General, 6
April, 1873; Col.-Comm., 60th Rifles,
24 Oct., 1872.
Henry, Viscount Melville, G.C.B.—
Ensign and Lieut., 18 Nov., 1819;
Captain, 1 April, 1824; Major, 11 July,
1826; Lieut.-Colonel, 3 Dec., 1829;
Colonel, 28 Nov., 1841; Major-General,
20 June, 1854; Lieut.-General, 5 May,
1860; General, 1 Jan., 1868; Col.-Com.,
60th Rifles, 1 April, 1863.

Lieut.-Colonels -

Charles Alexander Boswell Gordon—
Ensign, 21 April, 1843; Lieut., 13
June, 1845; Captain, 6 June, 1854;
Brevet Major, 6 June, 1856; Major,
18 Sept., 1860; Brevet Lieut.-Colonel,
1 Jan., 1868; Lieut.-Col., 9 Aug., 1871.
Hugh Parker Montgomery—2nd
Lieut., 21 Aug., 1849; Lieut., 28 Oct.,
1853; Captain, 17 Aug., 1855; Major,
10 Nov., 1869; Lieut.-Colonel, 13 Aug.,
1873.
Wykeham Leigh Pemberton—2nd
Lieut., 23 April, 1852; Lieut., 25 Aug.,
1854; Captain, 23 March, 1858; Major,
28 Oct., 1871; Lieut.-Colonel, 10
March, 1875.
Rowley Willes Hinxman—2nd Lieut.,
23 Nov., 1849; Lieut., 3 March, 1854;
Captain, 15 Jan., 1858; Brevet Major,
19 Jan., 1864; Major, 24 April, 1872;
Brevet Lieut.-Colonel, 7 Jan., 1874;
Lieut.-Colonel, 5 June, 1875.

Majors—

Francis Dundas Farquharson—2nd
Lieut., 18 Feb., 1853; Lieut., 23 March,
1855; Captain, 24 April, 1858; Brevet
Major, 5 July, 1872; Major, 1 Feb.,
1873.
James Durham Dundas - 2nd Lieut.,
3 March, 1854; Lieut., 23 March, 1855;
Captain, 22 June, 1858; Brevet Major,
12 Nov., 1870; Major, 1 April, 1873.
Herbert George Deedes, Private
Secretary to the Secretary of State for
War— Ensign, 11 Aug., 1854; Lieut.,
23 March, 1855; Captain, 2 July, 1858;
Brevet Major, 25 Sept., 1860; Brevet
Lieut.-Colonel, 30 July, 1871; Major,
5 July, 1873.
James Joseph Collins- Ensign, 25
Aug., 1854; Lieut., 23 March, 1855;
Captain, 19 July, 1859; Brevet Major,
5 July, 1872; Major, 5 July, 1873.

Majors (continued)—

Francis Vernon Northey—Ensign, 22 March, 1855 ; Lieut., 27 July, 1855 ; Captain, 18 May, 1860 ; Brevet Major, 12 Nov., 1870 ; Major, 5 July, 1873.

William Frederick Carleton—Ensign, 30 March, 1855 ; Lieut., 17 Aug., 1855 ; Captain, 18 Sept., 1860 ; Brevet Major, 23 Mar., 1873 ; Major, 13 Aug., 1873.

Cromer Ashburnham—Ensign, 20 April, 1855 ; Lieut., 26 Oct., 1855 ; Captain, 23 Jan., 1863 ; Major, 18 Oct., 1873.

Kennett Gregg Henderson—Ensign, 23 April, 1855 ; Lieut., 6 May, 1856 ; Captain, 30 June, 1863 ; Major, 27 March, 1874.

James Sturgeon Hamilton Algar— Ensign, 10 May, 1855 ; Lieut., 9 May, 1856 ; Captain, 17 May, 1864 ; Major, 10 March, 1875.

Rank and Name.	Rank or **Regiment**.
Captains—	
George Charles Keily	6 Oct. 1864
F. H. Anson Hamilton	4 Nov. 1864
Harry Robert Milligan	22 Nov. 1864
George Hatchell, Brigade Major, Chatham	23 Jan. 1865
James Kiero Watson	1 May 1865
Wm. Gerard Byron	3 Jan. 1866
William J. Everel Poole, Adj., 4th Middlesex Rifle Volunteers	3 April 1866
Newton Jones Pauli	5 June 1866
Wm. L. Knolch Ogilvy, Adjutant to Adam Buriel Aberdeenshire Rifle Volunteers	11 Dec. 1866
Reginald H. Beadon	16 Oct. 1867
Arthur Tufnell	24 Oct. 1867
John Charles	14 Aug. 1867
A. Fellowes Perry, Adj. 4th Ashby Battalion Rifle Volunteers	8 Dec. 1867
John Groft Cookle	20 May 1868
George Hewitt Trelvan	11 Jan. 1869
N. Willoughby Wallace	23 Jan. 1869
Arthur Morris	24 April 1869
C. Matthew Cameron	3 Feb. 1870
Rodiers Henry Bulfer, C.B., Deputy Assistant Adjutant-General	28 May 1870
Rank in Army, Lt. May. 1 April 1857	
C. Pierson Cramer	28 May 1870
L. Codlington Browning	20 April 1871
J. Henry Herbert Croft	9 Aug. 1871
Francis Wallace Grenfell, Aide-de-Camp to Sir A Cunynghame	28 Oct. 1871
Alex. Angus Airlie Knoloch, Deputy Assistant Adjutant-General for Musketry, Bengal Presidency	8 May 1870
Aubrey Vere O'Brien, Adjutant Chee. Militia	24 April 1872
Charles Louis Constantine de Roebeck	23 April 1872

Rank and Name.	**Rank and Regiment.**
Captains (continued)—	
Wm. Warren	1 Feb. 1873
Ph. J. H. A. Barne	12 Feb. 1873
George Thos. Whitaker	26 Feb. 1873
George Carpenter	30 April 1873
R. Collingwood Robinson	28 May 1873
George Lancelot M'Lean Farmer, Aide-de-Camp to the Governor-General of India	**5 July 1873**
E. W. Home Crofton	**5 July 1873**
Denis Bingham	**5 July 1873**
J. T. Durnley Crosbie, Aide-de-Camp to Brigadier-General Herbert	13 Aug. 1873
Walter Cowan	12 Nov. 1873
H. Donald Browne	27 Mar. 1874
Edm. Lemax Fraser	1 April 1874
Reginald Chalmer	2 April 1874
Henry Richard Ponsonby Lindesay	19 Sept. 1874
Wm. Tilden	10 Mar. 1875
H. Blackwood MacCall	1 April 1866
Benjamin Frend	12 May 1875
Amb. Humph. Bircham	13 May 1875
H. Affleck Houlton Ward	1 Dec. 1875
Lieutenants	
Hon. Cecil **Ralph Howard**	7 Aug. 1867
Percy Alex **John Hope** Johnstone	6 Nov. 1867
Alex. Ferdinand Henry Mitchell-Innes	20 Nov. 1867
Crawford Lewin Allan	25 Dec. 1867
Wm. Forster	9 April 1868
Arthur Pepys	10 April 1868
Robert Cradock Davies	30 June 1868
Henry Fh. Miles Wyhe	28 Oct. 1868
J. N. Blackwood-Price	11 Jan. 1869
F. J. Melbert Wood	23 Jan. 1869
Charles Hellel Smith	3 Feb. 1869
Henry Saville Marsham	17 Feb. 1869
Thomas Sydenham Clarke	24 April 1869
Ernest H. Thurlow	29 May 1869
J. Aubrey Williams	10 Nov. 1869
Hon. Keith Turnour	9 Feb. 1870
John Henry Burstall	28 May 1870
H. Somerville Hutton Riddell	4 Jan. 1871
Herbert James Hope-Edwardes	22 Mar. 1871
Thomas Prince Lloyd	29 Nov. 1864
Furnies Houghton Newton Dickenson	12 July 1871
Edward Thomas Henry Hatton	9 Aug. 1871
Fulbert W. Archer	9 Aug. 1871
Horace Walpole	27 Oct. 1871
John Dowling Howden	30 Nov. 1871
Charles Michell	28 Oct. 1871
Henry Ernest William Fetherstonhaugh	28 Oct. 1871
Francis Moore Ward	28 Oct. 1871
Ch. R. Brittan Thorne	28 Oct. 1871
Charles Hope (Interpreter)	28 Oct. 1871
R. S. R. Fetherstonhaugh	28 Oct. 1871
Godfrey Astell	28 Oct. 1871

Rank and Name.	Rank in Regiment.
Lieutenants (continued)—	
Humph. D. Parry Okeden	28 Oct. 1871
Nicholas Edw. de Berner	
Fenwick	28 Oct. 1871
Walter Henry Holbech ..	28 Oct. 1871
Wm. Sturrock Anderson	28 Oct. 1871
Fred. A. Beauclerk.. ..	28 Oct. 1871
Henry Alifrey..	28 Oct. 1871
Corbet Stapleton Cotton..	28 Oct. 1871
Henry Lowth Farmer ..	28 Oct. 1871
Robert Henley	28 Oct. 1871
Arthur George Addey	
Martin	28 Oct. 1871
Mordaunt Charles Boyle	28 Oct. 1871
Horatio Reginald Meuds	30 Dec. 1871
Montagu Chas. Brudenell	
Forestier Walker ..	6 Mar. 1872
Arthur Powys Vaughan..	29 May 1872
Geoff. Grim. Grimwood..	24 July 1872
Henry Vere	5 Oct. 1872
Ed. O. H. Wilkinson ..	9 Aug. 1873
Basil Templer Graham	
Montgomery	5 Oct. 1872
R. Ch. Dighton Wilson..	19 Oct. 1872
J. H. Carteret Carey ..	12 Nov. 1873
Hon. Alwyne H. Fulke	
Greville	9 Aug. 1874
Hubert Richard Lovett..	9 Aug. 1874
Frederick Savill Marsham	15 Jan. 1873
Edward Wm. Herbert ..	2 Dec. 1874
H. E. M. D. Clotworthy	
Upton	5 Oct. 1873
North More Nisbitt ..	6 Oct. 1875
Robt. George Buchanan-	
Riddell..	20 Nov. 1875
Hon. Conway Stratford	
George Canning.. ..	20 Nov. 1875
Sub-Lieutenants—	
George Greville Moore ..	21 Sept. 1872
Robert Story	12 Nov. 1873
E. Ayshford Sanford ..	12 Nov. 1873
Robert Erskine Wade	
Copland-Crawford ..	7 Jan. 1874
Greville Hylton Wells ..	28 Feb. 1874
Guy Thos. Campbell ..	28 Feb. 1874
Robert Henry Gunning..	26 Mar. 1873
Gilbert Samuel Baynes ..	11 Feb. 1875
Paymasters—	
Francis FitzPatrick, 2 March, 1855 —	
2nd Lieut.. 19 Oct., 1849; Lieut, 31	
May, 1851; Hon. Major, 2 March, 1865.	
Edward Charles Grant, 28 Dec., 1855	
—Hon. Major, 28 Dec., 1870.	
Wm. Fred. Nixon, 8 Jan., 1841 —	
Ensign, 3 Aug., 1830; Lieut., 22 Jan.,	
1836; Hon. Major, 1 Jan., 1860.	
Arthur Gore Anderson, 16 Aug.,	
1829 Ensign, 5 March, 1858; Hon.	
Major, 5 March, 1875.	
Adjutants—	
M. C. Boyle	13 Nov. 1875
E. T. Hutton	10 June 1874
T. S. Clarke	6 Nov. 1873
E. O. H. Wilkinson ..	1 Dec. 1875
Instructors of Musketry—	
A. G. A. Martin	10 June 1874

Rank and Name.	Rank in Regiment.
Instructors of Musketry (continued)—	
H. J. Hope-Edwardes ..	16 June 1873
P. A. J. Hope-Johnstone	19 May 1873
C. Michell	15 July 1876
Quartermasters—	
Wm. Holmes	17 April 1867
Wm. FitzHenry	6 July 1867
Wm. Robinson	12 Aug. 1874
Medical Officers—	
Adam Graham Young, Surgeon-	
Major; Surgeon, 20 June, 1865.	
Wm. Macnamara, M.D., Surgeon-	
Major; Surgeon, 16 March, 1867.	
Wm. Silver Oliver, M.D., Surgeon-	
Major; Surgeon, 3 Feb., 1872.	
Wm. Morton Harman, Surgeon,	
Assistant-Surgeon, 2 Oct., 1866.	

Regimentals—Green, facings scarlet.

Agents—Messrs. Cox and Co.

Irish Agents—Sir E. Borough, Bt., and Co.

1877.

Four Battalions.

England—India.

Celer et Audax.

Roleia, Vimiera, Martinique, Talavera, Fuentes d'Onor, Albuhera, Ciudad Rodrigo, Badajoz, Salamanca, Vittoria, Pyrenees, Nivelle, Nive, Orthes, Toulouse, Peninsula, Punjaub, Mooltan, Goojerat, Taku Forts, Pekin, Delhi.

Col.-in-Chief—
Field-Marshal H.R.H. the Duke of Cambridge, K.G., K.P., G.C.B., G.C.M.G., 3 March, 1869.

Cols.-Commandant—
Sir A. A. T. Cunynghame, K.C.B., Lieut.-General—2nd Lieut., 2 Nov., 1830; Lieut., 22 May, 1835; Captain, 17 Aug., 1841; Major, 8 Aug., 1845; Lieut.-Colonel, 3 Nov., 1846; Colonel, 20 June, 1854; Major-General, 20 April, 1861; Lieut.-General, 20 Oct., 1870; General, 1 Oct., 1877; Col.-Com. 60th Rifles, 2 Feb., 1876.

Freeman Murray, Lieut.-General— Ensign, 24 Feb., 1825; Lieut., 8 April, 1826; Captain, 21 Dec., 1832; Major, 20 Aug., 1844; Lieut.-Colonel, 5 Nov., 1847; Colonel, 28 Nov., 1854; Major-General, 13 Aug., 1862; Lieut.-General, 25 Oct., 1871; General, 1 Oct., 1877; Col.-Comm., 60th Rifles, 11 Oct., 1876.

Lieut.-Colonels—
Charles Alexander Boswell Gordon— Ensign, 21 April, 1843; Lieut., 13 June, 1845; Captain, 6 June, 1854; Brevet Major, 6 June, 1856; Major, 18 Sept., 1860; Brevet Lieut.-Colonel, 1 Jan., 1868; Lieut.-Colonel, 9 Aug., 1871.

Hugh Parker Montgomery 2nd Lt.,

Lieut.-Colonels (continued)—
21 Aug., 1849; Lieut., 28 Oct., 1853;
Captain, 17 Aug., 1855; Major, 10 Nov.,
1869; Lieut.-Colonel, 13 Aug., 1873.

Wykeham Leigh Pemberton—2nd
Lieut., 23 April, 1852; Lieut., 25 Aug.,
1854; Captain, 23 March, 1858; Major,
28 Oct., 1871; Lieut.-Colonel, 10 Mar.,
1875.

Majors—

Rowley Willes Hinxman—2nd Lieut.,
23 Nov., 1849; Lieut., 3 March, 1854;
Captain, 15 Jan., 1858; Brevet Major,
19 Jan., 1864; Major, 24 April, 1872;
Brevet Lieut.-Colonel, 7 Jan., 1874;
Lieut.-Colonel, 5 June, 1875.

James Durham Bomlow—2nd Lieut.,
3 March, 1854; Lieut., 23 March, 1855;
Captain, 22 June, 1858; Brevet Major,
12 Nov., 1870; Major, 1 April, 1873.

H. G. Deedes, Lieut.-Col., Private
Secretary to the Secretary of State for
War—Ensign, 11 Aug., 1854; Lieut.,
23 March, 1855; Captain, 2 July, 1858;
Brevet Major, 25 Sept., 1869; Brevet
Lieut.-Colonel, 26 July, 1871; Major,
6 July, 1873.

James Joseph Colnon—Ensign, 25
Aug., 1854; Lieut., 23 March, 1855;
Captain, 19 July, 1858; Brevet Major,
5 July, 1872.

Francis Vernon Northey, Ensign,
22 Mar., 1855; Lieut., 27 July, 1855;
Captain, 18 May, 1860; Brevet Major,
12 Nov., 1870; Major, 5 July, 1873

Cramer Ashburnham Ensign, 20
April, 1855; Lieut., 26 Oct., 1855;
Captain, 23 Jan., 1861; Major, 18 Oct.,
1873

Kennett Gregg Henderson, Ensign,
23 April, 1855; Lieut., 6 May, 1856;
Captain, 30 June, 1861; Major, 27
March, 1874

James Sturgeon Hamilton Agar, Ensign, 19 May, 1855; Lieut., 9 May, 1856;
Captain, 17 May, 1861; Major, 19 Mar.,
1875

H. R. Milligan, Ensign, 16 Feb., 1855;
Lieut., 23 Nov., 1855; Capt., 22 Nov.,
1861; Major, 11 Nov., 1876

George Hatch B., Ensign, 22 Oct.
1855; Lieut., 27 Sept., 1857; Captain,
24 Jan., 1865; Major, ?? Nov., 1876

Rank and Name
Captains—
J. K. Waller ...   1 May 1865
W. G. Bryer ...   3 Jan. 1865
W. J. E. Peel, Adj. Ich
    Middlesex Rifle Vols., 3 April 1866
N. J. Peel ...   5 June 1866
W.I. K. Ogilvy, Adjutant.
    1st Aberdeenshire R.V. 11 Dec. 1866
R. H. Bendon ...   16 Oct. 1867
A. Tufnell ...   23 Oct. 1867
John Charles ...   14 Aug. 1867
A. F. Terry, Adj. 5th Ad.
    Batt. Cheshire R. Vols. 8 Dec. 1867

Rank and Name		Rank in Regiment.
Captains (continued)—		
J. O. Crosbie ..	..	20 May **1868**
G. H. Trotman	..	11 Jan. **1869**
N. W. Wallace	..	23 Jan. **1869**
Arthur Morris ..	..	24 April **1869**
C. M. Calderon	..	9 Feb. **1870**
R. H. Buller, C.B., Dep.		
Asst. Adj.-General		**28 May 1870**
Rank in Army, Bt.-Maj.		1 April **1874**
C. P. Cramer ..	..	28 May **1870**
L. C. Browning	..	20 April **1871**
J. H. H. Croft	..	9 Aug. **1871**
F. W. Grenfell, A.D.C.		
to Sir A. Cunynghame		28 Oct. **1871**
A. A. A. Kinloch, Deputy		
Asst. Adjut.-General		
for Musketry, Royal		
Poulice ..	..	**8 May 1870**
A. V. O'Brien, Adj. Clare		
Militia		24 April **1872**
C. L. Crosbie de Roback		24 April **1872**
William Warren ..	..	1 Feb. **1873**
P. J. H. A. Barter ..	..	12 Feb. **1873**
O. J. Whitaker	..	26 Feb. **1873**
George Carpenter ..	..	30 April **1873**
R. C. Robinson	..	28 May **1873**
H. L. M'Jean, Farmer	..	5 July **1873**
E. W. H. Crofton ..	..	5 July **1875**
Percy Bingham ..	..	5 July **1873**
J. F. D. Crosbie A.D.C.		
to Brig.-Gen. Merthyr		13 Aug. **1873**
H. D. Browne ..	..	27 Mar. **1874**
F. L. Lesser ..	..	1 April **1874**
Roy Chalmer ..	..	2 April **1874**
William Eden ..	..	10 Mar. **1875**
H. R. Marshall, A.D.C.		
to Com.-in-Chief		1 April **1875**
B. Freud ..	..	12 May **1875**
A. H. Burcham ..	..	13 May **1875**
H. A. H. Ward ..	..	1 Dec. **1875**
Hon. C. R. Howard ..	..	5 Jan. **1876**
P. A. J. Heyer-Johnstone		24 June **1876**
A. E. H. Mitchell-Innes..		12 Aug. **1876**
P. A. R. Jones ..	..	17 May **1876**
C. L. Allen ..	..	11 Nov. **1876**
William Foster	..	29 Nov. **1876**
Lieutenants—		
A. Pepys ..	..	10 April **1868**
R. C. Davies ..	..	30 June **1868**
H. P. M. Wylie ..	..	20 Oct. **1868**
J. N. Blackwood-Price..		11 Jan. **1869**
F. J. A. Wood ..	..	23 Jan. **1869**
C. H. Smith ..	..	3 Feb. **1869**
H. S. Marsham ..	..	17 Feb. **1869**
J. S. Clarke ..	..	24 April **1869**
L. H. E. Row ..	..	29 May **1869**
Hon. Keith Turnour ..		9 Feb. **1870**
J. H. Russell ..	..	28 May **1870**
H. S. H. Russell ..	..	4 Jan. **1871**
H. J. Hope Edwardes ..		22 Mar. **1871**
T. P. Lloyd ..	..	29 Nov. **1871**
E. H. N. De Saxe ..		12 July **1871**
G. F. H. Hatton ..	..	9 Aug. **1871**
F. W. Archer ..	..	9 Aug. **1871**
Horace Walpole ..	..	27 Oct. **1871**
J. D. Howden ..	..	29 Nov. **1870**

Rank and Name.	Rank in Regiment.
Lieutenants (continued)—	
Chas. Michell	28 Oct. 1871
Henry E. W. Fetherston-	
haugh	28 Oct. 1871
F. M. Ward	28 Oct. 1871
C. R. B. Thorne	28 Oct. 1871
Chas. Hope (Interpreter)	28 Oct. 1871
R. S. R. Fetherstonhaugh	28 Oct. 1871
Godfrey Astell	28 Oct. 1871
H. D. P. Okeden	28 Oct. 1871
N. E. de Berner Fenwick	28 Oct. 1871
W. H. Holbech	28 Oct. 1871
W. S. Anderson	28 Oct. 1871
F. A. Beauclerk	28 Oct. 1871
Henry Allfrey	28 Oct. 1871
C. S. Cotton	28 Oct. 1871
H. L. Farmer	28 Oct. 1871
Robert Henley	28 Oct. 1871
A. G. A. Martin	28 Oct. 1871
M. C. Boyle	28 Oct. 1871
H. R. Meuds	30 Dec. 1871
M. C. B. F. Walker ..	6 Mar. 1872
A. P. Vaughan	29 May 1872
G. G. Grimwood	24 July 1872
Henry Vere	5 Oct. 1872
E. O. H. Wilkinson ..	9 Aug. 1873
G. G. Moore	27 Sept. 1872
B. T. G. Montgomery ..	5 Oct. 1872
Robert Story	12 Nov. 1873
E. A. Sandford	12 Nov. 1873
R. C. D. Wilson	19 Oct. 1872
J. H. C. Carey	12 Nov. 1873
G. H. Wells	28 Feb. 1874
Hon. A. H. F. Greville ..	9 Aug. 1874
H. R. Lovett	9 Aug. 1874
F. S. Marsham	15 Jan. 1873
R. H. Gunning	26 Mar. 1873
E. W. Herbert	28 Dec. 1874
G. T. Campbell	28 Feb. 1875
H. E. M. D. C. Upton ..	5 Oct. 1875
N. More-Nisbitt	6 Oct. 1875
R. G. Buchanan-Riddell	20 Nov. 1875
Hon. C. S. G. Canning ..	20 Nov. 1875
R. E. W. Copland-Craw-	
ford	7 Jan. 1876
Sub-Lieutenants—	
G. S. Baynes	11 Feb. 1875
G. C. Kitson	11 Feb. 1875
A. E. Miles	11 Feb. 1875
Lord Frederick Fitzgerald	11 Feb. 1875
H. Gore-Browne	11 Feb. 1875
W. P. Campbell	10 Mar. 1875
R. E. Golightly	28 April 1875
A. Davidson	10 Sept. 1875
L. W. G. Butler	10 Sept. 1875
H. C. Leigh	6 Oct. 1875
H. D. Banks	6 Oct. 1875
Paymasters—	
F. FitzPatrick, 2 Mar., 1855—2nd	
Lieut., 19 Oct., 1849; Lieut., 31 May,	
1854; Hon. Major, 2 Mar., 1865.	
E. C. Grant, 28 Dec., 1855—Hon.	
Major, 28 Dec., 1870.	
W. F. Nixon, 8 Jan., 1841—	
Ensign, 3 Aug., 1830; Lieut., 22 Jan.,	
1836; Hon. Major, 1 Jan., 1860.	

Rank and Name.	Rank in Regiment.
Paymasters (continued)—	
A. G. Anderson, 16 Aug., 1859—	
Ensign, 5 Mar., 1858; Hon. Major,	
5 Mar., 1873.	
Adjutants—	
M. C. Boyle	13 Nov. 1875
E. T. Hutton	10 June 1874
T. S. Clarke	6 Nov. 1873
E. O. H. Wilkinson ..	1 Dec. 1875
Instructors of Musketry—	
H. J. Hope-Edwardes ..	16 June 1873
Charles Hope	5 Jan. 1877
A. G. A. Martin ..	10 June 1874
C. Michell	15 July 1876
Quartermasters—	
W. Holmes	17 April 1867
W. FitzHenry	6 July 1867
W. Dixon	19 Jan. 1876
J. W. H. Riley	24 Feb. 1872
Medical Officers—	
A. G. Young, Surgeon-Major;	
Surgeon, 24 February, 1872.	
W. S. Oliver, M.D., Surgeon-Major;	
Surgeon, 3 Feb., 1872.	
W. M. Harman, Surgeon; Assistant-	
Surgeon, 2 Oct., 1876.	

Regimentals—Green, facings scarlet.

Agents—Messrs. Cox and Co.

Irish Agents—Sir E. Borough, Bt., and Co.

1878.

Four Battalions.

England—India.

Celer et Audax.

Roleia, Vimiera, Martinique, Talavera,
Fuentes d'Onor, Albuhera, Ciudad
Rodrigo, Badajoz, Salamanca, Vittoria,
Pyrenees, Nivelle, Nive, Orthes, Tou-
louse, Peninsula, Punjaub, Mooltan,
Goojerat, Taku Forts, Pekin, Delhi.

Col.-in-Chief—

Field-Marshal H.R.H. the Duke of
Cambridge, K.G., K.P., G.C.B.,
G.C.M.G., 3 March, 1869.

Cols.-Commandant—

Gen. Sir A. A. T. Cunynghame,
G.C.B. 2nd Lieut., 2 Nov., 1830;
Lieut., 22 May, 1835; Capt., 17 Aug.,
1841; Major, 8 Aug., 1845; Lieut.-
Col., 3 Nov., 1846; Colonel, 29 June,
1854; Major-General, 20 April, 1861;
Lieut.-General, 22 Oct., 1870; General,
1 Oct., 1877; Col.-Comm., 60th Rifles,
2 Feb., 1876.

Gen. Freeman Murray—Ensign, 24
Feb., 1825; Lieut., 8 April, 1826;
Capt., 21 Dec., 1832; Major, 20 Aug.,
1841; Lieut.-Col., 5 Nov., 1847; Col.,
28 Nov., 1854; Major-Gen., 13 Aug.,
1862; Lieut.-General, 25 Oct., 1871;
General, 1 Oct., 1877; Col.-Com., 60th
Rifles, 11 Oct., 1876.

Lieut.-Colonels—

Hugh Parker Montgomery* — 2nd Lieut., 21 Aug., 1849; Lieut., 28 Oct., 1853; Captain, 17 Aug., 1855; Major, 10 Nov., 1869; Lieut.-Colonel 13 Aug., 1873.

Wykeham Leigh Pemberton — 2nd Lieut., 23 April, 1852; Lieut., 25 Aug., 1854; Captain, 23 March, 1858; Major, 28 October, 1871; Lieut.-Colonel, 10 March, 1875.

Rowley Willes Hinxman — 2nd Lieut., 23 Nov., 1849; Lieut., 3 March, 1854; Captain, 15 Jan., 1858; Brevet Major, 19 Jan., 1864; Major, 24 April, 1872; Brevet Lieut.-Colonel, 7 Jan., 1874; Lieut.-Colonel, 5 June, 1875.

James Durham Dundas — 2nd Lieut., 3 March, 1854; Lieut., 23 March, 1855; Captain, 22 June, 1858; Brevet Major, 12 Nov., 1870; Major, 1 April, 1873; Lieut.-Colonel, 19 Dec., 1877.

Herbert George Deedes,† Private Secretary to the Secretary of State for War—Ensign, 11 Aug., 1854; Lieut., 23 March, 1855; Captain, 2 July 1858; Brevet Major, 25 Sept., 1869; Brevet Lieut.-Colonel 30 July, 1874; Major, 6 July, 1875; Lieut.-Colonel, 24 Aug., 1878.

James Joseph Collins — Ensign, 25 Aug., 1854; Lieut., 23 March, 1855; Captain, 19 July, 1858; Brevet Major, 5 July, 1872; Major, 5 July, 1875; Lieut.-Colonel, 24 Aug. 1878.

Majors—

Francis Vernon Northey, Ensign, 22 March, 1855; Lieut., 27 July 1855; Captain, 18 May, 1862; Brevet Major, 12 Nov., 1870; Major, 5 July, 1873.

Cromer Ashburnham, Ensign, 20 April, 1855; Lieut., 26 Oct., 1855; Captain, 23 Jan., 1863; Major, 18 Oct., 1873.

Kennett Gregg Henderson, Ensign, 23 April, 1855; Lieut., 6 May, 1856; Captain, 30 June, 1863; Major, 27 March, 1874.

James Sturges Hamilton Algar, Ensign, 10 May, 1855; Lieut., 9 May, 1856; Captain, 17 May, 1864; Major, 10 March, 1875.

H. R. Milligan,‡ Ensign, 16 February, 1855; Lieut., 23 Nov., 1855; Captain, 22 Nov., 1864; Major, 11 Nov., 1876.

George Hatchell, Ensign, 22 Oct., 1855; Lieut., 27 Sept., 1857; Captain, 24 Jan., 1865; Major, 29 Nov., 1876.

J. K. Watson, Ensign, 20 July, 1855; Lieut., 1 May, 1857; Captain, 1 May,

Majors (continued)—

1865; Brevet Major, 1 Oct., 1877; Major, 19 Dec., 1877.

William G. Byron—Ensign, 25 Sept., 1855; Lieut., 7 Sept., 1858; Captain, 3 Jan., 1865; Brevet Major, 1 Oct., 1877; Major, 29 June, 1878.

W. J. K. Ogilvy—Ensign, 15 May, 1856; Lieut., 21 May, 1858; Captain, 3 April, 1866; Major, 21 Aug. 1878.

Rank and Name.	Rank in Regiment.
Captains—	
W. J. E. Poole§	3 April 1866
R. H. Beadon	16 Oct. 1867
Arthur Tufnell	23 Oct. 1867
John Charley	14 Aug. 1867
A. F. Terry	8 Dec. 1867
J. G. Crosbie	20 May 1868
O. H. Trotman	11 Jan. 1869
N. W. Wallace	23 Jan. 1869
Arthur Morris	24 April 1869
C. M. Culderon	9 Feb. 1870
R. H. Buller, C.B.	28 May 1870
Rank in Army, Bt. Maj. 1 April 1876	
C. F. Cramer	28 May 1870
J. H. H. Croft	9 Aug. 1871
F. W. Grenfell	28 Oct. 1871
A. A. A. Kinloch	8 May 1870
A. V. O'Brien	24 April 1872
C. L. C. de Robeck	24 April 1872
P. J. H. A. Barne	12 Feb. 1873
G. T. Whitaker	26 Feb. 1873
George Carpenter	30 April 1873
R. C. Robinson	28 May 1873
O. L. M'Lean Farmer	5 July 1873
E. W. H. Crofton	5 July 1873
Denis Hinghan	5 July 1873
J. T. D. Crosbie	13 Aug. 1873
H. D. Browne	27 Mar. 1874
E. L. Fraser	1 April 1874
Reginald Chalmer	2 April 1874
William Talden	10 Mar. 1875
H. R. Mactall	1 April 1875
Benjamin Frend	12 May 1875
A. H. Bircham	13 May 1875
H. A. H. Ward	1 Dec. 1875
A. F. H. Mitchell-Innes	12 Aug. 1876
P. A. Robinson	17 May 1876
William Forster	29 Nov. 1876
Arthur Pepys	17 Jan. 1877
R. C. Davies	28 Mar. 1877
H. P. M. Wylie	30 June 1877
J. N. Blackwood-Price	8 Dec. 1877
J. J. Mallandane	11 Mar. 1877
C. H. Smith	19 Dec. 1877
H. S. Marsham	2 Mar. 1878
T. S. Clarke	5 July 1878
C. H. Thorlow	21 Aug. 1878
Hon. Keith Turnour	30 Oct. 1878
H. S. H. Riddell	30 Nov. 1878

* Retired on half pay on completion of 5 years command, 13 Aug., 1878.
† Retired on half pay, appointed Assistant under Secretary of State for War, 20 Sept., 1878.
‡ Retired on pension, with hon. rank of Lieut. Col., 29 June, 1878.
§ Retired on pension, with hon. rank of Major, 30 Oct., 1878.

Rank and Name.	Rank in Regiment.
Lieutenants—	
H. J. Hope-Edwardes	.. 22 Mar. 1871
T. P. Lloyd	.. 29 Nov. 1864
F. B. N. Dickenson	.. 12 July 1871
E. T. H. Hutton ..	.. 9 Aug. 1871
F. W. Archer	.. 9 Aug. 1871
Horace Walpole ..	.. 17 Oct. 1871
J. D. Howden ..	.. 30 Nov. 1870
Charles Michell ..	.. 28 Oct. 1871
Henry E. W. Fetherston-	
haugh	.. 28 Oct. 1871
F. M. Ward	.. 28 Oct. 1871
C. R. B. Thorne ..	.. 28 Oct. 1871
Charles Hope	.. 28 Oct. 1871
Richard S. R. Fetherston-	
haugh	.. 28 Oct. 1871
Godfrey Astell ..	.. 28 Oct. 1871
H. D. P. Okeden ..	.. 28 Oct. 1871
N. E. de B. Fenwick ..	.. 28 Oct. 1871
W. H. Holbech ..	.. 28 Oct. 1871
W. S. Anderson ..	.. 28 Oct. 1871
Henry Allfrey ..	.. 28 Oct. 1871
C. S. Cotton	.. 28 Oct. 1871
H. L. Farmer	.. 28 Oct. 1871
Robert Henley ..	.. 28 Oct. 1871
M. C. Boyle	.. 28 Oct. 1871
H. R. Mends	.. 30 Dec. 1871
M. C. B. F. Walker ..	6 Mar. 1872
A. P. Vaughan ..	.. 29 May 1872
G. G. Grimwood ..	.. 24 Jan. 1872
Henry Vere	.. 5 Oct. 1872
E. O. H. Wilkinson ..	.. 9 Aug. 1873
G. G. Moore	.. 24 Sept. 1872
B. T. G. Montgomery ..	5 Oct. 1872
Robert Story	12 Nov. 1873
E. A. Sanford ..	12 Nov. 1873
R. C. D. Wilson ..	19 Oct. 1872
G. H. Wells	.. 28 Feb. 1874
Hon. A. H. F. Greville ..	9 Aug. 1874
H. R. Lovett	9 Aug. 1874
F. S. Marsham ..	15 Jan. 1873
R. H. Gunning ..	26 Mar. 1873
E. W. Herbert ..	2 Dec. 1874
G. S. Baynes	11 Feb. 1875
G. T. Campbell ..	.. 28 Feb. 1875
H. E. M. D. C. Upton ..	5 Oct. 1873
N. More-Nisbitt ..	6 Oct. 1875
R. G. Buchanan-Riddell	20 Nov. 1875
Hon. C. S. G. Canning ..	20 Nov. 1875
R. E. W. Copland-Craw-	
ford	7 Jan. 1876
G. C. Kitson	11 Feb. 1875
A. E. Miles	11 Feb. 1876
Lord Fred. FitzGerald ..	11 Feb. 1876
Herold Gore-Browne ..	11 Feb. 1876
W. P. Campbell ..	.. 10 Mar. 1876

Rank and Name.	Rank in Regiment.
Lieutenants (continued)—	
Arthur Davidson ..	.. 10 Sept. 1876
L. W. G. Butler ..	.. 10 Sept. 1876
H. D. Banks	.. 6 Oct. 1875
H. J. Bolton	.. 17 July 1872
R. E. Golightly ..	.. 28 April 1877
Hubert C. Legh ..	.. 6 Oct. 1877
E. W. Brodie	.. 3 May 1876
Sub-Lieutenant—	
R. C. A. B. Bewicke ..	12 Feb. 1876
Second Lieutenants—	
E. J. S. Wortley ..	.. 13 Oct. 1877
D. C. W. Lysons ..	.. 23 Jan. 1878
H. J. Nevill	.. 15 Aug. 1877
C. H. T. Boultbee ..	.. 21 July 1877
A. P. Crawley	.. 13 Oct. 1877
A. C. B. Mynors ..	.. 11 May 1878
D. G. R. Ryder ..	.. 1 May 1878
G. C. B. Baker ..	.. 14 Sept. 1878
J. R. Garrett	.. 30 Nov. 1878
R. G. H. Couper ..	.. 30 Nov. 1878
C. E. Clowes	1 Jan. 1879
Paymasters—	
F. FitzPatrick, 2 March, 1855—2nd	
Lieut., 19 Oct., 1849; Lieut., 31 May,	
1857; Hon. Major, 2 Mar. 1865.	
Arthur J. Roberts ..	1 April 1878
E. C. Haynes	1 April 1878
A. G. Anderson, 16 Aug., 1859—	
Ensign, 5 March, 1858; Hon. Major,	
5 March, 1873.	
Adjutants—	
E. W. Herbert ..	.. 15 Sept. 1877
M. C. B. F. Walker ..	.. 29 May 1877
T. S. Clarke	.. 6 Nov. 1873
E. O. H. Wilkinson ..	1 Dec. 1875
Instructors of Musketry—	
W. H. Holbech ..	.. 23 Jan. 1878
C. Michell	.. 15 July 1876
A. G. A. Martin ..	.. 10 June 1874
C. Hope	.. 5 Jan. 1877
Quartermasters—	
William Holmes ..	.. 17 April 1867
James Ireland.. ..	.. 20 April 1878
William Dixon ..	.. 19 Jan. 1876
J. W. H. Riley ..	.. 24 Feb. 1872
Medical Officer—	
William Morton Harman, M.B.;	
Assistant Surgeon, 2 Oct., 1866.	

Regimentals—Green, facings scarlet.

Agents—Messrs. Cox and Co.

Irish Agents—Sir E. Borough, Bart., and Co.

STATEMENT OF OFFICERS' SERVICES.

For all Officers' Services the date of the List in which the Officer's name appears for the last time is shown.

COLONELS-IN-CHIEF.

1757.

The Right Honourable JOHN CAMPBELL, Earl of LOUDOUN, Lord MACHLIN, one of the 16 Peers of Scotland, a General in the Army, Governor of Edinburgh Castle, Colonel of the 3rd Regiment of Foot Guards, and F.R.S. Succeeded his father in 1732, and in 1745 was appointed Colonel of a new-raised Highland regiment, with which, in that and the following year, he took an active part in the Highlands against the rebels. In 1749 he was appointed Colonel of a regiment of foot. In 1756, being then Major-General, he was appointed Governor of Virginia, and Commander-in-Chief in North America. He arrived at New York on July 23. Lord Loudoun was superseded in his command in 1758, and appointed a Lieutenant-General.

1797.

The Right Honourable JEFFREY, Lord AMHERST, of Holmesdale, K.B., Privy Counsellor to His Majesty, Governor of Guernsey, a Field-Marshal in the Army, Colonel of the 2nd Regiment of Life Guards, and of the 60th (or Royal American) Regiment of Foot; received his first commission in 1731; was Aide-de-Camp to General Ligonier at the battles of Dettingen, Fontenoy, and Rocoux; was afterwards made Aide-de-Camp to the Duke of Cumberland, and, as such, was at the battles of Lauffeld and Hastenbeck; and continued with His Royal Highness till 1756, when he was appointed Colonel of the 15th Regiment of Foot. In 1758 he received orders to return to England, being appointed for the American service, and sailed from Portsmouth on March 16, as Major-General commanding the troops for the siege of Louisbourg. On the 26th of September, in the same year, he was appointed Commander-in-Chief of all the forces in America, in the room of General Abercrombie, and at the same time was appointed Colonel of the 60th Regiment. He was also made Governor of Virginia. He continued in the command in America to the latter end of 1763, when he returned to England. In November, 1768, he was reappointed Colonel of the 60th Regiment, and made chief officer of the Staff. In 1772 he was appointed Governor of Guernsey, and next year Lieutenant-General of Ordnance. In the years 1778, 1782, 1793, he held the post of Commander-in-Chief of the Army. In 1787, he was created Baron Amherst of Montreal, a title conferred in honour of the capture of Montreal.

1827.

H.R.H. FREDERICK, Duke of YORK, was born August 16, 1763. In 1780 he was appointed a Brevet Colonel in the British Army. In 1784 he was created Duke of York and Albany in Great Britain, and Earl of Ulster in Ireland, Bishop of Osnaburg, Knight of the Garter, First and Principal Knight Grand Cross of the Bath, Knight Grand Cross of the Guelphic Order, Knight of St. Esprit, a Field Marshal, Commander-in-Chief of all the King's land forces in the United Kingdom, Colonel in the 1st Regiment of Foot Guards, Colonel-in-Chief of the 60th or Royal American Regiment of Foot, and of the Royal Dublin Regiment of Infantry. In 1793 he was placed at the head of the British Army in Flanders, and after alternate successes was expelled from that country by the French. In 1799 he was employed in Holland, and was obliged to sign a disadvantageous convention. In 1809 he resigned the post of Commander-in-Chief. About two years afterwards he was reinstated in that office. He died on 3rd January, 1827, in his 64th year, having, with the exception of a short period in 1811–1812, been at the head of the British Army since 1795.

1854.

Lord Viscount BERESFORD, G.C.B., G.C.H., received the Gold Cross and seven Clasps for Corunna, Busaco, Albuhera, Badajoz, Salamanca (severely wounded), Vittoria, Pyrenees, Nivelle, Nive, Orthes, and Toulouse ; and the Silver War Medal with one Clasp for Ciudad Rodrigo.

1869.

Lord Viscount GOUGH, G.C.B., K.P., G.C.S.I., served at the capture of the Cape of Good Hope, and the Dutch fleet in Saldanha Bay, 1795. Served afterwards in the West Indies, including the attack on Porto Rico, the brigand war in St. Lucia, and capture of Surinam. Proceeded to the Peninsula in 1809, and commanded the 87th at the battles of Talavera, Barrosa, Vittoria, and Nivelle, for which engagements he received a Gold Cross. He also commanded the regiment at the defence of Cadiz and of Tarifa (slightly wounded in the head). At the battle of Talavera his horse was shot under him, and he himself afterwards was severely wounded in the side by a shell; for his conduct in this action the Duke of Wellington subsequently recommended that his Lieutenant-Colonelcy should be ante-dated to the date of his despatch, thus making him the first officer who ever received Brevet rank for services performed in the field at the head of a regiment. At Barrosa his regiment captured the Eagle of the 8th French Regiment ; and at Vittoria they captured the Baton of Marshal Jourdan. At the Nivelle he was again severely wounded. Commanded the land force at Canton, for which he was made a G.C.B., and during nearly the whole of the operations in China, for which service he was created a Baronet. On the 29th December, 1843, with the right wing of the army of Gwalior, he defeated a Mahratta force at Maharajpore, and captured 56 guns, &c. In 1845-46, the army under his Lordship's personal command defeated the Sikh army at Moodkee, Ferozeshah, and Sobraon, for which and previous services he was raised to the Peerage ; and, in 1849, he was created a Viscount after his crowning victory over the Sikhs at Goojerat (Medal and Clasps). His Lordship was also a Knight of Charles III. of Spain.

1878.

H.R.H. GEORGE W. F. C. Duke of CAMBRIDGE, K.G., K.P., G.C.B., G.C.M.G., commanded the 1st Division of the Eastern Army throughout the campaign of 1854, including the battles of the Alma, Balaklava, and Inkerman (horse killed), and siege of Sebastopol (Medal with four Clasps, and Turkish Medal). Field Marshal, 9th November, 1862 ; Commander-in-Chief, 15th July, 1856.

COLONELS-COMMANDANT.

1809.

Colonel-Commandant W. KEPPEL, Lieut.-General, October 6, 1805. Served in North America and West Indies. Was one of the Equeries to H.R.H. Prince Regent.

1812.

Lieutenant-General Sir G. PREVOST, Bart., 3rd Battalion, Colonel at Antigua, Lieutenant-Colonel, 1794.

1795. Went to Demerara and St. Vincent ; there attacked by the French ; was employed there in suppressing a Carib insurrection and French invasion, and commanded a column at the reduction of the Vigie, ordered to Jamaica to command troops.

1796. Resumed command of 3rd Battalion at St. Vincent's ; twice badly wounded in attacks to resist enemy's progress towards the capital ; after General Stewart's defeat at Colonarcy returned to England in 1809. Commander-in-Chief in America ; General, 1st January, 1805.

1815.

Lieutenant-General Sir HENRY CLINTON, G.C.B.

This officer served in Holland as A.D.C. to the Duke of York in 1793-94. Afterwards commanded the 66th Regiment in the West Indies. Served as Adjutant-General in India 1803-5, and was present at the battle of Lasswarree. Served as Adjutant-General to the expedition to Portugal under **Sir John** Moore, **including** Vimiera and Corunna. Appointed to the command of the 6th Division **of Lord** Wellington's army in 1811 (Colonel-Commandant, 1st Battalion, 60th Regiment, 20th May, 1813), and was present at Salamanca, Burgos, Pamplona, Nivelle, Nive, Orthes, Toulouse, and other actions, for which he received the thanks of Parliament. On the 4th June, 1814, he was promoted Lieutenant-General. The same year he was appointed Inspector-General of Infantry, and subsequently second in command of the Belgian Army. He commanded a Division at the battle of Waterloo, and for his conduct on that occasion was appointed Knight of the Austrian Order of Maria Theresa, Knight of the 3rd Class of the Russian Order of St. George, and Knight of the 3rd Class of the Wilhelm's Order by the King of the Low Countries. He afterwards commanded a Division of the British Contingent in France. On 9th August, 1815, he was removed from the 6th Battalion 60th Regiment to the Colonelcy of the 3rd Foot. Sir H. Clinton received the Gold Cross and Clasp for the battles of Salamanca, Nivelle, Nive, Orthes, Toulouse, at each of which **he** commanded a Division. Sir H. Clinton three times received the thanks of **Parliament**; first, on 10th February, 1814, for his services at Salamanca; **secondly, for** his services at the battle of Orthes; and, thirdly, for Waterloo.

1816.

Sir W. Pat. Ackland, K.C.B. (Lieutenant-General).
Cross and three **Clasps** for Badajos, Vittoria, Nivelle, **Nive, Orthes, Toulouse**; **Medal** and **Clasp** for **Maida** and Vimiera.

1817.

General Sir George Murray, G.C.B.
This officer, having served in the 3rd Guards the campaign **of 1793** in Flanders, in Egypt, and throughout the Peninsular War (Quartermaster-General, 1809), was appointed Colonel of the 7th Battalion 60th Rifles, and subsequently Lieutenant-Governor of Edinburgh Castle. He was a Knight Grand Cross of the **Bath**, and of the Hanoverian Guelphic Order, Knight Commander of the Tower **and Sword** of Portugal, and Knight of the Order of Leopold of Austria. He also **received** the Gold Cross and six **Clasps** for the Peninsular War.

1818.

General Sir James Kempt, G.C.B., &c.
Served the campaigns in Holland, 1799, and in Egypt. Commanded the Light Brigade at the battle of Maida, and having been present throughout the whole of the Peninsular War, was appointed a Colonel-Commandant in the 60th Regiment in 1813. Commanded a Brigade at Waterloo (severely wounded), was a Knight Grand Cross of the Bath and Hanoverian Guelphic Order, a Knight of the Austrian Order of Maria Theresa, of the 3rd Class of St. George of Russia, and of the 3rd Class of Wilhelm, of the Low Countries. He also received the Gold Cross and three Clasps for his services. He was successively Lieutenant Governor of Fort William, Lieutenant Governor of Portsmouth, and Governor of Nova Scotia.

1842.

Sir John Maclean accompanied his Regiment (the 92nd) to Holland, in 1799, and was present at the battle of the 27th August, the taking of the Helder, and the actions of the 19th and 19th September, and 2nd October, near Alkmaar, where he was severely wounded in two places. Accompanied the expedition to Egypt in 1801, and was present at the landing at Aboukir Bay, 8th March; at the battle of Alexandria, 21st March; and at every action which took place in Egypt during the campaign. Served in the expedition to Hanover, 1805-6, also in the expedition to Sweden, 1808. Embarked for the Peninsula in 1809; was present at the battle of Busaco; the action near Redinha; siege of Olivenza; siege of Badajoz, where he was severely wounded; the action near Canizal, where his battalion and the 10th Regiment attacked a column of the enemy double their number, and put them to flight; the battles of Salamanca, Vittoria, the Pyrenees, near Pamplona (wounded), Nivelle, Bayonne, Orthes, and Toulouse, where he was severely wounded, it being the fifth wound he received in the service of his country. Sir John received a Medal and two Clasps. Colonel-Commandant 60th, January 7, 1845.

1854.

Sir WILLIAM EUSTACE was at the battles of Ross and Vinegar Hill, and at Wexford, and all through the Irish Rebellion in 1798. Went to Naples with Sir James Craig; from thence to Sicily and Calabria, and was present at the action on landing in St. Eufemia Bay, the battle of Maida, and siege of Seylla. He was on board the *Loire* frigate when she captured the *Ganymede*. Commanded the Chasseurs Brittaniques, at the battle of Fuentes d'Onor, the siege of San Christoval, battle of Salamanca, capture of Madrid, defence of Oimos in front of Burgos, various engagements on the retreat from thence, actions in the Pyrenees (severely wounded 31st August), and various other affairs, in one of which he was wounded, and in another he had a horse killed under him. Sir William received a Gold Medal and one Clasp for Fuentes d'Onor and Salamanca, and the Silver War Medal and two Clasps for Madrid and the Pyrenees.

1856.

Colonel GABRIEL WILLIAM DAVY, C.B., K.C.H., Commanded the 5th Battalion 60th, in Spain and Portugal, and was present at the battles of Roleia, Vimiera, and Talavera, for which he received the Medal.

1857.

Lieutenant-General BUNBURY served with the storming party at Fort Frederick, and at the capture of Surinam in 1804; served in the campaign of 1814 in Holland, including the attacks on Merxem, and the bombardment of the French fleet at Antwerp. Served also in the American War.

1862.

Sir WILLIAM GEORGE MOORE, K.C.B., served in the Peninsula with the 52nd, and was present at the sieges of Ciudad Rodrigo, Badajoz, and St. Sebastian, at the battles of Salamanca, Vittoria, Nivelle, and Nive, for which he received the War Medal with seven Clasps. He was also at the repulse of the sortie from Bayonne, as Aide-de-Camp to Sir John Hope, and was severely wounded and taken prisoner with that general. He served also in the Waterloo campaign on the staff of the Quartermaster-General.

1863.

Lieutenant-General PATERSON served with a corps of cavalry as a Volunteer in the Rebellion in Ireland in 1798. He served in the Egyptian campaign of 1801 in the 26th Regiment, and was present in the actions of the 8th, 13th, and 21st March, as also at the capture of Grand Cairo and Alexandria. In 1805 he accompanied Lord Cathcart's expedition to the Continent. He served in the 77th in the Peninsula and south of France during the campaigns of 1811-14, including the affair at El Bodon, siege and capture of Ciudad Rodrigo and of Badajoz, investment of Bayonne and repulse of the sortie, besides various skirmishes. When the rebellion broke out in Canada, in 1837, he volunteered his services, which were accepted. Served five years in the West Indies. He received the Gold Medal from the Grand Seignior for the Egyptian campaign, and the Silver War Medal with three Clasps for Egypt, Ciudad Rodrigo, and Badajoz.

Major-General Hon. GEORGE UPTON served in the 1st Battalion Coldstream Guards throughout the Eastern campaign of 1854, including the battles of the Alma, Balaclava, and Inkerman (wounded and horse killed), and siege of Sebastopol (Medal and Clasps, C.B., Officer of the Legion of Honour, 3rd Class of the Medjidie, and Turkish Medal).

1876.

Lord TEMPLETOWN served throughout the Eastern campaign of 1854, and until March, 1855, in command of the 1st Battalion of Coldstream Guards; present at the battle of the Alma (mentioned in despatches); battle of Inkerman in command of the Brigade of Guards, which he brought out of action (wounded and horse killed); subsequently in command of the 1st Division; also present at the siege of Sebastopol (Medal with Clasps, C.B., Officer of the Legion of Honour, 3rd Class of the Medjidie, and Turkish Medal).

Lord MELVILLE commanded the 33rd during the suppression of the insurrection in Lower Canada in 1837, and also in repelling the attacks of the American brigands who landed near Prescott, Upper Canada, in 1838. Commanded the Bombay column of the Army throughout the Punjaub campaign of 1848–49, including the siege and storm of the town and capture of the citadel of Mooltan, battle of Goojerat, and subsequent operations (Medal with Clasps and K.C.B.).

1878.

Sir ARTHUR CUNYNGHAME proceeded to China in 1841 as Aide-de-Camp to Lord Saltoun, and was present at the storm and capture of Chin-Kiang-Foo (led the column of attack on the heights of Maknikiow) and at the investment of Nankin (Medal). In 1854 accompanied the army to the east as Assistant-Quartermaster-General to the 1st Division ; was present at the affair of Bulganac, battle of Alma, taking of Balaklava, affair of 23rd October on the Tchernaya, battle of Balaklava and Inkerman (served with the Guards in the Sandbag Battery and led into action a detached portion of the 20th Regiment), and siege of Sebastopol up to May, 1855 (Medal with four Clasps, C.B., Officer of the Legion of honour, Turkish Medal, and 4th class of the Medjidie). In March, 1855, was appointed local Major-General ; in May took command of a Division of the Turkish Contingent, and in August received the personal thanks of the Sultan, and was created a Lieutenant-General in the Turkish army. In October, 1855, sailed in command of 10,000 men to Kertch, and assisted to maintain that position throughout the second winter in the Crimea (Turkish War Medal and 2nd class Medjidie). In 1863 commanded at Lahore the reserve forces of the army employed in the Sittana campaign. On the 2nd and 23rd April, 1866, when in command of the Northern Division of Ireland, received the thanks of the Irish Government on the suppression of the Fenian rising. Elevated to G.C.B. Organised the military occupation of the Transvaal on its annexation in 1877. Commanded the combined forces on the Neer River in the war with the Galikas, and the rebellion of the Gaikas in Kaffraria.

LIEUT.-COLONELS COMMANDING.

1792.

Major-General STRUTT, Governor of Quebec ; Major 60th Regiment, 1783 ; General, 9th September, 1795.

1803.

Lieut.-Colonel Sir JOHN CAMPBELL, Knight, served with the Portuguese Army during the campaign in Portugal and Spain, and received the Order of the Tower and Sword of Portugal.

1804.

Lieutenant-General Sir FITZROY JEFFERIES MACLEAN, Bart.

Exchanged as Lieutenant from 29th Regiment to 4th Battalion 60th, 1788, and went to the West Indies, where he was actively employed for nearly six years, and was present at the capture of Tobago, the expedition against Martinique, at St. Vincent, &c. The 25th September, 1793, he was promoted to a company in the 60th, and on 8th September, 1795, to a Majority in the 114th Regiment. He afterwards exchanged to the 79th from which he was promoted into the 82nd, and removed to the command of the 2nd Battalion 60th, 5th February, 1801, which Regiment he again left for the 37th, Colonel, 25th September, 1803 ; Major-General, 25th July, 1810 ; Lieutenant-General, 4th June, 1814. He received Medal for capture of Guadaloupe, and a Baronetcy for his services.

Major-General ROBERT LITTLEHALES.

Entered the 4th Battalion 60th, at the age of 16, and joined his Regiment at St. Augustine, in East Florida, and in November 1778, he marched with the expedition into Georgia, under command of Major-General Augustine Prevost, and was present at the siege of Sunbury, when that place with its fort surrendered. He was promoted as Lieutenant into another Battalion which he joined at Jamaica, in August, 1780, and was for three weeks embarked with the Regiment in October, in Port Royal Harbour, for the Spanish Main, but owing to the mortality among the troops already on that service, the expedition did not take place. In 1786 his Battalion was removed to Nova Scotia, and thence to Quebec. He was promoted Captain in the newly raised 4th Battalion in England, and joining at Chatham, raised his company principally at his own expense, according to the conditions under which he had been appointed. On this Battalion embarking for Barbadoes, he exchanged back into the 1st Battalion in Canada, which he joined in November, at Niagara. In 1790 the Battalion moved to Montreal. In November of that year he was appointed A.D.C. to Lord Amherst, then Commander-in-Chief of His Majesty's Forces, which appointment he held till February, 1795, when he was nominated A.D.C. to the Marquis Townshend, and continued as such till his promotion to a Majority in the 3rd Battalion, in December, 1795. The year following he joined his Regiment, then on service in St. Vincent's, and was sent to command a post in the Carib Country. On the termination of hostilities by the surrender of the Vigie and the capture of the black General Marina, he proceeded to England and exchanged into the 2nd Battalion, which he joined at Montreal in November, 1798. In the following year the Battalion was ordered to be drafted, and the officers and non-commissioned officers to be sent to Barbadoes. In February, 1802, Major Lethbridge was promoted to the command of the 4th Battalion, serving in Jamaica; and in October, 1804, he was appointed Inspecting Field Officer, first of a recruiting district at Enniskillen, then at Shrewsbury, and in 1812, of Militia in Canada, where he served in that and the following year in the campaign against the United States until his promotion to the rank of Major-General.

1808.

Major-General GABRIEL GORDON.

Ensign, 60th Foot, 6 January, 1781; Lieutenant, 26th November, 1784; Captain, 10th July, 1794; Major, 16 May, 1800. After completing 20 years' service with the Regiment in the West Indies and Canada, Major Gordon obtained leave to come to England, and in 1803 returned to Jamaica. The 9th March, 1802, he received his Lieutenant-Colonelcy, and soon after his return to the West Indies was appointed to command and superintend the British settlement at the Bay of Honduras, and subsequently Deputy-Quartermaster-General on that station. He was present at the capture of Martinique and Guadaloupe, for which he received a Medal and Clasp. He was placed on half-pay 4th January, 1808.

1809.

Major-General LEWIS MOSHEIM.

This officer's first military commission was that of Lieutenant in the Würtemberg Regiment of Foot Guards, in 1789. In 1791 he left the Würtemberg service and obtained a Captain's commission in a Regiment of Riflemen raised by the Prince of Lowenstein Wertheim for the Dutch service, stationed at Maestricht, Vnets, and, lastly, at the fortress of Grave, during the siege of which place, in October, November, and December, 1794, he was entrusted with the command of all the light troops in garrison. He was taken prisoner with the garrison of Grave, and detained at the depôts of Lille, Amiens, Rouen, and Bernay, until released in June, 1795.

He rejoined the Prince of Lowenstein's Regiment, which, having entered His Britannic Majesty's service at the evacuation of Holland, was stationed at Winsen, near Harburg, to embark for England. In 1795 he proceeded with the Regiment to the West Indies in the expedition under the late Sir Ralph Abercromby. He served at the reduction of the Island of St. Lucia, St. Vincent, and during the expedition against Porto Rico in 1796 and 1797. He was appointed to do the duties of Major by Sir Ralph Abercromby, and the Regiment of Lowenstein Chasseurs having been formed into the 5th Battalion of the 60th Regiment on the 25th of December, 1797, he joined that Battalion as Major, his commission being dated 30th of December, 1797. He was next ordered from Barbadoes to take the command of a detachment of the 5th Battalion of the 60th Regiment, in the Island of Trinidad, where he remained under the command of the late Lieutenant-General Sir Thomas Picton, until ordered to join the 6th Battalion of the 60th Regiment in England. He sailed from Trinidad for England in November, 1799, in a running ship, which was captured by a French privateer and carried into Bordeaux, where he was detained a prisoner until permitted to return to England on parole. He was exchanged on the 7th of April, 1800, and joined the 6th Battalion of the 60th

Regiment in the Isle of Wight, from whence he sailed with the Battalion for the Island of Jamaica in December, 1800. The command of the 6th Battalion of the 60th Regiment having devolved upon him, he was entrusted with the same nearly five years, from 1801 to the 25th of July, 1805, when he obtained leave of absence to return to England for the benefit of his health. He was appointed Lieutenant-Colonel, by brevet, the 29th of April, 1802; and Lieutenant-Colonel in the 60th Foot, the 14th of September, 1804.

1812.

Général FRANCIS **Baron DE** ROTTENBURG.

This officer was appointed Major in Hompesch's Hussars, **25th December, 1795,** and Lieutenant-Colonel, 25th June, 1796, from which he was removed to a Lieutenant-Colonelcy in the 60th Foot, 30th December, 1797. The 1st January, 1805, he received the rank of Colonel; 25th July, 1810, that of Major-General; and 2nd September, 1813, the Colonelcy of De Roll's Regiment; and 12th August, 1819, the rank of Lieutenant-General. He served during the rebellion in Ireland, in 1798, in which year he formed the 5th Battalion of the 60th Regiment into a Rifle Corps, and submitted to H.R.H. the Commander-in-Chief the rules and regulations for the exercise of Riflemen and Light Infantry, and their conduct in the field; **which** having been graciously approved of, was published by authority, and made general for **the** Army. He was at the taking of Surinam, 21st August, 1799. In May, 1808, he was appointed Brigadier-General, and commanded the exercise and instruction of four Battalions of Light Infantry at the Camp **of** Instruction, on the Curragh of Kildare, **under** Sir David Baird. In the same year he was transferred from the **Irish to** the **English staff,** and stationed at Ashford, in Kent, and charged **with** the formation and instruction of three Battalions **of** Light Infantry, viz., the 68th, 85th, and 71st Regiments, assembled at Brabourne Lees Barracks. In 1809 he commanded the light troops at the attack on the island of Walcheren, **and** the siege of Flushing. In December of the same year he was at the evacuation of the island of Walcheren; returned with the troops to England, and was replaced on the staff in Kent. In May, 1810, he was transferred to the staff in Canada, **and** took the command of the garrison in Quebec on the 1st September of that year. In 1812, at the breaking out of the American **war,** he was appointed to the command of the Montreal district, and in 1813 took the command of the troops in the Upper Province, and was sworn in President of Upper Canada. In 1814 and 1815 he commanded the left division of the Army in Canada, and returned to England in September of the latter year.

Baron Rottenburg **was a** Knight Commander of the Hanoverian Guelphic Order.

1813.

Major-General Sir JOHN KEANE, K.C.B.

Major 60th, 27th May, 1802, and again joined the Regiment from the 13th Foot as Lieutenant-Colonel, 25th June, 1812; 4th June, 1814, promoted Major-General, and in August appointed Colonel on the Staff of the Army in Spain and Portugal, and was present at Vittoria, Pyrenees, Nivelle, Nive, and Toulouse, for which events, as well as for the capture of Martinique in 1809, he received the Cross and two Clasps and was also made a Knight Commander of the Bath. Sir John Keane also served in America, and was wounded in the unfortunate expedition against New Orleans, on recovering from which he joined the Army under Major-General Sir John Lambert on the coast of Louisiana.

1816.

Lieutenant-Colonel WM. WOODGATE, C.B.

Served in Spain and Portugal, and received the Medal for the battle of Fuentes d'Onor.

1817.

Major-General PAUL ANDERSON, C.B.

Removed as Lieutenant-Colonel from Nova Scotia Fencibles to 60th. Served as Deputy-Adjutant-General in the Peninsula under Sir John Moore, and afterwards, as Commandant at head-quarters, in which situation he remained till after the battle of Corunna, for which he received the Medal. Served as Assistant-Adjutant-General to General Graham's Division in the expedition to Walcheren, and was present at the siege of Flushing.

U 2

1825.

Major-General EDWARD CODD.

This officer entered the Army the 10th of December, 1789, as an Ensign in the 60th Foot; he obtained a Lieutenancy in the same corps the 20th of April, 1793; a company on the 15th of August, 1795; and a Majority the 25th of December, 1800. He served the whole of the above periods in North America and in the West Indies until June, 1804, when he obtained leave of absence, and returned to this country. The 26th of October of the latter year, he was promoted to a Lieutenant-Colonelcy in his Regiment. In September, 1808, he embarked with his corps for Spain, under Lieutenant-General Sir David Baird, and was present in the action of Corunna. He subsequently served in the West Indies. The 4th of June, 1813, he received the brevet of Colonel in the Army; and the 12th of August, 1819, that of Major-General.

The following complimentary honours were presented to this officer after the prompt suppression of the revolting negroes in Barbadoes, in 1816 :—

> " *Bay Plantation, 8th of August*, 1816.

" Sir,—By order of the House of Assembly, in a full house, when every member was present, I have the honour of transmitting to you the unanimous and grateful thanks of the House, and to the officers, non-commissioned officers, and privates of the garrison of St. Ann, for the eminent services rendered by you and them to this country, by speedily, and without waste of blood, putting a stop to the late dangerous insurrection of the slaves, which, in its commencement, threatened the destruction of the island. I cannot do justice to the high opinion which the House of Assembly entertain of your conduct, without conveying it to you in their own language; I therefore enclose copies of the votes of thanks, and request that you will be pleased to communicate the thanks of the House to the officers, non-commissioned officers, and privates of the garrison of St. Ann. The sentiments expressed in these votes are not confined to the House of Assembly—as far as my observations extend, they are the sentiments of every member in the community. Having long had the honour of your acquaintance, and no stranger to your exemplary conduct at the different times that you have been stationed in this island, and being also a witness to the promptitude and zeal with which you marched against the insurgents, I beg leave to assure you, Sir, that I feel highly flattered and gratified that it has fallen to my lot to be the instrument of handing to you this testimony of the regard and good opinion of the inhabitants of this country.

(Signed)   " JOHN BECCLES,
" Speaker of the House of Assembly.

" To Colonel Codd."

" Resolved unanimously—That the thanks of this House be given to Edward Codd, Esq., Colonel in His Majesty's Army, Lieutenant-Colonel of the 2nd Battalion of the 60th Regiment of Foot, Commandant of St. Ann's Garrison, and General of the Militia of the island, for the great and important services which he rendered to this island during the late unfortunate rebellion of the slaves, for his prompt and decisive measures, his vigilant and unremitted exertions, and his judicious arrangement of the forces under his command, by which good order, tranquillity, and security were, in a short time, restored; as well as for his humane interference, whereby all unnecessary effusion of human blood was prevented. That the thanks of this House be given to the officers, non-commissioned officers, and privates of St. Ann's Garrison, for the prompt, spirited, and efficient aid rendered to the inhabitants of this island during the late calamitous insurrection of the slaves.

" August 6th, 1816."

> " *St. Ann's, Barbadoes, 9th of August*, 1816.

" Sir,—I have had the honor to receive your letter, dated yesterday, conveying to myself, the officers, non-commissioned officers, and privates of this garrison the very favorable opinion which the House of Assembly has been pleased to express of our services during the late insurrection of the slaves, and I beg you will assure the House that we sensibly feel, and gratefully acknowledge this high distinction. The House of Assembly has much overrated my own efforts on that occasion. Prompt and energetic measures seemed to me necessary, and they were adopted equally to suppress the insurgents, as to spare the effusion of the blood of those who, from delusion, had been excited to acts of rebellion by mischievous persons. The expression of your own good opinion will ever be remembered by me with gratitude, and the favourable sentiments which you assure me so generally prevail in this community cannot but, and really do, prove highly satisfactory to my feelings.

" Honourable John Beccles,   (Signed)   " EDWARD CODD, Colonel.
" Speaker of the House of Assembly."

"*Barbadoes, August 14, 1816.*

"Sir,—It is a matter of the highest gratification to **me to** be the organ of the Honourable the House of Legislative Council to convey to you the enclosed resolutions. I cannot omit this opportunity to express, in addition to the well-deserved commendation of His Majesty's Council, my individual thanks for the good advice and ready co-operation I experienced from you during the late slave insurrection, and, as an eye-witness of your personal exertions and fatigue, I have sincere pleasure in testifying that this community must ever feel grateful for your services.

(Signed) "JOHN SPOONER,
"Colonel Codd." "President of the Council.

"Resolved—That the thanks of the Legislative Council be presented to Edward Codd, Esq., Colonel in the Army, Lieutenant-Colonel of His Majesty's 2nd Battalion 60th Regiment, and General of the Militia, for his zealous and meritorious services in the suppression of the late slave insurrection, and for his unremitted attention to the public interest while he commanded the Militia of this Colony. Resolved— That the thanks of the Legislative Council be likewise given to the officers, non-commissioned officers, and privates of the garrison of St. Ann, for the valour, steadiness, and good discipline displayed by them during the same period and **in** the **same** cause."

"*St. Ann's, Barbadoes, August 15, 1816.*

"Sir,—I have been honoured with your letter, conveying to me the resolutions **of** the Honourable the Members of the Legislative Council of this island, on **my** conduct and that of the officers, non-commissioned officers, and privates of **this** garrison, during the late insurrection of the slaves. It cannot but be flattering **to** the feelings of the officers, non-commissioned officers, and privates under my command on that occasion to have their conduct approved of by those who witnessed their exertions, which were rather fatiguing than dangerous; for myself I request you will convey my sincere thanks for the honour conferred upon me. It would, however, be unbecoming in me, if I did not declare, that the success which attended my measures was chiefly owing to the assistance **I received** on every occasion connected with the public welfare from yourself and **other** members of the Legislative Council, to whom I always applied with advantage in cases where their experience and local information were required; and I had ever the greatest pleasure in consulting with you, particularly when the interests of humanity required that the lives of deluded slaves should be protected from the punishments due **to** their **crimes,** into which mischievous persons had seduced them.

(Signed) "EDWARD CODD, Colonel.
"**His Honour** John Spooner, President of **the Council.**"

Colonel GEORGE MACKIE, C.B.

Colonel George Mackie was **appointed Major** in the 60th Foot on the 8th of March, 1802. He returned to England on account of his health, and in 1805 went again to the West Indies. In 1807 he came to England with the 2nd Battalion, 60th, and in February, 1808, was ordered to the West Indies to **take the command** of the 3rd Battalion of the 60th, of which he was appointed Lieutenant-Colonel, the 22nd December, 1808. He landed in the Bay La Trinité with 700 men; marched across the Island of Martinique, and was present at the siege and **surrender of Fort** Desaix. The 4th June, 1814, he obtained the brevet of Colonel. He has the honour of wearing a Medal for the attack and capture of Martinique, and is a Commander of the Order of the Bath. On leaving Martinique, the following **Brigade Orders** were issued:—

"*Fort Royal, 24th June, 1814.*

"Major-General **Wale,** after having three years' experience of Lieutenant-Colonel Mackie's merit as an officer, cannot omit, on the occasion of his leaving the island for England, to thank him for that uniformly steady support that the Major-General has ever received from that excellent officer. It was to Lieutenant-Colonel Mackie that the inhabitants of the town of St. Pierre were most indebted for their safety in the **partial insurrection of the black population in 1811.** It has been chiefly owing to his energy of character, joined to great urbanity of manners, in the execution of his measures, that the populous town of St. Pierre has been brought to that perfect state of tranquillity which it enjoys at the present moment, for which the Major-General, in his civil capacity as Governor, returns him his best thanks; and the Major-General assures Lieutenant-Colonel Mackie of his entire approbation of his conduct in the discharge of his duty as commanding the District **of St. Pierre,** and of the state of his garrison, both as to appearance in movements in the field, and as to general good conduct in quarters; and the Major-General can also assure Lieutenant-Colonel Mackie that in all his reports to head-quarters he has invariably remarked the happy art by which he has attained these essential objects, with the least possible coercion or severity, a circumstance which cannot fail to recommend him as much to the good graces of the Commander-in-Chief, as it must to the esteem and veneration of the soldiers who have had the happiness of serving under him, and who, with every officer and civilian who has known Lieutenant-Colonel Mackie, will join with the Major-General in wishing him welfare."

"To Lieutenant-Colonel MACKIE, Commandant of the Town of Saint Pierre.

"Sir,—The inhabitants of the town of St. Pierre learn with sensible regret that the state of your health compels you to retire from the command of this garrison, which you have held with such honour to yourself and so much to public satisfaction. They are ambitious to offer you, Sir, every respectful testimony of their approbation and admiration of your conduct generally in this command, but pointedly in a period of difficulty and apparent danger to the Colony at large, when personal confidence was restored by the exemplary order and discipline of the troops, resulting from the care and unwearied vigilance of the Commandant. They do not pretend to set forth in what high degree they appreciate your services in this command; they will, however, venture to solicit you to honour them by the acceptance of a piece of plate, of the value of one thousand dollars, as a testimonial of their regard, which will be flattering to them, in the hope it may recall to your mind, in distant time, the inhabitants of a town by whom you were so much esteemed. That your voyage may be prosperous, and its view filled to the plenitude of health, is their unanimous, their most anxious desire. Having been deputed by the inhabitants of Saint Pierre to present you this address, we assure you, Sir, that we pride ourselves in the opportunity it offers us of testifying to you our personal respect and attachment.

(Signed)   "LA GUIGUIGNERAYE.
                         "THOS. VILLEDEUIL.
                         "WILLIAM SMITH.
                         "JAMES MAHON.
                         "JOHN O'DELHORN.

"Saint Pierre, 22nd June, 1814."

(REPLY.)

"St. Pierre, Martinique, 22nd June, 1814.

"Gentlemen,—It has ever been my wish to deserve the confidence and esteem of the inhabitants of St. Pierre, and it is with feelings of the most lively gratitude that I now find, by the address that you have just honoured me with, that my endeavours have in so far succeeded; and it will ever, I assure you, be one of the happiest events of my life. The piece of plate, which you have requested my acceptance of, I receive with the greatest pleasure, and should circumstances place me again amongst you, I trust my conduct will prove that your confidence and liberality have neither been mis-placed nor forgotten. I feel much gratified by the anxious wish you express for the speedy re-establishment of my health, which a change to a Northern climate, I hope, will soon effect. To you, gentlemen, who are on this occasion the organs of this very respectable and populous town, I offer my most heartfelt thanks for the very flattering manner you have been pleased to convey their sentiments, and of which I shall ever retain a just sense.

(Signed)   "GEORGE MACKIE,
         "Lieutenant-Colonel 60th Regiment, Commandant of St. Pierre."

Lieutenant-Colonel JOHN GALIFFE, C.B.
    Appointed to 5th Battalion, 60th, from the York Rangers. Served in Spain and Portugal, and wounded at the battle of Talavera; also present at the battles of Nivelle, Orthes, and Toulouse, for which he received the Gold Cross. This officer had previously been in the French and Dutch services.

1857.

Lieutenant-Colonel BRADSHAW commanded the 1st Battalion of the 60th Rifles during the second siege operations at Mooltan; commanding, 28th December, 1848, at the battle of Goojerat (Medal), and with the Field Force on special service in pursuit of the fugitive Sikh army until its final surrender at Rawal Pindee. Commanded a Brigade of the Field Force west of the Indus in pursuit of the Afghan army beyond the Khyber Pass. Commanded the Field Force during the operations against the Hill Tribes in the Euzuffzie Country, on the 11th and 14th December, 1849, when the enemy, amounting to five times that of the British force, were routed with great loss, and the insurgent villages captured and destroyed. Commanded the advanced guard both in going to and returning from Kohat in the expeditions against the Affreedee tribe, in February, 1850.

1859.

Lieutenant-Colonel BROWN served with the 88th Regiment in the Eastern campaign of 1854-55, including the battles of Alma and Inkerman and siege of Sebastopol (Medal and Clasps, Brevet-Major, and Sardinian Medal, and 5th class of the Medjidie).

1860.

Lieutenant-Colonel DENNIS served with the 1st Battalion 60th Rifles, during the second siege operations at Mooltan, and commanded the Battalion, 27th December, 1848, when the enemy's outposts and suburbs of Mooltan were captured (wounded). He was afterwards present at the battle of Goojerat (Medal), pursuit of the fugitive Sikh Army, until its final surrender at Rawul Pindee, and expulsion of the Afghans beyond the Khyber Pass.

Lieutenant-Colonel PRETTYMAN served in the Eastern campaign of 1854-55 with the 33rd Regiment up to 20th February, 1855, when he was appointed Brigade Major to 1st Brigade, Light Division. He was present at the battles of Alma and Inkerman, siege of Sebastopol, and assaults on the 18th June and 8th September (Medal and Clasps, Brevet-Major, Knight of the Legion of Honour, and 5th Class of the Medjidie).

Lieutenant-Colonel BEDFORD served in the Kaffir war of 1851-53 (Medal), and received the brevet rank of Lieutenant-Colonel for services.

1861.

Sir John JONES, K.C.B., served the campaign of 1857-58 against the mutineers in India, commanded the 1st Battalion 60th Rifles, at the actions on the Hindun on the 30th and 31st May, battle of Badlee-ka-Serai and forcing the heights before Delhi on 8th June; throughout the siege operations before Delhi; action of the 19th June; attack on the Subzee Mundi on 18th July (commanded column of attack), and covering the assaulting columns at the storming of the city on the 14th September; commanded the left attacking column within the city from 15th to 20th September; forced through the city, blew open the gates and took possession of the Palace on 20th September, 1857. Commanded, as Brigadier-General, the Rookee Field Force throughout the operations at Roorkee from 17th April to 20th June, 1858, including the actions of Nagwallah and Nagena, relief of Moradabad, action on the Dojura, assault and capture of Bareilly, attack and bombardment of Shahjehanpore, defeat of the rebels and relief of the garrison, capture of the fort of Bunnai, pursuit of the enemy to the left bank of the Goomtee, and destruction of the fort of Mahomdee; commanded the Battalion at the action of Pusgaon. Received the thanks of General Wilson, of Lord Clyde, and of the Governor-General in Council (C.B., Colonel for distinguished services in the field, Good Service Pension, K.C.B., Medal and Clasps).

1864.

Lieutenant-Colonel BUTLER commanded the 2nd Battalion 60th Rifles, in the suppression of the mutiny in the Shalabad district of Bengal in 1858, and was wounded (Medal). Also served throughout the campaign of 1860 in China (Medal and two Clasps).

1865.

Lieutenant-Colonel BINGHAM served with the 1st Battalion 60th Rifles, during the second siege operations at Mooltan, including the siege and storm of the town and capture of the citadel. Afterwards, at the battle of Goojerat (Medal), pursuits of the Sikh Army and expulsion of the Afghan force beyond the Khyber Pass. Commanded the companies of the 60th engaged against the hill tribes in the Euzuffzie Country, 11th December, 1849, and was severely wounded in the head.

1872.

Colonel PALMER served with the 60th Rifles in the campaign of 1857-58 against the mutineers in India, including the siege operations before Delhi, from 22nd August, assault and capture of the city, with the final attack on and occupation of the Palace. Commanded the 1st Battalion 60th Rifles, throughout the campaign in Rohilcund, including the actions of Bagawallah and Nugena, relief of Moradabad, action on the Dojura, assault and capture of Bareilly, attack and bombardment of Shahjehanpore, defeat of the rebels and relief of the garrison, capture of the fort of Bunnai, pursuit of the enemy to the left bank of the Goomtee, and destruction of the fort of Mahomdee (C.B., Medal with Clasp). Commanded the 2nd Battalion throughout the campaign of 1860 in China (Medal with two Clasps for Taku Forts and Pekin).

Lieutenant-Colonel KENNEDY served with the 60th Rifles in the Punjaub campaign of 1848-49, and was present during the second siege operations at Mooltan (including the siege and storm of the town and capture of the citadel), battle of Goojerat, pursuit of the Sikh Army until its final surrender at Rawul Pindee ; the occupation of Attock and Peshawur, and expulsion of the Affghan force beyond the Khyber Pass (Medal with two Clasps). Served also in the expedition against the Affreedees in the Kohat Pass in February, 1850 (Medal and Clasp).

1873.

Colonel HAWLEY served with the 89th Regiment in the Crimea from the 31st December, 1854, including the siege and fall of Sebastopol and attacks of the 18th June and 8th September. Served as Deputy-Assistant-Quartermaster-General at Balaklava during 1856 (Medal with Clasp, Brevet of Major, Sardinian and Turkish Medals, and 5th Class of the Medjidie).

Colonel RIGAUD served with the 60th Rifles in the Kaffir war of 1851-53 (Medal). Also throughout the campaign of 1860 in China (Brevet of Lieutenant-Colonel, Medal with two Clasps for Taku Forts and Pekin).

1877.

Lieutenant-Colonel GORDON served as a Volunteer at the first attack upon Mooltan, and with the 1st Battalion 60th Rifles, through the Punjaub campaign 1848-49, including the siege of Mooltan and battle of Goojerat (Medal with two Clasps). Served as Assistant-Adjutant-General in the Turkish Contingent from June, 1855, to June, 1857 (8th Class of the Medjidie and Turkish Medal).

Lieutenant-Colonel MONTGOMERY served with the 60th Rifles in Kaffir war of 1851 (Medal).

Lieutenant-Colonel HINXMAN served with the 60th Rifles in the campaign of 1857 against the mutineers in India from 7th June, including the battle of Badlee-ka-Serai and taking the heights before Delhi, the subsequent siege operations, assault and capture of the city, with the final attack on and occupation of the Palace (Medal with Clasps).

1878.

Lieutenant-Colonel PEMBERTON served with the 60th Rifles in India during the mutiny, and was severely wounded, with loss of two fingers of left hand, at Cawnpore on the 27th November, 1857 (Medal).

Lieutenant-Colonel DUNDAS served with the 60th Rifles in the campaign of 1857 against the mutineers in India from 7th June, including the battle of Badlee-ka-Serai and taking the heights before Delhi, the subsequent siege operations to 6th August (wounded on 29th June); served the campaign of 1858 in Rohilcund, including the action of Bagawallah and Nugena ; relief of Moradabad ; action on the Dojura ; assault and capture of Bareilly ; attack and bombardment of Shahjehanpore ; defeat of the rebels and relief of the garrison, capture of the fort of Bunnai, pursuit of the enemy to the left bank of the Goomtee, and destruction of the fort of Mahomdee ; Oude campaign, including the action of Pusgaon and Russoolpore, attack and capture of Fort Mittowlee, and action of Biswah (Medal with Clasp), served in the Red River expedition of 1870 (Brevet Major).

Colonel DEEDES served with the 1ts Battalion 60th Rifles, the campaign of 1857-58 against the mutineers in India, including the actions of the Hindun, battle of Badlee-ka-Serai and taking the heights before Delhi, the subsequent siege operations (wounded on the 12th June) ; assault and capture of the city, **with the final attack on, and occupation of, the Palace.** Served as Aide-de-Camp **to** Brigadier-General Jones during the campaign in Rohilcund, including the actions of Bagawadish and Nugena ; relief of Moradabad ; actions on the Dojura ; assault and capture of Bareilly ; attack and bombardment of Shahjehanpore ; defeat of the rebels and relief of the garrison ; capture of the fort of Banian ; pursuit of the enemy to the left bank of the Goomtee, and destruction of the fort of Mahomdee ; served as extra Aide-de-Camp to Sir A. Wilson at the siege and capture of Lucknow, and as Orderly Officer to Brigadier Baker in the operation in Oude, from the 3rd December, 1858, to 1st February, 1859 (Medal with two Clasps), and brevet of Major.

OFFICERS.

1784.

Major-General THOMAS BARRON.

1778. Captain, 3rd Battalion 60th Foot. He was at the taking of Savannah, in Georgia, and in 1779 was appointed Major of Brigade to Major-General Prevost, and was present in that capacity at the defeat of **the** rebels at Briar Creek, in Georgia, and subsequently at the siege of Savannah. He served also at the siege and surrender of Charlestown, in South Carolina, under the command of Sir Henry Clinton. The following year he returned to the Regiment **at** St. Augustine, in East Florida. From thence the Regiment **was ordered** to New York, where he remained in service until the evacuation of the country. In 1782 he obtained leave of absence to return to England, and whilst there, owing to extreme ill-health, was obliged to go on half-pay. He subsequently served in the 63rd, the 5th and 6th West India Regiments. In March, 1809, he was appointed Brigadier-General on the staff **of the** Windward and Leeward Islands, and obtained the command of the Island **of** St. Christopher, and afterwards commanded the 2nd Brigade **of** the army **under** Sir George Beckwith on the expedition against Guadaloupe, for which he **received** a Medal. He **was** promoted Major-General, 4 June, 1811.

1794.

Lieutenant-General JOHN MATTHIAS KLAUS **served with 60th Regiment until** the commencement of the war of 1793 **; proceeded with it to the attack on Tobago.** On 25th October, 1793, **received the rank of Lieutenant-Colonel in the Army.**

1795.

Major-General Sir GEORGE TOWNSHEND WALKER, G.C.B.

Promoted from 10th Foot to a company in the 60th, 4 May, 1791. In 1793 he **went as a Volunteer with recruits to the Army in Flanders.** He was in the action **of 10 May, near Tournay**, and subsequently was employed by the Duke of York in **several important negotiations; and afterwards appointed Inspector of Foreign Corps, and employed** in the Black Forest and Switzerland, in the levy of De Rohe' Corps, and returned to England in 1796. In March, 1797, he was appointed Aide-de-Camp to Lieutenant-General Fraser in Portugal, and afterwards to the Prince of Waldeck, Commander-in-Chief of the united British and Portuguese Army; he returned home the following winter, and was appointed Inspecting Field Officer of the Manchester Recruiting District, and on 6th September, 1798, he was promoted Lieutenant-Colonel in 60th Regiment.

Lieutenant-Colonel ROBERT H. BURTON.

Rose from the ranks of 30th Foot, and appointed Quartermaster 60th. Served in America and West Indies, and was appointed Lieutenant 7th Foot, 31st December, 1794.

FREDERICK MAITLAND.

Promoted Captain in 60th (from Lieutenant, 30th Regiment), 2nd December, 1789. Present at the attack of Tobago in 1793, and afterwards returned to England, when he received the brevet of Major, and was appointed Aide-de-Camp to Earl Grey, whom he accompanied, first to the Continent, and was present at the siege of Nieuport, in 1793, and from thence to the West Indies. He was at the attack of Martinique, St. Lucia, and Guadaloupe in 1794 ; after which he was appointed

Deputy-Adjutant-General, and received the brevet of Lieutenant-Colonel. On the 2nd of October, 1791, he was promoted to a Majority in the 9th Regiment. He subsequently served as a Major-General at the attack of the Danish West India Islands in 1807 ; and commanded a Division of the Army under Sir George Beckwith at the attack of Martinique, in 1809, in which year he commanded the troops employed in the attack of Les Saintes and the French squadron there. In 1812, as a Lieutenant-General, he was appointed second in command in the Mediterranean ; he was Governor of Grenada from March, 1805 to 1812 ; and Lieutenant-Governor of Dominica, 30th January, 1813. He received a Medal for the capture of Martinique.

1796.

Major-General Francis Slater (Rebow).*
Ensign 60th Foot, 1788 ; Lieutenant, 1790; Captain, 1792. He served in the West Indies in each of the above ranks, and commanded the Grenadiers of his corps at the taking of Martinique, St. Lucia, and Guadaloupe ; at the latter place he was severely wounded through both his thighs. On 20th February, 1796, he was promoted Major, and exchanged to 2nd Life Guards 16th February, 1797.

1797.

Captain Jacob Tonson served with 60th in Antigua ; present at the insurrection at Tortola, in 1792 ; received the thanks of the Council and Assembly of the island ; proceeded with the Regiment to the attack on Tobago, 1793 ; served with the 60th at the reduction of Martinique, 1794. In 1795 was ordered to Demerara to take possession of the colony in the name of the Prince of Orange. Sailed for St. Vincent, and was present at the capture of the Vigie, when he was shot through the leg at the head of the Grenadiers, 3rd Battalion 60th Regiment.

1803.

Colonel Joseph Frederick Wallet des Barres.
Served for some years as Lieutenant-Governor of the Island of Cape Breton.

1804.

Major-General Sir J. Pringle Dalrymple, Bart.
Promoted to a Company in the 60th from the 90th Foot, 24th January, 1799. In 1818 he accompanied Major-General Pigou as Aide-de-Camp to the Mediterranean, and at the taking of Malta acted as Assistant-Adjutant-General to the expedition. After obtaining his Majority he went to the West Indies, but was shortly after transferred to the 48th Foot.

1809.

Major-General James Bathurst, C.B.
Appointed to a Majority from the 1st Royal Regiment. Served on the staff in England in 1803, and in 1804 went to Hanover on the staff of Lord Cathcart. In 1805 appointed to the staff of the King's German Legion, as Military Commissary. He served with the Russian and Prussian Armies, the campaign in Poland, and was present in most of the principal actions. Present on the staff of Lord Cathcart at the sieges of Stralsund and Copenhagen. He was next employed in the secret expedition under General Spencer, and joined the Duke of Wellington's army. In 1809 he served as Military Secretary, Aide-de-Camp to the Commander of the Forces, and subsequently as Assistant-Quartermaster-General. He was present at the battles of Roleia, Vimiera, Corunna, Talavera, and Busaco, for which he received the Gold Cross and C.B. Promoted Major-General 12th August, 1819.

1814.

Lieutenant-Colonel George Henry Zulke, C.B.
Employed with the 5th Battalion in Ireland during the Rebellion of 1798. In 1799 and three following years served in the West Indies, and was present at the capture of Surinam. From 1808-14, employed in Portugal, Spain, and France, and was present at the battles of Roleia and Vimiera, the taking of Oporto, and battle of Talavera, where he was severely wounded and taken prisoner. Escaping from the enemy he was appointed to the 2nd Battalion of Cacadores in the Portuguese Army, by the Duke of Wellington, and was engaged in the battle of Fuentes d'Onor, sieges of Badajoz and Ciudad Rodrigo, and battles of Salamanca, Vittoria, the Pyrenees, Nivelle, and Nive.

* This second name appears to have been taken afterwards.

Lieutenant-Colonel WM. FRASER.
Served in the West Indies in 1813 as Aide-de-Camp to Lieutenant-General Morrison, and in 1814 as Assistant-Adjutant-General on the staff in Jamaica.

1815.

Major JOHN WILLIAM HARRISON.
Exchanged from 67th into the Rifle Battalion, 60th; and in November, 1812, joined the British Army at Tordesillas, where he remained till 1814, when the Rifle Company was sent to the 1st Brigade of Guards, destined to invest Bayonne; shortly after which, in a skirmish under the walls, a musket-shot deprived him of his sight.

1816.

Major EDWARD FITZGERALD.
Served in the Peninsula, and appointed Major in the 60th in 1816. On Lord Liverpool communicating to the House of Lords in 1819 the reversal of the attainder of the relative of this officer, Lord Edward Fitzgerald, the Duke of Wellington observed, "That as one of the individuals on whom the act of grace would confer so incalculable a benefit had served for some time under his command, he would not let the present opportunity pass by without bearing testimony to the brave, honourable, and excellent conduct of the young man in question during the time that he had been acquainted with him."

1817.

Major CHARLES DE VIGNY.
Appointed Lieutenant in the Foreign Regiment of Wallstein's Light Infantry in the British service; sailed with it for Martinique, and was drafted, as Lieutenant, with his corps, into the 4th Battalion 60th, from 30th December, 1797. Joined that Battalion in Jamaica, promoted Captain in 5th Battalion, by purchase, but was not allowed to join that Battalion, being on the news of his promotion posted by Lieutenant-General Nugent, then Commander of the Forces on the station, to the 4th Battalion, and subsequently when that Battalion went home, in June, 1805, to the 6th Battalion, with which he remained until disbanded in 1817.

1818.

Major PHILIP MAUMIAGE.
Served on the staff in the West Indies as Deputy-Assistant-Quartermaster-General in 1813-14.

1823.

Colonel JOHN FORSTER FITZGERALD, C.B.
Extract from the "Times," November, 1877:—

"DEATH OF FIELD-MARSHAL FITZGERALD. Our Paris Correspondent telegraphs that the papers there announce the death, at Tours, of Field-Marshal Sir John Fitzgerald, of the British Army, at the age of 94 years. Sir John Forster Fitzgerald, G.C.B., Colonel of the 18th Royal Irish, was the son of Edward Fitzgerald, Esq., M.P., of Carrigoran, and was born in 1786. On the 24th October, 1793, when only seven years old, he obtained a commission as Ensign in an independent Company of Foot. On the 31st January, 1794, he was promoted to a Lieutenancy, and on the 9th May in the same year was promoted to a half-pay Captaincy in the old 79th Regiment, not the 79th Highlanders, which had been reduced in 1783. On October 31, 1800, he was brought on to full pay as Captain of the 46th Regiment. According to Hart's Army List he joined that regiment for duty in the following year, when, though only 15, he had already been a titular Captain seven years. The establishment of the 46th having been reduced in 1802, Captain Fitzgerald was again placed on half-pay, but on the 9th July, 1803, he was appointed to the new Brunswick Fencibles, and on the 25th September became Brevet Major when only 17 years old, being an instance of rapid promotion, we fancy, quite without parallel. On the 9th November, 1809, he was transferred to the 60th Royal Americans, now the 60th Rifles, and joined that corps in the Peninsula. He was present at the siege of Badajoz, and the battles of Salamanca, Vittoria, and the Pyrenees, together with many minor affairs. During part of the war he commanded a light battalion, and was at the battle of the Pyrenees in the command of a Brigade. He was taken prisoner by the French, as far as we can ascertain, at or after the battle of the Pyrenees, but subsequently exchanged. He received the Gold Cross for his services. On the 5th February, 1824, he was promoted to a Lieutenant-Colonelcy in the 20th

Foot, having received the brevet of Colonel in 1819. In 1830 he became a Major-General, and in 1811 a Lieutenant-General, having in the interval commanded a Division in the Bombay Presidency. In 1854 he became full General. In 1850 he obtained the Colonelcy of the 18th Royal Irish, and in 1862 was created G.C.B. On 28th May, 1875, Sir John was appointed Field-Marshal. Sir John Fitzgerald married first, in 1805, Mary, daughter of Mr. Hazen. She died in 1848; secondly, in 1850, Jean, daughter of Hon. Donald Ogilvy. She died in 1863. He sat as M.P. for Clare in the Liberal interest from 1852-57. Died at the age of 91 at Tours."

By the order of the Minister of War, the military honours paid to French officers of his rank were rendered to his remains, and the whole of the garrison escorted the body to the grave.

1829.

Major JOHN SCHOEDDE.
Served in the Peninsula, and received a Medal for Nivelle.

1839.

Captain RICHARD PASLEY was severely wounded at Bayonne.

Captain O'DELL served with the expedition to South America in 1807, and subsequently in the Peninsula, including the battles of Busaco, Fuentes d'Onor; actions at Sabugal and El Boden; first siege of Badajoz; siege of Ciudad Rodrigo; siege and capture of Badajoz; battles of Salamanca (wounded), Vittoria, Nivelle, Orthes, and Toulouse.

1841.

Major SLYFIELD embarked with the 84th Regiment, and joined the Army near San Sebastian, 16th September, 1813. Present at the crossing of the Bidassoa; battles of Nivelle and Nive (from 9th to 13th December); and sortie from Bayonne. Brevet Lieutenant-Colonel, 28 June, 1838.

1847.

Quartermaster BRANNAN served in the Peninsula, France, and Flanders, from July, 1809, to the end of the war, including the battle of Busaco; first siege of Badajoz; battle of Albuhera (severely wounded); actions of Arroyo del Molinos, and Castel Murrenito; battles of Vittoria (slightly wounded), the Pyrenees, 7th, 10th, 25th, and 31st of July; Nivelle, Nive, 9th December; and before Bayonne, 13th December (slightly wounded), St. Palais, Orthes, Lambeige, Toulouse, Quatre Bras, and Waterloo.

1850.

Mr. COWAN served with the force employed against the Rajah of Coorg, in April, 1834.

Lieutenant O'MOLONEY served in the campaign on the Sutlej (Medal) with the 50th, including the battles of Moodkee, Ferozabad, Aliwal, and Sobraon.

1851.

Captain J. F. JONES served in the 17th during the campaign in Afghanistan and Beluchistan, under Lord Keane, and was engaged at the storm and capture of Ghuzni and of Khelat. Accompanied the expedition from Aden which destroyed the Arab posts of Sheik Medi and Sheik Othman, and skirmished between those places on the 6th October, 1841.

1853.

Captain SIBTHORP served with the 1st Battalion 60th Rifles, during the second siege operations at Mooltan, including the siege and storm of the town (covering the advance of the storming parties), and capture of citadels. Afterwards at the battle of Goojerat (Medal), the pursuit of the Sikh Army, and the expulsion of the Afghan force beyond the Khyber Pass. Succeeded to the command of the companies of the 60th Rifles during the operations in the Hills in the Euzuffzie country, 11th December, and also on the 14th December, 1849.

Lieutenant GREVILLE served as Aide-de-Camp to Sir Harry Smith, and to Sir Cathcart in the Kafir war of 1851-2-3, and was present at the battle of Berea.

1854.

Major SPENCE ; Captains DOUGLAS, DARELL, CLAPCOTT, and HUTCHINSON, &c. ; Lieutenants TONGUE and BROOKE, served with the 1st Battalion 60th Rifles during the second siege operations at Mooltan, including the siege and storm of the town and capture of the citadel of Mooltan. Afterwards at the battle of Goojerat (Medal) ; pursuit of the Sikh army under Rajah Shere Sing until its final surrender at Rawul Pindee. Occupation of Attock and Peshawur, and expulsion of the Afghans' force under the Ameer Dost Mahomed beyond the Khyber Pass. Captain Douglas and Lieutenant Tongue served in the expedition against the Afreedees in the Kohat in February, 1851.

Major HOPE ; Captains SOTHEBY, BEACH SALMON, KENNY ; Lieutenants EARLE, MYER, H. J. ROBERTSON, COCKBURN, Assistant-Surgeon NICHOLSON, served in the Kaffir war of 1851-53.

Quartermaster BERRY, Doctor BOYES, and Assistant-Surgeon MACFARLANE, served in the Punjaub campaign of 1848-49.

1855.

Captain MACKENZIE served in the Kaffir war of 1851-52.

1856.

Lieutenant HUGHEY served with the 32nd Regiment in the Punjaub campaign of 1848-49, and was present at the second siege operations before Mooltan (including the storming and capture of the city, and surrender of the fortress), surrender of the fort and garrison of Cheniote, and battle of Goojerat (Medal and Clasps).

1857.

Captain COXEN served at the siege of Flushing in 1809, and subsequently in the Peninsula, the lines of Torres Vedras, actions at Pombal, Redinha, Morando de Corvo, Ponto de Rheza, Sabugal, and Almeida ; battle of Fuentes d'Onor, siege and storm of Ciudad Rodrigo, siege and storm of Badajoz, battle of Salamanca, capture of Madrid, actions of Zaragoza and San Munoz, battle of Vittoria, actions of Lesaca, Vera bridge and heights ; battles of Nivelle and Nive from 9th to 13th December, and Orthes ; and affair at Tarbes. Served also in the campaign of 1815, and was severely wounded in the knee at Waterloo. He received the War Medal and ten Clasps. Served in the Punjaub campaign of 1848-49.

Captains ST. JOHN and ANDREWS served with the 1st Battalion 60th Rifles during the second siege operations at Mooltan, including the siege and storm of the town, and capture of the citadel. Afterwards, at the battle of Goojerat (Medal), the pursuit of the Sikh Army, and the expulsion of the Afghans beyond the Khyber Pass. Also present during the operations in the Euzuffzie country, and capture of the insurgent villages on the 11th and 14th December, 1849.

1858.

Lieutenant Henry BRACKENBURY served in the Punjaub campaign of 1848-49 (Medal and Clasp), and was present at the battle of Goojerat, and with the field force in pursuit of the enemy to the Khyber Pass, in March 1849 ; expedition to the Euzuffzie country ; in action with the enemy 11th and 14th December, 1849 ; present at the capture and destruction of the insurgent villages of Luggos, Pallee, Zoormundie, and Thoorkano.

1859.

Captain HULL served in the Burmese campaign of 1852-53 (Medal). Served also at the siege of Sebastopol in 1855 (Medal and Clasp).

Captain McGILL served in the campaign of 1857 against the mutineers in India, including the actions on the Hindun, battle of Budlee-ka-Serai, and forcing the heights before Delhi ; the subsequent siege operations, assault and capture of the city, with the final attack on and occupation of the Palace (contusion on 19th June).

Lieutenant KING-HARMAN served in the campaign in Rohilcund in 1858, including the actions of Bagwallah and Nagous ; relief of Moradabad ; action on the Dojura ; assault and capture of Bareilly ; attack and bombardment of Shahjehanpore ; defeat of the rebels and relief of the garrison.

Surgeon INNES served as a Volunteer with the Army before Sebastopol, his regiment being in India, from the commencement of the year until August, 1855, and was engaged in the attack on the Redan on the 18th June (Medal and Clasp). Served in the 1st Battalion 60th Rifles in the campaign of 1857-58 against the mutineers in India, including the actions on the Hindun (contusion of right leg); battle of Badlee-ka-Serai, and taking the heights before Delhi; subsequent siege operations, assault and capture of the city, with the final attack on and occupation of the Palace; campaign in Rohilcund, including the actions of Bagawallah and Nugena; relief of Moradabad; action on the Dojura; assault and capture of Bareilly; attack and bombardment of Shahjehanpore; defeat of the rebels and relief of the garrison; capture of the fort of Bunnai; pursuit of the enemy to the left bank of the Goomtee, and destruction of the fort of Mahomdee.

Doctor LEWIS served with the Rifle Brigade in the expedition against the insurgent Boers, north of the Orange River, and was present at the action of Boem Plants on 29th August, 1848.

1860.

Captain WATERS served from 18th July, 1857, at the siege of Delhi, assault and capture of the city, and final attack on and occupation of the Palace; was wounded on the 6th August, and again at the assault on 14th September.

Captain MACQUEEN served in the expedition against the Affreedees in the Kohat in 1851, and was engaged with the mutineers near Cawnpore on the 26th and 27th November, and commanded a company of the 34th Regiment at the defence of Cawnpore, from 28th November to 24th December, 1857. Served with the 1st Battalion 60th Rifles, the campaign in Rohilcund in 1858, including the actions of Bagawallah and Nugena; relief of Moradabad, action on the Dojura, assault and capture of Bareilly, attack and bombardment of Shahjehanpore, defeat of the rebels and relief of the garrison; capture of the fort of Bunnai, pursuit of the enemy to the left bank of the Goomtee, and destruction of the fort of Mahomdee, attack on and capture of Shahabad.

Lieutenant Honourable R. PRESTON served in the campaign in Rohilcund in 1858, including the actions of Bagawallah and Nugena, relief of Moradabad, action on the Dojura, assault and capture of Bareilly, attack and bombardment of Shahjehanpore, defeat of the rebels and relief of the garrison.

1861.

Lieutenant ORCHARD served in the campaign in Rohilcund in 1858, including the actions of Bagawallah and Nugena, relief of Moradabad, action on the Dojura, assault and capture of Bareilly, attack and bombardment of Shahjehanpore, defeat of the rebels, and relief of the garrison; capture of the fort of Bunnai, pursuit of the enemy to the left bank of the Goomtee, and destruction of the fort of Mahomdee, attack on and destruction of Shahabad (Medal).

Lieutenant SHAW served in the Indian campaign of 1858, and acted as Field-Adjutant of Colonel Walter's column employed against the rebels in Shahabad (mentioned in despatches) (Medal).

Captain WILTON served in the 55th Regiment during the Chinese expedition (Medal), and was present at the operation before Nankin.

Captain K. CROWE served in the Eastern campaign of 1854-55 with the 93rd Highlanders, including the battles of Alma and Balaklava, expedition to the sea of Azoff, capture of Kertch and Yenikale, and siege and fall of Sebastopol (Medal and three Clasps, and Knight of the Legion of Honour).

Quartermaster FITZ-GIBBON served with the 46th Regiment in the Kaffir war of 1846-47 (Medal).

1862.

Lieutenant-Colonel MITTER served in the Punjaub campaign in 1848-49, including the siege and capture of Mooltan, battle of Goojerat, pursuit and surrender of Shere Sing, occupation of Attock and Peshawur (Medal and two Clasps). Served in the campaign of 1857-58 against the mutineers in India; commanded a wing of 60th Rifles at Meerut in suppressing insurgent villagers from 10th May to 26th of August ; present with the 1st Battalion on 6th September at the siege of Delhi, assault and capture of the city on 14th September, with the final attack on and occupation of the Palace on 20th September. Succeeded to the command of the attacking column on Kishingunge on 14th September, on the fall of Major Reid (Brevet Major). Served as Deputy-Assistant-Adjutant-General to the Roorkee field force under Brigadier Jones during the campaign in Rohilcund, including the actions of Bagawallah and Nugeena, relief of Moradabad, action on the Dojura, assault and capture of Bareilly, attack and bombardment of Shahjehánpore, defeat of the rebels, and relief of the garrison ; capture of the fort of Bunnai, pursuit of the enemy to the left bank of the Goomtee, and destruction of the fort of Mahoondee (Medal and Clasp, Brevet of Lieutenant-Colonel). Was **on** board the troopship *Eastern Monarch* when she blew **up** and was burnt on 3rd June, 1859.

Captains Hon. A. LIDDELL and KNOX-GORE served in the **suppression of the** mutiny in the Shahabad district of Bengal in 1858 (Medal).

Captain MEDHURST served with the 18th Regiment in **the** Sutlej campaign **in** 1846, and was present at the battle of Sobraon (Medal). Served in the Indian campaign of 1857-58, and was present at the mutiny of Dinapore and attempt to relieve Arrah in July, 1857 ; advance on Lucknow, and actions at Chanda, Umeerpore, Sultanpore, and Dourala, siege and capture of Lucknow, relief **of** Azimghur, operations in the Judgepore Jungle, and capture of that place ; subsequently commanded a detachment in garrison **at** Arrah, and was engaged in several skirmishes in its vicinity (Medal)

Lieutenant TREEVE served throughout the Oude campaign **in** 1858, including the actions of Poorgaon and Rissoolpore, attack and capture of Fort Mittowlie, and the action of Biswah (Medal). Served throughout the campaign of 1860 **in** China, including the actions of Sinho, taking of Tang-ku, and surrender of Pekin (Medal and Clasps).

Captain CHAPS served in the campaign in **Rohilcund in 1858, including the** actions of Bagawallah and Nugeena, relief of Moradabad, **action on the Dojura,** assault and capture of Bareilly, attack and bombardment **of Shahjehanpore,** defeat of the rebels and relief of the garrison ; capture **of the fort of Bunnai,** pursuit of the enemy to the left bank of the Goomtee, and **destruction of the fort** of Mahoondee (Medal). Served also **in the Oude** campaign **in 1858, including the** action at Rissoolpore.

Doctor DORAN served throughout the campaign of 1860 in China (Medal).

Quartermaster WALKER served with the 71st Highlanders at the siege of **Sebastopol** and expedition to Kertch and Yenikale, from 13th February, 1855 (Medal and Clasp, and Turkish Medal).

1863.

Captain COOKWORTHY served throughout the Eastern campaign of 1854-55, including the battles of Alma and Inkerman, and siege and fall of Sebastopol (Medal and three Clasps, and Sardinian and Turkish Medals).

Captain FLETCHER served throughout the campaign of 1860 in China (Medal and two Clasps).

Captain STOTHERD served with the 93rd Highlanders in the Eastern campaign of 1854, and up to the 14th July, 1858, including the battles of Alma and Balaklava, siege of Sebastopol, and expedition to Kertch (Medal and three Clasps, and Turkish Medal).

Lieutenant HEATHCOTE served in the campaign of 1857-58 against the mutineers in India, including the actions on the Hindan, battle of Badlee-ka-Serai, and taking the heights before Delhi ; subsequent siege operations, assault and capture of the city, with the final attack on and occupation of the Palace ; campaign in Rohilcund, including the actions of Bagawallah, and Nugeena, relief of Moradabad, action on the Dojura, assault and capture of Bareilly, attack and bombardment of Shahjehanpore, defeat of the rebels, and relief of the garrison, capture of the fort of Bunnai, pursuit of the enemy to the left bank of the Goomtee, destruction of the fort of Mahoondee, and attack and destruction of Shahabad (Medal and Clasp). Was wounded before Delhi 17th June, and has the Victoria Cross. He also served throughout the campaign of 1860 in China (Medal).

Lieutenant LEES served in the Royal Navy in the Baltic during the Russian war (Medal).

Quartermaster STOREY served with the 2nd Battalion 60th Rifles throughout the Kaffir war of 1851-53 (Medal). Also the campaign of 1860 in North China (Medal with two Clasps).

Dr. SPARROW served in the Kaffir war of 1847, and in that of 1852-53 (Medal). Was in medical charge of a strong force sent from Natal to aid Major Warden in the sovereignty, from Sept., 1851, to July, 1852. Served at the siege of Sebastopol in 1855 (Medal and Clasp, and Turkish Medal).

1864.

Captain CHEESE served with the 39th Regiment in the operations against Kurnool in 1839; and on 29th December, 1843, in the action of Maharajpore (wounded) (Medal). Served in 1855 at the siege and fall of Sebastopol (Medal and Clasp, and Turkish Medal).

Captain Hon. R. VEREKER served throughout the campaign of 1860 in China.

Captain EATON served in the campaign of 1857 against the mutineers in India from 3rd June, including the battle of Budlee-ka-Serai and taking the heights before Delhi, the subsequent siege operations (dangerously wounded on 10th September), assault and capture of the city, with the final attack on and occupation of the Palace (Medal and Clasp).

Captain HARE served in the campaign of 1857 against the mutineers in India from 7th June, including the battle of Budlee-ka-Serai and taking the heights before Delhi, the subsequent siege operations, assault and capture of the city, with the final attack on and occupation of the Palace (Medal and Clasp). Served also in the Oude campaign in 1858, including the action at Rissoolpore, attack and capture of Fort Mittowlee.

Captain LAWRENCE ARCHER served with the 24th Regiment throughout the Punjaub campaign of 1848-49, including the battles of Sadoolapore, Chillianwallah (wounded), and Goojerat (Medal and Clasps).

Captain BURSLEM served with the 67th Regiment throughout the campaign of 1860 in China, including the storming of the Taku Forts, being about the first Englishman who entered the fort, and was badly wounded in three places, and mentioned in despatches; also present at the surrender of Pekin (Medal and Clasps, and Victoria Cross).

Lieutenant COX was present in the action of Bunk-ka-Gong, the Oude campaign in 1858, including the action of Rissoolpore, attack and capture of Fort Mittowlee, and affair at Mahoundee (Medal). Served throughout the campaign of 1860 in China (Medal and two Clasps).

Lieutenant O'RORKE served in the Oude campaign in 1858 (Medal).

Ensign LONSDALE served throughout the Indian mutiny of 1857-58 in the Bengal Yeomanry Cavalry, with a Brigade of Sir Hope Grant's Division; present at the siege of Betwa, in Oude, actions at Amorah, 2nd March, Thilga (horse bayoneted), Amorah, 25th April, Debriah Dumeringunge, 26th November and 2nd December, and other minor affairs (Medal).

1865.

Major MARRIOTT served with the 82nd Regiment at the siege and fall of Sebastopol, from 2nd September, 1855 (Medal and Clasp, and Turkish Medal). Also served in the North West Provinces in suppressing the Indian mutiny in 1857-58, and was present in the operations at Cawnpore under Windham; defeat there of the Gwalior contingent; actions of Kala Nuddee and Khankur, siege of the gaol, and subsequent operations at Shahjehanpore (Brevet of Major and Medal).

Captain AUSTIN was engaged in active service in India in 1857 in dispersing insurgent villagers; served the campaign in Rohilcund in 1858, including the actions of Bugawallah and Nageena; relief of Moradabad, action on the Dojura, assault and capture of Bareilly, attack and bombardment of Shahjehanpore, defeat of the rebels and relief of the garrison, capture of the fort of Bunnai, pursuit of the enemy to the left bank of the Goomtee and destruction of the fort of Mahomdee; attack and destruction of Shahabad, and action of Bunk-ka-Gong ; Oude campaign, including the actions at Poosgaon and Russoolpore, attack and capture of Fort Mittowlee, and action of Biswah. (Medal).

Captain Honourable J. Colborne served at the siege of Sebastopol in 1855 (Medal and Clasp, and Turkish Medal).

Lieutenant Moodie served with the 2nd Dragoons the Eastern campaign of 1854–55, including the affair of McKenzie's Farm, battle of Balaklava, Inkerman, and Tchernaya, siege and fall of Sebastopol (Medal with three Clasps, 5th Class of the Medjidie, and Turkish Medal).

Ensign Visino served in the campaign of 1857–58, against the mutineers in India, including the actions on the Hindun, battle of Badlee-ka-Serai, and taking the heights before Delhi; subsequent siege operations, assault and capture of the city, with the final attack on and occupation of the Palace; campaign in Rohilcund, including the actions of Bagawallah and Nugena, relief of Moradabad, action **on the** Dojura, assault and capture of Bareilly, attack and bombardment of Shahjehanpore, defeat of the rebels and relief of the garrison, capture of the fort of Bunnai, pursuit of the enemy to the left bank of the Goomtee, and destruction of the fort of Mahomdee, attack and destruction of Shahabad (Medal **and Clasp).** Was also present in the action of Bunk-ka-Gong the Oude campaign, **including the** actions of Poosgaon and Russoolpore, attack and capture of Fort Mittowlee, **and action** of Biswah.

1866.

Colonel North was on service with the 6th Regiment at **the defence** of Aden against the Arabs in 1840–41. Served in **the** Punjaub campaign **of** 1848–49, including the second siege operations and **capture** of Mooltan, battle **of** Goojerat, pursuit of the Sikh Army until its final surrender at Rawal Pindee; occupation of Attock and Peshawur, and expulsion of the Affghan force beyond the Khyber Pass (Medal and two Clasps). Served during **the** Indian mutiny in 1857 with Havelock's Column from its formation, attached to 71st Highlanders, in the actions of Futtehpore, Aong, Pandoo, Nuddee, and Cawnpore, as Deputy Judge Advocate General from 21st July in the actions of Onao, Busseerutgunge (1st), Mungulwar, and Alum Bagh, and relief of Lucknow, defence of the Residency until relieved by Lord Clyde. Thanked by Governor-General in Council, and in **General** Outram's despatch "for the readiness and success with which he established **and** superintended the **manufacture** of Enfield rifle cartridges." This valuable **service was** rendered without **any** relaxation of his other duties, in the prosecution of which he met **with a wound** (Medal and Clasp. Brevet of Lieutenant-Colonel, and a year's service for **Lucknow).**

Lieutenant-Colonel Maguire served with the 55th Regiment in China, and was **present at the attack and capture** of Amoy, second capture of Chusan, attack and **capture of Chinhae, and operations up the Yangtz-ekiang (Medal). Served with the 60th Rifles throughout the** Punjaub campaign of 1848–49, including the siege and **storm of the town, and capture of the** citadel of Mooltan ; battle of Goojerat, pursuit **of the Sikh Army until its final surrender at Rawal Pindee; occupation of Attock and Peshawur, and expulsion of the Affghan force beyond the Khyber Pass (Medal and two Clasps).** Served throughout the campaign in Rohilcund, in 1858, including the **actions of Bagawallah and Nugena, relief of Moradabad, action on the Dojura, assault and capture of Bareilly, attack and bombardment of Shahjehanpore, defeat of the rebels and relief of the garrison, capture of the fort of Bunnai, pursuit of the enemy to the left bank of the Goomtee, and destruction of the fort of Mahomdee ; commanded a wing of the 1st Battalion 60th Rifles, at the attack and destruction of Shahabad (Brevet of Major) ; commanded the Battalion in the action of Bunk-ka-Gong (Medal); was three times mentioned in despatches, and recommended for an unattached Majority by Lord Clyde for service in the field, in lieu of which he subsequently obtained the Brevet of Lieutenant-Colonel.**

Lieutenant-Colonel Churchill served in the Kaffir war of 1846–47 (Medal) ; also the Eastern campaign of 1854–55, including the battles of Alma and Inkerman, and siege of Sebastopol (wounded in the trenches) (Medal and Clasp, Brevet Major, and 5th Class of the Medjidie, and the Turkish Medal). Served the campaign in Rohilcund in 1858, including the actions of Bagawallah and Nugena, relief of Moradabad, action on the Dojura, assault and capture of Bareilly, attack and bom-

X

bardment of Shahjehanpore, defeat of the rebels and relief of the garrison, capture of the fort of Bunnai, pursuit of the enemy to the left bank of the Goomtee, and destruction of the fort of Mahomdee.

Major WARREN served in the Kaffir war of 1851-53 (Medal) ; also in the Indian mutiny campaign in 1858-59, in the Shahabad district, and commanded detachments of the battalion in several engagements (mentioned in despatches) (Medal) ; and throughout the campaign of 1860 in China (Medal and two Clasps).

Major JONES served in the campaign against the mutineers in India from 3rd June, 1857, including the battle of Badlee-ka-Serai and taking the heights before Delhi, the subsequent siege operations until severely wounded on 23rd June. Served the campaign in Rohilcund in 1856, including the actions of Bagawallah and Nugena, relief of Moradabad, action on the Dojura, assault and capture of Bareilly, attack and bombardment of Shahjehanpore, defeat of the rebels and relief of the garrison ; capture of the fort of Bunnai, pursuit of the enemy to the left bank of the Goomtee, and destruction of the fort of Mahomdee ; attack on and destruction of Shahabad, action of Bunk-ka-Gong, campaign in Oude in 1858-59, including the action of Pusgaon, commanded the 1st Battalion at the battle of Rissoolpore, attack and capture of Fort Mittowlee (wounded) (Brevet Major, Medal and Clasp).

Captain MORGAN served in the campaign of 1857-58 against the mutineers in India, including the battle of Badlee-ka-Serai and taking the heights before Delhi, subsequent siege operations, assault and capture of the city, with the final attack on and occupation of the Palace ; campaign in Rohilcund, including the actions of Bagawallah and Nugena, relief of Moradabad, action on the Dojura, assault and capture of Bareilly, attack and bombardment of Shahjehanpore, defeat of the rebels and relief of the garrison, capture of the fort of Bunnai, pursuit of the enemy to the left bank of the Goomtee, and destruction of the fort of Mahomdee, attack and destruction of Shahabad, and action of Bunk-ka-Gong ; Oude campaign, including the actions at Pusgaon and Rissoolpore, attack and capture of Fort Mittowlee, and action of Biswah (Medal and Clasp).

Captain MORRAH (as Adjutant), Lieutenants BRERETON, CAMPBELL, BARRY, MEADE, PRUST, and BUTLER served throughout the campaign of 1860 in China (Medal and two Clasps).

Captain CURTIS served in the campaign of 1857 against the mutineers in India, including the actions on the Hindun, battle of Badlee-ka-Serai, and taking the heights before Delhi, subsequent siege operations, assault and capture of the city, with the final attack on and occupation of the Palace. Was wounded on the 12th June, and again at the attack on 14th September severely (Medal and Clasps).

Surgeon TODD served with the 71st Regiment in the Crimea in 1855, the greater part of the time in medical charge of the Regiment, including the siege of Sebastopol and expedition to Kertch (Medal and Clasp, and Turkish Medal). Served with the 99th Regiment throughout the campaign of 1860 in China, including the actions of the 18th and 21st August, and surrender of Pekin (Medal and Clasps).

Quartermaster HUNTER served in the Punjaub campaign of 1848-49, including the siege and capture of Mooltan from 28th December, 1848, to 22nd January, 1849 ; battle of Goojerat, pursuit and surrender of Shere Sing, occupation of Attock and Peshawur (Medal and two Clasps). Served the campaign of 1857-58 against the mutineers in India, including the actions on the Hindun, battle of Badlee-ka-Serai and attack of the heights before Delhi, subsequent siege operations, assault and capture of the city, with the final attack on and occupation of the Palace ; campaign in Rohilcund, including actions of Bagawallah and Nugena, relief of Moradabad, action on the Dojura, assault and capture of Bareilly, attack and bombardment of Shahjehanpore, defeat of the rebels, and relief of the garrison ; capture of the fort of Bunnai, pursuit of the enemy to the left bank of the Goomtee, and destruction of the fort of Mahomdee, attack and destruction of Shahabad, action of Bunk-ka-Gong ; Oude campaign, including the actions of Pusgaon and Rissoolpore, attack and capture of Fort Mittowlee, and action of Biswah (Medal and Clasp).

1867.

Quartermaster DUNCAN served in the Punjaub campaign in 1848-49, including the siege and capture of Mooltan, battle of Goojerat, surrender of the Sikh Army, and expulsion of the Affghans beyond the Khyber Pass (Medal with two Clasps); present at the capture of insurgent villagers in the Euzuffzie country in December, 1849; served in the Indian campaign in 1857, including the actions of the Hindun, battle of Badlee-ka-Serai, and attack of the heights before Delhi, subsequent siege operations, assault and capture of the city, with final assault on and occupation of the Palace (Medal with Clasp). Was granted a Medal for good conduct and long service; also a Medal and annuity of £15 for distinguished and gallant conduct in the field.

Quartermaster COLE served in the Eastern campaign of 1854-55, **including the** battles of Alma (wounded), Balaklava, and Inkerman, siege and fall **of Sebastopol** (Medal with four Clasps, and Turkish Medal).

1868.

Major ELLIS served **with** the 2nd Battalion 60th Rifles in the Kaffir war of 1851-53 (Medal); was Deputy Adjutant-Quartermaster-General at head-quarters of the Turkish Contingent in the Crimea from December, 1855, to June, 1856 (Turkish Medal). Also served in the Oude campaign of 1858, commanded a detachment of the 60th Rifles at the affair of Mahomdee, and was present at **the** action of Buwah. Commanded the 1st Battalion during the pursuit through **the** Khyreeghur jungles (Medal and Brevet **of** Major).

Lieutenant TURLE served in the campaign of 1857 against the mutineers in **India,** including the actions on the Hindun; battles of Badlee-ka-Serai, and taking **the** heights before Delhi; the subsequent **siege operations,** until dangerously wounded **on** 10th August (Medal and Clasp).

1869.

Major WICKHAM served **in** the Punjaub campaign **of** 1848-49, including **the** capture of the forts of Rungur, Nungul, and Morarie, affair at Ramnugger, passage of the Chenab, battles of Sadoolapore, Chillianwallah, and Goojerat, and with the field force in pursuit of the enemy **to** the Khyber Pass (Medal with two Clasps). Served during the Indian mutiny campaign in 1858-59, and acted as Orderly Officer to Brigadier-General Franks at the action of Nusrutpore, and commanded the 61st Regiment when forming part **of a column sent in pursuit** of Tantia Topee (Medal and Brevet of Major).

Lieutenant-Colonel WARD served as Aide-de-Camp to Colonel Viscount Melville during the campaign in the Punjaub of 1848-49, including the second siege operations before Mooltan and battle of Goojerat (Medal and two Clasps). Served with a detachment of the 60th during operations in the Euzuffzie country in December, 1849, and acted as Staff Officer to the European portion of the force sent against the Affreedees in the Kohat Pass in February, 1850.

Major BROOKE served with the 1st Battalion 60th Rifles during the second siege operations at Mooltan, including the siege and storm of the town and capture of the citadel of Mooltan; afterwards at the battle of Goojerat, pursuit of the Sikh Army under Rajah Shere Sing until its final surrender at Rawal Pindee; occupation of Attock and Peshawur, and expulsion of the Affghan force under the Ameer Dost Mahomed beyond the Khyber Pass; was wounded at Mooltan, 27th December, 1848 (Medal and two Clasps). Served also in the Kaffir war of 1851-53 (Medal). Served as Brigade Major to Brigadier-General Staveley during the China campaign of 1860 and the subsequent occupation of Tientsin and capture of the Taku forts (Brevet of Major, Medal with Clasp).

Surgeon W. W. MILLS served with the 63rd Regiment throughout the Eastern campaign of 1854-55, including the battles of Alma, Balaklava, and Inkerman; siege, **assaults, and** fall of Sebastopol, expedition to Kertch, bombardment and capture of Kinbourn (Medal and Clasps, and Turkish Medal).

Assistant-Surgeon R. O. HAYES served with the 60th Rifles in the suppression of the mutiny in the Shahabad district of Bengal in 1858 (Medal); also throughout the campaign of 1860 in China (Medal with two Clasps for the Taku Forts and Pekin).

1870.

Captain BLACK served with the 99th Regiment in the campaign of 1860 in North China, and was present at the surrender of Pekin (Medal and Clasp).

Captain JENNINGS served with the 60th Rifles the campaign of 1857-58 against the mutineers in India, including the actions on the Hindun, battle of Badlee-ka-Serai, and taking the heights before Delhi, subsequent siege operations, assault and capture of the city, with the final attack on and occupation of the Palace ; campaign in Rohilcund, including the actions of Bagawallah and Nugena, relief of Moradabad, action on the Dojura, assault and capture of Bareilly, attack and bombardment of Shahjehanpore, defeat of the rebels and relief of the garrison ; capture of the fort of Bunnai, pursuit of the enemy to the left bank of the Goomtee, and destruction of the fort of Mahomdee, attack and destruction of Shahabad (Medal with Clasp). Was also present in the action of Bunk-ka-Gong, the Oude campaign, including the actions of Pusgaon and Rissoolpore, attack and capture of Fort Mittowlee, and action of Biswah.

Captain TILFORD served with the 2nd Battalion 60th Rifles through the Kaffir war of 1851-53 (Medal) ; in the suppression of the Indian mutiny in 1868 in the Shahabad district (Medal). Also served throughout the campaign of 1860 in China (Medal with two Clasps).

Sir EDWARD CAMPBELL served with the 60th Rifles in the Punjaub campaign of 1849 (Medal and Clasps), and was present during the second siege operations at Mooltan (including the siege and storm of the town and capture of the citadel) ; battle of Goojerat, pursuit of the Sikh Army until its surrender at Rawul Pindee, occupation of Attock and Peshawur, and expulsion of the Affghan force beyond the Khyber Pass. Served with the expedition against the Affreedees in the Kohat Pass in 1850, as Aide-de-Camp to Sir Charles Napier (Medal). Served from 3rd July during the siege operations before Delhi, assault and capture of the city with the final attack on and occupation of the Palace on 20th September, 1858, and was thanked in despatch of Commander-in-Chief of India " for gallant conduct " when on the main picquet at Hindoo Raoo before Delhi (Brevet Major, Medal with Clasp).

1871.

Major BOWLES served with the 60th Rifles in the campaign in Rohilcund in 1858, including the actions of Bagawallah and Nugena, relief of Moradabad, action on the Dojura, assault and capture of Bareilly, attack and bombardment of Shahjehanpore, defeat of the rebels and relief of the garrison ; capture of the fort of Bunnai, pursuit of the enemy to the left bank of the Goomtee, and destruction of the fort of Mahomdee (Medal). Also served throughout the campaign of 1860 in China (Medal with two Clasps for Taku Forts and Pekin).

Captain BANBURY served in the campaign of 1842 in Affghanistan (Medal), including the forcing of the Khyber. Jugdulluck, and Tezeen Passes ; actions of Mamookhail, Tezeen, and Huft Kotul ; attack and capture of Istokliff ; the Sutlej campaign of 1845-46, including the battles of Moodkee, Ferozeshah, and Sobraon (Medal and two Clasps) ; the Crimean campaign, from 27th November, 1854, to 13th April, 1855, including siege of Sebastopol (Medal with Clasp, and Turkish Medal).

Captain MORTIMER served with the 60th Rifles in the campaign of 1857-58 against the mutineers in India, including dispersion of insurgent villagers in the Meerut district ; siege of Delhi from 7th September, assault and capture of the city, with the final attack on and occupation of the Palace ; campaign in Rohilcund, including the actions of Bagawallah and Nugena, relief of Moradabad, action on the Dojura, assault and capture of Bareilly, attack and bombardment of Shahjehanpore, defeat of the rebels, and release of the garrison ; capture of the fort of Bunnai, pursuit of the enemy to the left bank of the Goomtee, destruction of the fort of Mahomdee, attack on and destruction of Shahabad, action of Bunk-ka-Gong ; the Oude campaign, including the actions of Pusgaon and Rissoolpore, attack and capture of Fort Mittowlee, and action of Biswah (Medal and Clasp.)

1872.

Major STREATFIELD served with a detachment of the 24th Regiment at the defeat of the Jhelum mutineers, on the 7th July, 1857, and was severely wounded in both legs (right leg amputated) (Medal).

1873.

Colonel WILLIAMS served with the **1st Batalion 60th Rifles during the** second siege operations at Mooltan, including **the siege and** storm **of the town and** capture of the citadel; was afterwards present at **the battle** of Goojerat, the pursuit of the Sikh Army, and the expulsion of the Affghans beyond the Khyber Pass (Medal with two Clasps). Also present during the operations in the Euzuffzie country, and capture of the insurgent villages on the 11th and 14th December, 1849 (Medal with Clasp). Served in the campaign of 1857 against the mutineers in India, including the actions on the Hindun of the 30th and 31st May, battle of Badlee-ka-Serai, and taking of the heights before Delhi on 5th June, subsequent siege operations to 16th August (severe gun-shot wound and left thigh-bones broken on 19th **June**) (Brevet of Major, Medal with Clasp).

Major FITZGERALD **served** in **the 1st Battalion 60th** Rifles **during the second** siege operations at Mooltan, including the siege and storm of **the town and** capture of the citadel; was afterwards present at the battle of Goojerat, the pursuit of the Sikh Army, and the expulsion of the Affghans beyond the Khyber Pass (Medal with two Clasps). Also present during the operations in the Euzuffzie country and capture of the insurgent villages on the 11th and 14th December, 1849 (Medal with Clasp).

Major EUSTACE ROBERTSON served with **the** 1st Battalion 60th **Rifles during the** second siege operations at Mooltan, including the siege and **storm of the town and** capture of the citadel; was afterwards present at the battle **of Goojerat, the pursuit of the** Sikh Army, the expulsion of the Affghans beyond **the Khyber Pass** Medal with two Clasps). Served during the operations in the Euzuffzie country and capture of the insurgent villages on the 11th and 14th **December, 1849; also in the** expedition against the Affreedies in the Kohat **Pass in February, 1850 (Medal with** Clasp). Served on the Red River Expedition **of 1870.**

Lieutenant-Colonel TEDLIE, attached to the 53rd Regiment, was present with it in the operations against the mutineers in India in December, 1857, including the actions of Khodagunge and entry into Futtyghur; served as Deputy-Assistant-Quartermaster-General to the Roorkee Field Force under Brigadier-General Jones in the campaign in Rohilcund in 1858, including the actions of Bagawallah and Nugena, relief of Moradabad, action on the Dojura, assault and capture of Bareilly, attack and bombardment of Shahjehanpore, defeat of the rebels and relief of the garrison, capture of the fort of Bunnai, pursuit of the enemy to the left bank of the Goomtee, and destruction of the fort of Mahoudee (Brevet of Major). Served as Brigade-Major to the Shahjehanpore Brigade in 1858-59, including the action of Bunk-ka-Gong, under Sir T. Seaton, operations in Oude (Medal).

Captain CARLISLE served with the 60th Rifles from 12th November, 1857, against the mutineers in India, including the operations at Cawnpore on 26th, 27th, 28th November, and its defence till the defeat of the Gwalior mutineers on 6th December, and action of Kallee Nuddee; campaign in Rohilcund, including the actions of Bagawallah and Nugena; relief of Moradabad, action on the Dojura, assault and capture of Bareilly, attack and bombardment of Shahjehanpore, defeat of the rebels and relief of the garrison, capture of the fort of Bunnai, pursuit of the enemy to the left bank of the Goomtee, and destruction of the fort of Mahoudee, attack on and destruction of Shahabad, and action of Bunk-ka-Gong; Oude campaign in 1858, including the actions of Pusgaon and Russoolpore, attack and capture of Fort Mittowlee, and action of Biswah (Medal).

Captain YOUNG was engaged with the 1st Battalion 60th Rifles in active service in India in 1857 in dispersing insurgent villagers. Present at the action of Bunk-ka-Gong; also served the Oude campaign in 1858, including the actions of Pusgaon and Russoolpore, attack and capture of Fort Mittowlee, and action of Biswah (Medal). Served also on the Red River Expedition of 1870.

Lieutenant BODDAM-WHETHAM served with the expeditionary force under Brigadier-General Harley in British Honduras in February and March, 1867.

Doctor E. YOUNG served throughout the Eastern campaign of 1854-55, including the battles of Alma, Balaklava, and Inkerman, siege and fall of Sebastopol, and expedition to Kertch (Medal and four Clasps, and Turkish Medal). Served in the Indian campaign of 1858-59, including the actions of Dumoriagunje on 26th November and 3rd December, and of Toolsepore on 23rd December, 1858 (Medal).

1874.

Quartermaster JARVIS served with the 55th Regiment in the China war of 1841–42, and was present at the taking of Amoy, Chusan, and subsequent operations up the Ningpo river, and storming of Chin Kiang Fo (Medal). Has also the Good Conduct Medal.

1875.

Quartermaster TOOLE served with the 60th Rifles in the Punjaub campaign of 1848–49, and was present during the second siege operations at Mooltan (including the siege and storm of the town, and capture of the citadel), battle of Goojerat, pursuit of the Sikh Army until its final surrender at Rawul Pindee, occupation of Attock and Peshawur, and expulsion of the Affghan force beyond the Khyber Pass. Served in the Indian mutiny campaign of 1857–58, including the dispersion of insurgent villagers in the Meerut district, siege operations against Delhi from 28th August to 8th September, 1857; campaign in Rohilcund in 1858, including the actions of Bagawallah and Nugena, relief of Moradabad, action on the Dojura, assault and capture of Bareilly, attack and bombardment of Shahjehanpore, defeat of the rebels, and relief of the garrison; capture of the fort of Bunnai, pursuit of the enemy to the left bank of the Goomtee, destruction of the fort of Mahomdee, and action of Bunk-ka-Gong; the Oude campaign, including the actions of Pusgaon and Rissoolpore, attack and capture of Fort Mittowlee, and action of Biswah (Medal with Clasp). Served also on the Red River Expedition, 1870.

Dr. A. E. T. LONGHURST served in the Crimean campaign of 1854–55, including the siege of Sebastopol (Medal with Clasp, and Turkish Medal). Served also in the Indian campaign of 1858–59, and was present in the actions at Jugdespore (mentioned in despatches for "untiring zeal and courageous attention throughout the day") and Toolsepore (Medal).

Major FARQUHARSON served throughout the campaign of 1860 in China as extra Aide-de-Camp to Sir Hope Grant (Medal with Clasps for Taku Forts and Pekin).

1876.

Major CARLETON served with the 60th Rifles in the Indian campaign in 1858 in the Shahabad district (Medal).

Captain KELLY served with the 60th Rifles in the campaign of 1857–58 against the mutineers in India, including the actions on the Hindun, battle of Badlee-ka-Serai, and taking the heights before Delhi; subsequent siege operations, assault and capture of the city, with the final attack and occupation of the Palace; campaign in Rohilcund, including the action of Bagawallah and Nugena, relief of Moradabad, action on the Dojura, assault and capture of Bareilly, attack and bombardment of Shahjehanpore, defeat of the rebels and relief of the garrison, capture of the fort of Bunnai, pursuit of the enemy to the left bank of the Goomtee, and destruction of the fort of Mahomdee, attack and destruction of Shahabad and Bunk-ka-Gong; the Oude campaign; and officiated as Brigade-Major to a movable column under Colonel Dennis (Medal with Clasps).

1877.

Surgeon-Major A. G. YOUNG served with 2nd Battalion Rifle Brigade in the Crimea, and was present throughout the siege of Sebastopol (Medal with Clasp, and Turkish Medal). Served in Medical charge of the 2nd Battalion 60th Rifles throughout the campaign of 1860, in China (Medal with two Clasps).

Surgeon-Major OLIVER served in the campaign in Rohilcund in 1858, including the actions of Bagawallah and Nugena; relief of Moradabad; action on the Dojura; assault and capture of Bareilly; attack and bombardment of Shahjehanpore; defeat of the rebels and relief of the garrison; capture of the fort of Bunnai; pursuit of the enemy to the left bank of the Goomtee, and destruction of the fort of Mahomdee; attack and destruction of Shahabad; also present at the action of Bunk-ka-Gong, and served in the Oude campaign, including the actions of Pusgaon and Rissoolpore, attack and capture of Fort Mittowlee, and actions at Mehundee and Biswah (Medal). Served with the 1st Battalion 60th Rifles on the Red River Expedition of 1870.

1878.

Major ASHBURNHAM served with the 60th Rifles in the Indian mutiny campaign in 1857-58, including the actions on the Hindun, battle of Badlee-ka-Serai, and taking of the heights before Delhi ; subsequent siege operations ; assault and capture of the city, with the final attack on and occupation of the Palace ; campaign in Rohilcund, including the actions of Bagawallah and Nugena ; relief of Moradabad ; actions on the Dojura ; assault and capture of Bareilly ; attack and bombardment of Shahjehanpore ; defeat of the rebels and relief of the garrison ; capture of the fort of Bunnai ; pursuit of the enemy to the left bank of the Goomtee ; destruction of the fort of Mahomder ; attack on and destruction of Shahabad (Medal with Clasp).

Lieutenant-Colonel NORTHEY served the Oude campaign in 1858, with the 60th Rifles, including the capture of Fort Mittowlee and action of Biswah (Medal). Served also on the Red River Expedition of 1870 (Brevet of Major).

Majors HENDERSON and ALOCK served with the 60th Rifles in the suppression of the mutiny in the Shahabad district of Bengal in 1858 (Medal) ; also throughout the campaign of 1860 in China (Medal with two Clasps for Taku Forts and Pekin).

Major BYRON served with the 38th Regiment in the Indian campaign in 1857-58, and was present at the assault and capture of Meangunge ; siege and capture of Lucknow and action at Bunnai (Medal with Clasp).

Captain POOLE served with the 60th Rifles in the Indian campaign in 1858, in the Shahabad district (Medal).

Captains WALLACE, CALDEMON, ROBINSON, BINGHAM, FRASER, MITCHELL-INNES, and DAVIES; Lieutenants MARKHAM (as Adjutant). Hon. K. TURNOUR RIDDELL, ARCHER and HOLBECH served on the Red River Expedition of 1870.

Captain MOKKIS served with the 60th Rifles throughout the campaign of of 1860 in China (Medal with two Clasps).

Major BULLER, C.B., served with 2nd Battalion 60th Rifles throughout the campaign of 1860, in China (Medal with two Clasps). Served with the 1st Battalion on the Red River Expedition of 1870. Accompanied Sir Garnet Wolseley to the Gold Coast in September, 1873, and served as Deputy-Assistant Adjutant and Quartermaster-General, and head of the Intelligence Department throughout the Ashantee war of 1873-74, including the action of Essaman, battle of Amoaful, advanced guard engaged at Jarbinbah ; battle of Ordahsu (slightly wounded) ; and capture of Coomassie (several times mentioned in despatches) (Brevet of Major, C.B., Medal with Clasp).

Major FITZPATRICK served with the 2nd Battalion 60th Rifles through the Kaffir war of 1851-53 (Medal) ; in the suppression of the Indian mutiny in 1858, in the Shahabad district (Medal) ; also served throughout the campaign of 1860 in China (Medal with two Clasps).

Major NIXON served in the mutiny in India in 1857-58, and was present when the 81st Regiment, under Colonel Renny, disarmed at Meean Meer one Regiment of Native Cavalry, and three Regiments of Native Infantry, all disaffected and ripe for mutiny (Medal).

Major ANDERSON served with the 87th Fusiliers in the Indian mutiny operations in 1857-58 (Medal).

Quartermaster HOSKYN served with the 2nd Battalion 60th Rifles throughout the Kaffir war of 1851-53 (Medal) ; in the suppression of the Indian mutiny in 1858, in the Shahabad district (Medal). Also throughout the campaign of 1860 in China (Medal with two Clasps for the Taku Forts and Pekin).

Quartermaster HENRY served with the 60th Rifles in the Kaffir war of 1851-53 (Medal).

Quartermaster DIXON served throughout the Indian mutiny campaign of 1857-58, including the siege operations before Delhi ; assault and capture of the city, with the final attack and occupation of the Palace (wounded) ; campaign in Rohilcund, including action of Bagawallah and Nugena ; relief of Moradabad ; action on the Dojura ; assault and capture of Bareilly ; attack and bombardment of

Shahjehanpore, defeat of the rebels, and relief of the garrison; capture of the
fort of Bunnai; pursuit of the enemy to the left bank of the Goomtee, and
destruction of the fort of Mahomdee; attack and destruction of Shahabad; action
of Bunk-ka-Gong; the Oude campaign, including the actions at Pusgaon and
Rissoolpore; attack and capture of Fort Mittowlee, and action at Biswah (Medal
with Clasp); served on the Red River Expedition of 1870.

OFFICERS NOT SHOWN IN LIST.

Lieutenant-General J. Lord NIDDRY, K.B., 3rd October, 1805, Colonel, 6th
Battalion; General, 29th April, 1802.

Lieutenant-General G. Earl of DALHOUSIE, K.B., Colonel, 6th Battalion, 30th
August, 1809; General, 25th April, 1803.

Major-General BONHAM, Ensign, 4th Battalion; Lieutenant, 3rd Battalion;
Captain, 4th Battalion; General, 25th August, 1807.

Major Sir JOHN SCOTT LILLIE, Knt. Served in the Peninsula, and received a
Cross for the battles of the Pyrenees, Nivelle, Orthes, and Toulouse.

ROBERT OWEN. July, 1794; Captain-Lieutenant, 60th Regiment, and same
day Captain 56th Regiment.

DANIEL DODGIN. Captain, 60th Regiment, May, 1803; 66th Regiment,
9th July, 1803.

ROBERT JOHN HARVEY. Lieutenant, 60th, 24 March, 1804; 4th Dragoons,
14th September, 1804.

Major-General HENRY ELLIOT.
Promoted from Major, 70th Regiment, to the command of the 3rd Battalion,
60th Rifles, in 1808, with which Regiment he was present at the capture of the
Danish Colonies; and was left with his Battalion to garrison St. Croix; and on this
occasion the inhabitants of that colony made the accompanying flattering eulogium
on his conduct, and the discipline which the Battalion evinced under his command.

"The Burgher Council of the Island of St. Croix to Lieutenant-Colonel Elliot,
Commanding 3rd Battalion 60th Regiment.

"SIR,—The inhabitants of St. Croix have desired us to express to you their
warmest thanks for the friendly disposition that you have manifested towards them
during your stay on this island, and to request of you to testify to the 3rd Battalion
of His Majesty's 60th Regiment, now under your command, the esteem they entertain for them in consequence of the high discipline and exemplary conduct
exhibited by the whole of that corps when in garrison here. We beg leave to
assure you, that we are greatly flattered to be the organ through which sentiments
so congenial with our own are transmitted to you; and yielding to our wish to give
them as much publicity as possible, we hope you will not disapprove the freedom
we take of sending a copy of this letter to be inserted in the papers of the West
India Islands.

(Signed)   "By the BURGHER COUNCIL.
"In Burgher Council, 7th March, 1808."

On 25th November, 1808, Lieutenant-Colonel Elliot was transferred to the
96th Regiment.

OFFICERS OF THE 60TH ON THE STAFF OF THE ARMY AT WATERLOO.*

Lieut.-Colonel BARON TRIPP, } Aides-de-Camp to General H.R.H. The Prince
Capt. Lord JOHN SOMERSET, } of Orange, G.C.B.
Capt. SEYMOUR, wounded, Aide-de-Camp to Lieut.-General the Earl of Uxbridge,
G.C.B.
Capt. The Hon. E. S. ERSKINE, wounded, Deputy-Assistant-Adjutant-General.
Capt. BRUNTON, Deputy-Quartermaster-General.
Lieut.-General Sir HENRY CLINTON, G.C.B., Col.-Commandant, wounded.
Major Sir JAMES KEMPT, K C.B., Col.-Commandant, wounded.

* The above is extracted from "a Register of the Names of Officers employed at
Waterloo," by George Jones, Esq., Captain, Royal Monmouthshire Militia, 1817.

HARRISON AND SONS, PRINTERS IN ORDINARY TO HER MAJESTY, ST. MARTIN'S LANE.

REGIMENTAL CHRONICLE,

60TH ROYAL RIFLES.

ERRATA.

Subscribers are requested to place this errata in their copies, and it is suggested that those variations marked with an asterisk (which are considered important) should be noted on the pages on which they occur.

PREFACE.
* *Read* Charles Raikes Davy, *for* Richard Davy.

SERVICES.
*Page 14. Jan. 16, 1809. *Delete* 5th, *and read* 2nd Battalion formed part of.†

CHRONOLOGICAL TABLE.
* „ 48. 1805. 1806. *Read* augmented to, *for* augmented by.

LIST OF OFFICERS.
„	72.	*Delete* * *after* Pretyman.
„	154 to 193.	} *Read* J. Holmes Schoedde *for* John Schoedde (passim).
„	194 to 214.	} *Read* Sponge, *for* Sponge (passim).
„	196 to 203.	} *Read* Goldfrap, *for* Goldstrap (passim).
„	196 to 204.	} *Read* Gun, *for* Gunn (passim).
„	190.	*Read* Peyton, *for* Payton.
„	203 to 208.	} *Read* Bagot, *for* Bagott (passim).
„	205 to 208.	} *Read* Randal Rumley, *for* Randal Rumblier (passim).
„	208.	*Read* Sir R. Mahon, *for* Sir R. Mauou.
„	210.	*Read* Horell Thurlow, *for* Hovel.
„	211.	*Read* Cunyughame, *for* Cunyghim.
„	212.	*Read* Mark Wood, *for* Markwood.
„	216 and 231.	} *Read* Roe, *for* Rose or Rowe (passim).

† Since the publication of this work it has been ascertained from private sources that when on the line of march to Corunna, a counter order for 5th Battalion was received at Salamanca, and it returned to Lisbon. Hence the cause of its being included in some official returns as present at Corunna.

ERRATA.

Page 218 }
  to } *Read* Randle Joseph Feilden, *for* Randal Joseph Fielden (passim)
  230. }

„ 219. *Read* Earle, *for* Earl.

„ 223. }
„ 224. } *Read* Baynes, *for* Boynes (passim).

„ 223. *Read* Mure, *for* Muir.

„ 226. }
„ 228. } *Read* Heffernan, *for* Hefferman (passim).

„ 226 }
  to } *Read* Willes, *for* Willis Hinxman (passim).
„ 270. }

● „ 228. *Read* John Jones, *for* John James.

„ 229 }
  to } *Read* Cunynghame Ellis, *for* Cuninghame *and* Cunningham Ellis (passim).
„ 254. }

„ 233 }
  to } *Read* Grahame Young, *for* Graham Young (passim).
„ 280. }

„ 233 }
  to } *Read* McGrigor, *for* McGregor (passim).
„ 265. }

„ 234 }
  to } *Read* John Harrie Ker Innis, *for* John Harry Kerr Innes (passim).
„ 241. }

„ 235 }
  to } *Read* Phelips, *for* Phillipps (passim).
„ 237. }

● „ 238. *Read* Hon. Jenico Preston, *for* James Preston.
● „ 239. *Delete* V.C. and date, *after* Muter.
„ 247. *Read* Wykeham Leigh, *for* Whykham Leith Pemberton.
„ 255. *Read* Worswick, *for* Warwick.
„ 257. *Read* Davies, *for* Davis.
„ 271. *Read* Musketry, *for* Military.
„ 273. *Read* Mitchell-Innes, *for* M. Innes.
„ 273. *Read* Boddam-Whetham, *for* B. Whetham.
„ 273. *Read* Blackwood-Price, *for* B. Price.
„ 278. *Read* Copland-Crawford, *for* C. Crawford.
● „ 281. *Delete* Major, *before* Rowley Hinxman.
● „ 281. *Read* Major, *before* James Dundas.
● „ 283. *Read* Bt. Lt.-Col, 1st Oct., 1877, *after* Major Dundas, Major 5th July, 1873.
● „ 283. *Read* Bt. Lt.-Col., 1st Oct., 1877, *after* Major Northey, Major 5th July, 1873.

SERVICES OF OFFICERS.

● „ 235. *Read* 5th Jan., *for* 3rd Jan.
● „ 289. *Read* 83rd, *for* 33rd.
● „ 304. Lieut. Cox. *Read* affair at Mehunder, *for* Mahomdee.
● „ 307. Major Ellis. *Read* affair at Mehunder, *for* Mahomdee.
● „ 312. *Read* Major-General Sir J. Kempt, *for* Major Sir J. Kempt.
„ 311. *Read* Fitz Henry, *for* Henry.

www.ingramcontent.com/pod-product-compliance
Lightning Source LLC
Chambersburg PA
CBHW021118270326
41929CB00009B/942